HOFFMAN'S ARMY
THE 31ST VIRGINIA INFANTRY, CSA
1861 – 1865

DAVID W. WOODDELL

David W. Wooddell/CreativeSpaces

2015

This is a work of history based on primary documentary sources, as well as secondary sources. Permissions to publish quotes have been obtained where necessary. Factual errors are unintentional. If a reader finds an error of verifiable fact, and provides documentary evidence to support a correction, please contact the author with the information and I will attempt to make a correction in the next edition, time permitting, and resources available.

Published August 2015 by David W. Wooddell/CreativeSpaces

ISBN-13: 978-1515396994
ISBN-10: 1515396991

DEDICATION

This book is for my late grandparents, Harper S. Wooddell, and Ruby R. (Phillips) Wooddell. Each lost a grandfather in the Civil War.

Joseph E. Warwick Wooddell was mortally wounded May 19, 1864 at the battle of the Harris Farm, in the aftermath of the battle of Spotsylvania. He died later in Richmond, and is buried in the Confederate cemetery there, his grave marked with a headstone.

Charles Phillips disappeared in the mountains of West Virginia during the course of the war and his fate remains unknown.

This book is also for all their descendents.

ACKNOWLEDGEMENTS

This book about the 31st Virginia is in answer to my curiosity about my ancestor, Joseph E. Warwick Wooddell. With more than 30 years in the making, I have many to acknowledge for help, encouragement, criticism, and advice. My former colleagues at *National Geographic*: Bill Allen (former Editor); the late Dr. George Stuart, (resident archaeologist and civil war history buff); and Mark Holmes, former Art Director, who mentored me into the Macintosh age. To that list, I'll add author Tom Allen, whose opinion on my manuscripts I always value; Dr. Joseph W. A. Whitehorne, and Jan Hurgronje for comments and publishing advice; Gregg Clemmer, author of *Old Alleghany*, for encouragement and advice; David B. Kuhl, for sharing stories about his ancestor; and cousins Jim Wooddell, and the late Forest H. Wooddell, for sharing information about our many relatives who served in the 31st Virginia. At the West Virginia and Regional History Collection, David Bartlett was helpful with access to original documents in the Roy B. Cook Collection, long before they were scanned and put online. I had help from the Randolph County Historical Society, Virginia Military Institute, Library of Congress, and National Archives with access to original documents, microfilm, and sometimes typescripts. I spent hundreds of hours at the National Archives, where Mike Meier gave much needed help; and hundreds more at the Library of Congress, transcribing the entire Joseph C. Snider memorandum from microfilm.

I'd like to especially recognize and thank Kate Collins, and my son Daniel Lee Wooddell, for their many field trips with me to battlefields, and putting up with endless hours while I researched and wrote. Thank you to the late Paul Offner for comments on draft text; and Dick and Mary Collins, for endless hospitality. Thank you, Kat Forder, for the cover design, and for helping me in countless ways.

Several authors worked this ground before me, but especially John M. Ashcraft, Jr, *31st Virginia Infantry*, the starting point for my research. Others who wrote about the regiments in the Fourth Brigade include: Richard L. Armstrong, A. S. Bosworth, Roger U. Delauter, Jr., Robert J. Driver, Clayton R. Newell, and David F. Riggs.

This book was not possible without the voices of the men who served with the regiment. Most importantly for this book, Joseph C. Snider, the unsung diarist in Company C; William P. Cooper, John S. Hoffman, Alfred H. Jackson, William L. Jackson, John Cammack, Joseph Chenoweth, John G. Gittings, James E. Hall, Joseph F. Harding, William H. Hull, Christian Kuhl, John R. Phillips, Osborne Wilson, and brigade surgeon, Dr. Archibold Atkinson, whose comments on Colonel John S. Hoffman taught me more about the man than any other source.

SDZwkQkT3H

Order ID 104-4507613-8560264 - Order of July 2, 2016

Qty.	Item
1	Hoffman's Army: The 31st Virginia Infantry, CSA Wooddell, Mr. David W --- Paperback (** P-1-X176D53 **) 1515396991

Return or replace your item
Visit Amazon.com/returns

68/DZwkQkT3H/-1 of 1-//CLT5/second/11168003/0705-02:00/0704-01:35   V3

CONTENTS

MAPS

INTRODUCTION

This book is a history of the 31st Virginia Infantry, CSA, and the men who served in the regiment. The regiment was made up of volunteers when it was first formed, at a time very different from our own. Their ideas, especially of the politicians in the regiment, helped lead Virginia to civil war. It was their arguments over the rights of states versus national government, and the rights of property owners versus human rights that led to the conflict.

My family lost a lot of men in that civil war. We were a border family, and to all such families today, there remains a shadow of our personal loss. But other men, women, and children who had been slaves won their freedom in that war. I try never to forget the rightness of freeing a subjugated people. Yet, I believe we should also not forget those who served in the armies, Union or Confederate.

This history of the 31st Virginia is not about my beliefs in the rightness or wrongness of the South's defense of slavery and state's rights between 1861 and 1865. It does not, nor is it intended to defend slavery, which I consider indefensible and a crime against humanity.

Virginia seceded from the Union on April 17, 1861. Companies of volunteers were already forming to serve in an army to protect the state from possible invasion from the North. Late in June 1861, ten companies of volunteers were formed into a regiment designated the 31st Virginia Infantry. The regiment was immediately placed into service in the part of the state west of the Allegheny Mountains. Made up of new, untrained soldiers, with few men trained in the art of war, the companies of farmers, shopkeepers, lawyers, and politicians proceeded to march and drill, and do the many things that soldiers were expected to do near the middle of the 19th century. Some few of the recruits distracted themselves with their usual occupation of lawyering and politicking, something they were rather good at doing. Combined, the military amateurs and the professional politicians in the regiment made a double-threat, though not always to the Union Army, as should have been intended. They retreated from time to time in the beginning of the conflict, and for good reason: they were amateurs at war.[1]

The men in the 31st Virginia Infantry were from nine western Virginia counties that spread from west to east in a diagonal slash: Harrison, Marion, Barbour, Lewis, Upshur, Gilmer, Randolph, Pocahontas, Pendleton, and Highland counties. Most of the land in those counties was sparsely settled and untamed, with few towns of any size, and even fewer small cities. Only seven towns in western Virginia had more than a thousand people in 1860. Those who resided in the Allegheny Mountains lived among great tracts of forest, some of it wild and nearly impassable. The men who lived near the Ohio River were in an area that was a floodplain with rich soil that made agriculture possible. In between the mountains and the floodplain, hills rose up and rolled in a grassy landscape that was suitable for grazing cattle, and for some limited agriculture.[2]

Western Virginia in 1861 – now the state of West Virginia – was defined as those counties from the east front of the Allegheny Mountains westward to the Ohio River flood plain. Considerably isolated from Eastern Virginia, there were few good roads that crossed the mountains. When the Baltimore & Ohio Railroad was built in 1857, a faster means of transportation allowed better movement of goods and people. The railroad ran from Harper's Ferry on the eastern side of the mountains, to Grafton in the northwestern part of the state. It then branched off westward to the major port towns along the Ohio River, such as Parkersburg and Wheeling. The railroad's narrow transportation corridor became something to guard, as well as an asset to exploit with the rapid movement of troops. The rest of that part of western Virginia depended on roads that crossed the mountains and wandered here and there connecting towns, villages, and farms. The Staunton to Parkersburg Pike was one of the few major roads, but it was made of dirt and mud, and often nearly impassable.[3]

The Pike passed through miles of old growth forest with trees large enough to dwarf a man. So much untamed forest existed that large parts of the mountainous areas were considered primeval. Some of the early settlers in the forest lived in primitive and rude cabins, or structures that eastern writers said resembled woodpiles more than architecture. In one famous instance in Pocahontas County, in the early pioneer time of exploration, a settler turned a hollow tree into a place to live through the winter.[4]

Virginians prided themselves on their ruggedness, especially the hunters and outdoorsmen. Many were accustomed to firing muskets and rifles, and were horsemen by necessity, as well as sometimes by avocation or hobby. Their ancestors had fought Indians to defend against attacks as hunters from the two different cultures came into conflict with one another in what had been the mountainous hunting grounds of the native tribes from Ohio and the Carolinas. The forefathers of these western Virginians had also served as militia volunteers during the American Revolution, just four score and some odd years before.[5]

When the 31st Virginia reached the top of its form, its ranks included state legislators, former legislators, two judges, two newspaper editors, a pharmacist, several printers, a few teachers, one artist, a bevy of blacksmiths, a deputy sheriff, four men of the cloth, six carpenters, some shoemakers, a mechanic, three clerks, a coal miner, a plasterer, three cabinet makers, twelve adventurous students, one surveyor, five surgeons, one tinsmith, one saddler, a railroader, three tailors, an iron worker, a lumber-jack, four merchants, four painters, one academy professor, a college professor, and fourteen lawyers.[6]

Men served more faithfully if they had family and friends with them. The volunteers had brothers, uncles, fathers, and cousins of all kinds with them; first, second, and twice or three times removed. There were plenty of inlaws by marriage, too. More than 1500 men served in the 31st Virginia between the summer of 1861 and the spring of 1865. Hundreds died during the four years of war. Hundreds suffered wounds, some of them more than once. Disease claimed a heavy toll, and a few died in the harshness of prison camps. When General Robert E. Lee surrendered his Army of Northern Virginia to General Ulysses S. Grant at Appomattox on April 9, 1865, the 31st Virginia had just 22 arms-bearing men standing on the field.[7]

The regiment was formed on June 15, 1861 at Huttonsville, in Randolph County, and was initially placed in Brigadier General Robert S. Garnett's brigade in the Provisional Army of Virginia. The first commander of the 31st Virginia Regiment was Lieutenant Colonel William L. Jackson. A former lieutenant governor of Virginia, he was a lawyer and judge from Parkersburg with political pull and a commanding presence.[8]

In the spring of 1862, John S. Hoffman, a Clarksburg lawyer and legislator in the Virignia House of Delegate was appointed colonel of the 31st Virginia, and served in that capacity until he was dangerously wounded in February 1865. When the regiment surrendered at Appomattox, it was under the command of Major William P. Cooper, a former newspaper owner and editor, also from Clarksburg in Harrison County.[9]

Other field officers in the 31st Virginia included Lt. Col. Francis M. Boykin, Lt. Col. Alfred H. Jackson, Lt. Col. James S. Kerr McCutcheon, Major Joseph H. Chenoweth, and Major James C. Arbogast. The professional careers of the field officers offices were law/politics, publishing, and teaching. Of the field officers above captain, only Boykin and Chenoweth were trained in military affairs prior to the start of the war.[10]

With so few trained officers, the burden of command in battle at the start of the war rested heavily upon brigade commanders. The 31st Virginia served under several brigade commanders during their four years of war, including: Robert S. Garnett, Henry R. Jackson, Edward "Allegheny" Johnson, Arnold Elzey, Jubal Early, James Walker, William "Extra Billy" Smith, John Pegram, Robert D. Lilley, and Henry Kyd Douglas. Their own John S. Hoffman, lawyer-politician often served, as temporary brigade commander, and at times the brigade became known as *Hoffman's Army*.[11]

The regiment began service in the Western Virginia campaign of 1861, but transferred in the spring of 1862 to the Fourth brigade of Gen. Thomas "Stonewall" Jackson's Army of the Valley. Later, near the end of July of that year, the Fourth brigade was assigned to Richard S. Ewell's division, and became part of the II Corps of the Army of Northern Virginia. The 31st Virginia served in that division throughout most of the remainder of the war.[12]

The 31st Virginia participated in most of the major battles in Virginia, and more often than not, they were in the thick of the fighting. In one instance the regiment lost over half of its strength to casualties in a single day of battle. The list of major and minor battles/skirmishes in their war: Philippi, Laurel Hill, Corrick's Ford, Cheat Mountain, Greenbrier, Camp Alleghany, McDowell, Front Royal, 1st Winchester, Cross Keys, Port Republic, Gaines Mill, Malvern Hill, Cedar Mountain, Groveton, 2nd Manassas, Chantilly, Sharpsburg, Fredericksburg, Jones-Imboden Raid, 2nd Winchester, Gettysburg, Mine Run, Wilderness, Spotsylvania, Harris Farm, Bethesda Church, Cold Harbor, Monocacy River, Fort Stevens, Kernstown, 3rd Winchester, Fishers Hill, Cedar Creek, Hatcher's Run, Petersburg, Fort Stedman, Sayler's Creek, and Appomattox.[13]

When not in combat, the men in the regiment almost seemed at war with one another, but of a political kind. For all of the 31st Virginia's hard fighting, it was essentially *a political regiment*, with fourteen lawyer-politicians in its service. The officers thrived on legal arguments among themselves. Factional and sectional politics had created the situation in western Virginia that existed in the spring of 1861, leading to Virginia seceding from the Union and joining the Confederacy. Several of the regiment's officers played active political roles in their local areas, in the Virginia convention of 1860 and 1861, and in the state legislature. Some tried to calm the waters through compromise and reason. Others beat the drum loudly, and helped start the war. It should not be surprising that these politicians and lawyers continued to practice such behavior while in the regiment.

But what was the war about? John Letcher, the governor of Virginia spoke about this subject in his message to the extra session of the Virginia Legislature in January 1861:

"Many of the fanatics in the northern states are constantly calling attention to the fact, that the number of slave owners, as compared with the white population in the slave states, is small; and hence the inference that the non-slaveholder is not loyal to the state, and would not willingly defend the institution. This is a most serious mistake, and is well calculated to make an erroneous impression upon the northern mind. Such a representation does serious injustice to that loyal and patriotic class of our citizens. It is a reflection upon them, not warranted by their conduct, now or heretofore."[14]

"The northern states must strike from their statute books their personal liberty bills, and fulfill their constitutional obligations in regard to fugitive slaves and fugitives from justice. If our slaves escape into non-slaveholding states, they must be delivered up; if abandoned, depraved and desperately wicked men come into slave states to excite insurrections, or to commit other crimes against our laws, and escape into free states, they must be given up for trial and punishment, when lawfully demanded by the constituted authorities of those states whose laws have been violated.

"Second—We must have proper and effective guarantees for the protection of slavery in the district of Columbia. We can never consent to the abolition of slavery in the district, until Maryland shall emancipate her slaves; and not then, unless it shall be demanded by the citizens of the district.

"Third—Our equality in the states and territories must be fully recognized, and our rights of person and property adequately protected and secured. We must have guarantees that slavery shall not be interdicted in any territory now belonging to, or which may hereafter be acquired by the general government; either by the congress of the United States or a territorial legislature: that we shall be permitted to pass through the free states and territories without molestation; and if a slave shall be abducted, that the state in which he or she shall be lost, shall pay the full value of such slave to the owner.

"Fourth—Like guarantees must be given, that the transmission of slaves between the slaveholding states, either by land or water, shall not be interfered with...

"These guarantees can be given without prejudice to the honor or rights, and without a sacrifice of the interests, of either of the non-slaveholding states. We ask nothing, therefore, which is not clearly right, and necessary to our protection: And surely, when so much is at stake, it will be freely, cheerfully and promptly assented to. It is the interest of the north and the south to preserve the government from destruction; and they should omit the use of no proper or honorable means to avert so great a calamity. The public safety and welfare demand instant action...

"The number of persons in this state, in the year 1860, charged with taxes on slaves, was 53,874. The number of persons charged with taxes on lands in the same year, was 159,088. Most of the persons charged with taxes on slaves, are the owners of lands also; and others who own lands, own no slaves.

"The number of persons charged with taxes, other than owners of lands and slaves, is 201,000. All these parties have a common interest in the protection of persons and property, and each feels that in protecting the rights and property of the others, he is securing and protecting his own, whether of little or great value. As the chief magistrate, and as a citizen of Virginia, it is a source of pleasure to me to know that there is no jealousy or distrust, and that harmony and confidence exist between these classes. If the northern people entertain the opinion that the non-slaveholders of the south are not reliable and trustworthy in all respects, they are most grossly mistaken and deceived. I have seen it stated that in the empire city of New York the owners of real estate numbered less than 15,000. Do those who are not owners of real estate feel no interest in the property of the 15,000? Would they be unwilling to defend or protect it, if it were in danger of destruction? It might be charged with the same propriety, and with as much truth, in this instance, that feeling no interest in common with the owner, they would not risk their lives for the protection of his real estate, worth millions of dollars.

"They are interested—deeply interested in all that relates to the public prosperity. Their prosperity, their comfort, and the comfort of their families are dependent upon the protection of the rights of property of every individual in the community in which he lives. I have always reverenced the state rights doctrines of Virginia, as inculcated in the resolutions of '98 and the report of '99. I believe the doctrines therein asserted, and the principles therein affirmed, to be worthy of all acceptation. I cordially endorse them, and in so doing, endorse the doctrine of secession...

"I will endeavor in my administration to carry out the time honored state rights principles of Virginia. If at any time during my administration the federal government shall attempt to interfere with the rights and institutions of Virginia; if it shall at any time interfere with the rights of slavery or the rights of slaveholders in our state, I will be prepared, with the aid of the people, to resist any efforts to coerce us into submission. I will resist any attempt of federal troops to cross our line to execute such unjust, iniquitous and unconstitutional laws, either in Virginia or in any other southern state."

"I will regard an attempt to pass federal troops across the territory of Virginia, for the purpose of coercing a southern seceding state, as an act of invasion, which should be met and repelled. The allegiance of every citizen of Virginia is due to her; and when her flag is unfurled, it is his duty to rally to its support and defense. The citizen of Virginia who will not respond to her call, is a traitor to her rights and her honor."[15]

While the 1860 presidential campaign of Abraham Lincoln had turned up the heat on the issue of slavery, there were so many other voices on either side of the issue that Lincoln's voice was only one of many. The extra session of the Virginia legislature was full of discussion and proposed statements of support for Virginia's slave laws against possible intervention by the Federal government to prevent secession. [16]

Virginians had a strong loyalty to their state, of a type that is relatively unknown today. They believed that states had rights that were paramount over the rights of the Federal government. Who can say how many of the men in the 31st Virginia fought to maintain the right of citizens to own slaves? That is impossible to know. They did fight, and the reasons for the fight have been given in Governor Letcher's address. Some of the volunteers in the 31st Virginia fought to maintain states rights, and to repel what they saw as an unwarranted invasion of a state by Federal troops. Others may have joined the army simply because they felt like an adventure, without realizing the terrible price they would pay.

The war in Virginia's western counties was different than the war that was fought in eastern Virginia. In western Virginia there was true civil war of brother versus brother. Few other parts of the country saw such a degree of animosity and outright bloodshed within families between brothers, cousins, uncles, and neighbors. When a man from any other state volunteered to serve during the start of the war, he did not generally need to worry that his family might be murdered or turned out of their homes and robbed of their possessions by neighbors or relatives who claimed such actions were for the "public good." Men in this regiment lived with worry that terrible things were happening to their wives, children, and parents, and sometimes those depredations did happen to their family members back home. The soldiers in the 31st Virginia learned to fear bushwhackers, lawless partisan rangers, as well as over-zealous Unionist civilians.[17]

When the Union army announced it would turn Confederate families out of their homes and make them refugees, it was in western Virginia where the families first suffered this punishment against civilians. *Refugeed*, and *refugeeing* became new words and activities for people from Western Virginia who chose to follow the South in its war against the North. They thought of themselves as temporarily displaced, and when they could, they traveled to live with relatives or beg a bedroom from friends to the east of the mountains.[18]

Most of the men who served in the 31st Virginia were not slave owners, but nor were they disconnected from slavery. A few slave owners served in the regiment, or had family members who served in Virginia's army. Whether the other, non-slave owners who served in the 31st Virginia believed in slavery is difficult to determine from the journals, letters, and reminiscences available today.

When the legislature of Virginia voted in April 1861 to support secession, the political tension of the previous year had at last reached the breaking point and the forces of war were unleashed. As the residents of western Virginia expected, the path of Northern invasion was to be directly through their small towns and villages in northwestern Virginia, spreading south and eastward toward Pocahontas County. Union soldiers would invade from across the Ohio River and occupy the territory along the B&O Railroad to guard the railroad. Later, they used the muddy Staunton to Parkersburg Pike.

Virginia was not very well prepared to repulse such an invasion. The few small companies of volunteers were all that Virginia had on hand to repulse a Union force in the Northwestern section of the state. The counties there had little in the way of arms, and fewer experienced officers. Facing larger, more organized forces marching under the stars and stripes of the Federal government, carried by men from Ohio and Indiana, the western Virginia companies fell back and abandoned the very homeland for which they vowed to fight. They never got it back until the war was ended, and they could return as vanquished soldiers. Their home territory was controlled throughout most of the war by the Union army, and by citizens who defended the Union. Those Union supporters held strong feelings, too, and were able to move forward on another great issue, the breaking away of western Virginia into a new state.

Factions in western Virginia boxed the compass. In addition to men who supported issues of North and South, there had long been an East and West point of view. Citizens to the west of the Alleghenies had been discussing carefully their desire to break away and form their own state for nearly thirty years. In the confusion and disruption of the early months of the war, western Virginia politicians took advantage of the situation and forced secession from the state. Virginia was helpless to do much to prevent it, or to force the separated counties to return to the state.

After western Virginia was occupied by the Union army, and the supporters of the South had departed with their army, or had been arrested or otherwise forced to leave, the Federal government declared that the government of Virginia had abandoned its citizens by joining with the Confederacy, and so there was a need for the formation of a "Restored Government of Virginia." Delegates to the convention of western Virginians meeting in Wheeling elected Francis H. Pierpont, a politician from Marion County, to be the new governor of this Restored Government.[19]

The Federal government quickly approved the new Restored Government of Virginia. In the next two years, the Restored Government approved the discussion of formation of a new state, and a series of western Virginia conventions worked out the details of a new state constitution for the Virginia counties that were west of the Allegheny Mountains. By the summer of 1863 the convention had ratified the new constitution, the citizenry remaining in the western counties had voted to approve it, and the federal government recognized it. Arthur Boreman was elected to be the first governor of the new state, and a new star was added to the flag of the United States, representing the state of West Virginia. West Virginia was the only state created during the civil war.[20]

During the course of the war, men disabled by their wounds, or too sick to continue in the ranks were released to go home. Some were sent to prison camps, but released when the war ended. The few survivors of the 31st Virginia who fought to the end also returned to their homes in the spring and summer of 1865. They found themselves in a new state, under difficult circumstances, and governed by laws that were restrictive against the former Confederates. They were survivors, though, and had been in even more difficult positions during the past several years. They had marched hard and often under Gen. Stonewall Jackson and other generals, and had fought battles up and down the length of Virginia, on both sides of the Alleghenies, and even into Maryland, Pennsylvania, and the outskirts of the District of Columbia. They lost hundreds of men to death and disease, and hundreds more were lost to crippling wounds.

For some of those survivors, the situation held some quiet irony: they returned to the new state of West Virginia and took up their places at home with their families, secure in the knowledge that they had been in favor of a new state of their own for many years before the war. Eventually the difficulties remaining after the war, and the political reconstruction in its aftermath would fade.

Western Virginia 1861

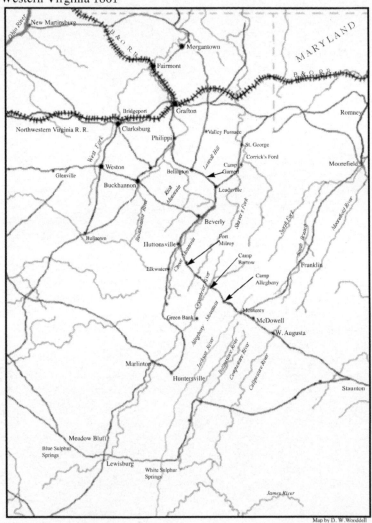

Map by D. W. Wooddell

1

SECESSION IN WESTERN VIRGINIA
January 1861 — May 1861

S*ecession or Union.* 1861 was a time of political choices. Politician and lawyer John S. Hoffman, 40-year-old state legislator from Clarksburg, in Harrison County resisted making such a choice for as long as he could. Hoffman was the elected representative in the House of Delegates for his county. In January, he was against secession unless the question of equitable taxation of slaves could be resolved. It was a thorny problem that had long plagued property owners in the western Virginia counties, where they owned great tracts of land, but few slaves. Land owners paid higher taxes on their property than slave owners paid on theirs.

On January 18, 1861, from the House of Delegates in Richmond, Hoffman wrote to his political mentor, best friend, and uncle, Judge Gideon D. Camden, "We have told Eastern men... that while we did not press our grievances at a time when all are in danger, that yet we did not see how our people could be expected to sanction secession that would result in war, heavy taxes, and ruin—all for the sake of slavery in which they have no interest—unless slavery should be taxed; and suggested to them that they would endear our people to them by instantly tendering uniform taxation, while they would only anticipate by a few years a necessary consequence."[21]

Hoffman's uncle Gideon Camden was a keen advocate of the Southern position on slavery, and an able politician in Western Virginia. He was a judge of the Twenty-first Circuit Court, and was a strong defender of Virginia's law against the encouragement of abolition. Under that law, it was illegal for any citizen to promote abolition: Judge Camden had gained some notoriety when he indicted newspaperman Horace Greeley for encouraging abolition through the pages of the *New York Tribune*.[22]

Although Camden owned two slaves in 1860, and bought another toward the end of the same year, yet he too was not convinced in January 1861 that Virginia should secede. "South Carolina has acted very unwisely," he wrote, "she should have waited and cooperated with the other Southern states in case Lincoln's administration was one of aggression on our rights. But we must see things as we find them, and our great object should now be to serve the Union if it can be done on honorable terms; if not, to preserve the shedding of blood."[23]

As events unfolded on the national scene, Hoffman and Camden changed their minds on the issue of secession. By April 1861, Camden was appointed a delegate to the Confederate convention, then meeting in Montgomery, Alabama. He was still serving as a judge and was unwilling to give up that position. Soon enough, the Confederate convention would move to Richmond, making a trip to Alabama unnecessary.

Judge Camden was also then particularly absorbed in the new oil business in his part of the state. Oil had been found in 1858 by the Karnes brothers at Burning Springs Creek, a tributary of the Kanawha River, several counties distant from Clarksburg. The Karnes discovery was followed in 1860 with new wells drilled by the Rathbone brothers, who owned land at Burning Springs. Later the same year, wells were dug and operated by a partnership that included Judge Camden. As one of the first speculators involved in this new, oily business, the Judge probably found the timing of the whole secession crisis most inconvenient.

Camden's partners in the petroleum operation were his nephew, Johnson N. Camden, and a couple of other men. They had purchased two acres of Rathbone land on Burning Springs Creek where they struck oil and gas in serious quantities in late January 1861. The oil began spilling out of the ground faster than they could collect it. Nor could they obtain sufficient barrels to store the black goo. At some wells, oil was producing at the rate of several hundred barrels a day.[24]

Lubricate the gears and wheels of industry and transportation, and the flow of commerce will follow—if the timing is right, and the price is competitive. Petroleum products were relatively new to the nation in 1861, the first wells being driven into the ground in Titusville, Pennsylvania just a few years before. Until then, mill gears, train wheels, and wagon axles were greased with rendered animal fat, or with vegetable oils, such as palm oil. And for illumination, parlors and offices used lamps filled with whale oil, or candles made from animal fats or beeswax. The forces of economics and commerce would change the situation: the oil and gas boom provided lubricants, and fuel for lighting at a cost well below the prices charged for whale oil, and provided a material far superior to animal fats or vegetable oils. Judge Camden was on the crest of a wave that would eventually sweep the world, and from which the world has yet to recover.

The oil boom was just one of the incentives for discussing the separation of western Virginia from Virginia. But the issue of tax equity for all property owners was the bargaining chip for the western Virginians: they would perhaps go along with secessaion, if the tax bases were equalized for landowners and slave owners alike.

But the issue of separation of western Virginia from eastern Virginia also hung over the legislature at this time. In January, from the Virginia legislature Hoffman wrote to his uncle Gideon, "The delegation from the North West have been exceedingly cautious, and I think prudent. We have been careful to say but little on the floor.... To our talks here of a division of the state, no hostility is impressed by any Western man to the East. We have all endeavored to cultivate friendly feeling."

Men from both sides of the national issue of slavery, state's rights and secession beloieved that western Virginia should separate from Virginia and become its own state. That issue went back decades in western Virginia. Owners of land, such as John Hoffman and Judge Camden claimed they received little return in their investment from the taxes paid on their property, while easterners paid a lower tax rate on their slave property, but received the majority of the benefits from the state government. In retrospect, the separation of western Virginia in 1861 was almost inevitable once the Union army invaded western Virginia.

President Lincoln called for volunteer regiments to defend Federal property in the South in March 1861. The circumstances that had been hanging in the balance were shifted. Volunteering to serve Virginia's stare forces became necessary, if the state was going to resist the Federal government. It was not a simple question for the men and their families, and in fact, many who wished to support the Union ended up volunteering for the secessionist army out of loyalty to their family and community.

With the crisis of secession gaining momentum in the South, and the military confrontation between the North and the South imminent, the resulting threat of a Northern invasion was enough to shift political alignments in western Virginia from centrist positions to those at either end of the spectrum. It then became a time of crisis, and regardless of the personal interest in forming a new state from Virginia's western counties, Hoffman and Camden chose to support the traditional states rights of Virginia. Hoffman volunteered for the army, but his uncle continued to serve in the role he knew best, behind-the-scenes politics.

Virginia was a border state. When the North sent an army to invade the South, it would have to cross Virginia on the way. Many predicted the invasion would come from Ohio, using the railroad. The prospect of their own state becoming a road for invasion brought Hoffman and many others to defend what they considered sovereign soil. Hoffman's hometown of Clarksburg was directly in the path of the storm: he wrote to Camden on March 13: "My views have much changed since I saw you. I then thought, beyond a doubt, that Virginia ought not under any circumstances to separate from the Union if constitutional guarantees could be obtained. I now think that the seceded states will not come back, and I see in our connection with the Northern states, even with guarantees, much that looks like mere provincialism on our part, and on the other hand many advantages to Virginia in a Southern connection which did not use to strike me. Yet I do not think Virginia can separate without North Carolina, Tennessee, and Maryland. Without the latter our condition in the Northwest would be interesting in the highest degree. I am therefore in favor of a concretion of the slave states."[25]

It was clear that most people in the northwestern part of Virginia would side with the Union. Hoffman wrote in one of his letters, "I have been very much mystified at the want of spirit and Black Republicanism sympathies that prevail to such an extent in Virginia and particularly in our own (Harrison) county. I am sorry to think partisan hatred by Bell & Breckenridge men of this Democratic Party have much to do with the present condition of Virginia and the Border States. A fair number of them in all parts of the state I am sure love the North better than the South—and I can attribute it to no other cause than the perhaps unconscious influence of party feeling."

Support for secession in the rest of the state, however, was overwhelmingly in favor of Virginia leaving the Union. Accordingly, on April 17, delegates at the Virginia Convention voted in favor of secession. Five days later in Clarksburg, a large crowd of Unionist supporters were holding a mass meeting, and were raising their voices on the Courthouse steps in support of holding the Federal government together, by force if necessary. Some reports said there were as many as twelve hundred Unionists at that mass meeting. Clearly, they were showing support for an invasion from the North. For secessionists in Harrison County, the threat was very clear. The crisis was finally there, on their doorstep.

Hoffman attended a select group meeting in Harrison County that same day, April 22, to discuss the crisis, and their need for military arms and support from the governor. Except for the local militia company, the county lacked substantial means with which to defend itself. Lt. Col. N. J. Coplan, commander of the 138th Regiment of Militia signed their letter to the governor, asking for muskets and ammunition. The small group included newspaperman William P. Cooper, James M. Jackson, Robert Johnston, Augustine J. Smith, and former governor Joseph Johnson. They added their endorsement to Coplan's letter, asking for the means with which to defend their homes.

"Of course you are aware of the general exposure of this section of the State, and especially the danger of an attempt to pass northwestern troops through upon our railroads," Coplan wrote to the governor. "We are almost entirely without arms... I beseech you to furnish for my disposal such arms as you can afford, and that you will authorize the military of this section to do what circumstances shall require to prevent the passage of troops through Virginia or other aggression or insult to the Commonwealth.[26]

The group of secessionists also wrote a plea that day for their fellow citizens to attend a rally of state rights supporters to counter a large Unionist rally then going on in Clarksburg. This call to Southern consciousness was designed to ensnare friends, neighbors, and anyone else willing to serve.

"To the Southern Rights Men of Harrison County—War is upon us! ... Free Men of Harrison! Will you stand by and permit this war to be waged without any interference or remonstrance? You are bound to assume a position: the fanatical North calls upon you; the outraged, injured and gallant people of the South call upon you; the honor, the independent State-rights men of Virginia call upon you, and you this day have to decide which voice you will obey. The Union is dissolved; it cannot be cemented again and made a Union by the spilling of blood.... We do not propose you to go to war, but we want the great heart of the people to beat audibly, as we know it does silently.... We are opposed to coercion — we deplore the necessity of revolution.... Come one! Come all! We may under the provi-dence of the God of Armies, make such a start that others may be induced to follow, or at least wipe out the stain and stigma of being looked upon as coercionists and the minions of the bloody crew who are preparing to destroy our homes, and worse than all, the liberties of the Commonwealth."[27]

It was not quite Shakespeare, but it was inspiring, and it brought out the crowd as intended. Richmond newspapers said that Harrison County, with this inflammatory call for volunteers, was the first county to openly declare itself in the controversy in northwestern Virginia. The states-rights meeting, held in Harrison County on April 26, voted to send copies of the meeting's proceedings to the Virginia Convention, the Maryland legislature, various Richmond newspapers, and to newspapers in several other counties to advertise their commitment to defend Virginia. Their proclamation gave support and approval to the governor's order to prepare volunteer regiments and companies.[28]

With the state rights men of Harrison County asking the governor for arms, the opportunity to use them would present itself soon enough. Jonathan M. Bennett, the auditor of public finance for Virginia, wrote to newspaperman Cooper to inform him that two or three hundred men would be stationed on the Baltimore and Ohio railroad, to repel a Union invasion, and to "carry on a guerrilla war if they attempt to pass before we are ready." The railroad town of Grafton was already being discussed as the natural place for establishing a force of Virginians to deny the rail line to the Union.

Bennett said that people in the government in Richmond were encouraged by the news from Harrison County, and the open declaration they had made in support of Virginia. "I have assured the people here that while you might differ in the politics, when the question arose for you to go North or South, or rather when they must fight for Lincoln or their own sunny South, they would find them true to all the great principles of states rights, and resist almost to a man the daring usurpations of the Federal Government, which would put Oliver Cromwell to the blush." If Bennett was confident that the voters in a special election would ratify secession, he was less certain of the safety of the banks in western Virginia if the North did invade. "Look after your Bank Vaults," he cautioned, "they will be first searched by Lincoln's troops."[29]

The volunteers in Harrison County were already planning to organize more than one company of secessionist militia. At Romine's Mill, recruiters set up on the green at the schoolhouse with some men playing drums and fifes. Several patriotic addresses were given, and then John S. Hoffman read to the crowd some extracts from abolitionist Horace Greeley, whose New York newspaper was one of the strident voices for abolition.

Hoffman promised the men at Romine's Mill that he was planning to enlist in the service of Virginia, though as he pointed out, the military was not something for which he was trained. "Gentlemen, I am a volunteer," Hoffman declared. "I am going with you. The trouble with me is that I am afraid I can't fight. I'm afraid I will run. I hope you will help me along and overlook my faults."

That was enough inspiration to get the young Cammack brothers to join, though John Cammack was then only 16 years old. He and his older brother, Lucius, signed on, and then went home to tell their parents. They were both living at home and helping their father work his farm. "Father and Mother were greatly worried," Cammack later wrote, "especially about my going, only 16 years and 4 months old. Well, they thought it over and finally mother said she would rather we went together than one alone, so finally to my great joy it was understood when the company marched away, I would be with them."[30]

Governor Letcher issued a proclamation on May 3, authorizing additional volunteers to be called out and mustered into the service of Virginia. On the western side of the Alleghenies, the volunteers would assemble at Grafton, in Taylor County, 23 miles northeast of Clarksburg.[31]

Grafton held the railroad. Situated in a steep valley of the Tygart's Valley River, the town was a haven for steam and steel. The Baltimore & Ohio Railroad had set one of its best workshops there in 1853 as a staging point for building the Northwestern Virginia Railroad. The machine shop, iron foundry, and bridge fabrication works were state of the art, equipped with forge, lathes, screw cutters, planing machines, and casting furnace for working with wrought and cast iron. Beginning in 1856, it was the focal point for construction of the Northwestern Virginia railroad line, including its many bridges.

Men and parts were sent out from the Grafton workshops to repair problems in the trains and tracks on both the main B&O line, and the Northwestern Virginia line. By 1861, with its half-round engine house and marshaling yard for making up trains, the Grafton facility was responsible for maintaining the track, engines, and rail cars on both lines to the Ohio River, and also helped maintain the track, bridges, and tunnels to the east toward Cumberland, Maryland.[32]

Harrison County's small military importance also derived from its location near other transportation networks. A major road, the Northwestern Turnpike, crossed the county, but more significantly, the Northwestern Virginia Railroad passed through Clarksburg as it connected Parkersburg, at the Ohio River, to the junction of the B&O Railroad at Grafton. From the junction at Grafton, the main east-west route of the B&O passed 11 miles north of Clarksburg, and ran in a northwestern direction to Wheeling on the Ohio River, where it connected with the Central Ohio Railroad. Eastward, the main line of the railroad ran from Grafton to Cumberland, Maryland, and then on to Harper's Ferry and Baltimore. Control of the railroad could delay an invading army, for the wagon roads in western Virginia were undependable and slow.

Twenty miles to the south of Clarksburg, at Weston in Lewis County, Major Francis M. Boykin was already under orders from Gen. Robert E. Lee to prepare enough volunteers to hold the northwestern section of the state against invasion. He was instructed to take command of the forces that would assemble at Grafton, or nearby, in order to protect the B&O. Boykin would later become major of the 31st Virginia, and by the end of the year, was promoted to lieutenant colonel.[33]

Francis Boykin was a graduate of Virginia Military Institute, class of 1856. "A genial, social and companionable gentleman," according to one of his schoolmates, Boykin joined the Coast Survey after graduation from VMI. He later turned to teaching to fulfill the contract VMI required of all students, two years of educational service to the state of Virginia. Though he was active in the Virginia militia, Boykin continued to teach beyond the two years, and was trying to encourage construction of a school at Weston.[34]

The 24-year-old Boykin worked as a private tutor for the children of Robert J. McCandlish, the cashier of the Weston branch of the Exchange Bank. The Exchange Bank was then in one room of the house where McCandlish lived. It was the only branch of the

Richmond-owned bank west of the Alleghenies. Jonathan M. Bennett, the auditor of public finances for Virginia, and former mayor of Weston, was one of the founding directors of the bank. Before the crisis in secession, Boykin had gone there, to the house on the corner of Center and Second Streets, to teach the McCandlish children. It is difficult to imagine the children, in their home school, had much of Boykin's attention in the spring of 1861.[35]

The oil rush at Burning Springs, inspired by the phenomenal success of the Rathbone and Camden wells, had drawn men away from Lewis County at an alarming rate, leaving Boykin's volunteer company at Weston with no one to drill. Boykin and McCandlish had visited the new oil wells, about 50 miles away in Wirt County. The tiny community had been transformed into turmoil of men and machinery. Sparsely populated with about 20 families in the spring of 1860, Burning Springs Run became a town of 6,000 persons. Boykin wrote to a friend, "Although we had a very rough time, we enjoyed the trip. I was partially prepared for what I saw there, but was astonished not withstanding, and could scarcely allow the witness of my own eyes."[36]

Boykin's concern at the disruption of his militia company was heartfelt. "Our Volunteer Company is a perfect failure," Boykin wrote on March 18. "I fear we will never get the scattered fragments together again. The oil excitement has carried off the best part of the Company, and we are now scarcely able to muster a Corporal's guard. I hope when the absent members strike oil, they will come back in uniform cheerfully. The town is duller than I have ever seen it — nothing talked or thought of but oil."[37]

The Editor of the Weston *Herald* complained in an editorial, "Our town will be drained of its fighting population, and not enough left to take care of the women and children in the event of a descent being made upon them by the Black Republicans. Our town, the loveliest on the plain, may soon be deserted."[38]

By the end of April, the secession crisis was overwhelming even the attraction of oil in Wirt County. Maj. Boykin was in Richmond on April 30, receiving orders from Gen. Lee. From there, he traveled to Harper's Ferry on May 5 to confer with Col. Thomas J. Jackson about how best to defend Virginia's northwest. From Harper's Ferry, Boykin took the train west to Grafton, where he arrived on May 6.[39]

His first priority was to determine the state of readiness in the nearby volunteer companies. From May 7 to 10, he visited various captains of those companies in the adjacent counties, ascertaining their situations, and encouraging greater efforts in forming the men. He discovered that few of the companies had muskets, rifles, or ammunition.

Making a trip to the Ohio River, Boykin went to Wheeling to recruit volunteers, but found few men willing to join. Most men living in Virginia's cities on the Ohio River were strong supporters of the Union, though there were some exceptions. One of those was Judge William L. Jackson, soon to become the first commander of the 31st Virginia.[40]

A resident of Parkersburg, Judge Jackson was especially recommended by Maj. Boykin to Gen. Lee as the best man to organize a defense at Parkersburg. Events would transpire to make a defense at the Ohio River impossible, but Jackson remained determined to serve his state wherever he could be most effective.

"Judge Jackson is a gentleman," Boykin wrote to Gen. Lee, "of very great personal popularity, not only with his own party, but with those who are diametrically opposed to him politically, and I am satisfied could exert more influence towards conciliating them than any other gentleman who could be appointed. I consider it unnecessary to say more of the Judge, as he is known throughout the State to be devoted to the interests of Virginia, and will stand by her to the last extremity. I have recently had a conversation with him, and he will accept the command if tendered him."[41]

Born in Clarksburg on February 3, 1825, a cousin of Thomas J. Jackson, he lost his parents at an early age and grew up as an orphan, a curious bond that he shared not only with his cousin Stonewall, who was orphaned at Clarksburg, but also with the regiment's second commander, John Stringer Hoffman, who was raised by relatives after his mother and father died in an epidemic.

William L. Jackson was very intelligent, with drive and an acquired skill in leadership which helped him to become a skilled lawyer, and later a politician. He was elected to the Virginia legislature, and later to the position of lieutenant governor of Virginia. In 1860, he was elected judge to the Nineteenth Circuit Court. With strong connections throughout the northwestern part of the state, Jackson knew both Hoffman and Judge Camden very well. In fact, he was one of the partners in Judge Camden's Burning Springs oil discovery, and stood to loose a great deal of future prosperity if he chose the wrong side in the political turmoil.[42]

Another cousin, Alfred H. Jackson, was at Weston. He was known as somewhat of a firebrand when it came to the secession question. In December he had argued at a mass meeting that Virginia already had sufficient cause for secession. He dissented strongly from the majority view held at the meeting, that secession would be unwise and destructive.[43] A son of a retired, professional military officer, Alfred Jackson had a law degree from Washington University at Lexington, Virginia. In 1861, he was 25 years old, with a wife, and 2 young children at home. The previous year, he was appointed Deputy U.S. Marshall, and was responsible for compiling the 1860 Federal census report for Lewis County.

Alfred Jackson resigned that post, and with Francis Boykin's help, started recruiting a company of volunteers. Calling the company the Lewis Rangers, they later became Company I of the 31st Virginia. By the time they were enlisted, on June 2, at Hall's Store on Skin Creek, the crisis in western Virginia was at hand. Alfred Jackson was elected the company captain, and later rose to lieutenant colonel.[44]

The Lewis Rangers lived in a county that was home to miles of prime, virgin forest. There were many cattle farmers, and the towns had merchants, and professional men such as doctors and lawyers. As with Harrison County to the north, some citizens in Lewis County owned a number of slaves. There were a total of 368 slaves in the county in 1860, according to the census. With a county population of almost 8,000 individuals, living in 1,533 households, Lewis County was not strongly involved in the slave business. Yet those who owned slaves were determined to protect their property, and played a role in urging war. To a man, the slave owners in the county either joined the 31st Virginia, or some other Confederate regiment, or they had a family member who joined.

The most prominent slave owner in the county was Jonathan M. Bennett, who owned 26 slaves. (His brother, Jesse, enlisted in the Lewis Rangers.) Dr. William Bland, soon to become surgeon of the 31st Virginia, owned 7 slaves; R. J. McCandlish, the banker, owned 3; Thomas W. Hoffman, a cousin of John S. Hoffman, and later the adjutant of the regiment, owned 1 slave. Other relatives at Weston, Emma and Eva Hoffman owned 4 slaves. Richard P. Camden, a brother of Judge Gideon Camden, owned a total of 5.

The issue of slavery may not have loomed largely in the economic background of most residents of Lewis County, but the racial fears among certain whites, of equality being granted to the Negro (see endnote [45]), were extreme in Lewis County. The threat to slavery cannot be ignored in estimating the reasons why men in this part of the state joined the Confederates. "The Black Republicans," as Lincoln's supporters were known in the South, were seen as an extreme threat.[46]

Although the secessionists had a good start at forming their company in Lewis County, there were Unionists there who were just as determined to take action. For instance, one block over from Dr. Bland's fine new home on Center Street was the law office Judge Camden and John Hoffman had once shared with J. M. Bennett. By 1861, the office was being used by Camden's son-in-law, Caleb Boggess, a strong supporter of the Union. Elected to represent the county at the Virginia Convention, he voted against secession, returned home, and later joined the Union army.[47]

Meanwhile, in Taylor County, where Virginia's volunteer companies had been ordered to assemble at Grafton to defend the railroad, the Provisional Army of Virginia had yet to form. Their new commander, Col. George Porterfield arrived by train at Grafton on May 14, expecting to be met at the station by the assembled companies of volunteers. Finding the secessionist companies absent from the staunchly Unionist railroad town, Porterfield spoke briefly with a sympathetic railroad worker and learned that a few men were waiting to enlist at the small village of Fetterman, about a mile west of Grafton. Renting a horse from the local livery stable, Porterfield set out to find these men, but shortly discovered the number of volunteers at Fetterman were nearly equal to the number of structures in the tiny hamlet, which could boast a post office, a store, a blacksmith, and a rough, log, one-room school house.[48]

Porterfield was a veteran officer of the Mexican War, but until recently had been living on his farm in Jefferson County. His bucolic life had been interrupted on May 4 when Gen. Lee gave him orders to go to Grafton and coordinate Virginia's volunteer troops.[49]

The paucity of volunteers in evidence at Fetterman disconcerted Porterfield. He rode a few more miles to Mahaney's Tavern at Pruntytown. There he met with a small group of secessionist leaders. Encouraged by this meeting, Porterfield hoped to soon bring at least a few volunteer companies into the immediate Grafton area.[50]

Soon after Colonel Porterfield's arrival, Maj. Francis Boykin joined him there to serve on the Colonel's staff, and was assigned to organize volunteers into companies. Around this time, Porterfield gained another VMI graduate to assist in the work at hand, Lt. John G. Gittings, VMI class of 1856. Gittings was a native of Clarksburg, and was yet another cousin of Thomas, Alfred, and William Jackson. A man of no real financial means, his father was a hard-working businessman whose legal acumen failed to prevent a swindle of most of his own assets. Shortly before joining the Provisional Army, young John Gittings helped his father straighten out the tangled business affairs, by which point his father was broke.

Nearly destitute himself, Gittings went to Richmond where he received a commission as a 2nd lieutenant. Then he borrowed from a friend the train fare back to Grafton and lost no time in reporting to Porterfield at Pruntytown. He was promptly made adjutant, a position he would also later hold in the 31st Virginia. "We were trying to raise recruits," Gittings wrote after the war, "but we had absolutely nothing. No money, no arms, no ammunition — no supplies of any kind."[51]

There were plenty of muskets in nearby Marion County, however. At Fairmont, the Marion Guards were already equipped with firearms and ammunition. Their captain, William P. Thompson was determined to make a reputation: he bought 175 muskets with his own money. Thompson began enlisting volunteers in the night of May 16, and continued the following day. The company was later designated as Company A of the 31st Virginia.

Thompson was a brash, young lawyer of 24. A brother-in-law of Johnson Camden, he had recently moved to Marion County from Wheeling, where his father, George W. Thompson was a judge of the Circuit Court. Thompson seems to have been an eager secessionist, and later claimed to be the senior captain of the regiment.[52]

Most of the Marion Guards were farmers, but the company also included several lawyers and prominent politicians, such as Alpheus F. Haymond. He was 38 years old, and had served two terms in the Virginia legislature representing the county. More recently, in the spring of 1861, he was elected as a delegate to the Virginia Convention, where he voted against secession, but later signed the Ordinance of Secession. When he departed from home, Haymond left behind a wife and several children. At the formation of the regiment, he was elected a captain on the 31st Virginia's regimental staff, serving as assistant commissary, in charge of procuring food for the regiment.[53]

Another of the county's lawyers was a young protégé of Haymond, William W. Arnett. He would be elected captain of Company A the following year, and his brother, Jonathan M. Arnett, also a lawyer, would become 1st lieutenant.[54]

James Neeson, another lawyer from the county also departed hastily after the Union invasion, along with the secessionist editor of the local newspaper. Neeson joined the Marion Guards and later Company A, but being a lawyer-politician-soldier, politics was dominant. Even though carried on the 31st Virginia's books as a soldier, Neeson spent much of the war serving as Marion County's representative to the Virginia Senate.

Marion County was sharply divided on the issue of secession, with a majority of the residents favoring the Union. Their leader was Fairmont's citizen, Frances Pierpont. On the night that Capt. Thompson called the company together to inform them to be ready to march the next morning, a number of the state rights men were placed under arrest by local Unionists and were temporarily prevented from marching away with the secessionist company.

The next morning, despite the missing men, Thompson gathered those who were ready to go and set off from Fairmont. They marched to Taylor Court House, at Pruntytown, a distance of 18 miles. At Pruntytown, Colonel Porterfield placed the company to guard the road, but ordered them to Fetterman the next morning, where they occupied a covered bridge to prevent its destruction by Union loyalists. A small company of Taylor County men who called themselves the Letcher Guards joined them there. The combined command totaled about 100 men.[55]

Other companies were even then being called on to march to Porterfield's camp. In Harrison County, John Cammack and his friends at Romine's Mill received the call to duty on May 20. "A horseman came rushing up the pike from Clarksburg," Cammack recalled, "and reported that an order had come from Col. Porterfield at Grafton for all the reinforcements that could be had — that the enemy were about to destroy his small force." The men from Romine's Mill, numbering 18 altogether, marched to Clarksburg right away, and met the small contingent of volunteers from Milford on their way into town. Joining together, they marched further until they met Clarksburg's company of volunteers, and were promptly enlisted. The Harrison Rifles were under command of their elected captain, Uriel M. Turner. He was a lawyer and former senator in the Virginia legislature. Norval Lewis was elected lieutenant, and so was newspaper editor Cooper.[56]

The scene in Clarksburg that night was tense, and dramatic. The Harrison Rifles were already forming in line with rifles on their shoulders when the men from Romine's Mill arrived around four in the afternoon. Later, they all marched down the street as a company under the command of Capt. Turner.

Harrison County's Union men were incensed over this show of arms at the county seat. The alarm bell at the courthouse rang out to call in the Unionist companies, and Capt. A. C. Moore, and Capt. J. C. Vance formed their two Union companies of volunteers in line to the rattle of a drum, the stars and stripes flying, and their men ready for action.

The Clarksburg standoff began, with neither side willing to fire first, nor neither side willing to back down. Around eight o'clock that night they reached an agreement: if the Confederates would stack their arms, they could remain the night in safety, and depart in the morning with their weapons. The muskets and rifles carried by the Harrison Rifles were placed overnight in the town jail under the watch of Waldo P. Goff, a prominent Union man.[57]

Many of the secessionists were sent to the homes of families who wanted to show their support for the South. John Cammack said his own good fortune in being sent to the home of a Circuit Court judge, George H. Lee, who was known in Clarksburg for generous hospitality.[58]

The next morning, as arranged, the firearms were returned to the Harrison Rifles, and the company formed in line in front of the town's principal hotel. Additional Union men were even then arriving in Clarksburg in response to the call to arms sent out the night before. Cammack later reported that many of the volunteers from the opposing companies stood forward to shake hands with friends and relatives, saying goodbye in a kindly way. These were men who knew each other from childhood. For all they knew, the next time they met they would be trying to kill one another.[59]

When the Harrison Rifles marched out of Clarksburg they passed a crowd that was gathered at the Walker House, at the corner of Second and Pike Streets. One observer wrote that the secessionists departed with, "No loud hurrahs nor waving of flags... some quiet good byes were said between those leaving and those remaining, and as they crossed Elk Bridge and rounded the bend in the street near the Catholic Church they were lost to sight. Very few of them ever saw their native town again."[60]

The Harrison Rifles marched as far as Bridgeport, a few miles away, where they paused briefly at the home of former governor Joseph Johnson to hear another political speech. From there, the company marched eastward, and arrived that evening at the town of Fetterman, where they joined the Marion Guards, and Letcher Guards in defending the railroad.[61]

By then, Colonel Porterfield had enough men to attempt a reconnaissance in force of the town of Grafton. There they met the mob of loyal Unionists, the hearty workmen of the B&O machine shops and fabrication yards. "We had about 250 in line," Private Cammack reported. "As we were moving into the west end of town we heard a tremendous noise of shouting which we thought was joy at our coming. It was not. Nearly the whole population was out on the streets, but they were not cheering. They were shouting and cursing and abusing us dreadfully. There were about 30 men on horseback, who followed immediately behind the infantry as we entered town...."

A scuffle ensued, and a chair was thrown at the men from a rooftop, but no one fired their weapons, and no serious harm was done. Maj. Boykin, in particular, was subjected to a great deal of abuse in the fracas, perhaps because he was better known in the county after his attempts at recruiting. As one of the few experienced officers, he probably also tried to control the situation by placing himself between his volunteers and the local, Irish toughs.

Porterfield's three companies eventually made their way through the scuffle to the railroad hotel and were formed in line on the platform. Cammack said they had about one officer for every six men, and none of the officers wanted the men to fire their weapons. "I think that was about the longest hour I ever spent," he later wrote.[62]

Grafton's citizens remained in the street calling the Confederates names. At the end of the day, Porterfield ordered the men back to Fetterman, and positioned sentries to guard the railroad bridge. In addition, sentries were placed for the night on the old bridge over the Tygart's Valley River. That night after dark, a member of a local Union company, Bailey Brown, was shot and killed by a Confederate picket guard at the bridge. John Cammack commented: "History began to make very rapidly after this."[63]

Porterfield had been promised a wagon train of supplies, muskets, and additional troops to arm his men. That wagon train departed Monterey in Highland County's mountains several days earlier. The wagons had to cross several mountains, including Allegheny Mountain that rose to 4000 feet and whose road was passable, but slow going for heavily laden wagons. These reinforcements arrived at Pruntytown on the 24th, at around 11 A.M. They included the Highland Sharpshooters, a company of infantry from Highland County commanded by Capt. Felix H. Hull, a middle-aged, successful, merchant-farmer. J. W. Myers was 1st lieutenant; Samuel A. Gilmore, 2nd lieutenant; and Jessie

Gilmore, 3rd lieutenant. Numbering about 200 men, they were later split into two companies in the 31st Virginia, Company E, and Company E#2.[64]

With them were a Pendleton County company called the Pendleton Volunteers, commanded by Capt. David C. Anderson. When the regiment was formed they were designated Company B, but their service in the 31st Virginia was destined to be troublesome, and by the spring of next year, they would transfer to another regiment.[65]

Pendleton and Highland were border mountain counties. Most of their residents supported the Southern cause, yet as with other border counties, both counties also had men who remained loyal to the Union. In light of those mixed loyalties, the Pendleton County Court took a bold step on May 10 when the county justices declared that the secession of Virginia meant they no longer were bound by the U.S. Constitution: they took an oath to support the Confederate States of America, then passed a resolution providing funds for outfitting their local Virginia volunteers.[66]

Hull and Anderson's companies departed Monterey with the wagon train. Capt. Robert Moorman, from Pendleton County, brought part of a second company with him. Helping to guard the wagon train, the Churchville Cavalry from Augusta County rode with the marching men. Heading westward on the Staunton to Parkersburg Pike, the men marched over Monterey Mountain to Hightown, a sparsely settled community in a high, mountain valley. At this scenic place, amid vivid green pastures overshadowed by steeper mountains to the west, they were given patriotic speeches by yet more politicians, according to one of the Highland County men, Osborne Wilson. "Immense cheering, waving of hats, and handkerchiefs," Wilson wrote later. From there, they crossed Lantz Mountain and marched to the top of Allegheny Mountain and stopped at the Wilfong house, where they heard more bombast by politicians.

Crossing over Allegheny Mountain, the men marched on to Traveler's Repose near the Greenbrier River where the wagon train stopped for the night. They proceeded to Huttonsville the next day and reached Beverly, in Randolph County, about one o'clock in the afternoon on May 21. "Ladies at most of the residences greet us with smiles and handkerchiefs," Osborne Wilson commented, obviously enjoying the kind attention of the fairer sex.[67]

At Beverly, Lt. Joseph H. Chenoweth had been waiting anxiously for the means to fight. Chenoweth would later serve as major of the 31st Virginia, after the reorganization of 1862, and gain distinction in the battles that June. For now, he was assisting the state in arming and organizing the volunteer companies, and was helping the county officials prepare for the May 23 special vote on secession. He was convinced the war would follow the secession vote.[68]

Chenoweth was a graduate of VMI in the class of 1859. After graduation from the state military school, Chenoweth gained an appointment as assistant professor at VMI. He taught mathematics and served as assistant artillery instructor there from 1859, but the following year accepted a position as professor of mathematics at Maryland Agricultural College. A sensitive young man, Chenoweth was uncomfortable in the civilian school, and resigned sometime after February 1861. He next received a commission as a lieutenant in the Provisional Army and was ordered to help with preparation for war in his home county.[69]

The ratification of Virginia's secession was an event of great importance. Chenoweth reported the local returns from the polls to his former mentor, Col. Francis H. Smith, the superintendent of VMI. Smith had been appointed by the governor to a small committee of advisors on the formation of Virginia's army.

"I am much fatigued after the day's work," Chenoweth wrote, "but I feel it my duty to send you the results of the election in this county, so far as heard from." Randolph County would support secession. "So will Tucker County, and Barbour," Chenoweth predicted. "Upshur will vote against." Chenoweth continued with a report on the military situation, including news of the wagon train and soldiers from Augusta, Highland, and Pendleton counties. Chenoweth said, "A great revolution was effected on the political feelings of the people in this and neighboring counties by the passage of our troops through here."[70]

The popular vote to ratify Virginia's secession passed overwhelmingly on the 23rd, and the nation was poised on the brink of war as the wagon train of supplies arrived with reinforcements for Porterfield at Grafton. Assigned the task of stopping an invasion, Colonel Porterfield was still assembling a scratch force of untrained, and untried men.

Reaching Pruntytown on the 24th with the Highland Sharpshooters, Osborne Wilson said that several of the men were complaining of fatigue as they formed ranks in front of the courthouse and sang "Dixie." The ever-present patriotic speeches followed before the company was divided into squads of 15 men, and were given dinner at the homes of local secessionists. Then the company was formed and marched to Fetterman, where the men were quartered overnight in a church.[71]

The next day, Porterfield formed his companies and marched them into Grafton, where they were once more met by a disorderly mob of outraged citizens. Altogether, the colonel had four infantry, and one cavalry companies when he entered the railroad town. Muskets had been issued to all of his men, though most of the weapons were old and barely functional. Still, it was a force equal to the task of intimidating the locals into withdrawing into their homes without bloodshed.

Porterfield was not comfortable with the tactical position. He reported to Gen. Lee, "The force now here is undisciplined, and I am greatly in need of officers acquainted with their duties. I have but two or three officers at all acquainted with their duty, and these can effect but little upon a mass of militia.... The cavalry companies require pistols or rifles. So far as the defense of this place is concerned, cavalry is useless. It can act effectively only in patrolling the county." He said that two of the cavalry companies were still without arms: he could equip them as infantry, or order them to return to their homes. Porterfield added to his list of shortages, "I am much in need of cartridge-boxes and cap-boxes, and instructions for the commissary and quartermaster's departments."[72]

Grafton then had a population of about 1,000 citizens. The town had mostly been built along a steep hillside, on the north side of the Tygart's Valley River, at the entrance of Three Forks Creek. The geography of this steep river valley led to construction of buildings and streets in a very scattered manner, the houses dotted up the hill's incline with narrow streets terraced in front of them, barely clinging in place, and looking as though a good strong push would tumble houses and street into the river far below. The B&O's railroad machine shop, foundry, engine house, and rail yard occupied most of the flat land available next to the river.

At the main passenger platform was the station and hotel, called Grafton House. It was a first class hotel, according to commentary of the day, with gas-lit dining rooms, a gourmet menu, and comfortable rooms. Grafton House was the place of choice for many of the Confederate officers. Among others, Capt. Thompson of the Marion Guards stayed there when the Confederates invaded Grafton on the 25th. Tom Surghnor, former editor of Weston's secessionist newspaper, the *Barbour Jeffersonian*, was also at the hotel.[73]

A minister visiting Capt. Hull's company from their home county came to preach to the men, and to observe the exciting events. The Highland Sharpshooters were quartered in a private house opposite the engine factory. The men drew rations of rolls, corn cakes, and a little beef, and they cooked in the back yard, sharing their facility with the Churchville Cavalry. The two companies from Pendleton County were occupying the engine factory itself, as well as a storehouse, and another brick building. During the day, the companies practiced drill, and the men were detailed for guard duty, and all the while waited for something of importance to happen. The local telegraph office was under guard, and civilian use of the telegraph had been cut off.[74]

Hoping for some assistance from the much better prepared, and equipped Virginia force at Harper's Ferry, Porterfield sent his adjutant, Lt. Gittings, to carry a message to Gen. Joseph E. Johnston. Gen. Johnston's force was already well organized, trained, and equipped with the contents of the Harper's Ferry armory. If sufficiently motivated, General Johnson could have sent a trainload of troops, weapons, and ammunition under Col. Thomas J. Jackson to assist Porterfield's force, a movement that would have taken less than a day with the aid of the railroad. Jackson had already suggested this, but had been rebuffed by the new commander at Harper's Ferry. Instead, Johnston chose to keep his men and material close to his own position, leaving Grafton unsupported in the face of what would be strongly armed and organized troops from Ohio.

Deflated, Adjutant Gittings took this opportunity to pay a call on his cousin, Col. "Tom" Jackson. Jackson was teaching at VMI prior to the secession crisis. Caught up on each other's familoy news, Gittings caught the train back to Grafton with the sorry news that Porterfield could look for little aid from Gen. Johnsons's force at Harper's Ferry.[75]

Military use of the railroad was of such importance that Porterfield was under orders to deny it to the North, even through sabotage if he found he could not protect it with his own force. When he received reports from sympathizers at Wheeling that the Union army was about to launch their invasion, he sent several men out to the west to burn key railroad bridges. The B&O was still running trains at this crucial time, for both the garrison at Harper's Ferry and at Grafton had been ordered to allow the railroad to operate between Baltimore and Wheeling.

Late in the evening of the 25th, William J. Willey, accompanied by newspaper editor Thom Surghnor and two others, rode a train on the main B&O line, bound for the railroad's terminus at the Ohio River. They jumped from the train about 36 miles west of Grafton and proceeded to set fire to two small bridges over Buffalo Creek, a few miles from Mannington. Then they made their way back toward Grafton.[76]

In addition to these bridges, situated between Farmington and Mannington on the B&O, Porterfield dispatched men westward on the Parkersburg line to burn bridges 50 and 60 miles from Grafton. A third bridge about 15 miles from Grafton was only partially burned: the railroad's workmen repaired it the next day.[77]

Meanwhile, in Grafton some of the civilians were evacuating, especially the town's families. Soldiers were tense, and wild rumors were passing through the ranks. Osborne Wilson wrote, on the 26th, "A rumor is out that we are to burn Grafton and murder the Union families, utterly unfounded. We momentarily expect troops from Ohio and other northern points to attack us. We mean to defend ourselves and sell our lives as dearly as possible."[78]

The Union army's invasion of northwestern Virginia began when Gen. George McClellan sent several Ohio volunteer regiments over the Ohio River on May 26, 1861. It was one of the first rapid deployments of troops by railroad in the Civil War. At the same time, other Union regiments already at Wheeling and Parkersburg were ordered by telegraph to move eastward on the railroad to protect the track and bridges from destruction.[79]

Colonel Benjamin F. Kelley commanded the First Virginia Infantry, a Union regiment formed in western Virginia. When Kelley started toward Grafton with his own regiment, he brought with him several companies from the Second Virginia Volunteers, also troops loyal to the federal government. Part of the Sixteenth Ohio Regiment joined Kelley's forces as they approached Grafton on the main B&O line. The rest of the Sixteenth Ohio regiment, as well as the Fourteenth Ohio, were moving via the Northwestern Virginia Railroad from Parkersburg, but were delayed by the burned bridges.

Gen. McClellan issued a proclamation to the people of western Virginia. "I have ordered troops to cross the river," McClellan wrote. "They come as your friends and brothers — as enemies only of the armed rebels that are preying upon you." The Ohio soldiers had been told that they could go home as soon as the Union men of northwestern Virginia were organized into an army. Their most advanced units, under Colonel Kelley, arrived at the burned bridges near Mannington on May 27. Mannington was about 30 miles by rail from Grafton — a couple of hours travel by locomotive.[80]

In Grafton, Colonel Porterfield received reports of the Union army's advance with a feeling of resignation that there was little he could do to stop the invasion. He sent a telegraph to Harper's Ferry, urgently seeking reinforcements, but the reply from Gen. Joseph Johnston was, as before, negative.[81]

The men in Porterfield's army were issued cartridges that day, and told to prepare themselves for an attack. They waited through the night, expectant of battle, but learned the following morning that the Union army had stopped to occupy Fairmont, in Marion County, just 20 miles away. Secessionists were being arrested by federal troops at Fairmont.[82]

"A report prevails among our men," Sergeant Wilson said in his diary, "that an overwhelming force is coming against us. The cavalry are on the scout all night, and at midnight we are ordered to prepare to retreat. Many of the men oppose it. Our company is excited and don't like to evacuate the place. We got our baggage ready, expecting to get orders to march immediately. We remain in the street before our barracks a long time, every moment expecting to start. All become impatient. At length, we march to the depot and remain on parade a long time."[83]

Fearing that his strength of about 550 infantry was not sufficient to hold Grafton, Porterfield decided to abandon this important point on the railroad and march south to Philippi, in Barbour County, taking with him the weapons and supplies. He reasoned that he should wait for reinforcements at a more easily-defensible place: he gave the order to withdraw and the infantry, cavalry, and their wagons started south toward the tiny hamlet of Webster.[84]

Lt. Gittings noted their commander's shortcomings. "I soon saw that Colonel Porterfield, though I believe personally brave, and very much of a gentleman, was not suited to have an independent command — he lacked will power — decision. An army officer, in time of war, must have an iron will." Gittings also commented that the early part of war was "the time to make a reputation."[85]

The men were scared and jumpy. As they marched beside the railroad tracks going south from Grafton, the sound of their own wagon train spooked the soldiers into thinking they heard a pursuing locomotive. "We were ordered to form in the timber and fire on them," Wilson observed. "We were all hoaxed, no enemy being near."[86]

Many of Porterfield's men were unhappy as they turned their backs on the invaders of their home state, and marched to Philippi. Others were relieved, for the Confederates in western Virginia were not yet ready for war.

2

LAUREL HILL
June 1861 — July 1861

The Provisional Army marched south; retreating over a road dwarfed by heavy forest, with enormous, old growth trees looming on either side. Occasionally, the soldiers passed isolated cabins in the woods, some half-hidden by climbing roses in full bloom. Their destination was Philippi, a small, Barbour County crossroads town amid high hills on the Tygart's Valley River. They would turn that town upside down by the time they were done with it.

There wasn't much to the place — a handful of houses, a hotel, a few stores, a couple of law offices, and a courthouse. An impressive covered bridge was built there in 1852, and a small store was operated at the east end of the covered bridge, with a tollgate, and a bridge keeper who slept in the store at night.[87]

Confederate sympathizers at Philippi had proclaimed their allegiance to the southern cause as early as the beginning of the year, when the Palmetto flag, symbol of South Carolina's defiance against Fort Sumter was raised over the courthouse. Here, the Unionists were less organized, and the secessionists more aggressive.[88]

The local company of Confederate volunteers called themselves the Barbour Greys. They were under the leadership of Capt. Albert G. Reger. A lawyer, Reger had served as a state senator for the Randolph and Barbour County district in 1850, and again in 1856. The company of volunteers enlisted on May 16, 1861 at the county courthouse, although they gathered unofficially as early as April 30. Second in command was Lt. Thomas A. Bradford, also a lawyer, and an active secessionist. The Barbour Greys would soon form the nucleus of Company H, 31st Virginia.[89]

The Barbour Greys had joined the wagon train of arms at Beverly, and accompanied it to Grafton. Now they were headed back to Philippi and their own county. "We suffered considerably... from the walk, and the want of food," one of Reger's men, private James Hall, commented about their march to Grafton. Hall was a 20-year-old former student from the Monongalia Academy in Morgantown. He had returned home to his father's farm near Philippi before enlisting. Hall's great ambition the first year of the war was to serve as an officer.[90]

Another of the men in the company was John A. Campbell. Also 20, Campbell had been apprenticed when he was 15 years old to Thomas P. Surghnor, Philippi's editor and publisher of the Barbour *Jeffersonian* newspaper. "The Philippi papers was the only one in all that section," Campbell recalled after the war. "Had a circulation of between 600 and 700, and was printed on a hand press. It took an entire day to run off the edition."[91]

In May, Campbell went directly from the print shop to the army, and welcomed the change. At the print shop, Surghnor provided him with board, clothing, and a little spending money, and while the former apprentice thought well of the editor, he had learned enough of the printing trade to know it was not what he wanted to do for a life's work.

The *Jeffersonian* strongly advocated the Southern cause. In March, the Editor had railed against the Unionist element attending the Virginia Convention in Richmond, and leveled this challenge, "The question now is where shall Virginia go? Shall she go to the North and be ruled by the pharisaical folly that has perverted one of the best systems of government, or shall she go with the South as her coequal and where she will be honored and loved?"[92]

Barbour County contributed more than one company to the 31st Virginia. The second company was known as the Mountain Guards, and was organized by lawyer Henry Sturm on May 18, at the small town of Meadowville. Set in the very rural, eastern part of the county, Meadowville, Nestorville, and Valley Furnace contributed most of the men in Sturm's company. They were nearly all farmers, with a few men from the local iron furnaces, and a few crafts and tradesmen. The Mountain Guards marched to Philippi and were mustered on May 21. Nathaniel Poling was 1st lieutenant; Jacob Hill, 2nd lieutenant; and Jacob Bennett, orderly sergeant.[93]

Henry Sturm was an old-fashioned type of individual, and a veteran of the war of 1812. While experienced as a soldier, he was not a trained officer, and did not pretend to be anything more than he was, an aging country lawyer who wore spectacles and carried a musket, powder horn, and shot pouch. At least one other in the company also carried some age — George Gainer was 62 years old when he joined as fife major. He was another veteran of past wars.

One of the younger men was John Riley Phillips, from a farm near Brushy Creek, a tiny hamlet not far from Valley Furnace. The iron foundry there gave the valley town its name, and it brought a fair amount of capital to the local economy. Many who worked in the foundry, and in the coal and ore mines, had earned enough money to buy their own farms, and have enough money to operate them successfully.[94]

Phillips was 22 years old in 1861, and had worked a variety of jobs in addition to helping on the family farm. He was a bricklayer when the courthouse at St. George was being built, and just before enlistment, was teaching school. "All the reading that I had done," Phillips wrote after the war, "was conducive to the idea that the states had all the sovereignty and that the union was but a creation of their construction. The states had a right to withdraw from that union when the compact was broken."

He took pride in being a Virginian. "My soul, my manhood were all wrapped up in my patriotism for the dear old state... I shouldered my rifle and hurried into her camp and offered myself as a volunteer." But he was dismayed to find how poorly organized, and equipped the army was. "Soon after our arrival at Philippi," Phillips recalled, "troops came in from Highland, Hardy, Randolph and Pocahontas. We were armed with old heavy rifles, rusted and out of order, guns that were useless. The most of the troops had old antiquated muskets. The locks had been changed from flintlock to cap lock — old guns from the factories of sixty years previous.... There were not ten guns in our company that would fire. We had not a single cartridge among us."[95]

Colonel Porterfield had only about a thousand cartridges on hand for the muskets that did work, but the percussion caps that had been sent were too small for the heavy muskets. His army at this time consisted of 9 companies of infantry, and 5 small companies of cavalry, totaling 775 men. He had sent home a company from Upshur County, as well as a third volunteer company of infantry from Barbour County, and also a cavalry company from Pocahontas, all because there were so few weapons, ammunition, and other material necessary to equip them.[96]

"Philippi was a pandemonium," Phillips commented. "No order, our drill foolishness. The whole thing a holiday, full of disorder, uproar, speeches and intense excitement. All kinds of rumors afloat. The imagination wrought up until the truth was too tame to be believed or readily exchanged for any kind of a highly colored falsehood.... Captains of the companies went when they pleased and returned when they pleased. The officers that could afford it stayed at the hotel. The troops occupied such shelters as could be obtained."[97]

The men were not always privy to the reasons behind their orders. Osborne Wilson in the Highland Sharpshooters observed the confusion in his company: "Go on parade under Sergeant Patterson for some duty not known to us," he wrote. "Sergeant Patterson is not well, and Corporal Ervin takes his place. After standing on parade in the sun, we are marched to the bridge, where the dust nearly suffocates us. Fifteen men were taken from all the companies as guards. We remain a short time.... Through some mistake of the officers we were marched over the river, and then back again. Our squad is marched and placed north of town as sentinels."

The courthouse grounds were used to drill squads and companies, while the cavalry from Rockbridge and Churchville patrolled the edge of town, or went out on scout duty. Sentinels were posted in the woods and hills around the town on picket duty. Others were posted at the courthouse, to guard headquarters.[98]

On the afternoon of Sunday, June 2, Colonel Porterfield received a warning that the Union army would attack Philippi within the next 24 hours. Once again, he chose to withdraw his small force, this time to the town of Beverly, about 30 miles to the south. He planned to use hired and impressed horses and wagons to carry the baggage and supplies, and he ordered the wagon train to be prepared to leave at midnight.

The rain was coming down in torrents that night, and visibility was very poor. The mounted scouts returned to town at eleven o'clock, in order to be ready for the midnight departure from Philippi. The picket guards had also returned to town by then, their ammunition soaking wet and useless because they had been carrying it in their pockets. No one had relieved them, and upon return to town they failed to inform Colonel Porterfield that the roads around Philippi were without guards. The wagons that had been loaded earlier in preparation for departure still sat there in the pouring rain, without the horses attached, and no one in evidence to get the wagon train on the move at midnight.[99]

Meanwhile, the Federal army was approaching from two directions, their progress concealed by darkness and rain. One force, under Col. Ebenezer Dumont, arrived on the road from Webster. The second force, under Col. Benjamin F. Kelley, was given the task of blocking the road that led to Beverly. The rain slowed his movement and his men did not arrive in time to block the Beverly Pike, an important exit from town.[100]

The Union artillery opened fire prematurely that morning, from two 6-pounder guns placed on an eminence overlooking the Confederate camp. Lt. Chenoweth, acting as an assistant to Colonel Porterfield, later reported the Confederates were completely surprised. "I was asleep myself," Chenoweth wrote, "taking rest after being up nearly all of the forefront of the night, when the enemy commenced cannonading, but the first discharges awakened me, and I went immediately to Colonel Porterfield's apartments and informed him that our foe was upon us with artillery. I found him putting on his pants. He ordered me to have the companies ordered from their quarters."[101]

With the commencement of the artillery, the Union army began to enter town. The heavy gunfire scared many of the Confederates as cannon balls knocked down tents, frightened horses, and generally created the right atmosphere for panic. After dressing hastily, Colonel

Porterfield mounted his horse and rode out, trying to assess the situation.

Porterfield wrote, "Whilst on the main street, I observed a company in blue uniform — a Union company — standing in line at the north end of the street, which I mistook for one of my own companies, having a similar uniform, and I rode down sufficiently near it to discover my mistake, when I turned and rode slowly away to avoid being recognized. Upon my return I was joined by Robert Johnston, Esq., of Clarksburg, acting adjutant, formerly Auditor of Virginia; and we were not discovered and fired upon until near the southern end of the street. We were the last of the command to leave the town."

The Union commander, Colonel Kelley was wounded as he was about to enter town. Capt. Hull's company, the Highland Sharpshooters, had formed a line in the orchard behind the school. As the Union officer approached on his horse, one of Hull's privates took aim and fired, bringing Kelley out of the saddle. This created a diversion that allowed the Confederates to retreat without pursuit for some moments. His officers carried the Union commander into one of the houses.[102]

Several of Porterfield's companies acted as rear-guard, including the Harrison Rifles, Marion Guards, and Pendleton Minutemen. A mile and half out of town, at a curve in the road near Henry Sturm's house, these companies made a stand and gave their pursuing enemy a volley of musketry. Lt. Thompson of the Marion Guards was mentioned in reports for his coolness as he formed his men in line and ordered them to fire.[103]

"We retreated in tolerably good order," Joseph Chenoweth claimed in his report, "considering the fact that our cavalry acted in such a manner as to inspire the infantry with a certain degree of terror. Our confusion was remedied before we had marched very far."[104]

The Franklin Guards and the Highland Sharpshooters had taken to the woods beside the road to ambush the approaching Federals. When they failed to appear, they made their way cross-country. "Capt. Hull ordered us to flank," Osborne Wilson wrote. "We flew to the timber intending to fire as they advanced, but they did not, and we continued silently to march through the woods for a long time. We had scouts out all the time. We got guides to show us the way."

The two companies marched together to Cheat River, and eventually arrived at Monterey on June 8, after six days of hardship and adventure, walking most of the way, and nearly broken down with fatigue. They had no provisions, but were able to stop at houses and ask for food. They used a church for a sanctuary one night, the men exhausted from rough marching on slim rations. They had no blankets to ward off the chill of the night. This was good practice for later on, when they would again cross the mountains with the Federals chasing on their heels.[105]

In Philippi, not long after the battle, Union soldiers raided Thompson Surghnor's newspaper offices. They broke up the press, and dumped the type down a well. Surghnor had retreated with the Confederates as they withdrew from the town. He was later enlisted in the Harrison Rifles by his friend, and fellow newspaperman, William Cooper, but was destined to die in a skirmish within the month.

Union troops also raided the Bank of Philippi, but the funds and other valuables had already been moved to Beverly. The soldiers blasted open the bank safe, but their only reward was the actual experience of blowing off the door.[106]

Casualties in the fight at Philippi were light in total, but heavy for two cavalrymen who suffered them. Colonel Porterfield recorded their material losses: "We lost our baggage, a few boxes of old rusty flintlock rifles and muskets, two kegs of powder and some lead — all the ordnance stores we had. We had neither medical, commissary's nor quartermaster's stores, except the tents of one cavalry company, the only company with the command which had tents. Our subsistence was procured from the surrounding country as needed, and our transportation was by hired or impressed teams."[107]

Most of Porterfield's army retreated on the road to Beverly. They stopped there long enough to refresh themselves with a meal at a tavern. "We were all beastly hungry," John Cammack wrote. "I remember we stood behind the chairs waiting for the men who were eating to get up." From there, the army marched on to Huttonsville, arriving at the foot of Cheat Mountain on June 6.[108]

Along the way, Capt. Currence's Company from Randolph County joined the retreating army. Capt. Jacob Currence was town constable of Huttonsville, a mountain community situated near the southern border of Randolph County. When his men were mustered into the regiment, Currence's Company became Company F of the 31st Virginia. The 33 year-old headmaster of the Huttonsville Academy, Jacob I. Hill, was 1st lieutenant. George W. Salisbury, also 33, was 2nd lieutenant. Enlisted in the company on May 24 were a number of former students from the school, including Joseph F. Harding, a 23-year-old lawyer; Oliver Hazard Perry Lewis, age 24; and Dudley Long, age 23. All three of these men eventually became officers, and Harding would later serve as captain.[109]

Other volunteer companies were even then hurrying to join Porterfield's command at Huttonsville, including the Pocahontas County Mountain Rifles, from one of the most rural and mountainous counties in the state. Capt. James C. Arbogast commanded the company. He was bachelor-farmer living on his mother's farm at Arbovale, near Green Bank in the spring of 1861. At 24, Arbogast was probably as well known then in Pocahontas as anyone could be. The Arbogast's were a large, established family in the Greenbrier Valley, related by blood to half the county; related by marriage to the rest.[110]

Feelings about the war were pretty clear in Pocahontas County, where voters responded in the special election with 360 in favor of Virginia's secession, and 13 against. County resident William H. Hull recalled, "By far the larger portion of our people were not original secessionists, but when coercion was threatened they cast in their lot with the South."[111]

The Pocahontas County court, on May 11, 1861 established a levy to pay for arms and equipment for local volunteer companies. The court set aside $15,000 to be used for equipping the volunteers, though some of the money was also designated to assist poor families whose men had gone to fight, or were killed, or disabled. Relief agents were appointed to administer those funds.[112]

Two companies were raised, one from the southern end of the county which later went into the 25th Virginia, and one from the northern end which went into the 31st Virginia. That company called itself the Mountain Rifles, and was enlisted on May 29 by Capt. Arbogast. George W. Siple was 1st lieutenant; James F. Gum, 2nd lieutenant; and Charles B. Ruckman, 1st sergeant. The privates in the company were mostly farmers.[113]

In previous centuries, Pocahontas County was a favorite hunting ground of the Shawnee. Buffalo were said to have ranged the mountaintops then, and elk were common. Panther stalked the great forests, and timber wolves numbered in the thousands. By 1861, buffalo and elk were long departed, and wolves and panther nearly so. Black bear, wild turkey, and whitetail deer continued in abundance, and the local woodsmen stalked all.

Farmers in Pocahontas County had all they could do to get their crops planted in the spring of 1861. They knew they would be called on to serve in the coming war, and they toiled long hours while they had a chance to get their fields ready, and the crop planted. Otherwise, the families might have nothing to live on while the men were away.[114]

When word finally came from the governor for the Mountain Rifles to join the Confederate army, Capt. Arbogast marched his company out of Green Bank. Their road took them northward, through a lovely green valley along the Greenbrier River. This was comparatively tame and productive land, good for cattle grazing, and was capable of some small amount of grain farming. Nearly all of the crops were intended for local mills and consumption. Their beef cattle were raised for sale in Staunton after driving the unlucky beasts in herds across the mountain on the Staunton to Parkersburg Pike. That road was the major link with the outside world, as there were no railroads in the county.

On June 2, the Mountain Rifles marched north to gain the turnpike, which they would take across Cheat Mountain to Huttonsville. They were accompanied by a small group of local militia. "Our music," William Hull reminisced later, "consisted of an old kettle drum, that had been used by the militia, and a fife. George R. Gum beat the drum, and Charles Phillips played the fife. At this stage of our experience we did most of our marching with our right foot. The left foot was carried along as a kind of silent partner. The right foot was raised up about as high as we could conveniently get it, and when we all came down together, which was not very often, it made quite a concussion. In order to get us together, in addition to the music, the officers "hepped" us a good portion of the time." The musicians played "Bonaparte Crossing the Alps", "Black Hawks March", and "Yankee Doodle."[115]

Much of the county then was heavy with forests draped over mountains; the woods filled with hardwood of chestnut, oak, hickory, ash, maple, poplar, birch, locust, and elm. Conifers included hemlock, pine, red cedar, and spruce. Abundant small shrubs such as dogwood, redbud, holly, and sassafras grew in harmony with the larger trees. Thickets of laurel were legendary for creating stands impossible to pass through.[116]

At one place along the road, the volunteers stopped to peel the bark from young elm trees, and the men "licked the succulent sap" as they walked. As William Hull recorded, they were enjoying themselves, "And what was the need of putting on airs away out there in the mountain where there was no one to look at us?"

The Pocahontas Mountain Rifles proceeded to Huttonsville, where they were mustered into the Provisional Army. When the 31st Virginia was formed, they became Company G and served the regiment for the duration of the war.[117]

To the west of Pocahontas County, residents of Gilmer County were deep in the oil craze that spring. Situated within the Little Kanawha River watershed, Gilmer County became a place of deep political division when the war came. Nearly half of the citizens sided with the Confederacy, the other half going with the Union: this created vicious discord in the citizenry. Partisan rangers and bushwhackers preyed on those who remained in the county, regardless of their political affiliation. Though not a populous county, it contributed nearly 700 men to both sides of the conflict. It has been claimed that bushwhacking was so dangerous in Gilmer County during the war that men joined the army to be safe.[118]

The county's gently rolling hills provided good pastures for cattle, while the bottom land's rich loam was excellent for growing crops. Thick forests underlain by bituminous coal, gas, and oil fields below the northern part of the county, though in 1861 those resources were mostly yet to be tapped. The county seat of Glenville was located at a ford over the Little Kanawha River, on the state road that ran from Weston to Charleston. Glenville was a relatively new town. Laid out in 1845, it nestled down in a valley, or glen, 53 miles from Clarksburg. [119]

The Gilmer Rifles were formed in Glenville on May 31: they would later become Company D of the 31st Virginia. Christian G. Kuhl, a 21-year-old farmer from Braxton County, along with his younger brother

John, were among those enlisted that day. They were sons of German immigrants who arrived in Baltimore in 1838. The family had lived in Weston a few years before moving to Braxton County, where they set to farming.

It was a family divided in its politics. Other than Chris, two Kuhl brothers eventually enlisted in the Union army, and a fourth brother was sent to Fort Delaware as a secessionist sympathizer. Their father was destined to die as direct result of the war.[120]

"There arose a cry," Kuhl later recalled, "the abolitionists are coming over from Ohio... overrunning our country, destroying property, compelling our men to enlist, taking horses, cattle, arms, ammunition, and insulting mothers and wives where the men had fled or refugeed.... We supposed their object to be the abolishing of slavery in Virginia and the rest of the south, which supposition proved itself true later on."[121]

They elected Reverend John Elam Mitchell as captain; Hezekiah McNemar, 1st lieutenant; and Samuel S. Stout, 2nd lieutenant. Rev. Mitchell was an eccentric man, an itinerant preacher noted for roaming the county on horseback, spreading the gospel of the Methodist Protestant Church to all who would listen in the Gilmer Circuit. He felt keenly about the secession question, which put him at odds with most of his fellow Methodist Protestant Church clergy: the M. P. Church was pro-abolition, anti-slavery, and anti-secession as well.

Mitchell mustered his company of volunteers, the Gilmer Rifles, at Glenville on May 31, and was said to thereafter wear a stovepipe hat, and a long, formal black frock coat as he put the company through drill. When the war started, he assembled sixty men for the company, along with all of the arms and ammunition they could find. Most of the weapons were squirrel rifles, but they also had a couple of unpredictable revolvers, and a few knives between them when they departed Glenville and marched eastward toward Stouts Mill.

The scene there remained with Chris Kuhl for life. "Many friends were at the way side to get the last glimpse of sons, husbands, fathers, and brothers, which was very affecting, but one case especially so. Mr. William Conrad, from Dust Camp, a middle aged man and an invalid, who had not been able to do any work for years, my near neighbor, had joined our company, ill as he was, and was marching along in ranks with rifle on shoulder. His wife, a mother of some six children — a very poor family — she grasped him around the neck — hung on as though she could not forbore, saying he could not, and must not go. But he was so intent that he dragged her for rods along in spite of her ponderous weight and his infirmity. He at last struck her off and went along all the same. This was heart rending. I heard several remark, 'He'll never get back again' and so I thought — and so it was."[122]

The Gilmer Rifles crossed into Braxton County that day, following the Little Kanawha River. That night they were at Skin Creek, in Lewis

County, where the company camped for the night. The next morning, the company joined forces with Capt. Alfred Jackson's company, the Lewis Rangers. From Skin Creek, the two companies marched into Randolph County, toward Beverly. Hearing of the rout of Porterfield at Philippi, they changed direction and proceeded to Huttonsville, in Randolph County, where they were mustered into the Provisional Army.[123]

Randolph County was the largest county in western Virginia, and was full of mountains. Anchoring the eastern side of the county is Rich Mountain, with a peak of 4275 feet. Going west from there, the next mountain is Middle Mountain (3200 feet), then Shavers Mountain (3600 feet), Cheat Mountain (4600 feet), and just to be confusing to everyone from outside of the county, another Rich Mountain (3660 feet). At the north end of this, more famous Rich Mountain is the Buckhannon Gap, followed by Laurel Hill, on the south end of Laurel Mountain. Surrounding the edges of the county are Middle Mountain, McGowan Mountain, Bickle Knob, Blue Rock Knob, Back Fork Mountain, Point Mountain, Elk Mountain, and the northern end of Back Allegheny Mountain. Between the major lines of mountains are several rivers, including the Elk, Tygart's Valley, Buckhannon, Middle Fork, and Cheat.[124]

Roads through the county meandered around and over the landscape, following river valleys, climbing through steep mountain passes, and running the gaps. Rivers or streams were generally crossed at fords where it was sometimes possible to drive a wagon through the stream of flowing water. For an army, churning up ruts as it went, those fords were never quick passages.

Huttonsville, near the southern end of the county, and in the midst of this geographic splendor, was a small town turned active by the arrival of the Provisional Army of Virginia. New volunteer companies were arriving daily; as were individuals who had made their escape from within the Union held areas of northwest Virginia.

Judge Jackson arrived at Porterfield's camp on June 9, and enlisted as a private. He was a man of great bearing and presence, six feet tall, and weighing around two hundred pounds. "He had unusually fine shoulders, head and face," one observer commented, "and was the most animated man that I had ever seen in conversation. His hair and whiskers were the deepest red that I had ever seen on the head and face of any man"[125]

Jackson still considered himself the only judge legally elected to serve the Nineteenth Circuit Court, and many of the men in camp continued to call him "Judge." Soon after his arrival at Porterfield's camp, he was appointed lieutenant colonel in the Provisional Army. "He has been very active, and will become a most useful officer," Colonel Porterfield reported to Gen. Garnett two days later.[126]

Other men, such as Joseph C. Snider arrived in small groups. A 22-year-old deputy sheriff from Harrison County, Snider had been under pressure in his home county to sign an oath declaring loyalty to the Federal government. Loath to do so, he made a hasty exit from the county on June 5, and traveled toward Huttonsville. Snider may have been a few steps ahead of a posse when he escaped town with only three hours notice.

Escaping in the company of two friends from home, Snider crossed Turkey Run on the southern border of Harrison County at around noon on the fifth, progressed to Lost Creek, and then spent the night outside of Buckhannon. On the way, suspicious citizens on the lookout detained the three men for secessionists trying to make their way south, but Snider and his friends talked their way out of the situation by claiming to be cattle merchants. They arrived at Huttonsville the following evening about sundown and enlisted in the Harrison Rifles.[127]

Brig. Gen. Robert S. Garnett had been given orders to take command of the forces in western Virginia, and was then on his way from Richmond to Randolph County. Garnett was 42 years old, and a graduate of West Point in the class of 1841. A veteran of the Mexican War, he had resigned his commission as major in the U.S. Army at the end of April 1861. Until posted to command the Provisional Army in western Virginia, Garnett was Adjutant General of Virginia Forces.[128]

Gen. Garnett arrived at Huttonsville on June 14, a day ahead of reinforcements in the form of 3 militia companies drawn from the counties of Pendleton, Highland, and Bath. He had a total of 23 companies on hand, mostly mustered into service, "In a miserable condition as to arms, clothing, equipment, instruction, and discipline," he reported to Gen. Lee.[129]

On June 15, Garnett chose 20 companies and formed them into 2 regiments of infantry: one was numbered the 25th Virginia, and the other the 31st Virginia. They were "sister" regiments, since most of the volunteers were drawn from within the same part of the state. Lt. Col. Jonathan M. Heck was placed in command of the 25th Virginia Regiment. Lt. Col. William L. Jackson was assigned command of the 31st Virginia Regiment.[130]

COMPANIES IN THE 31ST VIRGINIA
Company A: Marion Guards, Marion County, Capt. William P. Thompson
Company B: Pendleton Minutemen, Pendleton County, Capt. David Anderson
Company C: Harrison Rifles, Harrison County, Capt. Uriel M. Turner
Company D: Gilmer Rifles, Gilmer County, Capt. John E. Mitchell
Company E: Highland Sharpshooters, Highland County, Capt. Felix H. Hull
Company F: Currence's Company, Randolph County, Capt. Jacob Currence
Company G: Mountain Rifles, Pocahontas County, Capt. James C. Arbogast
Company H: Barbour Greys, Barbour County, Capt. Thomas A. Bradford
Company I: Lewis Rangers, Lewis County, Capt. Alfred H. Jackson
Company K: Mountain Guards, Barbour County, Capt. Henry Sturm

The 31st Virginia marched most of the night of June 15 to the Laurel Hill pass, 17 miles northwest of Beverly, where they arrived after noon on the 16th. Gen. Garnett came with them, along with part of Capt. Rice's battery of artillery. Meanwhile, the 25th Virginia Infantry, with the other section of Rice's artillery, was placed at the Buckhannon Pass of Rich Mountain.

The Union army was then holding Philippi and Buckhannon, the latter town with a small force. The Laurel Hill position, occupied by the 31st Virginia, was intended by Garnett to prevent the enemy from advancing from Philippi. The Rich Mountain position would guard the approach from Buckhannon. Garnett ordered work parties out along the road toward the northwest, where the men began to fell large trees, dropping them across the roads in a blockade.[131]

Laurel Hill's summit is about 15 miles south of Philippi, and about 13 miles north of Beverly. The nearest town is Belington. The Confederate defenses at Laurel Hill faced northward, overlooking the road that ran along the west face of a steep hill, and then turned at a hollow to skirt another hillside. Garnett placed his batteries on a hill overlooking the road just before the turn, and set other batteries on the opposite hill to command the portion of road below the turn. He had the men dig lines of trenches on the hillsides at right angles to, and overlooking the road, with breastworks of logs and piled-up dirt facing a potential foe. Farther along the road, as a second defense, he established more trenches and breastworks in a kind of redoubt to be used for a second defense, in case they were driven from the first position.[132]

Forage parties were sent to collect grain for the army's horses, and beef cattle to feed the troops. The officers and men were drilling in earnest whenever not engaged in other work. Maj. Francis Boykin, assisted by lieutenants Joseph Chenoweth and William R. Lyman, drilled some of the 31st Virginia's companies.[133]

A native New Yorker with many southern connections, William Remsen Lyman was close to his 23rd birthday. He had attended school near Baltimore before entering Harvard College in 1860, but evidently felt strongly about the coming crisis. Lyman later said that he seceded from Harvard and enrolled in the University of Virginia in 1861. At the university he joined one of the student military companies which was ordered to Harper's Ferry in April 1861.

Not long after, Lyman entered VMI for a special, short course of instruction, and from there he volunteered in June 1861 to go to Gen. Garnet's army to act as a drill instructor for the troops. Attached to Garnett's staff with the rank of 2nd lieutenant, Lyman was assigned to the 31st Virginia. "It was entirely undrilled," Lyman wrote long after the war. "We had officer's drill early each morning, for the regimental and company officers, and later in the day, company and regimental drill. Many were the "cussings them little spike-tailed cadets" got as the men stumbled over stumps and rough ground at Laurel Hill."[134]

For most of the men, marching and drill as a squad or a company was not unknown, but their experience with it was limited. They knew how to shoot hunting rifles and shotguns, but hunting was different from what was expected in the army. For instance, hunters rarely loaded their guns in steps, by command, to then fire in a volley.

There was a blizzard of new terms for the men to learn, such as the definition of a *regiment*, a body of troops composed of ten or twelve companies. Each regiment had its own field officers, such as the *colonel*, who was in command of the regiment; the *lieutenant-colonel*, next in rank to the colonel; and the *major*, who was next in command. At this time the 31st Virginia did not have a colonel. W. L. Jackson was the lieutenant colonel; and Francis M. Boykin was major.

Each regiment also needed a *staff*, which included the *adjutant*, an officer who discharged the duties of detail of a regiment or military post, communicated orders, formed the battalion (or regiment) for drills and parades, mounted the guards, and in the maneuvers assisted the lieutenant-colonel. The adjutant also often served in the role of the inspector-general, whose duty it was to inspect the troops and report the state of their discipline, and efficiency. Capt. Albert Reger seems to have briefly functioned as an adjutant, but was soon transferred to the 25th Virginia Regiment. Lt. John Gittings was the regiment's next adjutant, and continued in this capacity for about a year.

The *sergeant major* was the chief non-commissioned officer of the regiment. Parts of his duties were to assist the adjutant. John S. Hoffman was appointed sergeant-major on July 1, but he was apparently away from the regiment through most of 1861, serving in the legislature, and also frequently detailed to service with the adjutant general's office for the army, where Hoffman's legal expertise was at times considered indispensable.

Another position was *commissary officer*, who purchased and issued provisions for the troops. It is not clear who was acting as commissary for the regiment at this time. In January 1862, Capt. Alpheus F. Haymond was appointed to the position.

The *quartermaster's* duty was to supply the quarters, fuel, clothing, and transportation to the troops. Lt. Jacob J. Hill, from Company K, was eventually appointed assistant quartermaster. He also served as paymaster for the regiment. The men were to be paid every two months, though in practice it did not always work out that way. As the paymaster paid each man, he signed the pay book for his money, and a captain would witness the payment and also sign his name in the book along with the paymaster.

The medical department was made up of a *surgeon*, and *assistant surgeon*. William J. Bland was surgeon; Isaiah Bee, Smith Buttermore, and John T. Huff were assistant surgeons, although Isaac White replaced Huff in August.[135]

From Laurel Hill on June 25, Gen. Garnett made an assessment of the situation for Gen. Lee. The town of Beverly was the principal depot of supplies. He planned to establish a second, smaller depot at the foot of Cheat Mountain, with enough supplies to last the regiment for two days. That depot, six miles south of Huttonsville, would be garrisoned with three small companies that had yet to be assigned to a regiment.

Garnett had not given up on the original mission of the army in western Virginia, the protection, or destruction of the railroad. But getting to it would prove the problem. "The road from Saint George to Cheat River Bridge, on the railroad, is a country road, and scarcely practicable for wheels," he reported. "My best chance at getting at the railroad seems at present to be by the Morgantown road, a road which leads from Yeager's to Evansville."

The general was shocked by the attitude he found in the populace of western Virginia. "The Union men are greatly in the ascendancy here," he wrote, "and are much more zealous and active in their cause than the secessionists. The enemy are kept fully advised of our movements, even to the strength of our scouts and pickets, by the country people, while we are compelled to grope in the dark as much as if we were invading a foreign and hostile country."

Feeling isolated from the rest of Virginia, Garnett worried about the health of the men, for they were mostly without blankets or tents. The nights were cold, and the rain was frequent, and the men were sleeping rough in the camps, with little protection, and few comforts. They mostly did not know the first thing about cooking, and they lacked the proper utensils for cooking over open wood fires.[136]

Some had pen and paper, however, and could write to loved ones at home in their spare time. Lt. Col. Jackson's wife, Sarah had initially remained at Parkersburg after he departed for the army. Jackson wrote to her from Laurel Hill to reassure her that he was all right, and report that he was in command of a regiment. "I feel a presentiment that I will escape unharmed, and be with my dear wife and children again," he wrote. "I succeed well. Be certain that I will conduct myself, as a brave man should. Do not believe any rumors. I see men alive, who are in the papers represented as dead. Our reinforcements are coming, and we will drive the enemy out of our land."[137]

Unknown to him, however, Mrs. Jackson had already set out from their home in Parkersburg, and was then on her way south, to be closer to him. On June 21, Sarah Jackson was given a safe-conduct pass, and allowed to leave Parkersburg with their three children. The pass specified that she could travel with two buggies as far as Weston.[138]

Changes in the manpower of the regiment began early, and were unceasing through the years of war. Rev. Mitchell, captain of Company D, resigned on June 20. Some participants claimed that Mitchell then returned to Gilmer County to enlist more men. He never returned to the regiment. Rev. Mitchell became involved with the Partisan Rangers then operating in Western Virginia.

A guerrilla attack was made on the Union detachment at Glenville, in Gilmer County, in early July. This skirmish resulted in Glenville being occupied by the Seventh Ohio regiment. The Tenth Ohio regiment chased the guerrillas as far Bulltown, but the secessionist partisans escaped. The Tenth Ohio went on to Buckhannon to join the Federal garrison in Upshur County.[139]

The bushwhackers, or guerrillas who styled themselves partisan rangers proved to be a problem for nearly everyone in western Virginia. Their unregulated movements created havoc, murder, and destruction. No one was safe from such depredations. Rev. Mitchell evidently joined the partisan rangers after he resigned from the 31st Virginia. He claimed to hold the rank of captain, but his rank was probably just an honorific holdover from his short service as captain of the Gilmer Rifles. He was destined to die in 1862 while still practicing as a partisan ranger.[140]

Following Mitchell's departure from Company D, the company was without a captain until the beginning of August. In the interval, lieutenants McNemar and Stout were in command of the company. It was McNemar who came up with the solution for the nightly disruptions that were happening at one of the picket posts on Laurel Hill.[141]

Sentinels at a particular picket post had been firing in the dark on a regular basis, but it was unknown what was disturbing the men each night. To solve the mystery, Lt. McNemar placed Chris Kuhl and another man at the spot, and ordered them to hold their fire until certain of the target. Taking post at the big poplar where all the disruptions usually occurred, Kuhl and his friend each took a side of the tree and stood vigilant.

"We stood a short time," Kuhl wrote, "then we heard a great rustling in the leaves and foot steps on the hard beaten path, and apparently lots of them. So we got ready, one on the right, the other on the left of the tree. Said I, "Keep cool and stand your ground. Don't shoot until we see, and then let's be sure we get one apiece." It was very dark that night, and visibility so poor, they had to wait until an extended arm would practically touch the creatures, which turned out to be cows in a small herd, going down the hill to rest for the night in the leafy coolness of the forest.[142]

Soon after Gen. Garnett arrived at Laurel Hill with the 31st Virginia, the 1st Georgia and the 37th Virginia infantry reinforced him. Additionally, the 20th Virginia arrived, and was assigned to Rich Mountain. Its colonel, John Pegram, was senior in rank, and so took command of the Rich Mountain post.

By July 8, Gen. Garnett's total force numbered 4,615 men: 3,381 at Laurel Hill; 859 at Rich Mountain; and 375 at Beverly, guarding the Provisional Army's supplies.[143]

Garnett was worried that he did not have sufficient forces to hold the mountain passes, especially against the much larger forces that were building up in the Union camps. Reports of trainloads of Union troops arriving at Clarksburg, intended for the Cheat Mountain area, were particularly disturbing, though unconfirmed. He reported to Gen. Lee that if the reports were true, and if Union troops were able to threaten getting between his force and Richmond, that he would have to fall back at least to Leadville. Lee replied to this with information that Garnett would soon be reinforced again with troops already on the way, including the 44th Virginia. In addition, a large regiment from Georgia, commanded by Col. Edward Johnson, would soon be departing, as well as a North Carolina regiment. Once these troops were in place, Garnett should have enough men to hold the position.[144]

Unfortunately, they arrived too late. Garnett learned on July 6 that close to three thousand Union infantry had arrived at Parkersburg from Pittsburgh, via shallow draft river steamers. Those troops were then transported to Clarksburg by rail, and marched to Buckhannon. The same day that this intelligence came in, heavy skirmishing broke out at Rich Mountain as the Union forces under Gen. Rosecrans tested the strength of the Rich Mountain defense.[145]

"Heavy firing about midnight in every direction, but mostly near Belington," Osborne Wilson of Company E recorded on July 6. For the men on the ground, it was difficult to know what was really going on, but they found out the following day when it was their turn to skirmish. Pickets at Laurel Hill came under fire from sharpshooters, with one man taking a bullet through his cartridge box, coattail, and pants leg without receiving an injury to his body. Scouts were bringing in news that the enemy was coming, prompting Garnett to send the Georgia regiment out about three miles to fend them off. A man from the picket detail, provided that day by the 23rd Virginia, was killed in the resulting skirmish.[146]

Most of the 31st Virginia was farther back on Laurel Hill while this was going on. Two companies had gone out on picket or guard detail, leaving a sizable force back at the camp. They were there on July 8 when the Federals lobbed artillery shells into the camp, seemingly at random. The war was definitely spreading to Laurel Hill.

Snider experienced the falling, exploding artillery shells firsthand, but thought it was not very effective. He commented, "There was but little attention paid to them, except by our mules. They would neigh at them as they would pass over." Musket and rifle fire was also sporadic, though far from heavy. "There was about enough firing going on all day for about a dozen squirrel hunters... occasionally you would hear a small volley."[147]

Soon, they had other chances to be more intimately involved with skirmishing. About three quarters of a mile from the regiment's camp at Laurel Hill, a picket line was established at an old mill situated on the edge of a wood near the village of Belington. Seven companies from the 31st Virginia were sent down one night to the defensive line. "We were in an old mill race," John Cammack wrote, "which was dry and made very excellent breast works, and we were told that the enemy was only 300 yards in front and would attack and charge."[148]

Once more, Union skirmishers were "feeling" the situation, perhaps with the conclusion that driving the Confederates away from their position at the edge of the woods was not yet worth the trouble. They did some shelling of the woods with artillery, and a little light infantry musketry, and in return, the Confederate artillery did some shelling of their own.

But guard duty could be hazardous, even farther back from the front line, as part of Company H discovered on July 9. They had gone out with the 23rd Virginia, which was detailed to relieve the skirmish line. "We stopped a few hundred yards from the enemy's outpost," Hall wrote. After the 23rd Virginia continued on to the skirmish line, they became engaged in a hot firefight. Bullets zipped up the road toward Company H at its guard position. "We were sheltered from the balls by a huge log," Hall said. Company H remained there through the night, until, "The enemy's fire became so hot, we retired nearer our camp, but not out of range of their guns."

The Union artillery was just warming up to its work, however. It next tried to push the picket line and guards back with a concentrated fire of cannon balls, and exploding shot that lasted for nearly ten hours. The soldiers hid behind and under large trees. "Several of us came very near being struck by their balls, nevertheless," Hall wrote, "a few having the mud and dirt thrown over them by the explosion of shells. We picked up a few of their balls."

Meanwhile, the other side occupied a house near the road. Confederate artillery was brought up, and the guns fired six times at that Union refuge, destroying the house. At last, the Federal guns fell silent after hours of shelling the Confederate position.

On the 10th, Union troops were posted on the brow of a hill commanding the Confederate entrenchments, with the main body about a mile and a half from Laurel Hill. Their artillery was shelling Garnett's position on Laurel Hill at around noon, and once more the 12-pounder guns dropped explosive shells near the trench at the outer line of defense. The shelling continued sporadically throughout the day, but began to taper off as a severe storm began to hamper the gunners.[149]

The 31st Virginia was sent out on picket that evening around six o'clock, arriving in the rain while under rifle fire. Returning musket shots toward the source, the men could not tell right away if any of their bullets struck true. Later it was learned that they had killed a man

from the 25th Virginia who was part of the picket detail about to be
relieved. Company C's Snider said, "There was but few of us found it
out for some time, it being dusk and raining."

Flashes of light from the 31st Virginia's muskets had given their
position away to the Union gunners, and shells burst in the treetops
over their heads, sending branches and tree limbs falling onto the men.
Not long afterward, the fighting broke off for the day, leaving the 31st
Virginia on the picket line through a rainy and disagreeable night.[150]

On July 11, while the Union army was threatening Laurel Hill with
enough force to hold Gen. Garnett's attention, Gen. Rosecrans attacked
the Confederate force on Rich Mountain, cutting off a possible retreat
to Beverly. Colonel Pegram, the commander at that post, made an
assessment that they could not hold the position, and ordered the main
body of his troops, then still in their entrenchments, to retreat off the
mountain in an attempt to join with Gen. Garnett at Laurel Hill.[151]

News of Pegram's defeat reached Garnett's camp around 2 P.M. The
reports of Union troops threatening his position from toward
Buckhannon, and the concentrated force in his front made Garnett
believe that he could no longer defend Laurel Hill with any certainty.
His men already had two day's worth of cooked rations ready: Garnett
issued orders for the regiments to prepare to travel, and that night the
Confederates began their retreat from Laurel Hill.[152]

They started out slowly, around midnight July 11, their wagons
loaded heavily. About a half dozen sick and wounded men were too ill
to travel. Gen. Garnett posted a note with the sick men, asking the
Union commander to give them proper attention.[153] The camp had
accumulated too much material to carry quickly. They abandoned their
tents, and large quantities of flour. Several wagons full of supplies and
baggage were burned rather than leave them to the enemy.

Lt. Col. Jackson's trunk, containing $15,000, went up in the blaze
of one of those wagons, much to Jackson's horror when the mistake
was discovered. He was not the only one who lost personal baggage
when the wagons were burned, but his trunk was perhaps the most
expensive loss in the regiment.[154]

The 31st Virginia marched with the army through the night to a
crossroad west of Beverly, where Gen. Garnett discovered their enemy
had anticipated this line of retreat, and had blocked the road. Garnett
ordered the column's direction to turn north 20 miles, to the Cheat
River, using a rough mountain road that turned off at the church at
Leading Creek. Crossing a portion of Cheat Mountain, they came down
to Kaler's ford, the first crossing place over Shaver's Fork of the Cheat
River. They camped for the night in a pouring rain, the men cold, wet
and miserable, with the rearguard two miles away at Pleasant Run.[155]

Snider wrote in his journal, "After spending a very disagreeable
night, we started down the river about 7 A.M. The road being very

rough and muddy, we traveled slowly." The route heading north was now by a road that followed the course of Shaver's Fork, the main branch of the Cheat River. Three fords within three miles slowed them considerably. At each ford the wagons and cannon were forced through the streambed by manual labor, the horses often unequal to pulling the weight. Baggage and equipment suffered throughout the morning as wagons were lightened with disregard for the owners of the jettisoned gear.[156]

The 37th Virginia was head of the column, followed by the 31st Virginia, Hansbrough's battalion, Shoemaker's artillery, and a cavalry squadron. The baggage wagons followed next, and then the 1st Georgia, 23rd Virginia, another section of artillery under Lanier, and more cavalry bringing up the rear. They had just crossed the baggage wagons over the first ford above Kaler's when scouts reported the enemy following closely. The men in the 31st Virginia learned of this from a mounted messenger sent up the line to warn of the danger. The 23rd Virginia, still acting as rearguard, was already skirmishing. While the rest of the army marched on slowly, Garnet ordered the 1st Georgia to take a position in a meadow across from the river, and then support the 23rd Virginia as it withdrew. The Federal skirmishers were already shooting at them, and soon the rest of the Union companies had joined the fight, and a hot exchange of musket and rifle fire began.[157]

The 23rd Virginia and 1st Georgia continued to fall back in a leap-frog fashion, retiring upon eligible positions and stemming the enemy's thrusts until they reached Corrick's ford, which was unusually deep because of the recent rain. Some of the wagons became stuck in the mud and rocks of the river bottom, and were abandoned where they sat in the rushing waters.

The 23rd Virginia, meanwhile, was in another firefight, and this time the Union regiments were supported by artillery. Three artillery pieces replied from the Confederate side of the stream, while muskets from both armies zipped balls through the trees, and the smoke from gunpowder piled high at every discharge. By this time, about 30 men were either killed or wounded in the 23rd Virginia. They finally pulled back across the river at the ford, with the 1st Georgia once again in position to support them from the far side of the stream.[158]

Gen. Garnett was waiting there when the 23rd Virginia splashed across. Ten men and a lieutenant were chosen to stand skirmish, and were ordered into position by Garnett himself, while the rest of the 23rd Virginia withdrew around a bend in the road. Garnett was about to order the skirmishers to fall back when a Union bullet brought him down, killing him. One of the skirmishers fell next to him, but the other eight men and the officer made good their escape.

After the general's death, Colonel Ramsey, of the 1st Georgia Regiment, was the ranking officer in the brigade. Assuming command, Col. Ramsey ordered the column to continue the retreat. Behind them, at Corrick's Ford, the Federal soldiers had stopped at the ford after discovering the body of Gen. Garnett. He was the first general officer from either side to be killed in the war. Perhaps this stunned the Union commander, for he did not order his men to continue the pursuit right away, allowing the Confederates to retreat farther into the mountains, and eventually get away.[159]

The road from the ford was no less rough than before, and soon the men were worn and hungry, but the long march continued into the night, until they crossed over the Maryland line, and arrived at Red House about one o'clock in the morning. They stopped for the night there, the men falling to the ground at the roadside and slept until dawn.[160]

From Red House, the retreating Confederates traversed back into Virginia by way of Rocky River Bridge, the men very hungry now as the few provisions they had were almost all consumed. In fact, the chief recollection of the men in the 31st Virginia after this adventure was how hungry they were. They began to poach cattle discovered in farmer's fields, killing them on the spot and roughly cutting out chunks of meat and cooking it over a fire, using their ramrods as a spit. "We had neither salt nor bread to eat with it, but it tasted good," one of the soldiers recalled.[161]

The 31st Virginia had not lost any men in the fight at the fords, but it did loose a number of men who fell out of the line from exhaustion. The Federal cavalry that continued to follow from a short distance behind the retreating army captured nearly all of these stragglers. Snider was so desperately hungry on the morning of July 14 that he scrabbled in the muddy road for remnants of corn from where the horses had been fed, but did not feel much better after eating the dried grain. Even the roasted beef did not restore his strength, and he was in danger of falling out of the line when the march resumed. "I was so near given out that I took a nap before doing anything," he said. "Had it not been for Holden and West, (to) carry my gun and insisting so strong for me to try to keep up, I should have laid down and probably have been captured."[162]

Their shoes were falling apart, and they were hungry. Lucius Cammack was ill with whooping cough. Cammack sat down by the edge of the road, his brother by his side refusing to go on without him, when Lt. William Cooper came up, and asked if they had any money for food. The Cammack's hadn't a cent between. Cooper gave them all the money he had with him, a silver quarter. When the Cammack brothers came upon a private residence, they paid one of the kitchen servants for corn bread and buttermilk. Refreshed, the brothers were able to catch up with the regiment that night.[163]

On the 15th, the bedraggled army proceeded across the mountains until they could turn south toward Petersburg. Stopping at one place to have some of the horses shod with new horseshoes, some of the men were able to buy some provisions. The regiment camped a few miles short of Petersburg, and then continued to that town in the morning. The citizens there gave the soldiers bread and other food to eat, and some of the men had enough left over for the next day's breakfast. Leaving Petersburg in the afternoon, the 31st Virginia marched about ten miles and camped for the night, then got an early start on the 17th, and traveled into Pendleton County.

"We found plenty of bread and meat cooked by the good citizens," Snider wrote. They arrived at Franklin in the late afternoon, and camped for the night. Again, they were able to obtain food from the local citizens, who treated them well, and made sure they had enough for breakfast the next day. "Started at 4 P.M. and traveled 12 miles and camped within 13 miles of Monterey," Snider said on the 18th. The regiment arrived at Monterey, in Highland County, around noon the next day, the long retreat at an end. Their walk through the mountains had taken them a distance of 160 miles, from Laurel Hill to Monterey. Along the way, the 31st Virginia lost 17 men captured; and another 29 were listed as missing.[164]

3

GREENBRIER RIVER
Aug. 1861—Sept. 1861

Panics can sometimes be useful: they are short, force the mind to think and learn, and they bring out hidden strengths of men that might otherwise have been undiscovered.

So it was for Garnett's army, surviving the retreat from Laurel Hill, over mountain and through streams, crossing west to east to the foothills of the Alleghenies. When all seemed still to carry the infusion of failure, the soldiers discovered in themselves abilities they did not know they had, and endurance of hardships never before asked of them as men. Lt. Col. Jackson wrote to his wife, after bringing the regiment to safety, "It is true, in the retreat from Laurel Hill, I tried how long a man could do without food. I found that two days and two nights was about as much as I could stand, after having been previously very indifferently fed, and slept (afterward) for five days and nights."[165]

The 31st Virginia, with Jackson in command, had arrived at the small, crossroads, mountain town of Monterey, and there they slept for days, ate prodigious amounts of food, and tried to replace their clothing and other items of necessity lost in the retreat. Most of all, they found that they had gained a sense of accomplishment that transcended recent feelings of defeat. Within a week, they were ready once more.

Throughout the South, news of the disaster in Western Virginia brought embarrassment and chagrin. The defeat of Gen. Pegram at Rich Mountain, followed closely by the death of Gen. Garnett at Corrick's Ford, and the retreat of the Southern army from Western Virginia was the subject of gossip and newspaper articles. The losses there were blamed on poor leadership and disorganized, green troops.

Within days of the arrival of the 31st Virginia at Monterey, however, there was better news to cheer the South. On July 21, in northeastern Virginia, the battle of First Manassas had been fought and won by the Confederates under the leadership of Maj. General Joseph E. Johnston. A much larger retreat of the Union army took place there, as the North withdrew its forces nearly 25 miles, into the protection of Washington, D.C.

Brig. General Thomas J. Jackson, cousin of the regiment's own Jacksons, withstood the enemy at the battle near Bull Run, earning his nickname of *Stonewall*. His famous Stonewall Brigade became known as the elite of the Confederate Army. Nearly a year later, the 31st Virginia became part of Jackson's army (but was not in the Stonewall brigade).

The Southern strategy of defending the Shenandoah Valley, using Harper's Ferry as the initial base of operations, and then later with Winchester as the more important, strategic base, had proven effective. For the moment, the North had been turned back in its attempt to invade and control eastern Virginia, but in the western counties, across the Alleghenies, the Union army continued to hold the homeland of most of the soldiers in the 31st Virginia. That grasp by the North was ever tighter, and would not easily be removed, especially by demoralized men in the remains of Garnett's brigades. Before anything else, they must regain their spirit and their sense of purpose. Perhaps the news of the great victory at Manassas gave the men of the 31st Virginia some glimmer of hope.

George Morgan, in Company A, noticed on July 22, "Soldiers will be cheerful... sometimes under any circumstances. While I write this a party near here are playing cards merrily though nothing but a poor supper, rainy night, and wet blankets in store for them, but few of our company are sick, none seriously." On the 23rd, "We are all comfortably encamped near Monterey by the side of a little mountain brook with plenty of pure water, pure air, and all seem cheerful and happy. A soldier may be worn down and almost starved by long marches, and in a few days forget all and be ready and willing to go through the same again. This seems the case with our company more than any other."[166]

The Union army established a strong fort on top of Cheat Mountain, about 25 miles to the west of Monterey. The Confederates placed the main portion of their western army at Monterey, under the command of Gen. Henry R. Jackson of Georgia. A small brigade was also sent to Laurel Fork, on Allegheny Mountain, 12 miles to the west. Colonel Edward Johnson, of the 12th Georgia infantry, an experienced officer and West Point graduate, was in command of that brigade.

On July 25, the 31st Virginia received orders to march to Laurel Fork and join Johnson's brigade. While the 31st Virginia settled in at Laurel Fork amid hemlock spruce, black spruce, and other lofty trees in a dense, mountain forest, other regiments departed Laurel Fork and marched to the Top of Allegheny Mountain, where they began establishing a new camp.[167]

While in camp at Laurel Fork, on July 27, the 31st Virginia's Company E was divided into two companies. The largest company in the regiment, it had nearly 200 men, having gained 16 additional men a few days earlier. After this division, Company E retained its officers, with Capt. Hull still in command. The new unit, called Company E, No. 2, elected its own officers: Robert H. Bradshaw was made captain; William R. Keister, 1st lieutenant; Andrew S. F. Davis, 2nd lieutenant.[168]

The regiment was still gaining a few recruits. A significant gain for the 31st Virginia was James S. Kerr McCutchen, who arrived at the camp at Laurel Fork on July 29. Reporting to Colonel Jackson, he informed the Judge that he had escorted Mrs. Sarah Jackson, the Colonel's wife, from Lewisburg to Callaghan before coming on to join the army. Then he enlisted as a private in Company D, the Gilmer Rifles.

A teacher in Gilmer County before the war, McCutchen was a big man, six feet tall, with blue eyes, gray hair, and a concentrated seriousness that struck the men in his company. He was 31 years old. Company D was then in need of a captain, following the resignation of Reverend Mitchell, their first flamboyant commander. Four days after arrival in camp, James S. K. McCutchen was elected captain of Company D.

Their trust in him was not misplaced. A quiet man, born in Augusta County of a large family, McCutchen had several brothers and cousins serving in other regiments. Not a social man, and unmarried, he was studious and methodical in learning the essentials of company and regimental drill and had the will to apply them.[169]

When the regiment departed Monterey, the sick were left behind to recuperate. Disease such as measles and typhus was their other enemy that summer and fall, taking many lives among the soldiers. Private Snider, Company C, was one those who caught measles, but was lucky, and recovered near the end of the month. Others were not so lucky. Snider said grimly in his diary that one of the privates in Company H, Jacob Tolbert of Barbour County, had died at the hospital on the morning of the 25th. Those who recovered enough to re-join the regiment, including Snider, arrived at the regiment's camp on the morning of July 31. The walk from Monterey to Laurel Fork was not an easy one. "I was almost given out," Snider wrote, "not being over the measles yet."[170]

Snider and the other convalescents arrived at camp as the 31st Virginia was loading its wagons in preparation for their march to the Top of Allegheny, a rigorous hike of about four miles on a steeply climbing road. They set out soon afterward, and arrived later that day at Camp Allegheny, just over the line in Pocahontas County, on a farm owned by the Yeager family.[171]

On Allegheny Mountain, the 31st Virginia was camped in a field on a hillside. The men were without tents, and the rain commenced shortly after their arrival, and continued intermittently for the next several weeks. They were not given time to complain about fate casting them out onto the sodden mountain. On August 2, about 250 men from the regiment, including Company C, were sent to capture a group of Federals that seemed to be cut off by high water from the west side of the Greenbrier River. The regiment's patrol failed to make contact with the enemy that day, but saw evidence of their passing: many homes and farms in the valley had been vandalized and partially destroyed.

Measles continued to debilitate the army, spreading through the ranks at an alarming rate. Company C had twelve cases by August 6. Diarrhea was also striking the men: a soldier from Hansbrough's Battalion died from it on the 11th.[172]

The 31st Virginia finally received tents on August 12, another rainy day, as the men were cooking two day's worth of rations in preparation for another westward advance. Colonel Edward Johnson, commanding the brigade, notified Lt. Col. Jackson to have his regiment ready to move the next morning, "as early as practicable," but their departure was sadly delayed long enough to bury one of their privates. John M. Shoulders, Company I had died in the night from a fever. They buried him near a small stand of trees a little ways from the camp.[173]

The regiment marched with the brigade on the morning of July 13, on the Staunton to Parkersburg Turnpike. The other regiments marching with them were the 3rd Arkansas, 12th Georgia, and Hansbrough's Battalion. The road took them down the west face of Allegheny Mountain to the Greenbrier Valley. Not far from the foot of the mountain was a ford over the east branch of the Greenbrier River. The camp that Colonel Johnson established there, on the east side of the river was called Camp Bartow.[174]

The regiment arrived in mid-afternoon, and the men pitched their tents near the brow of a hill overlooking the river. Cold rain continued to fall, and the ground in their new camp soon turned to mud. They were, one of the men in Company H wrote, now in the land of "Yankees, rattlesnakes and bears."[175]

Scouts were needed to go into Union-held territory in the area of Valley Mountain, to discover the disposition of the other side's forces. The 31st Virginia's Company F was made up of Randolph County men who already had knowledge of the local terrain, and knew the local citizens and their loyalties. Accordingly, that company was detached from the regiment, and ordered to make an extended scout. Capt. Currence and his men marched toward Valley Mountain to see what information they could develop.[176]

With the weather keeping cool and damp, the rest of the regiment settled in at Camp Bartow. More reinforcements had arrived, including three pieces of artillery under the command of Capt. Shoemaker, which arrived on the 15th. To the east, the troops that were holding Monterey were also beginning to advance westward as far as Camp Allegheny. With such a large buildup of men in an area so far from the only major center of re-supply, at Staunton on the other side of the mountains, provisions were dwindling.[177]

Gen. Robert E. Lee arrived in the area around this time, to take command of the situation west of the Alleghenies, and to make certain the Confederate forces did not become too entrenched in their camps. The Governor of Virginia was afraid the campaign was going to bog down, and Lee's mission was to hurry things along. Accordingly, Gen. Lee set in motion the Big Scout.

It was intended to be an intense reconnaissance of Cheat Mountain and its various approaches, with the goal of finding a way to attack and carry the Federal stronghold that had been established on that high mountain. The Federals had gained considerable reinforcements by this time, and the more direct approaches were effectively blocked.

Colonel Albert Rust, commander of the 3rd Arkansas regiment, was placed in overall command of the venture. Around 1500 men volunteered to go on the scouting mission, including most of the 31st Virginia. The companies from the 31st Virginia, as well as from other regiments in the brigade, marched about 60 or more miles, searching in and around Cheat Mountain. They returned to Camp Bartow on August 22, after five arduous days in the field. The rain never seemed to let up during the scout, and the provisions the men carried with them were sodden and spoiled. For the last two days of the journey, the provisions were gone entirely, and the men did without.[178]

Those too sick to travel on the Big Scout, including the convalescents such as Snider, had been serving as picket at Camp Bartow while the rest of the men were away. On the 17th, more reinforcements arrived at the camp, the 23rd and 37th Virginia regiments. They were in time to help begin cooking rations, in anticipation of the army moving against Cheat Mountain in the near future, should the Big Scout prove a success.

On the 18th, with Confederate troops still out in the field in the area around Cheat Mountain, a contingent of about 50 Union cavalry probed the position at Camp Bartow, resulting in a little skirmish, the first at this location. They wounded a cavalry officer from Harrison County, and also one of the privates from the 31st Virginia, Lucius Cammack, catching both men out in the open. While no one was killed, it gave the men on picket a good scare, and the wounded Cammack was sent to a hospital in Harrisonburg. A bullet had passed through his right arm, a second slug creasing his right hip, and two more scoring his right shoulder. He eventually recovered from the wounds, but his arm was somewhat crippled, and to make it worse, he caught typhoid while at the hospital.[179]

By August 19, most of Henry R. Jackson's forces were brought over from Monterey. Gen. Lee was positioning his forces for the campaign against Cheat Mountain. Shoemaker's artillery departed camp that day, headed west, but was forced to turn back because of the rain and high water at the fords. On the 20th, part of the scouting party returned from their expedition. In camp, men were ordered to cook two day's rations as additional reinforcements, the 44th Virginia, arrived from the east.[180]

Returning to Camp Bartow, Colonel Rust reported to Gen. Lee that he had found a way of penetrating the Federal defenses on Cheat Mountain. With one of the local residents as a guide, Rust had searched until he was certain he had the right place to gain the rear of the Federal position. On the basis of this information, Gen. Lee began to refine his plan for a coordinated offensive against the Union army.[181]

The attack was delayed by several days, however, because conditions of the terrain, as well as among the soldiers of the Confederate forces, were not favorable. After six weeks of heavy rains, the roads were nearly impassable. The poor health of the soldiers was a more difficult problem, for measles, typhus, and diarrhea had struck nearly a third of the Confederate troops by this time. The 31st Virginia was particularly hard hit, leaving only 250 men able to serve in the regiment by mid-August.

A rifled artillery piece arrived at Camp Bartow on the 23rd, and a traveling preacher on the 25th. Reverend Emerson, a Presbyterian minister from Augusta County, preached from the Bible's Old Testament, 2 Kings, chapters 6 and 2, a most military portion of the scriptures to take as his text. Perhaps he emphasized the passages that suggest treating prisoners kindly, by feeding them, and then setting them free to return to their master. "And the Syrians came no more on raids into the land of Israel," the passage ends.[182]

The regiment's commander, Judge Jackson, was not at all satisfied with the progress the army was making in recapturing his homeland of western Virginia. On August 22, he wrote, "If, as I begin to suspect, we are merely here to guard this pass, and not to make any advance; if I cannot get a furlough, I will resign. To do nothing but ambush in the woods in constant cold rains is more than I can stand. There is a limit to human endurance and tough as I have been, I begin to realize the fact."[183]

Others in the regiment were also growing restless at the lack of progress in retaking their Union-occupied homeland. One of the soldiers in Company A said in his journal, "Here we are doing nothing as usual, about four regiments waiting for Gen. Lee to scatter the enemy, and then we expect to make a move westward...."

Most of the sick men from the regiment who had recovered were brought down to Camp Bartow on the 25th, but the regiment's surgeon, Dr. Bland, was so unwell that he remained up on the mountain, at the hospital. At Camp Bartow, the soldiers were finding the unceasing rain a terrible burden, perhaps prompting three Pendleton County men from Company B to desert in the night. Snider said, perhaps sarcastically, on the 29th, "We have only had about seventy-two hours rain in the last three days and still raining."[184]

Judge Jackson, having recently recovered from the measles himself, also complained of the rain and disease: "There never was such a climate as this," he wrote. "Our men sicken and many die. Indeed when the war is over it will be found that more have died in camp, than on the battle field."[185]

Despite these difficulties, their brigade commander was trying to fine-tune the operations of his command. Colonel Johnson issued an order on August 29 concerning the Grand Guard, which would in the future be mounted at 9 A.M. daily. The theory behind setting up the Grand Guard, and all of the other types of guards and pickets was to arrange concentric lines of defense radiating out from the main camp. As stated in *Gilham's* manual, which was one of "the books" for this army, "The ordinary arrangement of guards is such, that no matter how far the outer line may lie from the main body, it may rally from point to point, if driven by an advancing enemy, gaining strength each time, until it finally reaches the main body. Thus even the most advanced posts need never be cut off, while it would be impossible for the enemy to surprise the main body."[186]

There were a lot of small steps and procedures in going by the book, and many were probably seen by the men as overly officious, but being new soldiers they needed practice and a set of guidelines for their duties, and going by the book made certain they would not forget necessary steps. For instance, with the Grand Guard: men detailed for it from each company presented themselves on their regimental parade ground, where they were verified by the adjutant, and then marched to the brigade parade ground by the senior officer of the detail. The men were then inspected under supervision of the brigade's field officer of the day. As the new guard was preparing to go out, the old guard was returning and presented them for inspection. The officer commanding the old guard was required to pass along to the officer for the new guard, any orders, information, or instructions: the failure to inform the new guard of the password, for instance, could be disastrous.

Other attempts at regularizing the affairs of the regiments were also being made. At the end of the month, the 31st Virginia was mustered for a general inspection, in accordance with recent orders from the brigade commander: "All Captains of Companies will endeavor to collect, as far as possible, the data necessary to make out a correct muster roll of their respective companies by the 31st inst. The dates of the enlistment or enrollment, of death, discharges, furloughs, or cases of absence without leave, of detached service... must be accurately ascertained in the case of every officer and man, and noted on the muster roll in strict conformity with the printed form."[187]

In theory, companies and regiments were supposed to be inspected every two months, and the muster rolls forwarded to the adjutant for inclusion in the report of the regiment's inspection. Until this time, printed forms for the muster rolls had not been available to the 31st Virginia's officers. Many of the company commanders, or their sergeants, used blank pieces of paper to draw their own forms. Jackson said, "Many of my men are sick. They have every disease — measles, mumps, jaundice, dysentery, and typhoid fever. Out of about 500 men present, I have this morning only 231 men fit for duty. There has been much hardship and exposure."[188]

Eager for news concerning what was happening in the northwest, Jackson interviewed a man from Brooks County who had just come through to their lines from there. The Judge was not unhappy to learn that feelings were unsettled in that part of the state which continued to support the Union. Union supporters there had declared that the government in Richmond had absented themselves, and so declared they would form their own, "Restored Government of Virginia," with Francis Pierpont of Marion County serving as governor. Although approved by the Federal government, it was a legal fiction that was proving difficult for some people in the northwest of Virginia to accept, and the authorities had to apply some strong measures against individual liberties in order to prove they were in control.

"The Pierpont Government is becoming odious," Jackson wrote. "Union shriekers are panic struck, and many preparing to leave. Pierpont has his family in Washington, Pa., and stays there every night, going and returning by Hempfield Railroad.... Who is my successor as Judge? What a time I will have in trying him for treason! But he will have to be caught first."[189]

Jackson had not given up on re-claiming his position in Parkersburg as judge of the Nineteenth Circuit Court, but he was starting to worry that he had been too frank in letters to his wife concerning misgivings with the army. In particular, the Judge did not want Mrs. Jackson to tell anyone that he had already contemplated resigning from the regiment. Jackson wrote to her, cautioning, "I am now convinced that my regiment would go to pieces, were I to resign, besides there would be injurious reflections attaching to me through life. I am in for the war until I can hold court in my circuit, when there will be a necessity for my resignation. If before that period arrives winter should set in, and army movements here rendered impossible, I can then get a furlough."

Mrs. Jackson had been pressing for an opportunity to see him, and wanted to come to Camp Bartow. He tried what he could in a letter to dissuade her from it, but warned that he would not be permitted to take leave. "It will be impossible for me to get a furlough now as we are in the face of the enemy, and my health is improving, and an advance movement daily expected... Much as I would like to see you, yet you must not come. Within twenty miles of this place there is no place where you can stay. Those families who have been able to entertain have left for the interior, and those compelled to stay have the sick of the army crowded upon them with all manner of diseases. You cannot sleep in camp on dirty and sometimes wet straw. Such a trip might lose you your life. Stay where you are."[190]

Sarah Jackson was a person of strong resolve. She did not remain where she was, but instead traveled to Camp Bartow on September 5, forcing the Judge to request a short leave of absence. "My wife has arrived in the neighborhood," he wrote in his request to the brigade commander, "and is now within several miles of this camp. An event of so much importance compels me to ask leave of absence for several days. Besides, if required, Surgeon Bland, who will hand you this note, will certify that such leave of absence will be beneficial to my health...." Acquiescing to circumstance, Colonel Johnson approved the leave.[191]

Judge Jackson's fears for his wife's health were not unfounded. Men were dying on a daily basis now from measles and typhus. The regiments from Arkansas, Georgia, and Tennessee were particularly hard hit, but the 31st Virginia was also suffering losses. One of the men in Company D died on the 6th, and one from Company B on the following day. So many men were sick from Pendleton County at this time that all of Company B, along with other companies from that county were granted permission to go home to recuperate. They departed camp on September 7. Company F was still on detached service near Valley Mountain. The 31st Virginia had just nine companies present.[192]

The days of company and regimental drill were not over, but fortunately the drill also gave an excuse for the presence of the fairer sex to attend. Snider observed on the 7th, "This evening there was pretty girls rode out on the field to watch drill. Of course, we done our best." They needed the diversion, for many were growing morbid over their fears of death. Hall of Company H was more worried about dying in combat. He said in his diary, "If I should be so unfortunate as to be slain in any battle, and if any (black-hearted) kind Yankee should find this on my carcass while looking for other things of far greater value, of which I have not any amount, I will be much obliged to him to send it to Miss Emma I. Hall, Elk Creek, Barbour Co. Va."[193]

The regiment did not have its own chaplain at this time, but had a man of the cloth serving as one of the officers. Reverend Lt. Robert N. Crooks of Lewis County gained his nickname as the "Fighting Reverend" during this period. Near the beginning of the month, Snider observed that one impromptu church service also featured a young lady from Highland County who attended while visiting a brother or father, but the distraction caused by this lady was not lost on Rev. Lt. Crooks, judging by his choice of scripture that day, from James, chapter 4, and part of chapter 12, "From whence come wars and fighting among you? Come they not hence, even of your lusts that war in your members? Ye lust and have not; ye kill, and desire to have, and cannot obtain...." On September 8, Rev. Lt. Crooks again preached, this time from Mark, chapters 10 and 17, "Ye shall indeed drink of the cup that I drink of; But to sit on my right hand and on my left hand is not mine to give; but it shall be given to them for whom it is prepared." The weather did not cooperate that day: church service was interrupted by a shower of rain. Although the men had thought the weather could not possibly be any worse than the incessant cold precipitation, they were proved wrong later in the day when it snowed, the first baptism of winter for 1861 in those western Virginia mountains.[194]

Many of the regiments in the Army of the Northwest were given new brigade assignments at this time: the 31st Virginia was placed in the First Brigade, along with the 12th Georgia, 3rd Arkansas, 52nd Virginia, Hansbrough's 9th Battalion, the Danville Artillery, and a small unit of cavalry. Brig. Gen. Henry R. Jackson was commanding the brigade.[195]

The orders regarding the attack against Cheat Mountain disrupted these brigade assignments, however. Colonel Rust, commander of the 3rd Arkansas, was placed in command of a temporary brigade of 2,000 men drawn from several regiments, including the 3rd Arkansas, 23rd Virginia, 37th Virginia, and the 31st Virginia. They were ordered to attack at Cheat Mountain Pass on September 12, at daylight. The other regiments in the two brigades of their division would also advance, and occupy the eastern ridge of Cheat Mountain, directly in front of the Union fort. This would hopefully distract the Federals, while Rust's force slipped in the back way to turn the position, as the tactical movement was known. If Colonel Rust was successful in his attack at dawn on the 12th, the Confederate force directly in front of the enemy stronghold would press the attack in support of Rust's movement, and overwhelm the enemy.

Meanwhile, a second Confederate force under Gen. Samuel R. Anderson would approach Cheat Mountain from the direction of the Tygart's River and take control of the Staunton to Parkersburg Pike, on the northwestern face of Cheat Mountain.

Commanders of regiments were ordered to be certain that their men wore the right kind of identifying badge, to prevent being fired upon by their own men. With Lt. Col. Jackson away on leave, Maj. Boykin was in command of the 31st Virginia, and was specifically ordered to take command of his companies participating in the attack.[196]

Gen. Lee issued an encouraging order to the men on the 9th, urging great efforts: "The eyes of the country are upon you," he told them. "The safety of your homes and the lives of all you hold dear depend upon your courage and exertions. Let each man resolve to be victorious, and that the right of self-government, liberty, and peace shall in him find a defender. The progress of this army must be forward."[197]

The eyes of the country were indeed upon them. As isolated as this part of Virginia was, with mountain passes and roads nearly impossible to travel after weeks of rain and churning hooves, the press had sent correspondents to the area to report on the progress of the war. The Cincinnati newspapers, in particular, sent correspondents to explain to their readers why this out of the way corner of the country was so important. For the readers in the North, and perhaps even in the South, it must have been like receiving dispatches from a foreign country, the place was so unknown.[198]

The soldiers were issued four day's rations, and were confident, and in good spirits as they marched out of Camp Bartow at sundown on September 9, taking the Huntersville road southward for a few miles. They were traveling light, carrying their rations in haversacks, and blankets and waterproofs rolled and over their shoulders. They were issued plenty of ammunition. Colonel Rust was in command of a brigade of around 1,600 men, drawn from four regiments; the 3rd Arkansas, 23rd Virginia, 37th Virginia, and 31st Virginia. The brigade marched six miles before making camp for the rest of the night.[199]

The morning of the 10th, the brigade proceeded across the Greenbrier River at the turn-off from the road near Hevener's Store, then made its way across the south end of Shaver's Mountain (or more properly, Back Allegheny Mountain), and over the flank of Cheat Mountain. The column stopped when it reached First Fork, of Shaver's Fork of the Cheat River. The men made camp there for the night.

The following morning the going became substantially rougher as Colonel Rust directed the force to take to the stream of First Fork and follow it toward Shaver's Fork. The banks of the stream were choked with thickets of laurel, hemlock, and other brush, making it impossible to do anything but remain in the middle of the channel for three miles of cold water and slippery rocks. The officers were forced to send their horses back, and join the men in the watery trail. Some of the enlisted men took sly delight in seeing the more officious officer types grumbling at the harshness of the experience.

Massive patches of wet, green moss grew on the rocks, making the footing treacherous and dangerous in the rushing stream. When the head of the column reached Shaver's Fork, the men turned into it and waded for another two miles through rushing white water that varied from ankle-deep to pools that sent the men in up to their waists. At last, crawling out of the river, clothing soaked from the waist down, and mighty damp above the belt, the men silently made their way up the west face of Cheat Mountain to a high knob, where they found a flat place in the woods and made camp. It was near sundown, and they were about a half mile southwest of a Union encampment. No fires were permitted, and no conversation louder than a whisper. After a cold meal of salted meat cooked some days previous, the men tried to make themselves comfortable in their wet clothing, lying on the forest floor with few dry blankets to conserve body warmth. The rain began around nine o'clock. There was little joy in camp that night.[200]

They were weary and foot sore, and many slept on the uncomfortable ground until about midnight, when a dead limb fell from a high, old tree-top and landed on a man's head. Instantly, he sat upright and howled a blood-curdling scream of pain, but if the enemy pickets heard the noise, they did not respond, and may have taken it for a hound baying in the middle of the night.

"We was stirred up some time before the day," Snider wrote of their attempted silence in the blue-black dawn of September 12, "and was trying to get to the road, but it was so dark that it was impossible to keep together without holding fast to each other. At daylight, some four or five companies of us went down on the road leading to Huttonsville to intercept the pickets." This was where Rust's plan began to fall apart.[201]

Lt. Cooper was in command of Company C that morning as the soldiers crept along near the side of the road that ran towards Huttonsville. Their mission was to cut off the pickets from the fort, which was east of them. Hearing the sound of a Union picket guard coming along on the road, the Confederates scattered into the brush along the roadside and formed a line. When the Federals came opposite on the road, Company C gave them a volley of musket fire. This produced some undesired results in the form of a large number of Union reinforcements and a couple of artillery pieces issuing from the Union fort just up the road. The Confederates captured a number of prisoners, and sustained a few men wounded in their own ranks, but their situation looked to become quite difficult in the next hour as more Union soldiers came out to do battle.

Colonel Rust, brigade commander, questioned one of the wounded prisoners and was told that the Union camp had been heavily reinforced since his reconnaissance a few weeks earlier. Rust now made another quick reconnoiter of the defenses in person, moving close enough to see what was in store for them if they went forward with the attack. "A fort of block-house on the point or elbow of the road," he wrote later, "intrenchments on the south, and outside of the intrenchments and all around up to the road heavy and impassable abatis, if the enemy were not behind them.... We got near enough to see the enemy in the trenches beyond the abatis."

Pulling back to the waiting men, he consulted the other regimental commanders, Colonels Taliaferro and Fulkerson, of the 23rd and 37th Virginia; and Maj. Boykin of the 31st Virginia. They agreed the attack was too dangerous. Reaching a decision that would dash the hopes of the men in the 31st Virginia, as well as Gen. Lee's hopes, Colonel Rust ordered a withdrawal back down the mountain.[202]

Rust had been deceived by his captured prisoner about the strength of the Union fort, but would not learn about the deception until much later. For the moment, Rust and the other commanders believed the wise course of action was to withdraw, but it certainly made some of their men bitter. Chris Kuhl of Company D later wrote, "If I had been in command, orders or no orders, when we first got to the road behind them and had them in utter surprise, I would certainly have rushed the men right up the road into camp and took everything by storm. This might have been folly... I will say I would have been reckless enough to have done so, or else died in the attempt."

While Rust was having his adventure on the west side of Cheat Mountain, the other elements of Gen. Lee's advance were waiting in position, and ready for the attack that never happened. Gen. H. R. Jackson positioned his other forces, mostly comprised of the 12th Georgia and 52nd Virginia, on the first summit of the eastern side of Cheat mountain, ready to make a demonstration to hold the enemy's attention.[203]

On the southeastern side of the mountain, Gen. S. R. Anderson's Tennessee regiments were under orders to support Rust by positioning themselves between Elkwater and the gap. They repulsed a Federal company, cut the telegraph wire, and then fought off Union reinforcements that were sent after the first skirmish. Throughout the day, Confederate cavalry were on the flank of the Union force, waiting for a signal that never came.[204]

It was around noon when Lt. Cooper of Company C realized that Rust's brigade was withdrawing back down the mountain, and although he had not been notified of this, or ordered to follow, he put Company C in motion anyway. Colonel Rust had evidently forgotten to notify Cooper, whose company was still posted to stand guard some distance away from the main body of Rust's troops. Company C caught up with the rest of the regiment after hiking three quarters of a mile, but encountered Colonel Rust himself a little while later as the Colonel moved back to the rear of the column. In their haste to catch up with the regiment, Cooper and his men had left their knapsacks on the side of the road, back close to the Union camp, where they had taken them off before the anticipated battle. Rust ordered the company to return for the equipment.

"We were in the extreme rear of the command and in single file," John Cammack wrote later. "We about faced and started back, Sergeant Bill Taylor, being in advance. When we got down in sight of our baggage, I turned and looked back and there were only seven of us. So I looked again and everybody had gone but Bill Taylor and myself. The enemy was going up on either side of us and we would soon be entirely cut off. The Yankees were punching bayonets into our baggage and shooting holes in it. Taylor insisted on shooting at them, but I strongly urged that he should not do so. Finally I got Bill away and we caught up with the army."[205]

Colonel Rust brought the brigade out the same way it came in, down the mountain to the streambed of Shaver's Fork, and over mossy rocks, with the disadvantage that gravity was against them in the flow of rushing water, leading to slips downward on the rocks. The soldiers scrambled along gaining more sprains, abrasions, and twists in limbs, just as they had the day before. Their belief that the Union army was following, and might catch them at any moment kept the men moving in spite of the difficulties.[206]

After gaining the small branch they had taken the day before, the men crawled out of the stream at a place suitable to make camp for the night. "It was the dampest place that I ever saw," Snider said, "and had been raining for the last two days. It was next thing to impossible to get a fire made... we was all as wet as we could wring, being in the rain and wading the river for two miles. We was almost frozen. Thought that I would shiver to pieces, but I joined another one of my company and we cut some pine brush to lay on and covered with our wet blankets and slept pretty well."

The next day the brigade resumed its march at an early hour, back toward Camp Bartow, reaching Slaven's Cabin around one o'clock in the afternoon. Their wagons, horses, and some of their equipment and provisions had been left there, about six miles from camp. Taking these things with them, the column marched to the Greenbrier River, and after crossing, returned to Camp Bartow. Not a few of the men in the 31st Virginia felt they had made enormous sacrifice without having accomplished a thing except starve themselves once again on an overland march through difficult terrain.

With the camp nearly in sight, Chris Kuhl was walking beside Private Gough of Company D, who complained of hunger, and begged Kuhl to check to see if he did not have something in his haversack, even a crumb. "I had picked the bottom nearly out of it myself," Kuhl wrote, "but, said I, 'Here is an old raw meat rind from pickled pork.' I handed it to him. He just gnawed it like a dog, chewed the salt and grease out of it, and said, 'Oh, you don't know how that strengthens me. I was about to faint, but that helps me out.'"

Snider reported in his journal the worn condition of the men. "Some of them was crippled up with the rheumatism, and a great many of them came home barefooted. I lacked but very little of being barefooted myself." Perhaps the saddest note of all for Snider was the news he received upon their return to camp, that a good friend, Daniel Summer, the orderly sergeant for Company C, had died from a fever while Company C was on its mission to Cheat Mountain.[207]

The failure of Colonel Rust's attack on Cheat Mountain disrupted Gen. Lee's plans in the western Virginia campaign. Gen. H. R.

Jackson's troops had remained in possession of the first summit on Cheat Mountain, and were determined to hold their position. Gen. Lee was then in the vicinity of Elkwater with the portion of the Confederate army that had prepared to attack the Elkwater fort. When Lee did not hear the sound of an attack on Cheat Mountain, he ordered a withdrawal back to Camp Bartow.[208]

From his camp on Valley River, Gen. Lee issued a statement to the men, thanking them for their recent efforts. Lee departed not long afterward, to encourage other Confederate initiatives in different parts of Virginia. Gen. Loring remained in command of the Army of the Northwest: a power struggle had been played out, and was continuing between Lee, Loring, and others in the high command. Unfortunately, the effect of this was to allow Gen. Loring to become more isolated in his command. The uncertain movements of the 31st Virginia in the next few days were perhaps a reflection of that struggle for leadership between Lee and Loring, prior to Lee's departure for the Kanawha.[209]

Around noon on the 15th, the 31st Virginia and two other regiments were ordered to prepare to march that same afternoon to join generals Lee and Loring, on the other side of Back Allegheny Mountain at Big Springs, near Valley Mountain. They marched out of Camp Bartow around four o'clock in the afternoon, reaching the small town of Green Bank around nine in the evening. Camping for the night without tents, the men slept until the rain began sometime after midnight. They were still in their impromptu camp at nine the next morning when a messenger arrived with orders directing the regiment to return to Camp Bartow. Generals Lee and Loring had changed their minds, and did not need the 31st Virginia as reinforcements. The regiment reversed its course and marched back to Camp Bartow, arriving there around five o'clock in the afternoon. Once more the regiment's tents were pitched at Camp Bartow. They were, as Private George Morgan said, "Just where we were a month ago. Sometimes we think of crossing the mountains this winter, and sometimes we think it very doubtful."[210]

Joseph Snider, in Company C, was among those losing faith in their efforts to do any good at reclaiming their homeland from their enemy. He wrote that night, "I feel more despondent today than I have since I have been in the service, but still trust in the justice of our cause and the intervention of all-wise Providence."[211]

Their lives still had hazards, though they were not presently fighting a battle or skirmish. Inexorably, a few at a time, incidents and illness reduced the number of available men in the regiment. For instance, one of the picket guards from Company H managed to shoot himself in the left hand on the 17th: the surgeon amputated two fingers from Private William Holt's hand, a wound that would later earn the 21-year-old farmer from Barbour County a discharge with disability.[212]

Tempers also began to fray at Camp Bartow. Charles Campbell witnessed the difficulty that played itself out between Capt. Felix Hull, of Company E, and Capt. Shoemaker of the artillery. "Shoemaker fired at Hull," Campbell said in his diary on the 17th, "and was in the act of firing again when (Colonel) Johnson and others interfered. Hull was unarmed."

Later that evening, Capt. Shoemaker and his artillery departed in the rain from Camp Bartow, headed in the direction of Petersburg, in Pendleton County. The day after, the 3rd Arkansas, and the 37th Virginia followed for the same destination, only to return on the 19th when the order for their movement was countermanded.[213]

Meanwhile, the only part of the 31st Virginia that had previously joined Gen. Lee was about to be sent elsewhere. Company F was dispatched on detached service since early August, and were serving as scouts for Lee in the Valley Mountain area. Within a month of leaving Camp Bartow, however, typhoid fever struck the company, and Capt. Jacob Currence and many others in the company were too sick to continue serving in the field. On September 23, they were ordered to march to Huntersville, at the southern end of Pocahontas County, to recuperate and recover their strength. They would remain separated from the regiment until April of the following year.[214]

While the generals tried to decide on strategy, and disposition of troops, the commanding officer at Camp Bartow, Gen. H. R. Jackson ordered that the regiments be drilled. Accordingly, the 31st Virginia resumed its regular routine of drill, but this time without the assistance of their drillmaster, 2nd Lt. Lyman. He too had fallen ill with typhoid fever not long after the Cheat Mountain expedition, and was allowed to leave camp in an attempt to go home to recuperate. Lyman only got as far as Abingdon, where he was taken from the train, delirious, and was moved to a private residence where he remained for four months, too weak to be moved. He was able to travel after that, but could only move with the aid of crutches for about a month more, and would not be back with the regiment until April 1862.[215]

In Lyman's absence, Maj. Boykin drilled the men himself, and there is no doubt that they needed it, for the majority of this regiment was still without significant military experience or training. Judge W. L. Jackson, their lieutenant colonel, was untrained in such matters, and being pre-occupied with more weighty issues, never attempted to drill the regiment himself. He was not at all pleased that his regiment was still at Camp Bartow, guarding the Staunton to Parkersburg Pike, and he was trying to find a way to have the regiment ordered to join Gen. Lee at Valley Mountain. He commented on September 23rd, "I have no hope of such an order."[216]

Noting rumors, and allegations of mistreatment of women in Lewis County by the Union army, the Judge wrote that a friend had recently escaped from Lewis County, and had stopped at Camp Bartow on his way to Richmond. "He reports a frightful state of affairs in Lewis, Upshur, and Braxton. Detachments of the enemy who go out to kill or arrest secessionists have violated a number of women, among them the wife of Colonel Peterson, of Lewis, and Mrs. Ben Bassel of Upshur. Mrs. B. was violated twice. Ben Bassel is here, but does not know his misfortune. I believe it would set him crazy, and we therefore keep the information from him."[217]

During the day, the soldiers were kept warm by digging entrenchments on three levels of the hill at Camp Bartow. The entrenchments, or works, as they were sometimes known, were on the southeastern side of the Greenbrier River, and were arranged to face across the river, to the northwest. In case of battle, the 31st Virginia was assigned to occupy part of one trench, which was situated to the left of the Green Bank road, and another smaller trench to the other side of the road, splitting the regiment. There was one rifled artillery piece positioned behind them, between the trench on the right of the road, and the regiment's camp, which was farther back on the hill.[218]

It was in expectation that an attack might come any day that most of the sick men were sent to Crab Bottom, in Highland County, on the other side of Allegheny Mountain, where they would be safer. Some were too desperately ill to be moved, however, prompting Snider to note, "Whilst I am sitting in my tent I can hear the groans of a dying man on one side, and merry songs and laughing on the other amid the storm and rain."[219]

Army life was a practical exercise in contrasts for the men; one moment pleasant, the next disagreeable; one moment safe, the next full of danger. Snider remained philosophical, being a practical sort of man. Perhaps it was the only way to survive the rugged existence of army camp life and still retain a sense of balance. But sometimes the most trivial detail of civilian life took on great importance to the men in the ranks, such as the everyday problem of cooking and provisions. "We are all getting tired of biscuit, beef, and coffee without any change," James Hall complained, adding that the price of food charged by sutlers that visited the camp was incredibly high.

"Butter demands .25 cents per lb.," Hall wrote, "cheese .25 cents per pound; eggs .25 cents per dozen; chickens (cooked) .50 cents; turkeys (small) $2.00; corn bread .10 cents per lb.; apple butter .20 cents per pint; potatoes $1.50 per bushel. All the above are very scarce at those rates, but everyone purchases at any price. Sometimes we give them [the sutlers] a cursing and march them out of camp at double quick — and then half starve for the fun!" By contrast, Snider perceived food prices differently. "Country produce is quite cheap here," he wrote on the 27th, "cabbage 50 cts a head, eggs 40 cts per dozen, little green apples and peaches 25 cts per dozen."[220]

It was the day of the big storm, described by Snider as, "The most stormy rainy disagreeable day that I have experienced since I have been in the service." The river was already overflowing its banks, and the rain was slashing across the hillside camp with huge gusts of wind, knocking tents flat. The large hospital tent collapsed under the force of the wind, dousing the men inside with cold rain. The river remained high after the storm ended, and the pickets who had been serving that day on the other side of the river were cut off by the high water. Provisions were sent over to them in some manner.[221]

The end of the month was an improvement in the weather. With the temperature falling and big frosts in the night, the grass around their tents was coated so deep with frost the men had to wade through it. A Negro fiddler performed at their camp one night; and a sermon on the 29th from the Fighting Reverend, Lt. Crooks, featuring Job, chapter 21, and part of 15, "How oft is the candle of the wicked put out! And how oft cometh their destruction upon them! God distributeth sorrows in his anger. They are as stubble before the wind, and as chaff that the storm carrieth away."

Double excitement on the 30th, with a small skirmish at the picket posts, and the arrival of payday; the money was sorely needed. The officers had higher wages, but were expected to purchase their own provisions, uniforms, and horses. For officers the monthly pay was: colonels $195, lieutenant colonels $170, majors $150, captains $115, 1st lieutenants $105, and lieutenants $90. Privates were paid $11 per month, corporals $13, sergeants $17, and 1st Sergeants $20. The men received their pay at four-month intervals, though sometimes the interval was longer.[222]

The weather turned fine on the first of October, followed the next day by the more familiar cold rain for the Confederates at Camp Bartow. On the third day of the month, there was a battle.

In the night of October 2, the Union army approached from the south, on the Huntersville road. This road ran along the west side of the Greenbrier River, and just opposite the ford, made a sharp turn to cross the river. Around dawn on September 3, Federal skirmishers ran into the Confederate pickets, and both sides started firing their muskets. Colonel Ramsey of the 1st Georgia was in command of the picket, which had been chosen from several regiments, and included men from various companies of the 31st Virginia. Ramsey handled his men well in the face of overwhelming odds, pulling the pickets back to form a skirmish line.[223]

The picket slowly fell back on the road as far as the Burner house: Colonel Edward Johnson came up to join them there. He brought with him some hastily gathered reinforcements, including Company A of the 31st Virginia. The Federals pulled back a little, perhaps to regroup before another, stronger attack. Col. Johnson took advantage of this opportunity and led skirmishers forward to an ambush along the right-hand side of the road, about a mile from Camp Bartow's main lines. About 7 A.M., the Union skirmishers came up again. Johnson's small force took them by surprise, and held them back for over an hour in a hotly contested prelude to the larger battle. In the fighting, Colonel Johnson's horse was shot out from under him.[224]

To settle this preliminary firefight, Federal artillery pieces were brought to bear upon the skirmishers, and after the third or fourth discharge of the guns, the Confederates fell back. Some were able to cross the river, and gain the protection of their breastworks and entrenchments, while others took to the hillside west of the river. Cut off from their own army, they sought the security of the forest to wait the outcome of the fight. Hall, of Company H, and several other pickets were among those temporarily trapped in the woods. "We were engaged in a brisk fire," Hall wrote as he sat in the trees, "A large body got between us and the camp. We immediately took up the mountain. And now I am sitting beside a log. Am tired of the fight. What with the turn of affairs, how shall I ever write any more in my diary?"[225]

While Colonel Johnson skirmished with the enemy's advance west of the river, Gen. H. R. Jackson had time to get his brigades in line. The 1st Georgia was on the extreme right. Next to them in line was the 12th Georgia: Colonel Johnson would take command of this small brigade on the right as soon as he withdrew across the river. On the center of the line were the 44th Virginia, 23rd Virginia, and Reger's Battalion, under command of Colonel Taliaferro.[226]

Colonel Albert Rust was in command of the brigade on the left, made up of the 3rd Arkansas, 31st Virginia, and Hansbrough's Battalion. The ground there was a series of knolls on the hillside facing the river. Defensive entrenchments had been dug so that the brigade was somewhat scattered, with the Arkansas regiment placed in trenches on the extreme left, and next the 31st Virginia in two separate protected trenches. Two field pieces of artillery were placed on a knoll behind them, to enfilade the road across the river.

The 31st Virginia's encampment was farther up the hill. Most of the regiment's men were there when the fist shots were fired at daybreak. Company K had just started breakfast when a winded private ran up the hill and called out that the Federals were killing their men across the river.

Company K's aged captain, Henry Sturm, was doubtful, according to Phillips, who reported the old captain's preparations to fight. "The hell you say," said Sturm. A moment later, Adjutant Gittings arrived and ordered Sturm to have his company stand ready. "Git your guns," Sturm told his men, then put on his boots while they scrambled for their gear. "Where is my gun?" One of the privates handed his old, long hunting rifle to him. "By hell, I want my tackle." Someone else had the long ox-horn of powder, and shot pouch ready at hand, and stood by while the old man loaded and primed his piece. "Where's my specks?" Again, one of the men had the required article ready, and the captain could see to fight. "Let 'em cum, dam em," Capt. Sturm grumbled, and Company K was ready for the fray.[227]

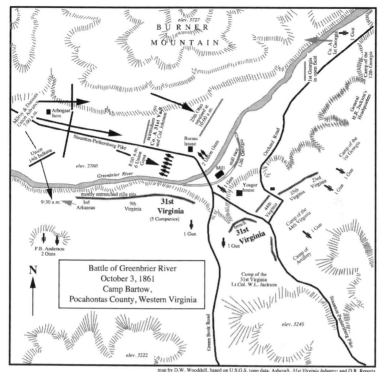

Battle of Greenbrier River
October 3, 1861
Camp Bartow,
Pocahontas County, Western Virginia

map by D.W. Wooddell, based on U.S.G.S. topo data; Ashcraft, *31st Virginia Infantry*; and O.R. Reports

In a little while, the company was ordered down the hill from their encampment, and was put in line on the left of the breastworks where part of the regiment was forming. "From our position," Phillips said, "we could see the preparation going on in the valley before us. The enemy was advancing in file by regiments." They watched the skirmish being played out across the river, and were ready when the main attack came after the Confederate skirmishers crossed back over the river.

About half of Company K, under Capt. Sturm, had been split off and sent to another knoll, to keep watch. Lt. Phillips was in command of the remainder of the company. "The enemy had no sooner advanced within range," Phillips wrote, "than our gunners opened with shot and shell upon their lines."[228]

The men of the 31st Virginia were much impressed by the terrible roar of the artillery, as they should have been — it soon grew into the largest artillery engagement between two armies in the course of the war to that date. The Confederates had seven guns firing for nearly four and half hours, and the Federals had nearly an equal number, though less well deployed or sited. The two Confederate guns positioned just behind the 31st Virginia's position fired 85 times. Another piece, sited in front of Judge Jackson's tent, fired 93 times. (It was later named "Colonel Jackson" in his honor.)

"The reports were deafening to me," Private Cammack recalled. "My hearing was badly injured by the noise." He said the bravery of one of their own gunners: "The enemy was throwing shells at us. One fell above the rifle pits and rolled down among the men before bursting. This gunner grabbed the shell and threw it out just two seconds before it burst. Had he not done this it would probably have killed and wounded a large number of our men."[229]

Closer to the river, Private C. W. H. Gough was standing guard at Yeager's Mill. The camp's commissary store had been established there, and Gough was on duty protecting the goods stored inside the mill. Three cannon balls came crashing through the mill, one of which clipped the barrel of Gough's musket, bending the steel and making the weapon useless. Gough had stood the shooting well enough to this point, but now felt compelled to leave his post and go in search of a replacement musket. He handed his damaged musket to an officer, and said that he would return to the mill, and guard duty, if someone would only issue him a musket that worked.[230]

While the artillery duel continued, the Federals attempted an infantry attack against the Confederate right. The river there was about 25 yards wide, and shallow enough for the blue-clad soldiers to wade across, but on the other side they came up against Colonel Johnson and the Georgia brigade. Confederate artillery, and rifled muskets hit them hard, and the Union men fell back across the river.

They next tried an infantry assault on the Confederate left, and were driven back by rifle fire from the 3rd Arkansas, which held that end of the Confederate line. The Federals turned two of their guns on the defensive works there, and with rapid fire, poured a large amount of canister and shell into the Confederate line, but did little damage to the Arkansas regiment, whose men were protected by a trench and breastworks.

Eventually, with his artillery proving ineffective, and the Federal infantry unable to cross the river without being cut to pieces by Confederate musket, rifle, and artillery fire, the Union commander withdrew his troops, leaving the field to the Confederacy. It was clearly a Southern victory.

For the men of the 31st Virginia, this was the first real test of battle in western Virginia in which their side came out the victors. As can be imagined, it was a tremendous boost for their morale, which had been somewhat low following the abortive Cheat Mountain affair. They also appreciated the praise of the commanding general, H. R. Jackson, for one of their men mentioned as "peculiarly distinguished" in the general's report of the battle. The severely wounded private was William W. Slayton, of Company G.

The regiment suffered a number of other casualties that day. Second Lt. Fred W. Bartlett, of Company A, also sustained a severe wound. Though carried on the company's roll until his resignation was accepted in March 1862, Bartlett's wound never allowed him to return to active duty.[231] Company A had the most casualties that day, as they had been part of the skirmish fight on the west side of the river at the start of the battle. The company's other wounded included Corporal Benjamin B. Shaver, who was dangerously wounded, and would take a long time to recover. Corporal Fred Exline, though wounded, recovered quickly by comparison. Private Jack Munford was killed outright. Munford was one of the few men in the regiment who was born in another country. An Englishman, he was a veteran of the Crimean War.[232]

Private James H. Alford, of Company K, was among the pickets who were taken prisoner: he was sent to Grafton, and from there, to Camp Chase, near Columbus, Ohio. Others captured that day included 1st Sergeant A. Ely Hoffman, and Privates Even Evans, Thomas West, James Ney, and George Morgan, all of Company A.[233]

Lt. Col. Jackson was overjoyed by the results of their battle. He called the engagement a grand artillery duel. "My men behaved nobly and sustained the reputation of Northwestern Virginians," he wrote to his wife. The next day, Jackson again wrote to her, "The terrible roar of the cannon, and the bursting of shells, was deafening. Before the enemy planted their pieces, our pickets and grand guards made a splendid fight. They were reinforced by two companies, one from my regiment, and every inch of the advance was fought. The display of musketry was splendid....

"Colonel Johnson, from being the most unpopular, has become the most popular officer here. He was everywhere, and had his horse killed under him.... We are now better prepared and our men in better spirits. Each man believes himself the nerve of the fight, or feels confidence in our ability to defeat any attack."[234]

The day after the battle, the Southern soldiers began picking up souvenirs of the conflict, including prying embedded Union cannon balls out of the dirt of their breastworks and the surrounding hills. From the start of the war, the men collected souvenirs and curiosities, most of which they lost in the course of the years to come, sometimes because they were too heavy to carry very far. The men also found more grisly evidence of the battle. "There was several dead Yankees found, which we buried," Snider said. "They took off most of their dead with them. We sent out pickets in the evening to their usual posts." Snider spent the day on fatigue duty, chopping timber.[235]

Private Hall had evaded capture during the battle while trapped in the woods on the far side of the river. He returned to camp afterwards, and glowed under the praise his comrades gave to the skirmishers and pickets. "We received the applause of the entire encampment," he wrote. "Some of the officers said they had never seen more gallantry in pickets — not even in the Mexican war. We were very pleased with their compliments."[236]

The weather had turned fine again, which was lucky for the men, since numerous tents were either destroyed, or seriously holed by the Federal artillery. The men were kept busy, and vigilant in case the Federals returned. Hall said, "On picket guard again. Extremely heavy duties have to be performed now. We are on guard every other night. Mr. James Campbell and I are on a post, and neither of us are allowed to sit down or sleep. The penalty for disobeying this martial law is death."

Private Snider and many others were put to work strengthening the fortifications. He wrote on the 6th, "The Yankees have been trying to get in with a flag of truce, they say to get their dead. They are quite thoughtful after four days about their dead. Colonel Johnson sent them word that he had buried their dead, and that he could bury the rest of them if they would come down. Gen. Jackson finally agreed to bury them in coffins, but would not let them in."[237]

4

ALLEGHENY MOUNTAIN
Oct. 1861 — Dec. 1861

Judge W. L. Jackson may have been ambivalent about his position as lieutenant colonel of the 31st Virginia, but being replaced in command of the regiment by a stranger who had not even been present when the regiment was formed was too much for Jackson's pride. On October 7, shortly after receiving notice from the War Department advising that Capt. Samuel H. Reynolds was promoted to colonel and assigned to the 31st Virginia, W. L. Jackson resigned.

"Under the circumstances, my self respect compels me respectfully but peremptorily to resign the position of Lieutenant Colonel of Virginia Volunteers," Jackson wrote in his resignation. "I will endeavor in some position consistent with my self respect to serve Virginia and the Confederate States."[238]

He sent a letter to his wife, Sarah, the next day: "Who Col. R. is, I do not know. He has not yet arrived. I have resigned my position, but will have to wait until my resignation is accepted." He told her that Colonel Johnson (their brigade commander) and the officers and men in the 31st Virginia supported him. "So warm are the protests made against the change, the War Department may rescind the order assigning Reynolds to the Command and reinstate me, by promotion," he wrote. "I fear the change will demoralize my regiment. I will not remain in this regiment in a subordinate position, having been in the command so long, in sunshine and storm."[239]

W. L. Jackson and Governor Letcher had evidently been at odds for some time, for Mrs. Jackson observed when she wrote back, "Of course, Letcher is at the bottom of this movement, what a miserable old brute he must be."[240]

Political upheaval in the regiment did not end with William L. Jackson's resignation. His cousin, Capt. Alfred H Jackson, of Company I, was also about to resign from the regiment. On October 11, Alfred

Jackson received an exciting invitation from their more famous cousin, Gen. Thomas "Stonewall" Jackson: "My Dear Alfred: If agreeable to you, please join me at once as a member of my staff. Please give my kindest regards to William L. Jackson. Sincerely yours, T. J. Jackson. P.S. Should you decline, please answer immediately."

Gen. Stonewall Jackson was at Centerville then, but would soon be transferring to Winchester, where he would take command of the Army of the Valley. Since he was not taking his famous Stonewall brigade with him, he needed additional new staff officers. A taciturn man, Stonewall Jackson was also a sentimentalist where his family was concerned, and found positions for many distant relatives, either on his staff, or elsewhere in the army. He was, however, particular about what type of person he would accept on his staff, preferring men who rose early in the day, and who had large amounts of energy and drive.

The position offered to Alfred Jackson was Assistant Adjutant General (AAG), a staff job on Stonewall's staff that involved a deal of administrative paperwork in the headquarters of the commander. It was, as one observer close to the scene described it, a rare and envied position. It appears that Alfred Jackson did not wait for formal approval before going to his cousin's headquarters. The son of a professional military officer, he may have realized that being ninth in order of seniority among the captains of the 31st Virginia would prove an obstacle to advancement. Experience on a general officer's staff would give him insights into the administration of the army, and might qualify him for higher office. He departed camp to join Stonewall right away, though the appointment did not become official until mid-November.[241]

The newly appointed commander of the 31st Virginia, Colonel Samuel H. Reynolds, arrived at Camp Bartow on October 12, but he didn't remain in command for very long. Reynolds was a 34-year-old graduate of West Point, class of 1849. A native of Lewisburg, Greenbrier County, Samuel Reynolds came to the regiment with 12 years of military experience: Reynolds served in the U.S. Infantry from 1849 to 1861 as a lieutenant. Enlisting in the Virginia state forces, he was given the rank of captain. Now he was promoted colonel and appointed to command the 31st Virginia. Being a professional military officer, he may have had little idea of the political and legal world that many of the officers of the 31st were accustomed to after years of politics and law. It was Reynolds's misfortune to become entangled for a while in the partisan politics of the 31st Virginia.[242]

On the 15th, the Confederates had a little brush with two companies of Federals who came up and surprised the pickets at Camp Bartow, capturing one of the men. Company C's Snider wrote that later in the day the Federal cavalry returned and nailed to the bridge over the Greenbrier River an invitation for Colonel Rust to pay them another visit on Cheat Mountain.

These were the opening moves in a series of light actions and skirmishes that would last from mid-October until mid-December. In that two-month period, there were 17 brushes, exchanges of shots, skirmishes, ambushes, and raids between the Federals at Cheat Mountain, and the Confederates. Most of the incidents took place at the picket posts outside of Camp Bartow, or at the nearby village of Green Bank.

The skirmish on October 15 prompted Gen. Henry R. Jackson to have the camp's sick men loaded in wagons and started toward Crab Bottom, in Highland County, where they would be safer, and probably receive better care. However, after the general realized the Federals were just skirmishing and scouting, he sent a messenger to stop the wagons, which had gone only as far as the easternmost picket post, and the sick men were brought back to camp. The seriously ailing Ben Snider died while in one of the wagons that day. It was a blow to his cousin Joseph Snider, who counted Ben his only blood relative in the army. Snider made certain his cousin was decently buried in a coffin the following day.[243]

The toll of disease was relentless. On the 22nd, Private William Conrad, of Company D, died from a fever shortly after arriving at Staunton Hospital. He had not been well even before joining the army, and as Chris Kuhl predicted when Conrad enlisted, a soldier's life in the field was too much for the older man.[244]

The Confederates sent their own scouting party out on the 19th, but meeting a larger force of Union cavalry on the same sort of mission, the scouts retreated back toward camp, passing within their own picket line where they waited the arrival of the Federal skirmishers. When the Federals approached, both sides traded shots, and then the Confederate scouts and pickets fell back to the next post. Instead of following closer, the Federals set fire to the Arbogast house, and then made their escape.[245]

The weather was warm with some fog gathered in low places in the mornings, but on the 23rd the feel of winter returned with a stiff wind and the smell of snow in the air. Company C was called out and formed in line as the distant sound of gunfire drifted over the river and up the long hill to their camp, but nothing major came of it, and the men were dismissed after standing in line a long while. They later learned that another skirmish had been fought with Federal cavalry, and this time the troopers pushed the Confederate pickets beyond the Arbogast house, which was up river from the camp by less than a mile. Once more, they set fire to the house before withdrawing.

The same day, the Federals also sent a raiding party to Green Bank, 12 miles south of Camp Bartow, where Capt. Arbogast's mother and many of his relatives lived. They robbed the post office and store, and confiscated as many horses and cattle as they could find. Several civilians were taken prisoner for being disloyal to the Union, including

Mr. Hevener, who owned and ran the store at Green Bank. They released Hevener along the road on the way back to Cheat Mountain; he'd evidently convinced them that he was not a secessionist.

Snider of Company C was outraged: "Quite a brave, bold act for a pack of thieves," he wrote, "to plunder a neighborhood after night, occupied principally by helpless women."[246]

In camp, politics were once more on the minds of several of the men who wanted to be elected to public office. A special referendum was called to replace Union men at the Second Virginia Convention. The election would also appoint men to serve in the Virginia legislature. On October 24, polling places opened at Camp Bartow. Several men from the regiment were elected: William P. Cooper, Stephen Morgan, and Augustine J. Smith were elected delegates to attend the Second Virginia Convention. William F. Gordon was elected for a seat in the legislature.[247]

A much more crucial referendum was under way farther to the west, where the question of division of the state of Virginia, and creation of a new state out of western Virginia was put before the electorate on October 24. The vote was held in counties that were known to be loyal to the Federal government, and even there the polling places were put under military guard to prevent interference from Confederate sympathizers. The result at the polls was resoundingly in favor of a new state: 18,408 voted for the measure, and 781 against. For the men of the 31st Virginia, this was cheerless news. Most of them were already physically cut off from their homes by the occupying Federal army. Now they would be even further removed politically from their families, businesses, and homes.[248]

They were about to be cut off from their former commander, too. Lt. Col. W. L. Jackson's resignation from the regiment had been accepted in Richmond, and would take effect from October 24. Jackson was confidant of how his men felt about him "This regiment does not lose my name," he wrote. "All call it, even now *Jackson's Regiment*. The piece of cannon still bears my name, and officers and men display an affection for me, so much so that it grieves my heart to leave them." Jackson departed camp in early November and traveled to Richmond, perhaps to see what could be done politically to alter his situation.[249]

Days and nights of freezing rain progressively brought the men closer to winter, with occasionally some snow. The soldiers were growing restless, and some turned to moonshine. "The boys are on a general drunk today," Snider wrote on the 30th, "and the guard house is full of drunken men."[250]

In the night, their pickets had a brush with the Federals. About thirty Union soldiers came up to the outside picket post around 9:30, but were checked when the pickets fired. The Confederates then fell back to their next picket post, and were ready about an hour later when the Union probe, now reinforced to a couple of hundred men, came up.

Once more, the pickets exchanged musketry with the Federals, and this time both sides fell back.

The Federals stopped when they came to the Arbogast house, and lit fires in the road, using fence rails from the much-destroyed property. The next morning, the brigade commander sent the pickets back out, reinforced with a regiment in case the Federals remained in strength. They found three wounded, and one dead Federal at the place where the last skirmish had taken place the night before. Later in the day they found another Union casualty who had crawled into the brush near the bridge over the Greenbrier River, but he was dead when they found him. Two of the injured Federals died from their wounds before nightfall.[251]

Tents were blowing over at Camp Bartow as the forceful winds of November drove cold blasts against canvas. Gusts brought chills to men standing guard. Those who were unfortunate enough to be sick with fever were given extra blankets by their friends. By the third of November, the distant treetops on Cheat Mountain were covered with ice and snow, glowing brightly in the sunlight, but the skies closed in and snow and freezing rain began falling later that day.

A handful of Union scouts came up in the late morning and exchanged a few shots with the pickets. Standing just at the curve of the road, within sight of the bridge, the Federals taunted the Confederates, obviously enticing them to a chase. "They remained several hours, "hussahing" for Lincoln and cursing the Damned Rebels," Snider said, "and I suppose that they was all drunk. Their firing annoyed us no little in camp."

The 31st Virginia was under orders, issued November 4 by their new colonel, to concentrate on learning drill, and did not need any distractions. For the soldiers in the ranks, this meant recitations from a drill manual each day from 9 to 10 A.M., followed by drill on the parade ground from 10:30 to 11:30 A.M., with more recitations in the afternoon from 2 to 3 P.M., and drill from 3:30 to 5 P.M. The recitations and drill were to be supervised by Maj. Boykin. Captains were specifically ordered to present themselves to Maj. Boykin at 6 P.M. every day, for additional special instructions. Non-commissioned officers were ordered to recite tactical drill and the army's regulations to the officers every morning from 7 to 8 A.M., also under the supervision of Maj. Boykin. All officers and non-commissioned officers were ordered to obtain copies of *Hardee's Rifle and Light Infantry Tactics*, one of the standard instruction books on tactics and the movement of troops on the field. It would keep everyone busy for the next few weeks, especially the hard-working Maj. Boykin.[252]

There were more distractions from drill. The Union Army was growing more active, making small attacks on the pickets at Camp Bartow and raids against the town of Green Bank on the 8th and 13th. Federal cavalry patrols rode into the area in an attempt to feel out

Confederate strength. On the 14th, Colonel Johnson sent two companies from the 31st Virginia, Companies A and G, two miles down the road to reinforce the pickets near the Widow Slaven's house. On November 19, the Federals raided Green Bank again.

Back in camp, some of the regiment's soldiers were getting edgy. Tempers flared, and sometimes the results were unfair. "We had a little fight in our company," Snider observed, "between Post and Smith boys of Clarksburg. They double teamed on Post, and hurt him considerable." Isaac J. Post was Drum Major of Company C, 26 years old, and a resident of Upshur County. There were no fewer than eleven Smith's in Company C, and it was no wonder they "hurt him considerable."[253]

Others in the regiment were looking forward to escaping their camp in the wilderness. William W. Arnett, William P. Cooper, and Stephen A. Morgan were soon to be on their way to Richmond. Arnett was a lawyer from Marion County. A recent graduate from Allegheny College at Meadville, Pennsylvania, he studied law before and after college in the offices of Alpheus F. Haymond, and had joined Haymond's law practice at Fairmont prior to the war. Arnett had been elected to represent Marion County in the Virginia legislature.

Cooper and Morgan had been elected to the Virginia Convention. They received furloughs that allowed them to attend the sessions in Richmond, and would be away from the regiment for several weeks.[254]

Changes in the regiment involved Felix Hull, captain of Company E, who transferred to the brigade quartermaster staff, leaving his company in need of a new commander. Lt. John W. Myers was promoted to captain to fill the position. He was 32 years old, and a lawyer from Monterey, Virginia. Company E had dwindled in size from illness and furloughs, and like the other companies, had only a handful of men present.[255]

Meanwhile, with the cold foothills of Allegheny Mountain coated with freezing rain and snow, illness was continuing to lower morale in the Confederate camp. A few men deserted at this time.

Others, such as Snider, spent a night of cold, raw wind and rain on guard duty. Once guard duty was over, he could return to camp, but being inside a tent was not always much better. He said on the 16th, "I awoke this morning and found my feet, and the most of my bed covered with snow, and a considerable pile drifted at the tent door." They had three inches of snow on the ground by the end of the day, and it was still snowing.[256]

Gen. W. W. Loring, the commander of the Confederate army in western Virginia, had decided to withdraw the army from Camp Bartow, in part because of the difficulty in supplying the isolated camp through the winter months. On the 18th, the 31st Virginia received orders to prepare to retire eastward with the brigade: their winter camp would be on the summit of Allegheny Mountain. They would be supported by several regiments posted at Laurel Fork, not far from Monterey to the east, and by a larger force camped at Monterey. Their primary mission was to deny the Staunton to Parkersburg Pike to the Federals. That would prevent the Union from reaching the Shenandoah Valley, and in particular, from reaching Staunton, which was the principal depot for Stonewall Jackson's Army of the Valley.[257]

Three brigades were transferred at this time from western Virginia to Gen. Stonewall Jackson's army. This transfer included the 1st Georgia, 3rd Arkansas, and the 23rd and 37th Virginia Regiments (Taliaferro's brigade); and the 21st, 42nd, and 48th Virginia regiments, along with the 1st battalion (Gilham's brigade); Anderson's Tennessee brigade; and Marye's battery of artillery.[258]

While preparations were being made to break camp in those brigades, some of the men of Colonel Edward Johnson's brigade, knowing they were going to be the front line of defense at an even colder place on top of the mountain were less than pleased. Private Hall of Company H disliked the idea of a winter spent guarding a lonely mountain pass. On the 18th, Hall said that he and a friend were sipping regularly on a two-gallon bottle of moonshine, obtained from one of the locals. Feeling a bit put-upon, Hall grumbled into his diary, "Not to save the life of Gen. Loring, and all the sons of bitches in the Confederate Army, would I volunteer again!"[259]

But the need for a strong guard on the road was obvious. On the 19th, more Union cavalry swept down on Hevener's store near Green Bank. They robbed Hevener of three horses before disappearing in the darkness, but were not chased because Colonel Johnson was preparing to break camp. He ordered civilian visits to camp be restricted to deny information about the planned movement from the Federals. When Union scouts continued to prowl the neighborhood, a southern sharpshooter with an Enfield rifle picked one of them off his horse from several hundred yards away. The wounded Federal was scooped up by his comrades, and carried away.[260]

New orders were issued to the brigade on the 22nd, detailing some changes to their previously announced winter dispositions. Gen. H. R. Jackson was on the point of departing for Richmond, having announced his intent to resign from the army so that he could serve with Georgia's state forces.

Colonel Edward Johnson was officially placed in command of the brigade, and also of Camp Allegheny, as their new location was to be called. The brigade's infantry would be composed the 12th Georgia, and the 25th, 31st, and 52nd Virginia regiments, plus Hansbrough's small battalion of a few companies. They would also have Flournoy's cavalry, and artillery batteries under Anderson and Miller.

The 44th Virginia, and Rice's battery, would man the outpost at Laurel Fork, on the road to Monterey. The 1st Georgia, 3rd Arkansas, and 23rd and 37th Virginia regiments would be at Monterey, under the command of Colonel Taliaferro.[261]

The Confederates struck their tents at Camp Bartow at 1:30 in the morning on November 22, and loaded them in wagons with other equipment and the soldier's baggage. The 31st Virginia marched out of camp at two o'clock that afternoon, serving as rear-guard, and arrived at Camp Allegheny around dusk the same day, having traveled over muddy roads churned up by marching feet and wagon wheels. The temperature warmed enough during the day for the roads to thaw, but as soon as the regiment reached the top of the mountain the weather changed again to freezing rain and snow. After pitching tents in the dark, the men used what rail fences they could find to make platforms to lie on, to keep themselves off the mud on the hillside.[262]

Camp Allegheny was at the top of the mountain, where the Green Bank road met the Staunton to Parkersburg Turnpike, otherwise known as the Pike. Overlooking the road junction were an incomplete set of trenches that had been dug around the crown of a knoll that the men named Battery Hill. That position had an elevation of about 4,260 feet above sea level, and although it overlooked the road, it was lower than the top of the opposite field, known as Church Hill. The Turnpike followed the base of Church Hill, winding around from the northwest, curving left to pass the Yeager House just beyond the road junction, then traversed generally eastward for about a mile, with the long, and high slope of Church Hill above it rising toward the mountain's top. A small church stood about a half mile east of the junction of the Pike and the Green Bank road.

The 31st Virginia made its camp above the road on Church Hill, a little ways east of the Yeager house. Situated about a quarter mile east of the 31st Virginia, on the same hillside were the tents of Hansbrough's Battalion. The other regiments in the brigade placed their camps below the road, at the eastern base of Battery Hill. This was the top of the head of Block Run. The stream was a mere rivulet until further down the hollow, meandering the declining terrain before being met by Sugar Camp Run, not far from Rattlesnake Hollow. From there, Block Run continued to wind its way down the mountain to Deer Creek, a tributary of the Greenbrier River.

The John Yeager house was just below the Pike near the present road junction. The family had lived there for many years, and their farm was well known to travelers going east and west, for the Staunton to Parkersburg Turnpike was the only major route across the mountain in that part of the Allegheny Mountains. The stagecoach from Staunton used this road on a regular basis for several years before the war, with one of John Yeager's sons employed as a driver.

Yeager, deputy surveyor of Pocahontas County, owned hundreds of acres on this mountain. A strong Virginia rights man, he welcomed the Confederate army to camp on his farm, and gave permission for them to cut the timber on Battery Hill, and also on large portions of Church Hill to give a clear field of fire. In all, five hundred maple trees were eventually cut for use in building cabins for the soldiers.

Treelimbs and brush were piled around the steep westward face of Church Hill, as a protective blockade to slow an approach to the camp. Another blockade of the same kind was placed to run up the face of Church Hill to the east of the 31st Virginia's camp.

The 52nd Virginia regiment had been stationed on the mountain for some weeks, supposedly preparing the camp, but when the rest of the brigade arrived on November 22, they discovered that few cabins had been erected, and most of those were just walls of logs, without roofs or floors. As a result, most of the 1,200 men in Johnson's brigade who were present at this time slept in tents through December.[263]

Canvas tents were scant protection against the winter elements on this exposed mountain hillside, as Snider discovered on his first morning at the new winter camp: "Awoke up early and found the snow two or three inches deep, and myself covered with it, being near the door. Still snowing away, and almost as cold as Greenland."

The hills on the old Yeager farm have no shortage of limestone rocks, a new crop is produced with every freeze and thaw as the substrata fractures and pushes the irregularly flat rocks to the surface. The army would need thousands of those rocks for chimneys and foundations for its cabins, as Snider discovered later that day, when three partially built cabins were assigned to Company C. They were structures that needed roofs and chimneys built, and the cracks between the logs sealed with mud. "We went to work immediately to carrying clapboards out of the woods," Snider said, "and rocks for our chimney, regardless of snow or cold."

Weather did not deter a small Union patrol from creeping up the mountain that day, around three o'clock in the afternoon, to investigate what the Confederates were doing on the mountain. They came as far as the Wilfong house, which was just below the Pike less than a mile west of camp as the road curved around the slope of the hillsides. Colonel Johnson had placed his outermost picket line at the road near the Wilfong house: they raised the alarm at the approach of the Federals, and fell back toward camp, but the intruders did not follow. As the Union scouts withdrew back down the road they set fire to some split rail fences that ran along the roadside. Later reports indicated they also set many fires at the brigade's old site at Camp Bartow.[264]

Not all of the picket posts were on the road, and with a substantial snowfall in the night on the 24th, the job of finding some of the out of the way picket posts to relieve the guard on duty was at times a challenge. The topography of their new mountain camp and its immediate surroundings was new to the men, and the number of ridges, hollows, and such were confusing. Snider said on the 26th, "Myself and three others were started east of camp last night after dark to relieve the pickets. We wandered about until eight o'clock, and came back to camp without finding them. We was again directed and started, but could find no pickets. We went to Mr. Varner's and stayed all night."

Snider and his comrades were in a very scenic, and out of the way place at the Solomon Varner farm. About a half mile east of camp, a farm track ran north from the Pike, up and over the summit of Allegheny, where it turned to the east toward the headwater of Little River and the Highland County line. The farm track ended at the Varner farm, which was situated on the very end of the ridge. From there, one could look toward the northwest and view the blue-green tops of the entire range of Allegheny Mountains, in line with one another as far as the eye could see. In the coming year, when the army marched away to fight the spring campaigns, there would be nine Varner men in the regiment.

"After breakfast, we again renewed our search, but in vain," Snider wrote. "After wandering about until about nine A.M., we started back to camp and met the officer of the guard, who took us back and posted us." While Snider was gone, his comrades finished work on one cabin and had moved in. The following day, they eagerly built the chimney out of Yeager's crop of flat rocks: once again, the weather turned nasty, with icy rain and snow blustering across the hillside and camp.[265]

The fireplace and chimney the men attached to their cabin was a mixed blessing, however, since the fire warmed the interior of the tent enough to allow the ground to thaw. On the 27th, Hall observed a vapor rising in his tent as the previously frozen but very wet ground became soft and turned to mud. It was Hall's 21st birthday, but he did not feel much like celebrating. "Never once did I suppose that in a country like this, a soldier would be so much exposed. Many times the mud has been shoe-top deep in and out of our tents. I was surely reared for a better destiny than this... the sleet and rain are falling incessantly. I am detailed to help load wagons out in the mountains. We are drawing logs for huts. The huts are not for us — but for the 12th Georgia Regiment!"

On the 29th, Company B returned to the regiment from Pendleton County, arriving in a freezing rain after marching difficult roads. The company had been granted an extended furlough to go home to recuperate, along with other companies from their county. They marched into camp along with one of the 25th Virginia's companies from Hardy County.

A wagon train of much needed supplies also arrived that day, carrying three men from Company C who had made the trip to Stribling Spring and back. The wagons brought some winter clothing for the men, including overcoats. Just as well since the temperature and snow were falling. Some of the men went on a spree. "We have had a general drunk on hand today throughout the camp," Snider said on the 30th. "It was wound up by Colonel Johnson sending two companies over to Wilfong's and pouring out (Wilfong's) whiskey. He sold his whiskey at five dollars a quart, and apples five dollars per bushel. The Guard House was filled with drunken men who had been fighting, and two or three of them was bucked and gagged. One Georgian was cut to pieces with knives and died instantly."[266]

It was a staggering way to end the month, but apparently not all of the whiskey had been poured out: five days later the men tried it again, with the weather warming, and the ground thawing enough to be slippery with mud. The thaw continued to the 7th, the roads opened up from the snow but very muddy. Four deserters were brought back to camp from Pendleton and Hardy Counties, and added to the crowd of drunks sitting in the guardhouse.

Colonel Johnson ordered work parties out on December 7. With several wagons, they slid and churned westward down the road to Hevener's store, near Green Bank, and loaded up with hay. Meanwhile, 25 men went to Camp Bartow to chase out the small force of Federals that had made an outpost at their old camp. With the Federals occupied near Camp Bartow, the teams and wagons safely returned to Camp Allegheny.

The sky threatened rain in the morning, and the temperature remained relatively warm. Brigade commander Colonel Edward Johnson sent another, larger patrol of about a hundred men down to Camp Bartow on the 9th, where they set up an ambush on the far side of the river. A few Confederate cavalry rode farther west, and waited. When a squadron of Union cavalry came down the road, the Confederate horsemen fired a volley and retreated, hoping to draw the Federals into the ambush. An over-eager rifleman in the ambush party fired too soon as the Union cavalry came around the bend of the road in hot pursuit. The other Confederates fired then, wounding an officer, and killing one of the Federals, but the main body of Federals escaped back toward their fort on Cheat Mountain.[267]

Ambush alone would not win the war. For the first time, the Confederate army in this part of Virginia was being drawn into an overall strategy devised by Gen. Stonewall Jackson, whose base of operations was to the east at Winchester in the Shenandoah Valley. Gen. William Loring and his western Virginia command were to be transferred to Jackson's control, and most of Loring's brigades withdrawn eastward to join with Jackson's forces. Late in November, four regiments that were camped at Monterey on the eastern side of Allegheny Mountain were ordered to march to Manassas, taking with them their ammunition, and camp equipage, which indicated a permanent move. At the same time, nearly all of the soldiers at Huntersville were also ordered to cross over to the eastern side of the Alleghenies, leaving that town in the hands of a small garrison made up of two infantry companies, about 400 cavalry, and the local militia. One of the infantry companies was the 31st Virginia's Company F, which remained detached from the regiment. Their mission was to guard the Confederate supply depot at Huntersville.[268]

On Allegheny Mountain, Colonel Edward Johnson's brigade remained the only force of any size standing between the Union army and the important railroad junction and Confederate supply depot at Staunton to the east. Johnson was uneasy about the situation and thought it only a matter of time before the Federals tried to dislodge him from this position straddling the Staunton to Parkersburg Pike. "I have all along contended," Johnson wrote in a report, "that this place would be occupied if we abandoned it." However, plans were already under way for his brigade's withdrawal. Johnson received orders, directing him to send his stores to Gen. Loring. By December 12, Johnson had complied with the orders, and most of his artillery ammunition was on its way in wagons to Staunton. If attacked now, Johnson's guns would barely have sufficient powder and shot to answer the need.

Under these same orders from Gen. Loring to prepare to withdraw from Camp Allegheny, Johnson was ordered to stop digging defensive trenches. Very little digging had been done before Johnson arrived to take command of the camp, and even then progress on digging the trenches was slow. The rocky soil on Yeager's farm made trench-digging an extremely difficult task. By mid-December, those trenches and defensive works were not very far along, and they were not very deep around the knoll of Battery Hill.[269]

Worried that the Union would soon attack, Johnson ordered all of the camp's sick men evacuated to Monterey, where they would be safer. They withdrew from camp on the 11th in a wagon train. Tepid rain fell on the road, turning it muddier as the day briefly warmed unseasonably. On December 12, after a frosty night, Johnson dispatched more wagons to proceed down to Camp Bartow under a heavy guard, to retrieve some baggage that remained after the brigade abandoned the Greenbrier River camp some weeks previous.

While this mission was being carried out, a scouting party of about one hundred Confederates went down the Green Bank road, with instructions to cross the Greenbrier River and set up an ambush two miles beyond Camp Bartow, on the Cheat Mountain road. This time, they made a perfect job of it as a squad of Union cavalry rode toward Camp Bartow. What was left of the Federal patrol pulled back at once, and the Confederates started after them, thinking to chase them down, but rounding a bend in the road they discovered a very large Union force on the Turnpike. It appeared that the cavalry patrol had been merely the leading element of a major offensive. The Southerners retreated back to Bartow, and then on to Allegheny with the wagons.[270]

What they had seen in the valley was the first indication of a changed Union command in that part of Virginia. On December 10, Gen. Reynolds was replaced at Cheat Mountain by Brig. Gen. Robert

H. Milroy, a native of western Virginia with some military experience gained in the War with Mexico. Milroy was determined to do more than just exchange skirmish fire and suffer ambush in the woods. By December 12, nearly all of Milroy's command was approaching Camp Allegheny with a combined force of about 1,900 men, drawn from several regiments garrisoned at Cheat Mountain, Beverly, Elkwater, and Huttonsville. Included were the following infantry: 700 men from the Ninth Indiana, 400 from the Twenty-fifth Ohio, 250 of the Second Virginia (Union), 300 from the Thirteenth Indiana, and 130 from the Thirty-second Ohio. He also had a handful of Indiana cavalry, and 75 artillerymen, who marched toward the Confederate camp without guns, hoping to capture and use the Confederate artillery on Battery Hill.[271]

Gen. Milroy's plan was to split his force into two bodies, one under his own command to advance on the Staunton to Parkersburg Pike up the west face of Allegheny Mountain, and then by a back trail around the crest of the mountain, and attack the Confederates from the east at dawn. Meanwhile, the other Union force would march through Green Bank before taking the narrow, secondary dirt road that ran from there up the southwest face of the mountain to come out near the foot of Battery Hill onto the Staunton to Parkersburg Turnpike at Camp Allegheny. The second force, under command of Colonel Gideon Moody, consisted of the Ninth Indiana and the Second Virginia (Union). They were ordered to attack the Confederate left as soon as Milroy's force made their assault on the Confederate right.

Before dawn on December 13, Colonel James A. Jones, and the Twenty-fifth Ohio Infantry arrived near the top of Allegheny Mountain with the Thirteenth Indiana and Thirty-second Ohio regiments close behind. Reaching a place on the road about a mile or more from the Confederate encampment, the Union soldiers turned left off the Pike and headed east on a trail toward Little River. This flanking move was intended to bring the Federals around the crest of the mountain to surprise the camp. As Federal skirmishers approached Camp Allegheny from the east, they stirred up the Confederate pickets, who fired and retreated toward camp with blue-clad soldiers hard on their heels.

The Union colonel ordered his men to follow at the double-quick, to take full advantage of surprise before a general alarm was given in the camp.[272]

It was about four A.M. when brigade commander Colonel Edward Johnson was awakened by the officer of the day, reporting the pickets being driven in. Johnson immediately ordered his entire force to turn out to meet the threat. The 31st Virginia and Hansbrough's battalion were ordered to form their lines on Church Hill, facing the Federals that was driving in the pickets.[273]

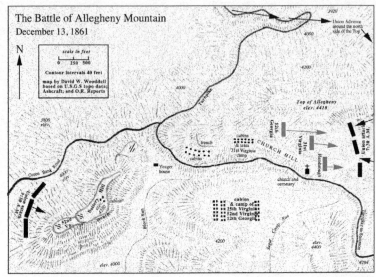

The Battle of Allegheny Mountain
December 13, 1861

Map by David W. Wooddell

Hansbrough's battalion was camped in the woods a little bit eastward on the hill from the 31st Virginia's encampment: they were that much closer to the Federals when the battle started. Hansbrough sent scouts out to the Pike below, and also towards Varner's, further up the hill toward the northeast. The 31st Virginia was still getting itself in line in the woods west of their camp, near the road, when they heard pickets firing, followed a few moments later by more gun shots, sounding closer this time as the Federals followed the southern pickets.

Colonel Hansbrough ordered his companies to advance toward the gunfire: they came within 150 yards of the Union line, which was still forming after chasing the pickets. Hansbrough recognized that he was facing a much larger force than he had on hand, and quickly sent a messenger to Maj. Boykin, urging him to hurry up the 31st Virginia. Hansbrough ordered his men to fire a volley and fall back, hoping the 31st Virginia would come up soon and join him on the hillside. The Federals returned the fire, but most of their lead passed over the heads of the Confederates as they backed slowly, re-loading and firing.[274]

There were no trenches on that part of the field, but a blockade had been made across the face of the hill out of slashed timber, a sort of abatis to slow an assault. In the dim light of morning, the 31st Virginia had its own difficulties negotiating the openings in the brush blockade. "We heard a heavy volley," Snider wrote, "some six hundred yards to our right, across a little point, which proved to be Hansbrough's Battalion. They poured a deadly volley into the Federals and then retreated. Our regiment was immediately ordered to their relief, but we had to pass through the blockade, and in doing so we got entirely disorganized and scattered.

"After getting through the blockade the balls was flying thick and fast over our heads, and the men was mixed up every way and could do nothing," Snider wrote. " Our Major begged us to form, almost with tears in his eyes." Boykin was in pain at that moment, having fallen roughly as they were going through the brush blockade, heavily bruising his left knee. It was the only injury he received that day.[275]

Company C began forming itself in two ranks, and as soon as a few men were in line, they started off toward the Federals as the rest of the company scrambled to fall in with them. Company A was also forming in line, and soon was marching to their left, and then the other companies formed themselves, and joined the moving line. "It was a bitter cold morning," Phillips recalled, "and the sun just up... when the first of the Federals appeared, coming six files deep at double quick. They were upon us, some within ninety steps. They were between us and the sun."

Company I's Lt. James Galvin said the effect as they came under concentrated fire from the Federals, "We went into the charge gallantly, losing five men wounded, including Lt. McNemar, in the first volley...." His company would lose six more men before the fight ended.[276]

As the regiment advanced, Hansbrough's companies were falling back and the two units soon became intermingled. "The fight here was almost hand to hand," Colonel Hansbrough reported, "the roar of musketry was incessant and deafening, but above the roar rang the shouts of officers and men. It must be admitted that not much order was observed. The men fought on their own hook, each loading and firing as fast as possible."

James Hall's youth, and all of the company drill had not prepared him for this day's fight on the hillside. "I hope never to witness such scenes again," he wrote. "I was particularly distressed with the sad fate of my esteemed friend, John Nutter, 1st Sgt. in Company C. Early in the battle I saw him raise his hands and fall. I hurried to his side, but saw he must soon die. I spoke to him, but he could only raise his eyes and smile a faint recognition. He asked very faintly for water, but I could not tarry longer with him."

About then, Colonel Hansbrough was wounded by a pistol ball, which entered his thigh as he stepped down from a log, where he'd been rallying the men to go forward. He was carried off the battlefield and back to the hospital tent.

Maj. A. G. Reger's 9th Battalion, made up of companies previously in the 25th Virginia, was forming at the blacksmith shop near the forks in the road. From there, they double-quicked about 200 yards and passed through the timber blockade, having to stop long enough to re-form their line. As they moved across the hillside, Colonel Edward

Johnson came up and ordered them back down the hill, to a position on a point of land just to the south of the road, to protect the right from being flanked.[277]

"A terrific fire commenced," Colonel Johnson reported afterward. "As soon as I heard the firing I ordered two companies of the 12th Georgia... who had at the first alarm been posted on the pike about a quarter of a mile in front down the mountain, to move up immediately to support our forces on the right." When the Georgians came up, they fell into line farther up the hillside, on the left of the 31st Virginia, and soon received a strong volley from the Federals. Colonel Johnson moved fearlessly up and down the hillside line of his own men, in the thick of the action, urging the men to rally and drive the Federals back. He carried a thick stick of wood, about two feet long, and waving it at the Federals, cheering on his men, "Give 'em Hell, boys, Give 'em Hell."[278]

Part of the 31st Virginia was taking heavy casualties and had fallen back under the intense rifle fire. Hearing the Georgians give a great shout as they moved up on the left, the 31st Virginia took heart and stepped forward again toward the Federals. Some of the Federals were using fallen trees, brush, and timber to shelter behind, and the 31st Virginia, according to Colonel Johnson, "Poured upon them a terrible fire. Our men were checked, but not driven back. They did not yield an inch, but steadily advanced, cheered and led by their officers. Many of the officers fought by the side of their men and led them on to the conflict. I never witnessed harder fighting."

Johnson was a few feet from Lt. Lewis Thompson, of Company A, when the lieutenant was shot, and watched the young officer fall mortally wounded as his comrades continued to load and fire.[279]

The Twenty-Fifth Ohio began falling back. Several officers rallied their men into returning to the line, and now the battle began to surge forward and back across the hillside, each side seemingly shattered by volleys and hails of individual rifle fire, then pulling together to return and repay the favor. "Our Company maintained the same position for near two hours, fighting hard all the time," Snider later wrote. "Our men kept closing in on our left and the enemy commenced giving back when we all raised the yell and took after them.

"There was three of my company of thirty killed in our first position...I was wounded in the left hand by a buck shot and had my gun shot and dented so badly I could scarcely get a load down her, and finally threw it down and picked up another. The first of the engagement I fought for more than an hour within a rod or two of my cabin mates, who lay weltering in their blood. It being a very cold frosty morning, a fog kept raising from their blood, and one of them asked for help. It would have been certain death to have undertaken to carry him off, besides we had all we could do to hold our ground."

At one point, as a portion of the Federal line fell back, the 31st Virginia followed too vigorously and lost contact with the regiment next in line. A little while later, part of a Union regiment tried to flank the 31st Virginia, swinging down to the road and coming up to the rear of the Virginia regiment. They were met by a fusillade from the 12th Georgia but managed to get among the tents and cabins for a brief time before they were driven back down toward the road. The 31st Virginia, hearing gunfire in their rear, fell back and took up a new position closer to the their cabins, with the Georgians on their left, and then began the process of clearing the field once more.

"In this move," Snider wrote, "I was slightly wounded in the right arm. By this time my left hand was almost useless, having a buck shot lodged in the joint of my third finger and fracturing the bone."[280]

The commander of the Twenty-Fifth Ohio later claimed that his regiment continued the fight until their ammunition was exhausted, which also happened to be around the time the Confederate artillery was turned on them from Battery Hill. Though the guns did not do the Federals much damage, their added weight to the considerable musket and rifle fire from the infantry on the hillside no doubt helped the Union commander decide when to withdraw, leaving the field to the Confederates.

A new phase of battle was just starting on the Confederate left, where the brigade's artillery had been placed on Battery Hill. The trenches there were not very deep, but they were some protection to the Southern soldiers who manned the hill (the 52nd Virginia, and several companies of the 12th Georgia.) From their high vantage overlooking the steep hill below, they repulsed a brief, and ineffective attack made by the Ninth Indiana and Second Virginia (Union) infantry, which had come up on the Green Bank Road from the southwest.

It was a contest made somewhat bizarre by the gray uniforms that were then being worn by Indiana's regiments. One of the Confederate officers lost his life when he first saw the approaching force, thinking they were Confederate reinforcements. The Hoosiers shot him down as he rode out to meet them. The Confederates opened such a strong, galling fire on the Federals that they almost instantly fell back, but rallied and kept up an exchange of rifle fire for some time. After reinforcements from the Confederate right arrived on Battery Hill, adding their weight to the firefight, the Federals withdrew from their attack there. Many retreated on the Pike, rather than retrace their steps on the Green Bank road. Confederate artillery continued to shoot at the retreating Federals on the Pike. Later, the gunners learned that they had hit a Union ambulance as it retreated past the Wilfong place, the cannon ball shattering the wagon, and killing a couple of the wounded men who were riding inside.

"*The Bloody 31st*," Colonel Johnson named the regiment after the battle. He said in his report the regiment's "unflinching courage throughout the struggle. This regiment suffered severely. Our victory has been complete, but dearly bought. " Johnson's first report, made soon after the battle, said the brigade had sustained 20 men killed, 96 wounded, and 28 missing in the battle.[281]

The 31st Virginia's casualties were: 6 killed, 5 mortally wounded, and 24 wounded. Those killed included Sgt. John A. Nutter (Co. C), Cpl. Ethelbert Smith (Co. C), James L. Smith (Co. C), Henry V. Springstone (Co. D), and George W. Whitman (Co. C).

Mortally wounded were: Cpl. Aldridge J. Cropp (Co. C), Daniel L. Cross (Co. K), Henry C. Nichols (Co. A), Isaac Sheets (Co. G), Lemon Tenant (Co. A), and Lt. Lewis S. Thompson (Co. A).

Wounded: George W. Beverage (Co. G), John W. Bird (Co. E), Patrick W. Bruffey (Co. I), Sgt. Thomas A. Compton (Co. I), Martin L. Dawson (Co. C), Robert Godwin (Co. K), Luther D. Haymond (Co. D), Samuel C. Higgins (Co. G), Lt. Isaac V. Johnson (Co. H), James S. Kerr (Co. A), Andrew J. Lockridge (Co. E), Robert W. McGlaughlin (Co. E), Sgt. Washington B. McNemar (Co. I), Samuel T. Peterson (Co. I), Lt. John R. Phillips (Co. K), Newton J. Powers (Co. I), John Pridemore (Co. C), Alfred Simms (Co. C), Nathan S. Smith (Co. I), Joseph C. Snider (Co. C), William S. Taylor (Co. C), Lt. David A. Toothman (Co. A), Jacob Tucker (Co. A), and Elisha Wilfong (Co. G).

The Yeager family was at their home throughout the battle. For nine-year-old Eveline Yeager it was already a sad winter. Her father, John Yeager, had died on the 2nd of December. A little more than a week later she was in the midst of a heated battle: "I remember the shots falling on the roof of our house like hail," she wrote. Their house was already being used as a hospital for some of the sick soldiers, and her mother and sister, Fannie had fallen ill not long before the battle. A spent rifle ball passed through the house, narrowly missing brother Henry, and his friend, Rachel Arbogast. During a lull in the battle, the commander of the 52nd Virginia Regiment had the children carried over on cots to his own cabin for safety, and they remained there during the day and through that night. Meanwhile, Mrs. Yeager allowed the second floor of their house to be converted into a ward for the badly injured men.[282]

Colonel Johnson's report said that the Federals had taken most of their wounded with them. "They carried off a large number, some ten or twelve ambulance loads of wounded," he wrote. This still left quite a few dead and wounded Union soldiers on the field for the Confederates to bury or take care of in the hospital.

"The night following the battle, I was dreadfully busy," John Cammack wrote. "We had to go over a field hunting for the wounded. I remember that up on the side of the mountain, about eleven o'clock, we found several wounded Yankees. One of them was shot through the thigh and groin. He swore frightfully, cursing every one of us and saying, 'If our men had all fought like I did, there would have been none of you left to tell the tale.' Poor fellow, he died the next day.'"

Corporal Cammack was the only officer or non-commissioned officer in Company C who was not injured (or absent), leaving Cammack in charge of the company for a couple of weeks. He helped bury six men from the 31st Virginia, and was in command of the party that fired a salute in their honor.[283]

The Staunton *Spectator* gave the regiment and Colonel Johnson's brigade high praise in its account of the battle of Camp Allegheny: "We venture to say that more gallant conduct was never exhibited upon any field than was shown on that occasion by our officers and soldiers."[284]

The Richmond newspapers noticed the 31st Virginia especially. One article quoted an observer, a prominent citizen, who had been present during the battle: "The 31st Virginia regiment suffered more severely than any other regiment in the fight of Allegheny Mountain.... The gallant 31st will now have its due honor! We call special attention, too, to the Harrison State Guards (Company C). Nearly one half of these brave fellows, whose homes are in the hands of the enemy, sealed their patriotism with their blood. Let such as accustom themselves to speak lightly of Northwestern Virginia, show an equal devotion with the Harrison Guards before they again indulge in indiscriminate censures." There would be more than enough chance in the following year, in the campaigns of Stonewall, for everyone to seal their patriotism with blood.[285]

On December 14, as reward for commanding the 31st Virginia during the battle, Maj. Boykin was promoted to lieutenant colonel. He had written to his brother, Solomon Boykin, the evening before to let the family know that he had passed through the battle relatively unharmed, and had noted that they expected a renewal of the attack on the morning of the 14th. They were, he said, remaining in the trenches overnight in case such a followup developed.[286]

Other promotions came on the heels of victory, and some held surprises. At this time, field officers were appointed by the governor, and in some cases, appointments were made more for political reasons than for reasons of sound military judgment.

The same day that Boykin was promoted to lieutenant colonel at Camp Allegheny, John S. Hoffman, lawyer, and deal-making member of the legislature, was in Richmond being appointed by the governor to the office of major of the 31st Virginia. Hoffman had not been at Camp Allegheny on the day of the battle, and in fact had spent very little time with the regiment since his enlistment in the Harrison Guards in May. He was dividing his time that first year of the war between duties as a serving member of the Virginia legislature, and as a legal expert. Hoffman was considered one of the foremost experts in the state on issues relating to ownership of property. The Judge Advocate General, and the Adjutant and Inspector General's offices in Richmond required his assistance in establishing precedents and regulations concerning property rights in Virginia during the war.

It is possible that John Hoffman used his influence with the governor to gain a promotion for Boykin, and an opening for himself on the regimental staff. It is also probable that his appointment to field rank was linked with the appointment of Judge W. L. Jackson, who was promoted two days later to colonel of the 31st Virginia, displacing Reynolds. With those two announcements, two of the leading politicians from the northwestern section of Virginia were placed in positions of authority in one of the few regiments to be formed from the northwest of Virginia. Their regiment had garnered glory in the recent Battle of Camp Allegheny.[287]

Governor Letcher was in debt politically to the men from the northwest, if nothing else than for their early announcement in April 1861 that they were publicly supporting the Southern cause of secession. Hoffman had implied, in a letter to Judge Gideon D Camden in early 1861 that his agreement to support the secession of Virginia would be repaid by the legislature with more favorable tax rates on land. Within months of his open declaration of support for secession, the thorny issue of property taxes that had been debated for close to two decades was resolved when the Virginia legislature made concessions, and changed the law, providing for uniform taxation of land and slaves.[288]

Although Col. Jackson and the governor had their differences, Hoffman may have helped broker a deal to have Jackson appointed to command in the key position as colonel of the regiment. With Francis Boykin serving as lieutenant colonel, they had at least one trained military officer in a position of leadership: with the Judge's cousin, Alfred H. Jackson, serving on Gen. Thomas "Stonewall" Jackson's staff in the Shenandoah Valley, they certainly had a voice close to an important headquarters of the army, which was desirable, though not absolutely necessary in cases of appointments to field command. Perhaps Alfred Jackson's later return to the regiment may also be viewed in light of the apparent political coalition in regimental leadership that seems to have occurred in the 31t Virginia.

Not everyone in the regiment was pleased with the announcements concerning Judge Jackson, Lt. Col Boykin, or Major Hoffman. The news of Hoffman's appointment sent Capt. Thompson into a fury of indignation. Thompson was never shy of self-promotion, or of demanding his own way: he declared that if Hoffman were to be made a major over him, and Boykin promoted to lieutenant colonel, then he was going to resign and go to Kentucky or Missouri and raise another regiment. On December 23, the brigade commander, Colonel Edward Johnson wrote a letter to Thompson, saying he understood if the captain felt compelled to resign.

Thompson's grievance was based on his claim of being the most senior captain in the regiment, and having drilled the regiment in its infancy. In a letter written at the end of the following summer to George W. Randolph, who was then the Confederate Secretary of War, Thompson gave his reasons for resigning from the 31st Virginia: "I had been in every engagement from its formation, the greater part of the drilling of the regiment had devolved upon me, and the regiment expected and was desirous that I should be made lieutenant colonel. The gentleman alluded to had never been under fire, had been but little with the regiment, and knew nothing of the drill, although he was a worthy gentleman and my personal friend. I conceived that his appointment over me was a grave reflection upon my character by the governor, who was then unfriendly to me, and under the advice of my military friends, I resigned. In this action I was sustained by every field officer with whom I have served."[289]

Near the end of 1861, other changes took place in the 31st Virginia, including the resignation of assistant surgeon Isaac White. The resignation of Alfred H. Jackson, captain of Company I, also became official on December 16, although Alfred Jackson had long ago departed to serve on the staff of his illustrious cousin. In his place, in February of the following year, Nathan Clawson was promoted from 1st lieutenant to captain of Company I.[290]

The regiment's wounded were sent down off the mountain on December 15, with Private Snider, of Company C, among them. A surgeon had removed buckshot from between his fingers, but warned that he might risk infection, and might be crippled in the hand.

A train of 20 wagons took the wounded men to Hightown, where they remained overnight; then traveled to McDowell on the 16th, and were quartered in a church. The following night found them farther east toward Staunton, at a fork of the road where they were quartered overnight in an old vacant house.

Snider began the morning of the 18th looking for some breakfast for himself and a friend, and ended up with a small adventure that illustrates the warm hospitality of the country people toward the southern soldiers. "At daylight we was stirred up and I started ahead to get a warm breakfast for myself and some milk for another of my comrades who was wounded in the foot, but I took the Warm Spring road and did not find out my mistake until I had traveled some two and a half miles." Persistently going on in search of food for himself and his comrade, he came across a house where the kind people gave him a breakfast, but when Snider walked on from there, he found that he was too far behind the wagon train to attempt to catch it that day.

"I came across Mr. Bears, who was fixing his mill dam," Snider wrote. "He invited me home with him for dinner, after which he invited me to stay all night, which I also accepted." The next evening, Bears visited his father's home, which was close by, and the elder Bears said that Snider should come and stay with them for a while, until his wounds were further healed.

Snider, the former deputy sheriff believed in following the rules. "I was afraid of being thought of as a deserter," he wrote, "and thought that I ought to get permission from the hospital to stay in the country. Old man Bears took me in a buggy and I tried to get off from the doctor to go back with him, but they said that there was danger of me loosing the one joint of my finger, and would not let me off."

Snider's friendship with the Bears family was well fixed by this chance encounter, and he would return to visit them several times in the next two years, when he had been wounded and needed a place to recuperate. They always took him in and doctored him up, as was the custom in that part of the country when someone was in need of assistance. For Snider, who was cut off from his own family in Harrison County, friendship was very gratefully received, and he seems to have almost considered himself an adopted member of their family.

By comparison to the cheerful home of his new friends, the hospital at Staunton was a grim and boring place for Snider, who remained at the hospital for more than two months while his injured hand slowly healed. "Nothing of particular interest occurred," he later wrote, "except I had three fragments of bone extracted out of my wound after being at the hospital some six weeks. After then my wound commenced healing, and in about two weeks after the doctor etherized me and broke my finger or the callous loose, and afterward worked my finger every day in order to make a (folding) joint, which was very painful for some time."[291]

Most of the wounded had been sent to another hospital at Staunton, so Snider did not have his own comrades nearby. Each company was supposed to provide two men to travel with their wounded, and act as hospital nurses, or attendants, to make sure the injured men received attention, and meals. Not all of the injured men from the 31st Virginia were sent to Staunton: some of the officers were taken to Sunny Side, the home of Edward Campbell, near the head of the Jackson River, in Highland County. Lieutenants Phillips, and Washington B. McNemar were among those from the 31st Virginia who were lucky enough to go to this gentle family's wonderful, and luxurious home, where they were cared for, entertained, and doted upon by the community's young ladies.

Campbell was a retired merchant with an elegant home and a prosperous farm and exceedingly fine blue grass for grazing horses and sheep. Mrs. Campbell was cultured, and refined, and the couple were blessed with several grown daughters who were educated, intelligent, and beautiful; and several younger children at home, who were well behaved, and healthy. Phillips would return to Sunny Side repeatedly throughout the war's dangerous course. They cared for Phillips and many other officers, helping them recover, and remaining at the side of the dying soldiers if that was their fate.[292]

Up at Top of Allegheny, the soldiers who had not fallen sick, or been wounded or killed, or were on leave of absence in Richmond or elsewhere were guarding the Staunton to Parkersburg Turnpike through the remainder of December's frigid winter. The men were put to work during the day digging the trenches deeper, and digging proper fortifications for the artillery on Battery Hill, making embrasures for the guns and barricades to protect the gunners. Private Hall said on December 18, "We are expecting another attack. I have been working on some batteries today. We have to sleep with our arms and accouterments fixed."

Hall was less than sanguine about his cold existence on Allegheny Mountain a week later, when he wrote, "This is Christmas, and as is common there must be some amusement and festivities going on. We are amusing ourselves hovering around a fire in our tent, which smokes us nearly to death. Though last night was Christmas Eve, I did not sleigh ride much! Instead of that, we were marched out with the regiment on the mountain, to guard the batteries and artillery. We spent our Christmas Eve very gaily, sure. We are still living in our tents, but we make them tolerably comfortable by constructing rude fireplaces in them. At night we do not fare so well. Some mornings when we awaken our blankets are wet with frost, and the inside of our tent lined with hoarfrost. Many times our hair is frozen stiff by congealed respiration, and our floor is covered with snow. This is a pleasant life, sure. I was at home this time one year ago."[293]

In Richmond, Stephen Morgan was bored with the Virginia Convention. He found ample time to take in the sights, read newspapers, attend the General Assembly, the Provisional Congress of the Confederacy, and visit with acquaintances. "I had patrolled the pavements until I had more corns than toes, and was ready to say this month was longer than either of the six that I had previously spent in the army," Morgan wrote.[294]

By the 19th of December, with his furlough about to expire at the end of the session of the Virginia Convention, it was time for Morgan, as well as William W. Arnett to return to 31st Virginia. Having made preparations, and obtaining passports from the War Department, they took the Virginia Central Rail Road to Staunton, where they met a number of men from the 31st Virginia, including Henry Sturm and Eli Chenoweth. Staunton was full of displaced people from the Northwest who were "refugeeing" away from their homes and the Union army. It also held many wounded and sick from the army. On the 20th, Morgan and Arnett visited some of their comrades from Company A at the Asylum for the Blind, which had been converted to a hospital.

"We spent some time with them, and examined some of their wounds," Morgan wrote. "Several persons in the hospital had been shot entirely through the body and yet survived. Among this number was Jacob Tucker of our company."

Morgan and Arnett departed Staunton on the 21st, and after a rollicking, and sometimes inebriated journey, arrived at Monterey in the night of December 24. They stopped the next day at Edgar Campbell's Sunny Side for a jolly evening with many friends. Campbell drove them in a buggy the next day to Camp Allegheny. "We arrived about four o'clock in the afternoon," Morgan wrote, "and we had the pleasure of again meeting our friends and comrades in arms." They were back in the army, in time to celebrate a cold New Year, perhaps remembering their comrades who had fallen on the field of battle or from sickness during the first year of civil war.[295]

5

COUSIN STONEWALL
May 1862—July 1862

Stonewall Jackson's army defended the Shenandoah Valley against Union incursion throughout the winter of 1861—62. In late March 1862, Gen. Thomas J. "Stonewall" Jackson fought an important battle at Kernstown, a few miles south of Winchester against a much larger Federal division under command of Gen. Nathanial Banks. It was not a victory for Jackson, but the strength of his attack convinced the Federals that the size of Jackson's army must be much larger than it was. Union HQ decided to keep a sizable force in that part of Virginia to prevent Gen. Jackson from moving north and threatening Washington.[296]

Farther to the west, in February, the war had turned in favor of the Union as Gen. Ulysses S. Grant attacked the Confederates in their western Tennessee defenses of Nashville. Taking both Forts Henry and Donelson and capturing Nashville, Grant had control of a key railroad junction to the west. In April, Grant combined his army with that of Gen. Don Carlos Buell to win for the Federals the largest battle of the war to that date, the Battle of Shiloh, Tennessee. Shiloh was a harbinger of things to come, with each side loosing more than 1,700 men killed, and 8,000 wounded in two days of hard fighting. It was a costly defeat for the Confederate army's Western Department, and it included the death of their commander, Gen. Albert Sidney Johnston, mortally wounded in the fighting. Succeeding him on the field was Gen. Beauregard, who subsequently failed to stem the flow of Union victories in many smaller battles in the war's western regions.

Further south the Union Navy was pressing attacks on Confederate strongholds along the Mississippi River. By the end of April, the Federals had captured New Orleans in a naval attack. Battles elsewhere along the eastern seaboard were bringing Union results in Georgia, North Carolina, and on the peninsula of Virginia at Hampton Roads. The Union Army, under Gen. McClellan, was invading Virginia from the direction of Yorktown. By early May, the Federals had assembled a large enough force of infantry and artillery to begin pressing the Confederate defense of Richmond, which was then under command of Gen. Joseph Johnston.

With the Federal invasion of the peninsula building for a campaign against Richmond, Confederate leaders felt it vital for Gen. Jackson's army in the Shenandoah Valley to continue distracting the Federal army under Gen. Banks, which was positioned north of Winchester, and to the west of Staunton under overall command of Gen. John C. Frémont. Gen. Jackson distracted Banks by a feint and some clever, secretive movements of part of his army in the Winchester area, but Frémont's force would have to be confronted and turned back into western Virginia.

The leading elements of the Union army under Gen. Frémont were brigades under command of brigadier generals Robert H. Milroy and Robert C. Schenck. With a combined force of 6,000 men, those two brigades held the small village of McDowell, Virginia on the morning of May 8. Opposing them were about 3,000 men in two brigades under command of Brig. Gen. Edward Johnson. In total, Johnson had six regiments of infantry, three artillery batteries, and a small force of cavalry. One of his infantry regiments that morning was the 31st Virginia.[297]

The Confederates marched west from Shaw's Fork at an early hour on May 8, with the 31st Virginia setting out in its place in the column at two o'clock in the morning. Lt. Col. Alfred Jackson and Maj. Chenoweth were in immediate command of the regiment as the men stepped out walking, since Col. Hoffman was violently ill that morning, and evidently rode in an ambulance during the first part of the day. Progress on the march was slowed by the artillery and wagons on muddy roads: Johnson's brigades did not come into contact with the Federal pickets until eleven o'clock, when Confederate skirmishers began pushing the Union pickets back.[298]

Brig Gen. Johnson was riding at the head of the column, with the brigade's scouts and skirmishers as they reached Sitlington's Hill, overlooking the village of McDowell. The hill stood on the left of the Pike as the Confederates approached, and was about a mile and half from the village. The main body of Johnson's brigade was still about two miles to the rear, on Bull Pasture Mountain, while Johnson and thirty men, including a few officers, crept up to the top of Sitlington's Hill for a reconnoiter. He found the enemy's position, spread out below at McDowell. Some Union troops also occupied a hill on his right, on the other side of the Pike, overlooking the road and the top of Sitlington's Hill.

Johnson ordered the 52nd Virginia to come up and act as skirmishers on the extreme left of Sitlington's Hill, and soon they were in contact with Federal skirmishers, who were sent up to engage the

52nd Virginia. A brisk fight ensued between the skirmishers, lasting until about four o'clock, and spreading the length of the hill and down the slope to the road. Meanwhile, Johnson was sending other regiments up from the backside of the hill, and was placing them in a line, but the terrain was too steep for artillery, and the guns were standing down on the road.

The 52nd Virginia continued to hold the extreme left, supported by the 58th Virginia. The 12th Georgia was placed at the center of the line, and the 44th Virginia positioned on the right, at the top of a fold in the terrain that ran down toward the road. There were no trees on the hill, except for a fringe along the right end, covering the descending slope. The 31st Virginia was ordered to hold the road and the base of the hill, and began the fight initially in the fringe of woods there, supported by the 25th Virginia. They were opposed by skirmishers from the Third (Union) Virginia infantry, who were using the cover of this woods to go up to the top of the hill, in order to attack the 44th Virginia.[299]

Enough of the Third (Union) Virginia made it up the hill on the right, using the concealment of the woods, to launch a strong attack against the 44th Virginia, sometime before five o'clock. Brig. Gen. Johnson was making a reconnaissance to the right of the 44th Virginia when the Federals came through the trees, forcing Johnson to move quickly into the protection of his lines to avoid being shot down or captured. The 44th Virginia and 12th Georgia returned fire, and forced the Third (Union) Virginia back down as far as the tree line, but the battle continued on the right, the musketry increasing in volleys, and Johnson ordered the 25th and 31st Virginia to come up to hold that end of the line. They went up in quick time, arriving at the top of the hill out of breath, and a little disorganized.

A few companies on the right were positioned down the hill, by the road. Their job was to stop the Federals who were grouped at the base in order to use the woods as cover to go up the hill. Snider said that he was among those who remained at the bottom, firing his musket at Union field officers on the road just below them.

Up on the ridge, Maj. Chenoweth got the men into line, but was in doubt if he was seeing the enemy as they emerged once more from the tree line. He asked Capt. Harding his opinion, and Harding told them they certainly were Federals. Chenoweth then ordered a volley, telling the men to fire low, then followed up by ordering the line forward, and led the charge toward the Third (Union) Virginia, pushing their opponents back further into the trees. As the two regiments came into closer contact, men from either side began recognizing one another, and started to halloo their former acquaintances from home, even as the battle raged. In this fight, Capt. Cooper managed to take prisoner a former neighbor from Clarksburg.[300]

Farther to the left, the battle had become general as more Union regiments were sent up the unprotected face of the hill against the

Confederate line. The 12th Georgia, in the center of the line, and slightly forward, came under intense fire. They were in a relatively exposed position, and suffered heavy casualties.

Taliaferro's brigade, arriving at the base of the hill, was ordered by Gen. Jackson to move up in support of Johnson's men. The 23rd and 37th Virginia climbed the backside of the hill, and then advanced to the center of the line, in support of the 12th Georgia. Meanwhile, the 21st Virginia was placed on the road at the bottom of the hill, taking over this position, and allowing the remainder of the 31st Virginia to climb the hill and join the fight with their regiment.

Campbell's brigade, along with the 10th Virginia, was behind the hill itself and around its right end on the road in reserve. Around 6:30, when some of Campbell's men were sent up the hill as reinforcements, they extended the line from the 31st Virginia, (with the 42nd Virginia in their reserve), down the slope to the troops holding the road.[301]

Relieved from guarding the base of the hill, Lt. Col. Jackson had gone up the hill by then, and was in command of the regiment until some point late in the day, when Col. Hoffman came up and joined in the fight. This was his first battle, having been away from the regiment during every other action of any size. Perhaps he had to gain a handle on his own fears, just as he had warned the volunteers from Harrison County nearly a year before, when urging them to enlist. He made it to the top of the hill in time for the battle's crescendo, as the regiment drove their enemy down the hill.

Brig. General Johnson was wounded in the leg around eight o'clock, and was forced to leave the field, turning command of the brigade over to Gen. Taliaferro to see the victory through to its conclusion. Around 8:30, a great shout of "Davis and Confederacy" rang out from the men on the right end of the line, and spread along the length of the Confederate line to the left. The Federals were retreating, and the battle was over, having raged with terrific violence for nearly four hours.[302]

Gen. Johnson was never shy about praising men, and later named many individuals "as having behaved most gallantly" in the Battle of McDowell, including Lt. Col. Alfred H. Jackson, and Col. John S. Hoffman of the 31st Virginia. The Confederate forces had won this battle, but at the cost of 498 casualties, most of them in the 12th Georgia and the 25th Virginia. Union casualties that day were 256 men killed and wounded.[303]

Casualties in the 31st Virginia were light, with the regiment loosing only 19 men, four of them mortally wounded: those included Asa Kelly, wounded in the thigh; William E. Lemon; John W. Wilson; and John Kuhl, wounded in the calf.

The other wounded in the 31st Virginia included: William L. Benson, in the hip; Franklin Bradshaw, in the side, and paralyzed in the lower limbs; William Chew, in the temple; John S. Griffin, in the left thigh; Andrew Mace, in the arm; Jacob C. Matheny, in the shoulder; Patrick Reilly, in the shoulder; George A. Rexrode, in the hand; George W. Rowan, in the foot; David Slocum, Jr., in the knee; David N. Spaur, in the thigh; James W. Wanless, in the arm; William Wright, in the arm.[304]

Sergeant Chris Kuhl later recalled his brother, John Kuhl. "He got a musket ball wound through the calf of one leg, a flesh wound, and (it) was not supposed to be serious. He held to his gun and everything. He left his musket to me, and said, 'Take good care of it, I'll soon want to use it again.' But not so. He was sent to the Staunton Hospital, and seemed to be getting on nicely, but from some careless nurse probing the wound, it began bleeding. It bled so he never rallied, and died." Chris Kuhl never saw his brother again.[305]

The 31st Virginia remained on Sitlington Hill until late in the night, sending a few men from each mess down to the wagons to cook rations. About one in the morning, the regiment came down from the hill in the darkness and ate, and then tried to rest. Meanwhile, the Federals retreated from McDowell in the night, abandoning several wagons filled with ammunition, many tents, and a lot of other equipment.

Johnson's brigades, including the 31st Virginia, took part in the pursuit of the retreating Union army. With Gen. T. J. Jackson in command, they chased the Federals for five days of rain and muddy roads, following the road that ran beside Straight Creek, and finally giving up the chase at the town of Franklin. The Federals under Milroy had reached the town in time to gain a strong, defensive position. During the chase, the brigade had several times been posted to guard artillery, and came under Union artillery fire on at least one occasion, but the 31st Virginia suffered no casualties.

Gen. Jackson decided the Union position at Franklin was too strong, and wasn't worth the cost in men in trying to attack. He turned his army around and marched it back to McDowell in the rain, stopping there to rest and give the men a chance to look over the battlefield. "There was two acres that was almost mowed by the bullets," Snider observed. "There was bushes six inches in diameter that was cut by bullets until they fell down."[306]

With Brig. Gen. Johnson wounded, Colonel Z. T. Conner, of the 12th Georgia, was in temporary command of the brigade. At ten o'clock, they once again marched as part of Stonewall's army. They crossed Shaver Mountain, and then turned at the road to Stribbling Spring, finally camping that night at Rutherford, a few miles from Jenning's Gap.

Private Hall, of Company H was marching barefooted that day because his shoes had given out the day before: "Still raining," he said that night in his diary. "Tried to get permission to ride, but could not. Marched about 15 miles and encamped somewhere — has no name, nor never should have — on the road leading to Harrisonburg."[307]

It was a disagreeably wet night, followed by a quiet, rainy day — a day of thanksgiving and prayer, set apart by Gen. Jackson, who was a great believer in prayerful worship. After another miserable night of rain, they marched at about eight o'clock on May 17, with the weather clearing and the day growing warm. They were heading northeast, down the valley toward Harrisonburg, the muddy roads churned deeply with hundreds of slogging feet. Around one o'clock they stopped for a rest on a hillside overlooking Mt. Solon.

"Soon after we stopped, the citizens began to bring in baskets of provisions and dividing it out amongst us," Snider wrote. "There was two young ladies came in with a wagon and a fine lot of bread and butter and pies... with a barrel of buttermilk. They cut and spread the bread with their own delicate little hands. I think they was the cleverest and best women that I have seen for a long time. We soon passed through Mt. Solon (seeing) lots of pretty girls."

They marched as far as Bridgewater, and camped opposite the town, on the other side of the North River. The brigade's camp was in George Gibbon's meadow, along the left-hand side of the road, and with the skies clearing, and the temperature seasonable, the men had a pleasant evening.[308]

The bridges at Bridgewater had been burnt, and the river was too full of spring runoff to attempt a crossing on the 18th, giving the men another quiet Sunday in camp. A number of the soldiers made it across the river in some manner, including Snider: "I was over in town to church and found it to be a very pleasant place," Snider wrote. "The stores was open and a good many of the ladies was engaged in sewing and cooking for the soldiers. I bought some goods and had me a fatigue shirt made. I had lost all of my clothes that were left at West View. In the afternoon, I returned to camp and washed my clothes, but by the time I got done, there was a shower of rain came up and I had to put them on to keep them from getting wet and dirty." Gen. Jackson and his mapmaker, Jed Hotchkiss paid a visit to the brigade's camp that evening to hear Reverend Dabney preach.[309]

Perhaps by then, Christian Kuhl of Company D had received tragic news from his home in Braxton County. His father, Henry Kuhl, had been arrested by the Federal army, and charged with shooting a uniformed Union soldier who had come into Kuhl's yard, and was confiscating Kuhl's private possessions.

One of Kuhl's descendants noted the results: "Henry Kuhl and Hamilton Windon were hung, 9 May 1862, from a scaffold built on the Court House lawn at Sutton. Their bodies were put into a single packing crate and they were buried at Town Hill cemetery in Sutton." Following Henry Kuhl's execution, his son Conrad was sent to Camp Chase, charged with disloyalty to the Union.[310]

Jackson's army crossed the North River on a bridge made out of wagons, and then marched through Harrisonburg on May 19. They camped several miles from town, and felt welcome by the smiles, and cheers of the local people. Along the road, the soldiers could see property that had been destroyed by the retreating Union army, which had passed through about a week before. The next morning, the 31st Virginia marched at about nine o'clock, stopping to camp for the night near New Market under a sky dark with clouds and promised rain. More evidence of Union destruction and ruin of civilian property angered the soldiers.

"A part of Gen. Ewell's Division is crossing Peaked Mountain, in sight of our camp below us," Snider wrote in the evening of the 20th. The next morning, they moved out once again at a late hour, 9 A.M., after waiting for a Louisiana brigade to pass. Then they followed in the wake of Ewell's Division, marching through New Market, and turning right onto a road that ran toward Front Royal.[311]

With this movement, Gen. Jackson brought all of his brigades into one force of two divisions. Taylor's Louisiana brigade was out in front, with the rest of Ewell's brigades following, and Jackson's brigades bringing up the rear. Weary after days of forced marches, Stonewall's army camped the night of May 22 at Cedar Point, on the South Fork of the Shenandoah.[312]

During the evening of May 21, the 31st Virginia, 13th Virginia, 25th Virginia, and 12th Georgia were assigned to the Fourth brigade of Ewell's Division. Their new brigade commander was Brig. Gen. Arnold Elzey, a 46-year-old career military officer who had been brevetted to captain for outstanding service during the Mexican War. In the spring of 1861, Elzey had resigned from the U.S. army, and was appointed colonel of the 1st Maryland Infantry. Promoted to brigadier general in July 1861, on the recommendation of Gen. Jackson, he had fought on Stonewall's left at the first Battle of Manassas.[313]

The 31st Virginia marched with Jackson's army on May 23, taking muddy roads in a cautious approach to Front Royal. Elzey's brigade was held in reserve in the late afternoon when the Confederates attacked a small Union force at Front Royal. Within two hours, Jackson had the Federals retreating in the direction of Cedarville on the Winchester Road. The Confederates captured more than four hundred prisoners that day, and all of the Union stores and supplies.

That night the brigade was posted to guard the Winchester Road, a few miles from Front Royal, near Guard Hill. They fought some skirmishes with Union cavalry in the morning, turning back the cavalry before marching in the rear of Jackson's two divisions toward Middletown. A large Union force commanded by Gen. Banks was there, but had already begun to retreat on the Valley Pike. Gen. Jackson sited his artillery on high ground and reduced the Federal wagon train to a shambles.[314]

The Union army continued to withdraw throughout the night, with the Confederates at their heels, pushing them to Winchester. Jackson attacked at dawn with a heavy artillery bombardment. The men of the 31st Virginia were eager for battle that day. "We marched forward until we had a splendid view of the fight," Hall wrote. "The cannonading was tremendous. In a short time the enemy commenced retreating, and in doing so set the town on fire." Elzey sent his brigade into Winchester, in pursuit of the retreating Federals, and with the 31st Virginia at the head of the column.

"Away we went on the double quick, nor halted until through town," Joseph Harding later recalled, "regardless of bursting shells, flying bullets, and the groans of the wounded. Men, women, and children thronged the streets."[315]

"The scene surpassed description," Lt. Col. Alfred Jackson wrote, "The streets were filled with women and children, and old and young, black and white, cheering, laughing, crying and shouting. Some were bringing water and food for our soldiers, others waving banners, and some of the ladies even went so far as to hug some of our boys in their delight. I assure you, I came very near being hugged several times in passing through the town, and you know how averse I am to anything of that kind."

The 31st Virginia, with Elzey's brigade just behind, passed quickly through the town and chased the Federals for five miles. The brigade stopped when it reached the Martinsburg Pike, and set up camp in the road to prevent anyone crossing without permission. Behind them, at Winchester, Jackson's other brigades helped put out the fires in town, and took possession of an immense quantity of stores, including $200,000 worth of medical stores, more than 200 wagons, 8500 guns, two artillery pieces, and 2,000 prisoners.[316]

The 31st Virginia remained camped near Winchester until May 28, when the regiment received marching orders on short notice, and marched until ten o'clock at night. They camped twelve miles from Charles Town. The next day was another of Gen. Jackson's famous early starts, shortly after two in the morning, and by that night they were a couple of miles past Charles Town.

With all of this hard marching and action, their brigade had spent precious little time at drill. To correct this defect, Gen. Elzey issued orders, on May 28, establishing times of day for drill and instruction in the Fourth brigade: from 8 to 9:30 A.M., 10:30 to 11:30 A.M., and 4 to 5:30 P.M. Commanders of regiments were charged with the execution of the order. Presumably drill would take place only on days when they were not marching, or fighting. The pace of Stonewall's campaign would leave scant time for drill.[317]

The regiment marched to Harper's Ferry on the 30th, Alfred Jackson recorded, "and were just about to attack the enemy who had made a stand there, when Gen. Jackson received intelligence that Gen. Shields, with 7,000 men, had entered Front Royal, and that Freemont, with 20,000, was marching to Strasburg, on the Capon Springs Road.

We immediately faced about and marched to Strasburg, reaching there on the morning of the first of June, (and) only beating Freemont (by) two miles."[318]

Freemont's army was on the Capon Springs Road, two miles from town, when the Confederates came up. After an hour's fight, Gen. Jackson repulsed Freemont, then turned his army toward Woodstock in the night, with Freemont's larger army following closely. Union cavalry skirmished with Jackson's rearguard, and captured the occasional stragglers from the Southern infantry. The 31st Virginia lost five men in this way, including John Josiah Spencer, a private in Company G. Spencer was luckier than many prisoners: the Federals confined him on board the steamer U.S.S. *Coatzacoalcos* until he was later exchanged at Aiken's Landing, Virginia.[319]

Stonewall's Army of the Valley continued its march on June 2, the rear of the army protected by Turner Ashby's cavalry. The lead regiments crossed the Shenandoah River near Mt. Jackson on June 3. Stonewall was moving rapidly now, his soldiers earning by sweat, fatigue, and blisters the title "Jackson's Foot Cavalry." In the early morning of June 5 the army passed through Harrisonburg and turned to the east, on the road to Port Republic.

"If I am doomed to fall during the war," Maj. Joseph Chenoweth had written in his journal, earlier in the war, "I hope it may not be until we are satisfied, beyond the doubt of the most timid, that we will gain our independence in the end. If it should be otherwise, I am resigned; God's will be done, not mine." Chenoweth was known as a sensitive man, and like many of his fellow soldiers, was deeply sentimental. "I could part from earth, were I doomed to die soon, far more willingly if I could once more behold the faces of father, mother, sisters, and brothers; but if this should be denied me, I have only to say that they need not weep for me, but be proud rather, and smile when they remember that I died on the battlefield trying to do my duty to my country, fighting for what I considered her rights."[320] The major had evidently made good on his vow to give up drink, and his efforts as an officer of the 31st Virginia were not unrecognized by friends, and fellow officers. Chenoweth made an entry into his diary, "Near Harrisonburg, June 6, 1862 — We camped here last night, and are marching towards Port Republic, but slowly over a rough road, made worse by long rain. I know not what our ultimate destination is, but I hope we will soon have time to rest awhile in camp."[321]

Their progress that day may have been slow, but in little more than one month Jackson's army, including the 31st Virginia, had marched from Staunton to McDowell; from there to Franklin; backtracked to McDowell and then east to Jenning's Gap; headed northeast through the valley to Harrisonburg; then to New Market; from there by way of Luray Valley to Front Royal; by way of Middletown to Winchester; then to Charles Town, and Harper's Ferry; returned up the Valley to

Strasburg and Woodstock; and finally arrived at Cross Keys, just over the river from Port Republic.

The past few days had especially been a race to arrive at Port Republic ahead of two separate forces of the Union army under generals Freemont and Shields. On arrival at Port Republic, Stonewall discovered Freemont had arrived ahead of him, and was positioned a few miles north of Cross Keys. "On June 7," Hall said, "we were awakened about two o'clock in the morning and ordered to cook one day's rations immediately, but before we could commence, everything had to be put in the wagon. About daylight we were marched back about 300 yards and formed a line of battle. We remained in line all that day — having momentarily expected the enemy to make his appearance. We camped near the same place." After their recent exertions in racing up and down the valley, staying in the same place for more than one day must have been a luxury to the soldiers. And they needed the rest, for on the next day, June 8, they would fight in a hotly contested battle.[322]

Cross Keys was a small village northwest of the town of Port Republic. Gen. Ewell placed his division just south of the town, to confront Freemont's Union army, while Jackson's other division held Port Republic, a few miles to the south. Ewell's line was facing Freemont's army of about 10,500 men. The 31st Virginia and the 12th Georgia were initially placed in reserve of Elzey's brigade, near the middle of the line, in support of the artillery. They were not far from the Mill Creek church, on a low ridge that overlooked a large, open field, and a small stream in front of them. There were woods on either side of the line, concealing their flanks. The road that connected Cross Keys to Port Republic bisected the field in their front, and continued through the center of Gen. Ewell's line.[323]

Part of the brigade was separated early in the battle, the 13th and 25th Virginia being detached to support Trimble's brigade on the right. Gen. Trimble, supported by the 13th Virginia, moved forward to try to take a Union battery that the enemy posted on the right, a half mile to the front. Before they arrived the battery was withdrawn, but in the meantime spirited skirmishing began and part of Trimble's force advanced to a place more than a mile from their original position. The battle was now fairly begun, and would continue for hours.

Around noon, Maj. Chenoweth wrote in his diary, "A heavy cannonade is being kept up on the side of us.... Some of our men have been wounded. I saw one going to the rear. The 31st is supporting the battery, which is engaged. I do not like our position, although it is a commanding one. We may possibly have our flank turned...." Maybe the journal helped to distract Chenoweth from the normal fears of soldiers in battle. "Later," he said, "There is a lull in the firing, I know not why." The smoke from artillery was fading. Chenoweth added a prayer for the success of his cause and the salvation of his people.[324]

In a while, Patton's brigade arrived from Port Republic as reinforcements, and was placed with Steuart's 1st Maryland on their left. They sent skirmishers out in front of the hill, to harass the enemy. After being moved around a little, as Gen. Elzey looked for the best place to put the 31st Virginia, the regiment was ordered to take a position to the left of the 1st Maryland regiment. According to Col. Hoffman, they were "in the edge of a wood on a bluff." The regiment was positioned to hold the extreme left of the line against Union skirmishers from Schenck's brigade.[325]

The 31st Virginia came under intense artillery fire there. Private Hall said, "We remained as silent and quiet as if inanimate, for some time, while the cannon balls, like winged devils, were flying around us. I noticed the countenance of the men. Some looked pale but calm, their eyes tranquil. The knitted brow and flashing eyes of others showed the more fiery spirit within. We remained in this position, occasionally moving around to the right or left. About two o'clock Lt. Whiteley of our company was killed—shot through the head."[326]

In the relative quiet between attacks on a warm June night, Capt. Harding and Maj. Chenoweth discussed their position. Chenoweth felt a premonition of his own death, and was fearful that he would never see his loved ones again, but he was not destined to die at Cross Keys.

A piece of artillery was brought up, and placed just to their left: it began firing at the Federals, and no doubt drew return fire from the Union guns. The 31st Virginia had also been firing their muskets, evidently at skirmishers who drew too close. By a little after six o'-clock, the fight had grown quiet. "Our regiment is lying down in line of battle," Chenoweth wrote, "in full view of the enemy's battery; the same battery which, only an hour ago, was pouring grape into the regiment. Noble soldiers! It tortures me to see them wounded. How many of them now, as they rest looking quietly and dreamily up into the beautiful sky, are thinking of the dear ones at home, whom they have not seen for twelve months! This is a hard life for us refugees who fight and suffer on without one smile from those we love dearest to cheer us up. But by the blessing of God the fires of patriotism will keep our hearts warm...."[327]

Col. Hoffman reported the regiment's casualties at Cross Keys: "Our loss was Lt. Whiteley, a brave and worthy officer, killed; and nine wounded." Their fallen comrade, Alexander Whiteley, born in Ireland, had been elected 2nd lieutenant of Company H just seven days earlier, on the first of May.

That night the 31st Virginia camped near the field of battle, but was roused at an early hour and ordered to march toward Port Republic. The Battle of Port Republic was about to begin. It would be one of the regiment's greatest trials in battle.[328]

BATTLE OF CROSS KEYS, JUNE 8, 1862

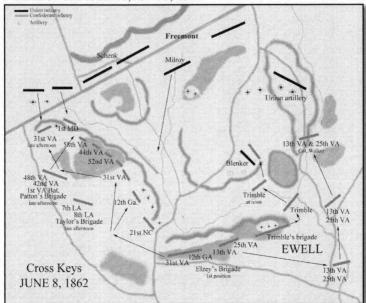

Map by David W. Wooddell

The bridge over the South River, in the town of Port Republic, had been burned on the previous day as a portion of Jackson's men skirmished with Union forces approaching the town from the south. The Federals had been held at bay while Ewell's division waged the fight at Cross Keys, but the next morning the Union army was back, south of Port Republic and in greater strength than on the previous day. They held a strong position further along the river, in a line of fenced grain fields, and were ready for the Confederates when the battle began.

Well before dawn on June 9, wagons were driven into the river and planks laid across for Stonewall's men to use as a bridge. In some places, the walkway narrowed to a single plank, and the passage of men began to falter. Among those crossed in this way was Col. Hoffman's regiment, the 31st Virginia, which was temporarily detached from Elzey's brigade. The regiment had grown small after all of the fighting and marching in the past weeks, and had only 214 officers and men present as it marched through the town of Port Republic in the dawnish hours, and made its way over the South River on the makeshift bridge.[329]

They followed in the trail of Jackson's division, and would be placed under Brig. Gen. Winder, in his brigade on the Confederate left. "The ball is open again, and we are, from what I can see and hear, to have another hot day," Maj. Chenoweth said in his journal at 8 A.M. "It is Shields this time. I may not see the result, but I think we will gain the victory, although I do not think our men have had enough to eat. I cannot write on horseback."[330]

This was the last entry in Maj. Joseph H. Chenoweth's diary. While the 31st Virginia moved forward, Chenoweth and Capt. Harding discussed his presentiment of death. By then, Gen. Winder was already placing various regiments and batteries on either side of the road, all the while under fire from several Union batteries. The Confederates were taking a heavy pounding by the Union guns, their ranks thinned and wavering. In response to Winder's call for help, the 7th Louisiana came up and was placed to the right of the line, with another regiment on their right. They were ordered to advance and drive the enemy, "at the point of the bayonet."

The Louisianans sprang forward with a cheer and drove the Federals back beyond a fence, and the Louisiana colonel halted his men behind the fence, which was their only protection in the face of heavy artillery and rifle fire. Next, a Confederate battery came up and was placed by Gen. Winder just behind the 7th Louisiana. Although they were receiving the brunt of the enemy's attack, Winder's force was holding out, but almost all of their cartridges were gone.

"The 31st Regiment Virginia Volunteers (Col. Hoffman) arrived about this time," Gen. Winder later reported, "to relieve Colonel Hays (7th Louisiana), who was ordered to join his brigade. This change it was impossible to effect, and I held Col. Hoffman in rear of the batteries for their security, as the infantry line began to waver under the storm of shot, shell, and balls which was being rained upon them." The line could not hold indefinitely, and with ammunition almost gone, some men panicked and rushed for the rear.[331]

Recalling tactical movement on the field of battle, after such a harrowing fight as the 31st Virginia was about to experience, was less important afterward to the men who survived than the experience, and the emotions of their ordeal. "Ordered forward through murderous hail of bullets," Capt. Harding recalled, "ardor carried us too far.... our position being a large wheat field, luxuriant with the ripening grain. We had scarcely gained our position, when the dense column of the enemy were thrown forward and we were subjected to a most deadly and destructive front and enfilading fire."[332]

Maj. Chenoweth's premonition of death was unfortunately on the mark that day. Capt. Harding said, "He had dismounted, and, in the commencement of the fight, taken his position immediately behind the center of the left wing of the regiment. As the battle progressed he passed down the line, around its left flank, and was advancing up the front, encouraging the men, and calling upon them to follow where he led, when he was shot, the ball entering just behind the left ear, and passing entirely though his head. He fell without a groan, his sword still in his grasp pointed toward the enemy, nobly discharging his duty."[333]

Others in the regiment had to find the balance between fear and courage, deciding to stay or run, and never knowing if they were heroes or cowards. William F. Gordon, former newspaperman from Company C, later recalled, "Under fire, in the midst of battle, hot with action, intoxicated with noise, the yells of comrades, the rattle of musketry, the whiz of miniés, whir of balls, and clatter of shells, the cheers of victors, the rush for position and desperate holding, the human passion of spiteful revenge and the roused taste for blood and carnage innate in the animal man—under fire in the phrenzy of fight is no test of courage. Many a man stands there, because he is afraid to run."[334]

The field at Port Republic was a fearful place. "We came near being annihilated, " Henry Yeager, of Company G later wrote. "Our company losing eighteen out of thirty-six men engaged in fifteen minutes, and but for the timely charges made by Taylor's Louisiana brigade (afterward Hays) the whole regiment must have perished."[335]

George Arbogast of the same company was severely wounded in the leg. William Hull helped carry Arbogast to a position of safety. "We were under a terrible fire of both musketry and artillery and were driven back some distance until the Louisiana brigade accomplished its flank movement on the right of our line," Hull recalled later.[336]

"We crawled up through that oat field on our bellies," William Gordon said their predicament, "rising to shoot, dropping again to load and advance. And every time we rose some comrades dropped to rise no more. We neared the crest until we could almost look down the black, sulfurous throats of those nine twelve-pounders that were belching grape and canister into our very mouths.

"Five times had our colors fallen... our tallest brave fellows, one after another, raised with the regimental flag, and fell, shot through the forehead. They had been picked off by the sharpshooters one after another, those gallant Western Virginia mountaineers.... The fifth had fallen. A sergeant jumped from Company C to raise the standard. *Better let that damned thing alone, Bill*, growled Lt. Cooper. *Use both hands with your bayonet next rise.*"[337]

A bullet clipped a sliver of a rib along the right side of Jeremiah Church's torso, as he was carrying a wounded comrade, James Stewart off the field. Church put the wounded man over his shoulders, and was heading back to safety amid the whizzing of bullets. The Federals were charging the position, and the regiment was giving way. Feeling the slam of a bullet snipping a piece of his side, Church dropped Stewart on the ground, telling him it was necessary to leave him there, to which Stewart agreed.

Church made a run for it, while the enemy shouted for him to halt where he was. "No," Church shouted at them, making up his mind, "to die rather than be captured and starve to death." He outran his enemy's aim, dodging every shot except the one that took the sliver of rib.[338]

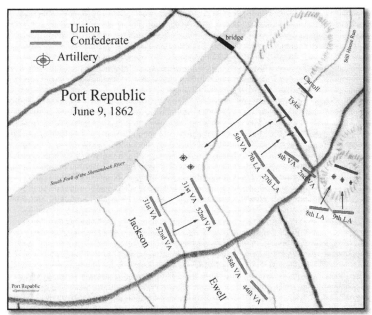

Map by David W. Wooddell

"The wheat was beginning to turn yellow," Sgt. Christian Kuhl recalled. "Harvest fields are generally hot places, but this was the hottest I ever was in. And the only one I had ever seen cut with bullets. There had been no previous provisions made, neither side had any fortifications, so an open wheat field was our only chance. Each minié ball seemed to cut its little swath, and the cannon balls a big one.

"We fought most of the time lying flat on the ground," Kuhl said. "My company lost one killed, (Charles W. H. Gough, and one wounded, Thomas J. McGinnis. McGinnis was a hero, and so was Gough. He had often said he wanted to die at his post of duty, and so it was granted. After some hours of hot conflict, we drove the enemy from the wheat field. But not much was left for the owner to reap that was not shot or tramped by us or the enemy."[339]

Gen. Winder later reported the tumult, and confusion that reigned while he tried to steady the men. "The batteries were moved to the rear and I tried to rally the men, placing Hoffman's regiment in line on which to rally; here I partially succeeded, but the enemy so greatly outnumbered us, and getting within such easy range, thinned our ranks so terribly that it was impossible to rally them for some time."

Gen. Winder held on in spite of the terrific losses. "I still endeavored to rally the remainder of this force, and succeeded in getting the 7th Louisiana, under Maj. Penn, the colonel and lieutenant colonel both being wounded, and the 5th Regiment, under Funk. I placed two pieces of Poague's battery in the position previously occupied, and again opened fire on the enemy, he having halted in his advance. A sharp fire from the wood on the right told (that) Gen. Taylor's and Allen's forces were engaged."[340]

Gen. Winder brought up regiment after regiment on the left, and after a flank attack on the right by the Louisiana brigade, was finally able to drive the Federals back. The Confederates chased the Federals for about 8 miles before Gen. Jackson recalled the remnants of Winder's force. The exhausted soldiers returned and camped near their wagons, around midnight.[341]

1st Lt. Lyman, of Company B, felt they had been used in a callous way. "We were simply "food for gunpowder" that day (along with one regiment from each brigade) while our main force went around, got in the rear of the enemy, and defeated him, but it was about the worst experience of the war for four regiments." Lyman's company lost 21 killed and wounded out of 40 on the field, including its Capt., Robert Bradshaw.[342]

Of all the battles fought by the 31st Virginia Volunteers, and there were many in the years to come, the battle of Port Republic was the regiment's highest percentage of casualties for a single engagement. More than half of the 31st Virginia's 214 arms-bearing men engaged in the battle became casualties, including 14 men killed, 76 wounded, 15 mortally wounded, and 4 men missing. Three of the missing were captured. "This was, I think, the bloodiest battle of the war," Lt. Col. Alfred Jackson wrote to his wife afterward. "Our regiment lost 114 killed and wounded... Four or five men were killed immediately (next to) me, but I was fortunate enough to escape unhurt."[343]

Killed: Capt. Robert H. Bradshaw, Maj. Joseph H. Chenoweth, Samuel Dawson, Charles W. H. Gough, John T. Hicks, Dallas Hudson, John H. Long, James A. Ruckman, James Steele, Jr., George W. Thompson, John W. Wellingham. Mortally Wounded: Lt. Jonathan F. Arnett, Peter H. Beathe, Josiah Gum, William Isner, John F. Leach, John Siron, James M. Steuart, John W. Sheffer. Wounded: George W. Arbogast, William J. Bonner, Lt. John M. Burns, John W. Carroll, Elam G. Corder, Noah Folks, Elam Gough, Houston F. Gwin, John S. Hicklin, Lt. Warwick C. Kincaid, Wilson Moore, Joshua W. Ness, Thomas Reed, John J. Stewart, Amos K. Sturm, Andrew J. Thompson, Washington Varner, Peter Wilt.

Some of the men would be away from the regiment for a very long time. Private George W. Arbogast was sent to a hospital, where he remained through the autumn of 1862, eventually receiving a furlough and going home to recuperate. He was still there, at Green Bank in Pocahontas County on February 11, 1863, when he was arrested by Union troops and sent to the small prison known as the Atheneum at Wheeling. From there he was sent to Camp Chase, Ohio, but was exchanged shortly after, on March 28, 1863. He was then just 23 years old, 5 feet, 9 inches tall, light complexion, gray eyes, light hair, and gave his occupation as farmer. His brother was Maj. James Arbogast.[344]

Capt. Harding mourned his fallen comrade, Joseph Chenoweth. "As a soldier he was brave and chivalrous; as a commander firm and generous; and as a companion kind, courteous, and true.... We buried him on the battlefield, where he so nobly fought and so nobly died, with no pillow save his soldier's knapsack, and no shroud but his soldier's blanket; and yet we left him shrouded in the glory of his own noble deeds that no time can obliterate."[345]

William Gordon later recalled Lt. Cooper's reaction to their narrow brush with death, noting that Cooper was "as brave a man as crawled back with our little regiment of 114 that day," Gordon wrote. "After we had reached safe quarters and were lying down to rest in the woods, he turned to me to ask: 'What were you looking up and down the line in there for, Bill?' 'Lieutenant,' was the answer, 'I was looking for a chance to run.' 'By, God, so was I! But damned if every fellow in the regiment wasn't looking right at me.'"[346]

On June 10, the 31st Virginia marched to a position near Mount Meridian, and was allowed to camp. Alfred Jackson wrote to his wife, Mary, "The enemy have fallen back to Strasburg. All is quiet now and our boys are resting after their severe labors; we have accomplished a great deal. We have captured millions of dollars worth of stores and brought them off safely. We have captured over 4000 prisoners and killed and wounded 6 or 7000 of the enemy. Stonewall Jackson is the Hero of the day and well does he deserve to be.

"Enclosed, I send you a piece of lace, and a Yankee shinplaster which some of the boys gave to me. The lace came out of a Yankee letter. Write often, dear Mary, and believe me ever your, Alf." Mary Jackson was then 20 years old. Originally from Lewisburg, in the Greenbrier Valley, they had married two years before the war, and had two small children, both daughters, by the time her husband went off to serve in the army. Throughout the war, she and the children were forced to refugee away from their home at Weston.[347]

The loss of Maj. Chenoweth required that the senior captain be promoted to take his place. Capt. Arbogast of Company G was the regiment's senior captain, and was given a field promotion to acting major on June 13. With Col. Hoffman sick much of the time in these months of the campaign, heavier duty and increased responsibility fell on Lt. Col. Jackson and Maj. Arbogast.[348]

There were other promotions in the 31st Virginia, resulting from the regiment's terrible losses at Port Republic. These included Lt. Lyman, who was elected captain of Company B to replace Robert H. Bradshaw, who had been killed in battle.

Private James E. Hall had worried through most of the first year with a sense of keen injustice at being a mere enlisted man. To replace their junior lieutenant, Alexander Whiteley, killed by a shot to the head at Cross Keys, Company H held an election about a week later, on June 21, and elected Hall as their new 2nd lieutenant, according to his diary. However, the election may not have been certified, and remained unconfirmed. Perhaps by then Hall had learned that the life of an officer was often short on the field of battle and did not protest too strenuously. Following so closely on the death of a comrade, Hall barely commented in his diary on gaining the new position.[349]

Stonewall's army had marched to a place near Weyer's Cave in Augusta County on June 16. The weather was refreshingly cool, and the men in need of rest, but they were not allowed to remain there for very long: the defense of Richmond required that Gen. Jackson move his two divisions to join with Gen. Lee in the fight against McClellan near the Confederate capital. On the 17th, the 31st Virginia received orders at ten o'clock to pack up their baggage at once. By eleven, they were marching toward Staunton. Capt. Phillips, of Company K, said, "Old mother rumor said we were going to the south."

They passed through Staunton on the way toward the Blue Ridge Mountains. On their way through town, one of the men from the regiment stopped in town and left a lasting impression on the county historian. "A member of the 31st Regiment, from northwest Virginia, came into our office this evening," Joseph A. Waddell wrote, "and meeting there an acquaintance from the same region, told with great glee that in the Monday's fight near Port Republic, he had shot the major in the First (Union) Virginia Regiment.... He manifested a savage joyousness in relating the fall, by his hand, of his fellow townsman."[350]

The regiment crossed the summit of the Blue Ridge at Jarmin's Gap, about four miles north of Waynesboro, around one o'clock that day. They were marching in the lead of Elzey's brigade, which was that day in the lead of Gen. Ewell's division. Behind them, stretching for miles was the entire column of Stonewall Jackson's army. When the 31st Virginia camped that night, on the roadside near Meechums River, about 10 miles from Charlottesville, the rest of the army was still strung out to the rear, and part of it remained on the flanks of the Blue Ridge, their campfires dotting the night up the mountainside.[351]

"All this was no small tramp for men," Sergeant Chris Kuhl recalled, "way worn, footsore, oft nearly or quite barefoot, hungry or scarce of rations, each one being his own baggage wagon, having to foot it day after day, carry his knapsack, haversack, canteen full and sometimes even worse, empty, and even sometimes haversack empty, and still worse stomach empty with little hope of filling. Besides carrying a heavy twelve pound gun, forty rounds of ammunition in cartridge box, cap box, belt, bayonet, scabbard, blankets, overcoats, (and) oil cloth."[352]

The regiment moved to Charlottesville on June 19, the day excessively hot, according to Hall. They were given a day of rest on the 20th, but the men continued to speculate on what next their fate would be. "A most beautiful day," Hall wrote, "The calmest and most serene day that I have seen for a long time. We are all much puzzled by this movement of the army. What it means, none can form the slightest conjecture. May abandon Virginia. May be a pitched fight."

While at Charlottesville, Brig. Gen. Arnold Elzey rejoined the brigade. He had been wounded at Cross Keys, but was recovered sufficiently to once more take to the field and command the brigade. But if he knew what Gen. Jackson intended, he kept it to himself.[353]

The 31st Virginia departed Charlottesville on the 21st, and marched 18 miles to Gordonsville, arriving at that railroad junction about eleven in the morning. The Virginia Central met the Orange and Alexandria Railroad at Gordonsville, leading the men to hope that they might get to ride for a change. Capt. Phillips said in his journal, "It is now almost sundown, and we have had nothing to eat since this morning. You can imagine much better than I can describe, the deep murmurs put up by the men. I heard today that two of the men of Company H had deserted, but I am not positive."

The next morning, a Sunday, the 31st Virginia "took to the cars" along with most of Ewell's Division, and rode a train to Louisa Court House. Their provisions had arrived, and they now had two days of cooked rations on hand. "Rumor says we are going to Richmond to guard prisoners," Phillips said. "I do not know where we are going."

While at Louisa Court House, with the regiment in camp, Phillips may have been afraid that his own resolve was crumbling. He took the time to reason through just why he was there, at such potential cost to himself. "When is the war to close? Must I go on day after day, and even year after year? I have studied my course of policy for hours and always arrive at the same conclusion that I would see this conflict through, if I was afterwards left to die a beggar. If I fall, I have but few to care for me, and there will be few tears shed for me."[354]

When the 31st Virginia moved out on June 23, the soldiers found sweet pickings in the cherry trees along the roadside as they marched. The regiment camped that night at Beaver Dam, a stop on the railroad, but broke camp early the following day for a long, and miserable 15-mile march toward Richmond, crossing rivers, and passing over mired swamps. In the afternoon, the skies opened with heavy rain, drenching the men, and turning the road to the well-known mud. After arriving at their destination, near midnight, Phillips wrote in his journal, "I believe I can say that the suffering this night excelled anything that I have ever experienced."[355]

The regiment marched again on June 25, leaving early on what was to be another long, dusty, and intensely hot day with little water, reaching Ashland by evening. Many of Gen. Jackson's brigades were without rations when they arrived at Ashland. Fortunately, the 31st Virginia had two day's rations baked by noon before beginning that day's march, and so they were able to set out with stomachs full, and haversacks loaded.

"The head of our column is still in the direction of Richmond," Capt. Phillips observed. "I do not know how far we are from the enemy. I think where ever they may be, we intend to attack them vigorously and in force, and I hope this will dry up the war.... Tomorrow undoubtedly our ears will be greeted by the sound of artillery. I think by every appearance that we will have a fight. Old Tom Jackson is not the man to lay still in the vicinity of an enemy."[356]

But they were too late for that day's small battle, at Oak Grove.

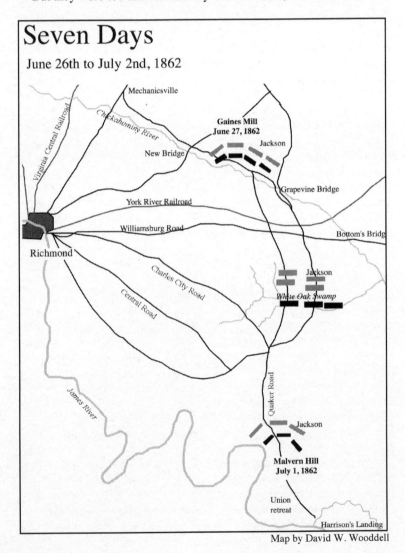

Seven Days

June 26th to July 2nd, 1862

Map by David W. Wooddell

The following day, after leaving Ashland, the 31st Virginia marched to Hundley's Corner, where a half-destroyed bridge slowed Jackson's army over the Totopotomoy Creek that had been set upon by retreating Federals. Whiting's division of Texans repaired the bridge so the men could cross, and the march resume toward Cold Harbor. At around noon that day, as they were taking a break, Phillips said that they were about eleven miles from Richmond. "We drive the Yankee pickets before us," he wrote. "We are passing over a low marshy country verging at times to huge swamps. Frog ponds and stagnant waters are plentiful... I am looking for a fight almost hourly."[357]

Late in the day, around four o'clock, they heard the sound of battle in the distance. "All at once, away on our right, burst out the deafening roar of artillery, causing the very earth to tremble," Phillips wrote. "Peal on peal, the artillery let out in the evening air. For a moment there would be a pause in the artillery, and then would come the sharp crack of thousands of muskets." They were listening to the guns and uproar as Gen. A. P. Hill's division attacked the Union right in the Battle of Beaver Creek Dam.

Elzey's brigade was marched rapidly down the main road until they were a mile from the Chickahominy swamps, and then formed a line of battle. "The sun looked like blood as its rays waded through dark clouds of smoke," Phillips wrote. "Our artillery took to position, and we expected to fight every few minutes, but the sun went down and we stacked arms for the night."

They slept where they were that night, muted swamp sounds mingling with the rumble of distant artillery until well after dark. While the 31st Virginia, and all but one of the other regiments of Elzey's brigade rested, the 13th Virginia under Colonel James A. Walker was assigned as skirmishers, along with the Maryland Line, and the 6th Louisiana.[358]

On the morning of June 27, the 31st Virginia crossed Beaver Dam Creek. This was another of the local swamps, named for a short stream that ran into the Chickahominy River. Beaver Dam Creek, according to Jed Hotchkiss, Stonewall Jackson's mapmaker, was "crossed by the main road from Mechanicsville down the north side of the Chickahominy, by way of Gaines' Mill, to old Cold Harbor. For about a mile from its mouth up to this road this swamp is well nigh impassable. Above the road a dam is thrown across it, making an extensive pond above it for the use of Ellison's mill on the north side of the road. This sluggish stream deeply trenches the plateau or high ground north of the Chickahominy."[359]

The Federals had placed earthworks for batteries and trenches for the infantry on the high ground that rose out of the water, facing north on the slope of the hill overlooking the swamp. They also cut most of the timber in their front, allowing the trees to fall haphazardly in an effective obstruction to the Confederate advance. But that wasn't what slowed Jackson's Army Corps.

Unfortunately, on the way to Gaines' Mill, Stonewall's army became lost, and a good part of the day was spent marching, and then countermarching over unfamiliar territory, looking for their destination. With Gen. Ewell's division in the advance, the route was south to Walnut Grove Church and the Old Cold Harbor Road, where the army turned east until it came to a turning for a small road through the woods that led south past Gaines' Mill near New Cold Harbor and intersected the Telegraph Road. Their guide led the army down that small road in the woods until they were near the headwaters of Powhite Creek, but there the mistake became apparent.

The army then turned around and retraced its steps along the same road until it could once again turn east on the Old Cold Harbor Road. This road made the turn to the south just a mile or two beyond the road through the woods, taking the army to Old Cold Harbor. Gen. Ewell's regiments did not reach the Telegraph Road, just west of Old Cold Harbor, until 3:30 in the afternoon. By then, A. P. Hill's Corps was pushing hard against McClellan's force, which was now defending itself from the heights south of Boatswain's Swamp.[360]

Gen. Ewell ordered the Fourth brigade, under Brig. Gen. Elzey, into the woods on the left of the Gaines' Mill road. Ewell's Seventh and Eighth brigades, under Trimble and Seymour, were sent into the woods to the right of the road. The brigades crossed the stream, and began to march in line of battle toward the first hill, the thick foliage of the woods making it impossible to see more than a few feet, or obtain a view of the enemy at the top of the hill.[361]

"On we rushed, cheered by the shrill voice of Elzey," Capt. Phillips later wrote. "Reaching the top of an eminence, and in full view of the enemy, here Maj. Howard said, 'Now boys, cheer!' but no one heard him. I then raised my voice to its full height and said, 'Now Cheer!' giving one loud cheer myself, and every man followed and such a cheer as never was went up before, rushing down the hill toward the enemy."

The swamp at the bottom of the hill slowed them, the men wading through the water and cheering, while a storm of exploding shell and musket balls flew into them. "Arriving at the summit of the second bluff, our men commenced firing, crash on crash went the musketry, and men fell everywhere... nearly an hour of the most terrific fighting that I ever saw, but our men were wasting away."

Gen. Elzey fell wounded and was taken off the field. On the left of the Confederate line, the Federals started a turning action, but Gen. Ewell sent reinforcements to push them back, and the situation was saved. Men sweated in heat and fear, the air thick and sticky with humidity. Incessant buzz of blood-sucking mosquitoes circled endlessly. Leeches clung wetly in crimson embrace on the soldier's legs.[362]

A maelstrom of gunfire stopped Seymour's Louisiana brigade, to the right of the Fourth brigade, and then Trimble's brigade came up through the confused remnants of the Louisiana troops. "These troops were attacked in front and flank by superior numbers, and were for hours without reinforcements," Gen. Ewell reported afterward. "The Louisiana brigade, having sustained a very severe loss in field officers, besides suffering in rank and file, was driven off the field, but the line was held by part of Trimble's brigade."[363]

When Elzey's brigade, on the left of Ewell's line, was sent in to the attack, they ran into Maj. Charles S. Lovell's brigade, composed of the Second, Sixth, Tenth, Eleventh, and Seventeenth U.S. regiments. Those soldiers were part of the Union's Second division, under the command of Brig. Gen. George Sykes, of the Union Fifth Corps, which was then commanded by Brig. Gen. Fitz John Porter.[364]

Ewell's Confederates continued the fight that day against a steady stream of Federal reinforcement, which came up into the Union line one regiment after another. The Confederates also fought well, considering how outnumbered they were by the Federals, who had the advantage of higher ground. Slowly, the Confederates gained ground and held on through the afternoon and into the evening.

BATTLE OF GAINES MILL, JUNE 28, 1862

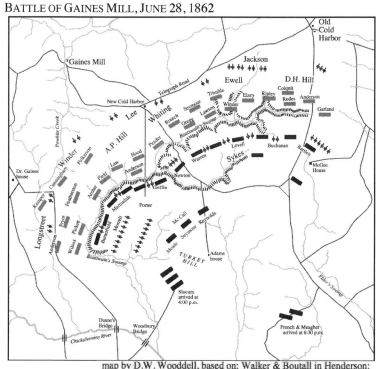

map by D.W. Wooddell, based on: Walker & Boutall in Henderson; Sears, *To the Gates of Richmond*; and O.R. Reports

Colonel James A Walker, the one they called "Stonewall Jim" of the 13th Virginia was temporarily in command of the Fourth brigade. Gen. Jackson rode up and ordered him to hold out until the Texas brigade could come to their support. The Texans were fresh, and they came with a rush toward the Federals, overwhelming the Union line and clearing the field.[365]

In that last charge, Elzey's brigade went forward onto the hill toward the Federals, through clouds of rifle smoke and artillery fire. The slope was 400 yards long and open, with tiny corn plants not much more than shoe-top high for the wounded to fall on and crush. When the 31st Virginia made it to the crest of the hill, the men were in a thin woods "Instantly we were engaged in a deadly contest at close range," one of the brigade noted, "some time almost together and at no time over fifty yards apart. The smoke became so dense that the men could only locate the enemy by the flash of their guns. The carnage was fearful on both sides. The volleys of musketry were so loud we could not distinguish the report of the cannon, but we could see the effect of the shot and shell as they cut down the trees around us."[366]

Capt. Phillips recalled the "wildest shouts that was ever heard by the ears of man" as the soldiers charged the Federal batteries. He saw the other side turn after five minutes of intense combat, turn and run for the safety of the swamp on the other side of the hill. "The day was won, but, oh horror, that miserable battle field behind,"

Phillips observed sadly when he wrote his memories of that day, "death with its ghastly paleness had over spread many a noble face and writhing upon the ground lay many another, groaning with mangled limbs. I withdrew to a neighboring grove, completely exhausted and almost dying of thirst, having been struck with a fragment of a shell on the right hip." It was but a temporary indisposition for Phillips, and he would be back up with the regiment before long.[367]

The other regiments in the brigade had suffered tremendous loss that day. Colonel Walker's 13th Virginia had 112 men killed and wounded, out of 250 men who went into the fight. Casualties in the 31st Virginia included 2 officers killed, 2 officers and 16 men wounded, and 2 men missing, for a total of 22 casualties. Considering the regiment's losses at Cross Keys and Port Republic, when nearly half of the regiment became casualties, the battle at Gaines Mill was another significant blow, physically as well psychologically. Even though many of the wounded later returned, the regiment was being used up at an alarming rate in proportion to the total number present.[368]

Colonel Hoffman was among the wounded that day. His health had been poor since May 1, when he was elected commander of the regiment, and although he remained with the army, he had often been too sick to command the regiment. Wounded in the fighting on June 28, he was forced to leave the regiment for several weeks to recover.[369]

The killed at Gaines Mill: George W. Harris (Co. I), and Lt. Isaac N. Reger (Co. I). Of the wounded, four later died of their wounds: Corporal Samuel H. Gibson (Co. I); James C. Moore (Co. G); 2nd Lt. Michael M. Rider (Co. H), shot through the left eye; and Richard H. Rider (Co. B). Some of the other wounded: Jacob Godwin (Co. K); Lt. Henry H. Jones (Co. B), with a ball through the right elbow leaving his arm permanently stiff; Thomas Wilson (Co. K); and William H. Wilson (Co. F).[370]

After dark, the 31st Virginia marched with the brigade to Beulah Church, about a mile north of Old Cold Harbor, where the men were able to fill their cartridge boxes with a re-supply of ammunition. The field hospital had been set up not far away: the regiment rested there through the night. They marched at ten o'clock, passing over the battlefield of the previous day. The dead lay everywhere, as well as the bodies of horses, abandoned small arms, and assorted military supplies abandoned by the Federals in their retreat.[371]

Gen. Ewell's division advanced down the north bank of the Chickahominy River, stopping at Dispatch Station to destroy some railroad track. The retreating Federal army had already burned the station and stores at that place. Ewell put the men to work prying up steel rails, bending the track out of shape and thus denying the railroad to the enemy. It was heavy, physical labor, especially in the intense heat of Saturday, June 28.

The next day the regiment was sent to guard Bottom's Bridge, but around six o'clock, Gen. Ewell was ordered to return the division to Grapevine Bridge. Junior Lieutenant James Hall made a grim note in his diary on that Sunday, the 29th. "Passed over part of the battlefield today. Saw a few dead Yankees. Some were as black in the face as the Ace of Spades. Let lie and rot, I expect. This is the Sabbath. I am awfully tired of this kind of life. Not changed clothes for a month, nor much prospect of doing so very soon."[372]

Gen. Jackson was at the head of the column, waiting for scouting reports when Brig. Gen. Jubal A. Early rode up and offered himself present and ready for assignment. They were somewhere on the road between White Oak Swamp and Malvern Hill, and it was the first day of July. Having recently recovered from a wound received in the fight at Williamsburg, Jubal Early was riding with difficulty that day, and was unable to mount his horse without assistance.[373]

The Union army found strong positions to defend itself on Malvern Hill, as Gen. Jackson and his officers discovered when the artillery opened fire on the head of the Confederate column, making Jackson and his staff ride back out of range. Jackson then gave Early his orders, assigning him to take command of the Fourth brigade of Ewell's division, which was bringing up the rear of Jackson's army. It was about ten o'clock by the time Early made his way back to Gen. Ewell, and once more reported ready to take command of the brigade.

Jubal Anderson Early was 45 years old, an experienced lawyer, county prosecutor, politician, and military man. He was sharp-tongued, with a penetrating, high-pitched voice. Not a religious man, he used strongly inventive, and descriptive language, and was a bachelor. Six feet tall, of medium build, with thinning hair that mostly disappeared from the top of his head; he had extra reason to wear slouch hats when having his photograph made. A graduate of West Point, he had served in the campaign of 1837—38 against the Seminole Indians, but participated in only one minor skirmish.

Later that year, Early had resigned and returned home to begin the study of law under N. M. Taliaferro, one of the prominent lawyers of his county. Obtaining a license to practice law in 1840, he was elected the next year to the Virginia Legislature, and served one term before becoming Prosecuting Attorney for Franklin and Floyd Counties, a position he held until 1851.

In 1847, the Mexican War brought Early back to the army as a volunteer. With a commission as a major in a regiment of Virginia Volunteers, his service in Mexico was uneventful, though he was often in command of the battalion, and for two months was military governor of Monterey, Mexico. The most significant effect of the Mexican campaign for Early was experience commanding volunteer troops in a foreign country, but at the cost of contracting rheumatoid arthritis, an illness that plagued him thereafter in life.

Early's legal career had blossomed in Virginia after the Mexican War. He was elected to represent his county in the Virginia Convention of 1861, and voted against secession, but when the war commenced, volunteered for service in Virginia's provisional army, and was appointed colonel, in command of a brigade. At the battle of First Manassas, his brigade played a crucial role, and he was rewarded with promotion to brigadier general. By the time that he was placed in command of the Fourth brigade, he had a reputation as an aggressive leader in combat, and a strong disciplinarian with his troops.

Now that he was partially healed from a wound received at Williamsburg, Early was eager to serve once again, though he was not very impressed by the Fourth brigade. Jubal Early, newly appointed commander of that brigade would have a profound influence on the lives of the men in the 31st Virginia Regiment, for they were under his command, one way or another, through much of the balance of the war.[374]

On July 1, 1862 the Fourth brigade was composed of fragments of seven regiments, numbering in all about 1,050 men present. "There was but one colonel present," Early reported, "Col. J. A. Walker of the 13th Virginia Regiment, and two lieutenant colonels (of the 25th and 52nd Virginia Regiments respectively), the rest of the regiments being commanded by captains."[375]

Major Arbogast was in command of the 31st Virginia that day; such as it was after their hard fighting in the past weeks. It was the size, approximately, of an over-large company. Of the company commanders, Captains Harding and Clawson were present, but Cooper, Arnett, and Gilmore were absent. The other regiments in the brigade were in similar condition. At one point in the confusing action that developed later in the day at Malvern Hill, Brig. Gen. Early found himself with three regiments from the brigade, and estimated the total number of men present as just above three hundred![376]

Battle of Malvern Hill, July 1, 1862

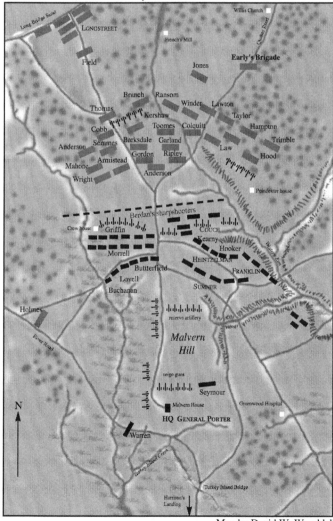

Map by David W. Wooddell

After taking command of the Fourth brigade, Early held the regiments in place for some time, awaiting orders to move forward and join the assault on Malvern Hill. When the order came, they marched past Willis Church, and came up behind the Confederate battle line. Early's regiments were assigned a position in the woods, just behind the Louisiana brigade, which occupied the center of the line. Trimble's brigade was to their left. General D. H. Hill's division was on the right of the road, and Whiting's division on the left, with Jackson's division held in reserve.

"The enemy soon commenced a heavy cannonade upon the positions where our troops were posted," Early later wrote, "and kept it up continuously during the rest of the day. From the position which I occupied, the enemy could not be seen, as a considerable body of woods intervened, but many shells and solid shot passed over us, and one shell passed through my line, killing two or three persons."[377]

It was late in the afternoon, nearly five o'clock when the brigade was ordered to advance to the right. "We were immediately moved along the edge of a huge swamp," Phillips wrote, "bordered by a high band which was over grown by cedars interspersed with old field pine and entangled briars and wild vines. Just as we were about to enter this thicket, we crossed a road running at right angles with the enemy's line of field works."

The light was falling, and the battle was at a crescendo to their left as the Fourth brigade came out into an open field. "The ground was strewn with wounded and dying men," Phillips recalled. Moving double quick, the brigade crossed open ground but ran into some ditches, which forced the brigade apart. The 31st Virginia scrambled up the face of a low hill and stopped at the summit, looking out over the battlefield. "The whole sky was lit up with bursting shell," Phillips said, "heavy cannonading and the hissing and hurling of bursting shells through the air, shouting murder in tones of demons. The horrible odor of brimstone was rolling up from the field of battle."[378]

The night was dark, and the forest thick with underbrush. Many of the brigade's men became lost in the darkness, separated from their new commander, much to Gen. Early's chagrin. Eventually, he was able to bring together the 31st Virginia, 25th Virginia, and 12th Georgia regiments, and under the direct orders of Gen. Ewell, who was with them, Early formed a line in a clover field next to Kershaw's brigade. Bright flashes of enemy artillery splashed the sky, but the Northerners were concealed from view behind a hill. Artillery shells burst in the air over the heads of the 31st Virginia's soldiers, and on the ground in front of them. "It was a magnificent display of fireworks," Early later recalled, "but not very pleasant to those exposed to it."[379]

Capt. Phillips was shaken by the experience. "The cries of the wounded and the groans of the dying made one of the most hideous pictures that I ever saw, and the most frightful, melancholy sounds that was ever heard. It seemed to me that hell itself was divided and all its demons in frightful rage was plying fire and apt to stir up human woe. The battle ended about ten o'clock, or that was about the time the gunboats ceased to shell us. We lay down in the mud and under drenching rain until morning."[380]

The brigade had been inflicted with constantly bursting artillery shells throughout much of the advance, and the men had been ordered to lie down in the field while the shells flashed thickly overhead. Near the end of this barrage, which the Union gunners used to allow their infantry to withdraw from the immediate front, the only other Confederate brigade in that portion of the field withdrew past the Fourth brigade, leaving it the leading force holding the line.[381]

The Federal retreated in the night, leaving behind parties of men who searched the field for wounded comrades. Early's three regiments, with a total of about 300 men, rested on their arms throughout the night, listening to the calls, cries, and groans of wounded men in the darkness. Small lights were moving around near the Federal line, as though men were searching for wounded comrades, and later they heard the sound of wheels as the Federals withdrew their ambulances and artillery limbers.

The sight of the battlefield the next morning was unforgettable. Jubal Early called it "appalling," the field before them "literally strewn with the dead and wounded, and arms were lying in every direction."[382]

Phillips was overwhelmed by death's remnants all around. "The gray dawn came stealing upon us and a sad spectacle met our eye," he wrote. "The earth was covered with still and stiff cold forms of hundreds of our dead braves. I went out amongst them. Here I saw all ages, murdered and mangled. Here was the old gray-haired sire, sleeping that long last sleep by the side of some young tender boy. My heart was too full to weep, and I do not remember to have spent so sad a day. To see so many of my poor country man sleeping in death's embrace was more than my young heart could bear."[383]

Federal cavalry came up and skirmished with them that morning, and then about ten o'clock the field of battle at Malvern Hill was entirely in the hands of the Confederates; with the exception that now both sides sent men forward to search for the wounded.

The report of killed and wounded for the 31st Virginia at Malvern Hill states that they had one officer, and three enlisted men wounded. Lt. Warwick C. Kincaid of Company B received his second wound in less than a month, having been wounded at Port Republic. Henry G. Britton, a Sergeant in the color guard was sent to a hospital in Richmond the following day with a piece of shell in his shoulder. Britton later returned to the regiment. Private James W. Quick of Company F, from Huttonsville, was 35 years old. Wounded in the fight, he was sent to a hospital at Scottsville, where he died in September, leaving a widow to grieve in Randolph County.[384]

All things considered, the 31st Virginia was lucky at Malvern Hill, but regiments in other commands, such as in D. H. Hill's division, suffered heavy losses. The Confederates sustained 5,355 killed and wounded: casualties in the Union army amounted to 3,000 killed and wounded.

On the road from Long Bridge to Westover, the regiment was near Charles City Court House on Thursday, July 3, and was involved on Friday and Saturday in skirmish fights while on picket duty. They camped in a pine grove on July 6 and listened to a chaplain preach, all the while expecting the battle to resume at any moment, but their rest was unbroken and they were allowed to remain in the pine grove until the morning of July 9, when the brigade marched toward Richmond with Ewell's division. The majority of Stonewall's army had started in that direction the previous day.[385]

Illness continued paring the regiment one death at a time: on July 5, Benjamin Aaron Wooddell, of Company G died in a Staunton hospital of a fever. He was then 28 years old, with a wife named Cynthia a few years younger, and three children. His younger brother, Warwick, remained with Company G through the month of July, but also came down with a fever in August, and was at a hospital for nearly two months.[386]

Illness and casualties reduced some companies more than others. After Gaines Mill and Malvern Hill, Company D had only 18 men present for duty on July 6. Discouraged by this, 2nd Lt. Sida H. Campbell sat down that day to write a resignation, giving the reduced strength of the company as his chief reason. Campbell's resignation was granted, but not until August 5, when he went home to Gilmer County for a visit, or perhaps even to recruit. Campbell's discharge papers served little to protect him when he was captured in Gilmer County by the Union army on October 18, and he was sent to Camp Chase, Ohio. Fortunate in his timing, he was transferred from Camp Chase to Cairo, Illinois on November 20, and was exchanged shortly afterward.[387]

The vastly reduced numbers in Stonewall Jackson's army at this time give an indication of what kind of hard campaign they had just passed through. By the beginning of August, Jackson's division numbered only 3,000 men present and fit for duty; Ewell's division numbered 7,550; A. P. Hill, 12,000; and they had 1,200 cavalry, for a total of 23,750 men present.[388]

There was one bright spot for the army then, however. Their supply of rifles had grown, and the smoothbore muskets the men began the campaign carrying were nearly all replaced by rifles and minié muskets, captured in battle from the enemy. With increased firepower in the line, the infantry in Jackson's army would become ever more effective, even with a reduced number of men standing in the line.[389]

6

EARLY'S BRIGADE
July 7, 1862—Dec. 1862

Early's brigade marched toward Richmond and went into camp near the city. They remained there until July 17, giving the men a chance to rest, patch up their wounds, and recover from various illness gained in the swamps during the Seven Days Fight, as the battles below Richmond were called. On the 17th, the 31st Virginia marched with the brigade to Hanover Junction, and camped for two nights, then marched to Gordonsville. From there, the regiment crossed the Rapidan River at one of the fords, skirmishing a little bit with some Union cavalry before marching to Liberty Mills, in Orange County. The brigade made camp near Liberty Mills, and remained there for nearly two and half weeks.[390]

The campaign in the Valley, followed by the battles to defend Richmond, had used up a lot of men in the Arm of Northern Virginia. Gen. Jackson needed to increase the number of conscripts in a hurry. On July 28, a new order was sent out from Jackson's headquarters, requiring each regiment to submit the name of one intelligent non-commissioned officer from each company. If approved, these individuals would report to the commander of Camp Lee, just outside of Richmond, and would help enroll conscripts into the regiments. By sending men to bring back the conscripts, or draftees, directly to the regiments, the army hoped to avoid evasions and exemptions.[391]

The regiment certainly was short-handed at this time. Company H had been particularly hard hit, losing all of its lieutenants. 1st Lt. Isaac V. Johnson, elected on May 1, had never recovered from wounds received at the battle of Camp Allegheny. "In fact, I am completely lamed," Johnson wrote on July 7 when he submitted his resignation, "and have been unable to keep up with my company in the various marches already made."[392]

2nd Lt. Alex Whiteley had been killed on June 9 at Gaines Mill, and Lt. M. M. Rider died on July 24 from wounds received at the same battle. Private Hall, who had thought himself elected to lieutenant on June 21, while the regiment was at Charlottesville, was not yet confirmed in the rank. He was now absent, however, having fallen sick on July 6. Hall was in a hospital in Richmond through the end of August.

However, the company had received a qualified man on June 22, when John W. Bosworth, former lieutenant in the 1st Virginia Battalion, known as the Irish battalion, enlisted as a private. He was apparently elected 2nd lieutenant shortly after enlisting in the company, and on July 30, was promoted to 1st lieutenant to replace Johnson, whose resignation was accepted that day, by Capt. McCutchen, of Company D, who was then in command of the regiment (all of the more senior officers being absent, sick or wounded.)

A native of Randolph County, John Bosworth had come to the regiment with strong recommendations. He was a graduate of VMI, class of '57, and had nearly a year's experience as a drill instructor, with the rank of 1st lieutenant. He had been a close friend of Maj. Joseph Chenoweth, and knew many of the other officers in the regiment. A former classmate from VMI, Walter Taylor, who was AAG for Gen. Lee, arranged Bosworth's transfer to the 31st Virginia. His 19-year-old brother, Squier Newton Bosworth, was already serving in Company F, having enlisted in March 1862. Newton was the regiment's fifer when he wasn't busy using his rifled musket in battle.[393]

In early August, most of the Union army under Gen. Pope was on the north side of the Rapidan River, but part of it had marched to Culpeper Court House. Learning of the Union force at Culpeper, Gen. Jackson decided to press an attack before the rest of Pope's men could arrive. One of Stonewall's maxims was "divide and conquer," and in this situation the Federals had obligingly divided themselves. Jackson moved his divisions from Gordonsville on August 7, and arrived within eight miles of Culpeper Court House on August 9.

This place, a short distance northwest of Slaughter Mountain, was known as Cedar Run. Col. Hoffman and Lt. Col. Jackson had returned to the regiment and were in command as the 31st Virginia took part in the battle that day. As luck would have it, the regiment was once more destined to fight in the heart of the struggle, in the front line where the casualties fell.[394]

With the 13th Virginia out in front as skirmishers, Early's brigade formed its line in a field north of a tributary of Cedar Creek, and to the left and somewhat oblique to the Culpeper Road. Stepping forward in line of battle, most of the brigade had to cross through a piece of woods as they marched toward the Culpeper Road. The brigade skirmishers were about 200 yards from the Federal line when the left wing ran into a small force of Union cavalry, which was driven back. The line continued to advance, while Union videttes on the Confederate right retired back to their own line, which was positioned in a field on the other side of the woods.[395]

The brigade crossed over the Culpeper road and came out into the open field beyond the woods, one end of the line swinging around to keep the men formed as they advanced parallel to the road. When the regiments came to a lane that ran on the right from Mrs. Crittenden's house to the Culpeper road, Early halted the line behind a fence for a few minutes. The skirmishers from the 13th Virginia were pulled back and that regiment formed on the left of the brigade's line. When it was ready, the fence in front of them was pulled down and the brigade advanced once more, up to a hillcrest that offered a full view of the field beyond.

The men had just reached the top of the hill when they came under artillery fire from three Union batteries. At the same time, Federal cavalry was spotted in a sizable body, obliquely to their left front, occupying part of a wheat field. Mindful of the hazards of the artillery fire they were starting to receive, Brig. Gen. Early ordered the men to step back a few paces so they would be just behind the crest of the hill, and lie down. "The hill sloped down in front," Gen. Early observed, "and farther on was a corn field running back to the crest of the next hill, along and behind which were posted the enemy's batteries, and it was evident there was a depression behind this hill in which large bodies of infantry might be concealed."[396]

The Third brigade came up on Early's left, which ended at the Culpeper Road, inside the woods. Several pieces of Confederate artillery came up around then and opened on the Federals. They were joined by artillery pieces from the other brigades, which were posted on the mountain. The artillery kept up its fire for nearly two hours, while the infantry lay down and tried to ignore shells bursting over their heads. The Federals sent infantry forward and to the left of Early's position, and then more Federals came up to the skirmish line, advancing across the cornfield toward the Fourth Brigade.

Early had placed the right of his brigade line so that it ended at a cluster of cedar trees, near some artillery pieces commanded by Brown and Dement. Federal infantry was advancing toward this portion of the line, and knowing that the hillside to that side was such a steep angle that the Union could appear suddenly from a masked approach and take his line by surprise, Early sent an urgent request to Gen. Jackson, asking for a brigade to be sent up to reinforce his right.[397]

Around three o'clock, the Federals charged on the left and broke part of the Confederate line. Capt. Phillips said, "There was hand-to-hand fighting and it was terrible." The brigade had been in danger of being flanked on the left. Early pulled his line back a little ways but the artillery of Snowden Andrews battery could not be withdrawn so quickly. Part of the 31st Virginia protecting the battery was in danger of being overwhelmed and captured. The 13th Virginia moved forward to come to the aid of the 31st Virginia, with other regiments rallying to the 13th Virginia. The situation degenerated as some men to their left began to fall back again, and then ran from the field in disorder.[398]

"The panic thus begun was communicated to two or three regiments on my right, which also fell back," Colonel Walker, 13th Virginia, later reported, "saving my regiment and a portion of the 31st Virginia, commanded by Lt. Col. Jackson, the only Confederate troops in that part of the field in sight of our position. Finding that one piece of artillery, which had been brought up on the right and a little in advance of my regiment, was thus placed in great jeopardy, I ordered my own and Lt. Col. Jackson's men forward to hold the enemy in check until it could be carried off. The men obeyed with alacrity, and advancing about 30 yards, opened a well-directed fire, which had the desired effect of checking the advance of that portion of the enemy's line directly in our front until the piece was removed."[399]

Lt. Col. Alfred Jackson rallied part of the 31st Virginia while their color bearer kept the battle flag of the old 31st Virginia waving in the face of the enemy. Forming a solid knot, a small group of the regiment's men advanced behind the color bearer, while next to them another determined group from the 25th Virginia were forming on their color bearer. They advanced into a maelstrom of rifled musket balls, with men falling wounded and dying all around them, the day growing hot under a bright sun. It was plenty hot just from flying bullets, Joseph Harding recalled later: they were loosing men steadily to the maelstrom of lead. "Color bearer Marks killed," Harding said. "Lt. O. H. P. Lewis wounded, John Lewis killed... color guard Martin Mulvey... brought our regimental flag, which I at once caught up and waved."[400]

About then, Alfred Jackson, cousin of Stonewall, lieutenant colonel of the 31st Virginia was dangerously wounded while urging his men to make even greater efforts. He was carried off the field to safety and the help of the regiment's surgeons, but Lt Col Alfred Jackson would never return to serve in the regiment.[401]

Gen. Early saw the dire situation, as part of the 31st Virginia, 13th Virginia, and 25th Virginia held on in the face of what seemed overwhelming odds. Several other regiments were also sticking to the fight, including the 12th Georgia, part of the 52nd Virginia, and part of the 58th Virginia. "These troops were then isolated and in an advanced position," Early said, "and had they given way the day in all probability would have been lost."[402]

Colonel Walker, in command of the 13th Virginia, discovered the Union infantry was flanking them: the Federals "had advanced under cover of the woods on our left, over the ground abandoned by the Third Brigade, and had crossed the road into the field considerably in rear of our position, and were pouring a very annoying fire into my left flank, and seeing no re-enforcements in sight, I ordered my regiment to fall back, and carried it off obliquely to the right and rear in tolerable order."[403]

Union cavalry suddenly appeared on the Culpeper Road, making their own charge. The 13th Virginia responded with a quick change of front and gave them a volley, breaking up the cavalry charge. Around the same time, the Federal infantry began to fall back along their line in the cornfield, and Early's brigade charged after them. The 31st Virginia started toward the enemy and kept going, Capt. Harding later recalled, "shooting and cheering, until we swept the enemy from the field."[404]

"Our army moved in the red glow of the sinking sun," Phillips wrote, "with bayonets, limbs of trees or anything we could fight with, cheering and chasing after the enemy. Our men chased them far into the twilight hours."

The day had been won at a terrific cost in men wounded and killed. "After this battle, we fell on the ground tired and hungry, but (there) was that terrible field in front of us. The leaves were gone from the trees, the wheat field a trodden chaff. Wounded and dead were everywhere... The day after the battle the time was spent in burying the dead," Phillips recalled.[405]

Lt. Col. Alfred H. Jackson's life was hanging by a thread, and continued so for a long time afterward. Other casualties in the regiment included the 1st Lieutenant of Company I, Hiram M. Marsh of Lewis County, who died two days later at Orange Court House. John M. C. Lewis was killed. Lt. Oliver H. P. Lewis, Capt. McCutchen, and Capt. George T. Thompson were wounded. The official report of killed and wounded for Early's Brigade in the battle showed the 31st Virginia lost 3 killed, and 17 wounded. The other regiments in Early's brigade also lost significant numbers of men: the 13th Virginia lost 2 killed, 32 wounded; the 25th Virginia, 1 killed, 24 wounded; 52nd Virginia, 3 killed, 10 wounded; 58th Virginia: 2 killed, 28 wounded.[406]

It had been a disturbing day on the field for their brigade commander, who tried afterward to understand why the regiments on the left had given way. He concluded that it did not occur until after Lt. Col. Jackson, and Maj. Higgenbotham of the 25th Virginia had fallen and were carried off the field. That meant the 31st and 25th Virginia regiments were without adequate commanders. As the brigade to the left of Early gave way, the 31st and 25th Virginia fell into confusion and the disorder spread to the right, to part of the 58th Virginia. "Colonel Walker, who was on my extreme left," Early said, "maintained his position with his regiment, and part of the 31st Virginia Regiment until they were left alone and the enemy were firing into their rear in the field. He then ordered them to retire, but he again formed them and brought them forward, and contributed very largely to the final repulse of the enemy, advancing as far as any of our troops were advanced until after the conclusion of the fight."[407]

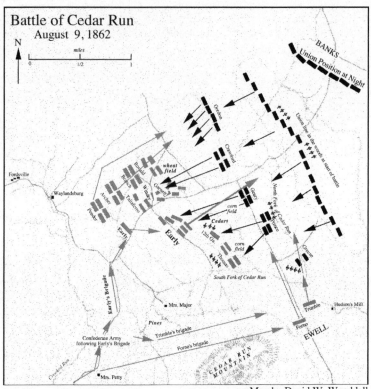

Map by David W. Wooddell

Following the battle of Cedar Mountain, the 31st Virginia returned to camp at Liberty Mills, about five miles west of Orange Court House on the Rapidan River. Around this time, it became apparent that 2nd Lt. Henry H. Jones of Company B was not coming back to his company any time soon. Jones had been 1st Sergeant when he was elected from the ranks in Company B, on May 1, 1862. He had served as an officer only a few weeks when he was wounded in the Battle of Gaines Mill. He was hit by rifle fire, Jones wrote, "the ball passing through my right elbow, rendering the arm stiff and disabled."[408]

Jones was lucky to have an arm at all. Against the human body, and human bone, the military weapons of the 1860's were a deadly menace when they actually hit their target. The minié ball often pulverized an entire section of bone; making it impossible for the surgeons to do much else other than amputate, as the bone rarely healed properly. Some men could not stand the shock of amputation, and lingered for days, or weeks on the edge of death before passing on. Infections often set in. Gangrene, one of the most dreaded of all conditions, took a heavy toll on amputees. Some of the wounded that later returned to the regiment were, like Jones, completely or partially disabled, making the casualty statistics of those who were wounded somewhat deceptive.[409]

Corporal Warwick C. Kincaid was later elected as replacement for Jones. He also had just returned to the regiment at the beginning of the month, after being wounded at Port Republic, and then again at Malvern Hill. By the end of August, his company was so short-handed from losses that Kincaid was signing the company's regimental return as "Corporal, commanding Company B." He was made 1st Lieutenant in September.[410]

Company I had suffered losses, too, and an election was held to replace its fallen officers. Capt. Clawson, who was temporarily commanding the regiment, supervised the election. Edward Bradbury, 4th Corporal, was elected 2nd lieutenant; and Patrick W. Bruffey became 1st lieutenant of the company.[411]

The regiment rested from August 11 until late in the evening of the 15th, when it quietly broke camp and marched to Mountain Run, near Pisgah Church, and Clark's Mountain. This movement put Jackson's division in place to defend Somerville, and Raccoon fords of the Rapidan River. Early's brigade gained one more regiment at this time, the 49th Virginia. That regiment was under the command of the colorful, and eccentric Colonel William Smith, former governor of Virginia.[412]

Capt. Sam Gilmore of Company E returned from the hospital on the 16th, although his illness would effectively keep him close to the sick list and eventually mean a disability certificate. Gilmore was suffering from chronic diarrhea, a terribly debilitating disease caused by bad water and poor sanitation around the camps.

For the first time in weeks, the men were well fed. There was plenty of beef from local farms, and corn from nearby fields. Unfortunately, eating green corn made chronic diarrhea worse, and Sam Gilmore was not the only man in the regiment affected by that disease. The same day that Capt. Gilmore returned, Adjutant John Gittings departed, too sick to keep up with the regiment.[413]

In the pre-dawn night of August 20, with a rising moon overhead, Jackson's division crossed the Rapidan River. Early's brigade crossed at Somerville Ford, then marched northeastward to bivouac in the night near Stevensburg in Culpeper County. From there, the regiment marched north the following day, and crossed over the Orange and Alexandria Railroad at Brandy Station. They turned northeast again to Saint James Church by way of a road that led toward Beverly Ford on the Rappahannock River. The ford was situated below the mouth of the Hazel River.[414]

During the day on the 22nd, the Fourth Brigade encountered some Union skirmishers, and was subjected to another artillery duel between Union and Confederate guns near Gaines' Farm. In this exchange of ordnance, Sgt. Thomas Alford, and Pvt. Granville Moore were hit by pieces of exploding shells. Alford's wound was mortal, and he would die two days later. He was one of Company K's original volunteers enlisted by Henry Sturm on 18 May 1861.

In the dark of night, the regiment sank down exhausted from their day's exertions, near St. James Church. Waiting on the other side of the Rappahannock River, the Union army was spread out from Hazel Ford, on the Union right, down as far as Kelly's Ford. The next morning, under Federal artillery shells in another heavy bombardment, the brigade was forced to cross the Hazel River on the milldam at Wellford's. Shells were falling to either side as the 31st Virginia crossed, and seven men were wounded. Private William Grogg, Company E, was killed.[415]

The regiment moved northward with the brigade, through woods and fields, the west bank of the Rappahannock River to their right. At a place just south of Warrenton Springs, the men crossed over the Rappahannock, again while Federal artillery dropped shells around them. It was also raining as the regiment crossed the river on another old and precarious dam, shoes and feet slipping on wet board, and then moved into the woods shortly before dark.[416]

The river was already swollen with rain, and was rising quickly. By the time that Early's brigade was across, the river was deemed too high to cross any more of the division, and the rest of Gen. Ewell's division remained where they were on the other side of the Rappahannock. About a mile farther upstream, at Warrenton Springs, the 13th Georgia Regiment, and Brown's and Dement's batteries also managed to get across the river. Brig Gen Early discovered a road running through the woods to Rappahannock Station below their position. "My left was posted on this road, the right extending to an old field just below where I had crossed. Pickets were put out in front and on the flanks."[417]

The rain had not stopped and the stream level was rising, with the chance of Early's brigade being cut off from Jackson's army, an un-crossable river at their back, and the Federals in their front. One of Early's staff, Maj. Andrew L. Pitzer encountered several Union cavalry in the darkness that night, but made an unobtrusive escape and reported the enemy's presence to the brigade commander. Early sent a message across to Gen. Jackson, and was ordered by reply to move toward Warrenton Springs to join with the other regiment there. The brigade accordingly marched toward the Springs, where their commander placed the 13th and the 31st Virginia on the road, to guard against a flank attack.[418]

After daylight, the men became aware of Union troops moving toward them in force, but Early pulled his men back to a position in the woods that was concealed by thick, wet foliage, leaving the Federals uncertain of the Confederate position. The 31st Virginia maintained silence throughout the day, moving around a little to change their front as Union troops came up, still unaware of the Confederate position in the concealment of the wet leaves and trees. The men was nothing to eat that day, nor had they eaten since the evening before, and would not eat on the next day either.

A small force of Confederate cavalry had moved two pieces of artillery onto a hill north of Warrenton Springs. They began firing on the Federals. A pair of Early's guns joined in with the artillery on the hill and a brisk cannonade went on between the Federals and the Confederates until dark, but without noticeable effect on either side. Early later said, "After the cessation of the artillery fire, a column of the enemy was observed to advance, it being then near dark and a mist rendering objects quite indistinct. Infantry was seen moving off to the left, and in a few moments the enemy delivered a volley into the woods where my infantry was posted and then gave three cheers, followed by a tiger regular style." The 31st Virginia, and 13th Virginia were then in the center of Early's line, facing the Federals. Early responded by running two guns to the left of his line and fired off a return charge of canister, after which the Federals withdrew.

During the night, Gen. Ewell ordered the brigade to withdraw across the Rappahannock on a rickety bridge that the engineers were then building. The 31st Virginia and the other regiments crossed this contraption in the dark, early hours of the 24th, but their withdrawal was followed at once by a fierce artillery fight between the Union and Confederate batteries. Only one man in the 31st Virginia was wounded.[419]

The regiment rested a while that morning, before coming under another artillery barrage from their opponents across the river. Reverend J. William Jones, chaplain of the 13th Virginia, was holding an impromptu prayer session for the brigade, thanking the Lord for seeing them safely back across the river, when the shells started exploding again. The chaplain's audience patiently waited the end of the prayer before continuing their withdrawal away from the river. Early's brigade retired to a place not far from Jefferson, to cook rations and patch up their wounds, and perhaps mourn losses sustained in the past few days.[420]

For the 31st Virginia, casualties from August 21 to the 24th were not so slight. The report of the Surgeon Gen. shows 8 casualties for the regiment during this interval—2 officers killed, and 6 men wounded. The medical records of the soldiers, however, show a few more. Thomas Alford and Granville Moore were wounded at Gaines' Farm on the 21st. On the 22nd, there were 8 casualties: William Grogg, killed; Fred Johnson wounded in the face; Thomas J. Jones, wounded; Jesse M. Moore, wounded in ribs and lung and permanently disabled; Cortland Phillips wounded; Henry Powers wounded by a shell; Sidney Ruckman, wounded in the leg; and Isaac Stockwell, wounded in the neck. Lt. William H. Wilson of Company F was struck in the temple with a fragment of a shell on the 24th, in the artillery barrage that followed their retreat back across the river. The lieutenant would be absent from the regiment for a long time.[421]

Manassas Junction: Waterloo Bridge was just south of the regiment's next crossing of the Rappahannock. It was August 25, and the men were moving through Orleans to camp the night at Salem, in Fauquier County. Capt. Nathan Clawson caught up with the regiment some time during the day, having been let out of a hospital at Lynchburg.

Col. Hoffman also returned on the 25th, but he wasn't yet fully recovered, and maybe should have remained longer at the private residence in Richmond that he favored when he was too sick to campaign. The Colonel would be with the regiment only until September 5, when he was once again compelled to retire to Richmond and try to regain his health.[422]

Before then, however, the regiment had a few more battles to fight. They made another early march that brought the brigade to Thoroughfare Gap with Ewell's division, and then to Gainesville, where the men embarked on "the cars" to ride the Orange and Alexandria Railroad to Bristoe Station. Early's brigade brought up the rear of the division on both days. On the 27th, as Trimble's brigade marched to Manassas Junction to capture the Union army's supply trains, the remaining three brigades in Ewell's division were posted in a defensive position. Lawton's brigade was on the left of the railroad, Hays's brigade posted to their right, and Early's brigade posted on the far right. They were not far from Bristoe, on a ridge in pinewoods, facing Warrenton Junction.[423]

The Union army advanced on them in the afternoon with a heavy column of infantry and artillery, but Ewell's division began to fall back defensively. Part of their artillery became engaged to hold the Federals at bay long enough to give the infantry time to withdraw. Federal infantry was advancing with a much larger force, trying to use the topography to mask a possible flank movement on the extreme right. If successful, the Federals would gain a position to the rear of Ewell's division, overlooking the river crossing at Broad Run.[424]

Gen. Stonewall Jackson ordered Gen. Richard Ewell to fall back to Manassas Junction without delay, in a defensive withdrawal of the force across Broad Run. By then, several Louisiana regiments had become engaged with the enemy and it would be difficult to withdraw without the Federals following too quickly on their heels. Early's brigade was given the task of guarding the retreat while the other brigades fell back under covering fire. "My own brigade was withdrawn from the pine woods," Early reported later, "and formed in successive lines of battle, so as to cover the ford at the bridge. The artillery was then brought over, as well as the 49th Virginia, which had been detached and crossed several hundred yards above the bridge."

The Federals were pressing on both sides of the railroad, skirmishers in front and artillery subjecting Early's brigade to constant bombardment. Early brought his regiments across one at a time, the 13th Virginia bringing up the rear, and moved to a high hill on the road toward Manassas, which was not quite a mile away. Meanwhile, Gen. Ewell withdrew the rest of the division toward Manassas Junction.

Early's brigade continued to guard the rear, employing a deception to fool the enemy into believing a large force was posted just behind the hill. It was a classic ruse. The colors from two regiments were put to marching back and forth with flags held high to give the impression of the arrival of reinforcements. While the enemy hesitated at this show of colors, Early pulled his brigade back after dark. The regiment moved toward Manassas Junction, with relatively light losses for such an active day.[425]

Out of 22 casualties in the brigade, only two men were wounded in the 31st Virginia. One of those was Samuel Tucker of Company A, a gray-eyed, 22 year old farmer from Taylor County. He was wounded in the thigh and permanently lamed. Tucker had joined his company at Pruntytown on 15 May 1861, before the first shot was fired, and had been at it ever since. After release from the hospital, Tucker was captured in Highland County and sent to Camp Chase, and was not let out until May 1865, a few weeks after the war ended.[426]

John Campbell, in Company H was one of the lucky ones in the regiment who profited on the 27th from captured Union supplies at Manassas Junction. "My brother and I were going along the railroad," Campbell recalled later, "and passed by a house that had been used as a hospital." Farther along, they spied one of the Union army's boxcars, which had been used to transport provisions. "We ran across a container of Vegetable soup, and as there was no one in sight we helped ourselves and proceeded to make soup. While we were making it, a Negro belonging to an Alabama regiment came up, called me by name, and offered me a half dollar for some soup to take to his Colonel. Of course, I gave him the soup but declined the money."

Lt. John Bosworth was then in command of Company H, and was standing nearby. "The incident worried him" Campbell said, "as he could not figure out how the Negro got my name, and it made him nervous, he said, as it did not look good for us." Campbell's soup probably tasted pretty good, nerves not withstanding.[427]

Provisions from the captured trains at Manassas Junction were officially passed out to the regiment at an early hour on August 28, before the men took to the road once more. The brigade marched to a bridge over Blackburn's Ford shortly after dawn. After crossing, it proceeded on the north side of Bull Run through some fields, going as far as the Stone Bridge, where it crossed the run. After taking the Warrenton turnpike a short distance, to a place near the Carter and Matthew houses, the brigade turned to the right and marched through more fields. Early said in his report, "My brigade was marched across the road running from the stone house on the turnpike to Sudley Church, and formed in line in the woods north of that road." They were not far from the battlefield of First Manassas, fought the summer before while the 31st Virginia was still locked in the mountain campaign in western Virginia.[428]

Map by David W. Wooddell

Early's brigade, leading Ewell's division, was ordered to move under cover of the woods towards Gainesville, following after Jackson's division. When they came across a railroad embankment, the brigade moved along the earthworks until the regiments stepped out from the cover of the woods. They turned to the right then, and formed a line of battle in the cover of some woods, with their left resting on the railroad, and the brigade's right tucked behind Starke's brigade, which was part of Jackson's division. Hays's brigade came up and formed its line just behind them, while Lawton and Trimble's brigades fell in to their right and were placed in line by Gen. Ewell. Brig. Gen. Early was directed to take command of Hays's brigade in addition to his own brigade.

While the day's light faded, the 31st Virginia rested in place, but before dark they were ordered forward to the army's front. Two regiments from the brigade, the 44th and 49th Virginia, were detached before moving up, and were ordered to reinforce Jackson's division.

A deep railroad cut had been dug across the landscape to their front, but the embankment was too steep for the men to cross. Early moved his regiments along the cut until he found a ravine that ran across it. By then, the battle had begun and they were under fire from artillery shells exploding overhead and around them. The brigade crossed the cut, and formed a new battle line just in front of the embankment, facing the enemy. To their right was Trimble's brigade, already in place, and suffering from the same hazard of exploding shell. The Union artillery was meant to mask the withdrawal of the Union infantry.

It was too dark to distinguish Confederate from Federal. Jubal Early called a halt to his brigade's movements: the men lay on their arms through the night, ready for battle to resume at any moment. Hays had halted his brigade behind them, on the railroad embankment.

Gen. Ewell was wounded late in the day. He fell on the field not far from Early's front line. Men from Early's brigade carried him off to a hospital. Ewell's wound was in the knee, and it was serious. It would cost him a leg before the surgeon's were finished.

Jackson's line of battle on August 29 extended along the unfinished railroad embankment that ran at an angle from the road to the northeast. That morning, on Stonewall's orders, the 31st and 13th Virginia regiments were detached from the brigade and marched to woods east of the pike. They were meant to serve as a buffer for the right end of the Confederate line, and were placed in a position where they would contact the Federals first as the Union army advanced from the east on the Warrenton turnpike. Brig Gen Early said later how successful the two regiments were in their mission: "The 13th Virginia Regiment, under Colonel Walker, and the 31st under Colonel John S. Hoffman, by skirmishing kept the body of the enemy's infantry... in check until the head of Gen. Longstreet's Corps made its appearance on the Warrenton turnpike from the direction of Gainesville."[429]

It was not meant to be a comfortable position for the two regiments, and the men's fears were just about realized by the day's action. Capt. Lyman was in command of the regiment's skirmishers during the fight. "If ever I quaked in my shoes," he wrote, "I did it that day." He had good reason—the 13th and 31st Virginia were facing nearly 40,000 men under Union Gen. Fitz John Porter. Early's men were once again deceiving the Federals into believing they were in contact with a much larger force. During the day, Lyman was struck in the knee by a spent ball and was removed from the field of battle by ambulance, which took him to a field hospital at Chantilly.[430]

Capt. Phillips of Company K later reported his men ran out of ammunition and were forced to gather a fresh supply from the bodies of dead men, friend and foe, while in the heat of the bloody firefight. The two scrappy regiments repulsed the Federals long enough for

Longstreet's divisions to come up, at which time Early sent word that he was ready to move his brigade to the left to rejoin Ewell's division. The much-relieved Walker and Hoffman brought their men back to the brigade in an orderly fashion, and in time to join Early's movement.

Passing behind Jackson's division, the brigade was placed behind the line already established by Gen. Lawton. Forno's brigade was then on Early's right, and the battle for the railroad embankment was about to begin.[431]

"About 3:30 P.M. Colonel Forno was ordered to advance to the front," Early later reported, "to the support of one of Gen. A. P. Hill's brigades, and he advanced to the railroad and drove the enemy from it and took position on it with his brigade." After Colonel Forno was wounded and removed from the field, A. P. Hill sent a courier to Early requesting support. Hill's regiments had exhausted their ammunition while making a stand.

"On reaching the railroad," Early wrote, "I found the enemy had possession of it and a piece of woods in front, there being at this point a deep cut, which furnished a strong defense." Two brigades of A. P. Hill's division were without ammunition, and had to be withdrawn a short distance, but were facing the enemy. Early's brigade, and the 8th Louisiana infantry were sent across the field to help them.

The men went to it with a will, driving the Federals from the woods. "The Federal troops were outnumbered," Colonel Walker of the 13th Virginia observed, "and taken by surprise, but they fought like devils."[432] The brigade not only chased the Federals out of the railroad cut, they chased them across the Manassas plain for three-quarters of a mile. "In this charge," Brig. Gen. Early reported, "which was made with great gallantry, heavy loss was inflicted on the enemy, with comparatively slight loss to my own brigade.... This was the last attempt made by the enemy on the afternoon of Friday, the 29th, to get possession of the line of the railroad."

At some point in the charge, a shell fragment struck Capt. Joseph Harding. He was found the next day, along with his brother Marion, about a mile in front of the regiment's position. Apparently knocked unconscious by the shell fragment, the captain fell before the regiment withdrew from that position and his brother stayed by his side to guard him through the night. Harding later recalled seeing, before he fell wounded, a Federal cannon ball strike and pass through the regiment's flag.[433]

As the 31st Virginia's men lay on their arms that night, two other regiments, the 12th Georgia, and the 8th Louisiana, shared the line with them. When the brigade came under fire from sharpshooters the next morning, August 30, Brig. Gen. Early realized his flank was exposed. "I soon discovered that the enemy's skirmishers were crossing the railroad to my left and advancing through a corn field...." Early sent a messenger to Gen. Hill, advising him of the enemy's approach, and Hill responded by reinforcing the line to the left of Early's brigade.

The brigade skirmishers repulsed an enemy column, and then the brigade was changed in its deployment as Hill's and Jackson's divisions positioned themselves on either side of Ewell's division. In making the change, there was room for only three of the brigade's regiments: the 31st, 13th, 25th, and 58th Virginia regiments were pulled back a short distance, as reserve.

A determined Union attack hit the line that day, but the Federals were once again repulsed. After this, as Gen. Longstreet was advancing, Early's brigade was sent forward. They went through woods to a field, where Early halted them a moment to allow the rest of Ewell's division to catch up. Gen. Jackson came past and ordered Early to take his brigade to the left flank, to forestall a Union movement that was reported there. Using the 13th Virginia as skirmishers, Early moved until he found the railroad embankment, then marched along the direction of the embankment to a field.

In the dusky light, some of Gen. Hill's men fired accidently on Early's brigade, but no one was hurt. In a little while the brigade returned to its original position on the line in Ewell's division. They found the men in other brigades asleep on the ground, and the soldiers of the 31st Virginia sank down with their muskets ready at hand. The cries of wounded, and smell of blood kept them company through the night.[434]

The report of killed and wounded in the 31st Virginia at Second Manassas included 5 men killed, and 20 wounded. For the rest of Early's brigade: 13th Virginia, 6 killed, 40 wounded; 25th Virginia, 1 killed, 28 wounded; 49th Virginia, 0 killed, 15 wounded; 44th Virginia, 1 killed, 14 wounded; 52nd Virginia, 10 killed, 51 wounded; 58th Virginia, 4 killed, 13 wounded.[435]

The past several battles had carved deeply into the 31st Virginia's manpower. On the 28th, Harrison Paugh, Co. H, 26 years old, a mechanic born in Barbour County, was wounded in the thigh. On the 29th, the heaviest day for the 31st Virginia in the campaign, they lost Lt. William J. West, Co. C, from Clarksburg, who was killed. The wounded on the 29th included: Capt. William Lyman, Co. B, wounded in the knee; John Bird, Jr., Co. E; Capt. Joseph Harding, Co. F; Lt. Patrick W. Bruffey, Company I, from Clarksburg; David Burrough, Co. I, from Lewis County, wounded in hand; John W. Carpenter, Co. G, wounded in arm; George M. Cookman, Co. C, from Clarksburg; David Dilworth, Co. H, from Barbour County, 22 years old; Francis M. Golden, Co. C; Jacob F. Clendennen, Co. E, 24 years old, from Highland County, gunshot wound to shoulder; John F. Lightburn, Co. F, 25 years old, from Randolph County, wounded in arm; Franklin F. J. Marshall, Co. H, from Highland County, wounded in the hip; Charles C. Steuart, Co. B, wounded in leg; William F. Varner, Co. H, wounded in the knee; and Elias Wilfong, Co. G, from Pocahontas County. On the morning of the 30th, George Harding, Company F, was killed: his body was buried on the field of battle, as was necessary, leaving his brothers Marion, and Joseph Harding to grieve in the regiment.[436]

Sunday morning, the last day of August, with Brig. Gen. Early in command of Ewell's Division, the 31st Virginia crossed Bull Run at Sudley's Ford before marching in the direction of Fairfax Court House. They marched through Pleasant Valley behind Jackson's division to Little River Turnpike, then on toward Germantown. Late that night, four miles west of Chantilly, the men were allowed to fall to the ground and sleep.

At dawn on September 1 they marched to Chantilly. Orders came down the line to change to columns. Artillery continued in the road as Early's brigade followed Lawton's brigade to the left, and Trimble's brigade advanced ahead of Hays's brigade on the right.

The Ox Road crosses the Little River turnpike at Ox Hill. There, Gen. Jackson halted the divisions and put the men in lines of battle. According to scouting reports, the enemy was moving in force toward them on the turnpike. Early's brigade was in reserve, along with Lawton's brigade, positioned in a woods behind Trimble and Hays. The Federals began firing artillery into the woods where the regiment stood in line, and soon their infantry attacked. It was raining, and the foliage was too thick to see through as Early moved his brigade forward, but the 31st Virginia and two other regiments were forced to remain where they were, fending off a sudden attack as Gen. Early disappeared in the distance with the rest of the brigade. The 31st Virginia was on top of a hill, just inside the tree line. Union marksmen kept up a steady musketry from inside another piece of woods on the far side of a field.

Suddenly, Union General Philip Kearny rode out of the woods on the other of the field. It was a fatal error, which Capt. Harding of the 31st Virginia later said was realized at once by all who saw the one-armed general on his horse. Harding ordered his men not to shoot, but others in the regiment, including Company E, which was directly opposite Kearny, fired their muskets, and the general fell mortally wounded.

Union riflemen were hitting the Confederates with punishing rifle fire, sending Hays's brigade into confusion by the fierceness of the Federal attack. His men started back through Early's regiments, but the Fourth brigade held on and repulsed the Federal attack, driving them back from the field. Capt. Harding was struck in the arm by a bullet. It was a dangerous wound this time. In delirium, while still on the field, Harding believed that Gen. Jackson came up and asked about his wound. The Captain was carried from the battle to a field hospital, where his arm was saved with great difficulty.[437]

When Harding arrived at the field hospital, Dr. Bland at first thought amputation was necessary. He delayed, and the arm was saved, but Harding was out of the fight, and away from the regiment for about six weeks. He was held together in a cast, or as noted on a regimental report, covered by heavy plaster, and held together by heavy linen.[438]

Near the last of the battle, Gen. Early returned to rejoin the other regiments of the brigade. It was essentially the end of a bloody day at Ox Hill, as the place was known, near the village of Chantilly. The reward for the efforts by men of the 31st Virginia was to lay on their arms, in the wet woods through a night without campfires.

There were only a few casualties for the 31st Virginia in that fight at Chantilly on September 1, with just seven men wounded, and one killed. Private William Tracy, Co. G, from Pocahontas County, was killed. The wounded included: Capt. Joseph F. Harding, Co. F; Corporal Henry G. Britton, Co. B; Eugenius Hutton, Co. H, wounded in leg; Sergeant Robert D. Leach, Co. B; Solomon J. McDaniel, Co. B; John M. Wilfong, Co. G; and Randolph Wise, Co. F, 19 years old and wounded in the left arm, which had to be amputated. Randolph Wise was discharged the following year and allowed to return to his farm.[439]

On September 2, the 31st Virginia was at the front again with the Fourth brigade a quarter of a mile beyond their position of the day before. The rest of the division was behind them by that quarter of a mile, with Hay's brigade connecting the left flank at an angle. Colonel James Walker, 13th Virginia, the senior officer in the brigade, was detached from his regiment at this time and assigned to the temporary command of Trimble's brigade. The men were issued boiled beef that day, but without bread, and without salt: provisions had once more grown scarce. Many of the soldiers augmented their dinner with ears of green corn, roasted over a fire.[440]

Gen. Lee was preparing to invade Maryland. Lee hoped the invasion of the North, although temporary, would cause the Union army to take its forces away from Richmond and the Valley of Virginia. It would also not be amiss if along the way the Confederate army found something substantial to eat.

The 31st Virginia departed Manassas on September 4. The men were in high spirits as they moved northward, Phillips said, "Wading rivers, columns of four, laughing, shouting, yelling and singing.... We are going to carry the war to the North."

They marched through Leesburg before camping for the night. Early the next day, the regiment marched to the Potomac River, arriving about ten o'clock in the morning at White's Ford, seven miles above Leesburg on the farm of Elijah White. The river's banks had to be dug out to widen the ferry so that wagons and artillery could cross. Infantry did what infantry usually does, crossed on foot, the men wading the river and giving themselves a moving wash at the same time. Still in good spirits, some of the men broke into song, offering "Maryland, My Maryland" as they crossed into the next state.[441]

At the canal on the other side of the river, the army captured a dozen canal boats loaded with feed grain. It would be put to good use by their horses and mules. Marching on, the brigade continued through Montgomery County, to Three Springs before bivouacking for the night.[442]

Colonel Hoffman issued an order on the 5th concerning company inspections: "Officers commanding companies will inspect the arms, accouterments, and dress of the men of their companies at two o'clock today, and at nine o'clock on each Sunday hereafter, when the same is practicable." They must have appeared bedraggled after so much marching and hard combat, but the general wanted the army to impress the citizens of Maryland. There were no more than 200 men present and able for duty in the 31st Virginia, and many were without shoes. Company E reported thirty men present, probably making it the largest company in the regiment on that day.[443]

Col. Hoffman's illness had returned, and by September 6, he was too sick to continue the march. Leaving the regiment in the command of Maj. Arbogast, Hoffman traveled once again to Richmond to recover from his debilitating illness. Capt. Cooper of Company C remained with the regiment, but was also too sick for duty that day.[444]

The Confederates occupied Frederick and Monocacy Junctions on the B&O Railroad on September 6, with Ewell's division covering the line of approach from the direction of Baltimore. The division remained in this area of operations until the 10th. The 31st Virginia was camped about four miles from the town of Frederick, but the commissary wagons had not caught up with them, and they were short of provisions. "We commenced to roasting corn," Capt. Phillips wrote, "and soon one may have seen the sweat pouring from the brow of man and officer as they bent over large fires and roasted corn. As I went past the Gen.'s quarters, I saw old Stonewall devouring some corn with as much concern as if it had been the ham of a turkey."[445]

An entertainment for the men was reading Northern periodicals as the men took their ease in camp. Commissary wagons had at last come up, and provisions were supplied to the companies. Some of the officers went into the town of Frederick.

While in camp there, Maj. Arbogast certified an election for a new 2nd lieutenant in Company I: Washington B. McNemar was elected to replace both Hiram Marsh, and N. G. Reger. He also approved the promotion of Patrick W. Bruffey, from 2nd lieutenant, to 1st Lieutenant. By this time, officials were questioning the validity of Bruffey's original appointment as an officer, as it had never been confirmed in Richmond. Bruffey had been collecting pay as an officer for quite some time, and the Richmond authorities were asking Col. Hoffman to cite by what authority he was being paid. Hoffman, aware of the inquiry, had allowed it to slip from the many details he had to take care of as colonel of the regiment.[446]

At some time in the next several days, Maj. Arbogast also was absent from the regiment, perhaps succumbing to the ravaging illness that was taking men out of the line of the 31st Virginia. Capt. Nathan Clawson, the senior officer, was in command as the regiment marched from Frederick on September 11. The brigade re-joined Ewell's division, between South Mountain and the village of Middletown. From there, the march took them through Boonsboro Gap, then re-crossed the Potomac River at Williamsport, with the men taking off their shoes, and in many cases trousers, carrying them in their hands as they waded the cool river. By evening, they were bivouacked for the night at the North Mountain depot of the B&O Railroad.

Martinsburg had been occupied until the day before by a small Union force: as Lee's army approached the town, the Federals retired, leaving the town open for the Confederates on September 12. The 31st Virginia camped after dark that day, near the banks of the Opequon River. They were part of the advance on Harper's Ferry which continued on the 13th: by nightfall, the day's march ended within sight of Union defensive works on Bolivar Heights, overlooking Harper's Ferry. Next day, Gen. Stonewall Jackson's troops began their attack on the town.

Ewell's division advanced along the turnpike through Halltown and was deployed in three lines of battle, with Early's brigade taking the rear-guard position. Brig. Gen. Early later reported: "We moved forward through some fields on the right of the road until we reached a woods on a hill called School House Hill, confronting the main works on Bolivar Heights, and in easy range for artillery."[447]

The artillery fell silent as the day ended. A. P. Hill's troops were pushed up close to the Union defenses, ready to make their assault at first light. As the Confederates readied their attack on the 16th, the Federals surrendered. The surrender saved many lives in both armies. Gen. Earl later wrote that his men would have to cross a wide expanse of cleared ground with a long approach up a steep hillside between School House Hill and Bolivar Heights.[448]

Gen. Alexander R. Lawton was given temporary command of Ewell's division after Ewell was wounded in the leg. As Gen. Lawton moved forward with his two other brigades, Early's and Hays's brigades were supplied with rations late in the day of September 15. Lawton was under orders from Gen. Jackson to follow the road to Boteler's Ford. That ford crossed the Potomac River below Shepherdstown. Early's brigade came up with Lawton before dawn the next morning, about four miles from the ford.[449]

Their division crossed the Potomac River once more, and marched to within a mile of Sharpsburg, Md before pausing for a rest in a piece of woods. Jackson's division had gone before them, and Hill's division was behind them. At this time, the rest of Gen. Lee's army, including Longstreet's corps was situated in a line from north of the town of

Sharpsburg, on the Hagerstown Pike, to Antietam Creek at the south. The Union army was massed along this line when Lawton's division, including Early's brigade and the 31st Virginia arrived on September 16. Skirmishing had begun, and it promised to be a large engagement.[450]

Their division rested in place for a few hours, awaiting developments. When later they were sent to the left, it was to follow Jackson's division through fields to the turnpike, which ran, between Sharpsburg and Hagerstown. Turning north there, they followed the road until they came to a small wood, just west of the pike. A Quaker Church was there; though it was mostly referred to by the term often used then, Dunkard Church. To their right was Hood's division. Early's brigade was placed immediately next to Jackson's division, to protect the left flank.

Day was nearing an end. In the falling light, the men of the 31st Virginia could hear heavy skirmish fire in the distance to the right. Jubal Early reported to Gen. J. R. Jones, in command of Jackson's division, and then moved his brigade to the left of Stark's brigade, which was posted in a woods to the west of the pike, and was the left of Jackson's line. There was a small road which came along behind the woods past Starke's left, and on this road Early placed his brigade, forming the line at right angles to Starke's line so that he could protect Starke's flank. Hays's brigade was placed in rear of Early's men, and later in the evening Lawton's other two brigades took their place in the main line, far to the right, where Hood had been skirmishing earlier. Gen. Early's two brigades were far from the supervision of their own division commander, but were essentially under the eye of Gen. Stonewall Jackson.

Rain fell in the night, leaving the woods wet and dripping in the hours of the pre-dawn morning, the air full of moisture and anticipation of the day to come. In the 31st Virginia's bivouac, men tried to catch a little sleep if they were not too soaked through by the rain. They were seasoned veterans now, entrusted to hold Stonewall's flank, but there were just not very many of them, less than 200 present in the 31st Virginia, hardly more than a couple of companies worth in numerical strength. They were perhaps worth a bit more than that in experience and grit.

The regiment's commander that rainy night before the battle of Sharpsburg was Capt. Nathan Clawson, a young man with dark eyes and dark hair, not overly tall at five feet, eight inches, and well liked by the officers and soldiers. The son of Reverend Samuel Clawson of the Western Virginia Conference, Nathan Clawson had an air of competence about him that went over well with the men of the regiment. On the following day, Clawson would lead the 31st Virginia through one of the bloodiest encounters of the war.[451]

"Early in the morning we moved to the extreme left of our position, not meeting the enemy at that point," Capt. Phillips later recorded in his diary, September 17. By then the Union artillery had opened on the Confederate line, exploding shells raining down on the soldiers with a deafening series of blasts. Federal infantry began to advance, threatening Pelham's horse artillery in Gen. Stuart's command, which was posted northwest of the Dunkard Church on a hill west of the Nicodemus farm. Stonewall sent Early's brigade to protect the horse-artillery from the Federal threat.

They ran into skirmishers in the wet morning light, Federals moving up close on the right. Gen. Early responded with a detail of his own skirmishers as the rest of the brigade pressed on to the north. "I found General Stuart about a mile from the position I had moved from," Early later wrote, "with several pieces of artillery in position on a hill." Stuart's cannon were banging away in a duel with some Union artillery when a body of Union soldiers were observed cutting across an opening. They threatened to intrude between Early's position and Jackson's left. Stuart decided to move his guns, and Early marched the brigade back toward Jackson's left, but swinging west of their former route to avoid other Union regiments until they reached a better position.

Using the cover of a strip of woods that ran off the northwest corner of the West Woods, Early began placing his men in a new line. Gen. Stuart passed on a message from Gen. Jackson: Jubal Early's presence was required at once. Gen. Lawton had been badly wounded, and Early was to take immediate command of the division.

"Leaving the 13th Virginia Regiment, numbering less than 100 men, with Gen. Stuart," Early wrote, "I moved the rest of the brigade across the angle made by the elbow (of woods) with the main body of the woods, through a field to the position I had started from early in the morning." This field was just north of Alfred Poffenberger's house.[452]

Early placed his brigade in line, along with a couple hundred men from the 27th Virginia and the 9th Louisiana, and moved them north to a position held by Gen. Stark the previous night, on a slight ridge of the plateau, just northwest of the Dunkard Church. Pressed by time to set up the situation in the west woods, Early finished the task and then went quickly to look for the remainder of the division. "Heavy bodies of the enemy were now discovered in the field beyond the woods moving up to it," Early wrote. "I left my brigade under the command of Colonel William Smith, of the 49th Virginia, with directions to resist the enemy at all hazards, and rode across the Hagerstown pike towards the right to find the brigades that had been engaged early in the morning."

Colonel William Smith, former governor of Virginia, known often as Extra Billy, was 65 years old, and full of fire and energy. Amid the limestone ledges that poke gray-black rims out of rich Maryland soil, the men of the Fourth brigade gave the aged and eccentric commander all they had. Jubal Early had told them to hold the position, and Extra Billy, the grand old man of Virginia politics, was there to see that they held. "Give it to them, my boys!" Smith shouted as a withering fire of Federal bullets threatened to sweep the brigade away. The 31st Virginia was on the left of the brigade line; the 49th Virginia was on the right. With the 13th Virginia detached to guard Stuart's artillery, the small brigade numbered about 900 men.[453]

Early was not gone very long: Stonewall sent him back to his brigade after consulting with the general because there was too little of the division left for Early to command. Only fragments of Lawton's other regiments had survived a heavy Union attack. Gen. Jackson promised to send reinforcements to Early and his brigade, if he could in the meantime hold the enemy back on the left, with his own brigade and any other units available, such as Grigsby and Stafford's 27th Virginia and 9th Louisiana. It was a daunting task: by the time Early returned to the brigade, the number of Federals in their immediate area had increased to a considerable number.

One of their comrades in the 49th Virginia later described a moment in the battle when the right of Early's Brigade was "at the foot of a long wooded slope with an ascending grade from their position, some three or four degrees for three hundred or four hundred yards. The growth on this gentle slope was... such that they could... easily see every movement upon it. The crown of this slope was occupied by the enemy in great force, and seemed to be moving and massing upon the 49th with a slow step. At this movement, a regiment much superior in numbers to our own, moved out from the body of the enemy at quick step to turn the flank from the 49th, the main body moving slowly as if desiring first to see the effect of the flanking movement."[454]

The men in Early's brigade were using the limestone ledges to screen them from view by the Federals, who were coming through the woods on their right. The brigade tried to keep pace with the Federals, still using the rocky screen to conceal their movement, but when the opportunity presented itself, the line quickly formed and gave their foe a volley of rifle fire. They followed this up by charging the surprised Federals.

The brigade's movements were fluid in its assigned area, responding to threats by the Federals, then changing front to deliver another blow to some other Union regiment as it passed through the confusion of woods, gun smoke, and terrain. Colonel Smith's memories of the action were vivid: "As the enemy swept around my flank, one of my men cried out from the ranks, "Colonel, they are surrounding us!" My answer was, "Men, you conquer or die where you stand."

Col. Smith ordered the small brigade "about face" to confront a Union force that was approaching their rear. "Around came the whole command... My great necessity was a crushing volley, and such a volley, I never heard! It is to this day with me one of the rich memories of the war," Smith wrote after the war. "The Yankees did not even return fire, but with a quick step retired on the line of their advance, and rejoined their advancing columns."[455]

The feisty old man held his soldiers back to keep them from following the Federals, then turned them again to another direction and used a large, low rock outcropping to partially shield the line, giving them orders, "Now take your position; fire at will; and give them hell." The men waited for the Federals to come closer.

'For a short time it was fast and furious," Smith noted, "a few volleys from our gallant boys, from their protected position, at a relatively small loss to them, into the masses of the enemy, soon covered the ground with their dead and wounded. The enemy finally broke, leaving, besides their killed and wounded, 350 prisoners on our hands." Col. Extra Billy Smith seemed to enjoy his moments of action, though he received several wounds. A courageous old man, he stood his ground well in spite of pain and loss of blood.[456]

He wasn't the only one wounded in the brigade. Capt. Phillips was hit in the right shoulder by a musket ball. Others in the regiment were wounded as well. The latest attack made on them was by Sedgewick's division, including the unfortunate One Hundred Twenty-fifth Pennsylvania. They received the brunt of the brigade's musket fire. By then, Pelham's guns were set up to the west, on Hauser's Hill where they had a clear field of fire against the rest of Sedgewick's division. Other Confederate units under McLaws and Walker also played an important role in repulsing the Federals at this part of the battlefield, sending the Federal division reeling away from the Dunkard Church area.[457]

"Gen. Early saw his handful of faithful men rapidly being wasted away. He threw himself as it was in the thickest of the fight and shouted, 'Boys, hold them, you have plenty of reinforcements coming, hold them!' And we did hold them. The aged and brave "Extra Billy" Smith with his snow-white locks waving in the morning breeze and his face as placid as the silver moon cried, 'Give it to them, my boys!' ...Gen. Early almost gnashed his teeth at times, then more calmly, 'Shoot! Take good aim.'

"Early ordered us to charge." Phillips recalled. "Springing forward in the direction of the enemy with almost terrific yells, in a few jumps we gained the foot of the hill on which the enemy was formed. The enemy unable to stand the fury any longer broke and fled, and at this period a ball struck me on the right shoulder. I was assisted from the field. After I gained the rear, I saw several prisoners being quartered back. I saw one man, J. H. Wilt, taking ten back."[458]

BATTLE OF SHARPSBURG, SEPTEMBER 17, 1862

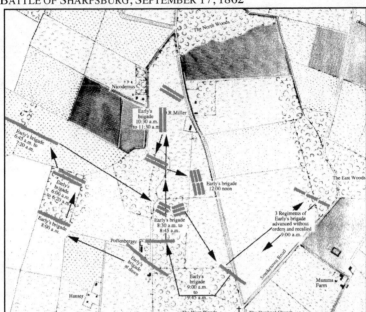

Map base from *War of Rebellion Atlas*

Brig. Gen. Early later wrote that he had not meant for the regiment to pursue the Federals at this time. "The brigade, however, without awaiting orders, dashed after the retreating column, driving it entirely out of the woods, and notwithstanding my efforts to do so, I did not succeed in stopping it until its flank and rear had become exposed to the fire of the column on the left."[459]

Colonel Smith of the 49th Virginia was wounded in multiple places in the final stages of their fight. Big. Gen. Early found him still standing, but too badly injured to move, and relieved him from duty so that Smith could be carried off the field on a stretcher. Early later said, "He was as brave a man as I ever saw, and seemed always insensible of fear."[460]

He certainly had helped keep the brigade effective in their movements on the left flank, and between Early's example early in the fight, and Smith's continued leadership, the little brigade had made a remarkable stand in holding off the Federals. As many as 2000 Federals from Sedgewick's division were said to have fallen as casualties there in less than thirty minutes of fighting in the West Woods. They included the One Hundred Twenty-fifth Pennsylvania, and Thirty-fourth New York, as well as other regiments in Gorman's, Howard's, and Dana's brigades.

So many Union men fell there, in fact, that after the battle, Federal reports claimed that Early had been in command of a division's worth of troops, entrenched in the area of the West Woods. What Sedgewick's division had encountered was not a division, but an augmented brigade, highly mobile, scared and full of fire, using the landscape to mask their movements at every opportunity. The brigade's desperate bid for survival in the face of seemingly overwhelming odds produced remarkable results. The survivors in the 31st Virginia were lucky to be alive afterward. [461]

The fight for the West Woods was only a small part of the greater battle of Sharpsburg. Although Early's brigade was through with their major effort for the day, the battle raged on to the right at Antietam Creek itself, where Burnside's bridge would earn its name by a Union commander's reckless mistake. It was hours before that battle on the right was over. Meanwhile, the men of the 31st Virginia could rest and recover, the worse part of their day finished by noon.

During the afternoon, they were posted in the Confederate line that ran along the Hagerstown Pike, north of the Dunkard Church. Through the balance of the day, while enemy shells sporadically exploded in the woods, the men held their position. Most of the shells passed over the lines and did little damage to the troops in their brigade line except shower them with tree branches and foliage that fell out of the trees onto the men as the artillery shells passed over. That night the regiment slept on the line with muskets at the ready.

The next morning, an informal truce was arranged for a few hours so the Federals could bring their most badly injured men from the field. After dark on that day, Early's brigade withdrew along with the rest of the division, now under command of Brig. Gen. Early. They marched that night toward the Potomac River, crossing at Boteler's Ford after sunrise on September 19. Formed in line of battle on the Virginia shore, the regiment remained through most of the day, guarding the ford. When the Union army finally appeared on the opposite shore with artillery and began to fire, Ewell's division retired towards Martinsburg, Va. It was, by then, very late in the day, and the men were weary.[462]

After all of the musket fire and exploding shells raining down on the regiment, casualties reported for the 31st Virginia after the battle of Sharpsburg amounted to no more than 1 man killed, and 7 men wounded. Of course, there were only about 200 men in the 31st Virginia at that battle, but by comparison, the 49th Regiment, on the right in the brigade, suffered 8 men killed, and 8 officers and 64 enlisted men wounded.[463]

The report of killed and wounded for the 31st Virginia at Sharpsburg included the regiment's color bearer, Corporal Allison D. Robinson of Company H, who was killed by an exploding shell. The wounded were: Laban R. Exline of Company A, badly wounded with two broken ribs and a terrible wound in the left arm, which was later amputated by their surgeon; Private Nathaniel Wilson, Co. A, wounded in the right leg, and was still in a hospital in April 1863, recovering from the wound; William. S. Lightner, Co. E, from Highland County; Elliot Jones, Co. H, absent recovering from his wound through November 1862; Harrison Paugh, Co. H, wounded for the second time in less than a month, would recover in time to be wounded again at Fredericksburg on December 13.

William. Warner, Co. I, 34 years old from Lewis County, received a wound that disabled him from carrying a rifle, but he volunteered to carry the colors after returning to the regiment, and was later appointed Ensign for conspicuous bravery under fire.

After Capt. Phillips was wounded in the right shoulder by a musket ball, he was taken to the Confederate hospital at Shepherdstown. He arrived there on September 18, along with many other wounded. Phillips recovered relatively quickly from this wound, and was able to report back to the regiment and command of Company K in October.[464]

Exchanges of prisoners occurred almost right away after the battle was over, for both armies had taken too many prisoners. The 31st Virginia had ten men captured at Sharpsburg. Of those, two took the oath of loyalty to the United States and were released at Sharpsburg to go home. This was not considered kindly by the regiment. William Bird and Nathanial Burns, both of Co. I, were later dropped from the regiment's rolls.

Manly Casto, Co. I was suffering from dysentery when he was captured. He died in a U.S. hospital at Harrisburg, Pa., on Oct. 20. The others were exchanged: Sergeant Valentine Gillespie, Co. G; William Gillespie, Co. G; Sergeant Nimrod D. Reger, Co. I, 19 years old; Marcus S. Rutherford, Co. A; Alfred Smith, Co. F, a saddler by trade; and Francis Waugh, Co. I.

At least one of the men, William S. Gillespie went home to Pocahontas County and never returned to the regiment. He was carried on the roll as "absent without leave" through November. Private De Witt C. Wellen, Co. I was granted a parole at Winchester on October 4, for later exchange under the same conditions.[465]

The 31st Virginia was sent to Boteler's Ford on September 20, along with the rest of Early's brigade, and Ewell's division. There they were, posted in the woods on either side of the road, within range of enemy artillery. They were to support A. P. Hill's division, which drove a small Union force back across the river almost as soon as it had crossed. Late in the day, the division once again marched toward Opequon Creek, where the men had a much-needed rest.

The division remained there until September 24, not far from where the mouth of Opequon Creek empties into the Potomac River, a few miles northeast of Martinsburg. By the 27th, the brigade was marching again. They crossed over the Opequon, and went into camp at Bunker

Hill. Their baggage wagons and supply train were at hand, and the men could refresh themselves on newly ground flour made from the Valley's wheat.[466]

Ewell's Fourth brigade was still called Early's brigade, although Gen Early was by then in command of Ewell's division while Gen. Ewell recovered from the loss of a leg at 2nd Manassas. In the 31st Virginia, there was speculation of a reassignment for the regiment, a matter that was already the subject of correspondence between Brig Gen John Imboden, in western Virginia, and Gen. R. E. Lee, in command of the Army of Northern Virginia.

Imboden proposed a plan to have the 31st Virginia, and their sister regiment, the 25th Virginia infantry transferred to his command on the western border along the Allegheny Mountains. General Lee said he was not opposed to the idea, but would have to think about it further. The rumor of this contemplated transfer of the two regiments reached the men in the ranks not long afterward. Except for an early end to the war, with a Southern victory, there was nothing most of the regiment would have liked better than to get closer to home.[467]

Plans were already afoot for their former commander, Col. William L. Jackson to form at least one regiment, and possibly two of cavalry to serve in the same area along the western border. With this in mind, Capt William Arnett submitted a letter of resignation from the 31sr Virginia on September 23: "The reasons I urge for so doing are: 1st, The reduced condition of my present command—there being not more than Fifteen (15) effective men remaining therein, nor has there been during the past two months; 2nd, The prospect of being able to raise a large company on the border from the northwestern counties of the state—the men of my section (N. W. Va.) now fleeing from their homes from fear of the Draft by the Federal Government." Arnett's resignation was approved and forwarded by Capt Nathan Clawson, commanding the 31st Virginia on that day. It was accepted at the end of October, and Arnett said his farewells to the regiment. He subsequently helped form a regiment of cavalry under Col. W. L. Jackson. [468]

Col. Hoffman returned to the regiment at the beginning of October. His illness seems to have been finally overcome and he was able to serve with the regiment through the balance of the year. Hoffman had a lot of paper work to catch up with, including figuring out what to do with the names of men who were known to have gone over to the enemy. A muster sheet for Company I, dated Oct. 1, 1862 has a notation signed by Hoffman: "Dropped from the roll five men for taking the oath while prisoners." Two of those men had been captured at Sharpsburg.[469]

Capt. George T. Thompson of Company H returned to the 31st Virginia at this time. Thompson, a 27-year-old farmer from Barbour County before the war, had been wounded in August at the battle of

Cedar Mountain. Enlisted in the summer of 1861 as a private in the ranks, the men in Company H elected him captain in May 1862.[470]

Many of the officers and men were away, on furlough or in hospital, and would continue so through the end of the year. The 31st Virginia continued to operate with about 200 men present and fit for duty, which was not a problem when they were not fighting, though it created more paperwork for Hoffman and his staff to keep track of where the men had disappeared to at this time.

During the second week of October, the brigade marched to Berryville and camped not far from town: they were about 12 miles from Winchester, and spent some days tearing up railroad track, each regiment having a turn. The 31st Virginia took its turn on the 11th as the brigade moved camp to a new place about two miles away. The army was moving camp every few days to combat illness in the ranks from bad water and raw sewage.[471]

The 31st Virginia marched from camp at Berryville with the brigade on October 19 and moved across the Shenandoah River to a camping place at Stonebridge, near White Post. They were there one day, and then continued to Port Royal, the brigade camping five miles from town. The 31st Virginia went on picket duty within sight of the town.

The remainder of the brigade passed by the next day on their way to tear up more of the B&O railroad: destroying railroad property seems to have been one of Stonewall Jackson's passions at this time. He wanted to disrupt as much of the railroad as his men could possibly manage. From soldiers, the men became railroad wreckers, their work hot and heavy as the men used pry-bars to pull up steel rails and then piled them on top of the old rail ties and set fire to the wood, trying to warp the rails out of all further use.

This was the rhythm of their lives in the autumn of 1862—camp for a night or two, move to a new location, tear up track, go on picket duty, move camp again. Between October 19 and November 18, the regiment was at Millwood, Stonebridge near White Post, Front Royal, Bunker Hill, Berryville, and Cedarville. They were benefiting from fresh air and exercise, and were regaining their strength. A new camp every few days meant the men were exposed to less bad water. Fewer men were on sick call. Wounded men, and those who had been sick, were returning from furloughs after prolonged recoveries in hospitals.

Many soldiers in the 31st Virginia had gone into the last campaign without shoes, and their feet had suffered considerably. Some had been forced to drop out of the line of march, unable to continue on bare feet. Now that there was a pause in the action, Capt. Cooper sent a stiff note to accompany a special clothing requisition for his company: "The men need the clothing badly and it cannot be elsewhere obtained." The requisition was for 21 pairs of pants, 19 pair of shoes, 4 shirts, 3 pair drawers, 2 uniform shirts, 1 jacket, and 1 cap. The other captains were sending similar requisitions in for their men too, trying to get the soldiers better equipped for the coming cold weather.[472]

The field and staff officers tried to keep up with the paperwork involved in settling affairs of business in the regiment. Every personnel requirement needed a piece of paper, it seemed: they processed requests and notices of discharges, transfers, resignations, disabilities, deaths, and hospitalizations. Nearly all of it was hand written with indifferent ink and poor handwriting on paper. Duty rosters had to be filled with details of men sent here and there for specific purposes; to hospitals as nurses, armories for ordnance requirements, homeward to counties on recruiting missions, or to round up the many strays who had gone home. Forms were sometimes hand drawn when the proper form was not obtainable from the regiment's adjutant.

On October 29, promotions in Company I were officially approved and the order published. Washington B. McNemar was promoted to 1st lieutenant. Lt. Bruffey's name was not on the list. Capt. Clawson later said that Bruffey was an efficient officer, and served bravely in combat, so the issue was not whether Bruffey was capable of being an officer, it was whether he was legally an officer. Eventually, Bruffey made the situation worse near the end of the year when he refused to carry out orders as a private. Capt. McCutchen, in command of the regiment that day was forced to forward charges against Bruffey for insubordination. No trial was ever held, however, and the issue remained unsettled.[473]

Irishman Dennis Bohner requested a discharge in November. Bohner had gone along with things in the army thus far, through thick and thin, although for him it was mostly the thin. From his point of view, there was a limit to what should be expected of him, a foreigner as he was. He was a coal miner and it was probably time to get back to work to provide for his family. Bohner's application for discharge was written on November 8, by Capt. Nathan Clawson, in their camp near White Post, and was forwarded up the chain of command. Even though he had enlisted at Huttonsville in June 1861, Bohner claimed to be a resident of Carbon County, in the state of Pennsylvania.

The 30-year-old Bohner was one of the few foreign-born men in the regiment, having been born in County Donegal, Ireland. In September 1861, he had been captured by the Federals and sent to Camp Chase, in Ohio, but had recently been released from captivity, and returned to the 31st Virginia. His application for discharge was returned to the regiment for clarification on whether he was, in fact a resident of Virginia, or if he owned property in the state. Capt. Clawson replied to the Adjutant Gen.'s query: "The applicant claims to have been a native of Ireland, not naturalized in any United or Confederate States, but domiciled in the State of Pennsylvania. His pretensions at the time he made the application are set forth correctly in the application and the endorsement made by the Colonel commanding. The said Bohner was known to several members of my company before the war, and I interrogated them as to whether he owned any property in Virginia, and they stated that to the best of their knowledge, he owned nothing but a gun and coal pick."[474]

Others in the regiment had troubles of another kind. Sergeant James Blair of Company C had learned some days before that his wife was dead. He wrote to his father in early November, complaining of the way that he learned of this tragedy. Blair was then 30 years old, a carpenter, six feet tall, with blue eyes and light hair, and weighed 195 pounds. "I heard on the 23rd of October that my wife was dead," he wrote to his father. "The news came so straight... which gave me the (most) terrible shock I ever had. I had just heard from G. M. Cookman and J. C. Snider. They had saw Peter and Canby's boys, and they said that Peter said she was well at the time they left home. I could not hear what was the matter, or when she died, all I could hear was that she was dead... I have come near deserting since I heard of the death of my wife... I want you to box up my books and take care of my other things. If my wife had lived, she would of taken care of things right, if she had lived. I hope the report I received of her death may prove false, like a good many other camp reports."[475]

Private W. B. Compton of Company A was in Richmond that day, November 10, staying at the "Virginia House." He had been given authority to raise troops for a new company for Jenkin's brigade, but the authority had not recognized the great reality of the situation in West Virginia: those who remained within the enemy's lines were far from willing to cross over just so they could be conscripted, or drafted, into whatever unit the government thought fit to place them. Clearly, men liked to pick the unit they were to serve in, usually one in which their relatives and friends served. Compton took the initiative to write to President Jefferson Davis, and had the audacity to point out these realities to the President of the Confederacy.

"The Secretary of War has authorized me," Compton wrote, "to raise a company of "Horse Artillery" to be attached to Jenkins Brigade of Cavalry in western Virginia, but had restricted me to enlistment of non-conscripts. There are a number of young men in West Virginia beyond our lines whom I could enlist and bring through the lines, but who are unwilling to run the risk of escaping from the enemy and be forced into service in any branch of the service and any regiment and company. Our western Virginians are already very much scattered in the different organizations of the army, and are thereby deprived of the credit of having more than two or three regiments in the field. I would respectfully ask Your Excellency for authority to enlist in my company such conscripts as I can pursued to "run the blockade"—as such will remain at home until placed within the power of the Govt. by the advance of our armies if not thus persuaded."

Jefferson Davis responded to this, as noted on the fold of Compton's letter: "In counties where the conscript act is suspended and that fact be sufficiently established, I see no objection to the proposition." Private Compton's commission to raise troops in western Virginia gave him the rank of Captain of the 31st Virginia, with authority to recruit, or so the papers he was carrying stated when he was captured the next year in Marion County, March 1863.[476]

Some of the men tried to visit their homes in western Virginia on furloughs, or as scouts to find out first-hand the situation in the occupied counties. Such a trip was dangerous, as discovered by the Harding brothers in early October. Capt. Joseph Harding was still recovering from a badly damaged left arm when he and Sgt. Marion Harding received permission to make a scout into Randolph County in late September.

On October 8, the brothers were south of Huttonsville, at Elkwater, just before daybreak. Traveling with two other Confederate soldiers and three of their civilian friends, they were scouting close to the old, and now abandoned, fortifications that had been established the year before on the knoll of Alexander Stalnaker's property. There were entrenchments there, below the main fortifications, and sometime just before dawn they ran into a party of Union soldiers who were being guided by Randolph County Sheriff J. F. Phares.

A blaze of gunfire sparked the dim, morning light across the entrenchments as the two parties gave battle. When the booming rifle shots faded, 24-year-old Marion Harding was dead from a wound in the thigh. One of the Union soldiers was also dangerously wounded: he was taken to the Stalnaker house by his comrades, where he'd be cared for while they sent for reinforcements. Capt. Harding, who was nothing if not bold, sent a message to the town of Beverly—the Union commander at that post could come and pick up their wounded soldier if he sent an ambulance and a doctor for the man, but without a guard, otherwise there would be a fight. Harding also insisted that the same ambulance must take his brother's body back with them to Beverly for burial. The Federals went along with the plan. The wounded man, and Marion Harding's body were collected by an ambulance under the watchful gaze of Capt. Harding. He started back to the regiment on October 15, arriving ten days later at their camp at Millwood, on the lower Shenandoah. He could tell them plenty about how things were at home.[477]

In anticipation of going into camp, on October 22, Col. Hoffman prepared an order for drill. Commanding officers from each company would drill their men on Tuesday, Wednesday, Friday, and Saturday, from ten to eleven in the morning. On Mondays and Thursdays, from ten to eleven, companies would be combined, and would drill together, with Capt. William Lyman drilling companies A, B, and C combined; Capt. McCutchen doing the same for companies D, E, and F; and Lt. Hiram McNemar putting companies G, H, I, and K through their combined drill. "The officer commanding the regiment, or some other, will drill it each day except Sunday, from four to five." Col. Hoffman was not in the habit of drilling the regiment himself.[478]

On occasion, men were discovered to have absented themselves from the regiment without leave. When caught, they were brought to camp to face punishment. The most pressing need was simply to get them back in the ranks, and carrying a rifled musket, as the army needed to increase its strength. One such soldier was Private Thomas J. Williams, of Company B. Williams had been recuperating from a wound at the Farmville hospital, and was given permission to go to his home in Highland County for three days on the way back to the regiment. For one reason or another, time seemed to slip away, and he was still at home on October 25, when he was arrested. He was brought into camp at Cedar Creek on November 7, under arrest and charged with being absent without leave. He was brought up on charges, found guilty, and sentenced to forfeiture of one month's pay. It was probably worth that much to Williams to have seen his family.[479]

The 31st Virginia crossed the Shenandoah River on November 15, and marched about six miles before camping for the night. They were at the Manassas Railroad, in the Manassas Gap. The following day the men tore up railroad track. "Our rations were out this evening," Hall commented in his diary, "but can not draw any until tomorrow. I went about one-half miles and got some corn." The next day, November 17, "Returned to camp today and cooked our rations, as we were nearly starved—had to roast hard corn."

They were on picket duty at Front Royal on the 18th; then marched at daylight to Strasburg on the 20th, a total of twenty-three miles. On the 21st, they were marching to Mt. Jackson; on the next day they marched another twenty-one miles. Twenty-two miles they traveled the day after that, bringing them to the eastern foothills of the Blue Ridge. November 24, they marched sixteen miles to Madison Court House, and there were allowed to rest for a few days. Many of the men in the division were still without shoes, their bleeding feet wrapped in rags as regiment marched.[480]

Politics and Resignation: Not all of the officers in the 31st Virginia were equipped to handle the type of criticism that was likely to be aimed by a very political body of men such as contained in their regiment. Maj. Arbogast certainly seemed to feel very keenly the criticisms, he wrote a terse resignation on November 25, 1862, at the regiment's camp near Madison Court House. "Having learned that some dissatisfaction exists among some of the officers and men of the 31st Virginia Volunteers, with regard to my holding the office I now hold, and having an opportunity of securing another situation in the service, I hereby resign any commission as "Major" of said regiment unconditionally and to take effect immediately." Arbogast had served as major of the 31st Virginia from June 9, 1862, when Joseph H. Chenoweth was killed, but it was only recently, on October 27 that his rank was officially confirmed. Why he felt so keenly the criticism of a few officers and men is not known, but his resignation was forwarded and approved very quickly.[481]

It was around this time, while the regiment was camped at Madison Court House, that moonshine became a problem once more. Capt. Joseph Harding later said they brought in their own moonshine still, and so many men were drunk that they called it "Camp Row." Harding claimed that Col. Hoffman sent for him one day to complain about the amount of drinking that was going on in the regiment. When Harding reported to Hoffman's tent, he saw a jug there: Harding told Hoffman he ought to "set a better example for the men."[482]

The regiment marched on November 27, taking the plank road along with the rest of Early's Brigade and Ewell's Division, arriving at Buckner's Neck, about fifteen miles below Fredericksburg on the Rappahannock River. "Our regiment went on picket while there," Hall said in his diary. "Had a long talk with the Yankees, as their pickets were on one side of the river and ours on the other."[483]

A. P. Hill's division, meanwhile, was at Hamilton's Crossing, protecting Longstreet's right. Longstreet occupied the heights above the town itself. This was the position of much of the army through the first part of December, immediately preceding the battle of Fredericksburg.

Hamilton's Crossing is just south of Fredericksburg, where the line of hills that run behind the town curve around, and the Richmond, Fredericksburg & Potomac Railroad makes a curve to pass at the base of the most southern hill. A country road ran through there to join the Telegraph Road with the River Road, south of town along the Rappahannock River. Pickets had been established in Fredericksburg, and also along the river above and below the town, to guard against a crossing by the Federals. Across the river, on the corresponding, but higher Stafford Heights, the Union army was waiting.

On the afternoon of December 12, Early's brigade received orders to march. Their camp was about 15 miles to the south of Fredericksburg. The brigade marched nearly all night to get to Hamilton's Crossing in time, and as the men neared the town of Fredericksburg, they could see the light of fires in the town. They bivouacked a short distance behind A. P. Hill's forces, sometime before dawn to allow the men a rest.[484]

A. P. Hill had moved his brigades forward from Hamilton's Crossing, and the end of his line was just in front of the most southern hill that ran down to the crossing itself. Many artillery pieces were posted on this small, cleared hill that faced the enemy. Archer's brigade was posted in front and to the left of the artillery, and Field's brigade was to the right of the batteries, to protect them from being flanked.

Ewell's division was posted along the ridge of the hills, some distance behind A. P. Hill's division, to form a reserve Confederate line. Their right rested on Hamilton's Crossing, and their left was adjacent to Jackson's right. The Fourth brigade, commanded that day by the senior colonel, James A. Walker of the 13th Virginia, was on the left of Ewell's line. The 31st Virginia was posted in woods so thick with trees and brush that the men could not see the enemy. At this time, the strength of the brigade was about 1,000 men.[485]

The battle of Fredericksburg began early on the morning of December 13. The men in the 31st Virginia had slept on their arms after arriving at Hamilton's Crossing, and were awoken early by the sound of skirmish fire to the front. "The morning broke clear and cold," Capt. Phillips observed. "Fog covered the countryside, the soldiers ate their scanty meal and calmly awaited orders. At nine o'clock the cannon began to boom and then the terrible contest began. When the sun broke through the fog (about noon), there stood the enemy, the sun reflecting off the snow on the bayonets"

Artillery shells began falling over the crest of the hill at Hamilton's, exploding over the men's heads in the tops of the trees. "It was here," Phillips said, "that Capt. Nathan Clawson and I were wounded by the same shell."[486]

BATTLE OF FREDERICKSBURG, DECEMBER 13, 1862

Map by David W. Wooddell

Waves of Federal infantry were then assaulting the Confederate lines in front of Hamilton's Crossing, but were being repulsed by furious artillery and rifle fire. The battle had been going on for some time when the Federals discovered a means of penetrating the Confederate line. A gap between two brigades at a low, marshy, wooded place near where the railroad crossed in front of the hill gave the Union an opening. Taking advantage of this gap in the line, the

Federals pushed forward, crossed over the railroad, and began to overwhelm the Confederates in that immediate area. Gen. Early received frantic requests for reinforcements. He sent Lawton's and Early's brigades, including the 31st Virginia to clear the Federals from the breach in the line.

Colonel Walker advanced the brigade at the double quick up and over the hill behind which they had been sheltering, and then sent them down the opposite slope to clear out the enemy at the crucial place. "Our brigade charged through two or three (Confederate) brigades," Hall wrote later, "and attacked the enemy with heavy firing." They drove the Federals out of the marshy woods, across the railroad, and into a field beyond.[487]

Just as this was accomplished, another Union force was coming up and crossing the railroad on their left. Walker sent the 13th Virginia over in that direction, using the woods as cover. The 13th Virginia, with the help of Thomas's brigade, repulsed that Union attack, while the rest of the brigade held their position in front of the railroad. They remained there until nightfall.[488]

With the breakthrough by the Federals repulsed, the battle on the right end of the Confederate line nearly came to a stop. The men in the 31st Virginia sank down on the marshy ground and waited out events, while far to their left, in the distance along Marye's Heights, the second phase of the day's battle continued to rage furiously for hours. When the day ended, the Confederates had won a major victory.

The Federal army lost 12,600 men as casualties at the battle of Fredericksburg, compared with 5,300 casualties in the Confederate army. Ewell's division lost 89 killed, and 639 wounded. In Early's brigade, composed of 5 regiments on that day, only 17 men were killed, and 114 wounded out of a total of 1,000 men who had gone into the battle. There were 17 casualties in the 31st Virginia, according to the report submitted by the brigade commander. Of that number, seven men later died of their wounds, a few of them within a day or two.

Edward Toothman, Co. A, a 21-year-old farmer from Marion County, died on December 13. Benjamin Wilson, Co. A, also died on the 13th: he was a 22-year-old ironworker by trade. Sergeant Cyrus Crouch, 26, of Co. F., from Huttonsville, died on the 14th. John A. Guildford, Co. G, would die within a couple of days. Wilson Moore, of Company K, previously wounded at Port Republic, and now again at Fredericksburg, also died on the 15th. David N. Spaur, Co. I, wounded by a musket ball, died on December 19, at Richmond.

Many others were wounded, and yet later recovered from their wounds. The list included George Arbough, William Barrett, Lt. Edward Bradbury, Capt. Nathan Clawson, Lt. Washington McNemar, Joseph Radosky, Marcus Rutherford, William Gay, Samuel Peterson, Capt. John R. Phillips, and Benjamin Varner. William Gay lost a finger on his right hand when a musket ball shot it off. Benjamin Varner got off lightly with a flesh wound to the right thigh.[489]

"Today is the anniversary of the battle of Allegheny Mountain," Capt. Phillips said in his diary that night, "and it has been fully celebrated by a hard fight."

The following morning, in the early hours before dawn of December 14, their brigade was relieved from the front as the Confederate line was adjusted to suit Gen. Jackson's plan of defense. Paxton's brigade relieved Early's brigade; Hays moved into the space vacated by Paxton; Hoke's brigade remained where it was; Lawton's brigade moved to the right of Hoke. Early's brigade was placed in reserve behind Hoke's command. Meanwhile, the Union army was gathered close to the river. An occasional rifle shot disturbed the relative calm of the battle's aftermath.

"I do not recollect to have suffered more any day in my life than I have today," Capt. Phillips wrote in his journal late in the day of the 14th. "My wound in my leg is very painful and I have had nothing to eat since yesterday morning, and it is now after sunset. I am so weak." Nathan Clawson and Riley Phillips were sent to Richmond in the same ambulance. At the hospital, Phillips said the kindness of the ladies caring for the wounded men. Eventually, he would be allowed to go to Edgar Campbell's "Sunny Side" in Highland County, to recover once more from his wounds.[490]

Private John A. Guildford, Co. G, was not so lucky. Mortally wounded, he was taken to a hospital, but there was little that could be done for him. Among his personal belongings, found at the hospital, was a sad letter he had written in early August to his parents in Pocahontas County. Perhaps he had been homesick when he wrote it, his parents being so far away; or maybe they had not supported his decision to enlist in the 31st Virginia. For whatever reason, the letter was never sent, and yet expresses the sentiment of many of these soldiers whose families were distant in the Union held territory of western Virginia. He lamented that he'd not received a letter from anyone at home, although he sent fifty dollars to them, via another soldier asked to deliver it for him.

"I have had some long marches since I left home, and have been in a good many fights, and have been spared to write home once more. We are expecting a fight soon...We have hard times here. I am tired of it.... If they don't give me a furlough to come home, I will take one. I don't know when. Soon it will be though. You needn't to look for me until you see me." But of course, Private Guildford never made it home to see his parents again. On December 15, 1862, he died from mortal wounds received in battle at Fredericksburg.[491]

The men at Fredericksburg suffered through torrential downpours of cold rain on December 15 and 16. The extreme weather masked the withdrawal of their opponents. Once it was realized that the Union had pulled back to the river, Ewell's division was relieved, and the men of the 31st Virginia moved to a spot in back of the hill at Hamilton's Crossing. They were once more in the reserve. That night, the Federals slipped quietly across the Rappahannock River, leaving the field of battle to the Confederates. Ewell's division was then sent down river to the vicinity of Port Royal, to guard against another crossing.

In the virgin wood on the hills back from the river, between an estate owned by John Taylor known as Hazelwood, and the neighboring property, called Camden by its owner, Mrs. Pratt, the regiment went into camp. This was to be their permanent quarters through a winter that was especially severe with heavy snows. The men built cabins to ward off the winter chill, and dug fortifications in the mud and the cold ground.[492]

In their new camp, Col. Hoffman wrote a note of praise for the men in his command: "The Colonel Commanding congratulates the officers and men of the Regiment upon their conduct and achievements in the last battle. If they continue to improve in discipline as they have done of late, he has no apprehension about their gallantry, which has ever been worthy of the cause in which they are engaged. With an army composed of such troops, inferiority of numbers is no impediment to success."[493]

A few days before Christmas, Lt. W. B. McNemar wrote a letter to the Editor of the Staunton *Spectator*, dated December 22, 1862, from their camp near Port Royal. The ladies of Augusta County, mostly from the vicinities of Mt. Sidney and Springhill, had sent 35 pairs of socks for the benefit of Company I. William Warner delivered the socks to the regiment, when he returned from recuperating in Augusta County from a wound he received in September, at the battle at Sharpsburg. McNemar thanked the kind ladies for the socks, and also acknowledged the receipt of a "visor" the ladies asked be given to the "bravest" private.

There being so many brave privates, McNemar replied to the ladies of Augusta County in his best hand, the visor had been given to a private who had gone through the recent fight barefooted.[494]

7

RAIDING WEST VIRGINIA
Jan. 1863—June 1863

Jubal Early was promoted to Major General after the first of the year, 1863. Early then commanded his own division, formerly Ewell's. The division was from that time called Early's division.[495]

The 31st Virginia was still in Early's brigade (also known as the Fourth brigade). They started 1863 camped about a mile from the town of Port Royal, on the Rappahannock River. Brig. Gen. William Smith of the 49th Virginia was the new brigade commander, promoted to brigadier general in early January. The brigade was then composed of five Virginia regiments, the 13th, 31st, 49th, 52nd, and 58th. From this point, it would be called Smith's brigade.

The 66-year-old Smith was absent from the brigade on a number of occasions in the next few months as he was still recovering from several wounds received at Sharpsburg. Former governor of Virginia, he was very involved in politics. He announced in mid-January that he would be a candidate for governor in the coming election. While he was away from the brigade the most senior officer present, Col. Hoffman of the 31st Virginia, was in temporary command.[496]

From January until April 9 the 31st Virginia was mainly engaged in incidentals such as serving in picket and guard details along the river. The regiment was detailed for picket duty in rotation with other regiments and normally served for 48 hours before turning the duty over to their relief, which was drawn from the division and not just their own brigade. The regiment went on picket: January 4, 16, and 26; February 5, and 18; March 12, and 24; and April 5.

Pickets were generally visible to one another on their respective sides of the Rappahannock River. When officers were not around the pickets talked with one another and exchanged items across the stream. Rarely did they do any shooting at one another. An exception was on February 6 when a Union picket fired at one of the 31st Virginia's companies, but did not hit anyone. It was such an exception to the rule of peaceful coexistence that it was commented upon in journals when someone did fire their musket across the river. It usually meant an over-eager officer was present and wanted to send a warning to the other side to not get too friendly.

The 31st Virginia was also frequently assigned to engineering duty during those winter months. Such duty consisted mainly in digging new entrenchments with picks and shovels along strategic portions of the river for possible later use in case the Federals decided to try crossing. The men also did some road building and repair. From the start of the year until mid-February the 31st Virginia was sent out on eight occasions on engineering duty, normally for just one day at a time. Some of their projects were repairing corduroy roads made of logs placed across the road in a tight-fitting layer that was supposed to help travelers overcome the constant mud of unpaved roadways. In one day they made about 125 yards of corduroy road. They were out digging in the mud with their picks and shovels on January 7, 12, 23, and 30; February 3, 8, 12, and 13.[497]

When not engaged on roads or entrenchments, or serving on picket details, the men could adjust their winter quarters, which were always a work in progress. Some of the soldiers built small log houses that would accommodate four to six men, covering the structure with their tent to make it more waterproof. This gave them more room than living in the tent, and was also warmer and more comfortable than living under thin canvas.[498]

Their rations had deteriorated, and by March 1863 some in the 31st Virginia began showing signs of scurvy with sore gums and loose teeth. Skin conditions caused by poor food and bad hygiene were reported by the medical staff. Various types of viruses and bacterial infections went through the ranks because the soldier's resistance was weakened by poor diet. Overexposure to harsh conditions was sometimes its own diagnosis. Many men lacked shoes and were kept in camp during bad weather as a result, or excused from going on picket or engineering duties because they were barefoot or had shoes in poor condition.[499]

Some who remained sick for too long were discharged from the regiment altogether. Three men were released from the 31st Virginia in the winter of 1863 after they became sick with typhus. Capt. Sam Gilmore resigned his commission on January 7, 1863, leaving Company E temporarily without a captain. His resignation was accepted the same day he wrote it and he was given a surgeon's disability certificate of discharge from the Army of Northern Virginia. He could return to Highland County and try to regain his health, which had nearly been ruined by typhus and diarrhea.[500]

On January 19, the quartermaster, Capt. Hill, paid and discharged Ashbel F. James. James was a druggist in Clarksburg before the war. Captured during the Battle of Camp Allegheny in December 1861, he returned to the army in January 1863 in poor health and suffering from typhus.[501]

Another typhus sufferer was Dick Everson in Company C: he was discharged with a disability on February 17. "On duty he was always a brave, willing, and subordinate soldier," Capt. Cooper wrote on his discharge certificate, but in reality he had spent more time in the hospital than present and fit for duty. The 24-year-old went home to Harrison County where he was later arrested in 1864 and sent to Cumberland, later to the prison at Wheeling where he was held until June 1865.

A few men were sent on details for duty elsewhere. Benjamin Corder, a 22-year-old private Company C was detailed to hospital duty at Staunton. Corder had been in poor health himself for some time. This job might aid his recuperate while still serving with pay, and without throwing him out of the service to his own devices.[502]

The men were paid in mid-January, which helped those soldiers who were worried about families at home in the Union-occupied counties of Virginia. Some of the men bought U.S. currency and sent it home to help their wives and children make it through the winter. Hard times had fallen on those at home.

The weather at their camp near Port Royal ran wet with heavy snowfall or freezing rain. On a couple of famous occasions the men organized snowball fights between regiments and brigades to have some exercise and light-hearted military maneuvers. At the end of January the 31st Virginia attacked the 13th Virginia with snowballs and "drove them half way across their grounds, when we withdrew."[503]

Letter writing, reading, and attending religious services were activities of note. Some turned to whiskey and moonshine, when they could get it, and at least one paid the price. Lt. Norval Lewis of Company C died on March 7 at Richmond from "intemperance." He'd been admitted to the hospital on March 5 for alcohol poisoning, and was buried at Richmond on March 8, much to the shock of the men in the regiment. A few were so saddened by this that they promised to abstain from drink: others held a wake and went on a drunken spree. Then the men of Company C held an election and replaced Lewis by electing James M Blair as lieutenant.[504]

Brig. Gen. Imboden had convinced Lee to allow his command to conduct a special raid through western Virginia in the spring. The 31st Virginia, made up of men almost entirely from that part of the state to the west was to be detached from Smith's (Fourth) brigade and temporarily loaned to Imboden's command. In preparation for the raid, several men from the 31st Virginia transferred to help form a new regiment of cavalry under their former commander, William L. Jackson, which would operate along the border of western Virginia as part of the Imboden raid.[505]

A handful of men volunteered to go on recruiting duty in western Virginia at this time, a dangerous endeavor if caught by the Union army. Three recruiters were captured in a Federal raid in Pocahontas

County: George W. Arbogast, George W. Cooper, and James G. Hamilton were sent to Camp Chase in Columbus, Ohio as prisoners of war after being captured in mid-February on recruiting duty. Despite the risk, others still volunteered to go to their home counties to recruit. Thomas Devericks was given an authority on February 23 to enlist conscripts in Pocahontas County. He was luckier than most, or perhaps more careful. A farmer from Highland County, he could slip back east over Allegheny Mountain and find friends to hide him from Federal patrols.[506]

Another on detached duty at this time was Private Hezekiah Holden of Company C, who quit the camp on March 6, 1863 to go to Salem, in Roanoke County to recruit from within the enemy's lines. His goal was to raise a company of men to join Lee's army.[507]

Capt. Phillips of Company K had returned to the regiment on March 4 after a prolonged recovery from his wounds. He was not entirely healed but his medical furlough had run out and he was anxious to see his friends at camp. However, not long after arriving back with the regiment, Phillips applied for a leave of absence to go recruiting in his home county. He departed camp on April 4 and spent several weeks successfully dodging the Federals in western Virginia. While there he even managed to enlist a few men. Mostly he just had adventures and visited family and friends.[508]

Except for a handful of men who were captured at Sharpsburg in September 1862 and paroled almost immediately, nearly all of the 31st Virginia's soldiers who were captured by the enemy between spring 1862 and spring 1863 were caught while visiting their homes in the west of Virginia. Even though they knew it was dangerous to go home, many of the men chose to go home soon after being discharged from the army with a disability. The records show 26 men from the 31st Virginia who were arrested in western Virginia between spring of 1862 and spring of 1863 and imprisoned by Union authorities. Although most were later exchanged, four died of disease while prisoners of war.[509]

Courts martial were held for those who got themselves in trouble. Mainly they were minor infractions such as absence without leave, but other crimes included misbehavior before the enemy, theft, drunkenness, and other sordid affairs. Two men were sentenced to 39 lashes, and to work on the fortifications for a year without pay for violation of the 25th Act of War—disobedience in the face of the enemy at the battle of Fredericksburg.

The regiment was mustered on March 6 to witness punishment for one of the pair, a grim reminder of what failing to follow orders could cost. "It seemed barbarous and inhuman, God never made a man to be treated so." Hall commented. The soldier who was yet to receive his 39 lashes no doubt felt the same way—he deserted in the night before he could be brought before the lash.[510]

Occasionally, the soldiers received news of terrible things happening at home to their families, such as the murder of Coleman Bowman's father in Barbour County. Animosities were sometimes acted out in violent ways at home in those occupied counties. Tragic chains of events resulted from single lawless acts. The murder of Coleman Bowman's father was such an example of the convoluted path that violence may take.

The kidnapping of James Trahern, the sheriff of Barbour County started it. Trahern was one of the newly elected county officials under the Union's reorganized "government of Virginia." Captured by a small detail of Partisan Rangers and taken to Richmond, Trahern was put into prison for several weeks. However, he was eventually released to go home to Barbour County. A few nights after returning to his home in western Virginia, two prominent citizens, Henry Bowman and Henry Wilson were murdered. Local Union supporters were under the impression that Bowman and Wilson had been somehow responsible for Sheriff Trahern's kidnapping and imprisonment at Richmond. The reality was that Brig. Gen. Imboden had sent a party of partisan rangers to Barbour County specifically to capture Sheriff Trahern in order to interfere with his duties.[511]

Henry Bowman was the father of the 31st Virginia's A. Coleman Bowman, a schoolteacher and law student before the war. A good friend of Phillips, Bowman had enlisted in May 1861 and served for a short while in Company K, but was taken prisoner during the retreat from Laurel Hill and sent to Wheeling and held as a prisoner of war. Released in March 1862, he was detailed to work in a government shop run by the Ordnance Department in Mecklenburg County, Virginia. He was there when his friend Phillips, still on furlough, wrote to tell him of the loss of his father, Henry Bowman.

"My dear old friend," Phillips wrote, "It is with a heart of unspeakable grief that your correspondent takes his pen to tell you an awful story. Capt. Ben Hill with some ten men went into Barbour County and arrested James Trahern, the bogus sheriff of our dear old county. The raid so enraged the vandal hordes of Lincolndom that they, in cold blood, murdered your father and Henry Wilson. They shot your dear old father full of holes in his own yard. Great God, how long is this damnable war to go on? I know how deep your grief will be. I know what a precious father yours was.

"Coleman, I have brewed my hands in the blood of my foes until I was tired of the butchery, but now again my anger comes in all its fierceness and now woe to the accursed cutthroats that fall in my path. Oh! Heavens avenge us.... You can't go home; if you do you will be hurried off to a prison; so remain where you are until spring."[512] It is understandable that Coleman Bowman had revenge in his heart after hearing the news of his father's death. Bowman wrote to John Letcher, the governor of Virginia, asking for help in carrying out his revenge.

He wanted permission to form a company of cavalry, and he received it—as captain of his own company, in Fontain's regiment of Partisan Rangers.

This was the essence of the civil war in western Virginia; wrongs never made right by violence and retribution, triggered by acts of revenge. The arrest of the sheriff was part of the official policy of the Confederate government to undermine civil authority in the counties that were occupied by the Union. From that action to a Union zealot's reaction in killing Henry Bowman to the son's wish to impose revenge on the murderers, and then into the Partisan Rangers, which was like throwing lamp oil on the fire to try to put it out.[513] Another of the 31st Virginia's men observed at this time, "No hopes are entertained for this war to end, at least while we live. Great men, to whom existence is not yet given, may cast a backward glance upon us as a people, and think there is something more in war than a poetical representation."[514]

On March 3, the 31st Virginia departed Port Royal and marched to Hamilton's Crossing to go into camp for a month. The weather was no better , and the food if anything was poorer in quality and quantity. The men were ordered to move into winter huts at this "new" camp, and complained of the fleas the previous occupants didn't take with them.[515]

Visitors to the camp, such as Judge Gideon Camden and his son Draper Camden, arrived now and then to see Col. Hoffman and talk politics. Hoffman had not forgotten that he was a politician. He requested leave on March 15 to attend the Virginia legislature after learning of a ruling that meant he was still a qualified member of the House of Delegates, but Gen. Early, perhaps wary of allowing Hoffman to escape to Richmond, denied the request. The Army was preparing for the spring campaign and needed its commanders.[516]

Others were also interested in politics: Capt. Luther D. Haymond of Company D was elected on March 28 to the Virginia House of Delegates to represent Braxton, Nicholas, Clay, and part of Webster counties.[517] Haymond remained in the regiment for many months afterward, but others departed, including their chaplain, Reverend S. H. Mullens, who resigned on March 19 and returned to his home in Augusta County. Earlier in the year, the 31st Virginia lost a few others who transferred to other regiments, including Private George Cookman, transferring to the 17th Virginia; and Dr. Isaiah Bee, assistant surgeon, who transferred to the 19th Virginia Cavalry. Incoming, they gained a fifer from the 17th Virginia, Private Enoch Yerkey who was placed in Company C.[518]

Brig. Gen. Smith returned to the Fourth brigade on April 6 and once again assumed command. Three days later, the 31st Virginia received orders detaching the regiment from Smith's brigade. Col. Hoffman was ordered to report to Brig. Gen. John Imboden at Shenandoah Mountain with the regiment to participate in the raid through western Virginia.

The regiment had about 250 men present and fit for duty when it took its leave from the Fourth brigade to participate in the Imboden raid.[519]

RAIDING WEST VIRGINIA, 1863

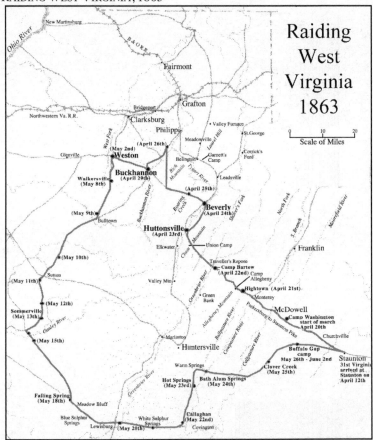

Map by David W. Wooddell

    The 31st Virginia marched from Hamilton's Crossing to Guiney's Station on the on the morning of April 10 and the men boarded the cars along with the 25th Virginia. "There was a great rejoicing by all of us," Hall wrote, "at once more getting together. We had been together for a long time and put a great deal of confidence in each other."[520]

    From Guiney's Station, the train switched back onto the main line and ran on to Hanover Junction, arriving there in the evening to stop for water and wood for the engine. From there it steamed through the night, passing Greenwood Station at dawn. It was not an uneventful trip. As Sgt Snider would write, at Greenwood, "Some of the boys got some whiskey... and two of them tried to fight on top of the cars whilst they was under full headway."[521]

The two regiments arrived at Staunton in the early afternoon, disembarked from the rail cars and marched along the railroad line for two miles before camping at Archie Stuart's farm. Snider was granted permission to remain in Staunton so that he could visit his brother Elmore, who was in the hospital with a disabling wound. They had not seen one another in quite a long while.[522]

Most of the others in the regiment were granted passes to go into Staunton and blow off some steam. The Provost Guard had its hands full as it attempted to maintain order during the visit of the 25th and 31st Virginia. The veteran soldiers of those two regiments were intent on having a rip-roaring good time before setting off across the mountains.

"Some of them got too much whiskey and got a little merry, but behaved themselves," Snider said. "The Provost Guard wanted to show their authority, and called for their papers, and in one or two instances tore them up and took them to the Guard House after a few of them got knocked down on both sides."

Lt. Col. John C Higgenbotham, commander of the 25th Virginia told the Provost Marshall that his men should be released immediately and be allowed to go where they pleased until their passes had expired. "Soon after they was released, they got to calling the Guard "conscripts" and cowards and the Guard was brought out to take some of them. The boys hollered, 'Fall in the 25th and 31st!' which they did and kept the Guards at bay. Finally, Colonel Higgenbotham came along and sent his men home."[523]

Hall was also in town that Sunday. Returning to the regiment's camp, he reported the fracas to Capt. William Cooper. "Am quite sick today," Cooper wrote in his journal that day. "I am fearful the coming campaign will be too hard for me. I am beginning to feel the effects of two years service." Cooper had started the year with a notation in his journal, "How many more times must we whip them before they will relinquish the contest?" Cooper's family was still in Clarksburg and he was even then looking for a means to arrange their release from within the Union lines and come south, or at least east where he could have more contact with them.

The 25th and 31st Virginia regiments marched from their camp near Staunton on April 13. "Start at sunrise," Cooper wrote, "and march to Calf Pasture River at foot of Shenandoah Mountain, twenty-three miles. Orders of Gen. Imboden... were quite complimentary." Brig. Gen. John D Imboden welcomed the men of the 31st and 25th Virginia back to the mountains. He gave them a chivalrous speech, telling them what heroes they were and how they would avenge all the wrongs that had been done to their families.[524]

Gen. Imboden went on to outline his plans for the next several days in the North West Virginia Brigade (as it was sometimes called) He ordered three days cooked rations to be prepared on the 14th. Colonels should have regiments ready to move at any hour after 4 A.M. on the 15th. All men too sick or physically unfit for immediate and active duty to be in the charge of an officer of the post at the camp and in the quarters of the 62nd Regiment. Baggage on the march to be limited to cooking equipment; other baggage to be placed in storage until the regiments returned from the raid. Each regiment was assigned one covered wagon and a team of four horses per every two hundred men; one four-horse wagon for ordnance for each regiment; two ambulances per regiment; and a two-horse wagon and team for the field staff. The ambulances would carry medical stores, and a brigade ambulance would carry the reserve medical supplies.[525]

One of the 31st Virginia's assistant surgeons, Dr. George Young was detailed to remain at Camp Washington as Post Surgeon under command of Capt. A. H. Nelson, who was Commandant of the 62nd Virginia's camp.[526]

Capt. Cooper said: "Prepare for the campaign by divesting ourselves of everything but arms, ammunition, a single change of underwear... a blanket, and cooking three days ration."[527]

Imboden issued written orders the following day. The brigade would take up the line of march on the 15th at six o'clock in the morning. The 62nd Virginia, a mounted infantry regiment would be in advance, followed by the 31st Virginia, and then the 25th Virginia. Regimental wagon trains were ordered to move immediately to the rear of their respective regiments and would be guarded at all times by regimental police guards. Brigade wagons and ambulances would follow immediately behind the train of the regiment marching in the rear of the column and would be guarded by the brigade's grand guard.

Straggling was specifically prohibited, and also riding in any wagon or ambulance unless a man had a pass from a surgeon stating he was too sick or broken down from the walk and had to ride to keep up with the brigade. "Leaving the ranks on the road to visit houses on the way, and all marauding or damage to private property are strictly prohibited," Imboden ordered. "All officers, but Commandants of regiments especially, are charged with a rigid enforcement of this order."[528]

The brigade set out on the morning of the 15th in a heavy rain that slowed the pace considerably: they traveled only as far as Shaw's Ridge on the Staunton Parkersburg Pike that first day. Seeing the streams too high to cross, and learning that a body of Federal cavalry was on the road ahead, the brigade reversed direction and went back as far as the Haymond farm on the eastern side of Shenandoah Mountain and camped for the night at a place their army had been using as a cavalry camp.

The April rain continued to fall heavily, and the next day the 31st Virginia was allowed to move into some cabins the cavalry had been using. They snugged down from the cold and wet. Remaining there through the 19th, "Receive orders to cook three days rations and be ready to move at four tomorrow morning," Cooper wrote, "Mr. Mullen preached in the morning, and Rev. Snider in the evening." Reverend Mullens had been the chaplain for the 31st Virginia until March, when he resigned, but was still with the regiment.[529]

While the regiment was at Camp Washington, on April 16, Lt. Sidney Ruckman of Company G submitted his resignation. Ruckman had been under arrest since December when Col. Hoffman preferred charges against him. Though Ruckman was the "acting" captain of the company, Ruckman had not been confirmed in the rank. At Camp Washington, he wrote, "Wishing to join another company in this brigade, I respectfully tender my resignation as First Lieutenant of Company G." Hoffman was not going to quibble over the resignation. When forwarding the resignation to Brig. Gen. Imboden for approval, Hoffman said that he was currently without copies of the paperwork with the exact charges preferred against Ruckman, and on that basis, he was recommending the resignation be accepted, and all charges dropped. Gen. Imboden went along with that, since no trial could possibly be held for months in the future. Since Ruckman had offered to enlist as a private in another company in a different regiment, Imboden approved the resignation, and transfer of Ruckman effective immediately.[530]

The brigade marched again on April 20, at six o'clock in the morning. The 18th Virginia cavalry, and J. H. McClanahan's battery of six guns had joined them by this time, and the combined strength of the brigade was 1,825 men. About two miles beyond the village of McDowell, after marching 19 miles on the Staunton to Parkersburg road, the brigade stopped for the night and camped.[531]

They were joined the next day by the 22nd Virginia infantry and a small battalion of dismounted cavalry, the 37th Virginia under the command of Lt. Col. A. C. Dunn. This brought the brigade up to strength of 3,365 men, out of which about 700 men were mounted infantry and cavalry. They had rations of flour for 13 days in their wagons, and were carrying a 30-day supply of salt. Imboden planned on purchasing local cows in western Virginia to furnish meat for the troops.[532]

The return of the Confederate army was an event the people of Highland and Pocahontas Counties had long awaited, and would long remember. As marching men and mounted riders made their way through the mountains, passing isolated houses and villages, people came out of their dwellings and stores to wave and cheer.

The regiments arrived at Hightown at the foot of Lantz Mountain with fair weather and good spirits. "You could see the joy in their faces," one onlooker commented later about the men in the regiments passing through his small village. The 62nd Virginia continued in the lead, followed by the 22nd Virginia, 19th Virginia cavalry, Dunn's battalion, 25th Virginia and finally the 31st Virginia bringing up the rear.

"Next came that war-worn veteran, Colonel John S. Hoffman, at the head of the "Old 31st..." wrote John McNeill, who'd been in Hightown that day expressly to see the southern army. "There were the first Confederate soldiers that I had seen marching with colors flying and to the step of martial music since Gen. Lee had fallen back from Valley Mountain in September 1861. A great many men who were refugees from Northwest Virginia had found out the secret of the raid and accompanied the raiders." McNeill was 19 years old and full of energy. Wanting to visit with his cousins and friends in the 25th and 31st Virginia, McNeill marched with them for the rest of the day, heading back to his home in Pocahontas County.

"The ranks of these two regiments had been fearfully depleted at that time," he said, "and what a change had come over the living. Their faces had grown old and careworn and while they looked strong and healthy, still their limbs were so stiff that not one of them I tried could mount "Billie" (his horse) from the ground. I managed to get two of my cousins on the horse at different times from a high bank, but it affected the hip and leg so they took cramp and had to get off immediately. No wonder! These were the legs that made up Stonewall Jackson's foot cavalry, and when you reflect what they had already done, how could they be anything else but stiff?"[533]

McNeill was not yet in the Confederate army, but his father had suffered the loss of more than 200 head of cattle in Pocahontas County and a number of fine horses at the hands of Federal cavalrymen in the past year. McNeill was determined to go along on the raid to see if he could recover some of his father's livestock.

The day grew cold and wet by the time the brigade reached the Top of Allegheny, where they paused to look over their old camp on the Yeager Farm. "The cabins at Camp Allegheny were many of them destroyed, my own among them," Capt. Cooper said. Continuing the march, they reached Bartow and the Greenbrier River later in the day, and slept that night at the regiment's old site at Camp Bartow, on the Greenbrier River, an eighteen-mile march from Hightown.

One of the "old veterans" of the 31st Virginia was 22-year-old Hall. Remembering fallen friends from long ago, Hall and his comrades paid their respects at the small cemetery at old Camp Bartow. "The hard, baked earth has given way to luxurious vegetation," he wrote, "and all over that broad camp a dead silence reigns, following the hum and stir of busy camp life. The graves of our soldiers who fell in that battle are all sodded over, and the green grass waves in beauty over those fallen heroes, as if it were enjoying the genial air of spring. As we stood around their graves we could almost envy their quiet, peaceful lot, when we remembered what we had undergone, and also thought of the probability of a still harder life to come."[534]

The brigade marched to Huttonsville, reaching that place on April 23. The rain had been nearly unceasing for all 70 miles of the journey, though it had become freezing rain on Cheat Mountain. A small unit of 30 Federal cavalrymen had withdrawn from Huttonsville, after learning of Imboden's approach, leaving the town to the weary Confederate soldiers when they arrived, thoroughly soaked, and in need of a rest. The mud on the roads had been particularly difficult to navigate for the past four days.

Imboden ordered the infantry to advance along the east side of the river on the morning of the 24th. They captured a Federal wagon train of forage, or animal feed, while the cavalry chased after some Union men on the west side of the river. By the time that Imboden got the infantry to Beverly, the Federals were prepared and disposed to make a fight.

Union artillery fired on the advancing Confederates when the head of the column was about a mile from Beverly. Imboden wanted to try flanking the Federals, who seemed to be strongly posted, so he sent his men on detours. Still, the infantry had to pass a gauntlet of skirmishers and a running fight ensued for the distance of about two miles, according to Imboden's report. The main body of Union infantry and cavalry managed to escape from the town while the Confederate brigade was setting up a flank movement and passing the skirmishers. By the time the brigade had circled around to the north side of Beverly, a third of the town was burning, set by Union soldiers in order to destroy as much of the stores as possible.

"I lost only three men," Imboden reported later, "so badly wounded that I had to leave them in Beverly in private houses, where they have fallen into the hands of the enemy. The enemy's loss was trifling, too, not over thirteen killed and wounded, and about the same number captured by us."

Apparently there was a bit of looting by the men when they reached Beverly, at least sufficient to prompt Imboden to issue a written order on the 25th specifically prohibiting the right to seize property from any citizen, and if a soldier was caught in the act it would be punished as though he had committed robbery. "In respect to the property of Union citizens useful and necessary for the army," Imboden wrote, "improvements will be made by the proper officers in legal form, and certificates given under Gen. Orders from these Headquarters."

Whether the payment of Confederate dollars would be acceptable to the Union citizens was questionable, but the intent was there to pay rather than openly steal. In the same vein, Imboden ordered that whenever the brigade entered a town the commanding officer of the first regiment was responsible for posting guards at every store, and for seeing that the private property of citizens in the town was not stolen.[535]

The 31st Virginia marched with the brigade on April 25th from Beverly, crossing Rich Mountain to Roaring Creek, a distance of about

9 miles. The rain stopped and the air was cool, according to Capt. Cooper, who said, "Colonel Jackson sent me authority to organize a battalion or regiment for his brigade. It was unsolicited and (I) consider it a compliment."[536]

Meanwhile, Sergeant Snider had been bringing up the rear in the way of an old veteran of Stonewall's foot-cavalry. He caught up with the regiment on the 25th near the foot of Rich Mountain. On the way, he came across a mortally-wounded man in the road: He'd been ambushed by Union scouts, the man told Snider, but they could do nothing for him and had to leave him where he was by the side of the road.[537]

On the 26th, the regiment marched early toward Buckhannon, but as Snider said, "Turned on the Philippi road and crossed the river and camped for the night between Buckhannon and Philippi." They were deterred by the burnt bridge at Middle Fork, but found a crossing through the stream about ten miles from Philippi. "Camped near widow Whiteley's after marching twenty miles," Cooper wrote in his journal.

The road to Philippi was impossible for wagons or artillery to travel over, with mud in some places up to the saddle skirts of their horses. Gen. Imboden had also received reports that the Union army under Brig. Gen. Roberts was in Buckhannon with a large force. The Confederate commander did not feel it prudent to go on to Philippi until the force on his flank at Buckhannon had been dealt with, so Imboden sent two companies of cavalry to try and locate Brig. Gen. William A. Jones, to see if he had destroyed the railroad bridges as planned.

Imboden held a conference of his highest-ranking officers, including Col. Hoffman of the 31st Virginia, Smith of the 62nd Virginia, Higgenbotham of the 25th Virginia, Patton of the 22nd Virginia, Jackson of the 19th Virginia, and Clairborne of the 37th Virginia Battalion. Patton showed Imboden one of Brig. Gen. Schenck's orders, which had been found in Beverly: this document revealed that six Union brigades were assigned the defense of the B&O railroad, leading Imboden and the others to suspect that Jones had not been able to disrupt the railroad.

The general listened to the opinion of his senior officers and later reported they all thought they were in a critical position if the Union still had use of the railroad. They worried about being cut off from a possible retreat, if one became necessary. "It was," Imboden wrote, "...the unanimous judgment of all my colonels, in which I concurred, that in the face of this new information, it would be extremely imprudent to advance farther or remain where we were, with the danger of being overwhelmed and cut off in a few hours."

Imboden decided to fall back to a place where they could retreat further if necessary. To some who had been with Porterfield and Garnett in the summer of 1861, it must have seemed as though the intervening two years had vanished. Retreat and withdraw. After the hard marching and tough fighting the 31st and 25th Virginia had experienced thus far in the war, to come back to West Virginia and then withdraw from the enemy must have been particularly galling.

The regiment struggled on through mud that coated men, horses, and wagons so thickly that the day was mostly gone before they traveled more than two miles in the direction of Roaring Run. They learned after dark that the enemy in Buckhannon had retreated, burning the bridges behind them at Middle Fork and the Buckhannon River. As Capt. Cooper said on the 27th, "The road we attempted to pass over was an awful one. A dog could hardly get over it."[538]

Snider was due for an adventure. On April 27th he was sent on a personal foray into enemy-held territory. "Myself and others were detailed to go to Harrison County to recruit for the regiment," Snider wrote. "We started... about 2 P.M. and came near to the Buckhannon River by dark, which we crossed on a raft of (fence) rails. We traveled several miles and put up for the day in an alder thicket a short time before day." One of the men going into Harrison County with Snider was Lt. James M. Blair.[539]

The 31st Virginia, meanwhile, was marching with Imboden's brigade to Buckhannon, camping four miles from town at White's Place. On the 29th they occupied Buckhannon. "Saw a number of old friends," Capt. Cooper wrote that day. "Everybody scared. Secessionists afraid we would not remain; and Unionists afraid of being harshly treated. The Confederate soldiers here have been represented as being terribly cruel. Quite a quantity of stores obtained. The Union sentiment seems to be predominant and Secessionists are very cautious."

Cooper returned to Buckhannon the following day, April 30. "The feeling is more quiet. A number of good arms, several hundred, have been found in wells and other places. A number of country people came into town, all of whom have tales of outrage, wrong, and tyranny to tell of the Yankees."[540]

The Federals had burned their army storehouses before leaving town, and when faced with leaving two pieces of artillery behind, had destroyed them, too. The Confederates set about collecting cattle and grain, impressing the local mills to grind as much grain as they could find, which was usually in very small quantities. They paid for the grain and the cattle: Brig. Gen. Imboden later maintained that they had paid the going prices, and that the locals were not unhappy at the currency used to pay for the supplies.

Brig. Gen. William E. Jones, whose force was making the raid into the northern part of the state in coordination with Imboden's raid further to the south, sent a letter to Imboden on the 27th, but the roads were so muddy that the letter did not arrive until the 29th. It informed Imboden that he had not been successful in destroying the railroad bridge at the Cheat River, which meant that the railroad was still operable by the Federals.[541]

The Union army was reportedly gathering a strong force at the village of Janelew, about halfway between Clarksburg and Buckhannon. Although Brig. Gen. Imboden urged his men to hurry up with collecting more cattle and corn on the 30th, Hall was able to visit for a short while with a cousin, M. E. Taft, in Buckhannon. No doubt others in the regiment used this opportunity to seek out family and friends, for time was at a premium and there was no telling when they would need to depart, or when they might be coming back.

Farther to the north, Snider's adventure had hardly begun, and yet he and his comrades were forced to hole up through the day on the 28th, and wait for darkness before proceeding. "We spent a long and wearisome day, having but little to eat," Snider said. "There was men working within talking distance of us all day. We struck out at dark and got to the edge of Harrison County before day, where we got something to eat and took up quarters in the woods for night." This was probably not the way that any of them had imagined returning home after two years of war, but if they revealed themselves to any but a few trusted individuals they would find themselves in the Atheneum prison at Wheeling quick as could be, maybe even before the day was out.

"Rained very hard in the evening," he wrote. "We started at dark and arrived at our destination before daylight. Our friends...very much surprised and glad to see us." Snider had the luxury of a roof over his head on the 30th: "In the house all day, which was in sight of a picket post that had been established in the morning. We learned that the enemy was fortifying on this side of Clarksburg and in the evening we concluded it would be most wholesome for us to fall back on Lost Creek. When we got into that neighborhood, we learned that our forces occupied Buckhannon and that some more of our boys had come home. We got some quilts and laid out till morning." They were well pleased to be home, even if they did have to scurry around and hide most of the time, like some kind of grown-up boy's game.

"We went to the house and got our breakfast, and then I went to Mr. Shoemaker's and got me a pair of shoes made and in the evening went to Rockford and back and staid all night in a house." This treat was spoiled by bad news from Lt. Blair's brother – Lt. Blair had been captured that day near Romine's Mills.[542]

James M. Blair was a large fellow, six feet tall, with blue eyes and fair hair, and was 31 years old when captured in Harrison County. He was more than a bit lucky after being captured. Sent to Wheeling and locked up in the Atheneum prison for a few days, he was then transferred to Camp Chase, the prisoner of war camp outside of Columbus, Ohio. He was in Camp Chase until May 13, when he was paroled and released. Lt. Blair was back in the army before the end of the month, a prison turnaround time that was difficult to equal.[543]

Brig. Gen. Imboden was still at Buckhannon with his troops on May 1. He sent a cavalry regiment to Weston to check on the town. Federal troops had destroyed their stores before leaving town to join the other Union command that was still rumored to be at Janelew. Imboden was about to move his troops toward Philippi on the morning of the 2nd when he learned that William Jones and his men had moved down to within six miles of Buckhannon.

By this time William L. Jackson's 19th Virginia cavalry had destroyed all of the bridges west of Fairmont for about thirty miles. They had also gone into the town of Bridgeport, in Harrison County, and destroyed a small railroad bridge, which would disrupt traffic north and south on the Northwestern Virginia Railroad.

Col. Hoffman and Capt. Cooper rode with the cavalry toward Weston. The rain from the past many days, and the movement of troops and citizens back and forth had created more mires of mud in the road. The mounted soldiers were thoroughly coated with Lewis County clay when they arrived at Jacob Bush's farm, four miles from Weston, on Saturday, May 1. They camped on the farm, and on the following day Hoffman and Cooper rode to Weston to visit relatives, old friends, and acquaintances.[544]

"The Secessionists seem more numerous and bold than at Buckhannon," Cooper wrote, "but there still exists the same low whispers and anxious looks around for eavesdroppers of an oppressed people." Capt. Cooper remained in town for the next two nights, staying with a friend. "Regiment did not pass through until evening," he said May 2. "It camped about half mile from town on Polk Creek. Am told that my family is well, by a person who saw them about two weeks ago. Thank God." On the following afternoon, Imboden allowed the men in the regiments to enter Philippi, a small town with a famous covered bridge crossing the Tygart River. The town's two-lane covered bridge on the Staunton to Parkersburg Pike was well known, and had even been mentioned in the *New York Times* report of the battle of Philippi in early June 1861. Now two years later the secessionists were back temporarily.

Imboden's scouts probed toward Clarksburg and came back with a tale of the Union army with several thousand troops fortifying against an attack at the railroad nexus. Clarksburg was a supply point for the Union army, and strongly held at this time. The Union brigades of generals J. R. Kenly and Benjamin S. Roberts were there, and two regiments under Colonel James A. Mulligan were at Grafton. Cattle pens, remount horses in corrals, and cowboys brought up to Clarksburg from Mexico to wrangle horses and cattle had combined with the thousands of Union soldiers from Ohio, Indiana, and other points west and turned the Harrison County seat into a more colorful place than it had been before the war. The smell of stockyards was not foreign to that part of the state, but the scope of the resulting waste and reek of the slaughterhouses necessary for turning cattle into salt beef for the soldiers made Clarksburg extra odiferous.

Brig. Gen. Jones had rounded up more than 1,200 horses. For the next day and night the principal occupation of the troops was gathering corn and cattle, of which there were plenty of cattle and not a great quantity of grain. Imboden's men gathered 2,000 head of cattle, which were sent eastward across the mountains under an armed guard. The rest of Jones's brigade arrived on the 4th and 5th of May. By then, the Federals were starting to probe the Confederate position.

The picket Imboden had sent to Janelew was attacked on the 5th by the Union army, with three men captured. This, according to Capt. Cooper, "Creating no little alarm among the citizens and new troops. The 62nd (Virginia) went down the road but it turned out to be a very small affair."[545]

"Still at Weston, but all very anxious to advance on Clarksburg," Cooper observed. He was as impatient as any. "I think I could make a right sharp fight there myself, to drive the enemy from my home and enable me to see my family." Cooper had not seen his wife, Margaret, or his children for two years.[546]

To the north, in Harrison County, Sgt. Snider and his comrades decided to return to the regiment. "I went to Rockford and got my dinner one mile above town," he said on May 2, "and immediately after dinner I learned that the enemy had been in Rockford...We took to the hills and struck back for the army, which we found had gone towards Weston.

Sgt. Snider was definitely in a martial mood, "On striking the pike, we traveled a few miles towards Weston and put up for the night in a barn." Snider caught up with the 31st Virginia on May 3, and then remained in camp for the next two days while they waited for the weather to clear. They must have had some stories of "home" to share with the boys who had remained with the brigade.[547]

Another of the regiment's recruiting officers, Capt. Phillips had gone home to Valley Furnace, in Barbour County, arriving on April 18. "There was a log rolling," he wrote when he was among his family and friends after a two-year absence. Phillips attended church on the 20th and heard a sermon by Rev. William Price. On the 21st, with his sister, he went visiting to "see the girls," and even visited at Meadowville, though he noticed there that the Union men recognized him. "The Yankees are watching," he wrote on May 4. A few days later, commenting on the Union men, "They are evidently afraid to attack."[548]

By May 5, Brig. Gen. Imboden's force had been reduced considerably. A few men who were too sick to travel were at Beverly and Buckhannon. Detachments of guards had been sent to travel with the cattle herds being driven back across the mountains to the east. They lost over 200 men from Dunn's battalion of dismounted cavalry when that unit learned they were not going to be able to steal horses along the way to use as mounts. Imboden's orders were to send all of the horses back to Gen. Lee—he was not going to tolerate theft or seizure of horses from local citizens for the use of individual soldiers. On learning this, the battalion of dismounted cavalry vanished during the night on sore feet.

The brigade dwindled to about 2,300 men. Imboden estimated that Jones had about 1,200 men, and with his force and Jones combined they would not have strength in numbers to defeat the Federals at Clarksburg. Reports now claimed Union forces there numbered about 5,000 infantry and 12 field guns, with reinforcements expected. On the 6th, Jones and Imboden decided to separate their forces, with Jones heading west to attack the Northwestern Railroad. Imboden would move south. Before marching out of Weston early on May 6, he sent his sick and wounded, and the stores he had captured at Buckhannon and Beverly to Monterey in the mountains.[549]

The roads had not improved, and the wagons only made 6 miles on the Bulltown Road before stopping. Snider said that day, after the regiment made camp, "We have had some of the most disagreeable days that I have ever experienced. Rained all night without intermission. We got into a field where there was some dead timber and made log huts and got along pretty well, taking everything under consideration. There was but very few of us that had anything to eat, our wagons being ahead."

The next morning, they sent men ahead to catch their wagons, and cook provisions for the hungry soldiers. The 31st Virginia caught up with their cooked provisions at one in the afternoon, and the men ate their dinners. Afterward, they marched two miles and made camp again. Some of the recruits that Snider and the others found in Harrison County began arriving during the day while the regiments camped at Mr. Bond's farm. "We passed over some of the worst roads that I ever saw," Snider commented that night.

The regiment marched ten miles on the 8th, camping close to Walkersville at the forks of the West Fork and Right Fork streams. More recruits from Harrison County caught up with them there. Capt. Cooper said, "Invited to stay at a Mr. Lewis's, but declined and cooked a rooster."[550]

Not all of the men were with the good fortune of a chicken dinner. "We drew and cooked some rations," Snider said, "coarse meal and beef and very little of that." On the 9th, even Cooper noticed provisions were getting scarce, with nothing but beef issued to the troops. The regiments marched at 8 A.M., taking the Bulltown Road, and were still close to Bulltown when they camped after dark. The roads continued as before, full of mud. The wagons could barely move, and the infantry trailing them were stuck in the mud waiting most of the day.

The new recruits from Harrison County were formed into two companies, and were mustered into the army on May 10. Three men from the 31st Virginia's Company C were appointed officers for the new recruits.[551]

"We drew no rations except beef last night," Snider complained. "Camped within seven miles of Sutton, an hour by sun and drew beef and meal, although part of the command got nothing but beef." They marched to Sutton the following day, arriving there around noon and rested until four o'clock. Sutton was in sad shape, the town badly damaged, and the local citizens nearly all gone. "The women remaining are of doubtful character," Capt. Cooper noticed. "The roads are getting better and I hope we can now get along faster." The regiment marched another eight miles to Little Birch, where the men were allowed to draw rations, one day's ration of flour and beef.[552]

Phillips was a bold adventurer at home at Valley Furnace. On May 6, in the midst of a county full of Unionists, he went on a "little spree" with several of his friends, R. K. Godwin, Martin Johnson, and Marion Talbot. On the 10th, after a send-off party, with "lots of pretty girls present to help cheer me on my way," Phillips said goodbye to his family and began traveling south to find the army. He stopped for the night at the home of another friend, but had to make a hasty escape when some Federals approached the place.

Phillips was going over a fence, and had just landed on the other side when a bullet split the top rail, showering splinters in every direction. He kept going and found another house to stay in the next night, farther south. "The Yankees are thick," he said on the 12th. "We are compelled to travel after night, much danger of arrest."

On the 13th, at a home in Upshur County, Phillips watched his enemy from indoor: they were obviously looking for him and his companions. "The Yankees are passing up and down the road rapidly," he wrote.[553]

The 31st Virginia was camped at Big Birch on the 12th. It was a former Union post with a burned-out blockhouse. There were good pastures there, and Brig. Gen. Imboden wanted to allow the horses to graze, to fatten them a little while there was an opportunity. Snider tried to supplement his diet that day. "I went a-fishing, but had no luck," he noted. Imboden's army was running low on consumables. That evening, the men were given only beef for dinner.

"Detail to go for salt," Capt. Cooper said in his journal. "Parkersburg company organized for Jackson's Brigades." A couple of days later, Cooper sent $250 to A. B. Young, with a message that he wanted Young to buy a horse. For Cooper, this was a major expenditure, but necessary if he was going to join the cavalry.[554]

Ahead of them 19 miles, the Confederate cavalry had captured the town of Summerville, and had confiscated a large amount of commissary stores, plus 200 mules and a number of wagons. The 31st Virginia marched early on the 13th, and arrived at Summersville before night.

The laden supply wagons captured at Summersville were much needed. The men had been on reduced rations for days, their daily allotment after leaving Beverly only a half-pound of meal per man supplemented by fresh beef. The salt supply was down to one day's ration for the entire command. Imboden's artillery and wagon horses were about worn out, but the mules that were captured were fresh. Imboden was able to switch the wagons and artillery to mules and refresh his horses. "We drew two day's rations of crackers, beans, etc," Snider wrote that night.[555]

To the north about 40 miles, Christian Kuhl of Company D had been on a furlough to visit his home in Braxton County. As he started back to the army, Kuhl traveled along the same route as the cavalry, and saw firsthand their activities, and the effect it had on the citizens.

Kuhl heard from friends that part of the Confederate army was not too far ahead. He set out to find them, but traveling up Cedar Creek found instead that the conduct of the Confederate cavalry was far from handsome. "They just literally stripped everything of the horse kind," he wrote. "Even took mares which had young colts at home, and that from our best friends."

"I soon overtook a lady, Mrs. Wilson Cutlip, and her little boy, Newton," Kuhl wrote. "She was in great agony because of the cavalry taking two of her horses, one of which had left a little colt at home." Mrs. Cutlip screamed and cried as Kuhl approached. "She knew me well, and soon told her woeful tale to my surprise and utter disgust. I must confess that by this time my confidence began to be a little shaky in regard to our goodness....

"Mrs. Cutlip was a very fleshy woman, and hot as the weather was, she was very red in the face, and had been running to overtake the Cavalry. I tried to comfort her, and soon stopped her by telling her if possible to do so, I would get her horse, and to let little Newtie to go with me, and she go back home and be quiet, which she did." Kuhl followed the cavalry to where they had camped for the night, and sought the officer in charge, but despite the man's statement that he would return the horse to young Newt, the promise was not kept, and the Cutlips were out of a good horse.

It was a sadly disillusioned Sergeant Kuhl who finally caught up with the 31st Virginia at Summersville. "On the morning after camping at Summersville," he wrote, "we prepared to leave our own dear West Virginia and set our faces towards Dixie again. Many of our refugees had gone back home a few days, had the pleasure of mingling with loved ones once more, and to tell them of some of our brief war horrors, only to be duplicated with more of the same, and even worse and longer ones."[556]

The men were ordered to cook their beef in a hurry on the morning of May 14. They marched at 11am, turning on the Coal Nob road, which would take them toward Huntersville. The infantry traveled about 10 miles before camping. The next day, they crossed the Gauley River, at the mouth of the Cranberry. Capt. Cooper said, "The ford was the roughest I ever saw. Came near losing two mules by stumbling over huge rocks and falling down."

"We had to wade it crotch deep," Snider commented, "and had great difficulty in getting our wagons across on account of large rocks and deep water. After which we traveled to the mountaintop and camped about 9 P.M. I was until after midnight drawing rations and only got one day's at that." The men cooked their rations early the next morning, then set out marching at eight o'clock, crossed the Cherry Tree River, and camped around three o'clock on the top of a mountain after marching only 10 miles. "We drew beef and a pint of beans to ten men, was all of the rations we got," Snider said.

They made an early start the next day, crossing through "a wilderness" on Bald Nob (Back Allegheny Mountain), and arrived at the McClung settlement in mid-afternoon. On the 18th, the regiment marched on to Falling Springs, arriving at two o'clock in the afternoon. "Capt. Cooper got a furlough for thirty days," Sgt. Snider said.[557]

"The commands of Gen Imboden and Col. (W. L.) Jackson separated at Falling Spring," Cooper wrote. "Jackson going toward Huntersville, and Imboden toward Franklin. I go with Jackson, leaving my company in command of Sergeant Snider. Camped at foot of Droop Mountain." Cooper was kind enough to allow Snider to ride his horse. Cooper borrowed a horse from a friend, intending to buy another for himself in the near future.

Cooper traveled with Jackson's command the following day to the Little Levels area of Pocahontas County, which he called, "fine grazing country, with many improvements." He stayed overnight with the cavalry, and met with three old friends, Robert Johnston, Charles Russell, and H. Fitzhugh, all seasoned politicians.

He was able to gain some advice from them concerning his own military and political aspirations. "As some of my friends think that by consenting to be a candidate for the Legislature, I impair my prospects for the command of Jackson's second regiment, I decline the election. An honorable position in the army is much preferable in time of war than any other civil office," Cooper wrote on May 22. He should have informed his friends in Company C, however.

On the 24th, he borrowed another horse and set out for Buffalo Gap in company with Colonel Thompson, his old comrade from the 31st Virginia, now in the 19th Virginia cavalry under William L. Jackson. The Honorable Mr. Russell rode along with them to the camp of Capt. Hutton, and then to the camp of Capt. Gilmer. Cooper discovered the prices for horses were "enormously high." He wrote in his journal on the 25th, "On my way to Monterey heard (I) could probably get a horse in Crab Bottom. Went over there and found some old rips in the hands of horse-thieving speculators at balloon prices. Did not buy. Stayed at Mr. Snyder's."

On the 26th, Cooper heard the sad news about Alfred Jackson's death. Alfred H. Jackson had been carried on the regiment's rolls as lieutenant colonel of the 31st Virginia since August 1862, when he was severely wounded. His injuries were too much for him and he was destined to never return to his regiment. "Regret it very much," Cooper wrote, after hearing the news, "although it probably makes me major of the Old 31st." Promotion by seniority meant that Maj. McCutchen would become lieutenant colonel. If he remained in the regiment, Cooper would be the regiment's major. The difficulty was that he was contemplating trying to transfer to the 20th Virginia cavalry and had hopes of being elected colonel of that new regiment, which would be part of Jackson's brigade.

While in Staunton, Capt. Cooper met several refugee ladies from the northwest of Virginia who told stories of being ejected from their homes. The Union commander, Brig. Gen. Benjamin S. Roberts, had sent them away. "Their treatment by the enemy was shameful," Cooper wrote, "and our soldiers swear vengeance. Do not hear of my family being on their way, but expect them."

Cooper waited in Staunton for several days expecting his family to appear from the northwest as refugees, but they did not arrive. He was sorely disappointed, and worried as he saw many other refugee families coming into town. Many of them were from Weston, where a number of secessionists had revealed their support of the South when Imboden's men were encamped there, and were forced to leave town after the Confederates withdrew.

The Federal army under Brig. Gen. Roberts went farther than just ejecting families in Weston from their homes. Their commander had ordered mass arrests of the citizens that he found objectionable. Edward Smith, the historian of Lewis County, would later report, "Sixty-three women and children, the wives and children and mothers and sisters of soldiers in the Southern army were sent through the lines, where they would help to consume the rapidly diminishing food supply of the Confederate states. About an equal number of prominent citizens were sent to Camp Chase to be interned until the close of the war."[558]

Capt. Cooper's wife, Margaret, and their four children remained at Clarksburg, just up the road from Weston. Perhaps they were not allowed to leave, or perhaps had chosen to stay where they were. Cooper's anxiety about them was profound, and he was torn about having to leave Staunton while there was a chance that they might yet come through from West Virginia.

If Gen. Lee's army was to do anything important in the summer campaign, it had to have provisions on which to march and fight. Altogether, Imboden estimated his buyers had purchased 3,100 head of cattle, most of them bought by Maj. W. M. Tate, chief cattle procurer.

As for new recruits, Colonel W. L. Jackson enlisted between 300 and 400 men, some for his 19th Virginia Cavalry, and the rest to go into the new companies that would make up the 20th Virginia Cavalry. Sergeant Snider and his companions from Harrison County recruited two companies of those men.

By comparison, Brig. Gen. Imboden gathered only about 100 recruits, which were divided between his regiment, the 18th Virginia, and the 25th and 31st regiments. On the negative side, Imboden lost a total of 16 men to sickness, death, and capture, and the 200 men of Dunn's battalion, who deserted as a group. Imboden did not say how many individual soldiers from other commands deserted while they were in the western counties, but it was not a small number. The recruits hardly equaled what he lost in total strength.

"In this respect, we were all disappointed," Imboden reported. "The people now remaining in the northwest are, to all intents and purposes, a conquered people. Their spirit is broken by tyranny where they are true to our cause, and those who are against us are the blackest-hearted, most despicable villains upon the continent.... I have heard scarcely a complaint of any wrong done to private rights of persons or property by the men under my command. They were nearly all Northwestern Virginians, and had much to provoke them to vengeance upon a dastard foe, who had outraged their unprotected families, but, with the willing obedience of the true Confederate soldier, every man obeyed orders to respect private rights, even of their traitor neighbors."

Not all the witnesses would agree to Imboden's report on the collection of cattle. John A. McNeill said, "No country could have been more abundantly supplied with live stock than all that fine grazing country of Northwestern Virginia was at that time, and all of this stock, independently of the sympathies of the owners, was brought back safely within the Confederate lines. Many and pitiable were the scenes of women, girls, and old men, pleading for their horses and cattle, but the Confederate soldiers that had been sent there to execute the orders of their government did it faithfully."[559]

A commentary on the raid appeared in the Wheeling *Daily Intelligencer*. Written on May 2 by an anonymous Union military officer at Winchester, the writer had some surprisingly good things to say about the leaders of the Confederate raid. "Imboden is a man of decided talent and a military turn of mind. He is moreover a man of decided character, having energy, will and firmness of purpose. (W.L.) Jackson and Jenkins are known to our people as politicians, and neither of them have manifested any great military ability, yet they are both possessed of talents of a peculiar character, are artful and cunning and having staked their all of earthly hope in the rebellion, and thus far being disappointed in its results, they may be fairly set down as being in that state of mind which we call desperate, and will prove to be ugly, troublesome customers."

As for citizens who may have helped the secessionists, the correspondent to the Wheeling paper voiced Unionist sentiments: "Gen. Milroy's doctrines that rebels have no right to anything but six feet of rope is the lone doctrine in theory, and all those spies and emissaries ought to have the benefit of a practical illustration of it. The aid of the militia ought to be invoked in every part of the state, to protect it against these raids, and every man who would refuse to aid in the militia service, should, at the very least, be banished to Dixie, and his property should be confiscated. By the aid of the militia fighting after their own fashion, laying in ambush for them at every practicable place, Western Virginia would be too hot a place for them to visit." The Confederates had been able to visit a few friends while on their raid, but they mostly made a lot of new, and more determined enemies while there.[560]

Hall was grateful for the short rest they had at Falling Springs. He said on May 14, "After so many long and weary marches, one day of rest is very gratefully received, and I have been asleep nearly all day under a low spreading cedar."[561]

The regiment was at Falling Springs when the men learned of Stonewall Jackson's death. Their great commander, Old Tom Jackson, their cousin and former neighbor had been mortally wounded on May 2 at a battle at Chancellorsville, and had died while the regiment that knew him so well was in the mountains of western Virginia. Having served under one of the best leaders on the field, the men were probably uncertain about the future, for who could take the place of Gen. Stonewall on the field of battle?

"We remained in camp and the most of the men put in the day in washing," Sergeant Snider wrote on May 19. They marched 20 miles on May 20, passing through Frankford, and Lewisburg to camp three miles outside of town on the Greenbrier River. "We marched early," Snider wrote on the 21st, "and the infantry crossed the river in a ferry while the train forded it below. We passed the White Sulphur Springs, a very grand, refined place where we watered and rested over an hour and then marched about one mile and camped about half past noon. (May 22) Marched early and came to Callaghan stand and took the Warm Spring road and camped about four miles from Callaghan. We have had a very hot day and dusty road."

On the 23rd, Snider had the luxury of a spa bath at the Hot Springs, after marching 17 miles on a hot, and dusty day. "I have washed in the hot spring bath," he said, as though it were one of his life's goals. "Things are fixed up very fine and there is several bathing houses." The respite was short enough, for the next day they were on the road early and passing through Warm Springs. "There is a considerable village at the Warm Springs. We passed close to the Bath Alum Springs and camped near the Cow Pasture River, traveling a distance of about thirteen miles." The rain returned that afternoon, with a thunderstorm, cutting the dust into mud and cooling the hot soldiers.

"Shoes have entirely worn out," Hall wrote on the 24th. "Got permission to remain in the rear. Commenced raining this evening, and I, with three other "poor soldiers" put up at a barn." The next day, Hall said he was allowed to ride for about three miles on Maj. McCutcheon's horse. They camped that night eight miles from the junction of the Staunton and Parkersburg pike."

The regiment reached Clover Dale on the 25th, and Buffalo Gap on the 26th. Snider was able to get a pass and go to the home of his friends, the Bears family, for some dinner and a change of clean clothes. The weather had cooled off once more, and though he had already traveled 20 miles that day, he probably didn't mind the ride back to camp after a home-cooked meal, and wearing clean clothes.[562]

Capt. Phillips, meanwhile, had returned to Barbour County, having missed connecting with the regiment before it crossed the mountains. "Gen. Imboden has retreated," he said in his journal, "and we are left to make our way through the enemy's lines." Phillips remained at his home on the 14th, and then continued the next day, stopping at Reason Johnson's residence overnight. He traveled through Randolph County with R. H. Godwin, Henry Lohr, Martin C. Johnson, Haymond Gainer, Monroe Wells, Marion Talbot, and Amos Ridgeway.

"The Yankees are all around us, but I do not doubt our ability to escape them," Phillips wrote on May 16. They crossed Cheat Mountain on the 18th, went through Crab Bottom, and arrived at Monterey in time to observe the local election on the 21st. Phillips and his companions finally reached Imboden's camp on the 24th, where Phillips was able to meet with his old friend, Coleman Bowman.[563]

Sergeant Snider had all of the best intentions in the world to help Capt. Cooper on May 27. This turn of events may illustrate the necessity for people of ambition to keep their allies informed of their plans. "I got a pass," Snider wrote in his journal, "and went to Staunton and to Jenkins Cavalry camp, below Staunton. I found the election excitement very high and my friend Cooper's name withdrawn. I returned to camp to ascertain whether it was an intrigue or not." The next day, doing his captain a huge favor—or so he thought; "I started at daylight for Jenkins camp and put Cooper's name on the books, not finding anyone authorized to withdraw his name. I returned in the evening in time to vote."[564]

The 28th was election day, and Cooper was still on a 30-day furlough. He visited the 31st Virginia's camp near Buffalo Gap and discovered that he had been voted for in the election, and whether he wanted it or not, a seat in the legislature was probably his for the taking. Within a few days he was almost positive that he had been elected to the Virginia legislature. Col. Jackson broke the news to him personally.

"This is certainly having greatness thrust upon me," Cooper said in his journal. His real desire was the position of colonel of the 20th Virginia, the new regiment formed by W. L. Jackson. Cooper knew he could count on several influential friends for assistance, including Charles Russell and Col. Hoffman, but there were others who wanted the position, and the last thing Cooper said was for something to stand in his way.[565]

Cooper's furlough allowed him to remain in the area for several more days, still hoping that his family would arrive. He arranged for money to be held with a friend, for their use should they come after he had departed. Cooper finally went to Richmond. He would return, on his way to William L. Jackson's cavalry camp, when he had an extension of his furlough. Cooper would serve as a volunteer with Jackson's 19th Virginia cavalry through much of that summer, while waiting for the decision about who would be appointed colonel of the 20th Virginia cavalry.[566]

Cooper's friend, Sergeant Snider said on the 29th, the day after the election, "I have a sore foot and am on duty and am staying at camp." With the use of Cooper's horse, Snider had time to visit his friends on the following day, and his brother in the hospital at Staunton on the 31st. On the first day of June, he stopped at the home of Reverend Lepps, and had dinner. Lepps would be joining the regiment as chaplain toward the end of the year.[567]

"In the evening," Snider said, "we received orders to cook three days rations and be ready to march at ten o'clock tomorrow morning." The 31st Virginia, and the 25th Virginia were under orders to return to Gen. Lee's army at Fredericksburg, with as little delay as practicable. Col. Hoffman, being senior to the 25th Virginia's Lt. Col. Higgenbotham, was in command of the two regiments while they were in transit. The quartermaster at Staunton would provide rail transportation for the men, and their baggage, as well as for their ordnance, medical stores, and the 14 horses belonging to the two regiment's officers.[568]

Capt. Lyman was detailed to remain behind to gather up any stragglers. From the depot at Staunton, he wrote a note to Lt. Swadley, in command of the regiment's Company E, informing him of this. "I am left, by order of Col. Hoffman, to collect the furloughed and straggling men of the 31st and 25th Regiments. My orders are to leave on the seven o'clock train in the morning if possible. As I understand you are near the town, you will move your company either tonight or tomorrow morning in time to reach here by (6:30) tomorrow morning. Send me the number of your command tonight if possible to facilitate the procurement of transportation."[569]

The 31st Virginia arrived at Staunton on June 2, and boarded rail cars for the journey to Hamilton's Crossing. The men hadn't been told their destination when the train pulled out of Staunton. They grumbled when it became apparent they were going back to Smith's brigade, but as Snider commented in his journal, they could do nothing about it, and soon became reconciled to the orders. "We had some rain," he said, "which made our ride very disagreeable, as the most of us had to ride on the top of the cars."[570]

"Our worst fears have been more than realized," Hall penned his disgust after arriving at their destination at Hamilton's Crossing in mid-afternoon on June 3. "We are now encamped on the same ground we occupied when we left Fredericksburg. Why did we come here? Surely there is no Providence that is concerned with the united wish of the people.... Although we have been here but an hour or two, everything looks as old and familiar as if we never had left. There is no boundary to one's vision here. And now far, far away northward, may be seen the tents of thousands of that hated race on whose account we have been called to this infernal region."[571]

Saying farewell to their comrades in the 25th Virginia as they arrived at Hamilton's Crossing, the 31st Virginia returned to Smith's brigade. In the Virginia elections that spring, Brig. Gen. William Smith had won the office of governor. His election meant another change of brigade commander, although he still intended to go with the brigade on their expedition to the north.

Competition for the position of brigade commander was stiff, and the political maneuvering had already begun when the regiment returned. Col. Hoffman was more than mildly interested in the position. He was not trained for that line of work, but it was nonetheless an ambition that would lead Hoffman on through the next several months, and perhaps in that regard was not a terrible thing. Many of them had political aspirations for after the war and it was apparent from the jostling for command positions that military rank would perhaps influence the voters when it was all said and done.

The regiments received orders to cook rations on the 4th, to prepare to march with the division. Officers received new orders on the issue of ammunition. In the past, men could load cartridge boxes with the prescribed forty rounds, and then add another twenty rounds to their pockets, even if it meant going light on rations. They preferred carrying plenty of bullets in a fight, but the army was short on ammo at this time. Gen. Ewell ordered: "Division Commanders will see that in future no more cartridges are distributed to their men than can be carried in the cartridge boxes, even if the boxes will not hold forty rounds."[572]

The same day, orders were issued by Gen. Early: "The Division will move tonight beginning at twelve o'clock, and will move up the valley of the Massaponax, on the South side, as follows: Smith's brigade, Hoke's brigade, Hays's brigade, Gordon's brigade. Each brigade will be followed by its train; the ordnance and provision trains will follow that of the rear brigade. Sick men who will be fit for duty in a short time and not able to march now will be sent on the cars via Gordonsville to Culpeper. Prisoners will be marched with their brigades under charge of a guard detailed for that purpose in each brigade. All details on Special, General, or fatigue duty will be called in at dark. The pickets will be relieved by the Corps of Gen. A. P. Hill."

8

GETTYSBURG
June 1863—Sept 1863

When Smith's brigade set out on the march, June 5, 1863, the 31st Virginia was in the lead of the division, followed by the 49th Virginia, 52nd Virginia, 13th Virginia, and 5th Virginia. They were on their way to Pennsylvania, and the town of Gettysburg.[573] They marched across the Telegraph Road, and passed Spotsylvania Court House. Around two o'clock in the afternoon, after traveling about ten miles, the brigade stopped and made camp.

"Revile was beat at 3 am," Snider said the following day, "but we remained in camp, I suppose on account of cannonading in our rear, which is said to be occasioned by us leaving, the enemy wanting to see if there was any troops left. They found plenty. About 7 am we was ordered to cook up two day's rations."

The regiment marched at three o'clock that afternoon. They camped seven hours later on the Plank Road. Rain in the evening made the roads sloppy, and they struggled to gain a mere six miles for the day's march. On June 7, they had an early start. Turning onto the Culpeper Road, the 31st Virginia marched until it was two miles from Culpeper Court House before camping. This march took the men past the Cedar Mountain battlefield, where Lt. Col. Alfred Jackson was so tragically wounded.

On the 8th, they marched through Culpeper Court House, but stopped three miles outside of town, and camped. It was still early in the day, just ten in the morning, but the men were ordered to cook three days' rations by noon, in anticipation of action with the Federals.

The next morning, the sound of artillery began early, and continued heavy until noon. "About noon we was ordered to pack up immediately and moved out to the road where we remained until 4 P.M." Brigade inspection was given to the men during the afternoon, Snider said. Then the brigade was ordered to reverse its course, and they marched back through town. The passed some prisoners and wounded men who were brought back from that morning's action. It was as close as they would get to the fight on that day. The regiment marched on before camping at sunset.

On the afternoon of the 10th, the brigade marched through Woodville. They crossed through Sperryville on the 11th; and camped that night after marching through the town of Washington (Virginia), a distance for the day of 21 miles. June 12, they had another early start on Gaines Mill road, and then turned onto the Front Royal road. The regiment marched through Flint Hill and Front Royal, crossing a little creek before making camp.

"At Chester Gap, ladies wave handkerchiefs, scatter bouquets on the road, and smile sweetly," observed Sergeant Osborne Wilson, of Company E.

"The ladies of Front Royal were very glad to see us," Snider wrote in his journal "and as clever as usual in bringing us water," he went on. "We waded through the river, although we had pontoons along. Jenkin's Cavalry joined us and went ahead. We camped and cooked one day's rations in the night."[574]

The regiment marched early on June 13, leaving behind a detail of men remain to cook two more days' rations, and then to follow. They ran into the Federals later in the day on the Newtown road, not far from Kernstown. The newly formed Maryland Line was leading the march that day. After skirmishing with Union pickets outside of town, the Marylanders stopped on a ridge overlooking Kernstown and waited for Gen. Early to come up and study the situation. Federal cavalry was in sight; with a Union infantry picket in Kernstown itself and some artillery on a hill near the town.[575]

Gen. Early placed his division in line of battle on either side of the turnpike, and after a delay for reconnaissance, sent Brig. Gen. Harry T. Hays's Louisiana brigade to the left. From there, that brigade could advance on Pritchard's Hill, where the Federal artillery had established itself. Gen. Hays soon discovered a force of Union infantry positioned just beyond the hill, to his left. He advised his Division commander, Gen. Jubal Early that he needed reinforcements. Brig. Gen. John B Gordon was ordered up to help, and moved to the left of Hays's. With both Confederate brigades on the attack, the Federal infantry and their artillery were driven from the hill. They withdrew across and beyond Cedar Creek turnpike.

Meanwhile, Smith's brigade, along with Hoke's brigade, under temporary command of Colonel Isaac Avery, formed a line to the right of the turnpike. From there, the two brigades were ordered to advance toward the town. Once the action was finished on the left, the Gen. Early shifted the brigades so that Smith's brigade took up the line on the far left; then Hays's brigade; next Gordon's brigade resting with his right on the turnpike; and Hoke's brigade to hold the right end of the line. They were just behind the crest of a hill, and south of Abraham's Creek.[576]

"The 31st Virginia Regiment was sent forward to hold a brick house and orchard near the road," Col. Hoffman reported, "and it being reported that the enemy was advancing in force, the residue of the brigade soon followed, and the whole formed near the house, where it was exposed to a few shell from one of the enemy's batteries; thence it moved to the left and forward, and formed on the southwest of the enemy's fortifications near Winchester, on the left of Gen. Hays' brigade, under a considerable fire of shell, which, however, passed over the command.

"Here the 13th and a part of the 49th Virginia Regiments were deployed and advanced as skirmishers. The brigade occupied this position during that evening and night... the 13th Virginia Regiment occasionally skirmishing with the enemy's sharpshooters." Four companies from the 31st Virginia were sent out in the darkness to stand picket guard, and there they remained through the night in a drenching rain.[577]

Dawn revealed Federal skirmishers holding Bower's Hill. The rest of the Union infantry and artillery had withdrawn quietly during the night. Generals Hays and Gordon were ordered to send a regiment each across the creek at the bottom of the hill to take the position, which they did after some skirmishing. Smith's brigade sent its skirmishers out to the left of Hays and supported the action as the Confederates advanced up the hill.

From the top of Bowers' Hill, Gen. Early and his commander, Lt. Gen. Richard S. Ewell could see Winchester and the Union forces defending the town. A hill to the northwest of the main defensive works had been occupied and fortified in the night by Federal infantry. Gen. Ewell ordered Early to move his division around to the left, to attack and take that hill. That would put his troops onto the enemy's flank and rear.

Early later reported that he led three of his brigades (Smith's, Hays's, and Hoke's) and two battalions of artillery to the left. "Following the Cedar Creek turnpike for a short distance, and then leaving that and passing through fields and the woods, which I found sufficiently open to admit of the passage of artillery, thus making a considerable detour... crossing the macadamized road... about 3 miles west of Winchester, and a half mile from a point at which the enemy had a picket the night before."

Brig. Gen. William "Extra Billy" Smith made quite a picture as he rode at the head of the brigade. In the sizzling afternoon, earlier, near the Pughtown Road, John W. Daniels of Early's staff delivered a message to the colorful general: the brigade commander rode at the head of his men, "The sun was hot, and he carried an umbrella over his head in one hand. He wore a citizen's hat, and an old fashioned standing collar. His horse was accoutered with a pair of saddlebags, and had nothing of the martial air about him. The general looked more like a judge going to open court than like a Southern brigadier, or fire-eater; and his smiling face and urban manners gave little inkling of grim-visaged war." He was 65 years old and would be the oldest Confederate general at Gettysburg.[578]

Former governor and judge turned military commander, Brig. Gen. Smith had a contingent of lawyers working for him that day in the various regimental commands. Col. Hoffman was a legislator at the start of the war, and one of the most skilled property lawyers in Virginia. Other lawyers who rode or marched nearby included Gen. Jubal Early, who had been a prosecutor in Franklin and Floyd Counties in Virginia.

In the 31st Virginia, most of the lawyers had departed the regiment by the summer of 1863. Killed, died, transferred, sent to the hospital, or detailed for other work. But a few like Hoffman and Capt Joseph Harding remained to see the men through the battles. In the brigade, Lt. Col. J. Catlett Gibson, in command of the 49th Virginia had practiced law in New York City before he returned to Virginia and enlisted in his regiment. Lt. Col. James H. Skinner rode at the head of the 52nd Virginia: he was a prominent lawyer from Augusta County before the war. With a brigade commander who was about to declare his candidacy for elected office soon again, redolent of politicians and jurisprudence, as well as the unwashed and ragged enlisted men and their sergeants and officers of lower rank, Extra Billy Smith's brigade made its way through the hot dusty march headed northward toward Pennsylvania.[579]

The men were about used up from the march, or so estimated Gen. Early after they'd marched about eight or ten miles without stopping for water. "I massed them in the woods in rear of the position, and gave them time to blow," he reported. Their wooded hill was called Little North Mountain, overlooking Mrs. Brierly's cornfield on one side, and an old orchard in another direction. It was about four o'clock in the afternoon.

Early formed the line with Smith's brigade on the left, on a ridge west of the Union defensive works, in rear of Hays's brigade. The division's artillery opened a bombardment around six o'clock on the Federal positions, and the Union guns replied. Brig. Gen. Hays led his brigade forward, assaulting the Union works under a severe storm of infantry and artillery fire, routing the defenders from their first line of entrenchments. Smith's brigade followed and supported the action, but by that time the hour was too late to take the Union's main line of defensive works, which Gen. Early estimated were very strong. Smith's brigade was lucky in loosing only two men wounded that day.[580]

Through the night, Smith's and Hays's brigades occupied the hill where the outer Union line had "protected" Winchester. The men spent the hours just before dark turning the captured Federal guns toward the town. Through the evening, Confederate artillery bombarded the main Union defenses.[581]

"I was awoke by heavy cannonading before daylight," Snider said on June 15th. The cannonade was evidently from Gen. Johnson's division hitting the Federals near the Martinsburg road, some distance away. "The fortifications was soon entered and found to be evacuated and the flag was taken down and ours run up and soon afterwards we was marched down to the Forks road, where the fighting had been. We kept meeting prisoners all along the road. There had been several killed, mostly Yankees, but the fight was very short and a good many surrendered, but (Union general) Milroy and a part of his force cut their way through and escaped. We camped on part of the battleground. Prisoners kept passing back all day."[582]

Smith's brigade was reduced by two regiments before the army went on to Maryland. The 58th Virginia Regiment was detached and ordered to escort a large body of Union prisoners to Staunton: altogether, they were put in charge of 108 officers, and 1,500 enlisted Federals who were captured at Winchester on June 14 and 15. (Gen. Ewell would announce the following day that the army had captured over 3,000 prisoners with less than 300 men killed, wounded and missing at this battle.) The 13th Virginia was also detached from Smith's brigade at Winchester and left to guard the town. It was a rare chance to sit out a major campaign for the men of the 13th Virginia.[583]

The army rested outside of Winchester through June 16 and part of the 17th. Some of the men went into the Union fortifications for a little foraging. At two o'clock in the afternoon on June 17, the 31st Virginia marched away from Winchester on the Harpers Ferry road and proceeded to a place near Charles Town, called the Big Springs before camping for the night. The following day they marched at an early hour to Leesburg, and from there to Darksville, on toward Shepherdstown, and went into camp about one in the afternoon. Their march was coordinated with the brigades around them, the wagon train of goods, cavalry, and columns of marching me as Lee's army headed north.[584]

The 31st Virginia was allowed three rainy days in camp cooking rations in anticipation of the next move, and waiting for their turn to cross the river. "All of our Corps are across the river except this division," Snider wrote on June 20. They received orders to march on the 22nd. "We was roused up at half past 3 AM," Snider wrote, "and marched at daylight, passing through Shepherdstown and crossed the river below town, which was waist deep." They marched through Sharpsburg, Earlysville and Boonsborough, and camped in the Sangerstown road, according to Snider. They were back in Maryland once again.

The few Maryland citizens who welcomed the Confederates seemed scared, according to Sergeant Wilson of Company E. "At Sharpsburg and Keedysville, people look very sour at us."[585]

The regiment marched at daylight on the 23rd, going through Keytown, Smithville, and Hedgesville. They camped that afternoon in Franklin County, near Waynesborough. "We find the people very clever, but it is from fear, not love," Snider observed. In the morning, they proceeded through Waynesborough to Quincy, Fantown, and almost to Greenwood. The Iron Works was a point of interest on the march in the afternoon, shortly before camping.

The next day, sergeant Snider reported, they were put on picket and informed the division would remain there for the day. "Some of the boys captured a runaway Virginia Negro out in the country," Snider recorded. He didn't say what happened to the runaway slave.

Snider was ordered to guard a private residence and was invited in to dinner and supper with the family living in the house. Evidently, not all of the local people were sour at meeting the men of the 31st Virginia.

The 31st Virginia's pickets were ordered back to camp around two in the morning on the 26th. Arriving there in the rain, Snider found the brigade had cooked two day's rations, which gave them a three-day supply. "We marched about 9 AM and passed through Greenwood and by the Iron Works, which we burned." The ironworks were owned by Thaddeus Stevens, and were located three miles east of Black's Gap, and fifteen miles west of Gettysburg, at Caledonia. Jubal Early had decided to burn the foundry in reprisal for destruction that had been done in the Valley of Virginia by the Federal army.[586]

After doing their destructive work, Early's division took to the road again, marching north through Bloomsburg, and stopped to make camp about 5 miles from Gettysburg. Their skirmishers were kept busy for part of the afternoon trading shots with a militia regiment, and capturing about 150 of the Union militiamen during the course of the afternoon.[587]

"We marched early, passing to the left of Gettysburg," Sergeant Snider said, June 27, "on through Hunterstown, where we paraded the prisoners, and through New Castle, Hampton and Berlin and camped close to town.... Whiskey was plenty and we had a good many drunken men."

Nothing like marching to cure a hangover. The 31st Virginia started early the next morning, taking the Dover road, and passed close to York. After crossing the river, the division rested for a while. The 31st Virginia was sent on picket, at Conigsburg, two miles from the main road on the railroad.

"We heard canon toward the river," Snider said, "and soon saw a big smoke, and we supposed the enemy have burnt the bridge to prevent us from crossing. We drew and cooked one day's rations and moved at midnight."

On the 28th, Smith's brigade entered York with their politician brigadier general bowing to all he saw on the side of the road. He'd ordered the brigade band to play Yankee Doodle as they came into town, the band leading the infantry in a display for the locals that was reported to be amusing. Then he stopped the brigade in the town square to make a speech, but was interrupted by the arrival of his division commander, who found it neither charming or timely. After Gen. Early entered York, Smith's brigade was ordered to camp about two miles north of town, along with Hays' brigade, close to some mills near the railroad. The 31st Virginia's Company C was sent to guard Small's Mill, which held a large quantity of flour. A family lived in the attached residence, but they had fled at the approach of the army, and by the time that Company C was posted to guard the mill, the house had already been vandalized and plundered.[588]

Gen. Early paid a call on the city fathers of York and demanded the city provide his army with $100,000 in cash; 2,000 pairs of shoes; 1,000 hats; 1,000 pairs of socks; and three days' rations. The merchants of York squirmed under Gen. Early's high-handed levy, but they did provide some of the general's requisition: $28,600 in cash; 1,500 pair of shoes; and all of the hats, socks, and rations that had been demanded. Gen. Early wrote later, "The shoes, hats, and socks were issued to the men, who stood very much in need of them." The money was used to buy cattle for beef.[589]

"It was here," the 31st Virginia's Capt. Harding later wrote, "that the boys, aided by an auger and a hole in the bottom of a nearby freight car, extracted a supply of liquid refreshment from a barrel which they had in some way located in the car; but next morning when their hilarity excited the suspicion, or cupidity, of our regimental and brigade officers and our camp was searched for some of the refreshment, none was found; nevertheless, the potency thereof with the resultant exuberance of the boys lasted until late on the evening of the next day."[590]

Sergeant Snider was assigned to another picket guard at a house on the road, on June 29. "We arrived at our post about 2 AM," he said, "and remained all day. We had a fine time and found plenty to eat, though the house had been plundered. There was a cow left, which we milked. In the evening we baked up two day's rations in the stove. Several of the boys have been nearly drunk, whiskey being plenty. About 11 P.M. we was ordered to report back to camp, arriving there about one o'clock."[591]

Snider was not used to such high living. "After getting to camp," he wrote, "I felt very sick and vomited all night, together with a cramp in my stomach. I got permission to ride in the ambulance for the first time since I have been in the service. We marched early, taking the back track, and passed through Berlin some three miles and camped." They were three miles from Heidlersburg when they bivouacked that night, according to Gen. Early.[592]

July 1, 1863: On the morning of July 1, Early's division marched through Heidlersburg before turning onto the Harrisburg Road.

Gordon's brigade was in advance, with Hays, Hoke, and Smith following with their brigades. Gen. Early learned during this march south that Ewell's other divisions were converging on Gettysburg, and that a battle was imminent. They hurried on toward Gettysburg.[593]

The fighting at Gettysburg had already begun by the time Early's division came within sight of town from the north. Gen. Early reported that the Federals had forces out on the Cashtown and Mummasburg roads, engaging brigades from Hill and Rodes's divisions. Those were the Federal cavalry under Gen. John Buford, the 1st Corps under Gen. Reynolds, and the 11th Corps of Gen. Oliver O. Howard.[594]

Snider noted, "Near Gettysburg, where our advance was engaging the enemy, about 3 P.M."[595]

Elements of the Union army, Barlow's XI Corps, were positioned on the west side of the Harrisburg Road, just north of Gettysburg's outskirts. Early sent Gordon's brigade forward, supported by Hays and Hoke. Extra Billy Smith's brigade was held in reserve, initially on the George Able farm to the east of the Harrisburg Road.

In front of them were Hoke's brigade, with a battalion of Confederate artillery posted directly in front of them. Early was at that time placing his brigades in line on the right flank of the Federal army. When the artillery in front of them, under the command of Jones began to fire on the town, the Union guns on Cemetery Ridge replied, bringing the infantry brigades under fire. Smith's brigade was "thrown back so as to present a line towards the York pike."[596]

Hays was positioned on the Harrisburg Road, and Hokes was to his left and back a short distance, east of the road. About a half hour later, Smith's brigade was moved forward, to a position to the rear of Hoke's brigade, on the Jonah Price farm. A battery of artillery under Jones was placed in front of Hoke, to enfilade the Federals, should they come from that direction.[597]

As the XI Corps fell back from Gordon's assault, three regiments and a battery of Coster's brigade, Union I Corps moved to a position beside the Harrisburg Road, a little closer to town. Hays's and Hoke's men pushed Coster's soldiers out of the way, and around 4 P.M., entered Gettysburg in pursuit of retreating Federals.[598]

Around then, Brig. Gen. Smith received reports of Union cavalry and infantry threatening the left flank, on the York Pike. Smith sent a message to Early, informing him of what he took for a threat, and then ordered his brigade to march eastward to investigate. This would become one of the more controversial military decisions Gen. Smith would make.[599]

Around 5pm, "The brigade moved to the left," Col. Hoffman later wrote in his report of the action, "crossing the Gettysburg Railroad and York Turnpike. The 49th Virginia Regiment was advanced as skirmishers." Their movement to the east put the brigade within range of Union artillery positioned on the northern end of Cemetery Hill. "On several occasions... the brigade was exposed to fire from the enemy's batteries," Hoffman wrote. Others reported that the regiment came under fire from Union sharpshooters, too.[600]

Gen. Early was surprised when he received Brig. Gen. Smith's message, and doubted the veracity of the report. Early sent Brig. Gen. Gordon and his brigade to investigate. On coming up with Smith's brigade, Gordon was to take command of both brigades.[601]

When Gordon's brigade arrived within sight of Smith's brigade, the 31st Virginia and 52nd Virginia were about two miles east of town, positioned in a line, with the 49th Virginia's skirmishers ahead of them. Gordon brought his brigade to a position about a mile west of Smith's brigade. By then, it was apparent that the cavalry threat from the east had disappeared.[602]

Desperate fighting continued elsewhere as the Confederate army began to form a line in a half-crescent around Gettysburg. Johnson's division would arrive that night, and lend support to Ewell's concentration on the Confederate left. To the west of Gettysburg, Gen. Longstreet's Corps brought reinforcements that would form the Confederate right.

In the twilight of July 1, Gen. Edward Johnson's division arrived after a full day's march. Under Gen. Ewell's orders, Johnson directed his brigades to form a line about a mile east of town, with one end of the line almost to Benner's Run, and the other end pointed at, and diagonal to the York Pike.

Capt. Phillips, in command of the 31st Virginia's Company K, wrote in his journal that night: "There will be hot work tomorrow, the enemy have the advantage of position. Three men in our regiment wounded."

The Federal army continued to arrive through the evening, filling the area south of Gettysburg, taking the high ground on and near Cemetery Hill.

While most of the troops slept with rifles at hand, Gen. Johnson sent pickets out well to the front, toward Culp's Hill. They found the crest of Culp's Hill already well protected.

July 2, 1863: At break of day on July 2, skirmishing began between the Federal right at Culp's Hill, and Johnson's skirmishers from the 2nd Virginia, of Walker's Stonewall Brigade. This attempted advance by the Confederates would eventually pull part of Smith's brigade down to the far left end of the Confederate line at Gettysburg.[603]

The 31st Virginia remained on guard against enemy cavalry. "Early on the morning of the 2nd," Capt. Joseph Harding later wrote, "we moved forward toward the enemy's entrenched position on Cemetery Hill until halted by a shower of grape-shot, from which we suffered but slight loss. We were then moved farther to the left, formed in line of battle facing said entrenchments, still in range of the Federal artillery, from the effects of which we were somewhat protected by the formation of the ground, and ordered to lie down in position. Here we remained, inactive, for some time, evidently awaiting, and expecting, Longstreet's attack on our right...."[604] They were in reserve, their day much less taxing than those closer to the firing line.

Around noon, July 2, Smith's brigade was sent out on the York Pike, along with Gordon's brigade, to guard the road. Reports had come in to Gen. Early that Federal cavalry was approaching on the York Pike, which would threaten the division's supply train. The 49th Virginia's skirmishers were deployed out in front on the two brigades.

Capt. Phillips was primed for the fight, noting in his diary about then, "Hell will be kicked up directly. I can see battery after battery getting into position. We are moved back and deployed to fight cavalry. I wish they would come. Oh! God be with our boys today. I am anxious for the battle to open. Oh, that we had them on fair ground."[605]

They may have seen the Confederate artillery moving into the wheat field on Benner's Hill. Johnson had ordered all of his artillery to fill one small flat field, putting them in the most effective place for bombarding the Federal guns on Cemetery Ridge, but the position also placed Johnson's guns under return fire from the Federals.

Nothing developed from the cavalry threat on the York Pike. A while later, Smith's brigade was detached from this position, and sent even farther to the rear, to act as support for Gen. J. E. B.'s cavalry, on the Hunterstown Road. Stuart had finally appeared, after joy riding around the eastern side of the Union army. Gordon's brigade had been guarding the pike: they were directed to move down to support Hays's brigade, near the railroad close to town. Smith's brigade was left to guard the cavalry.

Longstreet's artillery opened on the right at about four o'clock in afternoon on July 2, in preparation of his attack against the Union left. At nearly the same time, the Confederate artillery that had been brought into position behind Johnson's division, facing Cemetery Hill, and Culp's Hill, opened with their barrage. The Federal guns facing Johnson returned fire and inflicted heavy damage on Johnson's artillery. The combined sound, and reverberations were tremendous, and went on for about two hours.[606]

Capt. Phillips said the sensation of the artillery exchange, as from the 31st Virginia's position further back from the fight: "The artillery has opened, crash on crash. My God, this is hell on earth. The balls sing, whistle, and hurdle through the air like demons from hell, holding a carnival over the damned."

Some of the men in the 31st Virginia were frustrated, thinking they had been slighted in some way because they were held out of the infantry fight. "Four o'clock," Hall fretted in his diary. "The fight is now raging furiously. Awful artillery firing. We are not now engaged. I can not form an idea why we are not, for we have always heretofore been honored with going into every fight."[607]

Seeing that this unequal contest would result in the destruction of his own batteries, Johnson ordered his guns to withdraw, leaving only a battery of four pieces to cover the infantry. As Capt. Phillips said, "The musketry has opened. The ghost of both Confederate and Yankee are fleeing fast...." Phillips and the others in the regiment listened to the battle's sounds, noting that Longstreet was late once more.

"Gen. Smith is riding down our line," Phillips said a little later. There were concerns that Federal cavalry, under Gen. Killpatrick, were threatening the Brigade's position. "Killpatrick is making his appearance," Phillips wrote. "Now we will have it! A cavalry fight, let it come." But the Federal cavalry only made another feint.

Newton Bosworth, a 22-year-old private in Company F, was also making notes that day: "The sun is nearly down and is setting clear,' he wrote, "but the smoke from the battle is dense between it and us. The very hardest kind of a fight is going on, but we have not been ordered into it yet. I suppose we will have to go into the hardest place when we start."[608]

The infantry fight at Culp's Hill had been intense on July 2. The terrain included a rugged, and rocky hill covered with heavy forest of old growth timber. The Federals had dug in there, making breastworks and trenches part way up the hillside, and at the crest of the steep hill. Gen. Johnson had sent his brigades against the heavily defended positions, with the last of his regiments arriving at the base of the hill after dark.

Johnson's men were fighting George S. Greene's brigade, from the Second division of the Union XII Corps, was positioned on Culp's Hill, while the remainder of the XII Corps went to the aid of the Union regiments at the Peach Orchard, on the Union left. Late in the day, several units of the Union First, and XI Corps reinforced Gen. Greene's brigade. Many of Johnson's brigades were pulled back after dark to re-supply with ammunition, and then returned to the base of the hill in the pre-dawn hours of July 3.[609]

Smith's brigade, including the 31st Virginia continued to hold its position well to the rear, in support of Gen. J. E. B. Stuart's cavalry, which had finally arrived.

July 3, 1863: Sometime before dawn on July 3, Brig. Gen. William Smith, lawyer-judge-volunteer-soldier, and brigade commander received orders to bring his brigade to support Gen. Johnson's troops, but he could only do so with two of his regiments. The 31st Virginia had been detailed by Gen. J E B Stuart to support his cavalry while Smith marched the 49th Virginia and 52nd Virginia down toward Culp's Hill.[610]

Part of Walker's brigade was by then in position at the base of Culp's Hill, on the far left of the Confederate line, about 30 yards below a breastworks that had been captured late the previous day. Steuart's brigade occupied this breastwork. At daylight, the Federals began trying to retake the line of entrenchments they had lost the night before. Colonel James A. Walker, commanding the Stonewall Brigade, later reported, "Steuart's brigade, which was immediately in my front, became hotly engaged, and, on receiving a request from Gen. Steuart, I moved up to his support, and became warmly engaged along my whole line, and my right, extending beyond the breastworks, suffered very heavily."

Artillery was hammering the Confederate ranks: grapeshot, round shot, and exploding shell, joined by hails of rifle fire from well-placed infantry took a heavy toll on the Southern regiments. The Federals seemed to be trying to flank the Confederate line on the left, which would allow them to enfilade the Confederate regiments in the breastworks near the base of the hill. H. A. Brown's 1st North Carolina regiment was sent to push back this flank attack, and as a diversion, to attract the fire of the Federals, Colonel Nadenbousch sent one of the 2nd Virginia's companies to the southeastern side of Rock Creek, which was at their backs, making them more visible to the Federals. It was a desperate maneuver that could have resulted in many deaths because it was meant to draw Federal fire away from the men at the breastworks, and place it on the company as it made its diversion across the stream.[611]

Around this time, the 49th and 52nd Virginia regiments of Smith's brigade came up to the line. They had initially been placed in reserve, earlier that morning, but were now needed to support the left. Maj. Henry Kyd Douglas of Johnson's staff was sent to bring "Extra Billy" Smith's two-regiment brigade to the assistance of the Stonewall Brigade. Douglas offered to guide the Gen. to the assigned position.

"I lost no time in getting his column into line of battle and moved it to the rocky ascent," Douglas wrote after the war. "Artillery and musketry were filling the wood with the deadly din of battle, and columns of smoke were spreading through the trees and rising into the air through their tops."[612]

On the flank, the Federals continued to advance. They were the 1st Maryland (Potomac Home Guards), making a desperate charge across the meadow at the western base of Culp's Hill. Part of the left of their line entered the woods, and came within 25 yards of the 2nd Virginia's line at the breastworks, which was mostly a stone wall. The 2nd Virginia responded with "a heated oblique fire from the right of the regiment," and for a few moments those two regiments traded effective, close rifle fire. Suddenly, the Union regiment was ordered back by their brigade commander. He had received word that the 1st Maryland was in the way of another, larger body of Federal troops who were preparing to advance to their right.

"At this juncture," Colonel Nadenbousch wrote, "I detached some two more of my companies, and posted some at a bend of the creek, some sixty yards to the rear and left, and in full view of the enemy. The remainder I sent on the south side of the creek to reinforce Lt. Harrison, at that point engaging the enemy. With this concentrated fire, he was soon forced to retire in confusion.... About 7 AM the portion of my regiment... at the breastworks was relieved by Brig. Gen. William Smith's brigade."

Nadenbousch ordered the remainder of the 2nd Virginia to cross over Rock Creek, in support of the skirmishers he had sent out to keep the far left from being flanked.[613]

Maj. Kyd Douglas had foolishly ridden his horse into the front of the line: Federal sharpshooters spotted him directly and shot him with a rattle of rifle fire. While Douglas was being helped to the rear, Lt. Robert W. Hunter was assigned to act as Douglas's replacement.[614] Hunter later described the scene as Smith's brigade arrived. "They stood not upon the order of their coming, but came with a rush, the old governor in the lead, his voice rising above the din of battle, more potent than a blast from the bugle horn of Trelawney. Taking the highest position he could find, reckless of shot and shell, with bare head and sword in hand, pointing to the enemy, he harangued each regiment, as it double-quicked past into the arena of blood and fire."

Smith was never very good at remembering the prescribed commands for battalion drill. "I cannot recall his exact words," Hunter commented. Another witness later claimed that Smith ordered his men to *"pirouette on up there."*

Without a doubt, the old politician may have offered some choice language in his verbal orders that day. Ewell and Johnson may have foresworn swearing after Chancellorsville, but not everyone in the army had become so straight-laced.

"All that I know," Hunter wrote, "is that they were not in the conventional forms prescribed by Hardee, Upton, or Gilham.... Such, however, was the emphatic muscularity of his military dialect that there was never a moment's doubt or hesitation as to what he meant. His "boys", as he affectionately called them, knew and understood him, and off they dashed with a spirit and a vim that soon drove back the enemy."[615]

Smith's enthusiasm almost did them in that morning: he took his two regiments across the stone wall, and into Spangler's Meadow in a reckless charge against the distant Union lines just inside McAllister's Woods on the other side of the meadow, about 200 yards away. Federal rifles, and decisive artillery from a 20-gun battery slammed into Smith's two regiments, which began to falter under the withering fire.

The lieutenant colonel of the 52nd Virginia, John D. Ross told Smith they either had to continue the charge or withdraw to the protection of the stone wall. Faced with such a devastating onslaught of lead and the obvious effect on his men, Smith withdrew the small brigade behind the stone wall. In less than five minutes, 150 men had been killed or wounded in the 49th and 52nd Virginia regiments.[616]

CULP'S HILL, BATTLE OF GETTYSBURG, JULY 3, 1863

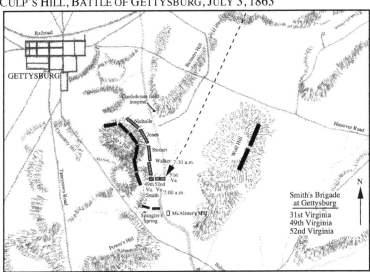

Map by David W. Wooddell

Once more behind the protection of the low, stone wall, the two regiments of Smith's brigade traded rifle fire with distant Union infantry while receiving plenty of Federal bullets from several angles. The enemy overlooked their position. All the while, a deadly crossfire of artillery shot and shell was hurled against them in one of the most terrible, prolonged shellings any in the brigade would ever encounter.[617]

While the rest of the brigade was getting shot up by plunging cross-fire, Col. Hoffman and the 31st Virginia were moving toward the base of Culp's Hill, finally having been relieved from guarding the cavalry. On the way, the 31sy Virginia skirted around hills, trying to keep out of the line of fire of the Federal artillery, but despite their caution the 31st Virginia received a severe shelling. They crossed over Rock Creek, perhaps about 8 AM, and came up on Smith's brigade line while the Federals continued their crossfire: the battle was at an intense pitch, according to survivor statements.

The low, stone wall ran from Rock Creek toward the base of the end of Culp's Hill, and was at right angles to most of Gen. Johnson's main line, which faced the hill. Steuart's brigade was positioned along the stone wall as it ran further up the hillside. Smith's brigade was aligned behind the wall, to Steuart's left, and was facing south across Spangler's Meadow, on the extreme left of the Confederate line.

Capt. Joseph Harding later wrote, "We lent some assistance and sustained some loss.... some of the Stonewall Brigade were on the line with us. We now faced the enemy at the distance of about three hundred and fifty yards, while our skirmishers, which were placed almost on our mainline, successfully fought theirs who occupied a position near their line." Harding said the men could see how individual shots landed against the Federals, but the Union artillery continued to pepper the Confederates with a harassing fire. Lt. W H. Wilson had his canteen shot up by the Federals, "yet, while he naturally did some flopping, he gallantly held his post and fought back as best he could."[618]

After some time of furious battle, the Stonewall Brigade was ordered to fall back from their close support of Steuart, and was placed closer to Rock Creek to re-supply with ammunition, and to clean their rifles. They were so engaged in this when Gen. Johnson came across them. "What in the — — — are you doing here?" Johnson demanded to know. When informed of the Stonewall brigade's need for ammunition, Johnson spoke with Brig. Gen. Walker and ordered the Stonewall brigade to move to the far right of his line, and take the place previously held by Jones. Walker lost no time in moving his men from such a dangerous position on the left and made his brigade ready to move forward in time for Johnson's third attack of the morning against the Union defenses on Culp's bloody hill. This was some time after 10 AM[619]

Smith's brigade continued to hold the far left of Johnson's line. A couple of hundred yards to their front, across the other side of Spangler's Meadow, two Union brigades began to prepare to attack Steuart and Smith's brigades. The 2nd Massachusetts, under Colonel Charles R. Mudge, and the 27th Indiana, under Colonel Silas Colgrove and Lt. Colonel John R. Fesler. They formed battle lines inside the woods on the far side of the meadow at around 10 AM On being ordered forward, the Federal regiments attempted to advanced across the meadow while every rifle that could be brought to bear from Steuart's and Smith's brigades took aim and fired, as fast as the men could load.[620]

The 27th Indiana only made it about half way across the field before being forced to turn back, losing about 100 men wounded or killed in a few brief minutes. The 2nd Massachusetts held on and advanced a little farther, and managed to gain part of the woods near the base of the stone wall before being driven away. During this foolhardy charge, within about ten minutes, the 2nd Massachusetts lost forty percent of its strength.[621]

The 31st Virginia was not in the line on the extreme left of Culp's Hill for very long, but several men were wounded in that brief span of time. Hall commented later, "It was a very trying place, as the grape shot and minié balls came to us at right angles. We had not remained in this line very long till I, with many others, was wounded. I was struck on the side of the knee."[622]

Company B came in for its share of the damage. Capt. Lyman's nearly charmed existence was threatened by a shell splinter that bloodied his cheek, "The same shell tripping up four men of my company," he said, "striking them on the calves of their legs." Capt. Elisha Wilfong of Company G had a minié ball fracture a bone in his arm. Fortunately, the broken arm was not so terribly damaged that amputation was necessary.[623]

Around then, Brig. Gen. Smith ordered the 52nd Virginia, and the 31st Virginia to withdraw and cross back over Rock Creek, to seem to threaten the Federal right flank. Col. Hoffman, next senior to Smith, took the two regiments over the stream, and marched them south-eastwardly and formed them in line so they could fire across at the Federal right. Private Newton Bosworth later wrote, "Our regiment acted as though they were on drill. Everyone seemed to be perfectly cool. Lt. Beverage of Company E had his leg shot off and died."[624]

Hoffman did not hold the two regiments in this position for very long. He soon ordered them to march back down the stream, to the north. Capt. Harding later complained that they had frittered away most of the day in useless marching. "We were moved a short distance further to the left, about faced, and under fire both from the enemy's artillery and musketry, marched back toward where we had neared their entrenchments in the morning. On this return march our loss was considerable. The writer was, himself, slightly hurt by a bursting shell.

"We had halted at the time and a little later one of the boys was struck, well forward on the left side, by a musket ball. He had been standing at my side and as he fell I caught and held him up on bended knee and arm. We could see where the ball had entered through his jacket, and upon inquiry he told us that it had passed through his body, and that he could feel the blood running down his back from the place of its exit.

"Upon further examination, however, we discovered the bullet had simply passed through his clothing in front of his body, upon which it left no mark.... our doctor, Bland, was inclined to think that the impact of the bullet with his clothing, aided by a vivid imagination, would have proved fatal but for our timely assurance that he was unwounded, and certainly his exhausted condition apparently sustained the doctor's opinion."[625]

The 49th Virginia next were ordered to rejoin the brigade and came up with them as Hoffman was marching the 31st and 52nd regiments back toward the Confederate right. There, Smith's brigade was placed once more in support of Walker's brigade. Things were no better on that end of the line, as reported by Brig. Gen. Walker, "The fire became so destructive that I suffered the brigade to fall back to a more secure position, as it was useless sacrifice of life to keep them longer under so galling a fire."

The only cover available was obtained by lying down, which the men were ordered to do. Phillips said in his diary the foolish behavior of his kinsman, Courtland Phillips. "Courtland and the rest of us were ordered to lay flat on the ground. Rations were short and we were hungry. Many soldiers would endanger their lives to appease their hunger. Courtland was hungry and he raised up and was sitting on the ground in a much-exposed position, eating a piece of bread that he had in his haversack. He was told, "You had better lay down or you will get shot there."

Courtland Phillips continued to devour his rations, and replied to his kinsman, "It's my hide that will get it." Capt. Phillips said, "Just then, he was struck by the ball of a Federal sharpshooter who had spied him, and he rolled down the hill in great pain. Some of his comrades said, "There, whose hide got it?"[626]

Walker's brigade was ordered to move forward again a couple of hours later to keep the enemy in check. He placed his men as well as he could, sheltering them with whatever was available. Desultory fire exchanged between the two sides through the rest of the day, and into the evening. Later, after it became apparent to everyone that they were not only not going to take Culp's Hill, but that they were loosing the battle entirely, the regiments under Johnson's command were withdrawn, including Smith's brigade, which had been on loan to Johnson's division for the day's action.

"It's now night," Capt. Phillips wrote in his diary. "We have lost several men today. Lt. Poling, Courtland Phillips, and Henry Lohr have been wounded. It is desperate... we will have to fall back, we are out of ammunition."[627]

The night of July 3, the 31st Virginia occupied nearly the same place they had slept on the night of July 1, beginning to withdraw to that place around 10 P.M., according to Capt. Harding. "Camped there for the night, taking position in line ready to meet the enemy should they advance, but they came not." The Federals seemed as exhausted as the Confederates and remained close to their own works through the night and into the next morning, doing very little harassment of their tired enemy.

The losses to the 31st Virginia at the Battle of Gettysburg could have been much worse, considering the places they had been sent during the last day of the battle. Reports of casualties killed and wounded in Lee's army were unsettled for a long time. There were so many other regiments fighting desperately in other areas, including the massive, and wasteful Picket's charge, that the experiences of the 31st Virginia at Gettysburg seem almost inconsequential. Even so, the 31st Virginia was lucky to have come out of the fray at Culp's Hill with so few losses.

Describing the hazards faced by Smith's brigade, Col. Hoffman's report sums up the day's action, "During most of the early part of the day the brigade was exposed to heavy fire of artillery, and during a part of that, of musketry also. The 49th Virginia Regiment suffered very severely, losing, indeed, more than two-fifths of its members. During the latter part of the day, the brigade was much annoyed by fire of the enemy's sharpshooters, protected by rocks."

The 31st Virginia had 1 man killed, 20 men wounded, and 7 captured or missing at Gettysburg. The men who were taken prisoner were all captured after the battle because they were wounded and unable to march and keep up with the regiment on the retreat. The losses in the 49th Virginia were 12 killed, 78 wounded, and 10 captured or missing; for the 52nd Virginia, there were 15 wounded.[628]

When the fighting ended that day, the battle at Gettysburg was essentially over. The following day, the Army of Northern Virginia had to extricate itself from the battle's aftermath while in the face of the enemy. Col. Hoffman reported, "On the morning of the 4th, (the brigade) formed westward of the town, on a ridge to the left of the Chambersburg turnpike, on the left of Gen. Gordon's, and right of Gen. Hays's brigade, where we remained during the day."

"We are fronting Gettysburg this morning, from a range of heights," Capt. Phillips said in his journal. "We are almost starved. I think we will commence a retreat to Virginia tonight."

Later in the day, Phillips went to visit his relative, Courtland, at a temporary hospital. "The old chaplain, some friends and myself went to see him, supposing he would die or be taken prisoner and we would never see him again. The chaplain gave him a silver dollar and a small testament. As we left the old chaplain said, 'We have to leave you and may never see you again. Here is a little book I give you to read.' As he took it in his hand, [Coutland] said, 'You'd better give me a chunk of meat and bread.' The fatherly old chaplain said to him kindly, 'It will be meat and bread for your soul.' As we left him the tears were running down his cheeks."

Courtland Phillips was later captured and sent to a Union hospital on David's Island in New York harbor, where he recovered from the flesh wound in the hip. He was back in the regiment by the end of the year, after being exchanged as a prisoner of war.[629]

Among the wounded at the temporary field hospital was Hall of Company H. Hall's knee had been hit by a musket ball, which penetrated from the side of the knee joint. Later, he wrote, "All the wounded that could walk had to follow the wagon train. We toiled on all day—suffering considerably. A short time before night my shoes gave out, and had to go it barefooted. When night came on four of us stopped at a straw pile on the side of the road. About two o'clock in the morning the enemy's cavalry came sweeping along the road with the wagons—shooting, yelling, and creating the greatest confusion. We heard the noise, and got up and ran back to the woods off the road. This morning we came down to a house, and are now waiting on the porch for breakfast. We are going to try the road again this morning."

Hall and the other wounded were captured about noon on the 5th, and as he said, "Sure, and it happened before I got breakfast."

As a wounded prisoner, Hall was taken to Frederick, Maryland to a hospital. He was later transferred to Fort McHenry, at Baltimore, and then to the prisoner of war camp at Fort Delaware. Months later, Hall was transferred yet again to the prisoner of war camp at Point Lookout, Maryland, where he remained in captivity until February 10, 1865.[630]

"Extra Billy" Smith's brigade was detailed as the rearguard of the army in the withdrawal to Virginia. Their homeward march began on July 5. Capt. Phillips wrote, "All night last night the rain poured down in torrents. We are miserable. Lee has moved, we are the rearguard of the army." They expected the wrath and fury of the Union army to come swift on their heels, and were puzzled that it did not come.

"We still guard the rear," Phillips wrote on the 6th. "Had an artillery duel last night at sunset. All is quiet this morning. We have a mountain to cross." He said the following day, "Left Waynsborough this morning and marched to Hagerstown, the enemy pursuing us."[631]

The 31st Virginia reached the swollen Potomac River at a ford just above Williamsport on July 7, and there the men were able to re-supply with ammunition. They had marched from Gettysburg with very little in their ammunition pouches, and until they reached the river, they would have been sorely pressed to fight.[632]

Their ranks continued to be nibbled away by attrition, even while they retreated. While at the 31st Regiment's camp just north of Hagerstown on July 8, the resignation of the long-missing 2nd Lt. Henry H. Jones of Company B was received by the regiment assistant adjutant. "I was wounded," Jones wrote in his application to be permanently discharged, "in the Battle of Gaines Mill, June 27, 1862, the ball passing through my right elbow, rendering the arm stiff and disabled. I have since, up to the 15th of last month, been away from my command for several months, being on Conscript and Recruiting duty. I am unable to endure the fatigue and exposure of field duty."[633]

The regiment continued to hold its position facing the Union army. Brig. Gen. Smith chose this time to resign from his command, leaving Col. Hoffman in command of the brigade. Capt. Phillips of Company K said in his diary on July 11, "We are now in line of battle about one and one-half miles south-west of Hagerstown. We came here at about ten o'clock last night."

They remained in line through the night, and on the following morning fought a prolonged skirmish action with the Federal infantry while under fire from artillery. Skirmishing continued through the day at other parts of the Confederate lines. Phillips said, shortly before dark, that they could see the skirmishing going on elsewhere. By this time, the 31st Virginia had dug some entrenchments and fortified small breastworks of logs and stone. The day's fight did not develop into much of a battle, but continued as ongoing skirmish fights into the next day, July 13.[634]

On the 14th, the 31st Virginia crossed the river at a ford above Williamsport, passing back into Virginia. The river had been fed by the rain for days, but was low enough for the men to cross. "Water nearly up to the armpits of the men, who had to hold their guns and cartridge boxes above their heads to keep them out of the water," Capt. Harding recalled. The soldiers had to lock arms with one another in a chain to avoid being swept away. "A good bath," Harding said, "which was not only refreshing, but much needed."[635]

The 31st Virginia marched south, arriving at Darkville on July 16, where they camped until the 20th as part of Ewell's Corps. The Army of Northern Virginia needed a rest as it attempted to come to terms with the number of casualties it has sustained in the recent campaign. As men straggled into camp after trailing along behind of the army, their presence needed to be reported as soon as possible so that the high command could discover exactly how many men had been lost at Gettysburg. Beginning on July 17, roll calls were held five times a day in Early's Division: at reveille, breakfast, noon, sunset, and tattoo. The orders stated: "All soldiers improperly absent on these occasions will be promptly punished."[636]

While at camp on July 17, 1862 near Darkville, the 31st Virginia's Maj. McCutchen wrote to the Adjutant Gen. to request a promotion for a young cousin of Col. Hoffman's. The regiment's adjutant position for a lieutenant was open following the resignation of First Lt. John G. Gittings. "First Sergeant Thomas W. Hoffman of Capt. Bland's Company, 17th Virginia Cavalry, is a fit and acceptable person to fill the vacancy," McCutchen wrote, "and accordingly I request that he be appointed first lieutenant for the position, and be assigned to duty as adjutant of the (31st Virginia)." The transfer, and appointment were approved within about a month for Thomas Hoffman.[637]

Smith's brigade marched to Hedgesville, then to Bunker Hill. And passed through Winchester on the 23rd; continued to Strasburg, Woodstock, and Mt. Jackson. After crossing the Blue Ridge, the brigade reached the Rapidan River around August 1, where they went into old camping grounds, about five miles east of Rapidan Station, near Pisgah Church.[638]

Their way to this camping place was one that was remarkable for the claims against Gen. Early and Col. Hoffman: "We were lost about half the time," Newton Bosworth complained later about their march to Pisgah Church, "General Early and Colonel Hoffman were drunk. Went into camp about ten at night. Men all mad!"

Their camping place was less than desirable, according to another of the men, who commented, "Water very bad, scarce, and inconvenient."[639]

Camp, drill, and prayer were their lot for the next while. The 31st Virginia began to drill again at their new camp, to restore order in the men, and to sharpen skills for the next campaign. As Col. Hoffman had done very little drilling of the regiment since taking command, he was sometimes at a loss for what term to use to give a command. It may have been that Hoffman had depended on Gittings to coach him with the commands. It appears that the nearsighted Col. Hoffman managed to blunder in front of the men one day when he could not recall the correct command during brigade drill.

Newton Bosworth commented, "Colonel Hoffman... had to call out Colonel Terrell to give a command for him." Hoffman's lack of expertise at drill did not serve to recommend him for higher rank, especially at a time when he was campaigning for promotion to replace Brig. Gen. Smith. Ultimately, he would need the approval of the division commander, Jubal Early, who was keeping his eye on Hoffman.[640]

That summer became a time of religious fervor among the offices and enlisted alike. Traveling preachers were with them, making sermons, giving baptisms, urging the men to find salvation before they met their end on the battlefield. They had seen what a killing game that warfare was at its heart. They were afraid of death and wanted reassurance that it was going to be all right, that they would live in the hands of their god.

Sergeant Osborne Wilson noticed on August 16: "Go to church 11 AM, at Mt. Pisgah, three miles from Rapidan Station, but the house is crowded and I have to stand by a window. Revival going on. Several come forward at close of sermon." The following day, nine men went forward to ask for baptism by immersion. All of this religious fervor kept the ministers busy.[641]

Reverend William Jones, chaplain of the 13th Virginia commented about the life of ministers at camp in Smith's brigade. "From the 1st of August to the 1st of October, I averaged two sermons every day, besides other work, and other chaplains were even more laborious, so pressing were the demands upon us; and I witnessed the professed conversion of hundreds of our own men."

The army was camped then along the Rapidan River from Liberty Mills, above Orange Court House, to Raccoon Ford. There were two churches close at hand for the men in Smith's brigade to use, the Mt. Pisgah Baptist Church, and a Methodist church in the lower part of Orange County. Rev. Jones, Rev. J. P. Garland, of the 49th Virginia, and Rev. Slaughter, of the 48th Virginia, combined forces to hold united church meetings. They invited guest speakers, including Rev. Dr. J. A. Broadus, Rev. F. M. Barker, and Rev. L. J. Haley. "There were 250 professions of conversion, and a revival among Christians, of the highest value," Jones wrote. He eventually became official chaplain for the brigade.[642]

The duties and activities of chaplains in the field were important to the men. Presbyterian minister, Dr. J. C. Stiles, another active chaplain with the army commented that in addition to forming churches for the men to attend, they also corresponded with churches in the home towns of the men, to keep them apprised of how they were doing in the army.

"These chaplains keep a minute record," Stiles said, "not only of the names of the whole regiment, but of all that may assist them either to save the sinner or sanctify the believer. Some of them have ten or twelve columns opposite the names of different companies of the regiment, so headed as to supply all that personal knowledge of the party, which might be serviceable in promoting their spiritual welfare. These columns they fill up gradually with such intelligence as they may be able to obtain in their pastoral visitations—when sick, wounded, or slain; when awakened, convicted, converted—all important information is conveyed by the chaplain to the family and the Church."

Rev. George B. Taylor of the 25th Virginia reflected that a chaplain, in order to do his job properly, had to be with the soldiers wherever they were. "If he sticks to the men as he ought, he must learn to say, "Tis' home where'er my oilcloth is," and may often be seen at dewy eve, selecting a clean place or smooth rail for his bivouac. He, too, must learn to eat once a day, to live on crackers, and may often be seen broiling his fat bacon on the coals, or making rye coffee in a tin cup."

Chaplains were forced to come to terms with the violence of the battlefield. Some were extremely brave, and several were noted for having assumed military positions beyond their duties as men of the cloth. The 31st Virginia, for instance, had its own "fighting reverend," Lt. Robert N. Crooks of Company I, who held services and preached to the men at times when they were short of a real chaplain.[643]

While the 31st Virginia was on the Gettysburg campaign, and immediately afterwards at the Rapidan, Capt. Cooper had remained in Pocahontas County with Jackson's cavalry. At the beginning of August, Cooper was still trying to gain the position of colonel in the newly formed 20th Virginia cavalry. Colonel W. L. Jackson had taken the muster rolls of the new regiment to Richmond for approval by the government. Once the muster rolls were approved, the election for colonel could take place. Meanwhile, politics in the cavalry camp in Pocahontas County grew thicker and more complex. On August 3, Cooper said in his journal, "Heard of a caucus prejudiced to me. Capt. A. and Lieut. N. went to see about it, but made no discoveries."

Preoccupied with worry about his family, who were not yet allowed to leave their home in Clarksburg, Cooper wrote to James McCann, a friend in Harrison County to ask that McCann look out for his family. Cooper was an intensive correspondent, and had mounted a letter-writing campaign to his friends of influence, asking for support in his bid to become colonel. He had already written to Col. Hoffman, asking for a letter of recommendation, and also to Robert Johnston and Jonathan M. Bennett. In mid-June, while on the road to Gettysburg,

Hoffman wrote a lengthy letter to the Secretary of War, full of praise for Cooper.

"His coolness and gallantry have always been conspicuous," Hoffman wrote. "A citizen of North Western Virginia, where his family yet remains, he has always had a burning desire to serve in that direction, and has thought much and formed, as I think, sound, practical opinions on that subject. Though I should greatly regret to loose him, I... recommend him to your consideration."[644]

Col. Hoffman's letter to the Confederate Secretary of War, James A Seddon along went with a letter from Robert Johnston, member of the Virginia legislature, who emphasized the correctness of Cooper's political leanings. "Capt. Cooper's labors, in inculcating sound political principles in North Western Va., his services in this war, his capacity and gallantry as a soldier, his resistance in the Unioncrat country from which this regiment comes, distinguish him among those who may be thought of for this appointment...Whilst the services of Capt. Cooper will be very valuable during the continuation of the present war, they will be no less so after the war, in settling the affairs of the divided and distressed region from which he comes."[645]

Col. William L Jackson returned to the camp on August 7 with approval from Richmond to form the 20th Virginia cavalry regiment, but on the 8th, politician Sam Woods arrived at the camp and made the situation more difficult yet by sending a letter to the Secretary of War, requesting that Lt. Colonel Thompson, of the 19th Virginia cavalry supersede the new colonel of the 20th Virginia in rank. Cooper went to Huntersville the next day, where he had letters waiting from James McCann in Harrison County, as well as from Capt. Uriel Turner. Turner, the original captain of Company C, was then serving as assistant quartermaster in Smith's brigade.

The political maneuvering for the new position of colonel in the 20th Virginia cavalry was finally resolved on August 14, with the election of Capt. William W. Arnett. A former officer from the 31st Virginia who had resigned to join Jackson's cavalry, Arnett had said previously that he was helping Cooper in his political campaign with the men in the 20th Virginia. This was a severe disappointment to Cooper: "When you wish to combine an interest in your favor, do not associate with an interest that militates against you."

Of the last minute changes in the voting blocks, and the election of Arnett to the position, Cooper wrote, "My friends are indignant. I would rather be myself defeated than Arnett elected by such means." Cooper started back to the 31st Virginia the next day, with this note in his journal, "I would like to have served in N.W. Virginia, and believe I could have been of more service here than there, but God's will be done."[646]

He reached Staunton on August 18 and made arrangements to obtain some personal items that he wished to take to camp, including a "camp box" to hold his possessions. Probably something smaller than his trunk, which was then stored at the residence of a friend in Staunton. Before leaving town, Cooper received an apology from Maj. Lady, who had been one of the contenders for the colonel's position in the 20th Virginia. It was Maj. Lady who switched his vote, and thereby the votes of his followers to Capt. Arnett at the last minute.[647]

Cooper rode out of Staunton on August 21, and arrived at the 31st Virginia's camp near Pisgah Church on August 24. "Find to my surprise, matters to be in anything but a pleasant situation." Politics were on the rise in the 31st Virginia once more, and Cooper would have no little involvement.[648]

At the beginning of the month, as commander of Smith's Brigade, Col. Hoffman submitted a list of men on detail or detached service for the brigade: 38 men from the 31st Virginia were then serving various positions away from the regiment. Several were at the Armory at Richmond. Others served as nurses at various hospitals. A few were wagoners; one at a government shoe shop; one was detailed brigade butcher; one was an enrolling officer in Pocahontas County; and one was a tailor at West View.[649]

Company D had been reduced to no more than fifteen men by mid-August. Luther Haymond, elected to the Virginia legislature in March, resigned as captain of Company D on August 11. For a man with one good arm, the other entirely disabled by a rifle ball early in the war, Capt. Haymond had done well. He was initially promoted to officer rank at the insistence of political connections, including Robert Johnston and George W. Lurty, but Haymond justified the support by serving as an effective officer. He had doubled as the acting assistant quartermaster at the end of 1862, when absentees reduced the regiment.[650]

Haymond's second in command, 1st Lt. John S. Heckert submitted his resignation around this time, on the 18th. Heckert gave no reasons, but when forwarding the resignation for approval, Capt. Haymond reported: "Lt. Heckert is a very excellent man and a gallant soldier, is fond of and uses the musket quite well. He does not consider himself competent to command. The company (is) also very small, having only 15 effective men." Heckert had started the war as a private in Company D, enlisting at the end of May 1861 at Gilmer Court House, and was promoted to 2nd lieutenant in May 1862.

Maj. McCutchen was less charitable than Haymond: "Lt. Heckert is an inefficient officer," McCutchen wrote, "and is willing to sacrifice his office in order to have the privilege of carrying his musket by the side of his brothers and other friends in another regiment." Heckert's resignation was accepted, and Capt. John H. Yancey subsequently replaced him.

This was the son of old Colonel Yancey, who had given Company D their first military feast as the company made its way out of Gilmer

County in June 1861. Yancey had enlisted in August of that year, and had been elected 2nd lieutenant. His promotion to captain in August 1863 was not confirmed until March of 1864.[651]

Company A also lost its captain in August 1863, though in a practical sense the 1st lieutenant had commanded the company since September 1862. Capt. Laban R. Exline had been absent from duty since Sharpsburg, when his left arm was broken by a serious gunshot wound, the ball pulverizing the bone to the extent that what bone was left would never heal. A surgeon had amputated the arm, and the stump healed well enough by February 1863 for Exline to go on recruiting duty. However, his broken ribs had not healed properly and they interfered with his lungs, leaving Exline seriously disabled from any exercise. Though he had been elected captain in December 1862, Exline had never been able to serve on active duty as such. He resigned on August 19, 1863, and was granted a discharge. For Exline the war was over, but the suffering was not: a resident of Monongalia County, West Virginia, this 24-year-old farmer was captured in Barbour County in November 1864 and sent to Camp Chase.[652]

On August 13, the thorny affair, if not to say controversy, over Patrick W. Bruffey's claim of being an officer in the 31st Virginia had to be dealt with by the regiment's overworked commanders. The claim of Bruffey as 1st lieutenant of Company I had been on the back burner for some time, but now the matter was forced as "Lt." Bruffey made his claim once more that he had been elected as junior lieutenant in 1862, but had subsequently been unfairly dropped as an officer by Col. Hoffman, who refused to recognize the legitimacy of Bruffey's supposed election.

By August 1863, the inquiry that Bruffey's protests began turned against him and included allegations by the Adjutant General's department that Bruffey had improperly collected the pay of a lieutenant since his supposed election. The government wanted him to pay it back, claiming that Bruffey had not been entitled to collect officer's pay.

Hoffman pointed out in his statement, on August 14, 1863, that while he did not think Bruffey was legally elected to the position, and had never been confirmed in it, making Bruffey's claim "counterfeit," Hoffman did think that Bruffey had done an admirable job while acting as a lieutenant, and in this way, had earned his pay. "I have no doubt that, in good faith, Bruffey acted and was entitled to, and drew his pay, and bought his subsistence and clothing as an officer," Hoffman wrote, "and I shall be glad if he can be relieved from accountability for the pay received, which he can ill afford to refund."[653]

The Bruffey affair would remain unsettled for some time to come, but meanwhile other controversies surfaced of a more damaging political effect on the 31st Virginia. Following the battle of Gettysburg, with its incredible number of casualties, the Confederate army was in serious need of reorganization. So many senior officers had been killed or wounded that the natural course of promotion of more junior officers would potentially result in serious difficulties. Accordingly, Gen. Lee made the recommendation for delaying any elections of new officers in the Army of Northern Virginia, especially of lower grades such as 2nd lieutenants, until after the companies grew with new recruits. The new policy was published as an order, through Gen. Ewell, on August 18, 1863. Gen. Early, in command of the division, apparently extended that order to include officers of higher rank, including lieutenant colonels, and majors.[654]

When Lt. Col. Alfred H. Jackson died in the summer of 1863, the most senior officer in the regiment under Col. Hoffman was Maj. McCutchen. Colonel Hoffman, had already forwarded his name to Gen. Early on August 1, 1863, with a recommendation for promotion to lieutenant colonel, but Gen. Early apparently held on to the paperwork, and McCutchen's new rank was not immediately confirmed. Hoffman would again submit McCutchen's name on October 12, 1863, but the promotion would not be approved until February 16, 1864.[655]

It was customary in the service, however, for an officer to assume the rank of his promotion before the new rank was confirmed. Upon the death of Alfred Jackson, Maj. McCutchen assumed the duties of lieutenant colonel in the regiment, but was scrupulously careful in signing all documents as major until his rank was confirmed. The assumed promotion of McCutchen to lieutenant colonel opened the position of major. Promotion should have been straightforward, going to the most senior captain in the regiment. But this was the 31st Virginia, a very political regiment. And a few did not agree on the seniority of the captains.

As Capt. Cooper said after learning of Alfred Jackson's death, the passing of their major would probably make Cooper the new major. However, upon returning to the regiment on August 24 he discovered that someone else was already claiming to be the senior captain. Nathan Clawson, the captain of Company I, was claiming the promotion to major, and he was supported in his claim by most of the company officers in the regiment. It became an explosive, and divisive controversy.[656]

On August 26, acting Lt. Col. McCutchen asked for statements from Cooper and Clawson, giving the reasons why each considered his own rank the most senior. Cooper's statement was rather long, meticulously written, and as it later turned out, was legally correct. Cooper stated that he had been elected captain on May 1, 1862, at the reorganization of the regiment: prior to that, he was 1st lieutenant, with seniority dating from May 7, 1861. Nathan Clawson was elected 1st lieutenant at this same election, on May 1, 1862. Cooper pointed out that when the officers of the regiment held an election a little later in the day, to choose field officers, Lt. Nathan Clawson had voted in that election as 1st lieutenant, and Alfred H. Jackson, who had been elected captain in the morning election, voted as captain of Company I. Cooper said that Clawson's name was subsequently published by the army as a 1st lieutenant, in a General Order dated May 3, 1862, announcing the new company officers of the regiment.

The complication came in when Capt. Alfred H. Jackson was elected lieutenant colonel in the field officer election on the afternoon of May 1, 1862. That meant a vacancy of captain in his company until Clawson was promoted to the position. Even though Clawson was promoted to the rank, with seniority dating from May 1, he was junior to Cooper because at the time of Cooper's election to captain, Clawson was elected a lieutenant. Cooper's legal reasoning was no doubt assisted by one of the regiment's many crack lawyers, and perhaps was even aided by his friend Hoffman. Cooper wrote, in his statement, "It may be claimed by Capt. Clawson that the law knows no fractions of days, but while it is not strictly the fact in the case of several legal papers, when the time of their issue is known, it is also a legal maxim that no fiction of the law shall be permitted to work an injury to any man. And if this or a like technicality is applicable to such as case as this, my promotion to the captaincy dates to the 16th of April, 1862, and his expressly to the 1st of May afterwards."

By comparison, the statement of Capt. Clawson was positively succinct. He based his claim on the fact that he had been promoted to captain in Company I in February 1862, following the resignation of Alfred Jackson, who had been the first captain of the company. In the election of May 1, 1862, he felt that although he was elected 1st lieutenant, which meant a reduction in rank, he would still hold seniority over Cooper because he had been a captain prior to the election. "I have been considered for some time the senior captain of the regiment," Clawson maintained in his statement, "and have, upon several occasions, during the absence of the field officers of the regiment, been put in command thereof. I therefore respectfully submit these facts for the decision of the commanding general."

Maj. McCutchen, still waiting for his promotion to lieutenant colonel to be confirmed so that there would be a vacancy for one of these two men to fill, noted dryly when forwarding the statements: "Approved and respectfully forwarded together with Capt. Cooper's statement, for the decision of the higher officers. Capt. Clawson and Capt. Cooper are either proper persons for promotion in the event of a vacancy in a higher office, and I would respectfully recommend that the officer decided to be the senior, be promoted when such vacancy occurs."

Major McCutchen was trying to revive the regiment's skills at drill, and hopefully bring the men up to a higher level of standards. While they had never spared themselves on the battlefield, over the course of the war the 31st Virginia still continued to fall behind other regiments in matters of drill. With Gen. Early sitting on McCutchen's promotion, it was no wonder he was putting the regiment—and himself—through the drill books.

Capt. Cooper noticed the change of attitude when he returned to the regiment. "I find that the rules and restrictions are more rigid than ever in this army," Cooper wrote on August 26. "Gen. Early is particularly severe. As a consequence the army is in a fine state of discipline and well drilled."

On the 27th, he commented, "Commence drilling with regiment and find that it has much improved, especially battalion drill." The following day, Capt. Lyman finished recitations from *Hardee* for the benefit of the officers. "Most of the officers are familiar with the different battalion evolutions," Cooper said. On the 29th, in preparation for a brigade review by Gen. Ewell, the Fourth brigade held a practice review, and then repeated the practice review on the 30th, and 31st. Hoffman and McCutchen were serious about making a good show for the general.[657]

Col. Hoffman was not above using political connections to become a brigadier general, but that didn't impress the one man he most needed to sway, Gen. Jubal Early. Hoffman received a letter from his Uncle Gideon Camden, dated August 19, which noted that he had given some thought to Hoffman's ambition, and would try to do what he could. Others were also trying to help: Hoffman received a letter on August 31 from politician Cyrus Hall, who said that Gen. Haymond, a veteran legislator at Richmond, had written to Gen. Lee on Hoffman's behalf. Although Lee's reply was complimentary to Hoffman, he said that the division commander had recommended another officer for the position. Jubal Early was the division commander, and obviously unless Hoffman could impress Early, no amount of political pressure would save the day. So the men in the regiment, and in the brigade practiced drill until they were worth showing in brigade review.[658]

Surgeon William J. Bland, and Maj. McCutchen had recently been elected to serve in the Virginia legislature. On August 30, Dr. Bland turned his Surgeon's Chest over to the assistant surgeon, Smith Buttermore. In some ways, it was one of the most important pieces of equipment in the regiment.[659]

Several days later, on September 4, Maj. McCutchen wrote an itemized ordnance invoice that indicated he had been serving as ordnance officer for the regiment.

The caliber of the small arms suggests that the 31st Virginia was then equipped with the Enfield .57 caliber rifled musket. The Enfield .57 cal. was considered accurate up to 1,000 yards and weighed 9 pounds each, measuring 53 inches in length. Manufactured in Great Britain, the Enfield was the standard-issue small arms of the British army. The quality of the rifle made it one of the most popular arms of the Civil War. Some experts estimate as many as 400,000 British

Enfields were smuggled into the Confederacy from England. Later in the war, the Confederacy manufactured its own Enfield pattern rifled musket at a factory in Georgia.[660]

Ordnance Invoice, 31st Virginia Regiment

257 Small arms, cal. .57	256 Cartridge boxes
199 Cartridge box belts	236 Waistebelts
147 Bayonet scabbards	240 Cap pouches
30 Gunslings	7 Ball screws
30 Screw drivers	20 Wipers
183 Haversacks	126 Knapsacks
135 Canteens	9430 Cartridges, Cal. .57
14000 Cartridges in Ordnance Wagon	

The Surgeon's Chest

1 Medicine chest	1 lb. Simple cerate
1/2 lb. Camphor	1/2 lb. Flax seed
1/4 lb. Ipecac	1 1/2 lb. Spirits of turpentine
1/4 lb. Calc magnesia	1 roll Adhesive plaster
1 lb. Heyd. chloride mitus	2 oz. Perls aprii
3/4 lb. Plumbi acetus	1/2 lb. Heydras cum creta
3 Spatulas	1 Scarificator
1 pair Bullet forceps	21 tin cans
1/4 lb. Emp. cantharides	1/2 lb. Resin cerate
1/2 lb. Mustard seed	1/2 lb. Peruvian bark
1 lb. Arrow root	1/2 lb. Patofsa chevras
3 ox. Perls Rhii (tusky)	1 bottle Bibson antidote
1/2 lb. Chloroform	1/2 lb. Cayenne pepper
1/4 lb. Blue mass	1 pill file
2/8 oz. Sulfer mossrhia	1 case Amputating Instruments (damaged)

With Maj. McCutchen preparing to depart for Richmond, Capt. Cooper was called on to command the regiment at drill on September 1. He said that day, "Although I have been absent some time, I find no difficulty in drilling with the regiment." Just as well, for on the 2nd, Gen. Ewell reviewed the brigade, prompting Cooper to observe, "The old General looks as well as ever and rides very well yet, notwithstanding his wooden leg."

The regiment was sent out on patrol duty on September 4 to round up stragglers. They marched as far as Clark's Mountain and returned that night with only one man found straggling from the army.

Dr. Bland and Maj. McCutchen departed for Richmond on the 5th to attend the Virginia legislature. Capt. Cooper was temporarily in command of the regiment while Col. Hoffman continued in command of the brigade.[661]

Early's Division had been sent a new artillery instructor, Lt. Thompson of Nelson's Artillery, along with a detachment of artillerymen to drill infantry companies in artillery tactics. Brigade commanders were ordered to select a company from each regiment for drill and instruction under Thompson. This drill and instruction resulted in Gen. Lee reviewing the troops on September 9. Three divisions formed lines of battle, each more than a mile in length. "Gen. Ewell had his Corps in a field near Orange Court House," Cooper wrote in his journal. "The spectacle was an imposing one and was attended by many ladies and other spectators."[662]

The matter of Cooper and Clawson's seniority reached Gen. Lee on September 11. From the general's remarks, it seems that he preferred Clawson to Cooper. Lee wrote, "In two papers forwarded on Sept. 4th and 5th, the question of seniority in the 31st Virginia Regiment between Capt. Cooper and Capt. Clawson is decided in favor of Capt. Clawson, and he is recommended for the majority of the Regiment. In case the Department sees fit to recuse their decision and promote Capt. Cooper, it is requested that his promotion be delayed until a Board of Examiners can be called to inquire into his fitness, which has been questioned. The fitness of Capt. Clawson for promotion has not been questioned and if the Dept. decides in his favor, there is no objection made to his promotion." Such comments from the commanding general did not reflect well on Cooper, or Hoffman.[663]

Clearly, Gen. Lee was not aware that the Adjutant General's office had already ruled in Cooper's favor, noting that his seniority as Captain dated from April 16, 1862, and Capt. Clawson's seniority as captain dated from May 1, 1862.[664]

Cooper still had to pass the Examining Board later in the year, but at least he had the weight of legal opinion from the Adjutant General's office on his side in the matter of seniority. Without a doubt, he would also have liked the good opinion of Gen. Lee. Perhaps with a foreboding of coming action, Capt. Cooper said that he had written to a friend at home, "To look after my family." By then, Cooper had not seen his family in Clarksburg for more than two years.

On September 13, the regiment received orders to march at sunrise the following day. The Federals were reportedly crossing the river at U.S. Ford. The men could hear the distant boom of artillery, a sign that something was in store for them when they marched out of camp early on the 14th. The previous year, they'd fought at Antietam in the bloody battle of Sharpsburg on September 17. It was the bloodiest day in American history, and they'd been present. Now it comes again, they were marching to the ford over a river.[665]

9

DISCONTENT AND REBELLION
Sept 1863 – Jan 1864

After marching at dawn to Somerville Ford on the Rapidan River, the 31st Virginia occupied a rifle pit overlooking the ford. The rest of the brigade took a position behind a nearby hill. Early's Division had been ordered to guard Somerville and Raccoon Fords, and his other brigades were positioned farther along the river. "The Yanks came up with cavalry and artillery, but we prevented their crossing," Captain William P. Cooper noted on September 14. The artillery exchange ran for nearly two hours, during which the regiment's Patrick Riley of Company H was badly injured.

Later in the day, after the artillery had subsided, some of the men decided to take the opportunity of being near water and have a bath and a swim. Stripping off their clothes, they went into the river and began to frolic. Soon enough, Federal skirmishers came up to the river and drove the men away from their clothes with well-placed rifle fire. Newton Bosworth observed from one of the rifle pits, "They have their guns and are now fighting manfully for their clothes."[666]

In the evening, the regiment was relieved by the 49th Virginia. The 31st Virginia marched back to join the rest of the brigade, which was concealed behind a hill. While there, Captain Riley Phillips mused in his journal on the effects of a recent visit to their camp from his father, "Who ever knew the nearness of relations until forced to part with them. I confess that the matter unmans me, but my temperament is a buoyant cast."[667]

"Brigade remained masked behind hill near the ford," Captain Cooper wrote on the 15th. "Frequent skirmishing was heard on the river, and our batteries frequently opened on the enemy." Later in the day, he noted that the men in the 49th Virginia struck up a conversation with Federal pickets on the other side of the river. The men were starting to exchange newspapers and other items of trade.

The brigade, including the 31st Virginia moved to another, enjoining hill and camped for the night, leaving the 49th Virginia on picket duty in the rifle pits. In the morning, a North Carolina regiment from another brigade came up and relieved the 49th Virginia. The day's action included watching as the North Carolina regiment gave the Federals a brush. "The Tar Heels made a dash at the enemy today," Cooper noted in his journal, "and a company drove a regiment out of their trenches. The batteries shelled them beautifully as they were leaving. The Yanks reinforced and drove them back."

In the evening, the men in Smith's brigade were entertained by Rev. Taylor, from Staunton, who came up to their camp and preached "a good sermon." The religious revival was ongoing, even on picket duty near the river. There was more skirmishing on the river on the 17th as part of Hays's brigade made another dash across the river, bringing back several prisoners. Companies D and E from the 31st Virginia were sent out on picket, but things had quieted down by then and the Federals were not crowding the river so closely. This held through the 18th as the weather grew chill and rainy.[668]

"The enemy seem to be moving down the river," Cooper noted on September 19. "The indications are that they will attempt to cross lower down instead of here. Deserters from their camp say that the impression there is that Lee's army is much depleted and now is the time to strike. If they come over they will find how it is."

A quiet Sunday was passed in camp on the 20th, the men watching Federal wagon trains move up and down the road on the other side of the river, and hearing their locomotives pulling past on the railroad. On the 21st, the regiment was ordered to relieve the 13th Virginia in the trenches at Somerville Ford, taking position around dusk. In the night, the men were put to work digging more entrenchments and by morning had increased the defenses with an additional 75 yards of rifle pits.

"The Yankees seem disposed to be sociable this morning," Cooper wrote on the 22nd, "and exhibit papers indicating a desire to exchange with us, but as we have positive orders to the contrary, we decline. Some North Carolinians get a *Washington Chronicle* from them containing the news of Bragg's victory over Rosecrans." Later in the day, the 31st Virginia was relieved by the 49th Virginia, and moved back to the camp on the hill, where they listened to a large artillery barrage from farther up the river, knowing that someone else was catching it that day.[669]

With Colonel Hoffman in temporary command of the brigade, and Major McCutchen in Richmond attending the legislature, the senior captains were in command of the regiment. Perhaps Cooper and Clawson had decided to share this duty? Clawson was in command on the 21st when he forwarded a recommendation for 2nd Sergeant Martin V. Stewart, of Company B, to be appointed to the office of ordnance sergeant for the regiment. Captain Lyman in command of Company B wrote a handsome recommendation, noting that Stewart was 2nd sergeant from May 1861 until the reorganization in the spring of 1862, when he was promoted to 1st sergeant. Stewart's night vision was diminished from some reason, and he had relinquished the position of 1st sergeant. He was serving as acting ordnance sergeant from November 1862, and had done an admirable job. "Upon an inspection of his books," Lyman wrote, "I find them well and carefully kept. Believing him, therefore, fitted for the position, I report him to you for the appointment." Captain Clawson added his full endorsement to the recommendation, and it was signed by Hoffman as commander of the brigade, and was subsequently approved on up the line. The Ordnance Department had final approval, which was granted near the end of the month.[670]

By this time, Colonel Hoffman was perhaps in receipt of an important letter dated Sept 13th from their former brigade commander, Governor William Smith. It only confirmed what Hoffman already knew, that he had very little chance of being promoted to brigadier general. "I had made nominations twice for my staff," Smith wrote, "which it seems General Early had not forwarded. But he was prompt to act, it seems, after I left, and even before I had parted with my command. I understood, in my own mind, who was at the bottom of the hasty and indelicate movement before I had any information upon the subject, but I never censured you. It was particularly indelicate of General Early, in every view, to interfere in these nominations, especially in reference to yourself, entertaining the opinion of you he did as an officer. But let all this pass and let us resolve to maintain ourselves manfully performing our duties."[671]

It seems that Hoffman may have forestalled his own promotion by trying to exert too much political pressure on General Early. With the new governor of Virginia advising to let it all pass, Hoffman had little recourse except through other political friends, and although those friends kept trying, it was to no avail. Unless the colonel could somehow convince General Early that he was the right man for the job, the promotion was never going to be made. There is no reason to believe that Jubal Early disliked Hoffman, but probably thought he was not cut out for higher military command. After all, Colonel Hoffman still had not fully mastered the manual of tactical drill.

Major James S. Kerr McCutchen was attending the legislature as a newly elected member when he wrote to Hoffman on September 15: "On yesterday I saw Judge Camden and (he) talked of visiting you soon, and thereupon I went to the book stores to get some military books to send out, but could get nothing but Jomini's *Practice of War*, and Hardee's 1st and 2nd Volumes." He forwarded the books to Hoffman, who was still rather new to the practice of war, in comparison to other, former regular army officers.[672]

On the 23rd, the men in the regiment heard more rumors about enemy movements across the river. Since all was quiet in their own sector, the 31st Virginia once more began to practice battalion drill, perhaps with Colonel Hoffman exercising his newfound knowledge from Hardee's manual.

Captain Cooper had time on his hands, and resumed his voluminous correspondence, in one day writing to W. L. Jackson, W. Arnett, Uriel Turner, Norval Lewis, O. C. Bond, Alpheus Haymond, Laban Exline, and Dr. Bland. On the 25th, Cooper received some comforting information: "Mr. Page visited us today. From him I heard good news from home. God bless those good friends who are kind to my family in my absence."[673]

On the same day, the quartermaster for the regiment, Lt. John M. Burns, was officially transferred to the 20th Virginia Cavalry. Burns had been wounded the previous year, and was slightly disabled. He'd been elected to the position of regimental quartermaster, but his wound had required some prolonged, and frequent absences. Perhaps he'd do better on a horse in Colonel W. Wiley Arnett's command: he left the regiment that day, and was replaced promptly by Captain Jacob J. Hill, the assistant quartermaster, who'd mostly been doing Burns's job anyway.[674]

The nights were clear and cold at the end of the month, with the regiment still camped near the fords of the Rapidan. On the 29th, they went on picket again at Somerville Ford. The Pioneer Corps, experts at pick and shovel, had been busy improving the defenses, establishing more sites for artillery, and enlarging the lengths of rifle pits for infantry. Across the river, it was apparent that the Federals were engaged in the same sort of thing, but despite the entrenchments, there was relative peace along the Rapidan for a few days. The 31st Virginia was relieved from picket duty on the 30th without incident.[675]

Responding to incomplete information, the regiment was sent to the river on the night of October 5, and placed in the trenches for a night of intense cold, without fires or blankets. Company C was posted on the bank of the river itself, waiting for something to develop, but the next morning the regiment was relieved by a North Carolina regiment and allowed to return to camp. It had been one more of the war's many false alarms.[676]

Three companies, B, C, and D were sent out on picket on October 7, on a wet, cold night. In the morning, Captain Cooper noted the Federals had drawn their picket post rather closer than before. "Discovering a picket post of the enemy this morning nearer our lines than our instructions permitted," he noted, "I ordered fire to be opened on it and drove them back. Colonel Coulter, Field Officer of the Day for the I Army Corps, as he called himself, came down to the river with a white handkerchief to know why it was done, and to communicate with our officers on the subject of picket firing. I sent word to camp and "Old Jubal" instructed me to tell him to keep out of range of our guns, and that the only communication that could be had was by a proper flag of truce from their commanding general."

The 31st Virginia was relieved from picket duty around 10 P.M. by a regiment from Georgia, and on returning to camp, discovered the army had moved during the previous day, about two and a half miles. On the 9th, the army moved again: this time the 31st Virginia marched with it, at sunrise, through Orange Court House, crossing the Rapidan River at Garnett's Ford, and camping in the woods after marching about eight miles in the direction of Madison Court House. They marched through Madison Court House on the following day, to the Robinson River, and towards Cedar Mountain.

"In the afternoon, the artillery and skirmishers opened in front," Cooper wrote. "Camped in a field at about an hour after dusk. The march today has been a tedious one and we have gone only about fifteen miles. Thank fortune I have a horse to ride."[677]

Colonel Hoffman received a letter from their regimental surgeon, Dr. Bland, who remained at the House of Delegates in Richmond. "General Pegram is here," Bland wrote. "Some of our friends has informed the department that if he is assigned to duty with the Fourth brigade, it will produce great dissatisfaction.... Your friends here hope that you will yet be appointed. If General Early would recommend you, there would be no difficulty." As with many of Dr. Bland's letters, the language was fairly informal. "Say to Captain Clawson his sister has just come through the lines.... Remember me to all the boys. I am very tired of Richmond. I am boarding on 5th (street), between Clay and Lee, at Mr. Chiles. Pay $125 per month, have good eating, no whiskey, whiskey has riz to $2 per drink—$45 per gallon. I did buy 1/2 gallon for $18—It's all gone."[678]

Brigadier General John Pegram arrived at Fourth Brigade headquarters on October 12 and assumed command of the brigade. Pegram was not unknown to the men of the 31st Virginia regiment. A graduate of West Point, class of 1854, he'd served in the regular army, and was a 1st lieutenant when he resigned to join the Provisional Army of Virginia. Pegram was subsequently in command of the forces on Rich Mountain that were overwhelmed in July 1861, and was taken prisoner along with most of his men, including the 25th Virginia regiment. He had come in for a great deal of criticism for the way he handled the situation on Rich Mountain, and had established himself in the eyes of the men there as less than gracious in his command style. He was not averse to telling subordinates who offered suggestions, or sometimes information concerning the enemy, to "mind their own business." As a lieutenant colonel of the Confederate army, he had insisted that his rank entitled him to command the forces on Rich Mountain, even though Colonel Heck of the 25th Virginia was there at the time. Pegram's reasoning was that a lieutenant colonel of the Confederate Army outranked a mere colonel of the Virginia volunteers. General Garnett allowed Pegram to have his way.

Following exchange as a paroled prisoner, Pegram went out west and served under General Beauregard and General Bragg, and was appointed brigadier general under General Kirby Smith in the autumn of 1862. He had combat experience at Lexington, Kentucky; Stones River; Gordon's Mills; and Chickamauga before he was transferred to the Army of Northern Virginia in the autumn of 1863.[679]

The brigade stopped at Bethlehem Church and cooked two days' rations before bedding down for the night. They marched again on the 12th, toward the Rappahannock River, passing through Jeffersonton; crossed the Hazel River at Rixeytown, and pressed onward. The Federals were withdrawing at the approach of Ewell's Corps, and the Confederates noted the presence of the abandoned Union camps as they marched past. Rumor had it that their army had captured 500 Federals in the past two days. At some point in the day, General Pegram came up with the brigade, and took command. That night, they made camp near the Rappahannock River.[680]

October 13, they pressed on to a place 2 miles beyond Warrenton, where they stopped to cook, preparing nearly a week's worth of bread, and one more day of cooked beef. There was skirmishing up ahead during the day, and when later they marched on, the regiment passed dead Federals and cavalry horses. The next day 31st Virginia marched at 4:30 A.M. and advanced to a position closer to Warrenton, where the army made a demonstration and spooked the Federals into retreating. General Ewell's corps followed toward Bristoe, the regiments going into the double quick to arrive there in time, and pitched into the Federals for an evening fight, but did not get the best of it. "The Yanks whipped a North Carolina brigade, and took a battery here today," Cooper noted.[681]

On the 15th, the regiment moved to a pine thicket, and the men cooked another day's ration of bread, and two of meat. The next day, the brigade was sent to the railroad to tear up track, and managed to destroy *nearly a mile of it* before dusk. Other brigades were doing the same sort of work that day, and altogether about 40 miles of track were torn up and the rails ruined, but the Federals would just rebuild the track.

On the 17th, they moved camp again, this time to a better site. They could hear gunfire from a skirmish going on near Manassas Junction, while rumor had it that their army had crossed Bull Run the day before. Evidently, that was far enough for General Ewell—they turned around the next morning and began marching back to the Rappahannock River. They stopped to camp near the river, and were hit by a tremendous storm of cold rain and hail on the 19th. Expecting the Federals to appear at any moment, the brigade went on picket on October 20 at a destroyed railroad bridge over the river, and were even reinforced by Steuart's brigade on the 21st, but the threat never materialized. The 31st Virginia was relieved from picket duty on the 22nd.[682]

Colonel Hoffman and his nephew, Lt. Thomas Hoffman were granted a leave of absence for a couple of days on October 22 to visit an uncle. While Hoffman was gone, Captain Cooper was in command of the regiment. The army had decided that the iron from the railroad track they had destroyed across the river would be useful, and had begun sending teams of wagons across to try to bring the iron back, but the Federals drove the wagons and guards back over the river on the 22nd and 23rd. On the 24th, the regiment had orders to march at dawn, at the head of the brigade. They ran the Federals back from the railroad and held them off long enough for 100 wagons and teams to cross: the iron was gathered and brought back to the Confederate side of the river, and the brigade returned to camp. They were ordered to cross the river again on the 26th, this time to support some of General Johnson's division, which had also gone over the river to gather iron.[683]

Earlier in the day on October 26, the examination of Captain William P. Cooper had begun to determine his competency for holding the office of major in the 31st Virginia. Cooper gave three hours of testimony to the board of inquiry that morning, but the proceedings were interrupted by the brigade being called out for an alarm. On the morning of the 27th, the examination board continued with six hours of testimony from Cooper that day, and more from him on tactics on the following morning. The board then heard testimony against Cooper, from Captains Harding, Lyman, Phillips, and Lieutenant McNemar. Lt. Blair, Major Haymond, Dr. Buttermore, and Colonel Hoffman gave supporting testimony. The examinations and statements were lengthy— Hoffman finished his testimony on October 31st, and afterward told Cooper that he was very confidant that the board would have a finding in Cooper's favor.[684]

On Sunday, November 1, the brigade moved its camp to a small woods two miles above Brandy Station. The men began building their winter cabins, but had not gotten very far when the brigade was ordered out on picket duty. The brigade was ordered to detail 500 men to dig entrenchments near the railroad bridge over the Rappahannock River; the rest of the brigade were ordered to stand by, armed, to protect them in case the Federals came up to skirmish. Colonel Hoffman was placed in command of the brigade, since General Pegram was serving as President of a Court Martial Board.

They marched to the railroad bridge on the 2nd: and the 31st Virginia was sent out as guards on picket post, within sight of the Federal pickets across the river. On the 4th, the brigade was relieved from picket and engineering duty and marched back to camp. Back at camp, some men had been left behind working on the winter cabins. They found a lot of timber had been cut in their absence, and the logs hauled.

The cabins were not large structures. For instance, Captain Cooper was planning to build a cabin ten feet by ten feet on the inside, "Which will be a snug little residence for four of us this winter," he noted after returning to camp. The men worked at cabin building on the 5th and 6th, by which time they had the walls erected and canvas roofs overhead on some of the structures.[685]

The Fourth brigade received a new assistant surgeon on November 6. Dr. Archibold Atkinson, Jr. was 31 years old, from Smithfield, in Isle of Wight County. He had served briefly with an artillery unit from his home county at the start of the war, but then had transferred to the cavalry for a more active service. Serving in the Wise Legion, which later became the 10th Virginia cavalry, Atkinson experienced the war in western Virginia. His ability to treat the sick and wounded was hampered by the unceasing movement of the cavalry, and decided to look for a better situation. Having a friend who was assistant quartermaster in the Fourth brigade, Capt. James H. Boughan of the 13th Virginia, Dr. Atkinson applied for transfer to Pegram's brigade. [686]

"I had not been assigned to any special regiment in the brigade," Atkinson wrote after the war, "so that soon after I had reported, Colonel Hoffman—then in command of the brigade and Colonel of the 31st Virginia—asked me to give especial attention to his regiment, which had no surgeon.... Dr. Buttermore was the assistant surgeon, and the men had very little confidence in his skill."

Atkinson was impressed with the 31st Virginia's reputation. "The 31st Virginia infantry regiment did itself great credit in the fight at Port Republic over the north fork of the Shenandoah river, where Turner Ashby was killed. It always made itself well heard from, for the men were brave, and the officers very trustworthy."

Hoffman and Atkinson seemed to strike up a good working relationship. Long after the war, when Atkinson wrote of his experiences and the people he knew in the course of serving in the Confederate army, he still seemed to hold Colonel Hoffman with some respect—as well as with some keenly pointed criticism. "Colonel Hoffman was a brave man, but he was near sighted," Atkinson recalled. "Men with defective eyes should not attempt to lead men in battle. General Pegram was near sighted, also. I have known Col. Hoffman to lead his brigade almost into the Yankee's, mistaking them for Confederates until the men would tell him of his misconception. You had to fight in woods, in bush, behind hills, and in every way, and the vision was not always the clearest. I have seen men from 200 to 500 yards away, and I could not know from the color of their clothes to which side they belonged. I would judge from the relative positions only. Many mistakes occurred from just this failure to distinguish friend from foe.

"Col. Hoffman had the reputation of being a great land lawyer, but in many of the affairs which concern us in the common mundane routine of life he was mentally slothful. He tried to be a disciplinarian but he did not know how to control, or to handle men. He became judge afterwards, and an able one I am told.

"He was fond of me, and tried to indulge me in *his own stumbling way*. If you asked him a favor, he would want to know if it was mentioned in the regulations, so after I had been a while with him, I took things in my own hand, or if I wanted anything, I went to Gen. Pegram, who commanded the brigade."[687]

With the addition of Dr. Atkinson to the brigade staff, Smith Buttermore of the 31st Virginia felt this was a good time for a furlough to replace some items in his wardrobe. He wrote from the regiment's camp near Culpeper Court House, on the 7th, requesting a leave of absence for fifteen days, "To go to Staunton, Va. to purchase myself some clothing suitable for the weather, which I need very much, and cannot obtain in camp. I will take the liberty to state I have been with this regiment on duty since 1861 and have never had a leave of indulgence. There is a surgeon with the Regiment."

Buttermore's wife was in Staunton then, having come over the mountains from western Virginia, and no doubt he wanted to see her. Colonel Hoffman approved the request and forwarded it, but for some reason Buttermore's furlough was denied by General Pegram. The surgeon would have to do without, or else find another way to obtain his new suit of clothes.[688]

He was not the only one in the army who was short on clothing, or food: this was a time of many hardships. Jubal Early noted after the war that the army was "now very much straightened for provisions, especially for meat, of which they were sometimes devoid for days at a time."

They were not short on activity on the Rappahannock River. On November 7, a Federal raid assaulted the picket line at the railroad bridge. Entrenchments had been dug on the opposite side of the river, and were occupied that day by a regiment from Hays's brigade. General Early received notice of the problem when a dispatch arrived from Colonel Penn of Hays's brigade, reporting the enemy advancing on his position at the river. The general responded by ordering all available men to march at once for the river. At the time, most of the men were out cutting timber for the cabins, or were in the process of building them. It took General Early a little while to gather a force of men, including part of the 31st Virginia under Captain Cooper, who was in camp working on the chimney for his cabin when the order came to march at once. Cooper put down his trowel and picked up his arms and marched with his men.

Colonel Hoffman caught up with Cooper and the regiment before they reached the river. Cooper was on foot because the horses had been turned out to pasture, but Hoffman evidently was mounted.[689]

General Early rode ahead to look over the situation, and while en route met a messenger from their picket at the railroad bridge. The

Federals were in line of battle, evidently prepared to move against the entrenchments held by Hays's brigade. There were also indications the Federals would try to cross farther up the river, at Kelley's Ford with a wagon train and a line of ambulances. Before long, General Lee caught up with Early and they went on toward the river, arriving a little after three in the afternoon.

General Early crossed over to the north side of the river and met with Colonel Penn, in command of the regiment holding the entrenchments there. Penn had his skirmishers out in front of his position, and a little to either side. They were facing a heavy force of Federal skirmishers who were slowly, and carefully advancing. The Federal line was formed about a mile away, supported by artillery.

Early withdrew across the river to report to General Lee. Not long after, Federal skirmishers began to push the Confederate skirmishers back to their entrenchments on the north side of the river. Some of the Federals came up to the river itself and were threatening to flank the Confederate position on the river.

General Hays arrived at four o'clock and took command of his brigade, and then more of Early's division began to arrive at the river to reinforce Hays. Hoke's brigade was sent across the river, to the entrenchments, while Gordon's brigade was positioned on Jamison's Hill, overlooking the bridge. Pegram's brigade was placed in reserve to the rear of that hill, to protect the men from artillery shells. The 31st Virginia was sent to occupy the entrenchments on the right, at the south end of the bridge. A cold wind was blowing as the daylight faded. The men had been dressed for working on their cabins when called to march to the river—they were not prepared for a night out in the elements. Captain Cooper noted they about froze while posted in the trenches that night.

The night became more interesting. Not long after they took position there, Federal artillery opened on them with a crossing fire, while a battery directly in front of the bridge joined in with more direct fire on the entrenchment's on the north side of the river. The wind was blowing stiffly from the south, and the sound of the artillery, as well as the ripple tear sound of small arms was blown back toward the Federals, making it difficult for Generals Early and Lee to hear what was going on as darkness fell on the Rappahannock.

General Lee believed it was too late for the enemy to try anything serious that night, and told General Early he was going to retire for the evening. Shortly after this, Early's aide, Major Hale, returned from across the river and reported the Federals were advancing. His report was followed quickly with a report that Hays's brigade was being driven from the trenches.

Early ordered the remainder of Pegram's brigade to move up to the south side of the railroad bridge, and also ordered his artillery to prepare to engage the enemy. Hays had narrowly escaped capture, but most of his brigade was captured, and Hoke's brigade was cut off from the river. The Federals were on the north end of the bridge itself. Pegram's brigade was sent to hold the south end of the bridge, and Gordon's brigade brought up in their rear, as reserve.

The Confederates could not use their artillery against the Federals in the darkness, for fear of hitting Hoke's brigade, and the 5th and 7th Louisiana regiments of Hays's brigade, who were prisoners by this time. General Early waited until he was certain that none of his men had avoided capture on the other side of the river, and then ordered the bridge to be set on fire, to deny it to the enemy. Volunteers from Pegram's brigade made their way onto the bridge. Some men went down to the river near its base in the darkness, while under fire from Federal sharpshooters. They managed to set it on fire, and burn enough of it to make it unlikely to be used by the Federals in trying to force a crossing.[690]

Around three in the morning of the 8th, General Early began withdrawing troops from the south side of the destroyed railroad bridge. They marched back to the camp, and quickly assembled their baggage, and then marched directly for Culpeper Court House. "The freeze last night affected my rheumatic knee," Captain Cooper noted later in the day, "so that I left the regiment to go to the wagon train with Criss and Blankensop. Couldn't find it and camped near the division command train." By the time he caught up with the regiment on November 9, it was already making camp near Somerville Ford, at their old campsite on the Rapidan River. Snow was falling heavily, and the temperature had plunged.

"Our quarters here are very uncomfortable, on a cold, bleak naked point," Cooper noted the following day. There was very little wood for the men's fires, and what they could obtain had to be hauled a long distance. "How I wish for the cabin I was getting so nicely fixed up at Brandy Station," Cooper grumbled, but he had good news on November 8, when he learned that the Board of Examiners had reported favorably on his competence to become major of the 31st Virginia, but the report had yet to be sent up to headquarters for approval.[691]

Shoes were hard to find in Lee's army that late autumn of 1863. The need was so pressing that on November 11, General Ewell issued an order: "As there is great difficulty in procuring shoes of proper sizes, Division Commanders will cause all shoemakers in their respective commands to be put to work at once, making and repairing shoes while in camp. They will be relieved from duty and kept constantly employed under the supervision of the officers, but will be required to participate in all engagements. Details will be forwarded for proper parties to go for leather, tools, etc."

The shoemakers were paid six dollars per pair of shoes, and that extra money would be useful for poor soldiers and their families.

Suddenly, it was popular to be a shoemaker, and from the number of men in the regiment who became engaged in this occupation, it seems that some were quick learners.[692]

Other shortages were not as critical, and yet were vexing. Lieutenant Thomas W. Hoffman, their adjutant, was having difficulties finding over shirts. He had several people in Richmond looking out for them at reasonable prices, but as a friend reported from the quarter masters office in Richmond, the over shirts were only for privates, and would not be sold by the clothing office to officers. The price for them in private stores was fifty dollars each.

The Virginia legislature adjourned, and Major McCutchen returned to the regiment, leaving behind Dr. William Bland, who was sick with a debilitating case of dysentery. Bland wrote to Lt. Hoffman from there, noting that he had been confined to bed for ten days, but was beginning to recover. "Richmond is a horrid place to be sick in, yet I ought not to complain. The family I board with… have been very kind to me. If I had been at a hotel I would have died."[693]

The 31st Virginia went on picket duty on November 11, under Major McCutchen. "I am quite lame, I remained in camp," Captain Cooper wrote from camp "Had a terrible time, the wind blowing the fire about so we had to put it out and freeze."

Returning from picket duty the following day, the field officers were busy with paperwork, making out clothing reports, the ordnance report, payrolls, and approvals for furloughs. The regiment's baggage came up from the division baggage train, but was sent back on the 14th, even though the regiments were in their winter quarters. This was, perhaps, an indication that General Early felt their position was either temporary, or threatened by the Federals. Certainly, the men wanted some of their personal possessions and minor comforts for the winter camp, but no one wanted the baggage to be destroyed by the enemy.[694]

The regiment went on picket again on the 16th, with Federal pickets visible across the river. They were relieved the next day by the 49th Virginia. The weather remained cold, and rainy, but the 31st Virginia went back on picket once more on November 22, relieving the 58th Virginia, and remained there on duty at the river until the 24th. Company C was posted at the Hume house, which had been their post on the previous picket duty. They found the Federals much more heavily reinforced on the other side of the river, but all seemed quiet, and there were no incidents between the pickets on those two days.[695]

On the 24th, the findings in Lieutenant Bruffey's courts martial case were announced in Bruffey's favor—he was cleared of the responsibility for repaying the government the wages he had collected as an officer. Bruffey would later attempt to resign from the regiment, choosing to serve elsewhere through the course of the war, as he said on his petition to transfer, but the resignation was not accepted until 1864.

The 31st Virginia was relieved from picket duty by the 49th Virginia and returned to camp on the morning of November 24. President Jefferson Davis planned to review Ewell's Corps that day, but heavy rain forced the review to be postponed. The brigade had marched as far as Moss Neck by the time the review was canceled. Pegram's brigade turned around in the pouring rain and began to march back toward Sommerville Ford, stopping that evening along the road to camp. To get off the road, the men crossed over a ditch swollen with runoff and tried as best they could to make camp during a downpour.

"In about half hour the men of the entire command were asleep, fatigued by their long march," Surgeon Atkinson wrote after the war. He had been riding with Colonel Hoffman that day. "I told the Colonel if he would favor me by sharing my couch for the night, I would make a gilt edge bed of leaves for us. I knew I should have to rake up quite a pile of the top leaves before I could get enough dry ones to form the top layer, and that he would never take the trouble to do so. I told him to build a fire leaving it to his good sense to build it away from the wind. I got my leaves together, and kept them in place by laying two short poles at the head and two longer ones at the sides. Then I spread the oilcloths on the leaves and then a blanket.

"We ate our cold supper of biscuits and boiled beef left from breakfast and a drink of water was our greatest need just then. I went off to look for some, and finding the ditch we had crossed shortly before, I filled our canteens, having drunk what I wanted.... Whilst I was away our bed of leaves took fire and the Colonel had much ado to save it." Hoffman had built the fire upwind from the bed and the burning embers had blown onto the leaves.[696]

On the 25th, orders arrived for Pegram's brigade to prepare to march at a moment's notice. Artillery was firing somewhere up the river, but as darkness fell, and no further orders arrived, the men were allowed to unpack a few things and settle down to sleep. The Union army seemed to be preparing itself for a campaign of some kind, and the Confederates were readying themselves to respond. They heard more artillery down the river on the 26th, and received orders to pack up and be ready to march. Rations were cooked and issued to the men, while over the river they watched part of a Federal wagon train, and some artillery, chased off the road by Confederate artillery.

This began the 31st Virginia's actions in the Mine Run campaign. The Federal army had crossed over the river further down stream, and General Mead's forces were seriously encroaching on Confederate territory. On November 27, the Fourth brigade under General Pegram marched on the Wilderness Road, or Old Turnpike, from Orange Court House toward Fredericksburg. "Formed line below Verdiersville—seven miles from Rapidan and Rappahannock," Captain Cooper wrote that day. "Enemy all round—made breastworks."[697]

The next day, the brigade was relieved from the breastworks and took a position two miles away in a pine thicket. In the afternoon, the regiment was marched a little ways and put into a line of battle in the woods, to protect an artillery battery in their front. The Federals shelled the battery, but the 31st Virginia came through unhurt, perhaps because they made some more breastworks in the afternoon to shelter behind. In the night, they marched toward Zoor Church, and camped.

On the 29th, Cooper discovered they were near the Vaux Cluse gold mine. "A long line of breastworks and battery fortifications have been made, leading from the river south," Cooper noted their position. The 31st Virginia was once again protecting artillery batteries, which were positioned on either end of the line. On the 30th, around nine o'clock in the morning, the artillery opened with a brisk fire, but the exchange stopped after a while and the men remained in their entrenchments. At some point in the day, Major McCutchen departed for Richmond: the legislature was back in session and McCutchen was preparing bills for consideration.[698]

"Received orders to be ready to move half an hour before daylight," Captain Cooper noted on December 1. "Marched some distance along the fortifications to the right and then returned. Bitter cold morning. Very quiet and cold today. Smoke excessive again." At three o'clock in the morning, December 2, their brigade was marched to the extreme right of the line, as part of Ewell's Corps, while Hill's Corps moved to the left to flank the Union army. They discovered the Federals had withdrawn in the darkness: Lee's army set out in pursuit, and followed the Union army to Germana Ford, and then past the Wilderness gold mine, but they gave up the chase in the morning. "Returned and camped near fortifications at about 9 A.M.," Cooper noted. "This has been a long and hard day's work."

The regiment marched at daylight on December 3 to a position near Somerville Ford, where the men were ordered to make shelters for themselves. They set to work gathering pine logs for cabins, but were interrupted with orders to go on picket in the morning. They relieved the 58th Virginia on picket the next morning with part of the regiment held in reserve. Captain Cooper, in command of the reserve, was ordered to bring the reserve up to the line after dark. "The enemy has advanced his posts during our absence," Cooper noted. "We fire on some of them, hitting one man (in front of) Captain Phillips' company."[699]

In the night, a work party was sent out to gather some logs to build a raft with which they could cross part of the regiment over the river. Finding the raft unable to carry the men, about 50 volunteers waded across the icy river in the dark and attacked the Federal picket, running them back from the river. They were supported in this by part of the 58th Virginia. "Five wagons came down and brought over some blacksmith's tools and forges, and building materials," Cooper wrote.

Relieved on picket by the 49th Virginia, the regiment returned to camp and went to work on their cabins, no doubt finding the tools they had captured the night before of some use. There was a shortage of pine logs at this position, however, and the cabins were less well built in consequence. The regiment remained in camp through the 11th, with the men working on the winter shelters.[700]

Captain Cooper's promotion to major of the 31st Virginia had been announced in Richmond on December 5, but was not received at their camp until December 12. Cooper was to take rank from August 1, 1863, the date of Alfred Jackson's death. He noted the arrival of the good news with a distinct lack of enthusiasm, for it caused tremendous amounts of trouble in the regiment.[701]

Thirteen of the 31st Virginia's company officers wrote resignations in protest, all giving essentially the same reason: they would not serve under Major William P. Cooper. Those officers were: Captains Lyman, Harding, Clawson, and Phillips of companies B, F, I, and K; Lieutenants Kincaid and Pullen (Co. B), Wilson and Long (Co. F), McNemar, Bruffey and Bradley (Co. I), Bryon (Co. K), and Stewart (Co. C), the last being from Cooper's own company. Colonel Hoffman was faced with a crisis in leadership that had been simmering for a long time.

Once before, in the autumn of the preceding year, the men of the regiment had driven one of their staff officers, Major James C. Arbogast to resign. Cooper had a thicker hide. Newspaper men of his day were accustomed to enduring hostile reactions on the controversial subjects of the day. Cooper was perhaps the best-equipped man in the regiment to receive the hostile opinion of his fellow officers, and the men who protested against his appointment may have failed to recognize this. After all, they had gotten their way with Major Arbogast in 1862.

W. R. Lyman later wrote, "Resigned from the infantry service because of the promotion to major of a man who had flanked out of every real fight we had, and who had overstayed a leave of absence covering our campaign in Pennsylvania, and come back under President Davis's amnesty proclamation." This was not accurate, at least in regard to Cooper's leave of absence during the Gettysburg campaign. The animosity between Cooper and Lyman was evidently extreme by this time.[702]

Colonel Hoffman was troubled by the protest over Cooper's promotion. Hoffman considered himself not only a fair man, but also one who went by the letter and spirit of the law. Though he and Cooper were longtime associates, it is doubtful if Hoffman would have forwarded Cooper's name for promotion had he seen anything wrong in it. It must have wounded Hoffman to discover that his own judgment in approving Cooper's appointment was not sufficient for the officers of the regiment. He did not back down, however, although he did try to smooth the troubled water.

The protest was supposedly based on Captain Clawson's claim to seniority, but that question had already been decided in Cooper's favor by the adjutant general's office. Nathan Clawson was clearly not the ringleader of the protest, although he was one of the thirteen officers who submitted resignations that day. It became evident that several officers in particular did not like Cooper, and were willing to cause trouble within the regiment via their resignations. Colonel Hoffman held the resignations for several days before forwarding them. Perhaps the officers would come to their senses.

On December 13, Cooper wrote in his journal, "I saw a letter from Major Watkins, Recorder of the Examining Board, to Col. Hoffman stating that I, 'Passed a very creditable examination and that in point of tactical knowledge and administrative ability, I compared favorably with officers of the Army of the same grade,' and of course I was much gratified."

WINTER CAMP 1864

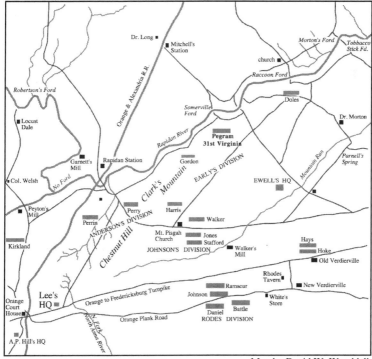

Map by David W. Wooddell

The regiment went on picket on December 14 and found the Federals had established their picket posts farther back from the river than before. They were on picket through the 15th and returned to camp December 16, after being relieved once again by the 49th Virginia. Back at camp, Major Cooper was allowed to move into the field officer's cabin that he would share with Colonel Hoffman and Lt. Col McCutchen.[703]

"Take up my quarters with Colonel Hoffman," Cooper wrote on the 16th. "Fix me up a nice bunk and I think we shall get along very comfortably and agreeably together."[704]

In response to the protest by the officers over Cooper's appointment as major, Colonel Hoffman wrote a lengthy statement on the back of Captain Lyman's resignation, explaining the trail of events that led to the crisis. Hoffman was clearly embarrassed at having thirteen of his officers resign at the same time. Hoffman's comments were forwarded on December 17 to brigade headquarters for General Pegram's approval. From Pegram it was bumped up to General Early, and then to General Ewell and General Lee.

After summarizing the chain of events concerning the claim of seniority, Hoffman wrote, "I had never heard any officer now in the regiment express dissatisfaction with Capt. Cooper, or dissatisfaction of his promotion. Soon after, most—not all, of the company officers of the regiment forwarded a protest against the promotion of Capt. Cooper, making charges. It was disapproved and forwarded by Major McCutchen. I made an endorsement of facts and forwarded it. It was returned with an endorsement made at the headquarters of the Army that Capt. Cooper be called before an examining board with reference to these charges.

"Accordingly he was called before the board appointed at the Army HQ for the Brigade. The testimony of as many of the protestants as were deemed material and of the witnesses called by Capt. Cooper as well, and a thorough examination was made. The Board honorably acquitted Capt. Cooper of all the charges except one, to which they attached no animosity, and found him qualified for the majority. The finding was forwarded and Capt. Cooper was promoted Major. At notice of the promotion... Capt. Lyman and several other company officers tendered their resignations. I herewith forward a copy of the protest, and the finding of the Board, in order to present the whole subject to the highest officers."[705]

Brigadier General John Pegram, their brigade commander, noted his approval on January 1, 1864: "Respectfully forwarded, with the recommendation that Capt. Lyman's resignation be accepted, as he is the leader of a move which in my judgment is highly prejudicial to the interests of the service." A few days later, on January 5, General Ewell's response was added to the back of Lyman's letter of resignation. The General was not inclined to accept this kind of behavior in his troops, and wrote, "I follow General Pegram's example in this affair, as he is probably more immediately acquainted with the circumstances and the officer's qualifications than I am, though my first impulse was to recommend the acceptance of all of the resignations and then conscription of the officers!"

In the end, Captain Lyman's resignation was approved as of February 3, 1864, but was not announced for some days afterward. When he was at last allowed to leave the regiment, Lyman immediately joined the Heavy Artillery, serving as a captain.

Another of the officers allowed to resign at this time was Captain Joseph F. Harding, of Company F. His resignation, also written on December 12, ran along the same lines as that of Captain Lyman. "My reason for so doing," Harding wrote, "is the appointment...of a man whom I cannot respect nor trust as a superior officer, feeling that it will be impossible for one to discharge the duties of a subordinate officer in an agreeable manner. I much prefer to serve in the ranks as a private soldier." If General Ewell had followed his inclination, Harding would have gone back in the ranks as *a conscripted private*.

Colonel Hoffman approved Harding's resignation, but held the letter until he had a response from headquarters on Lyman's resignation. On February 5, Hoffman appended the following note to Harding's resignation: "Most of the facts material to the considerations of this subject have been before the officers above me and I suppose are of accord with the tender of Captain Lyman's resignation, which I presume has been accepted." By then, however, Captain Harding had gotten himself into even deeper waters, as Hoffman also informed General Pegram. There was more to the situation than just a disagreement over who was going to be major, as would develop 1864.

Through the course of the next few months, as the controversy simmered and the response of the brigade and division headquarters was awaited, the officers continued to serve. Of the thirteen who submitted resignations on that December day, all but two remained in the regiment. After the two ringleaders, Lyman and Harding, were allowed to go on to other endeavors, the regiment seems to have settled down to its usual affairs. Nathan Clawson continued as he was, commanding Company I, and occasionally commanding the regiment when he found himself the senior officer present.

Meanwhile, on December 17, Colonel Hoffman was once again urgently called away from the regiment to assist the advocate general's office with a court case. Colonel Hoffman may not have been a skilled military leader, but when it came to the law he was still one of the best in the state. Throughout the war, Hoffman was repeatedly called away from the regiment to make available his expertise in the law. It was fairly shortsighted on the part of some of his feisty captains to try to get the best of their colonel in the law, or where army regulations were concerned. Hoffman's lack of zeal for drill perhaps had fooled them into thinking he didn't know the rest of the army's code.[706]

Major Cooper was in command of the regiment when he wrote to his wife, December 18, no doubt wanting to tell her the good news of his promotion. The following day the oath of office as major in the 31st Virginia was administered to Cooper by Thomas Davis, who was a Justice of the Peace from Harrison County.[707]

The 31st Virginia had been without its own chaplain for some months, following the resignation of Rev. S. H. Mullens in March 1863. On December 19, Rev. James Lepps, a Presbyterian minister preached to the regiment. From Parkersburg originally, Rev. Lepps had been living at New Creek, in Augusta County before being assigned to Ewell's Corps. Lepps was subsequently assigned to the 31st Virginia as chaplain and turned out to be a good preacher for the men, teaching many of the illiterate ones how to read and write.[708]

Winter camp had more than its share of difficulties for the 31st Virginia that year. On December 20, Private Aaron Rowan, of Company I, was charged with stealing rations of beef from the quarters of Private Henry C. Stewart. Rowan was found guilty of the charge, as he had been caught in the act, and was sentenced to march in front of the regiment, "with a placard upon his back with the word *"thief"* written thereon, at such time and place as the commanding officer may direct."[709]

Cooper continued in command of the regiment, with Hoffman assisting the judge advocate's office, and Lt. Colonel McCutchen also still in Richmond. Cooper noted that banditry was becoming common on the roads in the area, with one of the regiment's men, Hamilton Young, robbed near Orange Court House. "Almost every night somebody is waylaid," Cooper wrote on the 22nd.

Part of the regiment was sent on picket on December 24, with Cooper in command. They relieved the 58th Virginia and settled down for Christmas on the picket line, the air bitterly cold. With a report of movement across the river, Cooper increased his guard to watch over the frozen river. "No enemy made appearance other than the usual picket," Cooper wrote that day. "This is not so Merry a Christmas as some I have spent."[710]

December 26, he noted, "Relieved by Colonel Hoffman with a detail of one company of twenty men from each of the five regiments in the brigade." The regiment had received some boxes for the men, which were waiting for them at Orange Court House. Sending men to pick up the boxes and bring them to camp in the rain, Cooper discovered that one of the boxes was from their friends, the ladies of Fisherville, in Augusta County, with an assortment of provisions for the men of the 31st Virginia.

They had a visit from General Pegram on the 29th, and on the 30th the regiment was inspected. Colonel Hoffman mustered the regiment on the last day of the year, a very wet, muddy, and cold December 31st. The number of men present and fit for duty at this time was very small. For instance, there were 25 men present in Company C; 19 men present in Company D; 24 men present in Company E; and 27 men present in Company K.

An election had been held the previous day in Company C, with the men electing Joshua Radabaugh as their 2nd lieutenant, and electing James Blair captain from 1st lieutenant to replace Cooper. "1863 has been an eventful year to the writer, though in hardships and dangers, it has been nothing as compared with 1862," Cooper noted in his journal. The regiment was going to need every man for the coming campaign of 1864, and they were all going to need luck to survive the next year.[711]

1864 began for Colonel Hoffman with additional reasons for the veteran politician to rue the endless political and legal maneuvering of some of his officers. At their camp near Somerville Ford, the usual winter quarters had been built to protect the soldiers from winter's chill winds, but a stable was needed for the officer's horses. Accordingly, Hoffman ordered Captain Harding to detail a party of men for the work.

Aroused over what he called the impropriety of having the men build stables for officer's horses, Harding refused to detail the men for the task. Harding told the enlisted men that they had to build stables for government-owned horses, if there were any, but that they did not have to build stables for privately owned horses. Nearly all the horses ridden by the officers and staff of the regiment were privately owned, as that was standard in the Confederate army (unlike the Union army which provided horses for its officers.)

This was rebellion outright, and a legal dilemma for Colonel Hoffman. For the moment he seemed snared by the small legal trap. From the chain of events, it is clear that the trap became most dangerous to Harding himself, especially when the matter reached General Pegram at Headquarters of the Fourth brigade. Pegram was not a lawyer. He was a military officer and he expected obedience, not legal wrangling.

Captain Harding's timing for his little rebellion was not so good. An acting inspector from division headquarters happened to be present on the 13th when Harding raised his legal barrier. The Inspector told Hoffman that he would check at once if it was proper for the Colonel to detail men to work on stables for the officer's horses. In the meantime, Hoffman suspended any action regarding Harding or the enlisted men who had refused to work on the detail.

"Even though *I* suppose it unquestionable that the service required stables for the private horses in use, and its exigencies required that the men should build them," Hoffman reported to division headquarters, "I was indisposed to require any to do this duty against their will, and if I anticipated any trouble, would greatly have preferred to employ someone to do the work. Constituted as our army is, I regard it a very high duty on the part of officers to try any proper means to protect their men against abuse. I dislike exceedingly to make an issue of an officer against the alleged rights of his men... I would therefore gladly be spared the necessity of taking any action in this case, which discipline does not imperatively demand...."

Colonel Hoffman was not allowed that luxury, however: the response from General Pegram was hard and to the point.: "Brigadier General Pegram directs that you place Captain Harding in arrest by his order, and prefer charges against the privates for disobedience of orders, as he is of the opinion you have a perfect right to detail men for building stables."[712]

Colonel Hoffman had perhaps anticipated additional rebellion from his officers. On January 5, he wrote to Colonel R. H. Chilton, the Chief of Staff, asking for clarification on a point of law concerning courts-martial: "Paragraph 878 of the Army Regulations, which requires that proceedings of Regimental Courts-martial be transmitted to department Headquarters for supervision, is, I presume, beyond question unsuited to the present Army Organization, and I believe is generally disregarded; and yet it in terms remains in force, and leaves no power in the Commandant of the Regiment who ordered the court to act on the case. I would inquire whether the article is to be complied with, or the Commandant of the Regiment is at once to decide and order on the proceedings."

The reply came from Lt. General H. E. Young, of the judge advocate's staff: "The Sentence of a Regimental Courts-martial are confirmed and executed or mitigated or remitted by the Regiment's Commander. After he has acted on them, he forwards them for "supervision" only to Dept. Headquarters. By Order of General Lee." This interpretation gave Hoffman legal basis for using his own discretion in dealing with his obstructionist officers and men.[713]

Meanwhile, the occasional discharge of men with disabilities continued to reduce the regiment one man at a time. Christian Kuhl, Sergeant of Company D, was in command of his company on January 16 when Private Elam Gough was discharged from the army. Gough had been disabled in one arm by a gunshot wound at the battle of Port Republic in June 1862, and the broken bone had not healed, leaving him unable to do service since that time. Carried on the books of the company from then until January 1864, he was at last discharged after spending most of his war in hospitals. Before the war, Elam Gough had been a shoemaker by trade, but would find difficult times with only one arm.[714]

In order to replace the inevitable losses in the regiment, attempts were made to locate deserters and have them brought back to the regiment. Desertion by men who wandered away from the army to go home, or to join another regiment, had plagued the army from the start of the war. Accordingly, Washington W. Hevener was reported by Colonel Hoffman to the Conscript Office in Richmond as a deserter, with the information that the deserter would be found in the 62nd Regiment of General Imboden's brigade.

Washington W. Hevener was from Highland County, and was described as a ruddy-faced farmer, 23 years old, who had enlisted in March of 1862, but had deserted almost immediately and had later joined the 62nd Virginia. He preferred serving in the mountains along the border, and had not bothered with permissions and all of the paperwork; he simply transferred himself to Imboden's command. An order for Hevener's arrest was sent out on January 25. When caught, he would be returned to the 31st Virginia for punishment.[715]

The same day, a similar order was sent out for the arrest of James H. P. Wright, who was believed to have deserted the 31st Virginia Infantry for the 18th Virginia Cavalry, also of Imboden's command. On February 8, orders were sent regarding George Wilfong and Jacob Taylor, both from Pocahontas County, who were also to be found serving in the 62nd Virginia. Taylor and Wilfong were still on the roles of the 31st Virginia's Company G.[716]

The soldiers who deserted to serve with Imboden's command were not the only ones who were longing to be closer to their homes: most of the regiment continued to prefer service closer to West Virginia, where they might have a chance of reclaiming their homes from the Federals. Once again, the men wished to write a petition requesting that the regiment be transferred to the mountains. The petition was written, the men signed, and Colonel Hoffman forwarded it up the chain of command: he knew that the chances were slim that the 31st Virginia would be transferred anywhere. They were part of the division, and like it or not, that is where they would stay for many months to come.

"I am fully aware of the deep rooted desire of the men of this regiment existing from the first year of the war to the present to serve in the mountains near their homes," Hoffman wrote, on January 26, 1864 in his forwarding remarks. "While I am confident that they will fight well wherever they may be, if assigned they (will be) next to invincible in an immediate struggle to defend their homes. I concur in the opinion that if the regiment was on the border with the assurance that it would be allowed to remain there, it would recruit very considerably; while on the other hand, if it remains east of the Blue Ridge, I almost despair of an increase in its numbers. For the measure suggested, weighing other considerations, I earnestly approve the application if it be deemed that by granting it the public will be served as well as otherwise, and respectfully forward it."[717]

Major Cooper's statement, dated two days later, included the observation, "Since troops must be employed in keeping the enemy in check in that section, they claim the privilege of the service, and I hope it will not be found prejudicial to the service to grant the request." Thomas W. Hoffman, Adjutant of the 31st Virginia, and Smith Buttermore, Assistant Surgeon, added their endorsement to Cooper's letter.[718]

The petition was submitted with the signatures of the officers and men in the 31st Virginia. In particular, the officers were careful to endorse the petition, perhaps to prevent any doubt over the propriety of the men taking this on themselves, or any view of mutiny or threat of mass desertion. The officers prefaced the petition: "In view of the movement now being made by the enlisted men of this regiment looking to their transfer to North Western Virginia for future operations, we desire to assure the Department of our cordial approval of the object of the memorial, and to call attention to some facts bearing on the case, not thereon stated. We can not recruit the regiment while it remains in this army. Even while last spring, temporarily in North Western Virginia, comparatively few were added to this regiment because *it was* believed we would be ordered back here: while new companies were readily organized for service in those commands thought to be permanently assigned to that section. And indeed we are compelled to believe that there will be a depletion in our numbers unless some such action as that urged is taken, and this we cannot but contemplate with deep regret.

"Our regiment has so nobly stood together on the muddy battle fields of Virginia; has been so free from straggling and desertion, that we desire to have no effort untried to preserve its present strength and effectiveness. So deeply rooted is the prejudice in favor of service in the North West, that we fear many brave men at the expiration of their present term will be led into action that will cause trouble to themselves and the public service, and injury to the good name of the Regiment."

The arms-bearing enlisted men who were present signed by companies, with witnesses present and endorsing the validity of the signatures. The list of signatures, dated January 23, 1864, shows 305 men present in the 31st Virginia's camp, and was considered the regiment's effective strength on that day. It including 284 enlisted men, 17 company officers, and 4 field officers. The sizes of the companies ranged from 13 men, in Company D, to 45 men in Company B.

The response from the army was not unanticipated. General Pegram and General Ewell denied the request. On January 29, 1864,

General Lee noted, "I can understand the desire of the regiment to return to their homes. It has fought well and faithfully..." Praise was one thing, but the requirements of the army came before sentiment. Infantry was needed for the spring campaign, General Lee wrote: the request by the 31st Virginia was denied.[719]

10

WILDERNESS AND SPOTSYLVANIA
Feb. 1864 – June 1864

Rotating picket duty at Somerville Ford, taking their turn along with the brigade, occupied the men of the 31st Virginia through the winter of 1864. Most times, it was uneventful, although in early February they were engaged in one skirmish with the Federals. The 31st Virginia had just returned to camp from picket duty when the men were called back into the ranks by the long roll of the drum. They marched to Mountain Ford at the double-quick. The Union army had crossed and was pushing against the Confederate line. The following day, February 7, the regiment skirmished with the Federals, and suffered one man wounded. Between this time, and the end of April, they would go on picket on March 26, April 7, April 19, and April 29, most often at Somerville Ford.[720]

Meanwhile, personnel matters occupied a great deal of attention in the 31st Virginia. Resignations, leave of absences, elections of new officers and promotions, examination boards for officers, and a few punishments filled the time for the regiment's staff. The resignations of captains Harding and Lyman were finally accepted by Col. Hoffman, on February 5, and became effective on February 16, 1864. Both men were allowed to transfer to other units. Lyman joined Chew's battery of heavy artillery, commanded by Capt. Jim Thompson. He served as one of the artillerymen on a gun for several months before being detailed on Chew's staff. Harding joined Company C of the 20th Virginia Cavalry.[721]

Lt. James Blair, who had supported Maj. Cooper in the Examination Board hearings, was granted a leave of absence for 15 days at the end of February, to go to Highland County to obtain clothing for himself and for the men in his company. Although Blair was the only officer in Company C, with 11 men present, Col. Hoffman said that he could temporarily assign another officer to command the company in Blair's absence. The request was approved.[722]

Several replacement officers had been elected by the men in various companies, but under the new system instituted by Gen. Lee, all new officers were required first to pass an examining board to qualify in their new rank. Maj. Cooper, on March 8, wrote to the Adjutant & Inspector General to request an examining board to determine the fitness of 1st Lt. Warwick C. Kincaid for the position of captain of Company B. Following Capt. Lyman's resignation, Kincaid was next in line for promotion, but subsequently failed to pass the tactical portion of the exam, and was found unfit for promotion by the examining board. Henry B. Pullin, 2nd lieutenant of Company B, passed the examination, and was accordingly promoted to captain over Kincaid on March 16.[723]

The examining board was supposed to forward the paperwork directly up the chain of command, so that rulings could be made and the commander of the regiment informed before the individuals received the official results. This would prevent embarrassing individuals who had been superseded, but in the case of Kincaid and Pullin, the board's report went directly to the men. Hoffman protested afterward to the Adjutant and Inspector General's department that he was not given a chance to discuss the matter with either man before the findings were transmitted to them.[724]

The examining board for Kincaid and Pullin had raised some uncomfortable issues with Hoffman and Cooper. When Kincaid failed to pass the tactical exam, they were asked to give an account of how much instruction the men of the regiment had been given in drill and tactics. Col. Hoffman's reply gave no doubt that the men had been poorly prepared for their new rank: "The colonel of the regiment who preceded me and commanded it most of the time from its organization till its reorganization never drilled it at all," Hoffman replied in testimony. "Since I was called to its command, I—almost all of the time when it was not on active campaign, I have been on special service or in command of the brigade, and consequently I have drilled it but little. Other officers have drilled the regiment occasionally, but it has been drilled less than most other regiments that have been so long in the service. Last spring, during the greater part of the time when other regiments of the brigade were practically instructed, the regiment was moving in the northwest." This must have been painful for Hoffman, who had not yet given up entirely on his campaign for promotion to brigadier general.

Maj. Cooper was even more to the point: "The 1st year of the war our regiment was drilled a little by its then Maj. Boykin, a very competent officer. Since then it has been commanded by officers who have made no pretenses to a knowledge of military tactics, and has been drilled but little. At Hamilton Crossing in 1863, and Pisgah Church, Aug. and Sept. 1863, it was instructed in the drill by Lt. Col. McCutchen, and with the exception of a month's drilling in the summer of 1861, of some of the companies by then Cadet Lyman, and some rudimentary instruction at Laurel Hill and Philippi, (those) are substantially the opportunities the regiment has enjoyed of improvement."[725]

This testimony, as well as the visible results on the field when the brigade made a poor showing at drill, resulted in more practice at drill for the 31st Virginia. From the end of March, until the beginning of May, they were drilled on ten occasions. The army was trying to prepare for the spring campaign, and toward the end of April, the men were drilled nearly every day at either battalion drill, or brigade drill, or both on some days.

Cooper and Hoffman had another protest resignation to contend with in March, although this time it was not a protest against Maj. Cooper. 1st Lt. Matthew Carpenter, of Company A, submitted his resignation on March 11, and said he was not willing to serve under Albert Stringer, who was about to be promoted to captain of Company A. As with the protest over Cooper's promotion, there was more to the case than the fine points of law.

Matthew Carpenter had joined the regiment in 1862, when he was hired to take Stephen Morgan's place, which was legal at the start of the war, though later not allowed under the conscript law. Carpenter became commissary sergeant of Company A in July of 1862, and was elected 2nd lieutenant in August. He was elected 1st lieutenant shortly after Gettysburg, on July 10, 1863, but continued to serve as commissary for the regiment, which relieved him of duty with Company A. He was effectively on the staff of the regiment, but had not been confirmed in the position: Alpheus Haymond, though absent and performing duties of assistant quartermaster for the brigade, was still carried on the books as the regiment's commissary.

Albert Stringer had been acting sergeant major on the regiment's staff in September and October of 1862, but had returned to the position of ordnance sergeant. In September 1863, he was elected 2nd lieutenant in Company A, and was evidently popular with the men of the company. On March 23, 1864, Albert G. Stringer was elected 1st lieutenant to take Carpenter's place in Company A, in an election that was approved by Col. Hoffman. This qualified Stringer to be elected captain of the company in a second, hastily prepared election supervised by W. B. McNemar, and prevented Carpenter from qualifying as captain, as he had not put his name on the ballot. The maneuver was much desired by the men of Company A, who preferred Stringer as their captain. Matthew Carpenter's resignation as 1st lieutenant was accepted on March 25, 1864. The vacancy was later filled, near the end of April, when the company elected Edward J. Armstrong as 2nd lieutenant.[726]

Lt. Patrick W. Bruffey had been found innocent of the charges concerning his supposed illegal election as an officer, but submitted his resignation on December 12 as part of the protest over Cooper's promotion to major. When he again submitted his resignation in early April, Col. Hoffman sent it up the chain of command for approval. Bruffey said in this resignation, "Feeling that it will be impossible to discharge the duties of a subordinate officer in an agreeable manner, I prefer serving as a private soldier in the ranks." Bruffey got his wish, but apparently there were more problems to come.[727]

A number of men were charged with desertion, for leaving the regiment to join other regiments without official approval. "Sentence was read yesterday evening on three of our men," Private George Arbogast wrote on March 13. "Each one is to do twelve months of hard labor in Richmond with a ball not weighing over twelve pounds, and a chain not less than three feet long attached to their ankle. Two were taken from here this morning. Poor fellows, I pity them. It is generally thought they will have another hearing and be released. The Regiment dislikes it very much." The men were released back into the ranks before the spring campaign began in earnest, but ominously, another in the regiment noted on March 19 that a man had been shot for desertion.[728]

In early April, Col. Hoffman approved the election of William Warner, Company I, to the unique position of ensign of the regiment, a special mark of honor for an enlisted man. He had more than earned it, as Hoffman pointed out: "William Warner... having been wounded, and being unable to carry a musket without suffering, took the colors of the regiment, and has borne them gallantly to the present time. He is a man of character and a faithful soldier." Warner was wounded at the battle of Sharpsburg, and remained disabled in one arm. He then volunteered to serve as color bearer, one of the most dangerous duties in battle. Color bearers were often specially chosen targets in a battle, for a regiment's colors were its rallying point. Both Gen. Ewell, and Gen. Lee concurred in the appointment of Warner as ensign of the 31st Virginia.[729]

The old colors of the 31st Virginia were tattered and battle-scarred. On April 14, 1864, at dress parade, Col. Hoffman presented the regiment with a new flag sewn by a sister of John and S. N. Bosworth, Mrs. Rebecca Bosworth See. She had seen the tattered condition of the regiment's old flag while visiting their camp at Somerville Ford, and had returned home to Fisherville, in Augusta County to sew a new one. Col. Hoffman then ordered that the old flag of the 31st Virginia be sent to Mrs. See for safekeeping.[730]

That same day, the regiment's baggage, and all of their tents, were packed on the baggage wagons and sent to the rear, for storage. The army was preparing for the coming campaign by lightening up, and making quick marches more possible. The weather had not cooperated thus far for starting the campaign early, and the men without cabins were fairly exposed in the raw spring weather.[731] "This has been a cold, wet backward spring here, too bad for military operations," George

Arbogast wrote to his wife on the 18th. "I can see snow on the Blue Ridge and I am afraid you are out of wood or hay, but you must be contented while you have enough to eat or wear. We are doing pretty well here, though the rations doesn't come regular on account of the weather and the occupation of the cars by the troops. Sometimes we get one part of a meal a day, though generally have enough for two meals. We don't do much duty, go on picket once in three weeks, cook, and wash and carry wood near half a mile. I have gotten to making and baking very good bread, can cook very well. I wish you had some of the coffee that we draw here, and I had some rye and cream. When I was home I could not eat corn bread and coffee without cream, but here we have it nearly all the time and it is first rate. Hunger is a good sauce."[732]

The regiment went on picket on April 19, and listened to considerable cannonading from further down the river. The Union army was also preparing for the coming campaign, and had begun fighting sham battles, and working up the efficiency of its artillery. The Confederate responded by increasing the strength of the picket: on the night of April 20, the pickets for the entire brigade were called out at three o'clock in the morning, and kept on the line until after daylight. On the morning of the 21st, they heard the Federals firing their muskets across the river, and practicing mock charges. When the 49th Virginia relieved the 31st Virginia on picket that day, they were ordered to double the picket guard, and keep them on post day and night along the river.

The brigade was drilled on the 21st again, but the 31st Virginia made a poor showing in the afternoon in front of Gen. Pegram, who reprimanded Hoffman and the men, and told them that he would drill them himself on the following day. As promised, Pegram saw to it that the 31st Virginia was thoroughly engaged in drill on the 22nd. Snider, in Company C, said, "We was drilled according to the order by the General, and done a pretty good job, and he complimented us highly." They were drilled again in the afternoon, with the brigade, and "done tolerably well," according to Snider.

The 31st Virginia was relieved from drill on the 23rd because it was a Sunday, but the picket line was increased to two regiments from Johnson and Rodes's divisions. Across the river, the Federals were practicing their artillery again, and had begun moving batteries further down the river. Late in the day, Federal skirmishers came up to the river in force and drove the Confederate pickets away from their position, in order to fortify the Federal line with additional trenches and artillery. At Ely's Ford, the Union cavalry crossed over the river in the night, perhaps testing the Confederate line, but returned to their own side of the river by morning.

The regiment was now drilling in earnest, battalion drill in the morning, and brigade drill in the afternoon. On the 26th, their brigade drill was ended with a long mock charge, complete with the Southern yell. These remaining few days of April 1864 were the last peaceful days the regiment would have for months to come. They were busy days for some. On April 27, Sergeant Snider said, "I attended the North Carolina officer's drill in the morning, and then battalion drill at 9 A.M.; then drew and issued three day's rations, or as much as I could, and then finished it in the evening, and then attended brigade drill at 3 P.M., which wound up with two charges and big cheering as usual. I was about run down, and had the headache and aching in my bones."[733]

Perhaps unconsciously responding to the imminence of action, his body cringing away from the onset of their season of battles, Snider said on the 28th how miserably he had slept the night before. "I could neither lay, set, nor stand on account of pain in my head, back, and legs. I was excused from duty today and feel some better. The regiment drilled as usual. It is said that there was a great deal of firing going on across the river and suppose they are fighting sham battles. Raw, windy, clear day." He was well and back to performing duties again by the 30th.

The regiment went on picket again on the 29th, and on the 30th was due to be paid, but the money had not been delivered to the payroll officer. Perhaps the government knew the men would be too busy fighting to worry about a few Confederate dollars in their pockets.[734]

Some of the men, such as Snider, attended religious services more than once a day. On May 1, he noted that a chaplain from an artillery unit preached to them in the morning: in the afternoon, the men heard James Lepps, the 31st Virginia's chaplain. Across the river, their enemy had grown quiet, and the camps of the Confederate army were also relatively peaceful. They were treated to a considerable storm of rain and lightning the following day; and on May 3, the 31st Virginia was put through their paces at battalion and brigade drill, morning and afternoon.[735]

Lt. Gen. Ulysses S. Grant had taken command of the Union Army of the Potomac. That army began its spring campaign on May 3, when Gen. Meade's forces crossed from north to south over the Rapidan River, using pontoon bridges at Germana Ford, and at Ely's Ford. Meade's intention was to head east to flank the Confederates. Running parallel to the Rapidan River, between Lee's headquarters at Orange Court House and the fords, were the Orange Turnpike, and the Orange Plank Road.

Meade's army was pointed to cut across these roads, on the western border of the region known as the Wilderness. It was a scrubby, rugged, broken upland, full of ravines. Thickly wooded with dense brush, and closely spaced, second growth trees, the Wilderness was a tangle.[736]

The 31st Virginia's morning drill was interrupted on May 4 when orders arrived for the brigade to prepare to march at a moment's notice. None of the men were eager to commence battle, but the regiment had always been better at actual combat than they were at tactical drill, where everything was supposed to be by the book. "The enemy was said to be moving to our right," Snider said, "and we quit drill and went to cooking up our rations. About 4 P.M., orders came to move immediately, leaving a cooking detail behind. We marched in the direction of Mine Run a short distance, and stopped and drew two day's rations of hard bread." They crossed Mine Run, and continued for about two miles before camping along the road about nine o'clock that night, with orders to be ready to march at daylight.[737]

They were part of Gen. Ewell's II Corps, which in the morning would continue heading east on the turnpike. Stuart's cavalry was to their front, while over to their flank Hill's corps was coming up on the Plank Road. The men didn't rest well that night in the bushes by the roadside in the Wilderness tangle. "The enemy kept up such a strong scurming that night that we could not sleep much," George Arbogast wrote later.[738]

Some of the men felt pressed to write while there was still time, such as Will Yeager. "Mother, you need not send us any more clothing," he wrote on the 5th, "for we have sent away what we had except what we can carry, and you know we don't want much to carry this time of year, so we have plenty in that line." He was hopeful that they would win the coming fight. "I hope we will be able to give them a good thrashing," he wrote, "for on this fight depends greatly our future safety. I think if we are successful it may be one of the most important battles of the war. If we should be spared to see the fight through, I will write you immediately and give you the particulars."[739]

Early in the morning of May 5, Ewell's Corps continued advancing on the turnpike. The Federals were also advancing skirmishers from Charles Griffin's division (Warren's Corps) along the same road, protecting Griffin's headquarters at the Old Wilderness Tavern. Ewell's skirmishers began firing on them as the Confederates came up, and quickly, a battle developed with Ewell's skirmishers outnumbered. Ewell expected that any minute Longstreet's Corps would come up from the south to support him, but Gen. Longstreet had yet to arrive, and not all of Ewell's Corps was up to the front. The men of Ewell's Corps found themselves fighting a holding action, falling back a little at a time in the face of an overwhelming infantry force. The dense forest made it impossible for either side to use artillery.[740]

Pegram's brigade, including the 31st Virginia, was part of Ewell's reserve in the morning. They marched about seven o'clock to Locust Grove and were placed in line, farther back on the turnpike road. Up ahead, they could hear musketry and skirmishing, the intensity of the sound building until around ten o'clock, artillery began in the distance.

At the front, Johnson's and Gordon's Brigade were in a terrible firefight. Ewell's line was beginning to falter, with some regiments falling back under the onslaught of musket balls, when Gordon put a single regiment at the charge and followed up with the rest of his brigades in an audacious attempt to break the northern line. Gordon's charge was a success, and served to rally those parts of Ewell's line that had begun to fall back.[741] Reacting to this savage attack by Gordon, the Federals under Gen. Warren began to withdraw to some sketchy breastworks they had made the night before. Even when Sedgewick's Corps came up to support Warren, the Confederates continued their pressure. About four o'clock, they held the ground at the edge of a ravine, and began to dig in.[742]

Meanwhile, Pegram's brigade had been ordered to march to the front. Sergeant Snider said, "We left Locust Grove about 2 P.M. for the front, after we had religious service and arrived on the field about 8 P.M., where there had been heavy fighting for about 6 hours by Johnson's Division." The were ordered to form a line of battle to the left of Hays's brigade, and the men began scraping together some slight defensive breastworks. They used what fallen logs they could easily obtain, and scrapped dirt up with bayonets and pioneer shovels. One of the other men in the brigade commented on their defenses, "This was not bullet proof, but it helped a heap."[743]

Their turn at the action would come soon enough. Not long after dark, the brigade was assaulted by a tremendous charge by the Federals, and the two sides traded rifle fire for about a half hour before the Federals fells back a short distance. Capt. Phillips said in his journal, "Repulsed a charge of the enemy. Gen. Pegram wounded. Col. Hoffman in command of the brigade." Gen. Pegram's wound was in the leg, and was severe enough to disable him for several months.[744]

When all light in the sky was gone, and the fighting had stopped, both sides realized the battle was far from over. While Hoffman was busy sorting out the brigade, Maj. Cooper assumed command of the 31st Virginia. In the fighting that day, the regiment had suffered a number of losses. Jim Spencer of Company G, and John Doyle were captured and made prisoners. Lem Marks, who was wounded, was also captured, according to reports.

Among those killed were: William F. Gay, Lt. John W. Long, Francis M. Connolly, and Martin L. Dawson. The wounded included Allen A. Greenleaf, with a gunshot wound to the right arm; James Putnam, also wounded in an arm; John W. Rector, Jr., wounded in the hip; Martin Hall, whose leg was later amputated; Melvin N. Pullin; and William D. Townsend.[745]

The surgeon's work was unrelenting once the two armies tore into one another with determination. "There was a dearth of every thing except bullets, smoke and suffering," Surgeon Archibold Atkinson recalled after the war. He experienced the battle from an improvised field hospital in the brush, but being placed near enough to be useful to the brigade, it was also too far into the thicket to get ambulances, or supplies to it. [746]

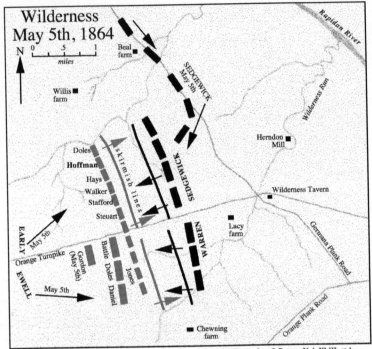

maps by D.W.Wooddell, based on Early, *Narrative of the War;* and on O.R. map Vol. XLIII, pt.1.

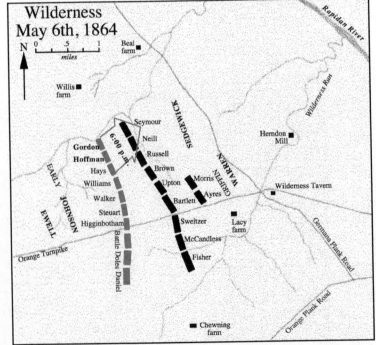

"We had to attend to our wounded in the midst of undergrowth so thick that we could scarcely move around," Atkinson said, "and no water to be had for washing off the wounded... it was very hot weather and the close brush of woods composed of small jack oaks twelve to twenty feet high, and rather larger than a man's arm, made the heat almost suffocating. Added to this the smoke from burning powder and leaves made every breath an effort. It was almost impossible to distinguish friend from foe. The firing was terrific and the carnage awful. The thirst was almost unbearable, and the whole surface of the earth afire with burning leaves."

Late in the day, Gordon's brigade was sent to the far left flank of Lee's army. Early's Division was for the first time entirely to the left of the road, with Johnson's division on their right. The men slept that night with their rifles close at hand, without leaving the front. The Confederate and Union forces faced each other along an irregular line five miles long, with Gen. Longstreet's men marching in the darkness to try to reach the battle before the next day. Skirmishing continued through the night.[747]

Pegram's brigade, under Col. Hoffman, was to the right of Gordon's brigade. Snider said that enemy pickets kept them up a good portion of the night. The men had made better breastworks this time, having learned that the Federals would attack in strength and come right up to the line.

On the morning of May 6, not long after daylight, Federal skirmishers came up supported by a heavy force prepared for an assault against Pegram's brigade, and drove back the brigade's skirmishers. Pavel Knisely of Company C was one of the 31st Virginia's skirmishers: he was about 75 yards out from the line when he was wounded, and remained on the ground, with bullets from both sides whizzing over him throughout part of the morning. Snider said that Knisely, "Was grazen on the shoulder and his clothes riddled." In a lull in the fighting, after the first large attack, he was brought back to their line, with flesh wounds in the thigh and shoulder, and a serious thigh wound that required amputation. He later died at a hospital in Charlottesville.[748]

Another of the skirmishers was John Campbell of Company H. "A Federal soldier shot my buddy and broke his neck," he recalled later. "The Yankee was hiding behind a large oak tree. I ran to a sugar tree and he shot at me seven times. One of two men behind the oak tree then ran out in the road and I shot him under the arm.... The other man took his arm out of the sleeve of his shirt and stuck it out from the tree as a target for me. I shot at it several times not knowing the sleeve was empty, and the fight between us continued.... It was like shooting squirrels, as we were not more than thirty yards apart."[749]

Not long after the skirmishers were pushed back, the Federal line came at Pegram's brigade with a ferocity that was met by equally determined Confederates. "We literally stayed them and but few of us was hurt as we had breastworks," Snider said.

"Yanks advanced within thirty yards of our breastworks when we opened on them. They stood one and one-half hours and broke..." Newton Bosworth wrote that day, "The ground is covered with their dead."[750]

Jacob Heater, Company D, recalled that when the Federals made their charge, they were in four lines, with colors flying, officers on horseback, and the men carrying loaded knapsacks that were tempting for the hungry Confederates. The Federals walked right up to within 30 yards of the brigade's line, while Hoffman and the other officers kept their men from firing until it was right in their enemy's faces. "Such a tumbling of knapsacks and broken ranks I had never seen," Heater wrote.[751]

"The Lord has saw fit to spare me through right smart danger," George Arbogast wrote to his wife a few days after the battle. "We let volley into them and they lay down and we fought them about three quarters of an hour and our guns got so hot that we were ordered to slacken our fire. The Yanks took advantage of the time and run, and the Yanks started to yell and we let a volley into them. There was about 100 Yanks dead. James Hamilton was wounded in the leg, Charles Moore scalped on the head, and James Sholes had his arm broken, the bullet entered his side and since then he died."[752]

After this fight early in the morning, the Federals returned, several times, against Pegram's brigade, and each time the 31st Virginia, and their comrades in the 13th, 49th, 52nd, and 58th Virginia stood their ground, and repulsed the Union infantry. Gen. Early later reported, "These attacks were so persistent that two regiments of Johnson's division were moved to the rear of Pegram's brigade, for the purpose of supporting it; and when an offer was made to relieve it, under the apprehension that its ammunition might be exhausted, the men of that gallant brigade begged that they might be allowed to retain their position, stating that they were getting along very well indeed and wanted no help."[753]

Ammunition had been a problem, but several men crawled back from each regiment and hauled up boxes of cartridges and spilled them out behind the soldiers at the breastworks, ready to hand for reloading. Many of the men fired more than 80 cartridges in the day's first attack.[754]

Phillips, Captain of Company K, was wounded late in the day. "The terrible roar of the cannon, the smoke of the guns, the groans of the dying men and the neighing of the horses filled the evening air," he wrote. "Twilight was setting upon the forest and suddenly, as if it came from nowhere, I was struck by a bullet in my right hip." Phillips was carried off the field of battle and taken to Charlottesville to a hospital where he lingered in pain for days, this wound perhaps the most damaging of all of his many wounds.[755]

Around 5:30 in the afternoon, Pegram's brigade still occupied the same ground on which they had started the day, with Gordon's brigade to their left. Brig. Gen. Gordon had come up with a plan to flank the Federals in their front. Sedgewick's Corps of the Union army had allowed the right end of their line to become exposed, which Gordon had discovered after scouting the situation.

Night had nearly arrived and the shooting had fallen silent along the front when Gordon's brigade launched its attack. Supported by frontal assaults from Pegram's brigade (under Hoffman), Gordon's men quickly rolled down the Federal line, creating panic and havoc especially in Seymour's brigade, and along the Union's VI Corps. The Federal line held by Seymour was forced back, as was part of Neil's brigade to the south. The Confederates captured many prisoners, including two Union brigadier generals.[756]

Col. Hoffman's orders had been to send his brigade forward as soon as he heard the sound of Gordon's attack. The ground to their front was full of standing water, with thickets of small trees and bushes crowding one another and making passage through the tangle nearly impossible in the falling light. After about a half-hour's march, the men waded out of the swamp, shoes and pants filled with mud and water, and began climbing up a bit of higher ground. They had thought their skirmishers were in front, but at some point, the skirmishers had veered one way or another, and the brigade was walking blindly toward the enemy when a voice called out of the darkness. "Boys, here we are!"

An explosion of muskets fired practically in their faces as the Union line rose up and let loose a volley that almost broke the Confederate line. Those not wounded or killed were blinded momentarily by the flash, and others were nearly deafened by the sudden explosion of so many muskets going off so close to their heads. Many of the men in the 31st Virginia dropped to the ground, and then scurried back from the line.

The brigade became disorganized in the darkness as the regiments lost contact with one another in the darkness. At one point, Col. Hoffman rode his bay horse up to a body of men, dimly seen in the night, and asked what regiment they were. "Sixty-first New York," was the answer. Hoffman wheeled his horse around while the Federals fired their muskets and called out for him to surrender. "I didn't volunteer to surrender," Hoffman yelled over his shoulder as the muskets lit the night.

Hoffman made a narrow escape, but his horse was killed by the rifle fire, and he had to jump off and run for safety. He later had a devil of a time getting the government to reimburse him for the full value of the horse. An officer in the 49th Virginia said that Hoffman lost his hat when he jumped from the horse. The next morning, one of the men gave him a Union cap with the bill burned off, which Hoffman wore for the next few days until he could obtain a proper hat.[757]

The Federals had fired too high in their first volley that night, and killed and wounded fewer men in the 31st Virginia than would have been the case if the Union infantry had aimed a bit lower. Eventually, the brigade was pulled together into a semblance of a line and the men began to dig in and wait for morning. Unknown to them was the fact that the Federals had also fallen back some time after their volleys, leaving some distance between the two lines once again. George Arbogast, of Company G, said they did not get much sleep that night, as they were fortifying their breastworks and worrying about a counter-attack by the Federals.

Sergeant Francis Golden in Company C was among the wounded that night. Company F had one man wounded, and Company G suffered several casualties, according to George Arbogast: "In this charge Mathias Moore was shot through the calf of the leg, (and) James Wanless was wounded slightly, making six wounded and one killed in the company."[758]

Early the next morning, May 7, the men were woken and told to prepare for an attack. "We went to work on our fortifications before daylight," Snider said. The Federals began shelling their position from a long distance away, the shells arcing up over the trees and exploding in the air over their heads. The brigade was ordered forward. "I certainly was frightened that morning," Jacob Heater recalled. "I would have given my right arm at the shoulder joint to have been in some safe place. When we came in sight of the breastworks that we had run against the night before, I imagined I could see bayonets and caps and almost clouds of smoke along the line. Several times I put my hand up to see if my cap was on my head. I think my hair must have been standing straight up. But when we approached the works, there was not a single live Yank behind them."

"I never was so not-anxious for an attack from the enemy in my life," wrote Snider, near tongue-tied with remembered fear. Occupying the Federal breastworks, the brigade rested until late in the day, with skirmishers out to their front most of the day, tangling with the Federal skirmishers. The 31st Virginia was ordered to be ready to move at around dark fall, and set out marching at around nine o'clock. They marched through the night, slowly traveling only about four miles before being told to lie down and sleep with their rifles ready at hand.[759]

The Battle of the Wilderness was over. The men were weary, and the Confederate army had taken heavy casualties in the past couple of days. "Had they known our situation," Gen. Early later wrote, "and charged us that night, they most certainly would have gained a victory." But the Union army had also taken heavy casualties in the fighting, and was in no position to press the fight longer. They had lost 17,666 killed, wounded, and missing. Confederate losses were somewhere around half of that many.

By May 7, Gen. Lee felt certain that the Union army would move next to Spotsylvania. Lee began making arrangements for his army to march there, in anticipation of Gen. Grant's next move, so that the armies would meet again very soon. There were some necessary changes to be made in the high command, however. Gen. A. P. Hill had fallen sick, and was unable to continue in command of his corps: Jubal Early was reassigned to command of Hill's Corps on May 7. Brig. Gen. Gordon, the most senior officer in the division, was promoted to Maj. Gen. and placed in command of Early's division. At the same time, Hays's brigade was transferred to Johnson's Division, where it was joined with another Louisiana brigade.[760]

The 31st Virginia remained in Pegram's brigade, though by now it was called Hoffman's brigade more often than not. For the 31st Virginia, the toll of battle for the past several days had once again been heavy. John W. Folks, Edward H. Kittle, John Long, and Uriah A. Tucker were killed outright.

Mortally wounded were Pavel Knisely, with right leg amputated (who would die on June 7); and James W. Sholes, who died later in the day on May 6. Other wounded included Edward Bradbury, Allen A. Devier, John W. Goodman, Francis M. Golden, Charles Moore, and Mathias L. Moore. Capt. Phillips was wounded in the right hip. Samuel A. Ralston, Chesley Simmons, and John S. Griffin, whose leg had to be amputated. The regiment had suffered a total of 13 casualties on May 5; and 15 casualties on May 6, not counting the Colonel's horse. The campaign was a week old, and already the 31st Virginia's loss was about ten percent of the men who signed the petition in January 1864.[761]

On the morning of Sunday, May 8, Will Yeager, private in Company G, dashed off a few lines to his mother and sister, to let them know that he and his brother Henry were all right. "Most of the wounded are doing well," he wrote, "and generally not seriously wounded except James Shales, who is mortally wounded. He is alive yet, but not expected to live. The rest of our neighbors are safe; Varner, Wooddell and all Mr. Wilfong's boys, including Daniel, also are safe yet. Our regiment fought nobly and has been highly complimented by the officers. We are still in line of battle and will likely have more fighting today. The Yanks have been badly whipped so far at all points. We have orders to move and must close, but will write again the first opportunity. This leaves us both well."

Without a doubt the folks in Pocahontas County were gladdened by Will Yeager's mentions that their relatives were safe after such heavy fighting. Warwick Wooddell was Will Yeager's cousin, and he was John P. Varner's brother-in-law. Warwick had not been home for quite some time now, and his wife Margaret was still on the farm at Green

Bank raising their child, Charlie. This news of Warwick may have been the last happy news that Margaret received of her husband.[762]

The 31st Virginia marched at nine o'clock on the morning of May 8, to the Plank Road, and across it, all the while following the line of breastworks. The day was unusually hot, dusty, and above all, smoky from the many forest fires burning on either side of the men as they marched toward Spotsylvania Court House. They arrived at their destination around five o'clock in the afternoon, exhausted and ready for sleep.

Part of Ewell's Corps had arrived earlier in the day, and had already fought at least one action with the Federals at Spotsylvania by the time that Hoffman's brigade arrived. The day's heat took a toll on the men as they marched, and a number of them were forced to fall out of line, too used up to move further. Most of them, such as Snider, caught up with the regiment and brigade the next day. "It was a very hot day, and a great many gave out and were overcome by heat and sun-struck," Snider said. "And I gave out, and laid all night, about eight miles from camp."

Surgeon Atkinson commented on the poor physical condition of the men that day. "As we were marching, men dropped like sheep along the road, while others were just able to drag their weary feet: poor half starved creatures trying to fight upon food hardly fit to sustain life...."[763]

Snider caught up with the regiment not long after daylight, in time to march with them at nine o'clock, when they were moved to the right flank and put in line. They began fortifying, digging a trench, and then adding breastworks. Skirmishing was heavy throughout that day as the men in Hoffman's brigade continued to strengthen the line. Late in the afternoon, as their division began to move out of their entrenchments, to try to make a flank movement on the Federals, they came under attack and were forced to withdraw to their entrenchments in order to repel the Federals.[764]

On the next morning, May 10, Hoffman's brigade once more was ordered to move out with the division, toward the right flank, and again the Union made an attack, this time with a furious artillery bombardment, which continued throughout the day. The battle ranged from place to place along the Confederate line that day. "We was moved from one end of the line to the other," Snider said, "in rear of the second line, frequently stopping when the shells flew thickest and began fortifying. About sundown we got to the extreme left of the line, where the enemy had been in the morning, and the right of our regiment was put on picket, where we remained until after dark and then was moved down the road to where we laid the first night. In the evening near our right flank, one brigade—Doles—run and let the enemy through our works, but they was charged back with great slaughter by Gordon's brigade."[765]

May 11 was the calm before the storm—although, in a literal sense, it was the calm during a tremendous rainstorm, as the brigade went on reserve and camped in an orchard. The men tried to rest, but their comfort was interrupted in the evening as the skies opened up with heavy rain that continued through the night.[766]

One of the deadliest contests of the war was soon to befall the men of Lee and Grant's armies, the battle of the bloody angle of Spotsylvania. The Confederates had established a line of entrenchments overlooking the Ny River valley. A huge inverted V was projected forward from the line, entrenched and fortified with high breastworks of logs and dirt, following the course of the high ground to the northeast about a mile, coming to a point, and then running another mile back toward the southeast. The base of the angle was about a half-mile across. Johnson's division occupied the crucial "angle" at the apex, or point. On the left, was Anderson's division. On the right, Gordon's division ran to the base of the entrenchments, and then ran across the base in a refused line, to prevent the enemy from flanking them in the salient.

Rain continued to fall through the night, and nearly all day on May 12. In the morning, around dawn, Hoffman's brigade was ordered to move to the left, in support of Hays's brigade of Johnson's division, which was in the entrenchments near the westward base of the angle, in an area the men began calling the mule-shoe.

An artillery position on a flattened platform of earth was close by as the 31st Virginia took up its position, but the rain had turned the ground into a mire of mud, and the Confederate artillery would have trouble throughout the day, getting stuck when they were needed elsewhere. As a result, their artillery was particularly ineffective on the 12th.

Not long after the 31st Virginia and the rest of Hoffman's brigade came up in support of Hays's brigade, the Federals launched a strong attack on Johnson's division. They took the Confederates by surprise, and overwhelmed the line, breaking through and capturing a great part of Johnson's division.

"Our brigade was ordered to fall in," Snider said, "and we was marched across the (angle) but soon after starting, the head of the column was fired on and we turned slightly to our right and moved out on the hill, where we was formed in line of battle with Gordon's brigade on our right." They were in a field, still close to the line that formed the base of the triangle, but had seen a force of Federals headed their way, from where the Federals had penetrated Johnson's line. In this field, the brigade stopped to catch its breath and form their line. They were engaged in this when generals Lee and Ewell rode along the line. "General Lee wanted to lead the charge," Snider said, "but General Gordon urged him to go to the rear."[767]

BATTLE OF SPOTSYLVANIA, MAY 12, 1864

Map by David W. Wooddell

Colonel Gibson asked Gen. Lee, as he rode by, "General, shall we give them the bayonet?" Gen. Lee gave his assent, but the closeness of the Federal infantry made a charge at once imperative, and the men were ordered to the charge without taking time to fix bayonets. "Forward," Col. Hoffman ordered his brigade, and they swept forward toward the line of entrenchments on the northeast section of the triangle.

Henry Yeager, in Company G, later recalled Col. Hoffman leading the men as they charged the enemy to recover their breastworks. "Never was a better charge made. The conflict became a hand-to-hand one at the breastworks, and many were killed with the bayonet. We lost heavily. I was wounded and left on the field... and know that all the timber was literally shot down or killed from the effect of musketry. Many of the dead were never buried. We lost seventeen men in our company."[768]

Colonel Hoffman was wounded at some point after they had cross the breastworks, and was forced to the rear for medical attention, leaving the brigade in the command of Colonel J. Catlett Gibson, of the 49th Virginia, who took charge of the brigade on the right, and Colonel

James Terrill, who took command of the two regiments on the brigade's left. Gibson reported that after they had crossed the breastworks and were pursuing the Federals through woods, "I found Colonel John S. Hoffman, of the 31st Virginia, in a thicket of bushes fingering the leaves at his feet, and asked him where he was hit. He said the bushes had knocked his spectacles off and he could not see. I told a man standing near him to find the Colonel's spectacles for him, and if he could not do so to lead the Colonel back to the rear, as he could not see a yard without his specks."[769]

The 31st Virginia had gone about 400 yards beyond the breastworks. There, the men fought lying down, and continued to fire at the Federals at close range. A while later, the regiment, and the brigade was ordered to pull back toward their line of entrenchments.[770]

Some of the men had become separated, after their charge into no man's land. Sergeant Snider found himself temporarily on his own. "I was on the extreme right in the woods, which was pushed back with Gordon's brigade into the hollow, and found I was cut off from my regiment and went a short distance to the left and got into the trenches, where I learned where the regiment was, and that they was out of ammunition." Snider shouldered a box of ammunition, and went forward to rejoin the regiment, picking up a fresh rifle on the way.

The Federals were not through for the day, however, and began pressing the brigade on the right. The brigade was ordered to pull back to the trenches, which it did, the men falling into the muddy, water-filled ditches and spending a good portion of the day soaking up Virginia clay and rainwater. The Federals had managed to turn some of the captured artillery further up the line, and fired through the rain and fog at the Confederates, but the trenches protected the men, and visibility was so poor that the Federals were just aiming generally in the direction they thought the Confederates were holding.[771]

Jacob Heater recalled the ditch for another reason. "When our lines entered the ditch at the edge of the timber, I noticed a Yankee officer lying on his back in the ditch, shot through the heart." The dead officer made a big impression on Heater. "I never expected to see the rising of another sun. How I have escaped death through so many perilous conflicts appears as a dream."[772]

Others were not so lucky as Heater. William Henry Hull, Company G, later wrote, "I found George W. Arbogast outside the breastworks, we having gone a short distance beyond the works in our charge and then falling back to the works, and with the help of two members of the company we carried him back to the works, and from there he was carried to the field hospital by the ambulance men. He said he was not taken by surprise and to tell his wife and friends he was prepared to go. He insisted that we should not go to the trouble or take the risk of trying to get him behind the breastworks, that his wound was fatal and that he could live only a very short time. I opened his clothes and saw that the ball had entered his body in the region of the heart." George Washington Arbogast's wound was mortal and he died the same day.[773]

The 31st Virginia lost a number of men wounded, killed, or taken prisoner on May 12, and in some cases, this led to a change of command in the individual companies. First Sergeant Christian G. Kuhl, of Company D, found himself once again commanding his company after that day. Kuhl continued to command Company D through the end of the summer, as all of the company officers had been killed, wounded, or captured. Fortunately for the company, Kuhl was a battle-hardened veteran with a steady disposition.[774]

The service records for the men in the 31st Virginia indicate there were 6 men killed on May 12, and 30 wounded. Of the wounded, 10 men later died from their wounds.[775]

Killed: Jefferson Arbogast, Adam Hevener, John W. Nottingham, Blackburn Piles, Lemuel Poling, and Joseph H. Stipe.

Mortally wounded: George W. Arbogast, Harvey Beverage, Thomas A. Compton, James S. Davis, R. Humphreys, Morgan Jolliff, John F. Leach, Charles C. Steuart, and James G. Wells.

The wounded included: Gideon Casto, William P. Cooper, Salathiel S. Dennison, Eldridge V. Ervin, William H. Hardman, Samuel C. Higgins, John S. Hoffman, James W. Hughes, George Keller, Lemuel Marks, Elam F. Poling, Joshua N. Ramsay, John M. Swecker, Zachariah Swink, John P. Varner, Wellington J. White, William G. Wilfong, Martin L. Williams, David O. Wilson, John H. Yancey, and Henry A. Yeager.

Battle had also taken its toll on the field officers of the regiment. Col. Hoffman's wound did not appear too serious, but Maj. Cooper's was more involved. Wounded by gunshot in the left hip, the ball passed through the muscles of his back, and lodged close to the spine. Cooper arrived at the field hospital around two o'clock in the afternoon. Surgeon Atkinson observed, "He was a fleshy man, which saved his back bone's being injured. The ball had lodged to the left side, and I cut it out. So the major did not have to report for duty for a long time." Maj. Cooper was later taken to Richmond and admitted to General Hospital #4, where he remained until the middle of June, when he was furloughed and granted leave. He chose to stay in private quarters in Richmond through the leave of absence.[776]

The Federals took prisoner a few of the men that day. One of those was Capt. Elisha Wilfong of Company G, captured during the fight and sent on May 17 to Old Capitol Prison in Washington, D.C. He was held there until June 15, and then was transferred to Fort Delaware, where he remained a prisoner of war until the end of the war.[777]

In the night, the Pioneer Corps began work preparing a new line of defensive entrenchments on a line that ran across the base of the salient. Around two o'clock in the morning, on May 13, the 31st Virginia and the brigade withdrew from the entrenchments on the angle, leaving a strong force of skirmishers in place there, and pulled back to the new line of entrenchments. The men went to work with a will to complete the fortifications, the brigade being positioned in a pine thicket. The rain continued through the day, and into the night, but the only fighting was along the skirmish line in the old entrenchments, but the skirmishers held the Federals back and the rest of the brigade could get some rest in their muddy trenches.

They were woken up several times in the night by volleys from their skirmishers, and early in the morning, before dawn on May 14, the regiment was woken and told to expect a heavy attack, but the Federals only opened on them with a heavy artillery barrage. In the afternoon, the Federals began shelling them once again. The Fourth brigade was protected by their trenches, and suffered little harm from it. They could hear a tremendous noise on their right, as late in the day Gen. Early charged the Federal positions with Hill's Corps, capturing several hundred prisoners, and re-taking the entrenchments they had lost the day before.[778]

The brigade surgeons had taken over the Wise house for the field hospital, pulling the planking off the walls to open it up for better light, and more ventilation. On the 13th, they asked the Pioneer Corps to clear the dirt and debris from a disused railroad track, and managed to have an old boxcar hauled to the hospital. They loaded it with the most seriously wounded, and then evacuated the men to Charlottesville on the boxcar.[779]

May 15, from Sergeant Snider's journal: "We had a tolerably quiet time last night and some little rain. We was roused up before daylight to be ready for any emergency, but there was nothing but skirmishing went on all day, with an occasional shell that would go clear over us. About noon we opened on them with several pieces of artillery at once and it was said to make them skedaddle badly. Our Chaplain gave us a short discourse. Rained occasionally through the day."[780]

While it was mostly quiet for the regiment, for those on the skirmish line the day had not entirely gone in their favor. Douglas H. Henson, private in Company F, was wounded on the 15th while on the skirmish line, and was captured by the enemy. The effects of his wounds were so serious that he died in a Union hospital on the 24th, with flesh wounds in the left hip and neck. He was 29 years old, a farmer from Randolph County who was enlisted in May 1861 by Capt. Harding. His health the first year had not been accommodating, however, and he was discharged in June 1862 for bronchitis verging on consumption. That had not kept him out of the fight for long, and by November of the same year he had enlisted again, at Port Royal, and was assigned duty as a nurse at Staunton General Hospital. Now in May of 1864, he had come back to Company F only to be fatally wounded.[781]

The regiment was engaged in skirmishing a little bit on May 16 and 17, with some artillery sporadically adding weight to the background noise of war. The Union army under Gen. Grant now included the V, VI, and II Corps under generals Wright, Hancock, and Burnside. They arranged their lines facing west, in a north-south line. On the 18th, Hancock and Wright again attacked the Confederates, but were repulsed in continuous, fierce volleys of minié balls, grape, and canister. As the Federals climbed over abandoned Confederate positions, they were exposed to a sweeping fire from new Confederate positions. "They began shelling us early," Snider wrote that day, "and run our skirmishers in, but did not advance on our works very far.... It was with great difficulty that their officers could get them to drive in our skirmishers, and the whole line fell back from our skirmishers a time or two. The officers would talk a while, and then curse a while and abuse them." By late evening, the Union army had once more withdrawn from the field, with the Confederate soldiers in the trenches no doubt making jokes at the expense of the Federal officers who could not get their men to advance.[782]

The 31st Virginia had nothing to joke about on the 19th, as the weary soldiers once again found the heat and heartlessness of war as fought in the front lines. Sergeant Snider wrote in his journal concerning May 19: "At daylight our skirmishers reported the enemy to have left our front and brought in a few standing guard. Our color bearer and some others was found and buried where they had been killed on the 12th."[783]

Gen. Ewell's II Corps was sent by Gen. Lee on a forced reconnaissance later in the day, their course taking the entire Corps around to the Fredericksburg Road to the northwest flank of Grant's army. The 31st Virginia moved from its position around two o'clock in the afternoon, climbing over their breastworks and deploying in line with the brigade as Ewell's entire Corps went for a cautious walk through the battered countryside.

"There was a good many of their dead laying between the breastworks unburied and half eaten up," Snider noted, "which was the unpleasantness sight that I ever saw."

About an hour after the 31st Virginia climbed out of the safety of its entrenchments, the men began to hear the rifles and artillery in the distance ahead, the noise rising in intensity very quickly. Ewell's force of 6,000 men had come into contact with the Federals, near the Alsop house and Harris farm, on the Fredericksburg Road northeast of Spotsylvania Court House.

Federal reserve troops under generals Kitching and Tyler had been positioned there, several regiments of untested, heavy-artillery-men who had been pulled out of Washington and brought to the front to fight as infantry. They were not at all pleased by the development, but they stood up to the fight once it began.[784]

BATTLE OF THE HARRIS FARM, MAY 19, 1864

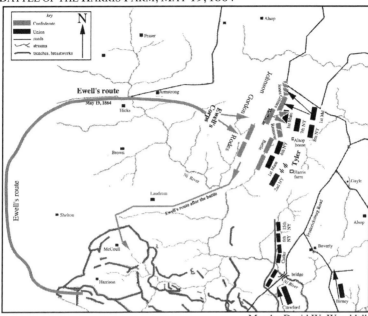

Map by David W. Wooddell

Gen. Ewell reported later that he was about to withdraw, having accomplished his mission of determining where the Union army's flank was located, when he was attacked. The Federals were formed up in the woods on a hill overlooking the Confederates, their line stretching between the Alsop house and the Harris house. They included the 4th New York Heavy Artillery, 1st Massachusetts Heavy Artillery, 2nd New York Heavy Artillery, and two guns from the 15th New York Independent Battery. The 1st Maryland Regiment (Union) also joined in the fight after it began. They were a veteran unit that had been pass-ing by and were attracted to the sound of gunfire.

Hoffman's brigade had been in reserve, but around 5:30 P.M., as Ramseur's brigade faltered when the brigade on their left fell back from the Union artillery, Col. Hoffman brought the old Fourth brigade up on Ramseur's left, and saved the situation from disaster. As the 31st Virginia splashed across a wet morass of swampy ground just in front of the Union line, the men were yelling and making as much noise as possible. "Our brigade made one charge and drove them back some distance and held our position," Snider commented.[785]

They were fighting green troops that day, but the Federals stood their ground, many of them in lines, as though on a parade ground, loading and firing by the numbers. The Confederates were mowing them down, but the Federals not only stood their ground after being driven back a little ways, they continued to give it back to the Confederate brigades under Hoffman and Ramseur.[786]

Gen. Ewell's horse was shot out from under him as he made his way to the front of the fighting. Several of Hoffman's soldiers had to help the one-legged general back onto another horse and get him turned around toward the safety of the rear where he belonged as their Corps commander. Rain continued falling steadily as Hoffman's men held their ground until after nightfall.[787]

Sergeant Snider said, "We was ordered to fall back, about 10 P.M., when we withdrew quietly. They was making a heavy force and artillery in our front and had a good position. We moved back to our original position, arriving about two o'clock that night, very near broken down. I think... our loss was light, but we had several killed and wounded, but none hurt in our company. We brought off several prisoners, and I think left some of our wounded behind on account of the roads being so bad that we could get no ambulances up."[788]

The cost in casualties for the 31st Virginia in holding the position on the evening of May 19 was light in total, but heavy for the individuals who suffered the wounds. Company E lost Capt. Jacob Matheny, wounded and destined to never return to the regiment. He was later discharged from the regiment, in July of 1864. 4th Sergeant Erasmus Hite, Company E, was wounded in the left hand and was admitted to a Richmond hospital on the 23rd, and later furloughed for 60 days.[789]

Warwick Wooddell, and Jacob Sheets, privates in Company G, were both severely wounded. They were carried off the field by their friends, and were later sent to Richmond in an ambulance and admitted to a hospital. Jacob Sheets recovered from his wound, but his recovery was slow and he remained absent through the summer.

Private Joseph E. Warwick Wooddell, of Company G, died at Winder hospital in Richmond on May 29, 1864. He was last paid at the end of December by Capt. Hill. A native of Green Bank, Pocahontas County, Warwick Wooddell was 27 years old when he died at the Confederate hospital. His widow, Margaret, and their three-year old son named Charles, were living on their farm.[790]

Gen. Ewell had gathered his intelligence concerning the whereabouts of the Union flank, but in the process, the "wooded hollows and little ravines" near the Harris farm were witness to a Confederate loss that day of about 900 killed, wounded, and missing. The Federal army's loss was slightly more than 1,500, mostly from the II Corps.

That same day, Capt. Phillips lay painfully wounded in the hip at the hospital in Charlottesville. "I am unable to help myself or even set up," he wrote in his diary. "I have suffered awful for the past several days. How I suffered in getting here! What I have endured. I am too weak to speak. I have heard nothing from my regiment. My wound is so painful. I hope soon that I will be able to set up. I sleep very little at nights. I am growing thinner every hour."[791]

The 31st Virginia had a restful day on May 20, Snider noting, "Everything has been remarkably quiet all day. We remained all day at our fortifications. Pleasant day." Compared to the evening before, when their regiment was fighting for its life, any day alive would have been a "pleasant day." The men must have needed the rest, and they were given a quiet night as well.

They marched on the 21st, as Gen. Lee sent Ewell's Corps to the southeast, to keep pace with a movement in that direction by Hancock's Corps of the Federal army. Snider said, "Soon after daylight we marched to the rear and a short distance and then along our line to the right, passing Hill's and Longstreet's Corps and marched on towards Guiney's. They moved out of Guiney's Station around one o'clock in the afternoon, and marched on the road to Hanover Junction, arriving there around eleven o'clock that night, within eight miles of the junction. This was not a short march, totaling about 25 miles on a hot day, after weeks of arduous fighting. Many of the men broke down on the march, and would trail in as stragglers the next day.[792]

The rains came again overnight, and the following morning the regiment marched again, setting out before daylight and reaching Hanover Junction about 11 A.M. The brigade was positioned in woods, and the men allowed to rest until sundown. They marched about a mile in the evening, and were told to camp for the night. On the 23rd, they were marched in the early afternoon, to a hill near the North Anna River, where they dug entrenchments and fortified them with breastworks. The Federal and Union armies were trying to gain an advantage over one another, and the regiments, brigades, and divisions were constantly being repositioned in response to the other side's movements. No sooner had the 31st Virginia finished its fortifications near the river, than they were moved about to a new position, and then again later in the day. In the evening, they were marched back to the same campground of the night before. They had heard artillery during the day, in the distance, and the regiment was ordered to march at three o'clock in the morning.

"We moved according to orders," Snider wrote on the 24th, "and passed the junction and about one mile further west, where we stopped along the Virginia Central Rail Road, moving along the line occasionally until we got near the left, in reserve, when at sundown we was moved back to the extreme right and went into some fortifications, and threw out videttes until Rodes Division put up new ones in a better position in rear of us. They worked all night. About dark we had a thunderstorm with some rain, which made everything very disagreeable. There was some really heavy fighting in the center in the evening and cannonading and skirmishing was kept up along the entire line. I saw 60 prisoners pass back in a gang in the morning.

Cannonading was principally, if not altogether, from our side, as there did not a shot pass over our lines that I know of."

The heavy fighting was mostly substantial skirmishing. Gen. Lee had placed his army in a very strong position, and the Union army was hesitating to attack in force against the strong fortifications along the North Anna River. "We had a very disagreeable night as the earth was soggy wet and we was in a low swamp," Snider complained on the 25th. "At daylight we tore down our old fortifications and moved back to the (Hanover) Junction where we remained until 5 P.M. and then moved on the extreme right, near where we first fortified and threw up fortifications, which we got done about 10 P.M. We had several showers in the evening, which made it very disagreeable. There was some cannonading up the line but things was pretty quiet all day."

They remained in position through the 26th, working on the fortification, with some skirmishing going on to their front and along the entire Confederate line that day. The regiment marched on the 27th at two o'clock in the morning, back to Hanover Junction, and then to their camping ground about a mile from the junction. They had lost a number of men to straggling since coming to this area, and during the morning of the 27th, tried to find them by marching their colors. "Our Regiment's colors passed three lines of fortifications in our front and found nothing but a few stragglers, which they brought back," Snider said. On these extended battlefields, where an individual could not take in even a fraction of the landscape, it was one of the few means of finding men who had become lost.

Around ten o'clock, the brigade marched again, this time crossing the Pamunkey River on the Virginia Central Railroad bridge. They marched southeastward, passing Hanover Court House, and then Merry Oak, and camped that night at rail station. The Federals were on the move, and Gen. Ewell's Corps was once again trying to keep pace with their enemy.[793]

They were coming closer to Richmond, and the only strategy that Gen. Lee could employ was to continue to position his army between the Confederate capital and Gen. Grant's army. The 31st Virginia had many wounded men in the hospitals in Richmond, from the fighting at Spotsylvania and the Wilderness. Among those at Chimborazo Hospital in Richmond was Sergeant Osborne Wilson, of Highland County. He had filled up his previous journal book and began one anew on May 27, while in the convalescent ward at the hospital. "Before this year is closed," He wrote, "or even this little book is half-filled with what occurs daily in my observation, I hope and pray that this cruel war may be over. A battle is expected. There is confidence in Lee and Johnson falling back. Chicken soup, mutton soup, beans, corn bread, and milk for dinner.[794]

Sergeant Snider's journal did not say what they had for dinner on May 28. "We marched before daylight and passed the station and left the railroad to our right and soon got on familiar ground that we had passed over, before the battle of Gaines Mill. (Near Shady Grove.) We passed where we laid on the night of the 26th of June '62 and stopped about 9 A.M., where we laid until midnight and then was moved a short distance and camped for the night."

Ewell's Corps, commanded by Gen. Early, was once more in the lead of Lee's army. The Union army was crossing the Pamunkey River that day, resulting in heavy skirmishing with Federal cavalry. The 31st Virginia had picket duty that night, with the left half of the regiment on duty, and orders to relieve them in the morning with the right half of the regiment. "Myself and six others of the company was stationed at a house where we got some peas and had a fine dinner," Snider said. "There was some heavy skirmishing by cavalry in the evening, and our brigade was moved to the front and drove them back, after which we was relieved and returned to the position that we occupied the night before. Our men had put up our fortifications in the evening... ready to move at daylight."[795]

The regiment marched out in the late morning of May 30, and put on a line and began fortifying a trench and breastworks, but a while later was moved to the right, to support Rodes's division, on the flank of the Union army, at Bethesda Church. "Colonel Willis of the 12th Georgia Regiment took command of the brigade about noon," Snider said. "Colonel Hoffman, who had command since the 6th of May, was absent sick."[796]

Colonel Edward Willis had been recommended for promotion to brigadier general, and the promotion had been approved. Col. Hoffman, who was senior to Willis, must have been more than a bit despondent over this turn of events. It was said that he had been bitten by a spider, and had become so sick that he was forced to leave the regiment on the 30th, to go to Richmond for medical attention. Lt. Col. McCutchen was in command of the 31st Virginia in his absence.[797]

The 31st Virginia, and the old Fourth brigade under command of Colonel Willis, were marched to Bethesda Church that day, arriving there around three o'clock in the afternoon. Rodes's division was already skirmishing with the Federals. The brigade formed a line with the rest of the division, parallel to a road, and rested for a while until their artillery could come up and begin shelling the Federals, who were positioned on the far side of a wide field, with a little bit of artillery showing. The Federal artillery did not respond to the division's guns, leading their divisional commander, Gen. Ramseur, to a false conclusion about the strength of the enemy.[798]

The Fourth brigade was in the lead of Ramseur's division that day. Archibold Atkinson later recalled Gen. Ramseur as a "careless daredevil sort of an officer." Atkinson remembered this day particularly well for a number of reasons, not the least of which was an artillery shell that landed directly under his horse, failing to explode, but frightening both Atkinson and the horse.

Gen. Ramseur requested permission from Gen. Early to send the Fourth brigade against a single gun that was visible in the Union line. "Gen. Early knew it would be a foolish thing to attempt," Atkinson wrote, " and that Ramseur would run any risk to accomplish the purpose. Early told him of the danger of great loss of men, but Ramseur insisted and Early said, "Well damn it, go on, Gen. Ramseur, but don't get all my men killed."

Unfortunately for Colonel Willis and the men of the brigade, the single visible gun was a decoy, and the brigade was being sent into an ambush. "Ramseur had what I think was the best fighting brigade in the army," Atkinson wrote later, "and put that in front of his division, and took the battery "in out of the wet," but oh! with what sacrifice of good men."[799]

The brigade's regular skirmishers had been detailed off earlier in the day, and had not yet returned to the brigade by this time. The 31st Virginia was sent forward as skirmishers. They were crossing a level, open field about a half mile across when massed artillery, concealed in the woods on the far side, and to the left and the right, opened on them in a furious bombardment. "As soon as we got out of the woods, they opened on us with grape, canister and everything else that are used in modern war," Snider wrote. The brigade was charging up behind the skirmishers by this time, and continued to charge through the 31st Virginia. Snider said that since they were not formed in a line, many of the 31st Virginia did not continue on with the main charge, but he went with the charge, coming to within 75 yards of the Federal line.

They found the Union infantry entrenched behind strong breastworks. "They enfiladed us from both flanks," Snider said, "and cut us all to pieces before we got near their works. But our men hung on and fought them for some time within 75 yards of their works."[800]

"The men who usually charged with the rebel yell rushed on in silence," Lt. Col. Charles B. Christian of the 49th Virginia wrote afterward. "At each successive fire, great gaps were made in our ranks, but immediately closed up. We crossed that field of carnage and mounted the parapet of the enemy's works and poured a volley in their faces. They gave way, but two lines of battle, close in their rear, rose and each delivered a volley into our ranks in rapid succession. Some of our killed and wounded fell forward into the enemy's trenches, some backward outside the parapet. Our line, already decimated, was almost annihilated. The remnants... formed and sheltered behind a fence partly thrown down just outside the parapet, and continued the unequal struggle, hoping for support that never came."[801]

Snider somehow lived through the fight, which has been called the bloodiest fight of the war for the old Fourth Brigade. Snider later wrote, "The colonel commanding (Willis) was wounded and the other two colonels was both wounded. Every field officer except our lieutenant colonel (McCutchen), and no one to order a retreat."

At some point in the wild battle near the breastworks, Col. Hoffman's young kinsman, Lt. Thomas W. Hoffman, the adjutant of the 31st Virginia, gathered the remnants of several companies together, and tried to storm a battery. A musket ball passed through his side and entered his liver, wounding him dangerously. He was carried off the field when the regiment withdrew.

"Finally, someone ordered us back," Snider said, "but few knew of the order, but the most withdrew one at a time before dark to the woods where Gordon's division was in support.... I laid by a fence and fought for some time within 75 yards of the works, and when I saw them falling back, and that we could do nothing more, I fell back to the woods. There was two of my company wounded, Lang and Young, from which Young died. There was one man fell dead running just before me as I came out. After coming to the woods I went back a short distance by request after Colonel Willis and helped carry him off the field. He was mortally wounded. The loss in the remainder of the Corps was very light. Our wounded was all brought away, that was got off the field. Some time after dark we fell back to our original line."[802]

The Fourth brigade was devastated in the day's action and would never be the same afterward. In addition to the death of Colonel Willis of the 12th Georgia, Colonel Terrill of the 13th Virginia was also killed. Command of the brigade passed to Lt. Colonel R. D. Lilley of the 25th Virginia, who was promoted to brigadier general and assigned command of the brigade as of June 2, 1864.[803]

Snider said, "Our regiment being on skirmish, a good many did not go up as they was not formed, and our regiment's casualties was much lighter than it would of been. There was 30 killed, wounded and missing in our regiment, and 233 enlisted men in the brigade, and 33 commissioned officers (casualties). Our lieutenant colonel (McCutchen) was the only field officer that escaped, except some of the staff."

After the battle, Lt. Hoffman was taken by ambulance to Richmond and admitted to General Hospital #9, but it was clear the wound was fatal. He was moved to the private residence of Alonzo Lorentz, formerly of Weston, who was then living in Richmond. Thomas W. Hoffman died there on June 4, 1864, ᵃnd was buried at Hollywood Cemetery, in a grave next to that of Norval Lewis of Company C, who had been his friend.[804]

Other casualties included Isaac Jones, and St. Clair McRea, both killed. The mortally wounded included: Milton Crouch, with a gunshot wound to the chest; William Jones, gunshot wound and leg amputated at hospital; and Asa Young, gunshot wound and fracture of occipital bone. Among the other wounded were: Peter W. Carpenter, gunshot wound to foot and ankle; Edward Jones Armstrong; Robert Bodkin, wounded in a shoulder; Morgan B. Campbell, severely wounded in the neck and hip, and captured; William Chew; Harvey Hevener; Silas B. Jones; Alstorpheus W. Lang, wounded in a thigh; and Hughard M. Pullin, wounded in an elbow joint.[805]

John Wilfong received a gunshot wound to both thighs at some time on May 31, and may have been the only soldier wounded that day from the 31st Virginia. The month's casualties had been heavy, and the regiment was now about half the size it had been at the start of the month. There would to be little rest as the campaign moved into the next phase, the battle of Cold Harbor. Fortunately for the Fourth brigade, they were spared the major fighting in that great battle.

The morning of May 31, the brigade was marched about a mile from the road, and went to work making fortifications. The men could hear the sound of considerable fighting going on to their left, but all was quiet in front of them. In the late afternoon, the sound of heavy fighting began far to their right, at Cold Harbor. It was Gen. Hoke's division, with Fitz Lee's cavalry, doing battle with Sheridan's Union cavalry for the town of Cold Harbor.[806]

"Sharp skirmishing began at daylight," Sergeant Snider said on June 1, "with an occasional bomb shell by way of change, which was pretty frequently, most of which passed clear over us. About 2 P.M. we was relieved by Hill's Corps from the extreme left and was moved to the right for a short distance... where Gordon's division had a considerable fight for the skirmisher's rifle pits, which the enemy gained whilst charging our troops.... About dark we laid down with accouterments on." The fighting at Cold Harbor continued throughout the day, the sound of the heavy fighting reaching the men in their fortifications on the left of the Confederate lines.[807]

The 31st Virginia was moved to the right at about two o'clock in the morning of June 2, in time for the early morning skirmishing at daylight. The day was relatively quiet, until around four o'clock in the afternoon, when their Corps was repositioned. Rain had begun falling around then, and would continue through the night. "The left of our Corps was swung around," Snider said, "turning their right flank which extended to our brigade, and we was moved out a short distance, and after dark threw up breastworks."

The 31st Virginia was moved from the right of the brigade's line, to the left of its line, to support a battery of infantry. "Our regiment had some men slightly wounded," Snider wrote. "Clark Queen returned to the Company."

The men spent the night fortifying breastworks in the rain, but June 3 was again relatively uneventful for the brigade. "Considerable fighting" was going on to their left, and a great battle was taking place on to their right. Ewell's division would continue in reserve, with a little skirmishing in the night, and then around two o'clock in the morning, they were moved back to a new line, in order to allow Heth's division to pass from their left, to the right. They continued to hold their position, with the rain again falling in the afternoon and continuing throughout the night of June 4. Snider said, "One third of us kept up as usual at a time through the night."[808]

"Rained in the fore noon, but we had a pleasant evening," Snider wrote on June 5. "Everything was unusually quiet today. We had religious service about noon. There was some cannonading on our extreme right in the evening, and after dark there was considerable of fighting along our line by the skirmishers, which we advanced and consequently we got but little rest."

On June 6, it became apparent that the Federals had withdrawn from the front, and the division moved forward, crossing the breastworks and advancing until they came across Federal skirmishers. "Captured near one hundred of them and forced the rest back to their breastworks," Snider said. "About 2 P.M., our Corps started on a reconnoitering expedition, getting partially in their rear. After marching about two miles, we was formed in line and our skirmishers drove the enemy back after having a considerable fight, when we shelled them until dark, when we withdrew and went back to our old position. In front of where we occupied and shelled from was a very bad swamp, by and which the enemy was very strongly fortified. We accomplished our objective, which was a reconnaissance and found their position. I have been quite unwell all day, occasioned by the bad water. There is but few of us that are almost dead with the diarrhea."

The Corps was sent forward on another forced reconnaissance on June 7, covering the same area as the previous day. "Our skirmishers drove them into their breast works. About 4 P.M. we moved a battery into position and shelled them for some time, when the battery withdrew. Our brigade was in support of the battery," Snider wrote.[809]

They had a real break in the action on June 8, the day unusually quiet. A few at a time, the men in the Fourth brigade were allowed to go to a stream and wash their clothes, a refreshment that must have made a world of difference to their appearance. They could hear some heavy skirmishing, and artillery far to their right, but in their area the day's peace continued. Most of the men were even allowed to sleep that night, with only a few sentinels posted.

On June 9, Ewell's Corps was moved farther to the rear by a few miles, and allowed to camp at a place not far from Gaines' Mill. They remained in camp for several days, the men recovering and resting. Gen. Jubal Early was still in command of Ewell's II Corps of the Army of Northern Virginia. On June 12, he received orders from Gen. Lee to move the Corps to the Shenandoah Valley, where he was to confront the Union forces under command of Gen. Hunter and Gen. Crook.

The men in the 31st Virginia were tremendously relieved at getting away from the living hell of Cold Harbor, and that part of the war still being fought against Grant's army. They were exhausted and about used up, and many of them had difficulty marching, but their hearts were still in it.[810]

"Our Corps was roused up half past one," Snider wrote on June 13, "and marched about 3 A.M. to Mechanicsville and turned off towards Louisa Court House and camped on South Anna River, about 5 P.M., marching about twenty miles. There was a great many broke down and I came very near it. There was heavy cannonading in our rear in the fore part of the day. (June 14) We marched early about daylight, crossing the river and camped (within) a few miles of Louisa Court House... the most of us stood it pretty well, being a cool day." The following day the regiment was two miles west of Louisa Court House, their march slowed by summer heat and the number of men who broke down on the march. On the 16th they camped five miles from Charlottesville, near the railroad, arriving at about five in the afternoon. From there the men were allowed to ride the rails, a blessed relief from marching in the June weather. The selection of rail cars was exotic, noted their surgeon, from passenger cars to box cars, cattle cars, and even repair cars.

They arrived at Lynchburg in the late afternoon of June 17, and were marched to a position about two miles from town, and put in line of battle, in time to join with part of Breckenridge's division, the 19th and 20th Virginia cavalry, which were engaged in a battle at the time. It turned out to be mostly skirmishing and artillery, which continued until after dark.[811]

Gen. Breckenridge had part of his southern forces in the Valley at this time, along with Gen. Imboden's cavalry and mounted infantry, and W. L. Jackson's 19th and 20th Virginia cavalry. Gen. D. H. Hill, and Gen. Hays were also there in force. When Gen. Early brought the II Corps into the Valley, he had about 8,000 men. In combination with Breckenridge, Jackson, and Imboden, this made a sizable threat to the Federals who had been raiding up and down the Valley under Gen. Hunter.

Unfortunately, nearly all of Early's men were on foot because the officer's horses could not be carried on the railroad. The men were on short rations, and Gen. Hunter had a head start on them. As Jubal Early observed in his memoirs, a stern chase by infantry is not a race that is often won, especially by hungry men who were already on the point of fatigue. "The enemy had left Staunton, moving south, which caused us to change our course," Snider said in his journal. "I judge it was our intention to get below them in the valley."

On June 18, around one o'clock in the morning, the Fourth brigade was moved to the right, and began fortifying their line, but were moved again before morning, and once more ordered to fortify the line. Both armies traded artillery shells throughout the day.

"About 4 P.M. they drove in our skirmishers and came up in range of our muskets," Snider said, "when we opened on them and they immediately stopped and laid down under a hill where they stayed a short time and then fell back quickly, leaving several dead and wounded on the field, all of whom was Virginian. Some of which our boys knew." Hunter's command was partly made of regiments formed in the counties of northwest Virginia. "If we had let them come up closer," Snider wrote, "we would of killed a great many more, but it is very difficult matter to keep our boys from firing at sight of a blue jacket."

Hunter's command withdrew in the night, and Gen. Early's Corps took up the chase, with the 31st Virginia leading the brigade, in advance of the division, in front of the corps. "Took several prisoners, (and) horses," Snider wrote, "and got near Liberty about one hour by sun, and found our skirmishers hotly engaged. Our regiment was deployed and moved forward, and finally the brigade came up by regiments and we had a sharp skirmish fight, but succeeded in driving them beyond town before dark, where we laid in line of battle all night.... We had four or five wounded in our regiment, one of them severely, and killed and wounded and captured several."[812]

Surgeon Archibold Atkinson noted their dislike of the Federal army's Gen. Hunter, who was believed to be responsible for so much destruction. The countryside was in ruins, the Union army having done its assigned task of laying waste the Valley of Virginia. Gen. Hunter's army had passed across the land as if they knew no compassion for the civilians living there. Houses and barns were burned, leaving women and children to fend for themselves by the side of the road. In many cases, the possessions of civilians were stolen or simply cut to pieces as though by a band of vandals. Families were without garments other than the clothes on their backs. They had nothing to eat after Hunter's men either carried it all away, or destroyed it to deny it to citizens and Southern army alike. The town of Lynchburg had been saved only because Hunter's men did not have enough time to destroy it.

"If ever a man was hated it was Hunter," Atkinson wrote after the war. "His men were scattered along the road, but we got his wagons and much of his artillery. He could not get it through the mountain pass at Beauford's Gap. We passed the Hollins Institute in Botetourt County near the Blue Ridge Springs." Atkinson had served in western Virginia at the start of the war, and knew the landscape well. "We fared badly on this trip for food, the cooking wagons coming up late at night. We started at 5 A.M. to march, stopping at ten o'clock at a big spring for breakfast. The biscuits were made with mutton suet instead of lard and could hardly be swallowed. It was like taking a wax impression for a set of false teeth."[813]

Gen. Early decided that Hunter had been chased enough at this point. He felt that Hunter would have difficulty from stopping his troops from withdrawing all the way through the mountains into West Virginia.

Early's Corps was allowed to rest on the 22nd. "We moved about 7 A.M. about two miles down the Pike," Snider wrote, "and camped for the day, and was ordered to wash up our clothes, which was very agreeable as we had not had clean clothes for near two months. I went about two miles off of the main road to a home and borrowed a pair of pants and got the Negroes to wash all of my clothes except my jacket."[814]

The regiment marched the following day to camp at a site near the Virginia town of Buchanan, and on the 24th marched again early in the morning, setting out at 3:30 A.M., passing the Natural Bridge. They camped several miles from the town of Lexington, at a site on Buffalo Creek, their day's march hot and difficult.

"We marched as usual," Snider said on June 25, "and passed through Lexington, and through the graveyard by Gen. Jackson's grave at reverse arms, and camped near Fairfield after having a very hard march. Sometime after dark my pass returned, that I had sent up to go on to Staunton to look for my brother, who was said to be wounded or killed in the battle near Staunton and I went on to Greenville, sixteen miles, and laid down by the spring until morning."

Sergeant Snider traveled in advance of the regiment with a pass that allowed him to look for his brother, Elmore, who was in a hospital at Staunton. "I started as soon as it was daylight," Snider said on the 26th, "and traveled about five miles and got some breakfast and arrived at Staunton about 10 A.M., and found my brother severely wounded in the thigh, but doing very well and was at the hospital.

"Immediately after he was wounded he fell into the enemy's hands, but says he was kindly treated and met many of his acquaintances, Capt. Mercer among them, who was very kind to him."

The 31st Virginia arrived at Staunton on June 27, where the men were allowed to rest for a day. Snider took advantage of this opportunity to get his clothes washed again. "I started before daylight to visit my Buffalo Gap friends... about 7 A.M. got my breakfast and changed apparel... and got all of my clothes washed."[815]

It is not difficult to imagine what clean clothes meant to the sergeant after weeks on the line at the Wilderness, Spotsylvania, Bethesda Church, and Cold Harbor; or how important it was, after the dangers experienced in this recent campaign, when he could write of visiting friends at Buffalo Gap near the end of June 1864.

11

Early's Valley Campaign
July 1864—Dec 1864

After chasing Hunter's Federals out of the Valley of Virginia, the 31st Virginia and the other regiments in Early's Corps rested one day at Staunton, and then began to march northward. Gen. Early had been ordered to make an advance on Washington, D.C.

In the south, the Union army under Gen. Sherman had begun a drive on Atlanta, beginning in early May at Chattanooga, Tennessee, and forcing the Confederate army under the command of Gen. Joseph Johnston to retreat, a step at a time, from Resaca, Georgia to Kennesaw Mountain. The situation there for the Confederacy was grim, and destined to grow worse daily until the inevitable fall of Atlanta in September, leaving Richmond ever more isolated as one of the last remaining Confederate strongholds. Gen. Early was sent north from the Shenandoah Valley to threaten the nation's capital in the hope that if his ten thousand-man corps could scare the politicians in Washington, they would draw part of Grant's army away from the Petersburg siege.

On June 28, Early's Corps set out on the Valley pike, reaching Winchester on July 2. The next day, Early split his army in two, and advanced toward Martinsburg, but his cavalry became engaged in a sizable skirmish near Leetown with Union forces under the command of Gen. Sigel. The Confederate cavalry was forced to withdraw to Leetown shortly after Ramseur's and Rodes's divisions arrived there, and the infantry was called on to assist in driving the Federal cavalry back. They did so, and the Federal army under Sigel withdrew to the Potomac River and crossed over to the Maryland Heights. The 31st Virginia participated in the skirmishes that day, and had several men wounded in the fighting, according to Snider.[816]

It was audacious for Gen. Early to consider marching his army across the Potomac River. He had little in the way of supplies, almost no shoes for the men, and the size of his Corps had dwindled through casualties in the hard fighting of the spring campaign. At Staunton, as he prepared for the Washington, D.C. campaign, Early's II Corps had three divisions, with about 8,000 infantry men present. The infantry divisions were each about the size of a normal brigade, and the brigades were smaller than full strength regiments.[817]

The Fourth brigade remained in Ramseur's division, but was exceptionally small by this time, with only about 200 men present, including the 31st Virginia. Col. Hoffman and Lt. Col. McCutchen were both present, but Maj. Cooper was in Richmond, recovering from the wound he received at Spotsylvania.[818]

The 31st Virginia marched at dawn on July 4, toward Charles Town, but passed that town and continued to a position just outside of Harper's Ferry, arriving there about ten o'clock in the morning. The regiment remained throughout the day as skirmishers went forward and occupied Bolivar Heights and the village of Bolivar. The Federals fell back to an inner line of defensive works closer to the river, protected by artillery on Maryland Heights on the far side of the river. Those guns occasionally shelled the Confederates, but many of the hungry skirmishers from the Fourth brigade took this opportunity to find as much to eat as they could, and regardless of Federal artillery, they continued to pass from their camp to Bolivar Heights. They brought back rarities such as coffee and sugar, of which they had been deprived because of the lack of supplies in the Confederacy. This continued through the night, and the following day of July 5.[819]

During the night, the Federals withdrew across the river to the Maryland heights, abandoning Harper's Ferry, and burning a railroad pontoon bridge behind them. By nightfall of July 5, the Federal artillery on Maryland Heights had given up, and both armies were given a quiet night.

The Fourth brigade marched on the morning of July 6 at 7 A.M., to a place on the Potomac River below Shepherdstown, where they waded the river and crossed into Maryland. Ramseur's division camped around one o'clock in the afternoon, and remained in camp through July 7, while Gordon's and Rodes's divisions skirmished with the Federal army. The Fourth brigade's new shoes arrived that day, and were passed out to the men. The roads of Maryland were hard compared to Virginia's soft dirt roads, and the shoes would make a welcome change.

Early's cavalry had gone ahead, crossing the mountains and making certain that the road was open. He ordered an early start for the infantry on the morning of July 8. "Rained some through the night," Snider said. "At 3 A.M. we took up the line of march, passed through Boonsboro (Gap) and camped about 3 P.M. on the hill, four miles west of Frederick, Maryland, but after dark was marched two miles nearer town, where we remained until morning. Cavalry fighting all the afternoon."[820]

The Federals had a large force under the command of Gen. Lew Wallace, positioned on the eastern bank of the Monocacy River, with fortifications to protect the railroad and highway bridges over the river, not far from Frederick Station. Ramseur's division was ordered to a position in front of the Federal entrenchments, skirmishing as they came up and pushing the Union skirmishers back across the Monocacy River. A while later, both sides opened with artillery, and a sharp cannon duel began. Ramseur's skirmishers continued to hold the attention of the center of the Federal line, while Gordon's division flanked the Federals on the right, and as the Federals began to fall back, Ramseur's division advanced across the Monocacy River on the B&O railroad bridge. The division assisted in the pursuit of the Federals until it was clear that they were retreating toward Baltimore.[821]

"About sundown," Snider said, "we moved back near the Frederick Station and camped for the night." They marched again on July 10, but since Ramseur's division was last in the column, the brigade did not set out until after noon. They marched hard the rest of the day, and eventually their division passed the other two divisions, and camped around eleven o'clock. They were about four miles from Rockville, Maryland.[822]

Despite a late arrival the night before, the Fourth brigade was ordered to march at an early hour on July 11, and by four o'clock in the afternoon, having taken the 7th Street pike, were within range of the Federal guns at Fort Stevens, part of the defenses of the nation's capital. "We had a very hot day and a great many gave out," Snider wrote, "Near half our brigade straggled. There was heavy skirmishing and some cannonading all evening."[823]

To their right was Rock Creek, which had been made impassable by fallen timber. The Union defenses appeared impregnable to Gen. Early, who wrote in his memoirs, "If we had any friends in Washington, none of them came out to give us information." Early's Corps could do little more than rattle sabers outside the Federal stronghold, making a demonstration in force, but it was an accomplishment for which few soldiers could boast.[824]

The Fourth brigade, once more part of the reserve, camped close to the home of Admiral Drum, near Silver Spring. Some of the brigade's men later confessed they took advantage of the situation that night to do a bit of foraging in the neighborhood—they "confiscated" ice from Montgomery Blair's ice house, and gathered molasses from the Admiral's cellars. It is even possible that individuals from the 31st Virginia participated in this foraging, but failed to mention it in their diaries.[825]

"We remained in our position until near sundown," Snider wrote on July 12, "when... our regiment moved out to support our sharp-shooters, but returned soon after dark. There was heavy skirmishing in the evening, about 10 P.M. We began our retreat on the same road that we came and traveled all night."[826]

The adventure at Washington, D.C. over, the army began its return to Virginia. The 31st Virginia passed through Rockville not long after dawn, and turned onto a road toward Poolesville, in the direction of the Potomac River. They stopped to rest around two o'clock in the afternoon. After dark, the army marched again as far as White's Ferry on the Potomac River, which they reached on July 14, at eight o'clock in the morning.

The regiment rested for about two hours, and then crossed the river and camped near Big Springs. At two o'clock in the afternoon, the 31st Virginia went on picket near Ball's Bluff. The Union cavalry had come up to the river and had a strong skirmish with Confederate cavalry still on the Maryland side of the river, but after dark the Federals crossed the river and even managed to shell the Confederate camp a little bit, but mostly found the range of the cooking details. On the 15th, the Fourth brigade was given a day of rest, followed by a brigade review.[827]

Early's Corps marched south on July 16, with the Fourth brigade bringing up the rear of the army, wearing coats of summer dust beneath a hot sun. Passing through Leesburg, they marched on the Winchester Road. About two o'clock in the afternoon, Federal cavalry attacked their wagon train, which was insufficiently guarded. The cavalry captured about 60 wagons, and destroyed many others. Later in the day, Confederate cavalry recaptured a number of those wagons, and the teams of horses and mules.

The regiment camped that night at Snickersville, and then marched on the following day to a place three miles below Berryville, and again went into camp. This night the sound of cannonading in the distance lulled the men to sleep. "We moved camp about two miles in the morning," Snider wrote, "down the valley, and a short time before sundown we moved back between Berryville and the river." Gordon's, Echols, and Rodes's divisions went into battle after the Federals crossed the Shenandoah River that day, but Ramseur's division was again in reserve. Both sides suffered substantial casualties in the fight.

"Everything seems quiet," Snider wrote on the 19th. "About 3 P.M. our division moved back, but a short time after dark... we moved back through Berryville, and traveled all night, and arrived at Winchester soon after sunup." Ramseur's division had been split off from Early's army, to confront Averell's Federal cavalry, which was threatening Winchester from the north.[828]

On July 20, Gen. Ramseur marched his men in the mid-afternoon, north on the Martinsburg Pike, toward Stephenson's Depot. He was deceived by the strength of Averell's force, and failed to take the necessary precautions before advancing into battle. The result was a much more difficult fight than Ramseur had bargained for.[829]

Ramseur put four pieces of artillery in front of his column that day, without first sending videttes out to ascertain the enemy's position. The 31st Virginia led the Fourth brigade, following closely behind the artillery as the division approached Stephenson's Depot. "The Yankees had found out that we were coming," Lt. John Bosworth wrote after the war, "and passing through a piece of wood... surprised the command (by) lying in wait. (They) captured the cannon in front, then opened fire from both sides of the road, having an enfilading fire and front fire, killing many of our men who were not yet deployed in line of battle, but made the attempt to line."

As though breathless from the scramble of battle, Snider said in his journal, "The skirmishing got heavy and fast, and we was moved some two miles from town and was rushed into the works by brigades in column, and the artillery in the same manner with empty guns, and our brigade was fired into before they got formed, which was in support of the other two brigades, and the one on our left gave back and left our flank unprotected, and we all had to fall back, which was done in the greatest disorder."[830]

The scene was one of confusion and panic. Godwin's brigade broke, and Robert Johnston's brigade panicked and fell back. Meanwhile, the Fourth brigade held its ground as well as it could, and suffered losses because of Ramseur's mistake. "Our artillery run into the line of battle and had the horses shot down before they could get in position, and here we lost four guns, and the rest came back in the greatest excitement..." Snider wrote.

Lt. Bosworth: "Colonel R. D. Lilly, seeing the danger of capturing our small brigade, and bullets coming from three directions, ordered a hasty retreat to save the brigade from being captured, as the enemy had ten times as many as we. During the fighting, orders were given to lie down, but a goodly number loaded and fought. Capt. (George T.) Thompson laid down, and refused to get up and take command. I then took command of the company.... The command was ordered to retreat—directly by my side Lieut. Bolinger of Co. K was killed, and Colonel Lilly before the retreat lost his arm. We were met a mile from there by Gen. Early, with reinforcements.... I heard Gen. Early give Ramseur some short talk for the manner in which he was marching without videttes in front."[831]

After dark, Ramseur's division was withdrawn toward Kernstown, and remained until daylight. The 31st Virginia had lost 31 men in the battle of Kernstown, the heaviest loss of any regiment in the division. Considering that the brigade only had about 200 men at this time, the number of wounded, killed, and missing was a staggering blow to the old 31st Virginia. Snider said the next day that only their own cavalry, charging the Federals on both flanks, had saved their division from even worse destruction.[832]

For the 31st Virginia, the casualties included: George R. Bolinger, killed; Edwin O. Hays, who died from wounds on August 3, and John V. Hupman, who died at Staunton hospital September 14. The wounded included: Elias Wilfong, Henry G. Britton (4th Sgt and Color

Guard), William P. Arnold (gun shot wound to right knee and disabled), Hampton B. Curry (gunshot wound to left thigh), Reuben K. Devier, David C. Gibson (gunshot wound involving elbow, and amputation of upper third of arm), Adam F. Gum, Robert Henderson (gunshot wound to left arm), Thomas H. McGinnis (wounded in the left leg and captured), Enoch Nay, and James C. Page. They also lost 13 men who were captured by the enemy, including Capt. George T. Thompson of Company H.[833]

All total, the Federals captured 267 unwounded officers and men that day in the fight against Ramseur's division. Four guns were lost from the artillery, and according to Union reports, 73 of Ramseur's men were killed, with another 130 wounded. The commander of the Fourth brigade, Brig. Gen. R. D. Lilly was severely wounded in the fighting, and later lost an arm to amputation. After Lilley fell, Col. Hoffman once again assumed temporary command of what remained of the old Fourth brigade.[834]

Sergeant Snider, July 21: "We moved back to Newtown and took position soon after daylight. Remained some time, when we moved back to Cedar Creek and went into camp about 3 P.M. (July 22) We moved out at daylight and to the right of Strasburg and was ... for some time on the road one mile from Strasburg, where we went into camp about 3 P.M. (July 23) We remained in camp all day. There was some skirmishing by the cavalry down the road and it is believed that they have quit pressing us."[835]

The 31st Virginia was part of the reserve on July 24, when Early's Corps fought Gen. Crook's "Army of West Virginia" in the battle of Kernstown. Crook's army included the commands of Hunter, Sigel, and Avery, composed of infantry and cavalry. "Ramseur's division was sent to the left, at Bartonsville, to get around the enemy's right flank, while the other divisions moved along the Valley Pike, and formed on each side of it," Jubal Early reported after the war.[836]

"We moved... down the valley at daylight," Snider said, "and soon heard artillery about Kernstown.... We pushed forward around their right flank, but did not get engaged except our skirmishers before they was routed." The Federals fell back from Early's Corps, leaving behind their wounded and dead, many of whom the men in the 31st Virginia recognized as former neighbors from home, who had been serving in Hunter's command. The Federals were pursued all the way back to Winchester, and the 31st Virginia went into camp that night just two miles from town.[837]

"Began raining in the night and continued... very cold and disagreeable," Snider said on July 25. "We remained in camp until about 5 P.M., when we moved to Bunker Hill.... The enemy had burned a great deal of their (wagon) train, particularly caissons, in their stampede. (July 26) We marched at daylight without rations and got to Martinsburg about 1 P.M. and went into camp near there. About 2

P.M.... our rations came up, and about 6 P.M. we marched onto the railroad, and tore and burnt it until after dark, when we went back to camp. The enemy had run our cavalry out of town last evening, but evacuated in the night and crossed the river."

The men were given a day off on the 27th. "We remained in camp all day," Snider wrote, "and was ordered to wash our clothes, which we gladly accepted." The next day, he said, "I went black-berrying in the morning, and tore up railroad about 3 hours in the afternoon. To be ready to move at daylight." Gen. Early had decided to make another raid into Maryland.

Ramseur and Rodes's divisions marched at daylight on July 29, reaching a ford near Williamsport, where they camped for the night. Their cavalry crossed in the early morning and raided Hagerstown, where they captured some Federals, sending the prisoners back across the river under guard. On the morning of the 30th, Ramseur and Rodes's divisions marched toward Hedgesville, and then turned to march back to their camp at Martinsburg, arriving there before noon. They marched again on July 31, to an old campground at Bunker Hill, arriving again before noon on a very hot day.[838]

Jacob C. Matheny, Capt. of Company E, had been elected on May 26 in Highland County for the office of clerk of the Circuit and County Courts. He was at that time recuperating in a hospital in Staunton from a wound received on May 19. Matheny wrote a resignation on July 26, while at the hospital, stating that he was sending the resignation direct to the Secretary of War because it was quicker than trying to catch up with the army in the Valley of Virginia.

Matheny apparently departed the hospital shortly afterward and returned home to Highland County to assume the office of clerk of the courts, no doubt with a well-earned sigh of relief. He had given of himself liberally while serving in the regiment.[839]

But others from the 31st Virginia were also still suffering in hospitals, such as Phillips. In early July, in his hospital bed at Charlottesville, perhaps delirious from the pain of his wounded hip, he wrote, "I have suffered desperately today, my wound still in bad condition. Colonel Hoffman paid me a visit today. I was very glad to see him."[840]

He was lonely, longing for a familiar face among the strangers at the hospital. The people who ran the hospital were very kind to him, especially Miss and Mrs. Coleston, who were in charge of the kitchen. Perhaps his delirium was the final crisis of a fever, for the next day his journal is clearly written, making observations about the University of Virginia, "...just a few hundred paces from the window of the room I occupy in Harris House Hospital." He noted the building had formerly been a boarding house for law students.[841]

On July 19, Phillips was transferred from the Charlottesville hospital to Sutherland's at North Garden, about 10 miles from

Charlottesville. While recuperating at Sutherland's, he was visited by several friends, including Lt. Coleman Bowman, and Lt. Elam Poling. By August 24, Phillips was well enough for a jaunt to Staunton to celebrate his birthday. "It is a dry place," Phillips wrote in his journal, "and has some hard nuts in it." Phillips remained at Sutherland's through the fall of the year, recovering strength and hearing of Gen. Early's army by way of letters from friends, and from reading newspapers.[842]

Sergeant Osborne Wilson was still at the hospital in Richmond, helping with the wounded. The prices Wilson recorded in 1864 are an excellent yardstick for the terrible inflation of the day: (June 20) $2.00 for a shave and a close haircut; (Aug. 17) $4.00 for peaches and melons; (Oct. 19) $5.00 for two pounds of tobacco; (Oct. 22) $8.00 for the fare from Richmond to Staunton; (Dec. 1) $5.00 for one dozen apples; (Dec. 30) $40.00 per bushel sweet potatoes. The soldier's meager pay for a month was paltry by comparison with those prices.[843]

While the 31st Virginia was camped at Bunker Hill, Jacob McLaughlin, of Company G, wrote to his cousin, Nannie McLaughlin. The McLaughlin's were a large and prolific family of Irish descent in Pocahontas County. Their ancestor, John McLaughlin had settled on Jackson's River, below Monterey in Highland County prior to the American revolution, and over time various members of the family had moved across the mountains to the Greenbrier Valley. Jacob had served as a private in the 31st Virginia since the spring of 1862, and had avoided major illness or wound. He was probably more than a little homesick, but was also reflecting on the hard campaign they had just fought, particularly since coming back to the Valley of Virginia under Gen. Early.

"It is lamentable to look upon," McLaughlin wrote concerning Company G, "for when we started out this spring we had fifty men, now we have only fifteen. The rest have been killed, wounded, and taken prisoners. I tell you it looks discouraging to fight under such circumstances; though through the mercies of God, I have been one of the few that have been spared, which I feel very thankful for and the kind mercies bestowed on me."

After noting the hard marches his regiment had made since arriving in the Valley, he wrote that he felt they had earned the right to a rest for some days. "I am sorry to inform you that both of your brothers are taken prisoners, and the whole 25th Regiment, excepting about fourteen, has been taken. Though we must expect to bear with many troubles in a war like this, you ought to be thankful that they are prisoners, instead of being killed, as there have so many poor soldiers fallen this summer. I think a prisoner now is much better off than we poor men that have to march and fight so much. At least now they are in less danger."[844]

The 31st Virginia remained in camp, quietly restoring their energy. On August 3, the regiment was sent on picket duty, not far from camp, and the weather being agreeable, they had "a very pleasant time,' according to Sergeant Snider.

It was around this time that Lt. John W. Bosworth of Company H had an odd little adventure of a different sort along the river. "My brother, Newton Bosworth, was with me," he wrote later, as though he needed confirmation of his own experience. "I was sent by order of Gen. Early, with about 100 southern soldiers, to make observation as to the movements of the northern soldiers not far from our camp, as we had driven them across the river.... Was ordered to remain there and if necessary report any movements of the enemy. No fighting was being done as the southern army had driven the Yanks across the river. While there, a regiment of Massachusetts soldiers stopped on the opposite side of the river. We could talk, as the river was narrow, and they were halted."

Bosworth discovered that one of the Union officers was from Northampton, Massachusetts, and shared the same name, John W. Bosworth. The father of John Bosworth of the 31st Virginia had grown up in Northampton, Massachusetts, but after serving in the War of 1812, had moved to Virginia. The coincidence of meeting a distant kinsman from the home of his father was remarkable. "I told him I had not seen my parents in over two years," the 31st Virginia's Bosworth wrote. "Well, he suggested for me to write home a brief letter and he would mail it to him, which he did, and after the war closed Pa told me he had received it at Beverly, Va. No war news in it—only our health."[845]

Sergeant Snider, August 4: "We was withdrawn before daylight and marched in the direction of Darksville after the brigade, and gained it on the Pike. The whole army was on the move." While Breckenridge and Gordon's divisions marched toward Shepherdstown, Ramseur's division moved to Big Spring, seven miles from Williamsport, and camped. They crossed the Potomac River again on August 5, and camped three miles below Williamsport. "About noon there was some whiskey issued that was got at Williamsport," Snider said. The issuance of whiskey to Confederate troops was extremely rare.[846]

"We had some rain this morning, which was very much needed," Snider wrote on the 6th. "Breckenridge's train began passing and directly his troops and we fell in the rear about noon and recrossed the river at Winchester, and took the back road and camped at Big Springs, near Hedgesville." They had been sent to the river to make certain that Breckenridge's cavalry could cross back into Virginia safely: the cavalry had made a dash to Chambersburg, Pennsylvania, where they burned the town in retribution for all of the property burned in the Valley of Virginia by the Union army.

The 31st Virginia marched again the next day with the brigade and division, and camped at their old Bunker Hill camp, remaining in camp on August 8, but on the 9th, they were roused out in a hurry. "About 8 A.M. we was ordered to fall in very unexpectedly," Snider wrote. "Marched though Winchester one mile and was moved one mile west on the back road, and our regiment put on picket." There was a cavalry fight that day, in which the Confederates repulsed a strong Federal cavalry unit.[847]

Ramseur's division marched at around five o'clock in the afternoon on August 10, and was placed to guard the road on the west side of town. They slept on their arms that night, about a mile outside of town. "Soon after daylight our cavalry advanced and found the enemy, which drove them back," Snider said on the 11th. "About 10 A.M. our brigade was pushed forward near two miles (on the Millwood Road), driving them back on their artillery and got eight or nine prisoners and killed and wounded several. One killed and one leg broken in our regiment... and one killed in the 49th regiment, after which we fell back to a good position near Newtown and remained until next morning."

While Ramseur's division was engaged in its heavy skirmish, Imboden and Vaughan's cavalry were involved in heavy fighting elsewhere, and Gordon's division was also engaged near Newtown. The Federal army in the Valley had recently gained a large reinforcement, and had been consolidated and renamed, the Army of the Shenandoah. It was now under the command of Gen. Philip Sheridan, an aggressive, professional soldier who was picked by Gen. Grant to carry out the destruction of all food and agriculture in the Valley of Virginia. His other mission was to endlessly harass and occupy Early, to defeat him if possible, but most importantly to press him so that none of Early's army would be released to go to the aid of Richmond. This Union commander proved to be a great problem for Early's Army of the Valley, and the nature of the fighting became much more intense, and costly.

For the men in Early's army, this meant constant movement: marching, skirmishing, and more marching, ranging up and down the valley through August and the first half of September without a major battle, but being used up in little ways, from wounds, and weariness.

The 31st Virginia marched to Fisher's Hill, south of Cedar Creek on August 12, and was engaged in skirmishing. They had more skirmishing on the following day, and again on August 15. On the 17th, they marched north again, to Kernstown, and helped drive the Federals through Winchester, and beyond. They continued northward to Winchester on the 18th, and camped.[848]

"The valley was filled with columns of smoke from the barns and stacks of grain," Snider noticed as they were marching north from Fisher's Hill. "All of which they (the Yankees) burnt and destroyed, the corn as much as possible." It was difficult on the soldiers to see the effects of the Union army's policy of denying food to the Confederate soldier and civilian. Without the harvest, there would be nothing to carry them through the winter.

Ramseur's division marched south on August 19 to Bunker Hill, and camped, and the following day the Fourth brigade was sent to Smithfield and back, in response to reports of a Union scouting party. They returned to Smithfield on August 21, and became engaged in a heavy skirmish action, with the Fourth brigade placed on the right of Ramseur's line. The 31st Virginia was sent out to support the skirmishers, and then served as rearguard as the army marched a few miles after dark and went into camp.[849]

They marched to Charles Town on the 22nd, following the Union army, and did some skirmishing with the Federal rearguard. The Federals had gone into strong defensive works, and had the support of heavy artillery. The 31st Virginia camped that night near Charles Town. The regiment was moved forward again on the 23rd, in support of the skirmish line, and then was deployed and drove the Federals back from their works. At dark, the 31st Virginia returned to the camp of the night before.

"We remained in camp until about 1 P.M.," Snider said on August 24, "when the enemy made a dash on our pickets with cavalry and infantry, and one (Confederate) regiment run and let the cavalry in, which was soon drove out by artillery, and our brigade was rushed up, but was not engaged. They got five prisoners, and killed one, and wounded a few, and fell back to their old position.... Forty of our regiment was left on picket with others from the brigade."[850]

"I was very unwell through the night," Snider complained on the 25th, " and about 9 A.M. we was relieved by Anderson's men, and our Corps moved toward Shepherdstown. The advance of Breckenridge's command found the enemy near Leetown and had a considerable fight with the cavalry, but drove them back across the river. Our division went to Smithfield, and then moved back about two miles and camped. I rode most of the day in the ambulance."

They marched back to Smithfield on the 26th, and camped. On the 27th, they marched to Bunker Hill and camped, and had a strong skirmish on August 28, near Smithfield. They were engaged again at Smithfield on the morning of August 29, with heavy skirmishing and a lot of artillery. "At the river, sharpshooters done the fighting," Snider said. The regiment was given a much needed rest on the next three days, allowing Snider time for such things as making out the payroll, one of his duties in Company C.[851]

With reports that the Federals were approaching Berryville on September 2, the army marched to Opequon Creek, four miles above Smithfield, but then turned around and marched to a position six miles below Winchester and camped. Ramseur's division marched the next day, with more skirmishing and chasing the Federals. They camped four miles from Opequon Creek that night.

On September 4, the division marched back to Berryville, where Anderson's division was confronting the Federals in some fortifications. The brigade's line of battle was formed about a mile from town, but was in reserve as Anderson pressed forward, taking the Federal position and capturing several hundred prisoners. On the 5th, Ramseur's division served as rearguard while Anderson's men marched toward Winchester. Ramseur's division followed in the afternoon, and by dark, the 31st Virginia was camped at Big Springs, four miles from Winchester.[852]

The regiment had a couple of days of rest in camp on September 6 and 7, the weather rainy. On the 7th, they received news that Atlanta had fallen to the Federals, a significant blow to the morale of the soldiers in Early's army. They knew that with the fall of that Confederate stronghold and port city, the Confederacy was weakened.[853]

Will Yeager wrote to his brother Henry on September 7, from their camp at Big Springs. Henry had been wounded in the Spotsylvania campaign, and after being released from the hospital, had gone home to Pocahontas County on a furlough. "You wished to know who is commanding our company," Yeager wrote. "Henry Hull is in command." William Henry Hull was the 1st Sergeant of Company G. They had used up all of their officers. "We received a letter from Lish," Yeager said. "He is at Fort Delaware, but knows nothing of any of the rest of our boys." Their captain, Elisha Wilfong had been captured in the fight at the Bloody Angle on May 12. "I must close, they are skirmishing now and we have orders to move. Tell Ma to send me a pair of pants the first opportunity. I'm almost naked and we can't get to stop long enough at one place to draw clothing."[854]

Others in the regiment continued on detached service, though the trend now was for men to be sent back to their regiments unless absolutely needed elsewhere. The regiments were thin in their ranks and could use every able bodied man. An exception to the policy was Private John A. Noel of Company E, who was put on detached service following a stay at the hospital at Staunton in November 1862 for epilepsy. He was detailed as hospital nurse through 1863 and into 1864, when he was transferred to Richmond in April as a guard.

Noel was 19 years old in 1864, dark-haired, with blue eyes, and stood close to six feet tall. On September 8, 1864, he was relieved from hospital guard duty at Camp Winder, and ordered to report to Capt. W. H. H. Coe, Commanding the President's Guard, for assignment. Private Noel, formerly of Company E, 31st Virginia, apparently finished the war as one of Jefferson Davis's bodyguards.[855]

A steady rainfall continuing through the day, September 8, gave the men another respite from war. They were sent out on picket on the 9th, along with the 49th Virginia, to a position between Gordon's Springs and the river. They returned to the brigade on September 10, as Breckenridge relieved the picket. The 31st Virginia marched with the Fourth brigade that day, to Bunker Hill, where they occupied the road by lying in it until near dark, and then went into camp. They marched again on the 11th, to a position four miles below Winchester, and camped. The men were given a day off on the 12th, and Snider said they were allowed to go to an orchard and pick apples. Around noon on September 13, Ramseur's division again marched, this time to guard a ford, where they skirmished some with the Federals. The 31st Virginia helped place a battery of artillery in position, and remained nearby to guard it during the artillery exchange.

"Our battery had two killed," Snider said, "and eight or ten wounded. At dark we moved back a short distance and camped on the Gordon's Spring road." They were allowed a day in camp on the 14th, but marched at dawn on the 15th, to a position a mile and a half east of Winchester, as Ramseur's division replaced Anderson's division.[856]

"About 10 A.M. we went on picket a short distance from camp," Snider said on the 16th. "Our Company was in the reserve. Everything quiet.... (Sept. 17) The cavalry was fired on before daylight and we was roused up to be ready for any emergency, but nothing more occurred. We was relieved and returned to camp about 10 P.M."

The notation for September 17, 1864 was Snider's last journal entry, and part of it could have been his own personal motto, had he survived the war: "We was roused up to be ready for any emergency." In the years since their enlistments in the army, Maj. Cooper and Snider had developed a rapport. Perhaps it was because Snider had become the orderly sergeant of Company C when Cooper was a captain. They were from the same town, Clarksburg, and were both public-spirited men, Cooper with his newspaper and occasional service in the city government; and Snider, though young, serving his county as a deputy sheriff. They had traveled a long road together since then, and perhaps had even become friends. Somehow it is not surprising that when Joseph C. Snider was killed in battle, William P. Cooper should take care of retrieving the journal that Snider kept faithfully and daily, and afterward fill in the missing days since Snider had last written, and explain the manner of Snider's death.

"September 18," Cooper later wrote, "The command remained in camp all day." The battle of Third Winchester awaited them on the following day.[857]

Gen. Sheridan had been trying for a month to corner Early's Army of the Valley in a position where the Federal Army of the Shenandoah could use its size, and firepower to break the Confederates. Through weeks of skirmish and movement, the two armies had moved back and forth through the Winchester area, until on September 19 the Confederates had at last positioned themselves in a line to the east of

Winchester that Sheridan believed was favorable to attack. Gen. Early's army was spread out, from Stephenson's Depot about four miles north of town, near the Martinsburg Pike, to the Berryville Road which ran east of Winchester to cross Opequon Creek. Gordon and Rodes's divisions were at Stephenson's Depot that morning, along with Breckenridge's cavalry; and Ramseur's division held the Berryville Road, about two miles east of town.

The Federals began their attack in the darkness of early morning as Wilson's cavalry division crossed the Opequon, with McIntosh's First brigade in the lead, armed with 7-shot breech loading Spencer repeating carbines, which were capable of laying down a tremendous amount of firepower in a short time. They drove in Ramseur's pickets while the rest of Wilson's division came up through a narrow pass where the road had been cut through a hillside. Deploying artillery, the Federals under McIntosh attacked Ramseur's line with mounted and dismounted cavalry, and pushed the confederates out of their breastworks. Ramseur's men fell back a short ways, reformed their lines, and began to counterattack.

Surgeon Archibold Atkinson recalled the early phase of the battle: "The first I knew of the nearness of the enemy, was the firing of cannon not far off, and thud came a ball falling about 20 ft. from the little knoll upon which the chaplain and I lay asleep. I paid little heed to the first, but when they began to be numerous, I awakened Mr. Lepps (the chaplain), and sent the "yellow" (negro) boy who attended us to catch our horses, which were down in an adjacent meadow. I pulled down the little tent, threw out the saddles which we had been using as pillows, and hearing the long roll, told the "parson" I would fall in with the regiment and go on and see what was to be done. The enemy had their artillery upon a hill, and our men were told to lie down and await developments."[858]

The Federals continued to pour more men through the pass on the Berryville Road, with Wright's Sixth Corps coming up around nine o'clock. Maj. Cooper reported, "Our brigade was placed in line of battle on the right. About ten o'clock it was ordered towards the left to support Johnston's brigade. Being out-flanked on both sides by vastly superior numbers, it was ordered back after inflicting severe injury upon the enemy. We established a new line farther in the rear and to the left and hastily threw up rail piles for defense." They had fallen back about half a mile, while waiting for Gordon and Rodes's divisions to come to their support.

"It was while bravely fighting behind these, that Sergeant Snider received a minié ball through the head and was killed almost instantly," Cooper wrote in Snider's journal. Joseph C. Snider had finally found the limits of fortune in his civil war. He died without marrying, leaving no children behind to remember him except a grieving mother in Harrison County, and a saddened brother in the hospital at Staunton.

Fortunately, Snider's brother, Elmore preserved his memory by saving Snider's journal. While far from elegant as literature, Snider's words were gained through incredible experiences and hard fighting on the field of battle with the 31st Virginia.[859]

Several other men from the 31st Virginia also became casualties that day. John Friel received a gunshot wound to the right fibula. Nicholas Poling, George W. Smith, and Warwick C. Kincaid were wounded and captured, Smith with a gunshot wound to the thigh.[860]

Ramseur's division, covering the road east of Winchester, held up the Union advance for five hours while Gen. Early brought his army into position to fight. The division's immediate threats that day were the Union's Sixth Corps, under Wright, and the Nineteenth Corps under Getty: Ramseur's division spent much of the day tangling directly with Getty's Corps.

The Federals attacked in force at 11:40 A.M., giving Gen. Gordon's brigades a rough time on the left, but Gordon's men fought them with intense musketry and the Union line fell back. Rodes's division came up and held the center of the Confederate line. Those two divisions occupied the ground between Ramseur's line, which was still astride the Berryville Road, to as far north as Red Bud Run, where the ground was nearly a swamp.

On the right, Hoffman's brigade was positioned near the center of Ramseur's line, probably on the road itself, but the pressure of too many Federal regiments finally forced their line back to Dinkle's farm, where they made another line and held. A spirited attack on the Union's right flank by Gordon and Rodes's divisions took the pressure off, giving the men a breather, although still engaged with the Federals, who continued to press.

Gen. Early was forced to consolidate his line in the afternoon, as the Federals began pressing from the north, northeast, and east. Early's line, by late afternoon, had assumed the shape of an angle, with Fitzhugh Lee, Breckenridge, and Gordon holding the northern part of the angle, just outside of the edge of Winchester. Rodes and Ramseur's divisions held the eastern line, the latter just barely positioned across the Berryville Road.

Around 4:30 P.M., Sheridan concentrated an attack against the northern part of Early's line, attacking from the north and against the angle where the Confederate line turned to the south. The sound of the battle brought the men in Ramseur and Rodes's divisions to their feet, to see what was happening. Men began to give way in Rodes's division, perhaps believing that something was going wrong on the left. As they fell back, something did go wrong and most of the rest of Early's line also began to fall back to entrenchments on the outskirts of the town.[861]

The 31st Virginia was placed on the right of Ramseur's new line. The men were getting themselves established, the brigade far from defeated, but probably discouraged, when Jubal Early received an incorrect message that his right was being pushed back. What had been seen were Hoffman's brigade and the other brigades in Ramseur's division deploying in the new line. Suddenly, the Confederate line began to fall apart as men panicked and turned toward town, in a rush that picked up speed. Early's army had become scared, and their retreat was hasty. They poured into Winchester, jamming the streets, and continued out through the southern edge of town, marching south on the pike. They had been defeated and routed.[862]

Throughout this phase of the retreat, however, Ramseur's division had held its line, and continued to block the Federal army from the eastern side of town while their compatriots made an escape through the town. Jubal Early later reported, "Ramseur's division, which maintained its organization, was moved on the east of the town to the south side of it, and put into position, forming a basis for a new line, while the other troops moved back through the town." Several pieces of artillery, under Wickham, guarded this movement, and held the Federal cavalry back until the new line had formed. Ramseur held his new line, on the south side, until after dark, when he withdrew up the Valley, as the rearguard to Early's retreating army.[863]

The Fourth brigade lost their best surgeon that day, as Archibold Atkinson was ordered to remain in Winchester to care for the wounded. "About 5 P.M. I was told to take my wounded into Winchester," he later wrote. "Upon striking the town, I went up Market St., and upon passing Mr. Conrad's house I saw many wounded men at a small hotel across the way. I stopped and found Tip Johnston and Collin Hackett doing what they could for the suffering soldiers. I soon had the hotel full of the wounded.

"The army came rushing by and I knew they were in retreat, so I told such men as could walk to get off as fast as they could. It is wonderful how fast a lame man can get over ground when he knows the enemy is after him." Surgeon Atkinson was ordered to remain in Winchester to care for the wounded men from the brigade. The wounded became prisoners of war by the end of that day, September 19. Those who gave a parole, swearing they would not attempt to escape or return to their army were allowed to remain in town until recovered.

Two new hospitals were established for the wounded Confederates at Winchester, using abandoned warehouses and factories: Dr. Atkinson's hospital was known as Baker hospital, while a second hospital run by Dr. Love was called the York hospital. The two surgeons were in charge of hundreds of wounded men for the next several months, but nearly all of the men, and the surgeons would be exchanged near the end of the year.[864]

A total of 775 men from Early's Army of the Valley were captured on September 19 at the battle of Third Winchester, according to the official Union reports, including 70 officers, 7 battle flags, and 2 pieces of artillery. Several men from the 31st were among those wounded and captured during the fighting, and were later sent to the prisoner of war camp at Point Lookout, Maryland. They were: John Friel, Company F; Sergeant Francis M. Golden, Company C; 1st Lt. Nicholas Poling, Company K; David H. Simmons, Company F; George W. Smith, Company C; John F. Taylor, Company F; and Corporal Jonas Wilfong, Company G.[865]

The Confederates fled south from Winchester on the Valley turnpike. They marched 20 miles that night to Fisher's Hill, a strong position about a mile south of Strasburg. The Federal cavalry had followed them only as far as Mill Creek, just outside of the Winchester town limits, before halting for the night to rest. By the time that the Federal cavalry next caught up with the Confederates, Early had placed his divisions in a line that extended across the valley on the Fisher's Hill ridge.

Early reorganized his command shortly after they arrived at Fisher's Hill. Gen. Ramseur was transferred to replace Gen. Rodes, who had been killed at Winchester. Gen. Pegram had returned to the army after recovering from a wound received at the Wilderness: he was given Ramseur's division, which included the Fourth brigade. Once these changes were made, Lomax's dismounted cavalry was placed on the left of the Confederate line at Fisher's Hill, with Ramseur next, then Pegram, Gordon, and Wharton. The right end of the line ended just east of the Valley pike. Beyond Wharton's division, and protecting that flank was the North Fork of the Shenandoah. Immediately in front of the line, at the foot of the ridge, was Tumbling Run, a shallow stream that could be easily crossed[866]

The Federal army began its pursuit on the morning of September 20, with the cavalry leading. Averell's division took the Back Road, while Merritt's division rode south on the Valley pike, and Wilson's division approached on the Front Royal road by way of Stevensburg. Sheridan's infantry and artillery marched south on the Valley pike, arriving near Fisher's Hill late in the day on the 20th.

Sheridan moved the various elements of his army carefully, using darkness on the 21st, and the natural cloak of topography to conceal the approach of his army. Gen. Crook's Eighth Corps had been sent around to a flanking position, on the Confederate left. About four o'clock in the afternoon, on the 22nd, while the Federal line held the attention of the Confederates, Crook's men stormed down upon Lomax's dismounted cavalry from the left flank and rear, pushing them into Ramseur's division. Ramseur tried to bring his line around to face Crook's flank attack, but could not hold. Pegram also attempted to change his line, including the Fourth brigade, but the movement was not successful, and his brigades were disordered. Crook's cavalry was quick to take advantage of the confusion in Pegram's lines, and pressed the attack. Gen. Early was forced to withdraw: in the evening, his army retreated through Woodstock to a place called Narrow Passage.

Following so quickly after the defeat at Winchester on the 19th, this battle and defeat at Fishers Hill was devastating to the morale of Early's soldiers. The Confederates lost 11 pieces of artillery at Fisher's Hill, and 1,235 infantry and artillerymen, most of them taken prisoner. The 31st Virginia had two men killed in the battle. One of the four wounded was Joshua Fast, with a gunshot wound to the right ankle. The list of men captured included: Jesse Bennett, Company K; John W. Bird, Company E; Henry G. Britton, Company E, 4th Sergeant and Color Guard; Sergeant James M. Burbridge, Company G; James A. Campbell, Company H; Alstorpheus W. Lang, Company C; John S. Robertson, Company E; John E. Rutherford, Company A; Hezekiah Wilson, Company B.[867]

Early marched his army to Mount Jackson on the 23rd, and skirmished a while with Averell's cavalry before marching to Rude's Hill, between Mt. Jackson and New Market. On the 24th, with Federal cavalry harassing their small army, the men remained in line of battle as they fell back to New Market, passing through the town, and taking a position at the split in the road, called Tenth Legion, nine miles from Rude's Hill. Federal cavalry harassed them all the way, and every two miles, Gen. Early had them stop and fire artillery, to discourage their enemy. The Federals went into camp just outside of the reach of the Confederate artillery. Early continued to hold at Tenth Legion until after dark, when he marched his army another five miles toward Port Republic.

Gen. Early informed Lee, on the 25th: "My troops are very much shattered, the men very much exhausted, and many of them without shoes." He marched them that day to Port Republic, and after crossing the two rivers there, took a position between Port Republic and Brown's gap. While there, Early was reinforced by Kershaw's division, which arrived on the 26th.[868]

Hoffman's Fourth brigade had been assigned the task of skirmish duty to protect the rear of the division on several occasions, including while they were in camp at Brown's Gap. Marching again on the 27th, and skirmishing frequently with the enemy, Early's Army of the Valley reached Waynesboro on September 28.

Pegram's division skirmished heavily with the Federal cavalry that day. "Pegram drove them to Dogtown by dark," Jed Hotchkiss reported in his journal that day, "and attacked them there just after Wickham drove them through Waynesboro from toward Rockfish Gap... Pegram had driven the Yanks three miles and a half. He gallantly attacked them after dark and drove them toward Fisherville and encamped where they had their camp on the Staunton road."[869]

The Fourth brigade, under command of Hoffman, had 663 men at this time, but more than two hundred of them were sick or wounded, and could not be counted as effective. They returned to Waynesboro after the fight at Dogtown, and rested for two days.[870]

Gen. Sheridan withdrew his cavalry not long after this, and began to employ his men in burning the fields and produce of the Valley. This was in response to the orders he had received from Gen. Grant, upon taking command of the Army of the Shenandoah, to deny all food to the Confederate army and civilian population. It was an activity that made refugees and paupers of entire families, who were forced from their homes and farms while their grain was burned, and animals killed. For the demoralized men of Jubal Early's army, who had suffered too many recent reverses of fortune on the field of battle, the knowledge that they could do very little to protect their treasured Valley farms from the torch was terribly depressing.[871]

Some of the men began to desert from Early's army. One of those was from the 31st Virginia, Private Aaron Rowan of Company I, one of the youngest men to serve in the 31st Virginia. He made it as far as Weston, in Lewis County, before being arrested on October 10, and was reported by the Union commander there as a rebel deserter. He was only 17 years old at the time, and had been serving in the regiment since May 1863. The Federal authorities allowed young Rowan to take the loyalty oath, and then released him to go home on October 14.[872]

Gen. Early was meanwhile on the move again. On October 1, in a cold rain, his army marched from to Mt. Sidney by way of the Valley Pike. They went into line along the North River, and there remained until the 6th, when Early began to follow the Union army down the valley as it withdrew from Harrisonburg. Early's men camped in a circle around the town, then marched the next day to New Market with Pegram's division in the lead. Camp that night was at the river on the Timberville road, where they remained through the 8th. Nasty hail and snow pelted the men, driven by a sharp wind.[873]

On October 12 the army moved again toward Narrow Passage, intending to cut off an attempt by the Federal forces to join with Grant's army near Richmond. The next day, the division made a reconnaissance in force, discovering that Sheridan had taken a strong position on the north side of Cedar Creek, and were occupying both sides of the Valley pike. Early settled his men at Fisher's Hill and watched the enemy fortifying their position.

On the 14th, Early took part of his army to Hupp's Hill, between Strasburg and Cedar Creek, to have a look at the enemy's lines. After Early stirred up the Federals with some artillery, Kershaw's infantry tangled with a Federal division and inflicted a number of casualties. Early withdrew his men back to Fisher's Hill, having discovered what he needed to know about the strength of the Federal force at Cedar Creek.

Col. Hoffman, in command of the Fourth brigade, reported the affair to Richmond on the 15th: "We skirmished with the enemy yesterday," Hoffman wrote, "Loosing probably 150 men, killing and wounding many of the enemy and taking about 50 prisoners. The enemy cavalry confronted us yesterday and (we) had slight skirmishing, and are before us today. It is supposed that Sheridan's whole army is at hand. Large encampments beyond Cedar Creek."[874]

In the regiment's camp at Fisher's Hill, on October 16, Will Yeager wrote to his sister Evelyn: "Dear Sister, I have neglected writing to you for some time, owing to the inconveniences of camp and our speedy movements. For the last few weeks, we have been kept pretty well employed keeping out of old Sheridan's range. He made us get up and dust from Fisher's Hill on the 22nd of last month.

"We fell back as far as Port Republic and Waynesboro, camped a few days near Waynesboro, then advanced again and drove the Yanks back almost as fast as they drove us.... The Yanks are camped about three miles from here, and nothing of importance is going on now between the two armies, only slight skirmishing, occasionally, which of late to us almost a daily occupation.

"We are all well and doing tolerably well, considering the manner in which soldiers have to live. We are getting tolerably good rations yet, though I fear we will have plenty little this winter since the Yankees have destroyed so much grain in the Valley. They have burned every barn and stack of grain from Staunton down as far as we have pursued them, and even burned the corn shocks in the field, besides many of the finest houses in the Valley, which they have destroyed and left families entirely out of house or home. I saw one field near Mt. Sidney, where they had shot down 10 or 12 cattle, and left them laying untouched. Another place, I saw a hog pen with 16 fine hogs burned up alive. Can the people ever prosper?

"Henry Wilfong returned yesterday. He brought me the two cakes you sent by him, and also the socks. I am thankful to you for the favor...."[875]

Gen. Lee had advised Early to use the concentrated force of his army, rather than divide his forces in complicated strategies. Despite these cautions, Early was determined to try a flanking movement to surprise Sheridan's army in its camp at Cedar Creek, near Middletown. He chose the Federal left flank, based on a report from Gen. John Gordon and Capt. Jed Hotchkiss, who had gone to a signal station to look over the situation.

"The movement was accordingly begun on the night of the 18th just after dark," Early later reported, "Gordon's, Ramseur's, and Pegram's divisions being sent across the river around the foot of the mountain, all under command of Gen. Gordon, and late at night I moved with Kershaw's division through Strasburg toward a ford on Cedar Creek just above its mouth, and Wharton was moved on the pike toward the enemy's front, in which road the artillery was also moved."[876]

The plan was for Kershaw to attack on the left flank, with a simultaneous attack against the enemy rear by Gordon's column. To get into position, Gordon's column had to march through the night, taking a narrow path through the brush and woods, to a position on the flank of Sheridan's army. With a unit of cavalry to lead the attack, Gordon gave the signal and the horses, and then the infantry splashed through the shallow, cold water of the Shenandoah's North Branch, the cavalry dashing forward and into the camp of Crook's Eighth Corps, taking the Federals by surprise. The infantry came next, at double quick, but stopped near the Cooley house to wheel into line, Gordon's division on the left, Ramseur's on the right, and Pegram's in reserve, following the line. Meanwhile, farther to the left, Kershaw's division was launching its attack on the Nineteenth, and also on the Eighth Corps camps.

Hoffman was in command of the Fourth brigade that day: Lt. Colonel McCutchen and Maj. Cooper commanded the 31st Virginia. Private Beverly of the 31st Virginia said that although Pegram's division was in reserve, it did not remain behind for long. The brigades stormed through the Eighth Corps camp, routing the Federals, many of who had been sleeping. "We crossed the Valley Pike and went by a large frame house on a hill. At the foot of the hill we stopped a short while at an old millrace which had no water in it. Just across a creek near by was the Union VI Corps, with a battery of six pieces of artillery. It was so foggy that we could hardly see one hundred yards. Fire belched forth from one gun, sending a shower of grape or shrapnel over us."

"Without waiting for a command, the 31st Virginia—and perhaps other regiments—poured a volley into them, and their men started to run. Sergeant John Pritt... who was carrying the flag... saw them running, and jumped out of the mill race and down to the creek, the regiment going with him."[877]

Capt. Buck of the 13th Virginia later reported, "Here, to my surprise, we were halted and ordered to reform. Colonel Hoffman could not see well, or he would not have stopped at this point; so I called him as he was passing, on horseback, and pointed out our danger, but he still insisted upon reforming before making a second charge. Seeing the enemy advancing upon their battery, which would be turned on us again, I urged Colonel Hoffman to allow me to move with a few men and hold the battery. To this he consented, and with about fifty men we charged across the river, captured the five guns, turned them on the enemy, and held them until Colonel Hoffman came to our assistance."

The 31st Virginia had moved too far forward in their charge, and were caught in a cross fire until Maj. Cooper ordered the men to fall back to the brigade's line. Hoffman sent the brigade sharpshooters out to flank a Federal unit, and soon they could move forward again. "From this charge," Capt. Buck recalled, "we gathered solidity and moved on, driving the enemy into and through Middletown. Here we were halted over right upon Valley Pike, north of the town and at the tollgate. We remained at this point all day waiting for orders to move forward."[878]

Early's surprise attack had been a grand success, his army capturing 18 pieces of Union artillery, and 1300 prisoners. But the Federals had more men than they had lost, and the Sixth Corps had withdrawn to a position of some strength, on higher ground. The remnants of the Eighth and Nineteenth Corps were also being gathered and formed, and by the end of the day would also pose a strong threat.

Some of the men from Early's hungry army had stopped in the Federal camps to look for plunder. One such individual was Sergeant Kuhl, of Company D, who later recalled, "My booty consisted of my own, and two full Yankee haversacks stuffed with Yankee bread, crackers, pickled pork, coffee, sugar, a Yankee frying pan, cup to make coffee in—enough to do me the rest of the day, and to give breakfast next morning to nine other comrades who were hungry and less fortunate."[879]

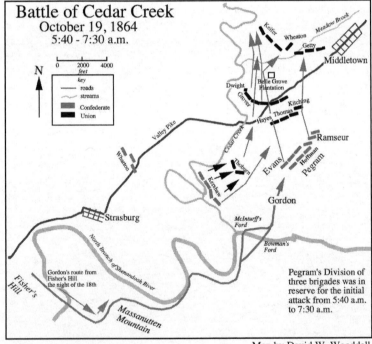

Map by David W. Wooddell

After the initial battle of the morning, Pegram's division, including the 31st Virginia and the Fourth brigade, was placed in a position on the western side of the Valley Pike, with Middletown on the immediate right, then Ramseur to their left, next Kershaw, and then Gordon holding the left end of the line. On the eastern side of the pike, Wharton was brought up to hold the right, but encountered Crook's Sixth Corps, which was holding a ridge to the northeast of Midletown. The Federals had artillery up there, and began to shell the Confederate line.

Another threat appeared shortly after, when a large force of Federal cavalry was observed coming down the Valley pike, and also from the northeast, but they were driven off by Early's artillery. Early next ordered Pegram's brigade to move north of Middletown, to occupy the Valley pike. Wharton's division, supported by Wofford's brigade, came up on the right of Pegram's division, and fought off several cavalry charges. On the left, Rosser's cavalry was outnumbered, but were temporarily holding the Federal cavalry from a concerted attack on Gordon and Kershaw's divisions.

Early began to advance his line toward the Federal infantry, but discovered that they were dug in behind entrenchments, and their position was strong enough to make Early hesitate. "It was now apparent that it would not do to press my troops further," Early wrote. "They had been up all night, and were much jaded." He also reported that the ranks had been thinned by men slipping away to plunder the Federal camps that had been overrun in the morning, and while Early had ordered the camps to be cleared of his men, it is doubtful how thorough that order was carried out.

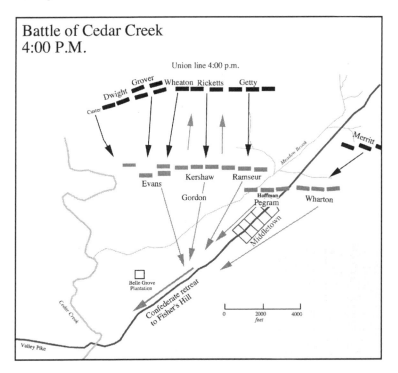

Meanwhile, cavalry charges made by the Federals against Early's line were repeatedly driven off with musket and artillery fire. Late in the afternoon, the Federal infantry advanced, in particular against the left of Early's line, and the clash between the two sides grew hot. The Federals found a break in the line, and managed to exploit it, causing Gordon's division to lose cohesion.

Confusion fell heavy as men turned to the rear in Kershaw and Ramseur's divisions, and soon the Confederate line was dissolving under the pressure of the Federal infantry on the left. A small body of men in Ramseur's division held on with the help of several pieces of artillery, but Gen. Ramseur was mortally wounded, and soon the Federals overwhelmed them.[880]

"Gen. Early was with us," Private Beverly later recalled, "when away on the left we saw our men give way. Soon our whole left wing broke and seemed to become panic stricken. Our brigade also started, but Gen. Pegram rode up just then and ordered us back to where we had been supporting a battery. We soon moved back in good order, even keeping step. We had not gone far before they came up, and we kept up a continual fire on them until we crossed Cedar Creek." By then, Gen. Early had ordered Pegram's division, which he said had maintained their order throughout the afternoon's fight, to withdraw.

Capt. Buck, of the 13th Virginia said, "We marched in line of battle from Middletown to Cedar Creek, where we had to break to cross the bridge. At Stickley's, south of the bridge, Gen. Pegram rallied about 100 men, and we again checked the enemy's cavalry; but soon a brigade charged us, and we made the best retreat we could."

"The men had slipped away one or two at a time," Private Beverly recalled, "and we had to deploy as skirmishers to keep them from flanking us. There was nothing but cavalry following us then, and when they came up Gen. Pegram said that we would fire on them and double-quick to the top of the hill.

"Someone remarked to the Gen. that we had better load at once or we would never get to the top of the hill. He paid no attention to that, but gave the command, "Right about, double-quick, march!" As soon as we started they charged through our line in column, and took after Gen. Pegram, Hoffman, and our adjutant." Col. Hoffman and Maj. Cooper escaped capture, though Cooper was wounded at some point in the day's fighting. He was eventually sent to the hospital at Staunton. Cooper did not like hospitals and did not remain there for long.[881]

Several men were wounded and captured that day from the 31st Virginia: Jacob C. McLaughlin, of Company G, was killed. Horatio N. Barker, Company A, received a gunshot wound to left thigh, and was captured: his left leg was amputated at a U.S. hospital the following day. Charles S. Kelly was gunshot in the left thigh; and Capt. Albert G. Stringer, Company A, was wounded in left hip and thigh, and captured. The others captured were: James K. Anthony, Co. F; S. Newton

Bosworth, Co. F, private and regimental fifer; Charles H. Chewning, Co. B; Adam F. Gum, Co. B; Cortland Phillips, Co. K; Melville N. Pullin, Co. E; William R. Stipe, Co. F; and Abel Siron, Co. B.

Private Beverly was also among the captured that day. "There was a house on the west side of the pike there, and as John Pritt went through the paling a Yank struck at him with his saber; but as he could get no further with his horse, he took up his carbine and shot at him several times as he crossed the garden.

"Pritt was rolling up his flag and paying no more attention to him, went on the other side, crossed the road, and got into some timber on the hill and got away. Pritt was a robust, stout man, and when he came to the river jumped in and swam across.... I was not able to keep up... and when I came to the river, not knowing that Pritt had crossed, I started to follow the river up above Strasburg. The road ran near the river, and just as I came in the edge of the town about twenty Yankee cavalrymen came down the road after two of ours. It was then dark and I lay down in the gutter and they all passed by me.

Private Beverly sought the refuge of a house nearby, but discovered there was only one door, and the house was full of wounded men. He decided to pretend to be a hospital steward, but a face covered with black powder from firing his musket in the fighting gave him away when the Federals searched the house. "That evening we were marched to Winchester and put into camp," he wrote. They were later taken to the isolated, and exposed prisoner of war camp at Point Lookout, Maryland.[882]

Total casualties for Early's Army of the Valley at the battle of Cedar Creek included 1,050 men captured, and 1,860 killed and wounded. The Federals had 644 men killed that day, 3,439 wounded, and 1,591 captured or missing.[883]

The remnants of Early's army retreated to Fisher's Hill that night, and then on the 20th, in the early hours, marched south with Rosser's cavalry protecting the rear. They marched to New Market and set up camp and defensive works, but were a thoroughly demoralized group of soldiers, their ranks thinned, and their supplies meager. With only a few exceptions, the 31st Virginia remained in camp at this place until early December.

Maj. Cooper returned to the regiment on November 25. He said as he prepared to leave Staunton, "My wound is not yet healed, but I prefer going to my regiment to going within gunshot of a Hospital Surgeon, and as my leave of absence is out tomorrow, I must do one or the other."[884]

Cooper arrived back to learn of another personnel dispute. Capt. James M. Blair had resigned after some disagreement with the regiment's commanders. Lt. Col. McCutchen wrote a biting comment on Blair's resignation, "I think the resignation of this officer would be beneficial to the service for the following reasons, viz. 1st, He never fails to grumble when required to comply with any order, no matter what its character may be. 2nd, He fails to enforce orders or discipline in his company, and 3rd, He finds fault with every body and every thing." McCutchen thereby approved the resignation, and passed it along to Col. Hoffman, who also approved it and passed it on to higher authority.[885]

Maj. Cooper said in his journal on the 26th, "This being Saturday, the usual company and battalion drills are dispensed with to enable the men to wash and police the camp. (November 27) Am detailed as Field Officer of the day. We go through all the forms of General Mounting and observe all the rules of guard duty. (November 28) Commence drilling. Our regiment is quite small, only about 100 men, and with its size, and my rustiness, it seems a little awkward. (November 29) The 49th regiment was united with ours in the drill today, which made it seem more like a regiment. It has been much recruited by detailed men ordered into ranks who are very awkward.

(November 30) Received orders to always drill the 49th (Virginia) with our regiment. A number of ladies accompanied by some of the officers of the Brigade, came to see us drill today. I don't know whither they were going and pretty or not, as I was too much engaged to notice them."[886]

"Officer of the Day again," he wrote on December 2. "Am handed a letter from my wife. It was received shortly after I was wounded and been kept by the Adjutant. It is dated October 9th, and brings me the gratifying news that all are well at home again. May God in his mercy continue to keep them so."

Gen. Lee's defense of Richmond was being hard pressed by Grant's army, and the need for additional men at that place was severe. Gen. Early's campaign in the Valley had ended in disaster, and by the beginning of December 1864, Gen. Lee had determined the best course was to leave Early, with a small body of troops in the Valley to harass the Federals: the rest of the Army of the Valley would be transferred to Richmond. On December 6, Pegram and Gordon's divisions were ordered to march to Waynesboro.

The 31st Virginia marched that day as far as an old campground, within three miles of Mt. Sydney, and camped for the night. The following day, they marched to Waynesboro, where Gordon's division boarded the cars on the railroad and were taken to Richmond. The 31st Virginia boarded the train the following day, after being issued new clothing. Many of the men did not like the idea of being sent back to defend Richmond, with its trenches and mud. According to Cooper's journal, 28 men from the 31st Virginia regiment deserted rather than board the train.

"I am surprised," he wrote. "I did not think we had a single man that would desert. They don't like the idea of going to Richmond. Sent Lt. Stephenson after them. Embarked on cars for Richmond."

On of the men who had not deserted was Will Yeager, of Company G. He wrote to his brother, Henry, on the 7th, as he stopped to visit a relative on the way to join the regiment in time to board the train. "I am now at Uncle Arbogast's," Will Yeager wrote. "Our army moved to Waynesboro today, two divisions, Gen. Gordon's and ours. Our destiny is supposed to be Richmond. It is rumored here now that they have been fighting at Richmond during the last two days. I had hoped we would get to winter in the Valley, but after all our hard working and fighting, we have to go to that awful place to share our fates.... Henry, I don't want you to come to the army yet. Wait until you hear from me again. If we go to Richmond, I don't want you to bring our produce until I write to you—and Henry, you know what a place it is; stay at home as long as you can.... I fear we will have some hard fighting to do."[887]

The 31st Virginia arrived in Richmond around eleven o'clock on the morning of December 9, and from there transferred to another train headed for Petersburg. The train dropped them off about four miles from Petersburg. The 31st Virginia marched to their assigned position on the right of the Confederate lines at Petersburg, a position recently occupied by Gen. Finnegan's brigade.

"Having left my horse to be brought with the wagon train," Maj. Cooper said, "I have a hard time marching on foot. Not being able to keep up, I turn the regiment over to the command of Capt. Clawson, and get along the best I can. Arrive in camp late at night, but fortunately find good quarters. The weather has been cold and stormy, making our trip very uncomfortable. Sleeting and snowing tonight."[888]

Lt. Colonel McCutchen had been granted permission to attend the Virginia legislature. He took his leave from the regiment on December 8, and was absent attending the legislature until after the end of January, through which time the senior captain, Nathan Clawson of Company I, was often called on to perform field officer duties to assist Cooper and Hoffman.[889]

On the 10th, the regiment moved to another position, occupying some cabins that were recently being used by McGowan's brigade. They were near Fort McCrea, at the breastworks. The regiment moved again on the 11th, to some cabins several hundred yards to the left. Not long after, however, A. P. Hill's Corps returned from an expedition, and Pegram's division was once again moved to a different position, this time going to the extreme right of their line, where they camped near the Sutherlands station on the South Side railroad. They were allowed to begin setting up their own cabins, giving the men some hope that they would not be moved again right away.[890]

According to an officer in the 13th Virginia, "Colonel Hoffman had it all done by rule and a very nice camp it was. All the huts were the same size and the grounds were well kept, fenced in by a brush fence all around the Brigade. We also had a large chapel built in which we would attend prayer meetings every Wednesday evening and prayer meetings were held every night in some of the huts."[891]

In their new camp, on the 17th, a private from Company K prevailed on Maj. Cooper to forward his request for a furlough. Private Isaac Stockwell, one of the designated sharpshooters for the brigade, was desperate to get home. His reasons were pressing, a worrisome letter from his wife, a letter she had written all the way back on September 20, from the town of Kasson, in Barbour County:

"Dear Husband, I take this opportunity to drop you a few lines, this leaves us all well and I hope it may find you enjoying the same. I received your letter this spring. I was glad to hear you was well, and you stated in your letter that you had not heard from me for over a year and you wanted to know how your children was and so we are all well at present.

"I have a hard time to get along. I am out of provisions and have got no crop and I will have to come to you; and I want you to meet me at Staunton. I will start to Staunton next week. I want you to meet me there, for I can't live here and the people is all in good health and June sends her love to you. Nothing more at present, Yours, Sarah Stockwell."

It was a heart-wrenching letter to receive, and certainly Maj. Cooper understood Stockwell's anxiety. When Colonel Taylor, Gen. Lee's Adjutant, sent the furlough request back with the question of how Stockwell intended to escape capture in Barbour County, Cooper's reply was that Stockwell lived in a part of the country that was often visited by Confederate scouts, and was considered a safe area to visit, since many of the residents there were Southern in their sentiments. "The applicant is a faithful man, and a good scout, and will not be easily captured," Maj. Cooper wrote to Taylor.

Col. Hoffman supported the request, and as he had pointed out in the original request when he first forwarded it, there were special domestic reasons for Stockwell to go home. Accordingly, Stockwell was granted his leave to go home to attend to his family.[892] He was arrested in Barbour County on January 15, while on his desperate mission to see his family. Sent to Camp Chase, where he remained a prisoner until May 16, 1865, Stockwell took the oath of loyalty to the United States. He was 35 years old, 6 feet fall, dark complexion, hazel eyes, brown hair, and a farmer. Enlisted in June 1861, he had served the regiment since that time, and had been wounded at least once, on April 22, 1862. He finished his service as a prisoner of war.[893]

On December 20, Col. Hoffman and Maj. Cooper rode horses along the lines in front of the position, and along the picket line. They had received orders for the regimental commanders to familiarize themselves with the position. "General Lee," Maj. Cooper wrote, "had taken great precautions to guard his right flank, and his preparations to meet a movement in that direction are characterized by the skill and judgment which so much distinguish him."

A cold, damp place full of breastworks, it was a long way from home for the regiment. Here, the horizon was scarred with winter-wet earth, and logs stained by the Virginia clay. "Being still sadly afflicted with rheumatism," Maj. Cooper wrote on the 23rd of December, "I go before the Medical Examining Board for a 30 days furlough, which is recommended and the application sent up. Most of the men have got in their cabins and we commence to make ours. Sent a cap and four letters to Colonel McCutchen by William L. Morgan."

"Christmas," Cooper wrote on the 25th, "and a dull Christmas it is! No social exchange of festivities among friends, or enjoyment of the innocent pleasures of the children over their little presents. I wonder if they have any Kris Kringle now? Doubtful! God speed the return of those happy days! We had service this morning, Mr. Lepps preaching an appropriate sermon."[894]

Gen. Gordon was assigned to command of the II Corps, Maj. Cooper said in his journal on the 26th. The following day, Cooper and Hoffman moved into their cabin. The men had occupied their own cabins a few days earlier. "Got about 12 ears of corn for our horses, after their doing without for three days," Copper said on the 29th. On the 30th, "My leave of absence came last night, and I start for Mr. Irly's in Lunenburg County. Get out of my course by several miles and stay all night with Dr. Richard Haskins, a wealthy planter, who with his wife treated me very kindly." At least, for Maj. Cooper, the end of this terrible year of 1864 might hold the promise of a warm bed and some caring friends to help him recover. For the rest of the men of the regiment the winter would only bring hardships.[895]

3rd Sergeant Robert Wolfenberger, Company G, found himself in command of the small company from Pocahontas County on the 31st of December 1864. He signed a special requisition for 8 jackets, 8 pairs of shoes, 6 pair of pants, 8 shirts, 11 pair of drawers, 5 pair of socks, 2 caps, and 8 blankets.[896]

Sergeant Wolfenberger made out the muster roll for the month, and the list of those killed through the past four years was now long, as was the list of crippled, discharged, and those in hospitals. There were few men who remained in the 31st Virginia, and those who were present were worn thin by the long struggle. Others returned in 1865, from hospitals and private homes where they were recuperating, or from furloughs. Those who returned had one or two more battles to endure.

12

FIGHT TO THE LAST
Jan 1865 – May 1865

Losses throughout the South continued to weigh upon the spirit of the Confederate army in Virginia. About a week after the November 1864 reelection of President Lincoln, the Union army marched to the sea from Atlanta; in December, it occupied Savannah, Georgia, one of the last remaining seaports available to the South. By mid-January, Fort Fisher, North Carolina would fall.

Desperate for replacement troops, and yet unable to properly feed the ones it had available, the Army of Northern Virginia was given a windfall of mixed blessings when the Union army released large numbers of prisoners of war back to the army. Among those released were 79 prisoners of war from the Fourth brigade, who were transferred from the hospital at Winchester in mid-December, and marched to Stephenson's Depot, where they were put on train cars.

The Fourth brigade's surgeon, Archibold Atkinson was with them as they traveled east for exchange. The train arrived in Baltimore during a heavy snowstorm, reaching Camden Station about nine o'clock in the evening. In Baltimore, the men were transported by ambulance to the West Buildings Hospital, on the Norfolk dock. "It was probable if they put us there for the night they would send us by the boat next day to Old Point, and we would be that much nearer exchange grounds," Atkinson wrote later. They slept that night in a large ward of 100 beds.

Atkinson had been worried that the men would be inflicted by lice in any of the military establishments in which they might be quartered, and their first night in Baltimore proved his fears. "Soon I felt crawlers on my face and turned my pillow over," he wrote. "Then again I pushed the pillow under the bed; next, I got up. The man next to me said 'There is no use in that, stand it like a man, and when they get enough, they'll let you sleep.' I was so tired out, I went to sleep, but the next morning the bloody sheet showed the results of the feast of the pests."

About one o'clock the next day, the brigade's prisoners boarded *Georgianna*, one of the Old Bay Line's boats. Arriving at Old Point at seven o'clock, the prisoners marched ashore and were placed in lines, guarded by Negroes wearing Union uniforms. They marched a short distance to a house where another line of prisoners were being processed for exchange. Some of those prisoners were also from the Fourth brigade, and included men who had been released from the Winchester hospital earlier, and had spent the intervening time in one of the prisoner of war camps. Learning that those prisoners were in the process of being prepared to board a steamer bound for Richmond, Dr. Atkinson was able to persuade the captain in charge of the proceedings to allow his group from the hospital to also sign their paroles and board the steamer *New York*, which was then ready to depart. They joined a great number of other prisoners, 700 men altogether, already on board the steamer.

"We were kept some two weeks about Dutch Gap, as Gen. Butler was shelling the men on the other side," Atkinson recalled. "The shells were mortar shells and resembled nail kegs, they were more noisy than dangerous. We were finally exchanged at Rockets in Richmond." The prisoners arrived there on January 6, 1865, and being entitled to a furlough following release from captivity, they did not report immediately to the brigade and their regiments.[897]

Maj. Cooper was in Richmond on a leave of absence from the 31st Virginia when some of the newly exchanged prisoners arrived, including private William F. Gordon, and Andrew Davis, who had been a lieutenant early in the war, but had been dropped as an officer in May 1862.[898]

Others from their territory back home also came through the Confederate capital. On January 12, Cooper said, "Saw J. H. Preston on his way back to Highland as a part of the detail from the sharpshooters from our regiment to arrest deserters from all commands in that and Pocahontas county." It was not a duty the soldiers would have chosen to do. Jacob H. Preston, from Bridgeport in Harrison county, was later captured in Petersburg, on April 3, and sent to the prisoner of war camp on Hart's Island, in New York harbor, remaining there until July 11, 1865.[899]

While in Richmond, Maj. Cooper was making preparations for the 31st Virginia's annual petition to be transferred to serve in the mountains on the border of Virginia and West Virginia. He visited a Richmond newspaper office on the 13th and obtained 36 copies of the regiment's 1864 casualty list. These had been prepared at his request, to accompany the petition. Brig. Gen. W. L. Jackson, still in command of a cavalry brigade, wrote to Cooper on the same day, "I can safely give the assurance that if the 31st Regiment Virginia Infantry is assigned to my brigade," Jackson wrote, "and authorized to act as mounted infantry or cavalry, the men shall be mounted. If the transfer can take place in the next 30 or 40 days, they shall be mounted in time for the early spring operation."[900]

Col. Hoffman had written a letter to accompany the regiment's request for transfer. The strategy this year was to carry the effort through the elected legislators for their home district. Hoffman's letter was addressed to Charles W. Russell and Robert Johnston, at the House of Representatives, Confederate States. He sent it to Cooper, in Richmond, to be delivered as part of the package of documents to go with the petition of the men of the 31st Virginia. Hoffman wrote, "Though I have at all times refrained from expressing any personal preferences on the subject, supposing I might serve my country best wherever my superior officers might designate—I have ever deemed it my duty, as it certainly has been my pleasure, to do any thing in my power to promote the wishes of the officers and men under my command, as far as these might be compatible with the general interest.... You need hardly be told that among the decorated and heroic men who have suffered and fought for our cause, none have suffered more, or fought harder than these from our own section of the country. None within my knowledge have deserved more at my country's hands."[901]

Cooper delivered the petitions, and the accompanying letters and list of casualties to Russell and Johnston on the 23rd. Included was a letter signed by all of the officers, in support of the regiment's petition. They noted that the men in the 31st Virginia did not like the prospect of being consolidated with other regiments from the eastern part of the state.[902]

The list of 1864 casualties in the 31st Virginia should have been enough to still the critics in Virginia, who were complaining that western Virginia had not contributed men to the defense of Virginia during the war. It showed that in 1864, the 31st Virginia had suffered a total of 327 casualties, including 30 killed, 28 mortally wounded, 178 wounded, 11 permanently disabled, and 70 taken prisoner. The total was just 19 men less than the entire strength of the regiment during that year. "This regiment was engaged in twelve regular battles, and twenty-nine skirmishes," Maj. Cooper reported in the summary. "The attention of those who are disposed to traduce the men from that section of the state is called to the fact that this is a Northwestern Virginia Regiment."[903]

After almost four years of war, there were only 121 men present for duty in the camp of the 31st Virginia to sign the petition for transfer to the mountains. Their statement was dated at Camp Godwin, Pegram's Brigade, January 20, 1865, and was directed to Russell and Johnston. 30 members of the Virginia legislature endorsed it. Russell and Johnston forwarded the petition to James A. Seddon, the Confederate Secretary of War, stating in a letter, "If these men, worn, stiffened, and disabled as they are by the privations, fatigues, and dangers of four years of hard service could be allowed the relief which a change to the cavalry service would afford them, it would doubtless be a great gratification to them, and one which they richly deserve. They are confident of being able to mount themselves and greatly to recruit their numbers, if allowed to serve for a time in the western part of this state."[904]

Unfortunately for the men of the 31st Virginia, this last request for transfer to the mountains bordering West Virginia went the same way as previous requests. Gen. Lee's army was fighting for its very existence, and could not afford to loose seasoned veterans.

"Rapid and heavy firing as I approached camp," Maj. Cooper wrote on January 29 when he returned to Petersburg and the 31st Virginia. "Found the men all well and in fine spirits and very anxious about their transfer." The men were huddled in shelters dug into the yellow Virginia mud. Mortars fired deadly bombs that sailed overhead, and marksmen sent minié balls after any part of a man's body that showed clear to the enemy.

Cooper must have been relieved when he was detailed for duty on a courts martial at this time, for it was certainly preferable to hunkering down in the cold mud at the end of January. "Took my seat on courts martial today for the first time," he noted on February 1. "Resolutions were passed unanimously by the regiment expressing their confidence in the government and its determination only to lay down their arms when our independence was achieved."

On February 3, the regiment received orders to be ready to march at daylight on the 4th, to counter a possible Union movement of three corps, but the day of February 4 remained relatively quiet and the Fourth brigade remained where it was.

The action started again on February 5. "The enemy's cavalry made a dash on our pickets, capturing a small number, and came nearly to Gen. Pegram's headquarters," Cooper said. The brigade was called to arms and set off in pursuit of the Federal horsemen, and somewhere along the way one of the regiment's soldiers, John Edmonds, was captured. The 31st Virginia returned to camp in the evening, without having caught the Federals, but they would meet them in a disastrous way on the following day.[905]

It was an hour before daylight on February 6, a bleak chill morning for the soldiers of Pegram's division to go out and reconnoiter the enemy. Col. Hoffman had command of the Fourth brigade. Gen. Pegram, in command of the division, rode nearby as they pushed forward, trying to find the Federals that had taken them by surprise the day before.

One of the brigades was near Hatcher's Run, while the others were moving along the Vaughan Road, farther to the right. When the Federals attacked, it was with a sudden blow from infantry and cavalry, taking the Confederates by surprise. In an instant, the reconnaissance turned into a pitched fight, with Pegram's division forced to give ground, though slowly, and grudgingly, to a large Union force.

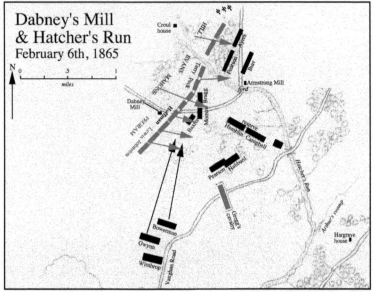

Map by David W. Wooddell

To the left, Gordon's division came up to send in its weight, charging and driving the Federals back, but only for the moment. There were too many Union soldiers rebounding at Gordon's men: his division was forced to fall back to its previous line, but then advanced once more as Pegram's division made its own brave charge. They pushed the Federals hard this time, the fight growing hot and close, rifles bruising shoulders, sabers flashing, gunfire ripping the air in a frenzy of lead. Gen. Pegram fell mortally wounded. When hit, he was riding immediately with the troops, in the thick of the action.

Then it was Col. Hoffman's turn. Struck on his left leg, the Colonel fell from his horse near Pegram. Hoffman's left foot was badly mangled. False rumors spread that he was dead. Nearby, the 31st Virginia's adjutant was also down, mortally wounded but not yet dead.

Some of the brigade's men lost their concentration, stopping to look and see for themselves if it was true that Hoffman was killed, and with the loss of attention, the Confederate line was thrown into confusion while their colonel was removed from the field. Hoffman, whose bravery had carried him through many tough fights with the help of his men, was clinging to life. And for the brigade, the fight raged on. Gen. Gordon later reported, "The battle had been obstinately contested for several hours, when Mahone's division arrived and was placed in position to fill a gap between Evans and Pegram. The whole line now advanced to the attack and drove the enemy in confusion to his works along the bank and creek."[906]

Maj. Cooper had remained at camp that day, complaining of rheumatism in his back. Later, he wrote sadly in his journal, "A severe engagement took place today. Our division attacking the rear guard of the raiders that went to Dinwiddie's Court House. Gen. Pegram was killed. Col. Hoffman and the adjutant wounded. Our regiment lost 5 killed, and 12 wounded. The enemy is thought to have suffered the most, but I believe retained possession of our works."[907]

Besides Col. Hoffman, whose life was hanging by a thread, the casualties included William A. Yeager, from Pocahontas County, Company G, who was killed and buried near the battlefield. William R. Oaks, and Henry C. Steuart, both of Company B, were also killed. H. A. Rexrode later died, on March 14. Other wounded included George A. Bagby, Andrew Lockridge, John B. Pritt, William W. Stockwell, and James P. Moss. The regiment's adjutant, Lt. Washington B. McNemar, died on February 17, while at the hospital.[908]

Surgeon Archibold Atkinson was then still on furlough. "Hearing I had been exchanged and was at New London, near Lynchburg, (Col. Hoffman) telegraphed me to go to him. I found two inches of the tibia bone protruding beyond the flesh. I rectified it." Without doubt, he saved Hoffman's life. The Colonel was sent to Richmond to recover, while Atkinson remained with the hospital, which was then situated near Mattoox.[909]

In Richmond, relentless war had not yet brought the people of Richmond to despair, though it was taking its toll. Sergeant Osborne Wilson reported, February 10, on the determination of the southern cause: "Mass meeting in Richmond in favor of prosecuting the war to the bitter end." On February 20 he said, "Only one man in one hundred is getting a furlough." The army was afraid that if the men were granted leave, they would not return.[910]

That same day, on the Confederate line with the 31st Virginia, Capt. Phillips received yet one more wound. The regiment was well dug in, with underground entrenchments, and roofed "bomb proofs" built into the earth to withstand periodic shelling. All approaches to the front lines had to be made with care to avoid being picked off by enemy snipers. At some point during the day, Phillips fell to the marksmanship of one of his enemies, hit in the abdomen and the shoulder. He was taken that day to the hospital at Charlottesville, the wounds dangerous and painful. He had been back on the line only a few weeks, after recovering from a wound received at the Wilderness, but this time he would not be returning to the regiment, though he would survive. The paperwork for a certificate of retirement was begun for Capt. Phillips, was approved and sent to Phillips on March 1, 1865.[911]

Maj. Cooper recorded in his journal, on February 17, "Adjutant McNemar died last night from the effects of his wound received on the

6th." Cooper went to visit Col. Hoffman on the 18th, and found the Colonel doing well. Judge Camden arrived on the 19th, and helped the Colonel's recovery no little bit, close friends as they were.

There were plans afoot to consolidate the 31st Regiment with other regiments that were also similarly reduced, but Maj. Cooper demurred when offered the command of such a regiment. "Told Capt. Wilson I was afraid my health would not permit me to do myself justice if assigned to command in a consolidated regiment," Cooper wrote on the 18th.[912]

Cooper arranged to send $100 home to his wife by way of Judge Camden, whose contacts could channel the money through to Clarksburg. "I sincerely hope she may get it," Cooper wrote in his journal on February 22.

The major had received a letter from a friend, advising him that a barrel of "eatables" had been sent to Cooper on the 15th, and from then until it arrived, he was somewhat fearful that some scoundrel would carry the treasure off. "Went to the depot to see about my barrel of provision," he wrote on the 25th. "Couldn't find it. It has undoubtedly been appropriated by some thieving skulker. I would like to get my eyes on him."

Lt. Colonel John G. Kasey of the 58th Virginia assumed command of the Fourth brigade. He held brigade inspection on the 26th, and the following day the brigades were ordered to prepare for active operations. All surplus baggage was made ready to be sent to the rear. Maj. Cooper's preparation included sending his diaries to a friend for safekeeping. The spring campaign had arrived early.[913]

Meanwhile, the petition from the 31st Virginia for transfer to Jackson's cavalry had been forwarded to Brig. Gen. James A. Walker, who was in command of the division following the death of Pegram. "Respectfully forwarded, disapproved," Walker wrote on March 8, "I cheerfully endorse all that is said in these papers about the gallantry, distinguished services, and patriotism of the officers and men of this regiment. There is no better, or braver set of men in the Confederate army, and they will do credit to any arm of the service they may be attached to, but my division is now very small and I would be very sorry to lose the true and tried men of the 31st from my command."

Walker sent the petition and letters to Gen. John B. Gordon, commander of the II Corps: he concurred with Walker's remarks and forwarded the documents to HQ, Army of Northern Virginia. Gen. Robert E. Lee gave his response to the regiment's request on March 9, 1865, and once again the needs of the Army of Northern Virginia were considered paramount to the desires of the men in the regiment. "Respectfully forwarded," Lee wrote. "This subject has been repeatedly considered and I am unable to come to any other decision than that previously stated—we require infantry as much, if not more, than cavalry. It is impossible to procure horses for the present cavalry, many of whom are now serving on foot. I feel assured these brave men are willing to serve their country wherever needed."[914]

Maj. Cooper had been assigned to serve on another Court Martial, but officers were needed on the line, and on March 9 Cooper was released from that Court Martial as all three officers being tried were returned to their regiments. Cooper's duty on Court Martial was not ended, however: on March 13, he was assigned to duty on another court. "Capt. R. I. Daniel of our brigade is Judge Advocate," Cooper wrote in his journal. "We tried one man for desertion. This is a very disagreeable duty, but it has to be done."

The Confederacy's prospects seemed dim at best. Jefferson Davis declared March 10 a "Fast Day." Reverend Lepps held three services that day for the men of the 31st Virginia. "I trust the God of battles will hear and answer the prayers ascending to Him today," Cooper said in his journal.

The regiment went on picket on the 11th, with Maj. Cooper assigned as Corps field officer of the day. The enemy remained quiet. "Not a drum was heard in their camp tonight," Cooper wrote. "A very unusual thing, I am told."[915]

On the 15th, the 31st Virginia moved with the brigade to a position east of Petersburg: "The left of our brigade resting on the Appomattox, relieving B. R. Johnson's division," Cooper wrote. "Looked about our new quarters," he said on the 16th. "Our breastworks are about 400 yards from the enemy's. We have two lines of cheval-de-frise in front of the breastworks. All the quarters are in bomb proofs. The enemy seem very anxious to exchange papers, etc. and practice many frauds. They exhibit a newspaper and then give the invitation to desert. They all want tobacco. The orders are to shoot every one that exposes himself. They were violated a little this morning, not being very well understood."[916]

March 18, Maj. Cooper: "The two lines shelled each other a while this evening. It was the first time I ever saw mortars playing. It really looked grand, the shells showing very distinctly in the dark." Cooper received his barrel of food, and being still a member of the courts martial board, said, "We have obtained a house in Blandford for our courts martial, and a quarter in the town. It is a suburb of Petersburg. The city is much worse injured than I supposed it was." The courts martial began its hearings on the day following, March 20, while Union batteries intensified the bombardment. "The enemy shelled furiously again today, our batteries replying. I have heard of no casualties on our side since we have been here, notwithstanding there is a good [deal] of picket firing, especially at night, besides the shelling."[917]

Lt. Hall rejoined the regiment on March 16, having been separated since Gettysburg, when he was captured and sent to a prisoner of war camp at Point Lookout. He was released from there on February 10, and given a furlough. When he rejoined the regiment, the 31st Virginia was still positioned just east of Petersburg. His diary said on March 22: "The lines of the enemy are only three hundred yards from us now, and a continual firing is kept up by both sides, especially at night. Our duties are very heavy—one third of the men all the time, and the whole [regiment] has to be up at four every morning. Our quarters are dug in the ground, and are very small and inconvenient—partially bomb-proof.... Mr. Mathews of Co. K accidentally shot himself today through the hand. His suffering was great, and his hand ruined."[918]

Elections were held on March 23 for seats in the Virginia Senate and the House of Delegates. "Very little firing along the lines today," Hall wrote. "Our men are quiet. I presume we will have to erect another chevaux-de-frise in front of our works.... We had a truce in front of our brigade this evening for a few minutes. I exchanged papers with a Yankee. Some of them gave our boys coffee, pocket knives, etc. The truce ended and both parties resumed the firing. The Yankee papers speak of our wavering people, and the inevitable overthrow, as if there were not a Southern soldier in existence."[919]

Hoffman's wound had required the amputation of his left foot. Late in March, he wrote to Colonel Walter Taylor, General Lee's Assistant Adjutant General. Hoffman said that he had been granted a furlough for medical reasons on February 24, and had departed from the regiment's camp to go to Richmond on March 2. "My wound has not yet healed and I am still confined to my bed.... As I am unable to write, this will be found to be in the handwriting of another." An extension for Hoffman's furlough was granted for an additional 60 days. He would be out of the war until its end.[920]

Lt. Colonel Kasey remained in command of the Fourth brigade, which included the 13th, 31st, 49th, 52nd, and 58th Virginia regiments. Since Maj. Cooper was still serving on the courts martial board, and was away from the regiment for much of the time, Capt. Nathan Clawson was in temporary command of the 31st Virginia.[921]

Cooper could count himself among the truly lucky: he was in a house, in Petersburg, as part of the courts martial board on March 25, when the Confederate army launched a forlorn hope attack on Fort Stedman. "By God's mercy I escaped," Cooper said in his journal. "The members of our courts martial quarter in town. I was with Mr. Lepps and Dr. Buttermore, and did not get word in time to join the regiment in the movement."[922]

The attack on Fort Stedman had been planned and led by Gen. Gordon, who was in command of the Confederate II Corps. Fort Stedman was one of the Union defensive works established during the siege of Petersburg: it was situated on Hare's Hill, less than a mile from the city. Opposite Stedman, on the Confederate side, there were two lines of soldiers in dugouts and trenches. Their lines were about 150 yards from the front of Fort Stedman. The advance pickets from each side were not only within sight of one another, they were close enough to converse.[923]

The men from Gordon's Corps were assembled after dark, and positioned in readiness to cross the lines and attack the fort just before dawn. A storming party armed with axes was placed in front, to cut the way through obstacles. White strips of cloth were tied across the breasts of the Confederates to aid identification of friend from foe. The men in the lead were in a cornfield from which the corn had not been gathered, and as they moved the dry cornstalks rustled, raising a query from the Union sentry. A Confederate replied that they were only gathering corn.

When the order was given to advance, "General Gordon fired three shots in rapid succession," and the Confederates in the advance party charged forward in silence. The Federal pickets responded by turning and running back to the fort, calling out the alarm that they were under attack. Hard on their heels were the advance team, following the pickets to see how to pass through the barriers of chevaux de frise.[924]

Reaching the enemy's breastworks, the Confederates begin cheering as loudly as possible to signal for the rest of the division to follow. They had been ordered, Brig. Gen. Walker said, "to fire as rapidly as they could reload, in every direction through the fort, to confuse the Federals and prevent them from rallying and forming before our main body should come up."

Reaching the obstructions, the Confederates were suddenly under a galling fire from muskets inside the fort, and several men were shot down in the short interval before the fort was taken. Meanwhile, the ax-men went to work and cut a way through the fort's defenses, and the Confederates began to pour inside the fort. Once inside, they fired at every blue coat they saw, and soon had carried the fort. Most of the garrison was taken by surprise, and a large number of Union prisoners were captured. These were sent back toward the Confederate lines as soon as they were organized and under sufficient guard.[925]

Holding the fort would prove to be the great problem. As soon as it was light, Federal artillery in Fort Haskell and at other positions overlooking Fort Stedman began to bombard the Confederates with a heavy barrage, turning the newly won ground into a killing zone of exploding shells. It did not take long for Gen. Gordon to decide that the fort must be evacuated, but by then the Fourth brigade and others had decided to try to force their way out of the fort, and advance on the Federals. They ran into a further storm of exploding shell and small arms fire.[926]

When generals Gordon and Walker began the withdrawal, they sent a messenger to the Fourth brigade, ordering the men back, but the messenger never arrived. By the time Lt. Colonel Kasey had determined to fall back, it was too late for many of the men in the brigade. Most were either killed, or wounded and captured. Lt. Hall of the 31st Virginia was one of the few officers in the regiment who managed to escape. "Strange things transpired today," he wrote in his journal. "The regiment lost over two-thirds of its entire number, killed, wounded and taken prisoner, and a fearful number are among the first. The dead are now being brought to our lines under flag of truce. One of my company has already been recognized. Mr. Frank Marshall, Drape Williamson, and Lt. Bosworth are among the missing, and I am actually afraid to hear from them. I fired over fifty rounds during the engagement and my shoulder is very sore from the rebounding of the gun."[927]

3rd Sergeant Robert Wolfenberger of Company G was dangerously wounded, a musket ball entering two inches forward, and exiting one inch below his right ear. He was so dazed by the wound that he was captured, and later sent to a hospital in Washington, where he recovered enough to be sent to Old Capitol prison, and was then transferred to the prisoner of war camp at Elmira, in upstate New York.[928]

Capt. John H. Yancey of Company D was captured and sent with many others to Old Capitol prison, and then to Fort Delaware. A native of Braxton County, he had been appointed captain on March 31, 1864.[929]

Sergeant Christian Kuhl was dangerously wounded in the right arm and captured. He was sent to a hospital in Washington. It was his fourth wound during war, and the most serious. He was not released from the hospital until near the end of June.[930]

Those in the regiment who were killed: Joseph H. Anthony, Company H; John W. Edmonds, Company I; Thomas Lewis, Company F. Listed as missing, and most assuredly captured—Franklin Marshall, and 1st Corporal Edwin Draper Williamson, both of Company H. Henry Yeager, W. H. Hull, and Jack Criss were also captured. The regiment's temporary commander, Capt. Nathan Clawson, accompanied them.[931]

The 31st Virginia lost 44 out of 81 arms-bearing men that day. "Colonel Kasey was captured," Cooper wrote afterward, "and I am left in command of the brigade; Colonel Tate being wounded, leaves me president of the Court Martial. My double duties are very onerous."[932]

Lt. Hall said on March 26, "Another truce today. Exchanged papers. Perry Talbott came to the regiment today. The first time I have seen him since I was captured at Gettysburg, July 5, 1863. He will probably be transferred to (the) cavalry in a few days, as he is disabled from infantry service. I feel mighty lonely since Drape's capture, but have much duty to do now, as I am appointed acting adjutant of the regiment."[933]

"The Yankees want to trade papers," Sergeant Osborne Wilson said on the 27th, "but our regiment permits no trade in our front." On the 29th, "Wakened soon after retiring by the report of heavy artillery and small arms. The sight is terribly grand. A magnificent display of fireworks. Never saw anything equal to it."[934]

On March 29, the brigade repulsed a feint from the Federals, with heavy rifle fire in the night. Several men were wounded in the Fourth brigade, and one man killed. There was more movement and massing of troops by the Federals on April 1, according to Cooper's journal. This was indication of a possible attack against the Confederate lines, and turned out to be the preparations for a decisive assault that would carry the Federals through the Confederate lines at Petersburg. Gen. Lee was forced to order the evacuation of Petersburg, and the retreat of his army.

"The assault came this morning," Cooper wrote on the 2nd, a Sunday. "A heavy attack was made all along our line, particularly on the right. They broke through the 13th [Virginia] regiment on the left of the brigade. I massed the 58th, 52nd, and 49th in the rear and drove them back, re-establishing our position before the assistance that was sent us came up. Bad treatment. They were not as successful on the right as we were and the enemy broke through, capturing many prisoners—some estimate our whole loss as high as 10,000. The enemy lost very heavily indeed in charging our works. Owing to the loss of our lines, Petersburg was evacuated tonight about nine o'clock. Marched nearly all night towards Amelia Court House."[935]

Before leaving Petersburg, details of Confederates were ordered to burn the supplies of the Army of Northern Virginia. The warehouse fires soon spread to other buildings, and the city of Petersburg went up in flames in the night as fires raged out of control. "The whole river front seemed to be in flames," one observer recalled, "amid which occasional heavy explosions were heard, and the black smoke spreading and hanging over the city seemed to be full of dreadful portents."[936]

Maj. Henry Kyd Douglas was assigned to command the Fourth brigade at this time, or as he called it in his memoirs, "the Light Brigade." Douglas later recalled, "While my brigade was waiting for its order to move, I rode to sundry houses to say goodbye. Before we got away, shells were bursting at places over the town and the air was now and then illuminated by the baleful light of mortars." Not long after daylight on April 3, Douglas was ordered to fall back with the brigade and become, as part of Gen. Walker's division, the rear guard of Gen. Lee's retreating army.[937]

They marched all day on April 3, and through the night. By April 5, the brigade was near Amelia Court House, and was placed on picket duty. Maj. Cooper said that day, "Marched all night. For the past week we have been under arms or marching day and night continuously, and the command is much exhausted. Rations very scarce."

Surgeon Atkinson had evacuated the wounded to Amelia prior to the fall of Petersburg. "I had a big hospital tent full of wounded men and officers who had been operated upon. We moved on to Amelia C.H. where we stopped to attempt reorganization, and where the artillery was parked. I met Dr. Dunn there and we were sitting upon the ground with our backs to a big tree, when there was a great explosion and up went the artillery into the air. The whole earth seemed to feel the shock and every thing was enveloped in smoke dust and debris."[938]

The regiment's new adjutant, Hall: "Wearied nearly to death. The enemy attacked our lines at various places, and could frequently be seen watching our movements. A few minutes ago they attacked our division, and we all thought a royal fight was coming, but a few rounds from a battalion of artillery drove them away—at least for the present."[939]

Late in the day, April 5, Cooper wrote: "After changing position several times to meet their advances, had a right sharp engagement with them and repulsed them handsomely. They renewed the attempt, and the left of the line composed of Grimes men broke. The line went to pieces and a number of ambulances and wagons captured. I mounted a mule belonging to one of the wagons and went a-kiting under a shower of bullets and shell. Our loss in captured was considerable." This battle was known as Sayler's Creek: Gordon's Corps had encountering the enemy at Perkinson's Mills on Sayler's Creek, while in the distance Sheridan's cavalry was overwhelming the fragmented commands that had been assigned to Gen. Ewell.[940]

Gordon's Corps was able to stave off their attackers, but became somewhat overwhelmed when reinforcements were sent to help the Federal II Corps. "The Yanks returned to the attack and drove our artillery from its position," Hall wrote. "The command immediately fell back and suffered considerably. Abandoned several wagons today on account of the mud."

Douglas, in command of the Fourth brigade: "Trying to hold the enemy in check as they moved against us from Amelia Court House, we were roughly handled and the loss in my brigade was very heavy for its size. We were driven back, but I had held the hill assigned to me until the trains and artillery of the division had crossed the stream in my rear.... After this battle my brigade did not number over 500 men."[941]

Lee's army continued the retreat, crossing over the Appomattox River on the High Bridge, a railroad trestle bridge that stood 150 feet over the river. The men crossed it by walking on the wooden ties. After the last of Gordon's command was across, the High Bridge was burned to deny it to the enemy.[942]

From Gen. Lee's report to Jefferson Davis: "Gordon, who all the morning (of the 6th), aided by Gen. W. H. F. Lee's cavalry, had checked the advance of the enemy on the road from Amelia Springs and protected the trains, became exposed to his combined assaults, which he bravely resisted and twice repulsed; but the cavalry having been withdrawn to another part of the line of march, and the enemy massing heavily on his front and both flanks, renewed the attack about 6 P.M., and drove him from the field in much confusion. The army continued its march during the night, and every effort was made to reorganize the divisions which had been shattered by the day's operations; but the men being depressed by fatigue and hunger, many threw away their arms, while others followed the wagon trains and embarrassed their progress."[943]

The next day, April 7, the retreating army stopped near Farmville for rations, but while they were being issued to the exhausted and hungry men, the Federals once again made their approach, and the fighting resumed, with the Federals nibbling away at the weary Confederates. Hall said, "Our artillery was quickly moved into position, and the infantry was seen stretching across the rolling fields. All at once the artillery opened on the advancing enemy, and the earth trembled with awful concussion. He was driven back, but only to come again at another point. This time he charged upon one of our batteries, and captured two pieces.

"Our Division being nearest, was hastily put forward to the rescue. When we came in sight, our artillery was galloping to the rear, with the Federal infantry yelling at its heels, not fifty steps in the rear. A sharp engagement ensued, the enemy was driven back, and the two captured guns recovered.

"The enemy exhibits an unusual bravery, so likewise do our own men, but it is rather the energy of despair, for everyone knows and feels that we are fighting against hope itself, when everything is even now lost forever. Our rations have failed and the soldiers live on raw corn and whatever the commissary can gather up in this war worn country."[944]

The following day was little better, though there was no fighting for the men of the 31st Virginia. With the James River to the north, and the Appomattox River to the south, on Saturday, April 8, Lee's army marched without the constant harassment from the enemy that had been their lot for the past several days. By this point, Gen. Lee had only two corps in his army, under generals Gordon and Longstreet.

"Made a very hard march and went into camp about two miles from Appomattox Court House," Maj. Cooper wrote in the evening, April 8. "Rations have been a little scarce for the last day or two, especially bread, and the men are completely exhausted and worn out." Cooper's command, the 31st Virginia, numbered just a handful of men.[945]

Nimrod Reger, Company I: "We were ordered not to leave camp and to take good care of all ammunition. Talk was rank of a big battle and of surrender."[946]

The Union army was closing in for the kill, and there was little that Gen. Lee could do to save the situation. His army was starving and the men were carrying on their persons all of the reserve small-arms ammunition of the Army of Northern Virginia. Once that was gone, there would be no more from an ammunition train to resupply. Archibold Atkinson, surgeon of the Fourth Brigade, recalled those final days of Gen. Lee's army. "We had neither food, strength, nor spirit left. Yet not one regretted the course he had taken."[947]

Walker's artillery was attacked in the night of the 8th, but managed to fight the enemy off: this was followed by a cavalry attack at Appomattox Station that was stopped by the infantry line. Fitz Lee's cavalry was sent to reconnoiter and determine the Federal infantry strength to his front, meanwhile breaking off the advance until morning if necessary.

The 31st Virginia was in it to the end, with 22 arms-bearing men present, according to a statement made later by Maj. Cooper. They did not spend the morning idle, or out of the action. The regiment had been active through the course of the war, from their start as some of the first volunteers in western Virginia, to this final solution of the conflict. In it from the start, they would help finish it on the day Lee surrendered.

Maj. Cooper said, on the morning of April 9, "Commenced marching at about five o'clock in the morning and marched to Appomattox Court House. In marching through town several shells passed harmlessly over us." The Fourth brigade was cautiously reconnoitering the enemy in cooperation with Fitz Lee's cavalry: "My brigade was sent with Fitz Lee so far out to the right that we were beyond sight of the army," Henry Kyd Douglas wrote, "and Fitz Lee, after giving me some instructions, moved further off to the right."

The 31st Virginia and the Fourth brigade were then just south of the village of Appomattox Court House, on Gordon's extreme right, when they encountered part of Gen. Ord's Corps. "Formed lines of battle and advanced on the enemy towards Lynchburg," Cooper said. "Drove them before us. An advance of the enemy was repulsed on our right by artillery."[948]

In this exposed position as skirmishers for Gordon's Corps, the brigade had found the enemy, and was engaging in a brisk firefight, with the scrappy, but weary Virginians holding their own. Some of Fitz Lee's men even captured two guns from a Union battery at about 8 A.M., but the massive Federal army was threatening to cut Gordon's Corps off from Longstreet, and Gen. Gordon was forced to pull his force back across the Appomattox River.[949]

This left the 31st Virginia, and the Fourth brigade, hanging in the air unsupported. Fortunately, the Union army was not pressing against them with the resolution and force that it was capable of making, and the brigade was allowed to withdraw to Gordon's line. Gen. Porter Alexander, in command of the Confederate artillery, later said, "About this time the pressure upon Gordon at the village had become so heavy that his line was falling back, and he sent urgent requests for reinforcements. On this, Gen. Longstreet directed me to select a line of battle upon which Gen. Gordon's force could fall back, and to form upon that line the whole force of infantry and artillery that could be mustered.... The country was open, which was favorable; for we had more guns in proportion than infantry. I found a very fair line, and made a very good show upon it, putting in every fragment of every command in the army, except the rear guard under Field. So that when Gordon united, our whole available force except the rear guard was in one unit."[950]

"Things look strange," Maj. Cooper said in his journal. The armies were in position, but no one was fighting, except for some occasional small clashes. "There was some contest with the Federal cavalry which was driven back, and there was moving and counter-moving," wrote Maj. Douglas. "After while, I observed some infantry skirmishers in my front, apparently with no special desire to advance, and they were soon retired, a few harmless shots having passed between us. I moved cautiously until I became aware of a solid body of infantry across the front, but motionless—it was Gen. Ord's Corps.

"Puzzled by the situation which I could not understand, I remained quiet, and very soon I saw a horseman riding toward me with great speed who proved to be Maj. Robert W. Hunter of Gen. Gordon's staff. With the good humor and facetiousness that never deserted him, he cried out, "Douglas, what is this racket you are making? Gen. Gordon wants to know whether you are in command of this army, or Gen. Lee—he has surrendered!"

"This accounted for the peculiar conduct of the enemy. But my little brigade had fired the last shot from Lee's army, and I sadly moved it back to its place in the division."[951]

Gen. Lee was even then in communication with Gen. Grant, and now the gray-haired Lee moved forward along the lines, expecting further word from Grant on the terms of a possible surrender. "I requested a suspension of hostilities until the terms could be arranged," Lee wrote in his report to Jefferson Davis. The famous meeting of the generals took place later in the morning.

"Saw three of the enemy's officers coming in with flag of truce," Maj. Cooper wrote in his journal as the regiment waited for something to happen. "Rumors that we are to surrender. Everybody gloomy." Their brigade commander, Maj. Douglas, had gone off by this time to attach himself to Gen. Lee's party as it made its way to the meeting with Gen. Grant. The men in the 31st Virginia were uncertain how to feel. Some were relieved that it was over. Others were ashamed they had lost. As Hall said, "The die is cast. The deed is done."

Gen. John Gordon, in command of the old II Corps, spoke to the men of his Corps that evening, telling them they had been good soldiers, and generally praising them as part of Lee's army. There were 7,892 Confederate infantry men present at Appomattox in the Army of Northern Virginia when Lee surrendered, and 63 pieces of artillery.

Cooper found it difficult to swallow. "The painful rumors confirmed and the whole army is surrendered to Gen. Grant. Officers are to retain their side arms and private property, and all are to be paroled and permitted to return to their homes."[952]

The fighting was over, but there were papers to be filled out, and certain formalities to be observed before the men could go home. The Confederates remained where they were, camped while the paperwork was prepared. Maj. Cooper was busy on the 10th, "making out rolls and preparing for the surrender." The regiment had 22 arms-bearing men on the field on the 9th, but others from the regiment were present but too sick or injured to fight on the last day. Maj. Cooper listed 56 men from the 31st Virginia as present at the surrender.

Their leader for the past several years, Gen. Robert E. Lee, issued a statement that day complimenting the men of the Army of Northern Virginia. He told them that they would be allowed to return to their homes, "After four years of arduous service, marked by unsurpassed courage and fortitude, the Army of Northern Virginia has been compelled to yield to overwhelming numbers and resources," Lee said. He took his leave from them then, bade them farewell, and went to Richmond.[953]

"The Corps was massed and addressed by Gen. Gordon, exhorting the men to be reconciled to their fate," Cooper wrote on April 11, adding Gordon's statements in summary form: "That the surrender was made because the army was out of ammunition and rations, and was overpowered by superior numbers. That Gen. Lee had only 8,000 infantry and 2,000 cavalry with which to meet hordes of the enemy. After Gen. Gordon's speech, the Corps stacked arms and accouterments and returned to camp."[954]

But the Union army wanted more of a ceremony than this simple speech by Gen. Gordon, followed by his men walking away from their arms. "About midnight last night," Cooper wrote on April 12, "We were notified that our manner of surrendering our arms last night was not satisfactory to the enemy, and to be ready to move at five o'clock in the morning to repeat this humiliating spectacle."[955]

Brig. Gen. Joshua Chamberlain was placed in command of the Union soldiers participating in the surrender ceremony on April 12. For sentimental reasons, Chamberlain requested that the men of his command at Gettysburg, the Third brigade, be included in the event, so on the morning of the 12th he placed three brigades of Union soldiers in lines to receive the veterans of Lee's army. (The Federal brigades included the First, Second, and Third brigades of the V Army Corps, First Division.) Gen. Chamberlain later wrote, "I placed the First brigade in line a little to our rear, and the Second on the opposite side of the street facing us and leaving ample space for the movements of the coming ceremony."[956]

Gen. Gordon rode at the head of the column of Confederate soldiers that day. They were all that remained of the Army of Northern Virginia at Appomattox. The regiments followed Gordon, each carrying its battle flag for the last time. The small number of men in the Confederate regiments caused the flags to be crowded together, making a mass of color as the units approached the waiting Federal soldiers. One by one, the regiments stacked arms, rolled up the colors, and placed them with the arms. Then the soldiers walked away, their ordeal of war at an end.

Brig. Gen. Chamberlain reported, "As each successive division masks our own, it halts, the men face inward towards us across the road, twelve feet away; then carefully dress their line, each captain taking pains for the good appearance of his company, worn and half starved as they were. The field and staff take their positions in the intervals of regiments; generals in rear of their commands.

"They fix bayonets, stack arms; then hesitatingly, remove cartridge-boxes and lay them down. Lastly—reluctantly, with agony of expression—they tenderly fold their flags, battle worn and torn, blood-stained, heart-holding colors, and lay them down; some frenziedly rushing from the ranks, kneeling over them, clinging to them, pressing them to their lips with burning tears. And only the flag of the Union greets the sky...thus all day long, division after division comes and goes, surrendered arms being removed by our wagons in the intervals, the cartridge-boxes emptied in the street when the ammunition was found unserviceable, our men meanwhile resting in place...."

The old Fourth brigade, including the 31st Virginia, came to the surrender in its turn. Maj. Douglas had asked Gen. Gordon if the brigade could be allowed the honor of being the last to stack arms. "In a little while my time came," Douglas wrote, "A heavy line of Union soldiers stood opposite us in absolute silence. As my decimated and ragged band with their bullet-torn banners marched to its place, someone in the blue line broke the silence and called for three cheers for the last brigade to surrender. It was taken up all about him by those who knew what it meant. But for us this soldierly generosity was more than we could bear.

"Many of the grizzled veterans wept like women, and my own eyes were as blind as my voice was dumb. Years have passed since then and time mellows memories, and now I almost forget the keen agony of that bitter day when I recall how that line of blue broke its respectful silence to pay tribute, at Appomattox, to the little line in gray that had fought them to the finish and only surrendered because it was destroyed." In total, the Fourth brigade numbered 304 men, with 42 officers, and 262 enlisted men present to stack their arms on the field of surrender.[957]

At the end, former newspaper editor Maj. William P. Cooper commanded the 31st Virginia. He was taciturn and grim that day, his cause brought to defeat out of desperation, and his words were spare and guarded of emotions. "At the appointed time, we stacked our arms in front of a line of Pennsylvanians, and then marched towards Lynchburg."

Nimrod Reger's recollection was much later: "The 31st, with its colors, was marched up in front of the New York Zouaves, noted for their blue jackets, red trousers and cap. They saluted at a distance of about 30 feet, sank on their left knee, remaining in this position until we stacked arms. Not a jeer or taunt was heard, and they seemed as sad as we were. Their colonel spoke to one of our officers. As I recall his words:

"I have heard much of the 31st Virginia. As I look over this line and think of how they have fought for four years I must say that their devotion to their cause places them among the noblest of men." Stepping to near the center of the line: "Good bye, boys, I wish you well; you have done nothing to which you may be ashamed."[958]

13

HOMEWARD
April 1865

31st Virginia's soldiers marched away from Appomattox as soon as possible after the surrender ceremony on April 12. Maj. Cooper said in his journal, "Saw several old acquaintances from Harrison (County) in passing through the lines." They made good time that day, and arrived at Lynchburg by evening, where the Federal army gave them an unlimited amount of rations and allowed them to sleep the night in Dudley Hall.[959]

Their chaplain took his leave on April 13. "Mr. Lepps left the regiment here, after an appropriate address and commending us all to the care of that kind Providence who has so often preserved us. We part company with the rest of the command here and pursue our way homeward alone," Cooper said.

Archibold Atkinson wrote many years later. "Mr. Lepps was one of the best men I ever knew. He was a learned man and spent much of his time in teaching. After I was transferred to infantry, I passed a good deal of my time with him.... Lepps was ever on the look out in what way he could help the men of his regiment. He knew most of them were ignorant and he would teach them reading, writing and arithmetic, and the advanced ones Latin, if they would come to him for instruction. He asked me to join him, and one winter we got the men to build a large log house in which we taught such as wished to learn."

Surgeon Atkinson said his farewells to the group at Lynchburg, on his way to the home of a brother-in-law, Rev. William A. Crocker, on the road from Campbell Courthouse to Concord depot, below Lynchburg. He recalled later that before leaving Appomattox, Dr. Grimes of the medical service insisted that the medical records be destroyed. "Even the archives of the brigade and divisions were burned. It was a foolish thing to do, as they told of as good medical and surgical service as could have been gathered from the archives of the Northern army, and would have perpetuated the work of the Confederate Medical and Surgical Departments."[960]

Atkinson set up a successful medical practice in Smithfield in September 1865. In 1873, following the deaths of his father and mother, Atkinson moved to Baltimore, Md. where he was physician to Barnum's Hotel, and later also to the Hotel Carrolton. Becoming one of Baltimore's most prominent physicians, specializing in skin ailments, Atkinson became a professor of dermatology, and ran the largest clinic for skin diseases in the city. In 1876, he was appointed resident physician for the resort at Jordan Alum Springs for the summer months, and later held a similar position, along with Dr. Moreman, at Greenbrier White Sulphur Springs, one of the nation's most famous resorts.[961]

VIRGINIA AND WEST VIRGINIA

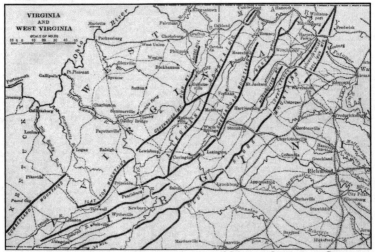

MAP FROM LIBRARY OF CONGRESS

From Lynchburg, Cooper and several others from the 31st Virginia continued toward Lexington, following the canal. "Get a boat about 12 miles from Lynchburg. Camp near the Big Island," Cooper wrote. The following day they arrived in Lexington, where they were quartered in the Washington College buildings.

The regiment's survivors split into more groups on the morning of the 15th. Some were returning home to Highland County by a shorter way. Hall said, "Today we separated. The majority of us will never meet again. All of us who live in North West Virginia have agreed to meet at Hightown on next Saturday, and go through the mountains with Maj. Cooper at our head. Eight of us started at noon and traveled about nine miles."

Cooper went to Staunton, arriving there on April 17. He met with Brig. Gen. Jackson and a few other acquaintances, and then went to Churchville to visit a friend. Jackson, former colonel of the 31st

Virginia, was among those who believed he had no alternative but to leave the country. When Cooper saw him in Staunton, W. L. Jackson had not yet personally surrendered. "Judge" Jackson eventually went to Mexico, but later returned to the United States and moved to Louisville, Kentucky. He was elected to office there, once more as a circuit judge, an office he held by successive elections until 1890.[962]

Capt. Joseph F. Harding was another of the regiment's former officers who would not surrender willingly. He was riding with about twenty-five other Confederates on their way home through the mountains of West Virginia on April 17 when they ran into a Union cavalry detachment commanded by Capt. Joseph Badger, of the 8th Ohio Cavalry. A shoot-out ensued, with the secessionists taking to the safety of the hills near Huntersville, where the cavalry could not follow.[963]

Harding was then 27 years old. The historian of Randolph county, A. S. Bosworth, knew Harding fairly well, and wrote the following description: "Harding has no characteristics of the man who yields, and after Lee's surrender, made an effort to reach the country beyond the Mississippi, where he believed the Confederates were still holding out, but on learning that all had surrendered, he wrote his own parole on May 23, 1865. Subsequent to the Civil War, Maj. Harding twice represented Randolph and Tucker counties in the State Legislature, and was a member of the Constitutional Convention of 1872. He was sheriff of Randolph from 1877 to 1881." Capt. Harding had, perhaps, fired the last shot of the war in West Virginia.[964]

Meanwhile, Maj. Cooper and a number of men had arranged to meet at Hightown, in Highland County on the 21st. From Hightown, they hoped to travel together in safety through the mountains. James Hall and Joseph West were in this group.

Cooper had been at William Vance's on Bull Pasture River the day before, and had taken the opportunity to say hello to Gen. Johnson as he passed by. "Went to Hightown, the place appointed for those to rendezvous who are going over the mountains home," Cooper wrote on the 21st. "The Yankee soldiers who were here day before yesterday say the Union men will not permit me to live in Clarksburg, but God can protect me."

They started over Allegheny Mountain on April 22. "Our party comprises 21 persons," Cooper wrote. "Capt. Radabaugh, S. Rutherford, R. Henderson, William N. Roberts, J. L. West, D. Slocum, P. M. Talbott, J. E. Hall, N. D. Reger, A. Spaur, J. W. Spaur, V. B. Flesher, S. B. Hardman, F. M. Waugh, F. C. Phillips, F. M. Johnson, and G. B. Moore, belonging to our regiment, and J. Shefford of the 10th Virginia Cavalry, D. Goff and Alex Jackson, son of Colonel Jackson, besides myself. Went today as far as White's on top of Cheat Mountain. Saw James A. Leeper as we were coming along."[965]

As anyone who has walked in those mountain will know, this was traveling at a good bit of speed for men on foot, or on horseback, and was a total of 31 miles, according to Hall. But their haste was understandable, for they were eager to be at home with their families. The party of former soldiers arrived at Beverly on the afternoon of the 23rd. "Plenty of ice and snow and the air very cold," Hall said of their journey.

"Without any mishap or particular annoyance," Cooper wrote on the 23rd, "having hoisted a white handkerchief and carried it all the way from the mountains. The Provost Marshall examined our papers and found our paroles all right. The letters given us to bring through were submitted to his inspection and part of them returned for delivery and the rest destroyed. My horse and saddles were taken from me. Being thus as it were set out on foot, I accepted the invitation of Mr. A. Crawford to stay all night with him. Beverly is occupied by the 74th Pennsylvania. Alex Jackson stayed with me. David Goff was confined in his home."

Hall and several others chose to walk a few more miles and camp. Hall said that the Provost Marshall took most of the horses they had with them. This was the first taste of the difficulties many of the former Confederates would have on returning to their homes after the war. Maj. Cooper did not waste time the next day, however, and went to visit Capt. Hoburg, the commander of the Union cavalry at Beverly, "Made a statement to him in regard to my horse... when he restored them to me. Went to Philippi and stopped with H. A. Barron. Found Maj. Sedders, 8th Ohio, commandant of post, a gentleman."

At Philippi, Hall stayed with an aunt, and then on the 25th he went home, accompanied by Capt. Radabaugh. "Powerfully glad to see the folks at home," Hall wrote on April 25. "It seems a little odd that I am here after being absent so long." After seeing Capt. Radabaugh off for home on the morning of the 27th, Hall celebrated his return to his home on the 28th by going fishing.

James E. Hall chose to remain on his parent's farm, and four years later married Elizabeth Wilson. They had one daughter, Lillian, who was raised on the farm that Hall purchased on Elk Creek, and then later in the town of Philippi itself, where the family moved in 1878. Hall promoted building a rail line connecting Grafton and Belington, and was manager of the line for several years. James Edmond Hall passed away in Philippi on January 1, 1915 at the age of 71.[966]

Although aware of threats that the Unionists in Clarksburg would not let him stay, Maj. Cooper traveled on to his home and was reunited with his wife, Margaret, and their four children, William, Irene, Darwin, and Hannah. It was a tremendous homecoming, for they had been separated for nearly four years. "Arrived at Clarksburg, found my family all well and humbly, but comfortably situated. I feel profoundly thankful to God for having preserved me through all the dangers of the past four years, and enabled me to be the first Confederate soldier to honorably go at large in Clarksburg.

"Reported to Capt. Ambrose, Provost Marshall. Met a number of old friends, some whom, though Union, treated me with great kindness, while others overrun with gall." Though Cooper, Hoffman, and the others of Company C had set out from there in the Harrison Rifles in May 1861, Clarksburg remained throughout the war a loyal Union town. "Wore my uniform up the street this morning," Cooper wrote the following day, "and then came back home and took it off, as I did not want to attract the attention it occasioned. My presence here has caused many bitter and disreputable remarks. All sorts of threats are made against me if I stay."[967]

"Received two letters warning me against remaining in Clarksburg," Cooper wrote on May 2. "One, without signature, advised me to find a place to bury myself, as I would be killed as sure as I now see a soldier. The other, from an old personal friend, Ira Hart, was of a better character. I have met too many brave men during the last four years to let cowardly assassins disturb my equanimity. I went to see Hart."

A county meeting was held at the Court House in Clarksburg, May 6, "To decide whether or not returned Confederates should be permitted to remain," Cooper wrote. "I am told rather peculiar resolutions were passed... I was the only person named." Cooper remained in Clarksburg, and on June 14, 1865, signed the oath of allegiance to the Unites States in the presence of Lucian Gray, Provost Marshall, Captain of the 2nd West Virginia Volunteer Infantry.[968]

Cooper lived in Clarksburg for some time after his troublesome return in June 1865, but traveled and engaged in various businesses, most of them outside the state. In September 1867, he was at Laurel Falls, North Carolina, where he and his brother, John A. Cooper, were partners in a factory with Peregrine Hays of Gilmer County. Hays had operated a cotton-processing factory in North Carolina late in the war, owning his own cotton farm there. William P. Cooper and his brother became part owners of that cotton processing factory. Cooper eventually settled in Fairmont, Marion County, West Virginia where he edited and owned the Fairmont *Index* newspaper. He remained in the newspaper business until his death on September 17, 1880, and was buried in Fairmont.[969]

Sergeant Osborne Wilson was still in the prisoner of war camp at Point Lookout on April 22, 1865. He said in his journal, "There is plenty to eat in the prison if I only had money to buy it." On May 5: "Suffer with hunger, sore eyes, and want of tobacco, and from lice. Sometimes there is nothing for breakfast." May 27: "Can find no place of comfort. Pea and bean soup generally thin. Sometimes eat all the crackers or cornbread at one meal. Mackerel and pickled beet."

"Mutton for breakfast," he wrote on June 22. "Take the oath of allegiance to the U.S. After long delays in the hot sun and spending three hours in the parole camp, are marched out, given hard tack and raw pork, then marched to the wharf and put on board the *Lizzie Baker* at 11 P.M. for Richmond." He was riding the train to Gordonsville on the 24th: "Country along the railroad enchanting. Never appreciated nature so much before." They were still very hungry. June 25: "Buy paper of French coffee and some sugar, and get milk and boil crackers for our breakfast. Boys [from the regiment] go to the fields for blackberries and huckleberries to eat with their crackers. Go at one o'clock to a citizen and get first rate dinner of vegetables...."

While still on the road to home, Wilson observed, "Crops and gardens look flourishing. Everything looks delightful, especially to men out of prison. [June 28] Ride on train from Staunton to Buffalo Gap. Reach the Cowpasture by sunset and have supper of bread, milk, and butter. [June 29] Things generally gone to ruin along the Pike. [June 30] The delightful scenery of my native land is more appreciated than ever since I came out of prison. (July 1) Four years of war ought and does give one an appreciation of civil life." Osborne Wilson arrived at his home in Highland County on July 2. "Get home at 1 P.M., and have corn bread, fried pork, currant pie, coffee, and milk for dinner."[970]

On Allegheny Mountain, near the Highland—Pocahontas County border, at the farmstead home of the Yeager family, young Eveline Yeager was a schoolgirl in 1865. She later recalled, "When the heavy fighting and cannonading was being done in Richmond and other points in Virginia, we would lie flat on the ground and listen to the rumble of the cannon. Anxiously we would wait for mail to hear if our boys were in those battles and were safe."

William Asbury Yeager, Eveline's brother, was killed at Hatcher's Run in February 1865. The stress of living through the conflict was too much for their mother, Margaret Arbogast Yeager. "Mother died May 11, 1865, they claim from worry and trouble during the war. She contracted brain fever following the news of Will's death during battle."[971]

Eveline's other brother, Henry Arbogast Yeager, returned safely and settled down on the farm his father had owned. The trenches were still there, on Battery Hill, as they remain today in faint recognition of the first winter of the war. Henry Yeager married Luverta Beard, of Greenbrier County, and they had several children, one of which was named Maud Lepps Yeager, after the chaplain of the 31st Virginia.

In the following years, Henry Yeager was elected to the West Virginia legislature, representing Pocahontas County, and was later appointed a special agent of the National Land Office at Cheyenne, Wyoming. Returning later in life to West Virginia, Henry Yeager was commander of the local post of the United Confederate Veterans in Pocahontas County, and contributed his knowledge of the war to Gen.

White for the volume on West Virginia in *Confederate Military History*. Henry Yeager died at Marlinton, West Virginia on January 9, 1902.[972]

Maj. Boykin, important to the regiment's existence in 1861, but dropped in the 1862 spring election, had served Virginia in other ways after leaving the regiment. He was captured at Sayler's Creek on April 7, 1865, and sent as a prisoner to Johnson's Island, remaining there until July 1865. He wrote to F. H. Smith after his release, "I returned from Johnson's Island about two weeks ago, and am anxious to make arrangements to get into employment as early as possible. I desire to teach mathematics in some high school, or the position of assistant in some college. I have had nearly five years experience in teaching, and if you can recommend me to any position, I shall always appreciate your kindness."

He taught school for several years in Norfolk, but following marriage to Ellen B. George, of Richmond, Boykin went into the tobacco business with her father, J. P. George. Later, Boykin established his own tobacco business at Richmond, and eventually became president of the Richmond Tobacco Exchange. He died May 5, 1906 at the age of 69 after a prolonged illness. Three children survived him: Hamilton Godwin Boykin, Miss Anna B. Boykin, and Miss Ellen P. Boykin.[973]

William P. Thompson, who resigned from the regiment because he was passed over for promotion, was rumored to have been arrested and jailed in Marion County not long after returning to his home in 1865, charged with "bridge burning," by the infamous Judge Thom. W. Harrison. With the help of his brother-in-law, Johnson N. Camden, the charge was dropped. Thompson became a partner with Camden in a venture called Camden Oil: they were one of the earliest manufacturers of refined petroleum in the United States. Standard Oil later bought them out.

Thompson became a Vice President of Standard Oil in Chicago, and later in Cleveland, but resigned from Standard Oil in 1887 and moved to New York, where he was director of a railroad. He died in Brookdale, New Jersey on February 3, 1896, and was reportedly worth 20 million dollars at the time of his death. While still with Camden Oil, he was an early advocate of marketing petroleum products to consumers, and is credited as one of the fathers of the modern gas station.[974]

McCutchen, a school teacher in Gilmer County at the start of the war, and Lt. Colonel of the 31st Virginia at the end of the conflict, moved in 1867 to California, along with several of his brothers and cousins. "He was a most heroic officer, survived the many conflicts in which his company, and regiment engaged, but he carried several battle scars still on his body," Sergeant Kuhl wrote.[975]

McCutchen, born in Augusta County, Virginia on June 6, 1830, died a bachelor in 1915 at Exeter, California. The *Exeter Sun* carried his obituary on the front page with this headline: "Another Pioneer Crosses Great Divide: Colonel McCutchen Answers Call to the Great Muster." The writer for the *Exeter Sun* said McCutchen was highly regarded in his community, and had "a natural commanding presence in which kindness and dignity were beautifully blended, so that to know him was at once to respect and admire him. A perfect type of the old Southern gentleman, kind and gentle... with both old and young; himself childless, yet a great lover of children, always taking an active interest in everything that pertained to their welfare and education." He had been living in the home of his cousin, Mrs. A. J. Buckman for more than thirty years, well cared for, and content at the end to depart this world.[976]

John G. Gittings, VMI graduate, and adjutant of the 31st Virginia, was in Marietta, Ohio by the summer of 1865. Following resignation from the 31st Virginia in June 1863, he became adjutant general of Jackson's cavalry brigade. Gittings ended the war a major in the 26th Battalion of Virginia cavalry, living in the saddle for days on end, and enjoying the adventurous life. He wrote in 1903, "After the war, I could not do anything in West Virginia, as I had no rights under the law, so I went west and taught school in Western Missouri and Southern Kentucky for four or five years, then came back and taught school in West Virginia. In the latter part of my active life, I was the city superintendent of the Clarksburg, W. Va. schools for ten years continuously, then out 2 years, and then back again for two years."

Heart problems forced Gittings to retire in 1897. He was the author of a book on music and songs of Western Virginia; and a book of essays, *Personal Recollections of Stonewall Jackson*. He remained a lifelong bachelor, and traveled to Europe twice on extended vacations. He had been lucky during the war, having escaped without a major injury. "I never received a wound to scar me," he wrote in 1903, "though my clothing and hair was cut by bullets at times, and once I was shot off my horse."[977]

William Henry Hull, captured at the storming of Fort Stedman in March 1865, was released from Point Lookout prisoner of war camp in mid-June. Born in 1844 at Anthony's Creek in Greenbrier County, Hull moved to Green Bank, Pocahontas County after the war. He operated a mercantile business, and was elected a Justice of the Peace. Hull married Rachel Curry, a daughter of Harvey Curry. When he died on March 5, 1930 at the age of 86 years, two daughters, Mrs. W. J. Yeager, Mrs. W. H. Arbogast, survived him. [978]

Capt. Phillips remained at Sutherland's until his parole papers were signed, on May 17, 1865. He departed Sutherland's on the 20th, and began the journey to his home near Valley Furnace, West Virginia.

He wrote after the war, "Let the circumstances speak. Did I do wrong? Before God and man I say today with the same train of circumstances before me, with the same light before me I would do the same as then, and if I did not, I would in my own sight be a hateful traitor." He was not alone in those sentiments—many of the soldiers later said they would do the same thing again in defending their state.[979]

"When I reached my home after the close of the war," Phillips recalled, "I took a calm deliberate survey of matters—I found my home almost in ruins and the briars spread over the long neglected fields. I saw wove around my affairs a web of difficulties that nothing but close attention and patient labor could untangle. I took a survey of myself and determined to improve my very defective education, to the extent of my means and opportunity.... We have peace; indeed, the sound of clash of contest has died away, no more bloody battles, no more outrageous murders. Our people are calmly mending their fortunes and repairing the way for an era of prosperity. Now we pick up our papers only to read of growing cities and proposed enterprises and we are glad that it is so. We have lived exciting times and deplored them. Now we welcome the calm sunshine of peace... let the old prejudices sleep in the grave of forgetfulness."[980]

In Washington, D.C., Sergeant Christian G. Kuhl, of Company D, was released from the Federal hospital on June 25, after taking the oath of allegiance. Standing 5 feet, 8 inches tall, with light hair, and blue eyes, the Braxton County native made his way back home. Though he never rose beyond 1st Sergeant in the 31st Virginia, Kuhl had often commanded Company D. He wrote after the war, "In nearly every battle my superior officers were wounded and left me in command of the company. So I headed my little company through many of the hotly contested conflicts.

"But I had always about double and treble duty to do. Not only that of sergeant, which was the company roll to call, rations to draw, and issue out, clothing to draw from commissary and divide among the men; all reports and details to make; company to report on dress parade, men to drill, and always to be present in camp or on the march and on the battlefield, as well as to head my company as captain when he was disabled.... I don't now remember of ever being absent at night on going into camp, no matter how long, hard, or muddy the miles were. I was always at my post to call the roll, no matter how few were there to answer.

"This scribe passed through the deadly scenes of some 32 or 33 regular hard fought battles, besides picket and skirmish fights, and under the great leadership of those great generals—Lee, Stonewall Jackson, Jubal Early, Ewell, Gordon, Pegram, and others, and usually came out victorious.

"We happened to be fortunate enough to find in the persons of Lee and Jackson material who could and would and did defend our capital to the last, until men, money, and rations were exhausted, and would dare to fight to the last." Christian G. Kuhl returned to Braxton County after the war, and became an ordained Methodist minister. Along with his brother, Conrad, Reverend Kuhl helped build Jobs Temple, in Gilmer County. He died in the influenza epidemic of 1918, and was buried in Burnsville, Braxton County, WV.[981]

Lt. John Bosworth returned to his parent's home at Beverly, Randolph County. He resumed the study of medicine with his father, Dr. Squier Bosworth, as preceptor. In 1865—1866, Bosworth attended lectures at Jefferson Medical College, and began practicing medicine in 1866, in Augusta County, Virginia. He married Martha E. Dold, daughter of Dr. Addison Dold of Fisherville, Augusta County, in 1866. Their daughter and only child, Anna Morrall Bosworth, was born March 15, 1869.

Bosworth moved to Philippi, West Virginia in 1868, where he set up a successful medical practice. He was associated with Dr. Elam D. Talbott, one of the pioneers of medicine in the Tygarts Valley. During the administration of Gov. A. B. Fleming, Bosworth was commissioned Surgeon General of West Virginia, and served through the term of office. When John W. Bosworth died at his home on Main Street, in Philippi, on Jan. 4, 1936 at the age of 99 years, he was the last Confederate veteran in West Virginia.[982]

Colonel John S. Hoffman was paroled by Col. D. M. Evans, 20th New York Cavalry, on May 9, 1865, while still in Richmond. Hoffman took the Amnesty Oath on May 22, 1865, giving his age as 43; residence Clarksburg, Harrison County; occupation lawyer.[983]

Hoffman's recovery from the amputation of his left foot was not yet complete, and he remained in Richmond for some time. His eyes were bothering him again, as they had often in the past. In the winter of 1861 his eyes had become so bad that he remarked on a number of occasions that it was the chief reason that he could do no writing or corresponding, and this at a time when he was a member of the Virginia House of Delegates, and in an intense season of political upheaval. "The worthlessness of my eyes," he wrote to Camden then, "has been the principle reason why my friends have not heard more from me this winter. This has not only prevented my writing, but has greatly dispirited me. I have no means of investigating or acquiring information on any subject, or attaining excellence in any pursuit or employment for which I have any taste."[984]

In the spring of 1865, he was without a foot, and once again his eyesight was failing him, making correspondence nearly impossible without the assistance of someone to write for him, and at times, also to read for him. For a man who lived by his intellect, and by ideas, this was undoubtedly a source of terror.[985]

Fortunately, John S. Hoffman had many relatives and friends to insure that he had good care and companions. He wrote to Gideon

Camden on May 19, "I am still where you left me. My wound is nearly healed and I walk a little in my room on crutches, though I will not be able to walk much for some time, owing to the tendency downward of the blood in my leg and its defective circulation." He said that visitors had brought him information concerning the county meeting in Harrison County, "in which after considerable discussion they pronounced us very odious and declared their opposition to our returning, but did not resolve that we should be driven away by violence, but on the contrary resolved that they would abide by the laws and military orders.

"I learn from the same source that a similar meeting was held in Weston on the 8th which resolved that those who had left home to participate in the rebellion should not return, and that they must leave, and resolved that lawyers should not defend suits against rebels and rebel sympathizers and learned that Judge Edmiston declared that he would not longer practice in the court. There is much feeling in Harrison, Lewis, and especially Marion against us—strong feeling against you and Capt. Sommers [one of Camden's son-in-laws] and others.

"A military order was issued by the Genl. Commanding the Department of West Virginia on the 6th inst. declaring that paroled soldiers residing in West Virginia had a right to return to their homes, and that a good faith required that they should be allowed to do so: that citizens having taken the amnesty oath might also return and remain unless their neighbors and the military authorities thought their presence dangerous and that soldiers might surrender themselves there upon the terms granted by General Grant to General Lee's army.

"The military authorities here have been eminently moderate, courteous, and conciliatory. No oath has been required except of those desiring to carry on business or travel on public conveyances or obtain license for some purpose. The best citizens of Richmond so far as I am informed, many paroled officers and all the people here from our section except myself have taken the oath.... The military order I spoke of required that persons holding State office desiring to return to West Virginia shall obtain permission from the Secretary of War."[986]

These were times of strain and tension for many of the former Confederates, particularly those who played any sort of leading role in the early stages, or who rose to prominence during the conflict. Many who returned home were given the cold shoulder, or worse, by former neighbors. Judge Camden remained in Brownsburg, Virginia, waiting until it was clear that he would not be arrested when he returned to Clarksburg. Some thought he was overly cautious, while others agreed the time was not yet right. And then it all turned into a farce—a serious, comic opera of a legal drama as Judge Camden, John S. Hoffman, and many others were indicted—en masse—for horse theft.

Barton Despard wrote to Camden from Parkersburg on June 18: "You and many others were indicted last term for horse stealing—I learn (but was not present) that Judge T. W. Harrison instructed the Grand Jury that every person connected (either cavalry or infantry) with the Southern Confederacy were (culpable) for the acts of any one person so connected, and horses having been taken from our citizens, the Grand Jury under these instructions found indictments—it is needless for me to say that nearly the whole profession were astounded and are decided in the opinion that the Judge's instructions were wrong."[987]

Camden received letters from several lawyers and judges, all friends of long standing, protesting the bogus indictments. Some thought Camden and others named in the indictment should merely shrug the charges off and return home; and if they were arrested, then post bail and take the matter to court. Others, such as Johnson N. Camden, felt Gideon should be more cautious.

Another friend, David Goff wrote to Camden from Weston: "Judge Tom Harrison, in his charge to the grand jury, instructed them that the stealing of horses or other property in a raid in the rebellion was a felony and that all persons who aided in the rebellion was equally liable. It seems to me that Judge Harrison knew better and therefore he must have acted corruptly, which is a sad state of affairs, when the Judiciary becomes corrupt our lives, liberties, and property are in danger. But I hope that such sentiments will be frowned down by the people.

"I heard whilst in Clarksburg on my first trip that Tom Harrison was opposed to the refugees returning and further said that if they were permitted to return they would want all the offices. I thought it was a mistake, but I presume such are his sentiments... and now he corruptly is using his office as Judge to prevent their returning...."[988]

Others, such as Gen. T. S. Haymond, of the Virginia Senate, had a little fun with Camden over it, appending to a letter of more serious import, "I should be benefited by the loan of one of your West Virginia horses, if you can spare one!"[989]

By late June, Camden's family had returned to Clarksburg, but the Judge remained away, waiting for the legal farce of "horse theft" to end. Hoffman was still in Richmond, his physical health bothering him no little, as James Neeson wrote to Camden from there on June 18: "Col. Hoffman's improvement after you left (was) soon very good and satisfactory. He was out on his crutches, which he used quite well. He was also out riding several times. But he has had a back-set. Which standing on his crutches in his room, one of them slipped so that he fell on the tender stump. This caused him some pain and loss of blood, as the skin was broken and the end of the stump opened. It was not re-garded as serious, however it kept him in bed.

"While there and fixed he was attacked by bilious fever, for which he is now under strongest treatment. Day before yesterday, being the first or second day after the attack, the doctor discovered *erysipelas* in his wounded limb, which as you know, is much to be dreaded. Yesterday the ladies of the house appeared greatly alarmed, from this cause, but in the evening when I saw the Dr. [Spence] any anxiety was much relieved, for he did not regard the *erysipelas* as very dangerous. He said it was [not] acute, and appeared not to dread its consequences. He said also that he would break up the fever.

"Today I visited the Colonel and found him improved, and the ladies much more easy about his situation. His situation is not at all what we could desire, though I think it is not alarming. At the best he must be confined to his bed or room for some time. He certainly will not be able to start home for some time, if he was inclined to go.

"Col. Hoffman requests me to say that he wishes you to ascertain and inform him what the records of Harrison, or other counties, show against him in the form of judgments or decrees, and what proceedings may be depending against him. He wishes also to know whether there is any indictment for treason against him, or any proceedings for confiscation."[990]

As soon as he was able, Hoffman went to Baltimore. Draper Camden reported home to Gideon on July 15 concerning his cousin. "He is staying with a Mrs. Egerton, who sent a special telegraph invitation to him, and where he is now much the lion and hero. He is much petted by the ladies and receives every attention that kindness and money can bestow.

"His leg is doing very well, not [hurting] any and he looks better than at any time since the war. His physician advises him not to stir much yet. He and I may go to Poolesville some time next week—if we do, I will write when we start."[991]

Hoffman was in Clarksburg by September, but soon returned to Baltimore. He wrote from there on October 29, informing Gideon that he had tried his "new leg," which he could wear "but a little at a time, but hope that with time I can walk very well again."[992]

In West Virginia, the Republican-controlled state legislature began squeezing the ex-Confederates. They would have liked to squeeze most of the former secionists right out of the state, and they tried several means. They made the former Confederates ineligible to vote. Lawyers who served in the Confederate army were prohibited from practicing in any of the state or county courts. Teachers who had served the Confederacy were prevented from teaching in the schools. Physicians were restricted from practicing medicine. There were some exceptions made by special arrangements with the governor of the state, but for the most part, the restrictions held the former Confederates in an economic grip that forced many to leave the state entirely for greener pastures. "The enforcement of this statute," wrote state historian Festus P.

Summers, "and the ratification of the constitutional amendment which automatically disqualified ex-Confederates, effectively disfranchised between fifteen and twenty thousand citizens and gave a semblance of permanence to the program."[993]

Hoffman began a life of travel on business, returning often to Baltimore, and later taking Philadelphia and New York into his sphere of West Virginia land transactions, acting as agent for buyers and sellers of large tracts of land throughout the new state. His expertise on land ownership, and willingness to go the extra distance in careful research of ownership was a benefit to individuals who became his partners and clients. Land that was for sale because of failure to pay taxes had long been one of Hoffman's specialties. In the years following the war, there were many parcels of land with unpaid taxes, some of it owned by former soldiers who had died in the past four years.

Pressed for money, Hoffman began to sell land in larger and larger quantities. He wrote to a business associate, in November 1868, explaining why he was involving himself in land transactions. "As I have not been allowed to practice my profession in the courts of this state since the war—though I practice in the United States Courts—I have been giving much attention to the lands of the county and been anxious to sell some of my own, or promote the sale of lands of others...." Earlier in the year, he had discussed selling 30,000 acres of land, possibly to be used for a colony, but said that he preferred to work within his specialty of land titles, rather than to be personally involved in promoting a colony of settlements.[994]

Hoffman remained a Democrat through the balance of his life. He was said to live a moral, and probably a self-contained personal life; he never married. Generous with his wealth, Hoffman had a feeling of responsibility for his former soldiers, as well as their families. He is said to have helped many of these ex-soldiers re-establish ownership of land that had been confiscated by others during the course of the war.

In 1872, when the repressive laws against the ex-Confederates were at last changed, John S. Hoffman ran for the office of Associate Judge of the Supreme Court of Appeals of West Virginia, the highest judicial position in the state. One endorsement, carried in the *Fairmont Liberalist*, said: "His merit alone entitles him to a seat on the bench of the Supreme Court of Appeals. But in addition the whole people owe him many obligations for his successful labors in bringing out of chaos the intricate land laws of this state, and reducing them to a systematic arrangement."[995]

George Atkinson, later governor of the state, knew Hoffman as a lawyer and judge, and also as a friend. Atkinson wrote, "At no time did he ever deviate from the paths of rectitude and virtue in his methods of living. His devotion to his profession and his success therein is a worthy example to young men in all callings of the present day."

Hoffman's health was never strong following the loss of his foot, and by 1876 he had to resign from his position as a justice of the Supreme Court of West Virginia. He died on November 18, 1877 at his home in Clarksburg, and was buried at the Odd Fellows Cemetery. His headstone carries a double inscription, for John S. Hoffman, and for his uncle, Judge Gideon D. Camden.[996] The *Wheeling Register* noted his passing, "He was a noble hearted gentleman, and warmly beloved by all who knew him well. In his death, the state loses one of its purest and most upright citizens."[997]

Judge Gideon Draper Camden eventually returned to Clarksburg, West Virginia after the war. With the assistance of his nephew, Johnson N. Camden, the Judge lobbied to rescind the proscription laws, but his political "usefulness was measurably impaired because of his war record." The members of the legislature, nearly all Republicans, refused to accede. Camden did not give up on his goal of restoring voting rights to the former Confederates. On December 18, 1867, he wrote to John Brannon and Jonathan M. Bennett: "Whilst at Charleston, Kanawha, a short time since, in conversing with some friends, it was thought best for a few of us disfranchised men to assemble in a quiet way in Wheeling about the 8th of January to consult upon the propriety of issuing an address to the people, or memorial to the Legislature to redress our grievances, or both, as might seem best. It was understood in that region that the members of the Legislature from that part of the State were in favor of repealing the restriction laws and would move on it, but wanted something from us to base it upon." When the restrictive laws were repealed, Judge Camden resumed practice as a lawyer. He was elected, in 1872, to the West Virginia Senate and served four years. It was his last elected office.

Gideon Camden's first wife, Sally Hoffman Camden, died in 1879 at Clarksburg. He remarried in 1883, to a widow, Mrs. Almira Horner Davis. Judge Camden traveled extensively in his later years, for pleasure and business. While visiting friends in Hot Springs, Arkansas on April 22, 1891, at the age of 86, the old Judge passed away.[998]

None from the regiment had become great generals, though W. L. Jackson had become a brigadier general. The men of the 31st Virginia fought as good a fight as any soldiers in either army, and a longer fight than most. Perhaps because they were from West Virginia, their story was seldom to be recognized by historians. Sergeant Christian Kuhl wrote after the war. "It might be charitable to say that we were not better men, generally speaking, than were in other regiments, but the fact that we were fighting for the cause we espoused, and our families and loved ones, our homes and property, was a double reason why we gained the reputation our regiment enjoyed."[999]

The deeds, failures, struggles, triumphs, and tragedies of Hoffman's Infantry, the old 31st Virginia Volunteers, remained mostly in the living memories of its veterans. Some were active after the war in veteran's groups; others simply wanted to forget. Only a few veterans from the 31st Virginia published memoirs of life in the service of the Army of Northern Virginia. Most seem to have adopted the idea that dredging the past could only bring harm to the present. There was too much bad blood remaining between men who were neighbors once, but had raised guns against one another in a civil war, and now were neighbors. Outside of the West Virginia, few knew the story of the 31st Virginia.

Warwick Wooddell's widow never remarried. Margaret Wooddell lived with her son, Charles, on the farm near Green Bank until he was a young man. She bought a farm on Buffalo Ridge, Allegheny Mountain, adjacent to the old Yeager farm, the site of Camp Allegheny. Charles Wooddell married Virginia Lee Spencer, a daughter of John H. and Frances J. Spencer. After the war, the Spencer's lived on the Yeager farm. Two of her older brothers, Jack and Jim, were veterans of the regiment.

For an only child, such as Charles S. W. Wooddell, whose father had died while serving in the 31st Virginia, the Spencer family must have seemed wonderfully large. Charles and Virginia Wooddell raised a large family on their farm on Buffalo Ridge, at the head of Long Hollow. Warwick's widow lived with them until her death in 1926.

While growing up, the children, grandchildren, and great-grandchildren of Charles S. W. Wooddell found ample time to play on the old battlefield at Camp Allegheny, turning up many relics from the war. Perhaps, without knowing it, they found traces of the old 31st Virginia Volunteers. Unfortunately, when the Wooddell home burned in the early 1940's, the family papers and artifacts were destroyed by the blaze, and were turned to ashes and dust. They are, like the war, faded memories.[1000]

THE END

BIBLIOGRAPHY AND SOURCES
Books & Journals
Alexander, Edward Porter *Military Memoirs of a Confederate: A Critical Narrative*, [1907; reprint, New York: Da Capo Press, 1993]

The Appomattox Roster: A List of the Paroles of the Army of Northern Virginia Issued at Appomattox Court House on April 9, 1865 [1887; reprint, New York, Antiquarian Press, Ltd., 1962]

Armstrong, Richard L. *25th Virginia Infantry and 9th Battalion Virginia Infantry* [Lynchburg, Va.: H. E. Howard, 1990]

Atkinson, Archibold, Jr., "Memoir of Archibold Atkinson, Jr.," Special Collections Department, University Libraries, Virginia Tech, transcribed by Dorothy Bodell and Stephen Zietz

Atkinson, George W., *Bench and Bar of West Virginia* [Charleston, W.Va.: Virginia Law Book Co., 1919]

Ashcraft, John *31st Virginia*, [Lynchburg, Va.: H. E. Howard, 1988]

"Battle of Gettysburg, First Day"
http://en.wikipedia.org/wiki/Battle_of_Gettysburg,_First_Day#cite_note-47

Bell, John W. *Memoirs of Governor Smith: His Political, Military, and Personal History* [New York: Moss Engraving Co., 1891]

Beverly, Private [S. N. Bosworth?], "Battle of Cedar Creek", *Confederate Veteran*, [14 11 Nov. 1906 501-502]

Boatner, Mark H. *The Civil War Dictionary* [New York: Vintage Books, 1988]

Bosworth, Albert S. *History of Randolph County, West Virginia* [Elkins, W.Va.: n.p., 1916]

Buck, Samuel D. "Gen. Joseph (sic) A. Walker," *Confederate Veteran* [10 1]

Buck, Samuel D. "Battle of Cedar Creek: Tribute to Early, " *Southern Historical Society Papers* [30 1902 104-110]

Bushong, Millard K. *Old Jube: A Biography of General Jubal Early* [Boyce, Va.: Carr Pub., 1955]

Caldwell, Willie Walker *Stonewall Jim: A Biography of General James A. Walker, C.S.A.* [Elliston, Va.: Northcross House, 1990]

Cammack, John Henry *Personal Recollections of Private John Henry Cammack: A Soldier of the Confederacy, 1861 - 1865* [Huntington, W. Va.: Marshall Library Association, 1991]

Chamberlain, Joshua L. *The Passing of the Armies* [New York: Bantam, 1993]

Conley, Phil (ed), *West Virginia Encyclopedia*, [West Virginia Publishing Company, 1929]

Cooke, James D., *A History of the Thirty-First Virginia Regiment Volunteers, C.S.A.*, [thesis, West Virginia University, 1955]

Cooke, John Esten *Wearing of the Gray* [New York: E. B. Treat & Co., 1867]

Cook, Roy Bird, *Lewis County in the Civil War, 1861-1865* [Charleston, W.Va., Jarrett Printing Co., 1924]

Curry, Richard Orr *A House Divided: A Study of Statehood Politics and the Copperhead Movement in West Virginia* [Pittsburgh: Univ. of Pittsburgh, 1964]

Driver, Robert J. *52nd Virginia Infantry* 2nd Edition [Lynchburg, Va.: H. E. Howard, Inc., 1986]

Douglas, Henry Kyd, *I Rode With Stonewall*, [1940; reprint, Simons Island, Ga.: Mockingbird Books, Inc., 1974]

Early, Jubal A. *Narrative of the War Between the States* [1912; reprint, New York: Da Capo Press, 1989]

Field Manual for the Use of the Officers on Ordnance Duty [Richmond: Ritchie and Dunnavant 1862]

Frasanato, William A. *Gettysburg: A Journey Through Time* [New York: Charles Scribner's Sons, 1975]

Freeman, Douglas S. *Lee's Lieutenants: A Study in Command* 3 volumes [New York: Charles Scribner's Sons, 1942 – 1944]

Funkhouser, Robert D. "Fort Stedman, So Near Yet So Far," *Confederate Veteran* [19 5 May 1911]

Gibson, J. Catlett "Battle of Spotsylvania Courthouse," *Southern Historical Society Papers* [32 1904 200-210]

Gilham, William *Manual of Instruction for the Volunteers and Militia of the Confederate States* [Richmond: West and Johnston, 1861]

Gordon, John B. *Reminiscences of the Civil War* [1903; reprint, Alexandria, Va.: Time-Life Books, 1981]

Gordon, W. F., "Under Sentence of Death," *Southern Bivouac*, new series, vol. 1, no. 10, [March 1886]

Hale, Laura V. and Stanley S. Phillips, *History of the Forty-Ninth Virginia Infantry* [Lanham, Md.: S. S. Phillips and Assoc., 1981]

Hall, Granville *The Rending of Virginia: A History* [Chicago: Press of Mayer and Miller, 1902]

James E. Hall, *The Diary of a Confederate Soldier*, edited by Ruth Woods Dayton, [Philippi, W.Va.: n.p., 1961]

Hardee, J. W., *Hardee's Rifle and Light Infantry Tactics*, [Philadelphia: J. B. Lippincott 1961]

Haymond, Henry *History of Harrison County, West Virginia: From the Early Days of Northwestern Virginia to the Present* [Morgantown, W.Va.: Acme Pub. Co., 1910]

Heater, Jacob "Battle of the Wilderness," *Confederate Veteran* [4 6 June 1906 262-264]

Henderson, George F. R. *Stonewall Jackson and the American Civil War* [1943; reprint, New York: Da Capo Press, 1988]

Hornbeck, Betty *Upshur Brothers of the Blue and the Gray* [Parsons, W.Va.: McClain Printing Co., 1967]

Hotchkiss, Jedediah *Virginia : Confederate Military History*, vol. 3, expanded volume [1899; reprint, Dayton, Ohio: Press of Morningside Bookshop, 1975]

Hotchkiss, Jedediah *Make Me A Map of the Valley* [Dallas, Southern Methodist University Press, 1973]

Hunter, R. W. "Gen. (Governor) William Smith at Gettysburg"

John Catlett Gibson V,

http://freepages.genealogy.rootsweb.ancestry.com/~opus/p2994.htm

King James Bible, Revised Standard Edition, [1870]

Krick, Robert K. *Lee's Colonels: A Biographical Register of the Field Officers of the Army of Northern Virginia* 4th Edition Revised. [Dayton, OH: Press of Morningside House, 1992]

Robert K. Krick, *Conquering the Valley: Stonewall Jackson at Port Republic* [New York: William Morrow and Company, Inc., 1996]

Lang, Crystal Wooddell, "C. S. W. Wooddell," in *History of Pocahontas County, West Virginia*

Lang, Theodore F., *Loyal West Virginia from 1861 to 1865*, [Deutsch Publishing Company, 1895 (hereafter Lang, *Loyal West Virginia*)

Letcher, John "Message to the Virginia Legislature," [Virginia General Assembly, House of Delegates [January 7, 1861] in *Journal of the House of Delegates of the State of Virginia, for the Extra Session* [1861] http://docsouth.unc.edu/imls/vadel61/vadel61.html

Long, A. L., *Memoirs of R. E. Lee* [1886; reprint, Secaucus, NJ.: Blue and Grey Press, 1983]

Mathews, Henry M. *Report of Cases Decided in the Supreme Court of Appeals of West Virginia* 6 [Wheeling, W.Va.: West Virginia Publishing Co., 1900]

Maxwell, Hu *History of Barbour County, West Virginia* [Morgantown, W.Va.: Acme Publishing Co., 1899]

Hu Maxwell, *History of Randolph County West Virginia* [Morgantown, W.Va.: Acme Publishing Co., 1898]

McClellan, George B. *McClellan's Own Story* [New York: Charles B. Webster Co., 1887]

McNeel, John A. "Famous Retreat from Philippi" *Southern Historical Society Papers* [34, 1906]

John A. McNeill, "The Imboden Raid and Its Effects," [*Southern Historical Society Papers*, 34, 1906]

Jones, John William *Christ in the Camp* [1887; reprint, Harrisonburg, Va.: Sprinkle Publications, 1986]

Moore, George E. *A Banner in the Hills*, [Appleton-Century-Crofts, 1963]

Morgan, George P. and Stephen A. Morgan, "A Confederate Journal." *West Virginia History* [22 4 July 1961]

Morton, Oren F. *A History of Highland County, Virginia* [1911; reprint, Baltimore: Regional Publishing Co., 1969]

Morton, Oren F. *A History of Pendleton County, West Virginia* [1910; reprint, Baltimore: Regional Publishing Co., 1974]

Murfin, James V. "The General's Tour of Antietam," *Blue & Gray Magazine*, [Aug.-Sept. 1985]

Newell, Clayton R. *Lee vs. McClellan: The First Campaign* [Washington, D.C.: Regnery Publishing, 1996]

Osborne, Randall and Jeffrey C. Weaver, *The Virginia State Rangers and State Line* [Lynchburg: H. E. Howard, 1994]

Peyton, George Q. "Pegram's Brigade at Spotsylvania," *Confederate Veteran* [38 2 March, 1930]

Pfanz, Harry W. *Gettysburg: Culp's Hill and Cemetery Hill* [Chapel Hill: Univ. of North Carolina Press, 1993]

Pocahontas County Historical Society, *History of Pocahontas County, West Virginia* [Marlinton, W.Va.: McClain Printing Co., 1981]

Price, William T. *Historical Sketches of Pocahontas County* [Marlinton, W.Va.: Price Brothers, 1901]

Price, William T. *On to Grafton* [Marlinton, W. Va.: Price Brothers, 1901]

Rice, Otis K. *West Virginia: A History* [Lexington, Ky.: Univ. Press of Kentucky, 1993]

Riggs, David F. *13th Virginia Infantry* [Lynchburg, Va.: H. E. Howard, Inc., 1988]

Sears, Stephen W. *To the Gates of Richmond: The Peninsula Campaign* [New York: Ticknor & Fields, 1992]

Stewart Sifakis, *Who Was Who in the Civil War*, [New York: Facts on File Publications, 1988]

Smith, Edward C. *A History of Lewis County, West Virginia* [Weston, W.Va.: Smith, 1920]

Stackpole, Edward J. *They Met at Gettysburg* [Harrisburg, Pa.: Eagle Books, 1956]

Edward J. Stackpole, *Sheridan in the Shenandoah: Jubal Early's Nemesis*, 2nd Edition. [Harrisburg: Stackpole Books, 1992]

Strother, David Hunter, "The Virginian Canaan" *Harper's New Monthly Magazine* [8 33, Dec 1853 18, 21, 25]

Strother, David Hunter, "Virginia Illustrated, Third Paper" *Harper's New Monthly Magazine* [11, 63, Aug. 1855, 289-311]

Strother, David Hunter, "The Mountains, " *Harpers New Monthly Magazine* [44, 263 April 1872 1863]

Stutler, Boyd B. *West Virginia in the Civil War* [Charleston, West Virginia Education Foundation, Inc., 1963]

Summers, Festus P. *Johnson Newlon Camden: A Study in Individualism* [New York: G. P. Putnam's Sons, 1937]

Thacker, Victor L. (editor) *French Harding: Civil War Memoirs* [Parsons, WV: McClain Publishing Co, 2001]

Trudeau, Noah Andre *Bloody Roads South: Wilderness to Cold Harbor, May-June 1864* [New York: Fawcett Columbine, 1989]

U. S. War Department, *War of Rebellion: A Compilation of the Official Records of the Union and Confederate Armies*, 69 volumes in 127 Books [Washington, D.C.: Government Printing Office, 1880-1901] (cited as OR)

Virginia, State of, Virginia Ordnance of Secession, April 17, 1861

Waddell, Joseph A., *Annals of Augusta County: From 1726 to 1871*, 2nd edition [1902; reprint, Harrisonburg, Va.: C. J. Carrier Co., 1986]

Walker, Charles D. *Biographical Sketches of the Graduates and Eleves of the Virginia Military Institute* [Philadelphia: J. B. Lippincott and Co., 1875]

Warner, Ezra J. *Generals in Grey: Lives of the Confederate Commanders* [Baton Rouge: Louisiana State University Press, 1959]

West Virginia: A Guide to the Mountain State [New York: Oxford Univ Press]

The West Virginia Encyclopedia [Charleston, W.Va.: West Virginia Publishing Co. 1929]

West Virginia Heritage Encyclopedia: supplement series of *Hardesty's Encyclopedia*, Edited by Jim Comstock [Richwood, W.Va.: Comstock, 1974]

West Virginia, *Acts of the West Virginia Legislature* (1865 and 1866), Joint Resolution No. 29 [1865 94]; and Joint Resolution No. 13 [1866 135-136]

Wheeler, Richard *On Fields of Fury: From the Wilderness to the Crater, an Eyewitness History* [New York: Harper Collins, 1991]

White, Robert *West Virginia, in Confederate Military History* 2 [1899; reprint, Secaucus, N.J.: Blue and Grey Press, 1975]

William "Extra Billy" Smith's Brigade, http://www.gettysburgdaily.com/?p=164

"William Lowther Jackson, Jr.," *The West Virginia Encyclopedia*, 1st edition [Charleston, W.Va.: West Virginia Pub. Co., 1929]

Williams, John A *West Virginia: A History* [West Virginia University Press, 2001]

Wilson, Osborne "Diary," in William T. Price, *On to Grafton* [Marlinton, W. Va.: Price Brothers, 1901]

Withers, Alexander Scott, *Chronicles of Border Warfare*, (originally published 1895 by Robert Clark Company) [McClain Printing Company, 1989]

Yeager, Henry A. obituary *Confederate Veteran* [10 6 June 1902]

Zembala, Dennis M. "Grafton Machine Shop and Foundry" [Washington, D.C.: Historic American Engineering Record, National Park Service, 1975]

Newspapers

Barbour County Jeffersonian [7 March 1861]

Morrison, Wilbur C., "Jeremiah Church," *Clarksburg Exponent Telegram* [3 May 1931]

Wilbur Morrison, "Aged Indian Fighter...(John A. Campbell)", *Clarksburg Exponent Telegram*, n.d., [in A&M 1561, ser. 2, box 2, vol. 1, 31st Virginia Papers, RBC]

The Clarksburg Register

"Another Pioneer Crosses Great Divide: Colonel McCutchen Answers Call to the Great Muster," *Exeter Sun* (California) [1 Oct. 1915]

John W. Bosworth, obituary, Lexington Gazette [4 Jan. 1936]

John W. Bosworth, *Lexington Gazette* [22 June 1910]

James A. Walker, *New Orleans Picayune*, 25 Oct. 1903

John Riley Phillips, "History of Valley Furnace," edited by Ilene Gainer White, serially in 15 parts, *Philippi Barbour Democrat* [31 July 1968, 7 Aug. 1968, 14 Aug., 21 Aug. 1968]

William H. Hull, obituary, *Pocahontas Times* n.d.

Richmond Daily Enquirer [31 January 1861]

"Harrison County in the Field," *Richmond Daily Enquirer* [April 24, 1861]

"States-Rights Meeting in Harrison," *Richmond Daily Enquirer* [7 May 7, 1861]

"The Right Spirit in Highland and Pendleton", *Richmond Enquirer* [21 May 1861]

Francis M. Boykin, obituary, *Richmond News Dispatch* [6 May 1906]

Virginia Free Press (Charles Town, Va.) [13 June 1861]
Weston Herald [18 February 1861]
Wheeling Daily Intelligencer [16 May 1861]
Wheeling Daily Intelligencer [20 May 1861]
"Exciting From Clarksburg!" *Wheeling Daily Intelligencer* [23 May 1861]
Granville Hall, *Wheeling Daily Intelligencer* [3 June 1861]
Wheeling Daily Intelligencer [17 July 1861]
Wheeling Daily Intelligencer [19 July 1861]
Wheeling Daily Intelligencer [3 Aug. 1861]
Wheeling Daily Intelligencer [7 and 11 Oct. 1861]
"The Rebel Raid in Western Virginia," *Wheeling Daily Intelligencer* [7 May 1863]
John S. Hoffman, obituary, *Wheeling Register* [19 Nov. 1877]

Documents

Library of Congress, Washington, DC
Snider, Joseph C. "Memorandum of Events Whilst Soldiering: Journal of the Civil War, 1861-1864," original diary owned by Maude Ladell Fletcher, microfilm, Library of Congress transcribed, unpublished, by David W. Wooddell

National Archives of the United States, Washington, DC
31st Virginia Infantry, Compiled Service Records of Confederate Soldiers Who Served In Organizations From The State Of Virginia, Record Group 109, Microfilm (M. 324) rolls 774-778 Transcribed (unpublished) by David W Wooddell from original and microfilm documents (cited as 31st Virginia CSR)

Letters Received by the Confederate Adjutant and Inspector General, National Archives, RG 109, M. 474, roll 14, item 2747-c-1862; roll 113, item 382-G-1864; roll 71, item 948-L; M474, roll 163, item 381/2V

Compiled Service Records of the Confederate General Staff, National Archives, M. 331, Roll 83
Report of casualties in 31st Virginia Regiment, Early's Brigade, 17 Sept. 1862 at Sharpsburg, Md.,

Confederate States Army Casualties, Lists and Narrative Reports, 1861-65, National Archives, M. 836, Roll 7

"List of Killed, Wounded & Missing in Early's Brigade in the Battle near Fredericksburg on 13 Dec. 1862," CSA Casualty & Narrative Reports, National Archives, M. 836, roll 5

Thomas W. Hoffman file, CSR, Confederate General & Staff Officers, National Archives, M331, Roll 129

Men of Smith's brigade on detail or detached service, with assigned duty, 4 Aug. 1863, RG 109, MS 3290

United States, Eighth Census of the United States, 1860, Slave Schedule, Virginia, Records of the Bureau of the Census, Record Group 29, National Archives (cited as U.S. Census, 1860)

Virginia Historical Society
Francis M. Boykin, Correspondence and Papers, Mary Ober Gatewood Papers, Virginia Historical Society, Richmond, in *Southern Women and Their Families in the 19th Century*, ser. D, part 2, microfilm, [Bethesda, Md.: University Publications of America, 1994]

Virginia Military Institute
Alumnus Records and Correspondence of the Superintendent, VMI Archives, Virginia Military Institute, Lexington, Va. (cited as VMI Archives).
Boykin, Francis M. Jr.,
John G. Gittings
Joseph H. Chenoweth
William R. Lyman
John W. Bosworth

West Virginia University, Morgantown, WV
31st Virginia Regiment Papers, A&M 1561, Roy Bird Cook Collection, West Virginia and Regional History Collection, West Virginia University (cited as 31st Virginia Papers]

Gideon D. Camden Papers, A&M 1199, West Virginia and Regional History Collection, West Virginia University Library (cited as Camden Papers, WVU)

John S. Hoffman Papers

William L. Jackson Papers

[1] Virginia Ordnance of Secession, April 17, 1861, affirmed by a citizen referendum on May 23, 1861; Robert S. Garnett to G. Deas, 25 June 1861, U. S. War Department, *War of Rebellion: A Compilation of the Official Records of the Union and Confederate Armies*, 69 volumes in 127 Books [Washington, D.C.: Government Printing Office, 1880-1901] (hereafter cited as *OR*)[2], 236; J. M. Heck, report, n.d., *OR* [2], 254-255; 31st Virginia Infantry, Compiled Service Records of Confederate Soldiers Who Served In Organizations From The State Of Virginia, [National Archives Record Group 109, Microfilm, M. 324, rolls 774-778] Transcribed by David W Wooddell from original and microfilm documents (hereafter cited as 31st Virginia CSR)

[2] John Ashcraft, *31st Virginia*, [Lynchburg, Va.: H. E. Howard, 1988], (hereafter *Ashcraft*) 1-3 - formation of companies in counties; James D. Cooke, *A History of the Thirty-First Virginia Regiment Volunteers, C.S.A.*, thesis, West Virginia University, 1955 (hereafter Cook *Thesis*); George E. Moore, *A Banner in the Hills*, [Appleton-Century-Crofts 1963], (hereafter *Banner*),

[3] *Banner*, 1, 4, 7 – the Northwestern Virginia Railroad was completed in 1857, but bought out by the Baltimore & Ohio by 1860.

[4] David Hunter Strother, "The Virginian Canaan" *Harper's New Monthly Magazine*, [8 33, Dec 1853], 18, 21, 25; David Hunter Strother, "Virginia Illustrated, Third Paper" *Harper's New Monthly Magazine* [11 63, Aug. 1855], 289-311; David Hunter Strother, "The Mountains, " *Harpers New Monthly Magazine* [44, 263, April 1872], 1863 – cattle trade in western Virginia.

[5] Alexander Scott Withers, *Chronicles of Border Warfare*, [McClain Printing Company, 1989 (originally published 1895 by Robert Clark Company)], 57

[6] 31st Virginia CSR; Ashcraft, *31st Virginia* 100, 112 - Lawyers and attorneys who served in the 31st Virginia: Jonathan F Arnett, William W Arnett, Coleman A Bowman, Thomas A Bradford, Joseph French Harding, Alpheus F Haymond, John S Hoffman, William L Jackson, Stephen A Morgan, John W Myers, James Neeson, Albert G Reger, William P Thompson, Uriel M Turner

[7] *The Appomattox Roster: A List of the Paroles of the Army of Northern Virginia Issued at Appomattox Court House on April 9, 1865* (1887; reprint, New York: Antiquarian Press, Ltd., 1962), 190-193. Estimates for the number of men who served in this regiment are based on this author's transcription of the Compiled Service Records of the 31st Virginia, with additional names added from other reliable sources. Many of the records of the 31st Virginia were destroyed, or lost during, or after the war. Ashcraft, *31st Virginia*, 109, cites 1232 men enlisted; *OR* [46 1 1277] cites the number of men paroled from the brigade at Appomattox. *The Appomattox Roster* cites 22 men in the 31st Virginia on the field on 9 April 1865, and 49 men and 1 officer paroled at Appomattox

[8] R. S. Garnett to G. Deas, 25 June 1861, *OR* [2 236]; Joseph C. Snider, "Memorandum of Events Whilst Soldiering: Journal of the Civil War, 1861-1864," [microfilm, Library of Congress] (hereafter Snider Memorandum), 15 June 1861; J. M. Heck, report, n.d., *OR* [2], 255; Henry Kyd Douglas, *I Rode With Stonewall*, (1940; reprint, Simons Island, Ga.: Mockingbird Books, Inc., 1974), 318-319; *OR* [46 1], 1270, 1277.

[9] "William Lowther Jackson, Jr.," *The West Virginia Encyclopedia*, 1st edition [Charleston, W.Va.: West Virginia Pub. Co., 1929], 439; Order #1, HQ, 1st Brigade, Valley Mills, Va., 3 May 1862, announcement of the election in the

re-organization of the 31st Virginia Volunteers, 31st Virginia Regiment Papers, [A&M 1561, Roy Bird Cook Collection, West Virginia and Regional History Collection, West Virginia University] (hereafter cited as 31st Virginia Papers, RBC)

[10]31st Virginia CSR – Boykin, Chenoweth, and McCutchen were teachers; James C. Arbogast, J. S. Hoffman, Alfred H. Jackson, and William L. Jackson were lawyers/politicians; William P. Cooper was a politician and newspaper owner and editor.

[11]Ashcraft, *31st Virginia*, 100-105 – Ashcraft gives an outline in these pages of the commanders of the 31st Virginia, and the brigade, division, and corps commanders through the course of the war

[12] *OR*, [1, 11 III], 648

[13] *OR* [1 7 II], 484, 787 – Report of casualties in Third Division, action of 9 June 1862 near Port Republic

[14] Virginia: John Letcher, Message to the Virginia Legislature, January 7, 1861, in Virginia. General Assembly. House of Delegates. (1861) Journal of the House of Delegates of the State of Virginia, for the Extra Session, [Richmond: William F. Ritchie, Public Printer, 1861], 306 http://docsouth.unc.edu/imls/vadel61/vadel61.html (hereafter Letcher, Message, Jan 7, 1861)

[15] Letcher, Message , January 7, 1861

[16]United States, Eighth Census of the United States, 1860, Slave Schedule, Virginia, Records of the Bureau of the Census, Record Group 29, National Archives (hereafter cited as U.S. Slave Census, Virginia, 1860). Analysis of the census of slave owners by this author indicates that nearly every slave owner from the counties in western Virginia that contributed to the 31st Virginia actively participated, or had a family member as an active participant in the Confederate army. This author believes they were in fact vigorously defending not just states rights, but specifically the right to own slaves as property; see also Letcher, Message, Jan 7, 1861 [49] for an argument that secession was over non-recognition of property rights in the states by the Federal government, especially slaves as property

[17] John A Williams, *West Virginia: A History*, [Morgantown: West Virginia University Press, 2001] 64-65; *West Virginia Heritage Encyclopedia*: supplement series of *Hardesty's Encyclopedia*, Edited by Jim Comstock [Richwood, W.Va.: Comstock, 1974] (hereafter *West Virginia Heritage*) [7], 8-10; Phil Conley (ed), *West Virginia Encyclopedia*, [Charleston: West Virginia Publishing Company, 1929], 382, 390-391 – division of sentiment

[18] Christian G. Kuhl, "Narrative, and Stonewall Jackson As I Saw And Knew Him," 31st Virginia Papers, RBC, [A&M 1561 2 2 1] (hereafter Kuhl Narrative; Charles D. Walker, *Biographical Sketches of the Graduates and Eleves of the Virginia Military Institute* [Philadelphia: J. B. Lippincott and Co., 1875] (hereafter Walker *VMI*), 113-114

[19]Roy Bird Cook, *Lewis County in the Civil War, 1861-1865* [Charleston, W.Va.: Jarrett Printing Co., 1924](hereafter, Cook, Lewis County), 9-10; Edward C. Smith, *A History of Lewis County, West Virginia* [Weston, W.Va.: Smith, 1920)](hereafter Smith, Lewis County), 281-282; Moore, *Banner*, 83

[20]Moore, *Banne*, 206

[21]John S. Hoffman to Gideon D. Camden, 18 Jan. 1861, Gideon D. Camden Papers, [A&M 1199, 5, D, West Virginia and Regional History Collection, West Virginia University Library] (hereafter cited as Camden Papers, WVU.)
[22]Festus P. Summers, *Johnson Newlon Camden: A Study in Individualism* [New York: G. P. Putnam's Sons, 1937] (Summers, *Johnson Newlon Camden)*, 155
[23]U.S. Slave Census, Virginia, 1860, Harrison County; Henry M. Mathews, *Report of Cases Decided in the Supreme Court of Appeals of West Virginia*, vol. 6 [Wheeling, W.Va.: West Virginia Publishing Co., 1900], 377-379; Gideon Camden, 3 Jan. 1861, Camden Papers, WVU [6]; Summers, *Johnson Newlon Camden*, 99.
[24]Summers, *Johnson Newlon Camden*, 84-87: The oil strike at Burning Springs Creek in January 1861, on the land they purchased on Dec. 18, 1860, led to further investments for the three partners, Gideon Camden, Johnson Camden, and John J. Jackson, Jr. Again with Johnson N. Camden, Judge Gideon D. Camden became part of a complicated land purchase of 200 acres of the Rathbone land, along with John J. Jackson, Jr., William L. Jackson, William L. Bland, and others. They hired a mechanic, Benjamin W. Byrne, to operate the drilling machinery.
[25]Hoffman to Camden, 18 Jan. 1861, and 13 March 1861, Camden Papers, WVU.
[26]N. J. Coplan to John Letcher, 22 April 1861, *OR*, [46 I], 25.
[27]"Harrison County in the Field," *Richmond Daily Enquirer*, [24 April 1861] carried advance notice of the meeting; see also Richard Orr Curry, *A House Divided: A Study of Statehood Politics and the Copperhead Movement in West Virginia* [Pittsburgh: Univ. of Pittsburgh, 1964] (hereafter Curry *House)*, 48
[28]"States-Rights Meeting in Harrison," *Richmond Daily Enquirer*, [7 May 1861]: "An immense meeting of the True Men of Harrison... held at their last (County) Court, at which resolutions were adopted pledging the county to the cause of Virginia in the present crisis of her fortunes...." Many others who attended the meeting on the 26th later served in the 31st Virginia, such as Uriel M. Turner, Norval Lewis, Aaron Criss, Eli Marsh, James Y. Harner, Isaac F. Randolph, Abel P. Bond, Jacob M. Eib, Elias Bruen, Alexander M. Austin, William M. Late, Jefferson B. West, and William F. Gordon. Gordon's ownership of *The Clarksburg Register*, purchased recently from William P. Cooper, was short-lived.
[29]Jonathan M. Bennett to William P. Cooper, 25 April 1861, 31st Virginia Papers, RBC [A&M 1561 2 1]
[30]John Henry Cammack, *Personal Recollections of Private John Henry Cammack: A Soldier of the Confederacy, 1861 – 1865* [Huntington, W. Va.: Marshall Library Association, 1991] (hereafter Cammack *Soldier)*, 14-15: John H. Cammack was born in Rockingham County, Virginia, Dec. 22, 1843, a son of John C. Cammack and Margaret A. (Gibbs) Cammack. There were 8 sons and 2 daughters, but 2 of the boys died as infants. Lucius Cammack was an older brother of John H. Cammack. The family moved to Harrison County in 1859 and began farming.
[31]*Richmond Daily Enquirer*, [7 May 1861] – Volunteers from the counties of Pendleton, Augusta, Pocahontas, Monroe, Highland, Bath, Rockbridge, Greenbrier, and Allegheny were to assemble at Staunton. Those from the

counties of Braxton, Lewis, Harrison, Monongalia, Taylor, Barbour, Upshur, Tucker, Marion, Randolph, and Preston were ordered to the town of Grafton.

[32]Dennis M. Zembala, "Grafton Machine Shop and Foundry" [Washington, D.C.: Historic American Engineering Record, National Park Service, 1975], 1-9

[33]Robert E. Lee to Frances M. Boykin, 30 April 1861, *OR*, [2] 790-791

[34]Francis M. Boykin, Jr., newspaper obituary, 5 May 1906, Richmond, Alumnus Records and Correspondence of the Superintendent, VMI Archives, Virginia Military Institute, Lexington, Va. (hereafter cited as VMI Archives). Francis M. Boykin, Jr. was the son of "General" Francis M. Boykin. Born on March 1, 1837 at Isle of Wight Courthouse, Virginia, he was schooled at Smithfield before entering VMI at 16.

[35]Cook, *Lewis County*, 9-22; Frances M. Boykin to Frances H. Smith, Weston, Lewis County, 5 Feb. 1861, VMI Archives. Superintendent of VMI, Colonel Francis H. Smith was one of three members of the Governor's Commission in charge of assigning personnel to various positions in the Provisional Army of Virginia. Boykin wrote to Smith, "I am informed, that my friends in Richmond are making an effort to secure for me an appointment in the Ordnance Department recently created by the legislature. Knowing that a letter from you will have great weight with Gov. Letcher, I must again trespass on your kindness and ask you to write him in my behalf...." Boykin was subsequently given the rank of major in the Provisional Army of Virginia, and was authorized to enlist companies of volunteers.

[36]Francis M. Boykin to Caleb Boggess, 18 March 1861, Camden Papers, RBC, [A&M 1199 6]

[37]F. M. Boykin to Boggess, 18 March 1861, Camden Papers, RBC

[38]Summers, *Johnson Newlon Camden*, 88-89, cites *Weston Herald*, [18 February 1861]

[39]R. E. Lee to F. M. Boykin, 30 April 1861, *OR* [2] 790; Frances M. Boykin to R. E. Lee, 10 May 1861, *OR* [2], 827; Thomas J. Jackson to R. E. Lee, 7 May 1861, *OR* [2], 815.

[40]*Wheeling Daily Intelligencer*, [16 May 1861]

[41]F. M. Boykin to R. E. Lee, 10 May 1861, *OR* [2], 827-828

[42]Robert White, *West Virginia, in Confederate Military History*, 2 [1899; reprint, Secaucus, N.J.: Blue and Grey Press, 1975], 17, 131; Ezra J. Warner, *Generals in Grey: Lives of the Confederate Commanders* [Baton Rouge: Louisiana State University Press, 1959], 154-155.

[43]Cook, *Lewis County*, 9-22, 27, 113-114; Summers, *Johnson Newlon Camden*, 96-97 –Alfred Henry Jackson was the son of Captain George W. Jackson and Hettie Taylor Jackson, both of Weston. Though his parents were both natives of Western Virginia, Alfred was born at McConnelsville, Ohio in 1836. His father, a veteran of the War of 1812, had retired from the U. S. Army and had moved his family to Ohio. Alfred Jackson graduated in 1857 with honors from Washington College in Lexington, Virginia, and in 1858 he married Mary Blair Paxton. They had two daughters, Ella Bennett Jackson and Mary Jackson.

[44]Cook, *Lewis County*, 13, 113-116

[45] **Negro** was the word most commonly used at the time of the Civil War for African Americans, or Blacks, as they are more commonly referred to today. I have tried to keep the language of this book in that of the time of the events

recorded, and in the words of the men who served in the regiment and others who reported. I have consciously avoided the more perjorative "N" word, as being inappropriate and disrespectful.

[46]U.S. Slave Census, 1860, Lewis County; Cook, *Lewis County*, 9-10; Summers, *Johnson Newlon Camden*, 88, 94.

[47]Cook, *Lewis County*, 12.

[48]Record of events, Muster Roll for Company A, 2 Sept. 1861, 31st Virginia CSR; Clayton R. Newell, *Lee vs. McClellan: The First Campaign* [Washington, D.C.: Regnery Publishing, 1996], 71; George Porterfield to Robert S. Garnet, Grafton, 14 May, and 16 May, *OR* [2] 843, 855

[49]White, *West Virginia: Confederate Military History* [2] 7-9; R. E. Lee to G. Porterfield, 4 May 1861, *OR* [2], 802-803.

[50]White, *West Virginia*, 115; Ashcraft, *31st Virginia*, preface

[51]R. E. Lee to G. Porterfield, 4 May 1861, *OR* [2] 802-803; John G. Gittings to Joseph R. Anderson, 23 Nov. 1903, VMI Archives

[52]Ashcraft, *31st Virginia*, 1; Summers, *Johnson N. Camden*, 67-68. Anne Gaither Thompson, daughter of George W. Thompson, married Johnson N. Camden in 1858. This Camden, a nephew of Gideon D. Camden, was a shrewd businessman, and became the most famous of the Camden family. A wealthy industrialist, late in life Johnson Camden became a Senator for West Virginia in the U.S. Congress. His brother-in-law, William P. Thompson, who served as a captain in Company A, 31st Virginia, was one of his partners shortly after the war in the oil refining business.

[53]George W. Atkinson, *Bench and Bar of West Virginia* [Charleston, W.Va.: Virginia Law Book Co., 1919] (hereafter Atkinson, *Bench and Bar*, 45-46

[54]31st Virginia CSR – William W. Arnett, and Jonathan Arnett; Atkinson, *Bench and Bar*, 337. Their parents were Ulysses N. and Elizabeth Cunningham Arnett.

[55]William P. Thompson, "Record of events to accompany the muster roll for Company A for the period July and August 1861," Camp Bartow, 2 Sept. 1861, Captions and Records of Events, Co. A, 31st Virginia CSR: *Wheeling Daily Intelligencer* [20 May 1861]; *West Virginia: A Guide to the Mountain State* [New York: Oxford Univ. Press], 328; G. Porterfield to R. S. Garnett, Grafton, 25 May 1861, *OR*, [51 2], 109; Richard L. Armstrong, *25th Virginia Infantry and 9th Battalion Virginia Infantry* [Lynchburg, Va.: H. E. Howard, 1990] (hereafter Armstrong, 25th Virginia), 1 - Pruntytown was the county seat of Taylor County until 1889, when Grafton became the county seat. General Robert S. Garnett was then Adjutant General of the Provisional Army.

[56]Cammack, *Soldier*, 15; Granville Hall, *The Rending of Virginia: A History* [Chicago: Press of Mayer and Miller, 1902] (hereafter Hall, *Rending*), 292; Theodore F. Lang, *Loyal West Virginia from 1861 to 1865*, [Deutsch Publishing Company, 1895] (hereafter Lang, *Loyal West Virginia*), 51-54; List of officers who served in the regiment, 31st Virginia CSR.

[57]"Exciting From Clarksburg!" *Wheeling Daily Intelligencer*, [23 May 1861]; Henry Haymond, *History of Harrison County, West Virginia: From the Early Days of Northwestern Virginia to the Present* [Morgantown, W.Va.: Acme Pub. Co., 1910] (hereafter Haymond, *Harrison County*), 316-317; Hall, *Rending*, 292. As seen from the date published in the Wheeling newspaper, the Harrison Rifles gathered in Clarksburg on May 20, and marched out of town on May 21.

[58]Cammack, *Soldier*, 15-16; *West Virginia: A Guide*, 214.
[59]"Exciting From Clarksburg!" *Wheeling Daily Intelligencer*, 23 May 1861, Cammack, *Soldier*, 16.
[60]Haymond, *Harrison County*, 316-317.
[61]Cammack, *Soldier*, 16-17.
[62]Cammack, *Soldier*, 18.
[63]Haymond, *Harrison County*, 322-323; G. Porterfield to R. S. Garnett, Grafton, 25 May 1861, *OR*, [51 2], 109: Hall, *Rending*, 287-288; Cammack, *Soldier*, 18
[64] Oren F. Morton, *A History of Highland County, Virginia* [Baltimore: Regional Publishing Co., 1911; reprinted1969] (hereafter Morton, Highland), 196-209. Company E, No. 2 later become Company B, following the transfer of the Pendleton Company to another regiment.
[65]"The Right Spirit in Highland and Pendleton", *Richmond Enquirer*, 21 May 1861; Oren F. Morton, *A History of Pendleton County, West Virginia* [Baltimore: Regional Publishing Co., 1910; reprinted1974] (hereafter Morton, Pendleton), 406.
[66]Morton, *Pendleton*, 107.
[67]Osborne Wilson, 18 May 1861, "Diary," in William T. Price, *On to Grafton* [Marlinton, W. Va.: Price Brothers, 1901], 36. (hereafter Wilson, "Diary")
[68]M. G. Harman to John Letcher, 20 May 1861, *OR* [51 2], 97.
[69]Charles D. Walker, *VMI*, 108-114; Joseph H. Chenoweth to Frances F. Smith, Maryland Agricultural College, 13 Feb. 1861, VMI Archives. Born at Beverly, Virginia, on April 8, 1837, Joseph Hart Chenoweth was a son of Lemuel and Nancy A. Chenoweth, his father being one of the noted bridge builders in Western Virginia. His mother was a great-granddaughter of John Hart, of New Jersey, one of the signers of the Declaration of Independence.
[70]Joseph H. Chenoweth to Frances H. Smith, Beverly, Va., 23 May 1861, VMI Archives
[71]Wilson, "Diary," 24 May 1861, 87.
[72]G. Porterfield to R. S. Garnett, 25 May 1861, *OR* [51 2], 109.
[73]Zembala, "Grafton Machine Shop and Foundry," 13-16; Granville Hall, *Wheeling Daily Intelligencer*, 3 June 1861.
[74]Wilson, "Diary," 25 and 26 May 1861, 87.
[75]J. Gittings to J. R. Anderson, 23 Nov. 1903, VMI Archives; Thomas J. Jackson to R. E. Lee, Harper's Ferry, 21 May 1861, *OR* [2], 863.
[76]Hu Maxwell, *History of Barbour County, West Virginia* [Morgantown, W.Va.: Acme Publishing Co., 1899] - Maxwell states, "Other parties were arrested and punished for burning the bridges who had nothing to do with it."; Moore, *Banner*, 70-71
[77]G. Porterfield to R. S. Garnett, 29 May 1861, *OR*, [2], 51-52.
[78]Wilson, "Diary," 26 May 1861, 87
[79]George B. McClellan, *McClellan's Own Story* [New York: Charles B. Webster Co., 1887], (hereafter McClellan *Story*), 50. McClellan's proclamation to the Union Men of western Virginia, and his Address to the Soldiers of Ohio are reprinted in full.
[80]McClellan, *Story*, 50, 53; Otis K. Rice, *West Virginia: A History* [Lexington, Ky.: Univ. Press of Kentucky, 1993], 125; see also White, *West Virginia*, 14-15. The Fourteenth and Eighteenth Ohio regiments occupied Grafton on May 30, and were reinforced by General Morris of Indiana, who assumed command

of the Union forces there. McClellan himself would arrive later. McClellan said that he sent the troops into Virginia entirely on his own, without receiving orders of any kind from Washington or the Lincoln administration.

[81]G. Porterfield to R. S. Garnett, 29 May 1861, *OR* [2], 51-52

[82]Wilson, "Diary," 27 May 1861, 87

[83]Wilson, "Diary," 27 May 1861, 87-88

[84]G. Porterfield to R. S. Garnett, 29 May 1861, *OR* [2], 51-52

[85]J. Gittings to J. R. Anderson, 23 Nov. 1903, VMI Archives

[86]Wilson, "Diary," 28 May 1861, 88

[87]Maxwell, *Barbour*, 245-248; *Wheeling Daily Intelligencer*, 3 Aug. 1861

[88]Maxwell, *Barbour County*, 245-248. The Palmetto Flag "remained there until hauled down by Union troops under Colonel Kelley on June 3, 1861."

[89]Maxwell, *Barbour County*, 247; *West Virginia Heritage* [4], 222-224; 31st Virginia CSR gives the date of May 16, 1861 for the day that Company H was first enlisted.

[90]James E. Hall, *The Diary of a Confederate Soldier*, edited by Ruth Woods Dayton, [Philippi, W.Va.: n.p., 1961] (hereafter Hall, *Diary*), 6, 11-12. James E. Hall was the son of John and Harriet Rightmire Hall.

[91]Wilbur Morrison, "Aged Indian Fighter...(John A. Campbell)", *Clarksburg Exponent Telegram*, n.d., in 31st Virginia Papers, RBC, [A&M 1561 2 2 1]

[92]*Barbour County Jeffersonian*, 7 March 1861

[93]Ashcraft, *31st Virginia*, 12; John Riley Phillips, "History of Valley Furnace," edited by Ilene Gainer White, serially in 15 parts, *Philippi Barbour Democrat* (hereafter cited as Phillips, *History*), 21 Aug. 1968.

[94]*West Virginia Heritage* [4], 225; Phillips, *History* 31 July, 7 Aug., 14 Aug., 21 Aug. 1968.

[95]Phillips, *History* Aug. 21, 1968

[96]Phillips, *History* Aug. 21, 1968; Maxwell, *Barbour*, 249. Colonel Porterfield had 600 infantry and 175 cavalry at Philippi on June 3: Infantry: Capt. Thompson, Marion County ; Capt. Anderson, Pendleton County ; Capt. Uriel Turner, Harrison County ; Capt. Felix H. Hull, Highland County; Capt. Alfred G. Reger, Barbour County ; Capt. Henry Sturm, Upshur County ; Capt. Robinson, Taylor County (9th Battalion); Capt. Stoffer, Pocahontas County; Capt. Moorman, Pendleton County; Capt. C.C. Higginbotham, Upshur County: Cavalry: Capt. W. K. Jenkins, Barbour County; Capt. McNutter, Rockbridge County; Capt. Robert McChesney, Rockbridge County; Capt. F. F. Sterrett, Augusta County; Capt. McNeel, Pocahontas County

[97]Phillips *Barbour*, 21 Aug. 1968

[98]Wilson, *Diary*, 30 May 1861, 38

[99]Findings of the Court of Inquiry, 4 July 1861, *OR* [2], 72-74; *Wheeling Daily Intelligencer*, 19 July 1861; *Virginia Free Press* (Charles Town, Va.), 13 June 1861; John A. McNeel, "Famous Retreat from Philippi" *Southern Historical Society Papers* [34 1906], 280-293; G. Porterfield to Hu Maxwell, Charlestown, 12 Aug. 1899, in Maxwell, *Barbour*, 250-251

[100]Maxwell, *Barbour*, 254-256

[101]Joseph H. Chenoweth to Frances H. Smith, Huttonsville, 12 June 1861, VMI Archives

[102]G. Porterfield to Hu Maxwell, Charlestown, 12 Aug. 1899, in Maxwell, *Barbour*, 250-251; McNeel, "Famous Retreat From Philippi," 289. McNeel

identified the Highland County soldier who shot Colonel Reynolds as John W. Sheffee.

[103]M. G. Harman to R. E. Lee, 6 June 1861, *OR* [2], 69; Cammack, *Soldier*, 21-22; Maxwell, *Barbour*, 257; Virginia Free Press (Charles Town, Va.), 13 June 1861.

[104]Joseph Chenoweth to F. Smith, Huttonsville, 12 June 1861, VMI Archives.

[105]Wilson, *Diary* 3 June to 8 June, 1861, 39-40.

[106]Maxwell, *Barbour*, 256-259.

[107]G. Porterfield to H. Maxwell, 12 Aug. 1899, in Maxwell, *Barbour*, 250-251.

[108]Cammack, *Soldier*, 22.

[109]Joseph F. Harding, "Narrative," 31st Virginia Papers, RBC [A&M 1561 2 2 1] (hereafter Harding *Narrative*); Harding, 31st Virginia CSR; Ashcraft, *31st Virginia*, 132, 147, 151; Albert S. Bosworth, *History of Randolph County, West Virginia* [Elkins, W.Va.: n.p., 1916] (hereafter Bosworth *Randolph*), 153, 338.

[110]U.S. Census, 1860, Pocahontas County, Virginia; William T. Price, *Historical Sketches of Pocahontas County* [Marlinton, W.Va.: Price Brothers, 1901](hereafter, Price, *Pocahontas*), 122-128; Pocahontas County Historical Society, *History of Pocahontas County, West Virginia* [Marlinton, W.Va.: McClain Printing Co., 1981] (hereafter, Pocahontas County), 220; Record of Events, Co. G, July and Aug. 1861, 31st Virginia CSR - James C. Arbogast was born at Arbovale, near Green Bank, in 1836. His mother was Jane Tallman Arbogast. By Pocahontas County standards, the family was probably considered moderately wealthy. In the 1860 census, Arbogast's real estate holdings were valued at $5,000, and his mother's real estate at $6,500. Jane Arbogast, age 49, had a personal estate valued that year at $11,300. In addition, Charles I. Arbogast, age 18, farmer, and Nancy J. Arbogast, age 16 were living in the household. William Arbogast, their father, was no longer living. James C. Arbogast's grandfather, Adam Arbogast (1759-1857), was known in Pocahontas County as "Adam, the Pioneer," and was considered a famous Indian fighter.

[111]William H. Hull, "Some Recollections of the Civil War," 31st Virginia Papers, RBC - [A&M 1561, 2 2 1] (hereafter Hull, *Civil War*) ;*Pocahontas County*, 25.

[112]*Pocahontas County*, 25 and 40.

[113]*Richmond Daily Enquirer*, 31 January 1861; *Pocahontas County*, 35-48; Hull, 31st Virginia CSR; Hull, *Civil War*

[114]Roy B. Clarkson, in *Pocahontas County*, 9-13; Hull, *Civil War*

[115]Record of events, Muster Roll of Company G for July and August 1861, 31st Virginia CSR; *Pocahontas County*, 40; Hull, *Civil War* - identified the militia as the 127th Virginia Militia, under the command of Capt. W. F. Bruffey, and Capt. William Arbogast. They met at the residence of Jacob H. Arbogast to organize their companies.

[116]Roy B. Clarkson, in *Pocahontas County*, 9-13.

[117]*Pocahontas County*, 40.

[118]*West Virginia Heritage* [7], 8-10.

[119]*The West Virginia Encyclopedia* [Charleston, W.Va.: West Virginia Publishing Co. 1929], (hereafter West Virginia Encyclopedia) 282; *West Virginia Heritage* [7], 8-10

[120]Kuhl Narrative, 31st Virginia Papers, RBC; David and Robert Kuhl, personal communications with author, 11 and 15 March 1998. Christian Kuhl (1839-

1918) was born in Baltimore, Maryland before the family moved to Weston. His father, Henry Kuhl (1802-1862) remarried after the death of Chris's mother, Catherine Yeagle (1804-1854). Chris's brother William served in the Tenth West Virginia; brother Henry was in the Third West Virginia. Their brother Conrad spent at least part of the war as a prisoner of war at Fort Delaware.

[121]Kuhl Narrative, 31st Virginia Papers, RBC

[122]R. B. Cook, "Notes on Rev. John Elam Mitchell," 31st Virginia Papers, RBC, [A&M 1561 2 2 1; Kuhl Narrative, 31st Virginia Papers, RBC

[123]Kuhl Narrative, 31st Virginia Papers, RBC

[124]U.S.G.S. Map of West Virginia, 1:500,000 scale.

[125]John A. McNeill, "The Imboden Raid and Its Effects," [*Southern Historical Society Papers*, 34, 1906] (hereafter McNeill, Imboden Raid), 301.

[126]William L. Jackson to Sarah Jackson, Traveler's Repose, 18 Oct. 1861, 31st Virginia Papers, RBC; G. Porterfield to R. S. Garnett, 11 June 1861, *OR* [2] 71.

[127]Snider Memorandum, 5-6 June 1861; Haymond, *Harrison County*, 330; U.S. Census, 1860 Harrison County, Va. By June 19, the Wheeling Convention had passed an ordnance that required all office holders to take a loyalty oath in support of the re-organized government of Virginia (Union). In mid-July, the Sheriff of Harrison County, James Monroe, had a "quo warrant" served on him to show cause why he should not be ousted from office for failing to sign the oath. Joseph Snider was a bachelor, and had been living in the home of James and Amanda Adams of Clarksburg; before that, he lived with the William P. Cooper family.

[128]R. E. Lee to G. Porterfield, 13 June 1861, *OR* [2], 71-72; Bosworth, *Randolph County*, 115; Stewart Sifakis, *Who Was Who in the Civil War*, [New York: Facts on File Publications, 1988] (hereafter Sifakis *Who*), 238. Robert S. Garnett's cousin, Richard B. Garnett was also a brigadier general in the Army of Northern Virginia at this time: he was killed at Gettysburg, during Pickett's charge

[129]R. S. Garnet to G. Deas, 25 June 1861, *OR* [2,] 239; J. M. Heck, report, n.d., *OR* [2], 254-255. Three other militia companies from Pocahontas, Randolph, and Barbour counties were sent home by Heck, "to take care of the crops, as our army had to be supplied principally from those counties."

[130]Snider Memorandum, 15 June 1861; R. S. Garnett to G. Deas, 25 June 1861, *OR* [2], 236; J. M. Heck, report, n.d., *OR* [2], 254-255.

[131]R. S. Garnett to G. Deas, 25 June 1861, *OR* [2], 236.

[132]*Wheeling Daily Intelligencer*, 3 Aug. 1861. Reprint of a letter from a correspondent in the *New York Times*, signed J. M. W.

[133]William P. Cooper, statement to Examining Board, March 1864 concerning instruction and drill in the 31st Virginia, Confederate Adjutant and Inspector General, Letters Received, National Archives, [RG 109, M. 474, roll 113, item 382-G-1864] (hereafter AIG Letters)

[134]William R. Lyman to J. R. Anderson, 29 Nov. 1915, VMI Archives

[135]William Gilham, *Manual of Instruction for the Volunteers and Militia of the Confederate States* [Richmond: West and Johnston, 1861]

[136]R. S. Garnett to G. Deas, 25 June 1861, *OR* [2], 236-238.

[137]William L. Jackson to Sarah Jackson, Laurel Hill, n.d., 31st Virginia Papers, RBC

[138]Safe conduct pass signed by R. L. McCook, Colonel, 9th Ohio Volunteers, Parkersburg, 21 June 1861, for Mrs. W. L. Jackson and her 3 children, 31st Virginia Papers, RBC

[139]R. B. Cook, "Notes on Rev. John Elam Mitchell" 31st Virginia Papers, RBC; Moore, *Banner*, 91.

[140]R. B. Cook, "Notes on Rev. John Elam Mitchell" 31st Virginia Papers, RBC - Reverend Mitchell was mortally wounded May 6, 1862 at Arnoldsburg, WV as he participated in a raid under Captain George Downs of the Partisan Rangers. Mitchell was shot through both hips, and died after capture by the 11th West Virginia Infantry

[141]31st Virginia CSR - Lt. Hezekiah McNemar commanded Company D from June 20 to July 25, when McNemar went on furlough. 2nd Lt. Samuel S. Stout was in command from July 25 to August 1, when James S. Kerr McCutchen was elected Captain.

[142]Kuhl, Narrative, 31st Virginia Papers, RBC

[143]Snider Memorandum, 17 June to 6 July 1861; White, *West Virginia*, 19.

[144]R. S. Garnett to G. Deas, 1 July 1861, *OR*, [2], 239: R. E. Lee, to R. S. Garnett, 5 July 1861, *OR* [2], 240.

[145]R. S. Garnett to G. Deas, 6 July 1861, *OR* [2], 240-241.

[146]Morton, *Highland*, 136; Wilson, "Diary," 6 July 1861; Snider Memorandum, 7 July 1861

[147]Snider Memorandum, 8 July 1861; Hall, *Diary*, 15.

[148]Cammack, *Soldier*, 27-28.

[149]Hall, *Diary*, 15 - Dr. Higler owned the house, according to Joseph Snider.

[150]Snider Memorandum, 10 July 1861

[151]White, *West Virginia*, 20; J. M. Heck, report, n.d., *OR*, [2], 254-259.

[152]Morgan *Journal*, 12 July 1861, 203.

[153]Snider Memorandum, 12 July 1861; *Wheeling Daily Intelligencer*, 17 July 1861.

[154]Thomas B. Camden, "My Recollections and Experiences of the Civil War," 5, Camden Papers, WVU (hereafter Camden Papers, Experiences)

[155]Morgan *Journal*, 12 July 1861, 203; *Wheeling Daily Intelligencer*, 17 July 1861; W. B. Taliaferro, report, 10 Aug. 1861, *OR*, vol. 2, 285-288. Additional details from Joseph Snider's journal

[156]Snider Memorandum, 13 July 1861; Bosworth, *Randolph County*, detailed map on page 12; see also the map in Douglas S. Freeman, *Lee's Lieutenants: A Study in Command* 3 volumes [New York: Charles Scribner's Sons, 1942 - 1944 1] (hereafter Freeman, Lee's Lietenants), 26; and the map in George F. R. Henderson, *Stonewall Jackson and the American Civil War* [New York: Da Capo Press, 1988] (hereafter Henderson *Jackson*).

[157]Snider Memorandum, 13 July 1861; W. B. Taliaferro, report, 10 Aug. 1861, *OR* [2], 285-288.

[158] W. B. Taliaferro, report, 10 Aug. 1861, *OR* [2], 285-288.

[159] W. B. Taliaferro, report, 10 Aug. 1861, *OR* [2], 285-288

[160]Snider Memorandum, 13-14 July 1861; W. B. Taliaferro, report, 10 Aug. 1861, *OR*, [2], 285-288.

[161]Cammack, *Soldier*, 29-30.

[162]Snider Memorandum,14 July 1861 - Snider's comrades, who helped him on the march, were Private Hezekiah Holden, and 2nd Sergeant William J. West, both of Company C.

[163]Cammack, *Soldier*, 31.

[164]Ashcraft, *31st Virginia*, 18; Snider Memorandum, 15-18 July 1861; Muster Roll, Company C, Camp Bartow, 31 Aug. 1861, 31st Virginia CSR

[165]W. L. Jackson to Sarah Jackson, Laurel Fork, Va., 30 July 1861, 31st Virginia Papers, RBC

[166]Morgan *Journal*, 21-23 July 1861, 204; Muster roll for Company I, 31 Aug. 1861, 31st Virginia CSR; W. R. Lyman to Joseph R. Anderson, 29 Nov. 1915, VMI Archives

[167]White, *West Virginia*, 32, 34, 40; Morgan *Journal*, 25 July 1861, 204.

[168]Muster rolls and record of events, Company E, No. 2, and Company B (2nd), 31st Virginia CSR; Morton, *Highland*, 120-121. Company E, No. 2 later became the 2nd Company B.

[169]James S. Kerr McCutchen file, 31st Virginia CSR; W. L. Jackson to Sara Jackson, 30 July 1861, 31st Virginia Papers, RBC; Robert K. Krick, *Lee's Colonels: A Biographical Register of the Field Officers of the Army of Northern Virginia* 4th Edition Revised. [Dayton, OH: Press of Morningside House, 1992] (hereafter Krick, *Lee's Colonels*), 249; U.S. Census, 1860, Augusta County, Va.; "Another Pioneer Crosses Great Divide: Colonel McCutchen Answers Call to the Great Muster," *Exeter Sun* (California), 1 Oct. 1915.

[170]Snider Memorandum, 25, 30-31 July 1861 - Jacob Tolbert does not appear on muster rolls of the 31st Virginia.

[171]Snider Memorandum, 31 July 1861

[172]Snider Memorandum, 1-6, 11 Aug. 1861

[173]Snider Memorandum, 12-13 Aug. 1861

[174]Order No. 23, Camp Allegheny, 12 Aug. 1861 by Col. Johnson, Commanding, 31st Virginia Papers, RBC; Mark H. Boatner, *The Civil War Dictionary* [New York: Vintage Books, 1988] (hereafter Boatner, *Civil War*), 49. The name of the camp was probably in honor of Colonel Frances Bartow, 8th Georgia regiment, who was killed leading the 2nd brigade of Joseph Johnston's army in a chivalrous charge at the battle of 1st Manassas.

[175]Snider Memorandum, 13 Aug. 1861; Armstrong, *25th Virginia*, 7, 169; Hall Diary, 18 - Lt. Colonel George W. Hansbrough, former schoolteacher and lawyer from Pruntytown, in Taylor County, was in command of the 9th Virginia Battalion, made up of several Western Virginia companies that had not gone into the 25th and 31st regiments. Later, the Battalion was absorbed by the 25th Virginia regiment.

[176]Harding Narrative, 31st Virginia Papers, RBC

[177]Snider Memorandum, 14-15 Aug. 1861

[178]Snider Memorandum, 16 Aug. 1861; Record of Events, Companies A, G, and C, 31st Virginia CSR; Hall *Diary*, 18-19; William L. Jackson to Sarah Jackson, 14 Aug. 1861, 31st Virginia Papers, RBC

[179]Cammack, *Soldier*, 34-35; Lucius Cammack file, 31st Virginia CSR; Snider Memorandum, 17-18 Aug. 1861

[180]Snider Memorandum, 19 Aug. 1861

[181]Price, *Pocahontas County*, 450.

[182]Snider Memorandum, 22 and 25 Aug. 1861; *King James Bible*, Revised Standard Edition, 1870.

[183]W. L. Jackson to Sarah Jackson, Camp Bartow, HQ 31st Regt. Va. Vols., Travelers Repose Post Office, 22 Aug. 1861, 31st Virginia Papers, RBC

[184]Snider Memorandum, 25 Aug. 1861; Morgan *Journal,* 25 Aug. 1861, 206.

[185]W. L. Jackson to Sarah Jackson, Camp Bartow, 29 Aug. 1861, 31st Virginia Papers, RBC

[186]Gilham, William *Manual of Instruction for the Volunteers and Militia of the Confederate States* [Richmond: West and Johnston, 1861], 470.

[187] General Order issued by Col. Edward Johnson, HQ, Camp Bartow, 29 Aug. 1861, 31st Virginia Papers, RBC

[188] W. L. Jackson to Sarah Jackson, Camp Bartow, 1 Sept. 1861, 31st Virginia Papers, RBC - The lack of accurate muster rolls for the 31st Virginia through this early part of the war makes it difficult to establish the number of men who were present for duty. Only a few of the early muster rolls have survived.

[189] W. L. Jackson to Sarah Jackson, Camp Bartow, 1 Sept. 1861, 31st Virginia Papers, RBC

[190] W. L. Jackson to Sarah Jackson, Camp Bartow, 3 Sept. 1861, 31st Virginia Papers, RBC

[191] Pass written on 2 Sept. 1861 by Bob Moorman, Greenbrier Cavalry, for Mrs. Jackson to visit her husband, 31st Virginia Papers, RBC; Request for leave, from W. L. Jackson, HQ 31st Regt. at Camp Bartow, 5 Sept. 1861, 31st Virginia Papers, RBC

[192]Snider Memorandum, 6-7 Sept. 1861; 31st Virginia CSR, Addison Moyers - Moyers, Company B, died on Sept. 7. He had enlisted on May 18, 1861 in Pendleton County.

[193]Snider Memorandum, 7 Sept. 1861; Hall, *Diary,* 19.

[194]Snider Memorandum, 1 and 8 Sept. 1861

[195]General Orders No. 10, Army of the Northwest, Valley Mountain, 8 Sept. 1861, *OR* [51 2], 283-284.

[196]C. L. Stevenson, Confidential Memo, HQ Valley Mountain, 8 Sept. 1861, *OR*, vol. 51, part 2, 282; Special Orders No. 113, HQ Monterey Line, Northwest Army, Greenbrier River, 9 Sept. 1861, *OR* Vol. 51, part 2, 285. There were several more elements to this plan, involving the movement of General Donelson's brigade; placement of the artillery, which would be supported by Major Munford and Colonel Gilham; the advance of Colonel Burke's brigade; and the coordination of the regimental supply wagons.

[197]*OR*, vol. 5, 192.

[198]*Wheeling Daily Intelligencer,* 7 and 11 Oct. 1861.

[199]Morgan *Journal,* 9 Sept. 1861, 206; Snider Memorandum, 9 Sept. 1861; Kuhl, Narrative, 31st Virginia Papers, RBC; Albert Rust, report, Camp Bartow, 13 Sept. 1861, *OR* [5], 191-192. Colonel Rust estimated between 1500 and 1600 men were in his column. Other sources cite as many as 1800.

[200]Snider Memorandum, 10-13 Sept. 1861; Kuhl, Narrative, 31st Virginia Papers, RBC .

[201]Snider Memorandum, 10-13 Sept. 1861

[202]Albert Rust, report, Camp Bartow, 13 Sept. 1861, *OR* [5], 191-192.

[203]Kuhl, Narrative, 31st Virginia Papers, RBC - That morning, General H. R. Jackson's men had a minor skirmish with the Union picket at the first summit of Cheat Mountain, resulting in the death of a Union officer, Captain Junod, and one of Junod's soldiers.

[204]White, *West Virginia,* 41-42.

[205]Cammack, *Soldier*, 37.
[206]Cammack, *Soldier*, 37-38.
[207]Snider Memorandum, 10-13 Sept. 1861; Kuhl, Narrative, 31st Virginia Papers, RBC ; Daniel E. Summer, from the Compiled Muster Roll of Company C, and the Record of Killed, Wounded, and Died for the regiment, 31st Virginia CSR.
[208]White, *West Virginia*, 41-42.
[209]R. E. Lee, Valley River, 14 Sept. 1861, *OR* [5], 192-193.
[210]Morgan *Journal*, 15 Sept. 1861, 206; Snider Memorandum, 15 Sept. 1861
[211]Snider Memorandum, 16 Sept. 1861
[212]William F. Holt file, Company H., 31st Virginia CSR; Snider Memorandum, 17 Sept. 1861
[213]Charles L. Campbell, 17 Sept. 1861, "Diary of Charles L. Campbell," In William T. Price, *On To Grafton*, 56 (hereafter Campbell Diary); Snider Memorandum, 17 Sept. 1861
[214]Harding, "Narrative," 31st Virginia Papers, RBC.
[215]W. R. Lyman to Joseph Anderson, 29 Nov. 1915, VMI Archives.
[216]John S. Hoffman, and William P. Cooper, proceedings of Examining Board, March 1864, AIG Letters, National Archives, M474, roll 113, item 382-G-1864; W. L. Jackson to S. Jackson, Camp Bartow, 23 Sept. 1861, 31st Virginia Papers, RBC.
[217]W. L. Jackson to S. Jackson, Camp Bartow, 23 Sept. 1861, 31st Virginia Papers, RBC.
[218]Ashcraft, *31st Virginia*, 21-22, and map, 14.
[219]Snider Memorandum, 25-26 Sept. 1861
[220]Hall, *Diary of a Confederate Soldier*, 24-25; Snider Memorandum, 27 Sept. 1861, "Memorandum of Events Whilst Soldiering."
[221]Snider Memorandum, 27 Sept. 1861; Hall, *Diary of a Confederate Soldier*, 26.
[222]Hall, *Diary of a Confederate Soldier*, 27; Snider Memorandum, 28-30 Sept. 1861, Boatner, *Civil War Dictionary*, 624-625; Lt. O. C. R. Lewis and 1st Lieutenant Jacob Matheny, record of payments, 1863, 31st Virginia Papers, RBC.
[223]Hall, *Diary*, 28; Snider Memorandum, 3 Oct. 1861,
[224]Morgan *Journal*, 3 Oct. 1861, 207. Stephen A. Morgan, a nephew of George P. Morgan, also lived on a farm in Rivesville. Born in 1835, he was educated at the Fairmont Seminary before reading law at the offices of Judge James Neeson of Fairmont. In 1860, Stephen A. Morgan was admitted to the Marion County bar. Politically active, he also joined the "Marion Guards" as a volunteer when it was formed by Captain Thompson. Two of his brothers, Edward and William, served in the same company. On October 3, 1861, after George P. Morgan was taken prisoner, his nephew Stephen decided to continue the journal.
[225]Hall, *Diary*, 28.
[226]Henry R. Jackson, reports, 7 Oct. 1861, *OR* [5], 224-229.
[227]Phillips History, 4 September 1968. Phillips was promoted to lieutenant around the first of July.
[228]Phillips History, 4 September 1968.
[229]Cammack, *Soldier*, 38.

[230]Kuhl, Narrative, 31st Virginia Papers, RBC; Cammack, *Soldier*, 39.

[231] James H. Alford, and Frederick W. Bartlett files, 31st Virginia CSR.

[232]Jack Munford file, 31st Virginia CSR; W. L. Jackson to S. Jackson, Travelers Repose, 4 Oct. 1861, 31st Virginia Papers, RBC.

[233]Morgan *Journal*, 202, 207; James H. Alford file, 31st Virginia CSR.

[234]W. L. Jackson to S. Jackson, Travelers Repose, 3 Oct. 1861, 31st Virginia Papers, RBC; W. L. Jackson to S. Jackson, Travelers Repose, 4 Oct. 1861, 31st Virginia Papers, RBC.

[235]Snider Memorandum, 4 Oct. 1861

[236]Hall, *Diary*, 29.

[237]Snider Memorandum, 6 and 10 Oct. 1861

[238]Resignation of Lt. Col. William L. Jackson, Camp Bartow, 7 Oct. 1861, 31st Virginia Papers, RBC.

[239]W. L. Jackson to Sarah Jackson, Traveler's Repose, 8 Oct. 1861, 31st Virginia Papers, RBC.

[240]S. Jackson to W. L. Jackson, Tuckwillers (Va.), 16 Oct. 1861, 31st Virginia Papers, RBC.

[241]Cook, *Lewis County*, 118; A. H. Jackson file, 31st Virginia CSR. Alfred H. Jackson was appointed Assistant Adjutant General on Nov. 12, 1861, and ordered to report to General T. J. Jackson. Alfred Jackson's resignation from the 31st Virginia did not become official until December 10, 1861.

[242]Krick, *Lee's Colonels*, 318; W. L. Jackson to S. Jackson, Travelers Repose, 12 Oct. 1861, 31st Virginia Papers, RBC.

[243]Snider Memorandum, 15-16 Oct. 1861

[244]Snider Memorandum, 22 Oct. 1861; William Conrad file, 31st Virginia CSR.

[245] The house was owned by Jacob Arbogast, an uncle of Captain James Arbogast of Company G.

[246]Snider Memorandum, 19-24 Oct. 1861

[247]Snider Memorandum, 24 Oct. 1861; Morgan *Journal*, 2 Nov. 1861, 207.

[248]Moore, Banner, 133-135.

[249]Special Order No. 188, 24 Oct. 1861, 31st Virginia Papers, RBC; W. L. Jackson to S. Jackson, Travelers Repose, 27 Oct. 1861, 31st Virginia Papers, RBC. He wrote to her again on Nov. 2 that he had not received a reply from the Richmond authorities.

[250]Snider Memorandum, 26-30 Oct. 1861

[251]Snider Memorandum, 31 Oct. 1861 - Of the two men mentioned by Snider Memorandum for their bravery, one was probably Aldridge J. Cropp, corporal of Company C. However, it is difficult to say which Smith is meant here, as there were no fewer than 11 Smiths in Company C.

[252]Snider Memorandum, 1-4 Nov. 1861; Special Order signed by S. Reynolds, HQ 31st Regt. Va. Vols., Camp Bartow, 4 Nov. 1861, 31st Virginia Papers, RBC; Hardee, J. W., *Hardee's Rifle and Light Infantry Tactics*, [Philadelphia: J. B. Lippincott 1961]

[253]Snider Memorandum, 8-19 Nov. 1861; William D. F. Jarvis file, 31st Virginia CSR.

[254]Morgan *Journal*, 14 Nov. 1861, 208; George W. Atkinson, *Bench and Bar of West Virginia*, 336-337; Krick, *Lee's Colonels*, 38.

[255]Snider Memorandum; John W. Myers file, 31st Virginia CSR. His promotion was confirmed to date from November 24, 1861.

[256]Snider Memorandum, 16 Nov. 1861

[257]Special Orders No. 163, Headquarters, First Division, Army of Northwest, Camp Bartow, Va., 18 Nov. 1861, *OR* [51 2] 382.

[258]White, *West Virginia*, 52-53.

[259]Hall, *Diary*.

[260]Snider Memorandum, 19 Nov. 1861

[261]General Orders, No. 21, HQ 1st Division, Army of the Northwest, Camp on summit of Allegheny, 22 Nov. 1861, *OR* [51 2], 388.

[262]Snider Memorandum, 22 Nov. 1861

[263]White, *West Virginia*, 44-45; *Pocahontas County*, 43-45.

[264]Snider Memorandum, 23-24 Nov. 1861

[265]Snider Memorandum, 26 Nov. 1861; *Pocahontas County*, 499 and 450. A stone memorial to the Varner family is on the location of their farm. One of Solomon Varner's daughters, Margaret Varner (1837-1926), was married to Joseph E. Warwick Wooddell (1837-1864), of Green Bank. (They were this author's great-great grandparents.)

[266]Snider Memorandum, 27-30 Nov. 1861

[267]Snider Memorandum, 1-9 Dec. 1861

[268]R. G. Cole to Gen. H. R. Jackson, 25 Nov. 1861, *OR* [51 2], 389; W. W. Loring, Staunton, report, 17 Dec. 1861, *OR* [5], 459-460; Henderson, *Stonewall Jackson*, 142-143.

[269]Edward Johnson, report, 13 Dec. 1861, *OR* [5], 460-464.

[270]Snider Memorandum, 11-12 Dec. 1861; Edward Johnson, report, 13 Dec. 1861, *OR* [5], 460.

[271]Boyd B. Stutler, *West Virginia in the Civil War* [Charleston: West Virginia Education Foundation, Inc., 1963], 136-137.

[272]James A. Jones, report, 13 Dec. 1861, *OR* [5], 457-458.

[273] This part of the battlefield was considered the Confederate right.

[274]Edward Johnson, report, 19 Dec. 1861, *OR* [5], 462; G. W. Hansbrough, report, 16 Dec. 1861, *OR* [5], 465-466.

[275]Snider Memorandum, 13-14 Dec. 1861; Solomon H. Boykin, to "sister", Richmond, 16 Dec. 1861, relating information received in a letter from their brother, Francis M. Boykin, 13 Dec. 1861, in Francis M. Boykin, Correspondence and Papers, Mary Ober Gatewood Papers, Virginia Historical Society, Richmond, in Southern Women and Their Families in the 19th Century, ser. D, part 2, microfilm, (Bethesda, Md.: University Publications of America, 1994.)

[276] R. B. Cook, *Lewis County*, 1861-1865, 114; Lt. James Galvin, Summary of Events, 31 Dec. 1861, Muster Roll, Co. I, 31st Virginia Papers, RBC; Phillips History, 4 Sept. 1968.

[277]Hansbrough, report, 16 Dec. 1861, *OR* [5], 465-466; Hall, *Diary*; A. G. Reger, report, 16 Dec. 1861, *OR* [5], 466-467.

[278]Edward Johnson, report, Dec. 19 1861, *OR* [5], 462; Cammack, *Soldier*, 42.

[279]Johnson, report, Dec. 19 1861, *OR* [5], 462-463; Lewis Thompson file, 31st Virginia CSR. Colonel Johnson, in his report of the battle, incorrectly names him as George T. Thompson.

[280]Snider Memorandum, 13-14 Dec. 1861

[281]Johnson, reports, 13, 15, and 19 Dec., *OR* [5], 460-464; Henry A. Yeager to Gen. Robert White, Crickard, W. Va., 21 Oct. 1898, A&M 1561, ser. 2, box 2, vol. 1, 31st Virginia Papers, RBC.

[282]Casualty list, 31st Virginia, from CSR; Betty Hornbeck, *Upshur Brothers of the Blue and the Gray* [Parsons, W.Va.: McClain Printing Co., 1967], 78. Mrs. Eveline Yeager Beard of Arbovale, West Virginia in an interview on 4 Nov. 1926 (transcript in possession of the late Rev. W. W. Sutton, of Victoria Street, Buckhannon, West Virginia.) There were allegations that John Yeager had been murdered with poison, but nothing was ever proven. Later that winter, John Yeager's father, Jacob Yeager, also died in their home.

[283]Johnson, report, 13 Dec. 1861, *OR* [5], 461; Cammack, *Soldier*, 42.

[284]Hull, 31st Virginia Papers, RBC, quoting an excerpt of a Staunton Spectator, 24 Dec. 1865.

[285]Solomon H. Boykin, to "sister," 16 Dec. 1861, Richmond, and newspaper clippings, Gatewood Papers, VHS, in Southern Women and Their Families in the 19th Century, ser. D, part 2.

[286]Solomon H. Boykin, to "sister," 16 Dec. 1861, Richmond, and newspaper clippings, Gatewood Papers, VHS, in Southern Women and Their Families in the 19th Century, ser. D, part 2; Francis M. Boykin file, 31st Virginia, CSR.

[287]Special Order No. 267, Adjutant and Inspector General's Office, Richmond, 16 Dec. 1861, 31st Virginia Papers, A&M 1561, ser. 2, box 2, vol. 1, RBC.

[288]Hoffman to Camden, 18 Jan. 1861, Camden Papers, WVU.

[289]William P. Thompson file, 31st Virginia CSR; W. P. Thompson to George W. Randolph, 28 Aug. 1862, 31st Virginia CSR; Letters of recommendation from William L. Jackson, Edward Johnson, Francis M. Boykin, and John S. Hoffman, 31st Virginia CSR; Armstrong, *25th Virginia*, 243.

[290]Nathan Clawson, 26 Aug., 1863, Examining Board hearing, AIG Letters, National Archives, M474, roll 71, item 948-L.

[291]Snider Memorandum, 13-19 Dec. 1861 - Joseph C. Snider's journal stops on Dec. 19, 1861 and resumes on Feb. 21, 1862.

[292] Phillips History, 18 September 1968.

[293]Hall, *Diary*.

[294]Morgan *Journal*, 19 Dec. 1861, 214.

[295]Morgan *Journal*, 19-26 Dec. 1861, 214-216.

[296]

[297]Jedediah Hotchkiss, *Virginia : Confederate Military History*, vol. 3, expanded volume [1899; reprint, Dayton, Ohio: Press of Morningside Bookshop, 1975], 226.

[298]Snider Memorandum, 8 May 1862; Edward Johnson, report, 17 May 1862, *OR* [12 1], 482-484.

[299]Johnson, report, 17 May 1862, *OR* [12 1], 484; W. C. Scott, report, 12 Aug. 1862, *OR* [12 1], 485-487; Snider Memorandum, 8 May 1862

[300]Harding quoted in Walker, *VMI*, 110; Snider Memorandum, 8 May 1862,

[301]R. H. Cunningham, report, 18 May 1862, *OR* [12 1], 476; B. W. Leigh, report, OR [12 1], 480. Leigh noted that this was not, at this time, a principal scene of action, and mentions only one man who was shot in his command, and that was by accident.

[302]Lang, *Loyal West Virginia*, 54; Hornbeck, *Upshur Brothers*, 82-83; S. Hale, report, *OR* [12 1], 478-479. The 48th Virginia was posted on the left near the 12th Georgia.

[303]Freeman, *Lee's Lieutenants* [1], 354; *Civil War Battlefield Guide*, 47-49; Jedediah Hotchkiss, *Make Me A Map of the Valley* [Dallas, Southern Methodist University Press, 1973] (hereafter Hotchkiss, *Make Me A Map*), 40; Edward

Johnson, report, 17 May 1862, *OR* [12 1], 484; Return of Casualties, *OR* [12 1], 476.

[304]Casualties compiled from 31st Virginia CSR.

[305]Kuhl, Narrative, 31st Virginia Papers, RBC .

[306]Snider Memorandum, 9-14 May 1862, Alfred H. Jackson to Mary Jackson, 13 June 1862, 31st Virginia Papers, RBC.

[307]Snider Memorandum, 15 May 1862; Hall *Diary*; Hotchkiss, *Make Me a Map*, 45,46; *OR*, map vol., plates XCIV, 1-2.- Hotchkiss identified this place as Lebanon White Sulphur Springs.

[308]Snider Memorandum, 16-17 May 1862; W. C. Scott, report, 2 Aug. 1862, *OR* [12 1], 487.

[309]Snider Memorandum, 18 May 1862; Hotchkiss, *Make Me a Map*, 46.

[310]David and Robert Kuhl, personal communication with author, 1998.

[311]Snider Memorandum, 19-21 May 1862

[312]Freeman, *Lee's Lieutenants* [1], 374.

[313]*OR* [11 2], 484; Freeman, *Lee's Lieutenants* [1], 369; Henderson, *Stonewall Jackson*, 236; David F. Riggs, *13th Virginia Infantry* [Lynchburg, Va.: H. E. Howard, Inc., 1988], 12 (hereafter Riggs, *13th Virginia*); Sifakis, *Who Was Who* - Riggs indicates the transfer of the 31st Virginia, 25th Virginia, and 12th Georgia to Elzey's brigade was the evening of May 21. The Fourth brigade later gained three more regiments, the 44th Virginia, 52nd Virginia, and 58th Virginia, in time for the Seven-Days Battles near Richmond. Previously, Brig. Gen. Arnold Elzey had been in command of a brigade consisting of the 1st Maryland, 3rd Tennessee, 13th Virginia, and 16th Virginia. By the middle of May 1862, transfers of three regiments to other brigades left Elzey with just one regiment, the 13th Virginia.

[314]Alfred H. Jackson to Mary Jackson, 13 June 1862, 31st Virginia Papers, RBC; Riggs, *13th Virginia*, 13. The Union troops encountered on the 23rd were under the command of Colonel John R. Kenly.

[315]Freeman, *Lee's Lieutenants* [1], 389; Hall, *Diary*, 58; Harding, Narrative, 31st Virginia Papers, RBC.

[316]Alfred H. Jackson to Mary Jackson, 13 June 1862, 31st Virginia Papers, RBC; Harding, Narrative, 31st Virginia Papers, RBC.

[317]General Order No. 13, HQ Fourth Brigade, 28 May 1862, 31st Virginia Papers, RBC.

[318]Alfred H. Jackson to Mary Jackson, 13 June 1862, 31st Virginia Papers, RBC.

[319]Ashcraft, *31st Virginia*, 30; John J. Spencer file, 31st Virginia CSR; *Pocahontas County*, 451. John Josiah Spencer was exchanged at Aiken's Landing on June 26, 1862 and returned to the regiment.

[320]Walker, *VMI*, 112.

[321]Walker, *VMI*, 110, 112.

[322]Hall, *Diary*, 60.

[323]Thomas J. Jackson, report, 14 April 1863, *OR* [12 1], 713.

[324]Walker, *VMI*, 112-113.

[325]John S. Hoffman, report, Camp at Brown's Gap, 12 July 1862, 31st Virginia Papers, RBC; Thomas J. Jackson, report, 14 April 1863, *OR* [12 1], 713.

[326]Hall, *Diary*, 60.

[327]Walker, *VMI*, 113-114.

[328]Hoffman, report, 12 July 1862, 31st Virginia Papers, RBC; Alexander Whiteley file, 31st Virginia CSR.

[329]Robert K. Krick, *Conquering the Valley: Stonewall Jackson at Port Republic* [New York: William Morrow and Company, Inc., 1996], 382-384 (hereafter Krick, *Conquering the Valley)*; James A. Walker, report, 14 June 1862, *OR* [12 1], 791-793; Ashcraft, *31st Virginia Regiment*, 31. Col. Walker noted in his report that the actions of the 31st Virginia Regiment were in a separate report, but the compilers of the *OR* stated that the report of Col. Hoffman was not found.

[330]Walker, *VMI*, 114.

[331]Freeman, *Lee's Lieutenants*, [1], 455-456; Charles S. Winder, report, 15 June 1862, *OR* [12 1], 739-742.

[332]Harding Narrative, 31st Virginia Papers, RBC.

[333]Walker, *VMI*, 111.

[334]Gordon, W. F., "Under Sentence of Death," *Southern Bivouac*, new series, [1 10, March 1886], 589-592.

[335]Henry A. Yeager to Robert White, Crickard, W.Va., 21 Oct. 1898, 31st Virginia Papers, RBC.

[336]William H. Hull to the Pocahontas Times, 31st Virginia Papers, RBC.

[337]Gordon, "Under Sentence of Death," 589-592.

[338]Morrison, Wilbur C., "Jeremiah Church," *Clarksburg Exponent Telegram*, 3 May 1931.

[339]Kuhl, Narrative, 31st Virginia Papers, RBC .

[340]Charles S. Winder, report, 15 June 1862, *OR* [12 1], 739-742. The commanders of regiments in the brigade were Col. H. T. Hays, 7th Louisiana ; Col. Grigsby, 27th Virginia; Lt. Col. Funk, 5th Virginia. Colonel Hoffman and the 31st Virginia were part of Winder's brigade for this fight only, and afterward returned to Elzey's Brigade.

[341]Krick, *Conquering the Valley*, 475.

[342] W. R. Lyman to J. Anderson, 29 Nov. 1915, VMI Archives.

[343] Alfred H. Jackson to Mary Jackson, 13 June 1862, 31st Virginia Papers, RBC; Casualties in the Third Division, Fourth Brigade, *OR* [12 1*J*, 787; Yeager to White, Crickard, W.Va., 21 Oct. 1898, 31st Virginia Papers, RBC; Ashcraft, *31st Virginia*, 31. Note that the total does not match the number of killed and wounded reported by Lt. Colonel A. H. Jackson in his letter to his wife, which was 114.

[344]George W. Arbogast file, 31st Virginia CSR.

[345]Walker, *VMI*, 112.

[346]Gordon, "Under Sentence of Death," 592.

[347]Alfred H. Jackson to Mary Jackson, 13 June 1862, 31st Virginia Papers, RBC.

[348]Special Order dated HQ, 31st Regt. Va. Vols., 13 June 1862, by order of Lt. Col. Jackson, 31st Virginia Papers, RBC.

[349]Hall Diary, 61.

[350] Phillips History, 11 Sept. 1968; Joseph A. Waddell, *Annals of Augusta County: From 1726 to 1871*, 2nd edition [1902; reprint, Harrisonburg, Va.: C. J. Carrier Co., 1986], 473.

[351] Phillips History, 11 Sept. 1968; Hotchkiss, Make Me a Map of the Valley, 57.

[352]Kuhl, Narrative, 31st Virginia Papers, RBC .

[353] Hall Diary, 61; Thomas J. Jackson, report, 20 Feb. 1863, *OR* [12 1], 552559.

[354] Phillips History, 18 Sept. 1968.

[355] Phillips History, 18 Sept. 1968; Hall Diary, 62.

[356] Hotchkiss, *Virginia*, 285; Phillips History, 18 Sept. 1968.

[357] Phillips History, 18 Sept. 1968.

[358] Jackson, report, 20 Feb. 1863, *OR* [12 1], 553; Phillips History, 25 Sept. 1968.

[359] Hotchkiss, *Virginia*, 286-287.

[360] Stephen W. Sears, *To the Gates of Richmond: The Peninsula Campaign* [New York: Ticknor & Fields, 1992], (hereafter Sears, *Gates of Richmond*) 227-228, and the maps on 198,220, 231.

[361] Richard S. Ewell, report, *OR* [12 1], 605-607; Sears, *Gates of Richmond*, 231.

[362] Phillips History, 25 Sept. 1968.

[363] Ewell, report, *OR* [12 1], 605.

[364] Sears, *Gates of Richmond*, 231, 382.

[365] Willie Walker Caldwell, *Stonewall Jim: A Biography of General James A. Walker, C.S.A.* [Elliston, Va.: Northcross House, 1990] (hereafter Caldwell, *Stonewall Jim*), 54-55.

[366] Caldwell, *Stonewall Jim*, 50-51.

[367] Phillips History, 25 Sept. 1968.

[368] Caldwell, *Stonewall Jim*, 51, 53; List of killed, wounded, and missing in the Fourth Brigade, Third Division, Army of the Valley District in the battles of Cold Harbor (Gaines Mill), 27 June and Malvern Hill, 1 July, 1862, Brig. Gen. Elzey commanding, *OR* [12 1], 608.

[369] John S. Hoffman, statement, HQ, Smith's Brigade, 15 Aug. 1863, AIG Letters. Although it is clear from other sources that Colonel Hoffman was at times absent from the regiment between May 1, 1862 and June 28, 1862, he was not absent the entire time, and served as commander of the regiment when he was physically able, as allowed by his illness. In giving a statement relating to another matter entirely, in August of 1863, Colonel Hoffman had reason to recount his presence with the regiment in June of 1862, and stated that he had been unwell from around May 1, 1862 until "on the 28th of June, I was compelled to leave the regiment injured."

[370] Casualties derived from 31st Virginia CSR.

[371] James A. Walker, report, 2 Aug. 1862, *OR* [12 1], 610-611; Caldwell, *Stonewall Jim*, 55.

[372] Hall Diary, 62.

[373] Jubal A. Early, *Narrative of the War Between the States* [1912; reprint, New York: Da Capo Press, 1989] (hereafter Early *Narrative*), 78; Jubal A. Early, report, 2 Aug. 1862, *OR [12 1]*, 611-613.

[374] Early, *Narrative*, xvii-xxvi, 77-78; John Esten Cooke, *Wearing of the Gray* [New York: E. B. Treat & Co., 1867], 96-112; Jubal Early file, Compiled Service Records of the Confederate General Staff, National Archives, M. 331, Roll 83; Millard K. Bushong, *Old Jube: A Biography of General Jubal Early* [Boyce, Va.: Carr Pub., 1955].

[375] Freeman, *Lee's Lieutenants*, [1], 588; Early, *Narrative*, 78.

[376] Regimental Return for July 1862, 31st Virginia CSR. James C. Arbogast is listed as Adjutant Major. At this time he was newly promoted to fill Joseph H.

Chenoweth's position, but his promotion was not officially confirmed until Oct. 27, 1862. He signed the July return as commanding the regiment on that date, presumably the last day of July.

377Early, *Narrative*, 79. A private in the 44th Virginia, and a volunteer in Walker's 13th Regiment were the two men killed.

378 Phillips History, 9 Oct. 1968.

379Early, *Narrative*, 79-84.

380 Phillips History, 9 Oct. 1968.

381Early, report, 2 Aug. 1862, *OR* [12 1], 611-613; Early, *Narrative*, 82.

382Early, *Narrative*, 79-84.

383 Phillips History, 9 Oct. 1968.

384List of killed wounded and missing in the Fourth Brigade... Brig. Gen. Arnold Elzey commanding, *OR* [12 1], 608; Warwick C. Kincaid, Henry G. Britton, and James W. Quick files, 31st Virginia CSR; Ashcraft, *31st Virginia*, 118,148.

385 Phillips History, 9 Oct. 1968; Early, *Narrative*, 88.

386Benjamin A. Wooddell, Green Bank, Pocahontas County, Va., U.S. Census, 1860; Warwick Wooddell file, Confederate Archives, Ch. 10, File No. 34, p 126, 271.

387Sida H. Campbell file, letter of resignation, 31st Virginia CSR; Acceptance of S. H. Campbell's resignation, Special Order #181, 5 Aug. 1862, 31st Virginia Papers, RBC. Sida Campbell's other reason for resigning was to join a new regiment, the 19th Virginia cavalry, which was being formed under the 31st Virginia's former colonel, William L. Jackson.

388Henderson, *Stonewall Jackson*, 403. Henderson points out that one effect of this weeding out process of the sick and disabled was that the remaining men present were tough, experienced soldiers who had proven their ability to endure the rigors of war.

389Early, *Narrative*, 90.

390 Phillips History, 9 Oct. 1968.

391Special Orders No. 245, Major General T. J. Jackson, 28 July 1862, 31st Virginia Papers, RBC.

392Isaac V. Johnson file, 31st Virginia CSR.

393Resignation of Isaac V. Johnson, approved by James S. Kerr McCutchen, Commanding the Regiment, 30 July 1862, Isaac V. Johnson file, 31st Virginia CSR; John W. Bosworth file, 31st Virginia CSR. Bosworth was recommended for the regiment by A. G. Reger, and C. W. Newlon: they wrote on his behalf to Charles W. Russell in Richmond, who represented their home county in the Confederate House of Representatives. Russell wrote to the Secretary of War, and the transfer was granted.

394Robert E. Lee, report, 18 April 1863, *OR* [12 2], 176-179.

395Jubal A. Early, report, 14 Aug. 1862, *OR*, [12 2], 228-233; James A. Walker, report, 14 Aug. 1862, *OR*, [12 2], 233-235.

396Early, report, 14 Aug. 1862, *OR*, [12 2], 228-233.

397Early, report, 14 Aug. 1862, *OR*, [12 2], 228-233.

398Samuel D. Buck, "Gen. Joseph (sic) A. Walker," *Confederate Veteran* [10 1], 34-36; Phillips History, 9 Oct. 1968.

399Walker, report, 14 Aug. 1862, *OR*, vol. 12, part 2, 233-235.

400Harding, "Narrative," 31st Virginia Papers, RBC.

401Early, report, 14 Aug. 1862, *OR*, [12 2], 228-233.

⁴⁰²Early, report, 14 Aug. 1862, *OR*, [12 2], 228-233.

⁴⁰³Walker, report, 14 Aug. 1862, *OR*, [12 2], 233-235.

⁴⁰⁴Buck, "General Joseph A. Walker;" Early, report, Aug. 14, 1862, *OR*, [12 2], 228-233; Harding, "Narrative," 31st Virginia Papers, RBC.

⁴⁰⁵ Phillips History, 9 Oct. 1968.

⁴⁰⁶Lafayette Guild, Report of Killed and Wounded, *OR*, [12 2], 179-180.

⁴⁰⁷Early, report, 14 Aug. 1862, *OR*, [12 2], pp. 228-233.

⁴⁰⁸Henry H. Jones file, 31st Virginia CSR. 2nd Lieutenant Henry H. Jones of Company B wrote his resignation on July 8, 1863, while at the 31st Regiment's camp near Hagerstown, Md. After being wounded on June 27, 1862, Jones had spent a long time recovering in a hospital. "I have since, up to the 15th of last month (June 1863), been away from my command for several months, being on Conscript and Recruiting duty. I am unable to endure the fatigue and exposure of field duty." The resignation was approved September 19, 1863.

⁴⁰⁹*Field Manual for the Use of the Officers on Ordnance Duty* [Richmond: Ritchie and Dunnavant, 1862], 70-71.

⁴¹⁰Robert H. Bradshaw, William C. Kincaid, and Henry H. Jones files, 31st Virginia CSR.

⁴¹¹Hiram M. Marsh, and E. Bradbury's files, Statement by Nathan Clawson, witness to the election of officers, 31st Virginia CSR.

⁴¹²Henderson, *Stonewall Jackson*, 422-423; Early, *Narrative*, 105-106.

⁴¹³Ashcraft, *31st Virginia*, 35, 127.

⁴¹⁴Jubal A. Early, report, 12 Jan. 1863, *OR*, [12 2], 704-716.

⁴¹⁵Thomas Alford file, 31st Virginia CSR; Early, *Narrative*, 106; Early, report, 12 Jan. 1863, *OR*, [12 2], 704 ; William Grogg file, 31st Virginia CSR.

⁴¹⁶Early, report, 12 Jan. 1863, *OR*, [12 2], 704. Warrenton Springs was also known as Sulphur Springs, and appeared that way on many maps.

⁴¹⁷Early, *Narrative*, 107; Early, report, 12 Jan. 1863, *OR*, [12 2], 705.

⁴¹⁸Early, report, 12 Jan. 1863, *OR*, [12 2], 705.

⁴¹⁹Early, *Narrative*, 107-113; Early, report, 12 Jan. 1863, *OR*, [12 2], 706-708.

⁴²⁰Early, *Narrative*, 113; Riggs, *13th Virginia*, 21.

⁴²¹Casualties in the Third (Ewell's) Division, Jubal A. Early, Brig. Gen. Commanding, on the Rappahannock., 21-24 Aug. 1862, *OR*, [12 2], 716-717; Thomas Alford file, 31st Virginia CSR; Harding, "Narrative," 31st Virginia Papers, RBC.

⁴²²Nathan Clawson file, 31st Virginia CSR; John S. Hoffman, 15 Aug. 1863, AIG Letters.

⁴²³Early, report, 12 Jan. 1863, *OR*, [12 2], 708.

⁴²⁴Early, report, 12 Jan. 1863, *OR*, [12 2], 709.

⁴²⁵Early, report, 12 Jan. 1863, *OR*, [12 2], 710; Report of Casualties, *OR*, [12 2], 716.

⁴²⁶Samuel Tucker file, 31st Virginia CSR.

⁴²⁷Morrison, "Aged Indian Fighter," 31st Virginia Papers, RBC.

⁴²⁸Early, report, 12 Jan. 1863, *OR*, [12 2], 710.

⁴²⁹Early, report, 12 Jan. 1863, *OR*, [12 2], 711.

⁴³⁰William R. Lyman to Joseph R. Anderson, 29 Nov. 1915, V.M.I. Archives.

⁴³¹Ashcraft, *31st Virginia*, 37.

⁴³²Early, report, 12 Jan. 1863, *OR*, [12 2], 712; Caldwell, *Stonewall Jim*, 70.

[433]Early, report, 12 Jan. 1863, *OR*, [12 2], 712; Harding, "Narrative," 31st Virginia Papers, RBC.

[434]Early, report, 12 Jan. 1863, *OR*, [12 2], 713.

[435]Lafayette Guild, Killed and Wounded at Manassas Plains or Second Manassas, 28-30 Aug. 1862, *OR*, [12 2], 560-562.

[436]31st Virginia CSR; Harding, "Narrative," 31st Virginia Papers, RBC. After the war, George Harding's body was moved to a cemetery in their home county by his brother, Joseph Harding.

[437]Harding, "Narrative," 31st Virginia Papers, RBC.

[438]Harding, "Narrative," 31st Virginia Papers, RBC; Return of the 31st Virginia, July 1862, 31st Virginia Papers, A&M 1561 vol. 3, Box 1 of series 2, RBC.

[439]Casualties in Ewell's Division, *OR*, [12 2], 716; 31st Virginia Infantry, CSR.

[440]Early, *Narrative*, 134.

[441] Phillips History, 9 Oct. 1968.

[442]Early, *Narrative*, 134-135.

[443]General Order, HQ, 31st Reg. Va., 5 Sept. 1862, signed by John S. Hoffman, 31st Virginia Papers, RBC.

[444] John S. Hoffman, statement for Examining Board, 15 Aug. 1863, AIG Letters; Ashcraft, *31st Virginia*, 38.

[445]Early, *Narrative*, 134-135; Phillips History, 9 Oct. 1968.

[446]James C. Arbogast, 15 Aug. 1863, AIG Letters.

[447]Early, *Narrative*, 136.

[448]Early, *Narrative*, 137.

[449]*Civil War Battlefield Guide*, 473.

[450]Early, *Narrative*, 140.

[451]John W. Bosworth to Roy Bird Cook, 6 Dec. 1926, 31st Virginia Papers, RBC; Phillips History, 16 October 1968.

[452] Phillips History, 16 October 1968; Early, *Narrative*, 142.

[453]Laura V. Hale and Stanley S. Phillips, *History of the Forty-Ninth Virginia Infantry* [Lanham, Md.: S. S. Phillips and Assoc., 1981], 52; Early, *Narrative*, 147.

[454]John W. Bell, *Memoirs of Governor Smith: His Political, Military, and Personal History* [New York: Moss Engraving Co., 1891], 47.

[455]Bell, *Memoirs of Governor William Smith*, 47.

[456]Bell, *Memoirs of Governor William Smith*, 47; Ashcraft, 31st Virginia, 40.

[457]James V. Murfin, "The General's Tour of Antietam," *Blue & Gray Magazine*, [Aug.-Sept. 1985], 22.

[458] Phillips History, 16 October 1968.; Hale and Phillips, *History of the Forty-Nine Virginia*, 53.

[459]Early, *Narrative*, 147

[460]Jubal A. Early to Robert Stiles, 5 March 1888, in Bell, *Memoirs of Governor Smith*, 48-49

[461]Murfin, "The General's Tour, Antietam," 22; information on Union units from Antietam National Battlefield Park, National Park Service.

[462]Early, *Narrative*, 150-153.

[463]Nathan Clawson file, 31st Virginia CSR; Report of casualties in 31st Virginia Regiment, Early's Brigade, 17 Sept. 1862 at Sharpsburg, Md., Confederate States Army Casualties, Lists and Narrative Reports, 1861-65, National Archives, M. 836, Roll 7.

[464]Ashcraft, *31st Virginia*, 150; Phillips, "History of Valley Furnace," 16 Oct. 1968.

[465]Compiled by author from 31st Virginia CSR.

[466]Early, *Narrative*, 163.

[467]Armstrong, *25th Virginia Infantry*, 51

[468]W. W. Arnett file, 31st Virginia CSR.

[469]Special Order #254, 30 Oct. 1862, 31st Virginia Papers, RBC.

[470]George T. Thompson file, 31st Virginia CSR.

[471] Hall Diary, 64.

[472]William P. Cooper file, 31st Virginia CSR.

[473]General Order No. 1, Early's Brigade, 29 Oct. 1862, AIG Letters.

[474]Dennis Bohner, and John G. Gittings, 8 Nov. 1862, AIG Letters; Nathan Clawson, 1862, AIG Letters.

[475] James M. Blair to J. D. Blair, at Camp near Front Royal, Warren County, Va., 10 Nov. 1862, 31st Virginia CSR

[476]William B. Compton to Jefferson Davis, 10 Nov. 1862, William B. Compton file, 31st Virginia CSR.

[477]Hu Maxwell, *History of Randolph County West Virginia* [Morgantown, W.Va.: Acme Publishing Co., 1898], 304-305; Joseph F. Harding and Marion Harding files, 31st Virginia CSR; Harding, "Narrative," 31st Virginia Papers, RBC.

[478]Orders dated 22 Nov. 1862 at HQ 31st Va. Regt., at Camp near Cedarville, 31st Virginia Papers, RBC.

[479]Charges preferred against Pvt. Thomas J. Williams, Company B, at camp near Cedar Creek, 11 Nov. 1862, 31st Virginia Papers, RBC.

[480] Hall Diary, 65-66; Early, *Narrative*, 163.

[481] James C. Arbogast file, 31st Virginia CSR.

[482]Harding Narrative, 31st Virginia Papers, RBC.

[483] Hall Diary, 66; Early, *Narrative*, 166.

[484]Early, *Narrative*, 166, 170.

[485]Early, *Narrative*, 170.

[486] Phillips History, 16 October 1968.

[487] Hall Diary, 66.

[488]Early, *Narrative*, 173-174.

[489]James A. Walker, "List of Killed, Wounded & Missing in Early's Brigade in the Battle near Fredericksburg on 13 Dec. 1862," CSA Casualty & Narrative Reports, National Archives, M. 836, roll 5; and individual soldier records, 31st Virginia CSR.

[490] Phillips History, 16 October 1968.

[491]John A. Guildford to his parents, from camp near Gordonsville, 1 Aug. 1862, John A. Guildford file, 31st Virginia CSR.

[492]Ashcraft, *31st Virginia*, 44; Harding Narrative, 31st Virginia Papers, RBC.

[493]J. S. Hoffman, HQ, 31st Va. Reg., Camp near Port Royal, 17 Dec. 1863, 31st Virginia Papers, RBC.

[494]31st Virginia Papers, RBC.

[495]Early, *Narrative*, 184,186,188.

[496]Bell, *Memoirs of Governor Smith*, 54, 116; Hale and Phillips, *History of the Forty-Ninth Virginia*, viii, 50.

[497]William P. Cooper, 1-6, 16, 26 Jan.; 3, 8, 13 Feb.; 12, 24 March; 5 April 1863, "Journal," A&M 1561, ser. 2, box 2 [5], 31st Virginia Papers, RBC; Snider Memorandum, 6, 12, 23, 30 Jan.; 3, 12, 13, 18 Feb.; 12, 24 March; 5 April 1863,

[498]Snider Memorandum, 9 Jan. and 4 March 1863; Hall Diary, 69.

[499]Snider Memorandum, 16 Jan., 3 Feb., 13 Feb. 1863; Hall Diary, 72-73. Hall noted that his mouth was very sore, and men were showing signs of scurvy.

[500]Samuel A. Gilmore file, 31st Virginia CSR.

[501] Ashbel F. James file, 31st Virginia CSR.

[502]Cooper, 31 Jan. 1863, "Journal," 3, 31st Virginia Papers, RBC; Benjamin F. Corder file, 31st Virginia CSR.

[503]Snider Memorandum, 31 Jan. 1863

[504]Hospital records, 5 and 7 March 1863, Norval Lewis file, 31st Virginia CSR; Snider Memorandum, Hall Diary, 71-72.

[505]John D. Imboden to R. E. Lee, 2 March 1863, OR, [25 2], 652-653; Lee to Imboden, 11 March 1863, OR, [25 2], 661; Sam Jones to John B. Floyd, 8 March 1863, OR, [25 2], 660; Lee to Jones, 11 March 1863, OR, [25 2], 661; Jones to Imboden, 4 April 1863, OR, [25 2], 704; Jones to W. L. Jackson, 4 April 1863, OR, [25 2], 704-706; Jones to James Seddon, 5 April 1863, OR, [25 2], 705-706; Jones to George S. Patton, 5 April 1863, OR, [25 2], 707. Patton's 22nd Virginia was ordered from Lewisburg to meet with Imboden at Huttonsville on April 15.

[506]Thomas M. Devericks file, 31st Virginia CSR. The 26-year-old Devericks had the authority to enlist recruits renewed on August 12, 1863.

[507]Notification of authority for Hezekiah Holden to raise a company from within the enemy's lines, 23 Feb. 1863, 31st Virginia Papers, RBC; Hezekiah Holden file, 31st Virginia CSR; Snider Memorandum, 4 and 6 March 1863

[508] Phillips History, 23 October 1868.

[509]Prisoners of War, 31st Virginia derived from the 31st Virginia CSR.

[510]Snider Memorandum, 6-7 March 1863 - Private Jacob Runyon received punishment on March 6; Zadoc Griffith, scheduled to receive the same punishment, deserted that night.

[511]Maxwell, Barbour, 267.

[512]Phillips to A. Coleman Bowman, Monterey, 29 Jan. 1863, in Phillips History, 11 September 1863.

[513]Hornbeck, Upshur Brothers of the Blue and the Gray, 104-105; Record of Events, Company K, 31st Virginia Papers, RBC; Randall Osborne and Jeffrey C. Weaver, The Virginia State Rangers and State Line [Lynchburg: H. E. Howard, 1994], 155.

[514] Hall Diary, 68.

[515]Snider Memorandum, 3 March 1863, Hall Diary, 72-73.

[516]John S. Hoffman, request for permission to attend the Virginia legislature, 15 March 1863, 31st Virginia Papers, RBC.

[517]Luther D. Haymond file, 31st Virginia CSR.

[518]Snider Memorandum; George M. Cookman, Isaiah Bee, and Enoch Yerkey files, 31st Virginia CSR; W. P. Cooper, Journal, 6, 31st Virginia Papers, RBC; William P. Cooper to A. P. Mason, Assistant Adjutant General, Early's Brigade, 27 Dec. 1862, concerning request for Enoch M. Yerkey to transfer to the 31st Virginia from Jenkins Brigade of cavalry, and George M. Cookman to transfer from the 31st Virginia to Jenkin's Brigade, and related approvals by

Walker, Early, Jackson, and Lee, AIG Letters, National Archives M474, roll 14, item 2747-c-1862.

[519]W. P. Cooper Journal, 9 April 1863, 31st Virginia Papers, RBC. Strength of regiment, between 250 and 350, is estimated from the existing muster rolls for 30 April 1863, 31st Virginia Papers, RBC.

[520] Hall Diary, 74; Snider Memorandum, 10 April 1863, "Memorandum of Events Whilst Soldiering."

[521]Snider Memorandum, 10-11 April 1863

[522]W. P. Cooper, Journal, 11 April 1863, 31st Virginia Papers, RBC; Snider Memorandum, 11 April 1863 - This location was probably Archibold Steward's place, according to a note on the typescript of Cooper's journal.

[523]Snider Memorandum, 11 April 1863, "Memorandum of Events Whilst Soldiering."

[524]W. P. Cooper, Journal, 12-13 April 1863, 31st Virginia Papers, RBC; General Orders No. 11, HQ N.W. Va. Brigade, 15 April 1863, 31st Virginia Papers, RBC.

[525]General Orders No. 12, HQ Northwest Virginia Brigade, 13 April 1863, 31st Virginia Papers, RBC.

[526]Extract from Special Orders No. 36, Northwest Virginia Brigade, Camp Washington, 14 April 1863, 31st Virginia Papers, RBC.

[527]W. P. Cooper, Journal, 14 April 1863, 31st Virginia Papers, RBC.

[528]General Orders No. 13, HQ N.W. Va. Brigade, Camp Washington, 14 April 1863, 31st Virginia Papers, RBC.

[529]W. P. Cooper, Journal, 15-19 April 1863, 31st Virginia Papers, RBC.

[530]Sidney Ruckman, resignation, Camp Washington, 16 April 1863, with John S. Hoffman's comments, and John D. Imboden's comments on the fold, Sidney Ruckman file, 31st Virginia CSR.

[531]W. P. Cooper, Journal, 20 April 1862, 31st Virginia Papers, RBC; John D. Imboden, 1 June 1863, OR [25 1], 98-105.

[532]Imboden, 1 June 1863, OR [25 1], 98-105.

[533]McNeill, "The Imboden Raid and Its Effects," 294-312.

[534] Hall Diary, 75.

[535]Imboden, 1 June 1863, OR [25 1], 98-105; General Orders No. 20, HQ N.W. Va. Brigade, Roaring Run, Upshur County, Va., 25 April 1863, 31st Virginia Papers, RBC.

[536]W. P. Cooper, Journal, 25 April 1863, 31st Virginia Papers, RBC.

[537]Snider Memorandum, 24 April 1863

[538]Snider Memorandum, 26 April 1863; W. P. Cooper, Journal, 26-27 April 1863, 31st Virginia Papers, RBC.

[539]Snider Memorandum, 27 April 1863

[540]W. P. Cooper, Journal, 29-30 April 1863, 31st Virginia Papers, RBC.

[541]Jones to Imboden, Evansville, 27 April 1863, OR [25 1], 105.

[542] Hall Diary, 75; Snider Memorandum, 27 April - 1 May 1863

[543]James M. Blair file, 31st Virginia CSR.

[544]Imboden, 1 June 1863, OR [25 1], 102.

[545]Imboden, 3 May 1863, OR [25 1], , 98.

[546] W. P. Cooper, Journal, 3-4 May 1863, 8, 31st Virginia Papers, RBC.

[547]Snider Memorandum, 2-5 May 1863, "Memorandum of Events Whilst Soldiering."

548 Phillips History, 23 Oct. 1968. Log Rollings are lively discussions in which everyone is talking until the entire sound fills the room like a log rolling down a hill.

549Imboden, 1 June 1863, *OR* [25 1], 98-105; Snider Memorandum, 7 May 1863

550 W. P. Cooper, Journal, 8 May 1863, 31st Virginia Papers, RBC.

551 W. P. Cooper, Journal, 9-10 May 1863, 31st Virginia Papers, RBC.

552Snider Memorandum, 10 May 1863; W. P. Cooper, Journal, 11 May 1863, 31st Virginia Papers, RBC.

553 Phillips History, 30 Oct. 1968.

554Snider Memorandum, 12 May 1863; W. P. Cooper, Journal, 12 May 1863, 31st Virginia Papers, RBC.

555Snider Memorandum, 13 May 1863 - Imboden reported the 19th Virginia Cavalry attacked the Ninety-First Ohio, and two companies of Union cavalry, capturing 23 prisoners, 28 wagons loaded with supplies, and 168 mules with harnesses.

556Kuhl, Narrative, 31st Virginia Papers, RBC .

557 W. P. Cooper, Journal, 14-15 May 1863, 31st Virginia Papers, RBC; Snider Memorandum, 14-30 May 1863

558Smith, *History of Lewis County*, 313.

559McNeill, "The Imboden Raid and its Effects," 294-312; Imboden, 3 May 1863, and 1 June 1863, *OR* [25 1], 98-105.

560"The Rebel Raid in Western Virginia," *Wheeling Daily Intelligencer*, 7 May 1863. On May 13, the Wheeling Daily Intelligencer carried an article written by the special correspondent of the Philadelphia Inquirer. He sent a very well written, detailed analysis from Grafton on May 8. The author credits Colonel Mulligan of the Union army as his primary source.

561 Hall Diary, 77-78.

562Snider Memorandum, 19-26 May 1863; Hall Diary, 77-78.

563 Phillips History, 30 Oct. 1968.

564Snider Memorandum, 27-28 May 1863

565 W. P. Cooper, Journal, 28-30 May 1863, 31st Virginia Papers, RBC; William P. Cooper file, 31st Virginia CSR; John S. Hoffman to James Seddon, 16 June 1863, 31st Virginia Papers, RBC.

566 W. P. Cooper, Journal, 31 May 1863, 31st Virginia Papers, RBC.

567Snider Memorandum, 30 May - 1 June 1863

568Special Orders No. 37, HQ N.W. Virginia Brigade, Buffalo Gap, 2 June 1863, 31st Virginia Papers, RBC.

569William R. Lyman to Adam F. Swadley, Staunton, 2 June 1863, 31st Virginia Papers, RBC.

570Snider Memorandum, 2 June 1863

571 Hall Diary, 80.

572Gen. Orders No. 41, HQ, 2nd Army Corps, 4 June 1863, 31st Virginia Papers, RBC.

573Circular, Headquarters, Early's Division, 4 June 1863, 31st Virginia Papers, RBC.

574Snider Memorandum 5-12 June 1863; Osborne Wilson, 12 June 1863, from "Diary" in Morton, *History of Highland County*, 137.

575Snider Memorandum, 13 June 1863

576Jubal A. Early, report, 22 Aug. 1863, *OR*, [27 2], 459-473.

[577] John S. Hoffman, report, 4 Aug. 1863, *OR*, [27 2], 488-490; Snider Memorandum, June 13, 1863

[578] Early, report, 22 Aug. 1863, *OR*, [27 2], 461; John W. Daniel to Thomas Smith, William Smith's son, in Bell, *Memoirs of Governor Smith*, 117; William "Extra Billy" Smith's Brigade, http://www.gettysburgdaily.com/?p=164

[579] Haymond, Henry, *History of Harrison County*, p. 250; Driver, Robert J. *52nd Virginia Infantry*, p. 1 and 150; William "Extra Billy" Smith's Brigade, http://www.gettysburgdaily.com/?p=164; John Catlett Gibson V, http://freepages.genealogy.rootsweb.ancestry.com/~opus/p2994.htm

[580] Early, report, 22 Aug. 1863, *OR*, [27 2], 462; Hoffman, report, 4 Aug. 1863, *OR*, [27 2], 488-489. The 31st Virginia had no wounded that day.

[581] Early, report, 22 Aug. 1863, *OR*, [27 2], 463

[582] Snider Memorandum, 15 June 1863

[583] Hoffman, report, 4 Aug. 1863, *OR*, [27 2], 490.

[584] Snider Memorandum, 16-17 June 1863

[585] Snider Memorandum, 18-22 June 1863; Wilson, 23 June 1863, "Diary," in Morton, *History of Highland County, Virginia*, 137.

[586] Snider Memorandum, 23-26 June 1863; Freeman, *Lee's Lieutenants*, [3], 31.

[587] Snider Memorandum, 26 June 1863

[588] Snider Memorandum, 27-29 June 1863; Early, *Narrative*, 259; Driver, *52nd Virginia Infantry*, 30 – interesting that Early does not mention this incident.

[589] Early, *Narrative*, 259, 261.

[590] Harding, "Narrative, 31st Virginia Papers, RBC.

[591] Snider Memorandum, 29 June 1863

[592] Snider Memorandum, 30 June 1863; Early, Jubal, *Narrative*, 264

[593] Harry W. Pfanz, *Gettysburg: Culp's Hill and Cemetery Hill* [Chapel Hill: Univ. of North Carolina Press, 1993], 40 (hereafter Pfanz, *Culp's Hill*).

[594] Early, Jubal, *Narrative*, 266

[595] Snider Memorandum, 1 July 1863 - Joseph C. Snider's journal stops here, and does not resume until several months later.

[596] Early, *Narrative*, 267

[597] Ashcraft, *31st Virginia*, 52-53.

[598] Pfanz, *Culp's Hill*, 40-41; "Battle of Gettysburg, First Day" http://en.wikipedia.org/wiki/Battle_of_Gettysburg,_First_Day#cite_note-47 - "of Coster's 800 men, 313 were captured, as were two of the four guns from the battery"

[599] Driver, Robert, *52nd Viginia Infantry*, 39-40; Pfanz, *Culp's Hill*, 77-78; Early, *Narrative*, 270-271

[600] Driver, *52nd Viginia Infantry*, 39; Hoffman, report, 4 Aug. 1863, *OR* [27 2], 489; Pfanz, *Culp's Hill*, 55-56. The Federal artillery on Cemetery Hill was part of Reynolds's force, under command of Breck; and on Culp's Hill, that of Stevens.

[601] Driver, *52nd Virginia Infantry*, 40, 102 Others shared General Early's doubt about the report sent by General Smith. Lieutenant "Bent" Coiner of the 52nd Va noted that by the time they received reinforcements, it was obvious even to General Smith that the supposed enemy was no longer in evidence.

[602] Pfanz, *Culp's Hill*, 95-96.

[603] Phillips History, 30 Oct. 1968; Edward Johnson, report, 18 Aug. 1863, *OR* [27 2], 499-506; J. Q. A. Nadenbousch, report, 30 July 1863, *OR* [27 2], 521-522; James A. Walker, report, 17 Aug. 1863, *OR* [27 2], 518-519.

[604]Harding, "Narrative," 31st Virginia Papers, RBC.

[605] Phillips History, 30 Oct. 1968.

[606]Early, *Narrative*, 272-273; Johnson, report, 18 Aug. 1863, *OR* [27 2], 499-506.

[607] Phillips History, 30 Oct. 1968; Hall Diary, 82. - Phillips noted the artillery opened at 3:00 p.m.

[608] Phillips History, 30 Oct. 1968; Ashcraft, *31st Virginia*, 54.

[609]Edward J. Stackpole, *They Met at Gettysburg* [Harrisburg, Pa.: Eagle Books, 1956], 214; Boatner, *The Civil War Dictionary*, 194. Greene's brigade was numbered the 3rd Brigade of J. W. Geary's (2nd) division. The Twelfth Corps was commanded by A. S. Williams at Gettysburg. H. W. Slocum commanded the Union right wing.

[610]Hoffman, report, 4 Aug. 1863, *OR* [27 2], 489.

[611]Walker, report, 17 Aug. 1863, *OR* [27 2], 518-519; Nadenbousch, report, 30 July 1862, *OR* [27 2], 521-522.

[612]Douglas, *I Rode With Stonewall*, 241.

[613]Pfanz, *Culp's Hill*, 292-293; Early, *Narrative*, 275; Nadenbousch, report, 30 July 1863, *OR* [27 2], 521-522.

[614]Douglas, *I Rode With Stonewall*, 241.

[615]Bell, *Memoirs of Governor Smith*, 52-53; R. W. Hunter, "Gen. (Governor) William Smith at Gettysburg."

[616]Robert J. Driver, *52nd Virginia Infantry* 2nd Edition [Lynchburg, Va.: H. E. Howard, Inc., 1986], 40-41.

[617]Pfanz, *Culp's Hill*, 338-339; Driver, *52nd Virginia*, 40-41.

[618]Harding, Narrative, 31st Virginia Papers, RBC.

[619]Pfanz, *Culp's Hill*, 314.

[620] Was the 31st Virginia on the line with them at that point? Sources seem to differ and I've not decided, but see much evidence of it being before Hoffman arrived with the 31sr Virginia.

[621]William A. Frasanato, *Gettysburg: A Journey Through Time* [New York: Charles Scribner's Sons, 1975], 136-139.

[622] Hall Diary, 83.

[623]William R. Lyman to Joseph R. Anderson, 29 Nov. 1915, VMI Archives; Elisha Wilfong file, 31st Virginia CSR. The wound took Wilfong off the active list for a while. He was sent to Richmond to a hospital, and then furloughed on August 3rd for 60 days, apparently to go home to see his family in Green Bank, Pocahontas County.

[624]Ashcraft, *31st Virginia*, 55.

[625]Harding, Narrative, 31st Virginia Papers, RBC.

[626]Walker, report, 17 Aug. 1863, *OR* [27 2], 518-519; Phillips History, 30 Oct. 1968.

[627] Phillips History, 30 Oct. 1968.

[628]Harding, Narrative, 31st Virginia Papers, RBC; Return of Casualties in the Army of Northern Virginia at the Battle of Gettysburg, Smith's Brigade, 1-3 July 1863, *OR*, [27 2],340; Hoffman, report, 4 Aug. 1863, *OR* vol. 27, part 2, 490. The official casualty report does not tally with Hoffman's report, which was written in August, nearly a month later. Hoffman reported, "During the

three days of the battle, the loss of the brigade was 3 officers and 12 men killed, 5 officers and 105 men wounded, and 17 men missing."

[629]Hoffman, report, 4 Aug. 1863, *OR* [27 2], 490; Phillips History, 30 Oct. 1968; Courtland Phillips file, 31st Virginia CSR.

[630] Hall Diary, 83.

[631] Phillips History, 30 Oct. 1968.

[632]Harding, Narrative, 31st Virginia Papers, RBC

[633] Henry H. Jones file, 31st Virginia CSR. The resignation was approved on 19 Sept. 1863.

[634]Ashcraft, *31st Virginia*, 56; Phillips History, 30 Oct. 1968.

[635]Harding, Narrative, 31st Virginia Papers, RBC.

[636]Driver, *52nd Virginia Infantry*, 43; Early, *Narrative*, 283; General Orders No. 13, HQ, Early's Division, 17 July 1863, 31st Virginia Papers, RBC.

[637]Thomas W. Hoffman file, CSR, Confederate General & Staff Officers, National Archives, M331, Roll 129. The request was forwarded to Head Quarter's, Smith's Brigade on July 17, and was approved and forwarded by Colonel John S. Hoffman, Commanding Brigade. Subsequently it was approved on August 24, 1863, to take rank from July 17, 1863.

[638] Phillips History, 30 Oct. 1968; Ashcraft, *31st Virginia*, 57.

[639]Ashcraft, *31st Virginia*, 57; Morton, *History of Highland County*, 137.

[640]Ashcraft, *31st Virginia*, 57.

[641]Morton, *History of Highland County*, 137.

[642]John William Jones, *Christ in the Camp* [1887; reprint, Harrisonburg, Va.: Sprinkle Publications, 1986], 319.

[643]Jones, *Christ in the Camp*, 226.

[644]John S. Hoffman to James A. Seddon, 16 June 1863, William P. Cooper file, 31st Virginia CSR; W. P. Cooper, Journal, 3 Aug. 1863, 31st Virginia Papers, RBC.

[645]Robert Johnston to James A. Seddon, 23 June 1863, William P. Cooper file, 31st Virginia CSR.

[646] W. P. Cooper, Journal, 7-15 Aug. 1863, 31st Virginia Papers, RBC.

[647] W. P. Cooper, Journal, 18-21 Aug. 1863, 31st Virginia Papers, RBC.

[648] W. P. Cooper, Journal, 21-24 Aug. 1863, 31st Virginia Papers, RBC.

[649]List of men of Smith's brigade on detail or detached service, with assigned duty, submitted by Colonel John S. Hoffman, Commanding Brigade, 4 Aug. 1863, RG 109, MS 3290, National Archives.

[650]Luther D. Haymond file, 31st Virginia CSR.

[651]31st Virginia CSR. At the beginning of the microfilm roll is a compilation of the officers who served in the regiment, giving dates for resignations and in some cases, appointments; John S. Heckert file, 31st Virginia CSR.

[652]Laban R. Exline file, 31st Virginia CSR.

[653]Statement by John S. Hoffman, 14 Aug. 1863, H.Q. Smith's Brigade, AIG Letters.

[654]Order from HQ, 2nd Army Corps, 18 Aug. 1863, 31st Virginia Papers, RBC.

[655]James S. Kerr McCutchen file, 31st Virginia CSR. McCutchen began functioning as lieutenant colonel in early August 1863, and is referred to as such by some of the men; and yet McCutchen himself continued signing documents as Major, and is referred to by Captain Cooper as "Major

McCutchen" until late in the autumn of 1863. When McCutchen's promotion was confirmed, his seniority as lieutenant colonel dated from August 1, 1863.
[656] W. P. Cooper, Journal, 24 Aug. 1863, 14, 31st Virginia Papers, RBC.
[657]Statements on seniority by William P. Cooper, and Nathan S. Clawson, 26 Aug. 1863, AIG Letters; W. P. Cooper, Journal, 26 Aug. 1863, 31st Virginia Papers, RBC.
[658]Gideon D. Camden to John S. Hoffman, 19 Aug. 1863, Camden Papers, WVU; Cyrus Hall to John S. Hoffman, 31 Aug. 1863, Hoffman Papers, WVU.
[659]Surgeon Smith Buttermore, A List of Medicines, Instruments and Hospital supplies, 30 Aug. 1863, 31st Virginia Papers, RBC.
[660]J.S. Kerr McCutchen, Invoice of Ordnance and Ordnance Stores, 4 Sept. 1863, 31st Virginia Papers, RBC.
[661] W. P. Cooper, Journal, 1-5 Sept. 1863, 31st Virginia Papers, RBC.
[662]Circular, HQ Early's Division, 8 Sept. 1863, 31st Virginia Papers, RBC; W. P. Cooper, Journal, 9 Sept. 1863, 31st Virginia Papers, RBC.
[663]R. E. Lee to Samuel Cooper, 11 Sept. 1863, AIG Letters; W. P. Cooper, Journal, 9 Sept. 1863, 31st Virginia Papers, RBC. The records of this Examining Board were given to Cooper near the end of the war.
[664]Edward A. Palfrey to Robert E. Lee, 10 Sept. 1863, AIG Letters.
[665] W. P. Cooper, Journal, 13 Sept. 1863, 31st Virginia Papers, RBC.
[666]Ashcraft, *31st Virginia*, 58; Morton, *History of Highland County*, 137; Early, *Narrative of the War*, 302; Cooper, 14 Sept. 1863, "Journal," 31st Virginia Papers, RBC.
[667]Phillips, "History of Valley Furnace," *Barbour Democrat*, 30 Oct. 1968.
[668]Cooper, 14-18 Sept. 1863, "Journal," 15, 31st Virginia Papers, RBC.
[669]Cooper, 19-22 Sept. 1863, "Journal," 15, 31st Virginia Papers, RBC.
[670]William R. Lyman, and Nathan Clawson, 21 Sept. 1863, recommending Martin V. Stewart for the office of Ordnance Sergeant, AIG Letters.
[671]William Smith to John S. Hoffman, 31st Virginia Papers, RBC.
[672]James S. Kerr McCutchen to John S. Hoffman, 31st Virginia Papers, RBC.
[673]Cooper, 23-25 Sept. 1863, "Journal," 16, 31st Virginia Papers, RBC.
[674]Transfer for John M. Burns, 31st Virginia CSR; Jacob J. Hill file, 31st Virginia CSR.
[675]Cooper, 29-30 Sept. 1863, "Journal," 16, 31st Virginia Papers, RBC.
[676]Cooper, 5-6 Oct. 1863, "Journal," 16, 31st Virginia Papers, RBC.
[677]Cooper, 7-10 Oct. 1863, "Journal," 17, 31st Virginia Papers, RBC.
[678]Dr. William J. Bland to John S. Hoffman, 9 Oct. 1863, 31st Virginia Papers, RBC.
[679]Armstrong, *25th Virginia*, 14-22; Boatner, *The Civil War Dictionary*, 629-630.
[680]Cooper, 11-12 Oct. 1863, "Journal," 17, 31st Virginia Papers, RBC.
[681]Cooper, 13-14 Oct. 1863, "Journal," 17, 31st Virginia Papers, RBC.
[682]Cooper, 15-21 Oct. 1863, "Journal," 17-18, 31st Virginia Papers, RBC.
[683]Cooper, 22-26 Oct. 1863, "Journal," 18, 31st Virginia Papers, RBC.
[684]Cooper, 26-31 Oct. 1863, "Journal," 18-19, 31st Virginia Papers, RBC.
[685]Cooper, 1-5 Nov. 1863, "Journal," 19, 31st Virginia Papers, RBC.
[686] Atkinson was given permission to join the brigade on November 6, 1863.
[687]Archibold Atkinson, Jr., "Memoir of Archibold Atkinson, Jr.," Special Collections Department, University Libraries, Virginia Tech, transcribed by Dorothy Bodell and Stephen Zietz; Riggs, *13th Virginia Infantry*.

[688]Early, *Narrative of the War*, 332; Smith Buttermore to R. H. Chilton, 7 Nov. 1863, 31st Virginia Papers, RBC. When the request was returned, denied, attention was directed to a circular from HQ of the 2nd Army Corps dated 11 Nov. 1863.

[689]Cooper, 7 Nov. 1863, "Journal," 19, 31st Virginia Papers, RBC.

[690]Jubal A. Early, report, 11 Nov. 1863, OR, vol. 29, part 1, 618-626.

[691]Cooper, 8 Nov. 1863, "Journal," 19, 31st Virginia Papers, RBC.

[692]Circular, HQ Early's Division, 8 Sept. 1863, 31st Virginia Papers, RBC.

[693]Mayburry to Thomas W. Hoffman, 3 Nov. 1863; Dr. William J. Bland to Thomas W. Hoffman, 7 Nov. 1863, 31st Virginia Papers, RBC. - Bland was staying with Mr. I. O. Chiles and family in Richmond.

[694]Cooper, 11-12 Nov. 1863, "Journal," 19-20, 31st Virginia Papers, RBC.

[695]Cooper, 16-24 Nov. 1863, "Journal," 20, 31st Virginia Papers, RBC.

[696]Cooper, 24 Nov. 1863, "Journal," 20, 31st Virginia Papers, RBC; Atkinson, "Memoir of Archibold Atkinson, Jr."

[697]Cooper, 25-27 Nov. 1863, "Journal," 20-21, 31st Virginia Papers, RBC.

[698]Cooper, 28-30 Nov. 1863, "Journal," 20-21, 31st Virginia Papers, RBC.

[699]Cooper, 1-4 Dec. 1863, "Journal," 21, 31st Virginia Papers, RBC.

[700]Cooper, 5-6 Dec. 1863, "Journal," 21-22, 31st Virginia Papers, RBC.

[701]Cooper, 12 Dec. 1863, "Journal," 21-22, 31st Virginia Papers, RBC; William P. Cooper file, 31st Virginia CSR. Cooper was appointed Major on Dec. 15, 1863, and the rank was confirmed Feb. 16, 1864 following the protest and resignations. He was to take rank from August 1, 1863.

[702]Cooper, 12 Dec. 1863, "Journal," 21-22, 31st Virginia Papers, RBC; William R. Lyman to Joseph R. Anderson, 29 Nov. 1915, VMI Archives.

[703] . McCutcheon's promotion to lieutenant colonel had still not been approved officially, but he was functioning as such, and with Cooper officially recognized as major it seems confusing to continue calling McCutchen a major.

[704]Cooper, 13-16 Dec. 1863, "Journal," 22, 31st Virginia Papers, RBC.

[705]John S. Hoffman, 17 Dec. 1863, and other documents relating to William R. Lyman's resignation, 31st Virginia CSR.

[706]Joseph F. Harding, resignation, 12 Dec. 1863, and J. F. Mercer to John S. Hoffman, 31st Virginia Papers, RBC.

[707] In order to send the letter to his wife, Cooper had to make arrangements for the letter to be carried across the lines by a flag of truce.

[708]Cooper, 18-20 Dec. 1863, "Journal," 22, 31st Virginia Papers, RBC; Atkinson, "Memoir of Archibold Atkinson, Jr."

[709]Charges Preferred against Private Rowan, 31st Virginia Papers, RBC.

[710]Cooper, 21-25 Dec. 1863, "Journal," 22, 31st Virginia Papers, RBC.

[711]Cooper, 26 Dec. 1863, "Journal," 23, 31st Virginia Papers, RBC. William P. Cooper's journal ends here and does not resume until November 1864.

[712]John S. Hoffman, report, 15 Jan. 1864, and Gen. Pegram's order, dated Jan 17, signed by R. W. Wilson, AAG of Pegram's Brigade, 31st Virginia Papers, RBC.

[713]John S. Hoffman, 5 Jan. 1864, and Gen. Young's reply, 31st Virginia Papers, RBC.

[714]Elam Gough file, 31st Virginia CSR.

[715]J. J. Shields, Conscript Office, Richmond, 31st Virginia Papers, RBC.

[716]J. J. Shields, Conscript Office, Richmond, 31st Virginia Papers, RBC; Extract, Special Order No. 37, HQ, Dept. of Northern Virginia, 8 Feb. 1864, 31st Virginia Papers, RBC.

[717]John S. Hoffman, Sommerville Ford, 26 Jan. 1864, on the subject of a petition from the men of the 31st Virginia requesting a transfer of the regiment to western Virginia, and the desirability of such a move, AIG Letters.

[718]William P. Cooper, 28 Jan. 1864, on the subject of a petition from the men of the 31st Virginia requesting a transfer of the regiment to western Virginia, and the desirability of such a move, AIG Letters.

[719]R. E. Lee, 29 Jan. 1864, reply to the petition by the men of the 31st Virginia for transfer to the mountains, AIG Letters.

[720]Ashcraft, *31st Virginia*, 61.

[721]William R. Lyman to Joseph R. Anderson, 29 Nov. 1915, VMI Archives; Joseph F. Harding file, 31st Virginia CSR; Harding, "Narrative," 31st Virginia Papers, RBC. Captain Harding later wrote that General Lee upheld him about the matter of the stables, following a letter Harding wrote to General Lee. The official paperwork does not bear out Harding's claim.

[722]James M. Blair, 29 Feb. 1864, 31st Virginia Papers, RBC.

[723]Examining Boards for Warwick C. Kincaid and Henry B, Pullin, 8 March 1864, AIG Letters, National Archives, M474, roll 113, item 382-G-1864.

[724]R. E. Lee, 16 March 1864, AIG Letters.

[725]John S. Hoffman, and William P. Cooper, statements at Examining Board for Warwick C. Kincaid and Henry B. Pullin, 8 March 1864, AIG Letters, National Archives, M474, roll 113, item 382-G-1864.

[726]Matthew Carpenter file; and Albert G. Stringer file, 31st Virginia CSR; Papers relating to the election of Albert G. Stringer, in the W. B. McNemar file, 31st Virginia CSR; Special Order No. 26, 28 June 1864, Pegram's Brigade, confirming Edward J. Armstrong as 2nd lieutenant, Edward J. Armstrong file, 31st Virginia CSR.

[727]Patrick W. Bruffey file, 31st Virginia CSR.

[728]George W. Arbogast to Ellen Arbogast, 13 March 1864, 31st Virginia Papers, RBC; Morton, History of Highland County, 137; Snider Memorandum, 11 April 1864

[729]John S. Hoffman, letter of recommendation, 1 April 1864, William Warner file, 31st Virginia CSR.

[730]Snider Memorandum, 14 April 1864; Ashcraft, *31st Virginia*, preface. The old 31st Virginia flag, which is said to have been presented to the regiment by Stonewall Jackson on May 5, 1862, had been made by the ladies of Beverly. The flag was given to S. N. Bosworth by his sister after the war, and was later handed down through his family to Mrs. E. D. Talbott, who preserved it in a mothproof frame. "In 1970 the family gave it to the United Daughters of the Confederacy. It hangs in their Memorial Building in Richmond as the "Stonewall" Jackson flag."

[731]Snider Memorandum, 14 April 1864

[732]George W. Arbogast to Ellen S. Arbogast, 18 April 1864, 31st Virginia Papers, RBC. "Croff" referred to in this letter was probably James C. Arbogast, former captain of Company G.

[733]Snider Memorandum, 19-27 April 1864

[734]Snider Memorandum, 29-30 April 1864

[735]Snider Memorandum, 1-3 May 1864

[736]Richard Wheeler, *On Fields of Fury: From the Wilderness to the Crater, an Eyewitness History* [New York: Harper Collins, 1991], 4, 38, 78.

[737]Snider Memorandum, 4 May 1864

[738]George Arbogast to Ellen Arbogast, camp near Spottsylvania Court House, 9 May 1864, 31st Virginia Papers, RBC; Early, *Narrative*, 344-345.

[739]Will A. Yeager to Margaret Yeager, 5 May 1864, 31st Virginia Papers, RBC.

[740]Early, *Narrative*, 345-346. Ewell's 2nd Corps had three divisions at this time, under Johnson, Rodes, and Early -- and Early had three brigades, under Hays, Pegram, and Gordon.

[741]Early, *Narrative*, 346; Richard S. Ewell, report, 20 March 1865, *OR* [36 1], 1069-1075.

[742]Wheeler, *On Fields of Fury*, 99-100, 105-106; Noah Andre Trudeau, *Bloody Roads South: Wilderness to Cold Harbor, May-June 1864* [New York: Fawcett Columbine, 1989], 65-66.

[743]Snider Memorandum, 5 May 1864; George Q. Peyton, "Pegram's Brigade at Spottsylvania," *Confederate Veteran* [38 2 March, 1930], 58-62 - George Peyton was a private in Company A, 13th Virginia Infantry.

[744]Phillips History, 6 Nov. 1968; Early, *Narrative*, 346

[745]Casualties derived by author from 31st Virginia CSR.

[746]Atkinson, "Memoirs of Archibold Atkinson, Jr."

[747]Early, *Narrative*, 346-347; Wheeler, *On Fields of Fury*, 119.

[748]Snider Memorandum, 6 May 1864; Pavel Knisely file, 31st Virginia CSR.

[749]Morrison, "Aged Indian Fighter," 31st Virginia Papers, RBC.

[750]Snider Memorandum, 6 May 1861; Ashcraft, *31st Virginia Infantry*, 64.

[751]Jacob Heater, "Battle of the Wilderness," *Confederate Veteran* [4 6 June 1906], 262-264 - Jacob Heater was a private in Company D, 31st Virginia.

[752]George W. Arbogast to Ellen Arbogast, 9 May 1864, 31st Virginia Papers, RBC.

[753]Early, *Narrative*, 347-348.

[754]Hale and Phillips, *History of the Forty-Ninth Virginia*, 107-108.

[755]Phillips History, 6 Nov. 1968.

[756]Wheeler, *On Fields of Fury*, 143; John B. Gordon, report, 5 July 1864, *OR* [36 1], 1077.

[757]Hale and Phillips, *History of the Forty-Ninth Virginia*, 109-110; John S. Hoffman, Headquarters, Pegram's Brigade, 2 Oct. 1864, John S. Hoffman file, 31st Virginia CSR. The officers of the regiment placed a value on the horse of two thousand dollars. Many letters went back and forth between Hoffman and the Confederate government in Richmond, and it does not appear that the matter was ever settled. The officers who attested to the value of the horse were James S. Kerr McCutchen, W. P. Cooper, and Surgeon Smith Buttermore.

[758]Snider Memorandum, 6 May 1864; George W. Arbogast to Ellen Arbogast, 9 May 1864, 31st Virginia Papers, RBC.

[759]Snider Memorandum, 7 May 1864; Heater, "Battle of the Wilderness"

[760]Early, *Narrative*, 351; Wheeler, *On Fields of Fury*, 145,150.

[761]Casualties derived by author from 31st Virginia Infantry CSR.

[762]Will A. Yeager to his mother and Fannie Yeager, 8 May 1864, 31st Virginia Papers, RBC. The Wooddell mentioned was probably Warwick Wooddell. At that time, he was the only one of his direct family still in the regiment.

[763] Snider Memorandum, 8 May 1864; Atkinson, "Memoir of Archibold Atkinson, Jr."

[764] Snider Memorandum, 8 May 1864

[765] Snider Memorandum, 10 May 1864

[766] Snider Memorandum, 11 May 1864

[767] Snider Memorandum, 12 May 1864; Heater, "Battle of the Wilderness," - There are many versions of the story of "General Lee to the Rear." Jacob Heater later claimed, "when General Gordon turned General Lee's horse around, he was standing nearly in front of the colors of the 31st Virginia."

[768] Henry A. Yeager to Robert White, Crickard, W.Va., 21 Oct. 1898, 31st Virginia Papers, RBC; J. Catlett Gibson, "Battle of Spottsylvania Courthouse," *Southern Historical Society Papers* [32 1904], 200-210. Henry A. Yeager spent two months in a field hospital, recovering from his wound.

[769] Hotchkiss, *Virginia: Confederate Military History*, 890; J. Catlett Gibson, quoted in Hale and Phillips, *History of the Forty-Ninth Virginia*, 120.

[770] Heater, "Battle of the Wilderness," 262-264.

[771] Snider Memorandum, 12 May 1864, "Memorandum of Events Whilst Soldiering."

[772] Heater, "Battle of the Wilderness," 262-264.

[773] William H. Hull, "Some Recollections of the Civil War," 31st Virginia Papers, RBC.

[774] Company D, muster roll dated 1 Sept. 1864; Christian G. Kuhl file, 31st Virginia CSR.

[775] Casualties derived by author from 31st Virginia CSR.

[776] William P. Cooper file, 31st Virginia CSR; Atkinson, "Memoir of Archibold Atkinson."

[777] Elisha Wilfong file, 31st Virginia CSR.

[778] Snider Memorandum, 13-14 may 1864

[779] Atkinson, "Memoir of Archibold Atkinson."

[780] Snider Memorandum, 15 May 1864

[781] Douglas H. Henson file, 31st Virginia CSR.

[782] Snider Memorandum, 16-18 May 1864

[783] Snider Memorandum, 19 May 1864

[784] Ewell, report, 20 March 1865, *OR* [36 1], 1072.

[785] Snider Memorandum, 19 May 1864

[786] Trudeau, *Bloody Roads South*, 206.

[787] Ewell, report, 20 March 1865, *OR* [36 1], 1072.

[788] Snider Memorandum, 19 May 1864

[789] Jacob Matheny file; and Erasmus Hite file, 31st Virginia CSR.

[790] Jacob Sheets file, 31st Virginia CSR; Warwick Wooddell file, 31st Virginia CSR, cites Confederate Archives, chap. 10, file no. 8, 271; and file no. 34, 126. - Warwick's only child, Charles Stewart Warwick Wooddell carried on the family line. Warwick Wooddell was this author's direct ancestor.

[791] Phillips History, 6 Nov. 1968.

[792] Snider Memorandum, 20 May 1864

[793] Snider Memorandum, 22-27 May 1864

[794] Wilson, Diary, 27 May 1864, in Morton, *History of Highland County*, 137.

[795] Snider Memorandum, 28-29 May 1864

[796] Snider Memorandum, 30 May 1864

[797]Freeman, *Lee's Lieutenants*, [3], p. 502; A. L. Long, *Memoirs of R. E. Lee* [1886; reprint, Secaucus, NJ.: Blue and Grey Press, 1983], 370; Driver, *52nd Virginia*, 60. Colonel Hoffman had been "bitten by a spider" according to Lt. Colonel C. B. Christian of the 49th Virginia.

[798]Snider Memorandum, 30 May 1864

[799]Atkinson, "Memoir of Archibold Atkinson, Jr."

[800]Snider Memorandum, 30 May 1864

[801]Driver, *52nd Virginia*, 60.

[802]Snider Memorandum, 30 May 1864

[803]Driver, *52nd Virginia*, 61.

[804]Thomas W. Hoffman file, CSR, Confederate General & Staff Officers; Confederate Archives, chap. 1, file no. 86, 457; R. B. Cook, *Lewis County*, 119. - Lorentz was then working for J. M. Bennett in the Auditor's Office. Lorentz lived at 113 Broad Street, on the west side of the street. The Battle of Bethesda Church has also been called the Battle of Mechanicsville Road.

[805]Casualties derived by author from 31st Virginia CSR.

[806]John Wilfong file, 31st Virginia CSR; Snider Memorandum, 31 May 1864

[807]Snider Memorandum, 1 June 1864

[808]Snider Memorandum, 2-4 June 1864

[809]Snider Memorandum, 5 June 1864

[810]Early, *Narrative*, 370-371.

[811]Snider Memorandum, 13-17 June 1864

[812]Snider Memorandum, 17-19 June 1864

[813]Atkinson, "Memoir of Archibold Atkinson, Jr."

[814]Early, *Narrative*, 378-379; Snider Memorandum, 22 June 1864

[815]Snider Memorandum, 23-27 June 1864

[816]Snider Memorandum, 3 July 1864; Early, *Narrative*, 380-383.

[817]Freeman, *Lee's Lieutenants* [3], 559; Early, *Narrative*, 382; Douglas, *I Rode With Stonewall*, 293.

[818]William P. Cooper file, 31st Virginia CSR.

[819]Snider Memorandum, 4-5 July 1864; Jubal Early, *Narrative*, 384.

[820]Early, *Narrative*, 385; Snider Memorandum, 6-8 July 1864

[821]Early, *Narrative*, 387; Snider Memorandum, 9 July 1864

[822]Snider Memorandum, 9-10 July 1864; Early, *Narrative*, 389.

[823]Snider Memorandum, 11 July 1864; Early, *Narrative*, 389.

[824]Early, *Narrative*, 390-391.

[825]Riggs, *13th Virginia*, 54.

[826]Snider Memorandum, 12 July 1864

[827]Snider Memorandum, 13-15 July 1864

[828]Snider Memorandum, 16-19 July 1864; Early, *Narrative*, 397.

[829]Douglas, *I Rode With Stonewall*, 288; Early, *Narrative*, 397.

[830]Snider Memorandum, 19-20 July 1864; John W. Bosworth to Roy B. Cook, 21 July 1927, 31st Virginia Papers, A&M 1561, ser. 2, box 2, vol. 1, RBC.

[831]Snider Memorandum, 19-20 July 1864; Bosworth to Cook, 21 July 1927, 31st Virginia Papers, RBC.

[832]Snider Memorandum, 19-20 July 1864

[833]Casualties derived by author from 31st Virginia CSR; Ashcraft, *31st Virginia*, 73.

[834]Boatner, *The Civil War Dictionary*, 795; Freeman, *Lee's Lieutenants* [3], 570.

835 Snider Memorandum, 21-23 July 1864

836 Early, *Narrative*, 399.

837 Snider Memorandum, 24 July 1864

838 Snider Memorandum, 25-31 July 1864

839 Jacob C. Matheny file, 31st Virginia CSR. - Certification of Matheny's election was signed by A. Stephenson, Clerk of the Highland Court, on July 6, 1864.

840 Colonel Hoffman was at Monocacy, Maryland that day. The pain of Phillips's wound was giving him visions, perhaps.

841 Phillips History, 13 Nov. 1968.

842 Phillips History, 13 Nov. 1968.

843 Wilson Diary, in Morton, *History of Highland County*, 138.

844 Jacob C. McLaughlin to Nannie McLaughlin, Camp Bunker Hill, 1 Aug. 1864, in Price, *Historical Sketches of Pocahontas County*, 321-323.

845 John W. Bosworth, to Roy B. Cook, (1930?) 31st Virginia Papers, A&M 1561, ser. 2, box 2, vol. 1, RBC.

846 Snider Memorandum, 4-5 Aug. 1864

847 Snider Memorandum, 6-9 Aug. 1864

848 Snider Memorandum, 10-18 Aug. 1864; Early, *Narrative*, 406-407.

849 Snider Memorandum, 17-21 Aug. 1864

850 Snider Memorandum, 22-24 Aug. 1864

851 Snider Memorandum, 25-29 Aug. 1864

852 Snider Memorandum, 2-5 Sept. 1864

853 Snider Memorandum, 6-7 Sept. 1864

854 Will Yeager to Henry Yeager, 7 Sept. 1864, 31st Virginia Papers, A&M 1561, ser. 2, box 2, vol. 1, RBC.

855 John A. Noel file, Transfer, 8 Sept. 1864, 31st Virginia CSR. - Noel was later captured, paroled, and took the oath of allegiance at Charlotte, North Carolina, on May 4, 1865.

856 Snider Memorandum, 8-15 Sept. 1864

857 Snider Memorandum, 16-17 Sept. 1864; William P. Cooper, 18 Sept. 1864, in Snider Memorandum

858 Early, *Narrative*, 420-422; Atkinson, "Memoir of Archibold Atkinson, Jr."

859 William P. Cooper, 19 Sept. 1864, in Snider Memorandum - Cooper carried Snider's journal with him through the end of the war, and gave it to Elmore H. Snider after the war. Elmore made a notation that Cooper had filled in the last two entries, and requested the journal be given to their mother.

860 Casualties derived by author from 31st Virginia Infantry CSR.

861 Freeman, *Lee's Lieutenants* [3], 580.

862 Early, *Narrative*, 426.

863 Early, *Narrative*, 426.

864 Atkinson, "Memoir of Archibold Atkinson, Jr."

865 Prisoners of war derived by author from the 31st Virginia Infantry CSR.

866 Edward J. Stackpole, *Sheridan in the Shenandoah: Jubal Early's Nemesis*, 2nd Edition. [Harrisburg: Stackpole Books, 1992], 231, 234-235; Jed Hotchkiss, 20 Sept. 1864, "Journal," in *OR* [43 1], 574.

867 Stackpole, *Sheridan in the Shenandoah*, 250-255; Hotchkiss, 20 Sept. 1864, "Journal," in *OR* [43 1], 575; Ashcraft, *31st Virginia*, 79; Casualties and prisoners of war derived by author from 31st Virginia Infantry CSR.

868Jubal A. Early to R. E. Lee, 25 Sept. 1864, *OR* [43 1], 558; Hotchkiss, 23-25 Sept. 1864, "Journal," in *OR* [43 1], 575.
869Hotchkiss, 28 Sept. 1864, "Journal," in *OR* [43 1], 574; Driver, *52nd Virginia*, 69.
870Hale and Phillips, *History of the Forty-Ninth Virginia*, 165
871Hotchkiss, "Journal," in *OR* [43 1], 577; Stackpole, *Sheridan in the Shenandoah*, 266-267.
872Aaron Rowan file, 31st Virginia CSR.
873Hotchkiss, 1-8 Oct. 1864, "Journal," in *OR* [43 1], 577-578.
874Hotchkiss, 9-14 Oct. 1864, "Journal," in *OR* [43 1], 574; John S. Hoffman, report, near Strasburg, 15 Oct. 1864, 31st Virginia CSR.
875Will A. Yeager to Evelyn Yeager, 16 Oct. 1864, 31st Virginia Papers, A&M 1561, ser. 2, box 2, vol. 1, RBC.
876Jubal A. Early, report, 21 Oct. 1864, *OR* [43 1], , 561; Hotchkiss, 18-19 Oct. 1864, "Journal," in *OR* [43 1], 580-582.
877 Organization of Forces under Lt. Gen. Jubal A. Early at Cedar Creek, 19 Oct. 1864, *OR* [43 1], 565; Private Beverly [S. N. Bosworth?], "Battle of Cedar Creek", *Confederate Veteran* [14 11 Nov. 1906], 501-502 - this article was written by an anonymous veteran of the 31st Virginia Regiment who lived at that time in Beverly, W.Va. For reasons of attribution, I have identified him as "Private Beverly." I suspect that this writer was S. N. Bosworth, brother of John W. Bosworth.
878Samuel D. Buck, "Battle of Cedar Creek: Tribute to Early, " *Southern Historical Society Papers* [30 1902], 104-110.
879Kuhl, Narrative, 31st Virginia Papers, RBC
880Early, *Narrative*, 446-449.
881Beverly, "Battle of Cedar Creek", 501-502; Buck, "Battle of Cedar Creek: Tribute to Early, " 104-110; Inspection Reports for Pegram's Brigade, 29 Oct. 1864, 31st Virginia Papers, RBC; William P. Cooper file, 31st Virginia CSR. - Cooper returned in November and was present for the Inspection Report on Nov. 29, near Harrisonburg.
882Casualties compiled by author from the 31st Virginia CSR; Beverly, "Battle of Cedar Creek," 501-502.
883Stackpole, *Sheridan in the Shenandoah*, 340.
884 W. P. Cooper, Journal, 24-25 Nov. 1864, 31st Virginia Papers, RBC.
885James S. Kerr McCutchen, camp near New Market, 4 Nov. 1864, forwarding James Blair's resignation, James M Blair file, 31st Virginia CSR.
886 W. P. Cooper, Journal, 26-30 Nov. 1864, 31st Virginia Papers, RBC.
887 W. P. Cooper, Journal, 2-8 Dec. 1864, 31st Virginia Papers, RBC; Will A. Yeager to Henry Yeager, 7 Dec. 1864, 31st Virginia Papers, A&M 1561, ser. 2, box 2, vol. 1, RBC.
888 W. P. Cooper, Journal, 9 Dec. 1864, 25-26, 31st Virginia Papers, RBC.
889 James S. Kerr McCutchen, Leave of absence granted by General Early, Special Order no. 120, 29 Nov. 1864, James S. Kerr McCutchen file, 31st Virginia CSR.
890 W. P. Cooper, Journal, 10-15 Dec. 1864, 31st Virginia Papers, RBC.
891Driver, *52nd Virginia*, 71, quoting Capt. Samuel D. Buck.

[892]Sarah Stockwell to Isaac Stockwell, Kasson, W. Va., 20 Sept. 1864; William P. Cooper request for furlough for Stockwell, 17 Dec. 1864, approved and forwarded by John S. Hoffman, Isaac Stockwell file, 31st Virginia CSR.

[893] Isaac Stockwell file, 31st Virginia CSR.

[894] W. P. Cooper, Journal, 20-25 Dec. 1864, 31st Virginia Papers, RBC.

[895] W. P. Cooper, Journal, 26-30 Dec. 1864, 31st Virginia Papers, RBC.

[896]Robert Wolfenberger file, 31st Virginia CSR. - The number of blankets probably did not represent all of the men in the company, but it probably can be taken as an indication of those who were in camp.

[897]Atkinson, "Memoir of Archibold Atkinson, Jr."

[898] W. P. Cooper, Journal, 6-10 Jan. 1965, 31st Virginia Papers RBC; Andrew S. F. Davis file, 31st Virginia CSR. - Davis had transferred to another regiment, but apparently was returning to the 31st Virginia.

[899] W. P. Cooper, Journal, 12 Jan. 1965, 31st Virginia Papers RBC; Jacob H. Preston file, 31st Virginia CSR.

[900] W. P. Cooper, Journal, 13 Jan. 1965, 31st Virginia Papers RBC; William L. Jackson to William P. Cooper, 13 Jan. 1865, AIG Letters, M474, roll 163, item 381/2V.

[901]John S. Hoffman to Charles W. Russell and Robert Johnston, 16 Jan. 1865, AIG Letters, M474, roll 163, item 381/2V.

[902] W. P. Cooper, Journal, 23 Jan. 1865, 31st Virginia Papers, RBC.

[903]31st Virginia Regiment, Petition by the men of the 31st Virginia for transfer, with list of casualties from 1864, AIG Letters, M474, roll 163, item 381/2V. - The totals on the aggregate of the accompanying casualty list do not seem to add up, and without doubt, the system of adding the casualties for each company defies simple math. However, as a list of killed, died, wounded, captured, and missing, it is a valuable document, though perhaps somewhat flawed.

[904]Robert Johnston and Charles W. Russell to James A. Seddon, 20 Jan. 1865, AIG Letters, M474, roll 163, item 381/2V.

[905] W. P. Cooper, Journal, 29 Jan. 1865, 31st Virginia Papers, RBC.

[906]John B. Gordon, report, 9 Feb. 1865, OR, [46 1], 390; E. O. C. Ord to the U.S. Secretary of War, 10 Feb. 1865, OR, [46 2], 522. General Ord reported Colonel Hoffman as mortally wounded.

[907] W. P. Cooper, Journal, 6 Feb., 1865, 31st Virginia Papers, RBC.

[908]Casualties compiled by author from the 31st Virginia CSR; W. P. Cooper, Journal, 17 Feb., 1865, 31st Virginia Papers, RBC.

[909]Atkinson, "Memoir of Archibold Atkinson, Jr." - Mattoax is about 25 miles west of Petersburg.

[910]Wilson Diary, 10 and 20 Feb. 1865, in Morton, History of Highland County, 139.

[911] Phillips History, 13 Nov. 1968; W. P. Cooper, Journal, 1 March 1865, 31st Virginia Papers, RBC.

[912] W. P. Cooper, Journal, 17-19 March 1865, 31st Virginia Papers, RBC.

[913] W. P. Cooper, Journal, 22-27 Feb. 1865, 31st Virginia Papers, RBC.

[914]James A. Walker, and John B. Gordon, 8 March 1865; and R. E. Lee, 9 March 1865, concerning the request of the 31st Virginia for transfer to Jackson's cavalry brigade, AIG Letters, M474, roll 163, items 381/2 v.

[915] W. P. Cooper, Journal, 9-11 March 1865, 31st Virginia Papers, RBC.

[916] W. P. Cooper, Journal, 15-16 March 1865, 31st Virginia Papers, RBC.

[917] W. P. Cooper, Journal, 18-20 March 1865, 31st Virginia Papers, RBC.

[918] Hall Diary, 128.

[919] Hall Diary, 128.

[920] John S. Hoffman to Walter Taylor, 27 March 1865, 31st Virginia CSR.

[921] Freeman, *Lee's Lieutenant's* [3], 628-629; William P. Cooper and Nathan Clawson files, 31st Virginia CSR.

[922] W. P. Cooper, Journal, 25 March 1865, 31st Virginia Papers, RBC.

[923] John B. Gordon, *Reminiscences of the Civil War* [1903; reprint, Alexandria, Va.: Time-Life Books, 1981], 374; Freeman, *Lee's Lieutenant's* [3], 628-629.

[924] James A. Walker, *New Orleans Picayune*, 25 Oct. 1903, in Hale and Phillips, *History of the Forty-Nine Virginia*, 201-202.

[925] James A. Walker, *New Orleans Picayune*, 25 Oct. 1903, in Hale and Phillips, *History of the Forty-Nine Virginia*, 201-202.

[926] Robert D. Funkhouser, "Fort Stedman, So Near Yet So Far," *Confederate Veteran* [19 5 May 1911], 217.

[927] Hall Diary, 129.

[928] Robert Wolfenberger file, 31st Virginia CSR.

[929] John H. Yansey file, 31st Virginia CSR.

[930] Kuhl, Narrative, 31st Virginia Papers, RBC; Christian G. Kuhl file, 31st Virginia CSR.

[931] Hall , *Diary*.

[932] W. P. Cooper, Journal, 25 March 1865, 31st Virginia Papers, RBC.

[933] Hall Diary, 129.

[934] Wilson Diary, 27 March, in Morton, *History of Highland County*, 139.

[935] W. P. Cooper, Journal, 29 March 1865, 31st Virginia Papers, RBC.

[936] Edward Porter Alexander, *Military Memoirs of a Confederate: A Critical Narrative*, [1907; reprint, New York: Da Capo Press, 1993], 519.

[937] Douglas, *I Rode with Stonewall*, 315-316.

[938] W. P. Cooper, Journal, 3-5 April 1865, 31st Virginia Papers, RBC; Atkinson, "Memoir of Archibold Atkinson, Jr."

[939] Hall Diary, 134.

[940] W. P. Cooper, Journal, 5 April 1865, 31st Virginia Papers, RBC.

[941] Douglas, *I Rode With Stonewall*, 316.

[942] W. P. Cooper, Journal, 6 April 1865, 31st Virginia Papers, RBC.

[943] R. E. Lee to Jefferson Davis, 10 April 1865, *OR* [46 1], 1266.

[944] Hall Diary, 135.

[945] W. P. Cooper, Journal, 8 April 1865, 31st Virginia Papers, RBC.

[946] R. B. Cook, *Lewis County*, 117.

[947] Atkinson, "Memoir of Archibold Atkinson, Jr."

[948] R. E. Lee to Jefferson Davis, 10 April 1865, *OR* [46 1], 1266; W. P. Cooper, Journal, 8-9 April 1865, 31st Virginia Papers, RBC; Riggs, *13th Virginia*, 66; Douglas, *I Rode With Stonewall*, 317.

[949] Alexander, *Military Memoirs of a Confederate*, 534; Lee to Davis, 10 April 1865, *OR* [46 1], 1266.

[950] Alexander, *Military Memoirs of a Confederate*, 534.

[951] W. P. Cooper, Journal, 9 April 1865, 31st Virginia Papers, RBC; Douglas, *I Rode with Stonewall*, 317.

[952] Lee to Davis, 10 April 1865, *OR* [46 1], 1266; W. P. Cooper, Journal, 9 April 1865, 31st Virginia Papers, RBC.

[953] W. P. Cooper, Journal, 10 April 1865, 31st Virginia Papers, RBC; General Orders No. 9, HQ Army of Northern Virginia, 10 April 1865, *OR* [46 1], 1267:

[954] W. P. Cooper, Journal, 11 April 1865, 31st Virginia Papers, RBC.

[955] W. P. Cooper, Journal, 12 April 1865, 31st Virginia Papers, RBC; Joshua L. Chamberlain, *The Passing of the Armies* [New York: Bantam, 1993], 194.

[956] *OR* , [46 1], 1277 - The Union regiments present for the Appomattox surrender ceremony were: First Brigade -- 185th New York, and 198th Pennsylvania regiments; Second Brigade -- 187th New York, 188th New York, 189th New York regiments; Third Brigade -- 1st Maine Sharpshooters, 20th Maine, 32nd Massachusetts, 1st Michigan, 16th Michigan, 83rd Pennsylvania, 91st Pennsylvania, 118th Pennsylvania, and 155th Pennsylvania regiments. These veterans had been part of Major General G. K. Warren's Corps until April 1, at which time Bvt. Major General Charles Griffin was given command of the Fifth Corps, and Bvt. Major General Joseph J. Bartlett was given command of the First Division. Brig. General Chamberlain was technically in command of only the First brigade, while Brig. Gen. Edgar M. Gregory commanded the Second brigade, and Brig. Gen. Alfred Pearson commanded the Third Brigade. For the ceremony, however, Major General Bartlett deferred to General Chamberlain and stood back to allow the young, former college professor to accept the arms of the Confederates.

[957] Chamberlain, *Passing of the Armies*, 194; Douglas, *I Rode With Stonewall*, 318-319; *OR* , [46 1], 1270, 1277. - Commanders of the regiments in the Fourth brigade that day were: Capt. George Cullen, 13th Virginia; Major William P. Cooper, 31st Virginia; Capt. William D. Moffett, 49th Virginia; Capt. Samuel W. Paxton, 52nd Virginia; and Lieut. Robert L. Walrond, 58th Virginia.

[958] W. P. Cooper, Journal, 12 April 1865, 31st Virginia Papers, RBC; Nimrod Reger in R. B. Cook, Lewis County, 117.

[959] W. P. Cooper, Journal, 12 April 1865, 31st Virginia Papers, RBC; Hall Diary, 137.

[960] W. P. Cooper, Journal, 13 April 1865, 31st Virginia Papers, RBC; Atkinson, "Memoir of Archibold Atkinson, Jr."

[961] Atkinson, "Memoir of Archibold Atkinson, Jr."

[962] W. P. Cooper, Journal, 13 April 1865, 31st Virginia Papers, RBC; Georgia J. Holton (granddaughter of W.L. Jackson) to Roy Bird Cook, 30 Jan. 1938, 31st Virginia Papers, RBC; "William Lowther Jackson, Jr.," *The West Virginia Encyclopedia*, 439.

[963] Joseph Badger, report, 23 April 1865, *OR* [46 1], 1310-1314.

[964] Bosworth, *History of Randolph County*, 350.

[965] W. P. Cooper, Journal, 18-22 April 1865, 31st Virginia Papers, RBC.

[966] Hall Diary, 6, 139, 140; W. P. Cooper, Journal, 23-24 April 1865, 31st Virginia Papers, RBC

[967] W. P. Cooper, Journal, 25-26 April 1865, 31st Virginia Papers, RBC.

[968] W. P. Cooper, Journal, 2-6 May 1865, 31st Virginia Papers, RBC; William P. Cooper, oath of allegiance to the United States, Clarksburg, 14 June 1865, 31st Virginia Papers, RBC.

[969] Krick, *Lee's Colonels*, 99; W. P. Cooper to Peregrine Hays, 9 Sept. 1867, Hays Family Papers, RBC.

[970]Wilson Diary, 22 April, 5 May, 27 May, 22 June-2 July, in Morton, *History of Highland County*, 139.

[971]Eveline Yeager Beard, in Hornbeck, *Upshur Brothers of the Blue and the Gray*, 79.

[972]Price, *Historical Sketches of Pocahontas County*, 466-467; Henry A. Yeager, obituary, *Confederate Veteran* 10, no. 6 (June 1902), 275; Henry A. Yeager to Robert White, 21 Oct. 1898, 31st Virginia Papers, RBC.

[973]Francis M. Boykin to Francis H. Smith, 14 July 1865, VMI Archives; Francis M. Boykin, Alumni Files, File Summary Sheet, VMI Archives; Francis M. Boykin, Obituary, *Richmond News Despatch*, 6 May 1906.

[974]Summers, *Johnson Newlon Camden*; Krick, *Lee's Colonels*, 371; Hall, *Rending of Virginia*, 229.

[975]Kuhl, Narrative, 31st Virginia Papers, RBC - James S. Kerr McCutchen was born 1830, and died in 1915, which dates the manuscript by Christian Kuhl to circa 1910-1915.

[976]Obituary for James S. Kerr McCutchen, "Another Pioneer Crosses Great Divide," *Exeter Sun* (California), [13 39, 1 Oct. 1915].

[977]John G. Gittings to Joseph Anderson, 23 Nov. 1903, VMI Archives.

[978]William H. Hull, Obituary, *Pocahontas Times*, 31st Virginia Papers, RBC.

[979] Phillips History, 31 Aug. 1968.

[980] Phillips History, 13 Nov. 1968.

[981]Kuhl, Narrative, 31st Virginia Papers, RBC ; David B. Kuhl to David W. Wooddell, 6 March 1998. David B. Kuhl is a great-great grandson of Christian Kuhl, and is the owner of Kuhl's narrative of the war. In 1997, David Kuhl donated the Sergeant's jacket, complete with bullet holes, to Beauvoir Museum, in Biloxi, Mississippi.

[982]John W. Bosworth to Roy Bird Cook, 6 Dec. 1926, 31st Virginia Papers, RBC; *West Virginia Heritage Encyclopedia*, [4], 222; John W. Bosworth, obituary, 4 Jan. 1936; *Lexington Gazette*, 22 June 1910, VMI Archives; Joseph H. Chenoweth to Col. Francis H. Smith, Beverly, Va, 24 May 1861, VMI Archives; Biographical Information from John W. Bosworth, supplied to VMI, undated, but from context written in 1903, VMI Archives; Dr. John W. Bosworth to Joseph R. Anderson, Philippi, W. Va., 9 Feb. 1909, VMI Archives.

[983]Report of Paroles Given to Prisoners of War by D. M. Evans, Col. 20th New York Cavalry from 1 to 15 May 1865; Register of the Provost Marshall, District of Henrico, HQ Richmond, John S. Hoffman file, 31st Virginia CSR.

[984]John S. Hoffman to Gideon D. Camden, 13 March 1861, Camden Papers, WVU.

[985]John S. Hoffman to Walter H. Taylor, 27 March 1865, John S. Hoffman file, 31st Virginia CSR. - Hoffman noted in this letter that it was in the hand of another person because he could neither read, nor write at this time.

[986]John S. Hoffman to Gideon D. Camden, 19 May 1865, Camden Papers, WVU.

[987]Barton Despard to Gideon D. Camden, 18 June 1865, Camden Papers, WVU.

[988]David Goff to Gideon D. Camden, Camden Papers, WVU.

[989](General) T. S. Haymond to Gideon D. Camden, Cumberland, Md., 22 June 1865, Camden Papers, WVU. - "Judge Camden, My friend, I desire you make an application for me, to the President in such form as you may deem proper,

and send it here. I desire to be restored to all my rights, civil & political. You know (how) to do it. Enclose to me."

[990] James Neeson to Gideon D. Camden, 18 June 1865, Camden Papers, WVU.

[991] Gideon D. Camden, Jr. to Gideon D. Camden, Baltimore, 15 July 1865, Camden Papers, WVU.

[992] John S. Hoffman to Gideon Camden, 27 Sept. 1865, John S. Hoffman Papers, WVU; John S. Hoffman to Gideon D. Camden, 29 Oct. 1865, Camden Papers, WVU.

[993] Summers, *Johnson Newlon Camden*, 122,123, cites Acts of the West Virginia Legislature (1865 and 1866), Joint Resolution No. 29 (1865), 94; and Joint Resolution No. 13 (1866), 135-136.

[994] John S. Hoffman to B. Franklin Clark, 7 April 1868, and 12 Nov. 1868, John S. Hoffman Papers, WVU - Hoffman's land business involved many of the most prominent individuals in the state, including John S. Carlile, J. M. Bennett, Cyrus Hall, and Governor Pierpont. Much of that land, hundreds of thousands of acres, had been purchased by Hoffman and his associates, including Gideon D. Camden, at tax auction prior to the war.

[995] *Fairmont Liberalist*, 1874, John S. Hoffman Papers, WVU.

[996] Atkinson, *Bench and Bar of West Virginia*, 60-62. - George W. Atkinson, later the governor of West Virginia, served on the Supreme Court, and knew John S. Hoffman personally, and counted him as a friend.

[997] *Wheeling Register*, 19 Nov. 1877.

[998] Atkinson, *Bench and Bar of West Virginia*, 122-123; Summers, *Johnson N. Camden*, 125-126, cites Camden to John Brannon and Jonathan M. Bennett, 18 Dec. 1867, Bennett MSS; "Line of Gideon Draper Camden," Camden Papers, WVU. - Following Gideon Camden's death, his widow married George W. Atkinson.

[999] Kuhl, Narrative, 31st Virginia Papers, RBC

[1000] Crystal Wooddell Lang, "C. S. W. Wooddell," in *Pocahontas County, West Virginia*. Charles Steward Warwick Wooddell was a great-grandfather of this work's author, David W. Wooddell. Charlie Wooddell was the only child of Joseph E. Warwick Wooddell, who was mortally wounded on May 19, 1864 in the Battle of the Harris Farm, near Spotsylvania, Virginia.

***

© Daniel Lee Wooddell

About the Author:

David W. Wooddell is a writer, photographer, and editorial researcher in Baltimore, MD. Following a 20-year career at *National Geographic* magazine, retiring as a Research Editor, David has been writing history books, making photographs in the studio, and enjoying the renaissance of information in this new age of self-published fiction and non-fiction. An avid reader of history and fiction, he spends countless hours in archives and libraries, searching for the telling facts and anecdotes in primary sources that bring his stories to life.

Currently, David is working on a history of the municipal inspection steam tugboat *Baltimore*, (forthcoming from History4All Publishing in spring 2016), telling the story of Baltimore harbor through the focus of two city-owned steam tugboats named *Baltimore*, from 1857 to today.

David lives in Baltimore with his wife, and their two shelties. He remains one of the family owners of the Wooddell Farm on Buffalo Ridge of Allegheny Mountain, next to Camp Allegheny, where his ancestor, Warwick Wooddell enlisted in Company G, 31st Virginia.

Made in the USA
Lexington, KY
02 July 2016